THE PAPERS OF
WOODROW WILSON
VOLUME 30
MAY 6–SEPTEMBER 5, 1914

SPONSORED BY THE WOODROW WILSON
FOUNDATION
AND PRINCETON UNIVERSITY

THE PAPERS OF

WOODROW WILSON

ARTHUR S. LINK, *EDITOR*

DAVID W. HIRST AND JOHN E. LITTLE

ASSOCIATE EDITORS

EDITH JAMES, *ASSISTANT EDITOR*

SYLVIA ELVIN, *CONTRIBUTING EDITOR*

PHYLLIS MARCHAND, *EDITORIAL ASSISTANT*

Volume 30

May 6 – September 5, 1914

PRINCETON, NEW JERSEY

PRINCETON UNIVERSITY PRESS

1979

Note to scholars: Princeton University Press
subscribes to the Resolution on Permissions of
the Association of American University Presses,
defining what we regard as "fair use" of copyrighted works. This Resolution, intended to encourage scholarly use of university press publications and to avoid unnecessary applications
for permission, is obtainable from the Press or
from the A.A.U.P. central office. Note, however,
that the scholarly apparatus, transcripts of
shorthand, and the texts of Wilson documents
as they appear in this volume are copyrighted,
and the usual rules about the use of copyrighted materials apply.

Publication of this book has been aided by a
grant from the National Historical Publications
and Records Commission.

Printed in the United States of America
by Princeton University Press
Princeton, New Jersey

INTRODUCTION

As this volume opens, Wilson has just accepted the mediation of the Veracruz incident by the ambassadors to the United States of Argentina, Brazil, and Chile. The peace conference opens at Niagara Falls, Canada, on May 20, 1914, against the background of the steady advance of the Constitutionalist armies toward Mexico City. Wilson, in direct and usually daily telegraphic communication with the American commissioners, rebuffs all suggestions by the A.B.C. mediators and Victoriano Huerta's delegates for the formation of a provisional Mexican government composed even in part of leaders of the old regime. Wilson insists, instead, that the mediators recognize the inevitability of the triumph of the Constitutionalists and their First Chief, Venustiano Carranza, and agree to the establishment of a Mexican government dedicated to sweeping social and economic reforms. While Wilson drags out the sessions at Niagara Falls, Carranza moves ever closer to the Mexican capital. The Mexican and American delegates finally sign an ambiguous protocol on July 2, and the conference adjourns. The doomed Huerta abdicates on July 15 and flees to Spain. The remnant of his government surrenders to Carranza on August 13, and the First Chief enters the City of Mexico on August 20.

Wilson's friends hail the Constitutionalist victory as a signal triumph for him. However, continued perplexities lie ahead, for the Mexican revolutionary forces have already divided between Carranza and his supporters and Francisco Villa and his powerful Division of the North. Wilson does what he can to reconcile the two factions, but prospects for peace in war-torn Mexico are not hopeful as this volume ends.

Meanwhile, antitrust legislation, already under way as this volume begins, moves slowly through the two houses of Congress. The documents printed herein fully reveal Wilson's determinative role in leading divided and often confused Democrats on Capitol Hill to accept a Federal Trade Commission with strong regulatory authority as the chief instrumentality for the protection of competition. The documents also reveal that it was Wilson himself who presided over the weakening of the heretofore almost Draconian provisions of the Clayton antitrust bill.

This volume ends with the occurrence of two devastating tragedies for Wilson and the world. His wife dies after a lingering illness on August 6, and Wilson is inconsolable in his grief. Only a few days before, war has erupted in Europe between the

Central Powers and the Triple Entente. Wilson offers his good offices of mediation to no avail. The end of this volume finds him, his advisers, and congressional leaders laying the foundations of American neutrality and meeting the unprecedented crisis at home caused by the disorganization of world trade and a near paralysis of domestic and foreign exchanges.

We reiterate that we reproduce documents *verbatim et literatim* and correct typographical and spelling errors in square brackets *only* when necessary for clarity or ease of reading. Names misspelled in the texts of documents are printed correctly in the footnotes identifying these persons. We continue to read Swem's transcripts of Wilson's speeches and press conferences against Swem's shorthand notes and other texts of speeches and to correct Swem's mistakes silently. Since *The Papers of Woodrow Wilson* is a continuing series, persons and events identified and annotated in earlier volumes are not usually re-identified in subsequent ones. Many of the typographical devices (angle brackets, square brackets, double square brackets, italics, etc.) used to show changes in documents made by Wilson and others will not, in this volume and hereafter, be printed in the list of symbols. The use of these special typographical devices will be explained in the annotation accompanying these particular documents. Finally, the names of persons mentioned casually in documents (for example, obscure Mexicans) and not identified in the notes will be printed in full in the Index whenever it is possible to find their full names.

We still find untranscribed items in Swem's notebooks. We are grateful to Mr. Jack Romagna for continuing to transcribe these notes with his customary dispatch and accuracy. We thank Miss Katharine E. Brand and Professors John Milton Cooper, Jr., and William H. Harbaugh for reading Volume 30 in manuscript and for many helpful suggestions. We also thank our editor at Princeton University Press, Judith May, for her constant assistance.

In this volume, we say farewell to Ellen Louise Axson Wilson, whom, over the past years, we have come to know, admire, and love. We are happy to include twelve pages of her charcoal portraits and paintings in the illustration section, and we dedicate this volume in loving memory to her.

THE EDITORS

Princeton, New Jersey
December 8, 1978

CONTENTS

CONTENTS

Collateral Materials

ILLUSTRATIONS

Following page 298

Portraits and Paintings
by Ellen Louise Axson Wilson

The Rev. Dr. Isaac Stockton Keith Axson
  Charcoal on arches, 24" x 17"
  Independent Presbyterian Church, Savannah, Georgia

The Rev. Dr. Joseph Ruggles Wilson
  Charcoal on arches, 20" x 17"
  Woodrow Wilson Birthplace Foundation

William Ewart Gladstone
  Charcoal on arches, 20" x 17"
  Woodrow Wilson Birthplace Foundation

Prospect Gate
  Oil on canvas, 9⅞" x 13⁵⁄₁₆"
  Princeton University Library

Prospect Gardens
  Oil on canvas, 12" x 16"
  Woodrow Wilson Birthplace Foundation

Scene Near Old Lyme, Connecticut
  Oil on canvas, 12" x 16"
  Woodrow Wilson Birthplace Foundation

"Autumn," 1910
  Oil on canvas, 18" x 24"
  Woodrow Wilson Birthplace Foundation

Pastoral
  Oil on canvas, 12" x 16"
  Woodrow Wilson House, Washington

Woods and Fields, 1911
  Oil on canvas, 18" x 24"
  Woodrow Wilson House, Washington

Apple Orchard
  Oil on canvas, 16" x 20"
  Woodrow Wilson Foundation

Moonlight Scene
  Oil on canvas, 12" x 16"
  Woodrow Wilson Birthplace Foundation

Landscapes
  Oil on board, 7⅜" x 9¼"
  Woodrow Wilson House, Washington

ABBREVIATIONS

ALI	autograph letter initialed
ALS	autograph letter signed
CC	carbon copy
CCL	carbon copy of letter
CCLS	carbon copy of letter signed
CLS	Charles Lee Swem
CLSsh	Charles Lee Swem shorthand
CLST	Charles Lee Swem typed
EAW	Ellen Axson Wilson
EMH	Edward Mandell House
FR	*Papers Relating to the Foreign Relations of the United States*
FR-LP	*Papers Relating to the Foreign Relations of the United States, The Lansing Papers*
FR 1914-WWS	*Papers Relating to the Foreign Relations of the United States, 1914, Supplement, The World War*
hw	handwriting, handwritten
HWLS	handwritten letter signed
HWCL	handwritten copy of letter
JPT	Joseph Patrick Tumulty
JRT	Jack Romagna typed
LI	letter initialed
LMG	Lindley Miller Garrison
MS	manuscript
OGV	Oswald Garrison Villard
RG	Record Group
RL	Robert Lansing
T	typed
T MS	typed manuscript
TC	typed copy
TCL	typed copy of letter
TL	typed letter
TLI	typed letter initialed
TLS	typed letter signed
TS	typed signed
WHP	Walter Hines Page
WJB	William Jennings Bryan
WJBhw	William Jennings Bryan handwriting, handwritten
WW	Woodrow Wilson
WWhw	Woodrow Wilson handwriting, handwritten
WWHwLI	Woodrow Wilson handwritten letter initialed
WWhw MS	Woodrow Wilson handwritten manuscript
WWsh	Woodrow Wilson shorthand
WWT	Woodrow Wilson typed
WWT MS	Woodrow Wilson typed manuscript
WWTLI	Woodrow Wilson typed letter initialed
WWTLS	Woodrow Wilson typed letter signed

ABBREVIATIONS FOR COLLECTIONS
AND REPOSITORIES

Following the National Union Catalog
of the Library of Congress

AGO	Adjutant General's Office
CDR	Commerce Department Records
CtY	Yale University
DLC	Library of Congress
DNA	National Archives
FO	British Foreign Office
GFO-Ar	German Foreign Office Archives
KyBB	Berea College
MH	Harvard University
MHi	Massachusetts Historical Society
MoSW	Washington University
NcDaD	Davidson College
NjHi	New Jersey Historical Society
NjP	Princeton University
PRO	Public Record Office
RSB Coll., DLC	Ray Stannard Baker Collection of Wilsoniana, Library of Congress
SDR	State Department Records
TxHR	Rice University
WC, NjP	Woodrow Wilson Collection, Princeton University
WDR	War Department Records
WP, DLC	Woodrow Wilson Papers, Library of Congress
WU	University of Wisconsin

SYMBOLS

[June 4, 1914]	publication date of a published writing; also date of document when date is not part of text
[*May 28,1914*]	composition date when publication date differs
[[June 5, 1914]]	delivery date of speech if publication date differs
* * * *	text deleted by author of document

THE PAPERS OF

WOODROW WILSON

VOLUME 30
MAY 6–SEPTEMBER 5, 1914

THE PAPERS OF
WOODROW WILSON

To Richard Olney

My dear Mr. Olney:　　　　　The White House May 6, 1914

I need not tell you how deeply disappointed I was that you felt that you could not accept the governorship of the Federal Reserve Board. I felt so strongly that your presence at the head of the board would secure the confidence of the country and was so anxious to be associated with you that I am exceedingly loath to accept your decision.

But, of course, I must do so. I realize that your decision in the matter has been arrived at after full consideration, and I have no right to follow my inclination, which would be to urge you to reconsider it.

I wonder if you have been thinking of the matter of the personnel of the board and would give me the benefit of any suggestions you may have.

　　　　　Cordially and sincerely yours,　Woodrow Wilson

TLS (R. Olney Papers, DLC).

From Franklin Knight Lane

My dear Mr. President:　　　　　Washington May 6, 1914.

I have seen Mr. Underwood and he does not hold out much hope of being able to get our conservation program through at this session, because he says that with the appropriation bills, the trust bills and the rural credit bill the time of the House will be fully occupied. He has told Mr. Ferris,[1] however, that he would cooperate with him in any way that he could to get action on some of the measures. He will have to resist in caucus any effort to make these measures a party program, because he says this will open the door for a lot of other bills. I believe that when you next see Mr. Underwood it would be helpful if you were to urge him to do all in his power to secure the passage of these measures; or if you would drop him a brief note, saying that you desire that these measures should pass, that would be equally helpful.

I have also written to Senators Kern, O'Gorman, Lea, Johnson[2] and Hoke Smith, asking them to advance this program. I wish very much that either in conversation or by letter you would urge them to a conference as suggested by you to-day.

Cordially yours,   Franklin K. Lane

TLS (WP, DLC).
[1] Scott Ferris of Oklahoma, chairman of the House Committee on Public Lands.
[2] Charles Fletcher Johnson, Democrat of Maine.

Walter Hines Page to William Jennings Bryan

London, May 6, 1914,
Rec'd 5:20 p.m.

209. Sir Edward Grey sent for me this afternoon and we had the most solemn conversation we have ever held about Mexico. Carden has telegraphed Grey that Villa and Zapata are sure to take Mexico City and that they will sack it, killing foreigners and destroying foreign property. Grey expresses earnest hope that the United States is prepared to prevent destruction of property and loss of foreign lives. He said: "To put it plainly if your Government is not so prepared foreign Governments must prepare to protect their Nationals which they are unwilling to do provided they can rely on the United States." He did not make formal demand but in effect he asked what are the plans of our Government in case Zapata and Villa overthrow Huerta and secure Mexico City and the government; and he thinks the time is come which makes such a question proper.

He repeated with much emphasis what I have already reported namely that if Villa succeed Huerta this succession will be a horrid anticlimax and that the British Government will demand satisfaction of Villa for Benton's death the moment they can get at him.   Page.

T telegram (SDR, RG 59, 812.00/11838, DNA).

To William Cox Redfield

My dear Mr. Secretary: The White House May 7, 1914

I have yours of May fifth containing a copy of the suggestion made to Senator Newlands by gentlemen connected with the lumber trade of the Northwest with regard to permitting certain forms of combination and association in foreign trade. It is a matter which has very seriously engaged my thoughts, and any suggestion is most welcome.

Cordially and sincerely yours,   Woodrow Wilson

TLS (CDR, RG 40, Office of the Secretary of Commerce, General Corr., File 71774, DNA).

From Charles William Eliot

Cambridge, Massachusetts,
Dear Mr. President: 7 May, 1914.

Your note of May 4th emboldens me to make another brief report to you. I attended, night before last, a meeting of two or three hundred serious-minded men who were listening to an exposition of the Mexican situation based upon nothing but official documents, proceeding either from the Department of State or from the Executive.[1] Most of these documents, of course, were the product of your Administration, but there were a few which belonged to earlier administrations.

After the very competent lecturer had finished his address there was much conversation, the lecturer taking part. I tried to get at what the Quakers call "the sense of the meeting," and this is what I arrived at: There were many opinions as to the correctness or wisdom of the series of your acts, and I could discern no general agreement on the more important points. The majority seemed to think that you should have recognized Huerta, & a decided majority thought that the Tampico incident was no satisfactory cause for War. Many seemed to feel that the policy of the Administration with regard to the embargo on arms had been uncertain and changeable. Many thought that the term "pacific blockade" had no application to your dealings with Mexico. All wondered that American troops, holding an important Mexican city, could declare martial law in that city when the American government was affirming that there was no war with Mexico, and no declaration of war had been made. Your instructions to Mr. Lind were read to the meeting, and, so far as I could judge, there was not a man in the room who thought it possible for any Mexican government to accede to the terms therein laid down. It appeared clearly that the official documents, on which the lecturer relied, had never been printed in any Boston paper, and were new to almost all the gentlemen present.

The conclusion of the lecturer was to the effect: Stand by President Wilson and this most fortunate mediation; and let us hope that the Administration will drop all earlier issues or subjects of contention, and try to get three rules of action in North and South America established: (1) When an American republic gets into trouble with a neighbor, an appropriate combination of other republics shall be called in to settle the difficulty; (2) No American republic shall acquire any territory from another republic by force; (3) No American republic shall protect or support by force of arms its citizens who venture of their own accord into the territory of another republic, either with or without capital, to teach, trade, manufacture, mine, hunt, explore, or travel,—such citizens to be assumed to have placed themselves and their property, if any, under the protection and control of the government of the country into which they go.

No dissent from these conclusions was expressed by any person present, and, so far as any one could see, the conclusion was acceptable to the audience. The lecturer was a thorough student of international law, and a man of experience in international negotiation. I do not know to what political party he belongs.

I am, with highest regard,

Sincerely yours,   Charles W. Eliot

TLS (WP, DLC).

[1] George Grafton Wilson, Professor of International Law at Harvard, spoke on "The Mexican Situation" to the Harvard Club of Boston on May 5. There was no report of the event in the Boston newspapers.

From Henry Smith Pritchett

Dear Mr. President: New York May 7, 1914.

President Frost of Berea College has shown me your letter of April 30. I send a line simply to say that I have sought in every way to show Mr. Carnegie that the question involving the development of Berea College was a very much larger one than that of giving moderate assistance to the ordinary college. It is not an easy matter to get Mr. Carnegie to give the time to appreciate this problem, but I hope sincerely that it may in time, at any rate, be taken up seriously by the Carnegie Corporation.

Sincerely yours,   Henry S. Pritchett

TLS (WP, DLC).

From the Diary of Colonel House

Washington, May 7, 1914.

At 5.45 we went to the White House for the wedding. There were no guests outside the family and Cabinet. The service was simple and very beautiful. The President and Mrs. Wilson bore up bravely, but Nona McAdoo[1] broke down and had to be taken home. Refreshments were served at small tables in the State

Dining Room. When Eleanor and McAdoo left the White House all the guests ran out on the south porch to see them off excepting the President and myself. He seemed to lack the heart to see the last of her. I think he loves her better than any member of his household.

A little later he sent for me and we sat in the hall while the guests were leaving, and we talked of his coming trip to New York. He is to lunch and dine with me Monday so that we may finish up everything before my departure for Europe. He wishes to appoint my brother-in-law, President Mezes, as one of the Mediators in the Mexico matter. I admitted Mezes' fitness for the work, but I protested against his giving it to him. I did not want my brother-in-law to occupy such a position, and did not think he should take a man from Texas, particularly since our Governor[2] has been so rabid in his talk concerning Mexico. I was sure it would make a bad impression if a Texan was selected for so important a place.

We talked of Hamlin for the Federal Reserve Board and I told him how much McAdoo desired it. He said he simply could not do it and for the reasons given before. I told him Harding had accepted. This, of course, was news to him as Harding's letter had not reached him.

We all left the White House by 8.30. Loulie and I drove with Mr. and Mrs. Tumulty down to Potomac Park. Tumulty said he was thinking of resigning, that he could not live on the money he was getting. I can see that he is influencing the President toward conservatism. He has been doing everything possible to have the railroad rates increased and also he has been doing what he could to have the President meet the big financiers of the country. He spoke of himself as a "conservative progressive"! My opinion is that he might eliminate the last word.

T MS (E. M. House Papers, CtY).
  [1] McAdoo's daughter.
  [2] Oscar Branch Colquitt.

From Lindley Miller Garrison

My dear Mr President: Washington. May 8. 1914

I am writing so as to avoid a misunderstanding and to be able to act advisedly.

After the Cabinet meeting this morning Secretary Lane informed me that he had a talk with you and that he understood you to say that I was authorized to make all necessary preparations to assemble and transport to Vera Cruz whatever troops etc were necessary in view of the possibilities we discussed at Cabinet. I inquired whether this related to the 1st Division which would embark from N. Y. as well as to the 2nd which embarks at Galveston—and he said he so understood it. He also said he understood that you felt you had given me carte blanche to get the necessary forces at Vera Cruz.

I did not feel that you and I had had any such explicit understanding and I, therefore, write to ask you to give me definitely just what you wish me to do in the premises.

By way of information I add—that the 2nd Division complete, with the marines would aggregate between 14000 & 15000: that the 1st Division would add about 11000 that the ships for the 2nd Division (i.e. the one at Galveston) have been chartered are being filled up and will be all assembled at Galveston as soon as possible—details as to time required were given you in yesterday's memorandum.[1] Ships for the 1st Division (i.e. the one at & about N. Y.) have not been chartered—but readily could be—the time for refitting and loading would be approximately the same as already given.

If we have to go to the City we will certainly need as many men as this total if we keep any line of communication whatever.

When you have opportunity—please advise me of your conclusions.   Sincerely yours   Lindley M. Garrison

He also said you were in doubt whether to authorize me to send out and guard the San Francisco Bridge.[2]

ALS (WP, DLC).
  [1] James B. Aleshire, Quartermaster-General, "Memorandum for the Secretary of War," May 7, 1914, TS memorandum, enclosed in LMG to WW, May 7, 1914, TLS (WP, DLC).
  [2] A railroad bridge on the Interoceanic Railroad, about twenty-five miles northwest of Veracruz. The American military authorities feared that Huerta's troops would destroy it to prevent the advance of American forces toward Mexico City. *New York Times*, May 5, 1914.

To Asbury Francis Lever

[The White House] May 8, 1914.

I had the great pleasure of signing the bill today.[1] I congratulate the country on its passage and you most sincerely on the important constructive part you played in framing it.

                         Woodrow Wilson.

T telegram (Letterpress Books, WP, DLC).
  [1] The Smith-Lever Act, providing federal funds for agricultural extension work through the land-grant colleges.

From Walter Hines Page

Dear Mr. President: 8 May, 1914. London

The news that reaches London through every channel that I hear of—governmental, financial, and newspaper—indicates not only the early downfall of Huerta but the gravest fears for the lives and the property of foreigners in Mexico City especially but throughout the whole country as well. I cannot guess to what extent these fears may be the result of the opinion that has prevailed here till now—that Huerta could never be dislodged by the "rebels"; and, of course, I have no data to form any opinion of my own.

But I report this universal fear of anarchy & murder & plunder because of its bearings on governmental relations. Sir Edward Grey is thoroughly alarmed. His advices are that such a state of things may follow as will endanger foreign lives & property everywhere in Mexico; and they (members of Parliament and others) are already asking this Government what assurances it has from us or what preparations is it making in common prudence, on the eve of the approaching catastrophe? And nobody here—from Sir Edward down—looks on Villa and Zapata except as scourges—thoroughly unprincipled brigands and murderers. Carranza they know next to nothing about. But with Villa or Zapata as a conqueror, they will consider rank anarchy come. Are we in a position then to protect foreign lives & property? Will we take this active task in hand? I am asked this on all sides.

This I send you for whatever it may be worth—nothing, or little, or much.   Yours Sincerely,   Walter H. Page

P.S. The newspapers and certain question-asking members of Parliament keep saying that we have laid so much emphasis on the elimination of Huerta that we seem to have forgotten the larger problem of order & security in Mexico. This is as persistent as it is irritating.   P.

ALS (WP, DLC).

To Walter Hines Page

Washington, May 9, 1914 11 a.m.

In response to your [May 6, No. 209], please say to Sir Edward Grey that *the President's position may be stated as follows:*[1] we share the grave solicitude of his government with regard to possible events at Mexico City; that we fully realize our responsibility with relation to the protection of the lives of foreigners and the property of foreign governments there; and that we are making every preparation possible in the circumstances to act promptly and effectively should the necessity arise.

As for what might follow the success of the forces at the north we of course have no favourites and no individual personal choice of our own. We shall merely try to secure an orderly reorganization of the government of Mexico and a choice of president by the Mexicans themselves as nearly as may be in accordance with the provisions of the national constitution. The new government set up will of course, we assume, admit its responsibility for all national obligations which may have been incurred under international law during the prevalence of revolutionary conditions.

Bryan

WWT telegram (SDR, RG 59, 812.00/11838, DNA).
1 Italicized words in the body of the telegram are WJBhw.

From Carter Glass

Confidential.

[Washington] Saturday, May 9, 1914

My dear Mr. President: 12:40 p.m.

At 11:30 today I learned very definitely, from the expert of the committee and from Mr. Brown of West Virginia,[1] a member of the committee, that Mr. Bulkley has today avowed his intention to introduce the Agricultural credit bill on Monday with the government aid provision,[2] and that his purpose is to give the bill to the press tomorrow for release on Monday morning. Mr. Brown tells me that Mr. Bulkley has not made it plain to the members of the sub-committee that you are unalterably opposed to the government aid provision, but represents to his colleagues that your frame of mind is such that you may be brought to favor the provision. Mr. Bulkley, as I am told by Mr. Brown, proposes to project this bill before the public and to introduce it in Congress without consultation with the majority members of the Banking and Currency Committee.

I am endeavoring to prevail with members of the sub-committee to combat him on this point, and some of them have promised to do it. I am communicating this information so that you may, if you please, take some action in the matter.

Very respectfully yours,   Carter Glass.

TLS (WP, DLC).
1 William Gay Brown, Jr., Democratic congressman from West Virginia.
2 The Hollis-Bulkley bill was introduced in both houses of Congress on May 12. It provided for a system of rural credits in which the national govern-

ment would be required to establish twelve federal land banks with a minimum capital of $500,000 each and to purchase their bonds up to a total of $50,000,-000, if private investors failed to do so. See the *New York Times*, May 13, 1914, and Arthur S. Link, *Wilson: The New Freedom* (Princeton, N. J., 1956), pp. 261-64.

A Memorandum by Lindley Miller Garrison

May 9, 1914

President 'phoned for me at 12:30 & I went to Ex. office & saw him—conversation ab't 20 min.

In substance he said

That he tho't that by recruiting up, we had or would have 20 000 at Vera Cruz, i.e. that the 2d Division assembled up would make that Number. That he felt to assemble the transport necessary to take down the 1s Division in N. Y. would be impossible to accomplish without unexplainable criticism from both Constitutionalists & Huerta. That we could assemble, as already ordered, the transports at Galveston for 2d Div. without these undesirable effects because we had begun our maneuvers from there & preparation there to send rest of that force would be differently viewed.

He said that he would not authorize the assembling of ships at N. Y. or elsewhere for 1s Div. nor would he authorize me to load & transport the balance of the 2d Div. at Galveston. That I should get everything assembled at Galveston for 2d Div. & wait for further orders before anything could go.

He seems to feel that under whatever arrangement we make with the A.BC's we could not send more men to Vera Cruz—& that to prepare the 1st Div. would also be in contravention of spirit of our understanding in this respect.

As to this he said he would get Mr Bryan to see the ABC people & find out their attitude toward our properly preparing by having troops at Vera Cruz for what might happen in City of Mexico; & that he would also get an opinion from Mr. Lansing as to our legal & ethical rights under the existing situation.

He said he had replied to Sir E. Grey by saying that "We recognize to the full our obligation & responsibility, and that as to Villa we were playing no favorites." I was to do no more after assembling ships at G. & having them fitted up until further directions from him. The net result was that I was to go ahead as previously directed & as just stated & then await instructions.

LMG

P.S. He referred to attitude Constitutionalists would take if we seemed to be preparing for a considerable move & saw it might unite them to unfriendly action. He also referred to force now there as sufficient to go thru to City. I told him I would not take such a responsibility—in my view entirely insufficient & peril one should not be invited. I said 10 000 least I will start with & they to be immediately followed up. Spoke of inability with that No. to keep open communications—& occupy towns en route.

We of course spoke of apprehensive conditions in re Zapata & also of Villa, suggesting that enough should be sent in for probability of not expected contingency of both turning vs us as well as what was left of Huerta's forces.

P.S. No. 2. He said he felt we could not in Honor reinforce under the armistice. I said then he had no field for choice— no alternative. It was not a question of what was wise or prudent to do but of what we had promised not to do. I of course said I could not say anything if this was the situation. He said it was the situation.

Hw MS (NjHi).

To Mary Allen Hulbert

My dearest Friend,   The White House 10 May, 1914.

I despair of *finding* time to write to you: there literally *is* no time that I have the right to call my own; I must simply *steal* what I use for the purpose. I used to reserve here an hour, there a morning or an afternoon, for my own use and renewal, but little by little the crowding events and duties have swept everything into their domain and I am not free to think of myself or of the things that are nearest to me personally any more. Of course my thoughts steal away to them upon the slightest occasion or opportunity, but they are truants from this hard school when they do. You do not know how I need these moments with dear friends or what deep refreshment they mean to me when I get them.

I *must* write you to-day just a line or two about the wedding. But, first, of your sweet thoughtfulness in sending me the necktie, which is not only really beautiful but whose value to me far exceeds its looks and its mere material, for it is the thought of a dear friend. And I know how the dear little bride appreciated the embroideries you sent her. She will write, I know, when the first leisure of thought and emotion comes. Ah! how desperately my heart aches that she is gone. She was simply part of me, the only delightful part; and I feel the loneliness more than I dare admit even to myself. The wedding was as simple and beautiful as any

I ever saw or imagined and she has married a noble man, who I feel sure will make her happy and proud, too. But just now I can realize, in my selfishness, only that I have lost her, for good and all. She will love me as much as ever, but she will not be at my side and every day in my life, and I am desolate. But, never mind that! Life is all burden (and the privilege and resulting strength of bearing it) as one passes fifty and faces towards his reckoning! I must rejoice in her happiness and be quiet. Have I not the best and truest and sweetest friends that ever a man had; and can I be dow[n]hearted so long as they live and thrive and I can subscribe myself, as now,

Your devoted friend,   Woodrow Wilson

I am very well indeed; and the blessed dear ones who love me grow all the sweeter companions as we draw nearer in the narrowing circle!

WWTLS (WP, DLC).

A Memorial Address[1]

[May 11, 1914]

Mr. Secretary: I know that the feelings which characterize all who stand about me and the whole nation at this hour are not feelings which can be suitably expressed in terms of attempted oratory or eloquence. They are things too deep for ordinary speech. For my own part, I have a singular mixture of feelings. The feeling that is uppermost is one of profound grief that these lads should have had to go to their death; and yet there is mixed with that grief a profound pride that they should have gone as they did, and, if I may say it out of my heart, a touch of envy of those who were permitted so quietly, so nobly, to do their duty. Have you thought of it, men? Here is the roster of the navy—the list of the men, officers and enlisted men and marines—and suddenly there swim nineteen stars out of the list—men who have suddenly been lifted into a firmament of memory where we shall always see their names shine, not because they called upon us to admire them, but because they served us without asking any questions and in the performance of a duty which is laid upon us as well as upon them.

Duty is not an uncommon thing, gentlemen. Men are performing it in the ordinary walks of life all around us all the time, and they are making great sacrifices to perform it. What gives men like these peculiar distinction is not merely that they did their duty, but that their duty had nothing to do with them or their own personal and peculiar interests. They did not give their lives for themselves. They gave their lives for us, because we called upon them as a nation to perform an unexpected duty. That is the way in which men grow distinguished, and that is the only way, by serving somebody else than themselves. And what greater thing could you serve than a nation such as this we love and are proud of? Are you sorry for these lads? Are you sorry for the way they will be remembered? Does it not quicken your pulses to think of the list of them? I hope to God none of you may join the list, but if you do, you will join an immortal company.

So, while we are profoundly sorrowful, and while there goes out of our hearts a very deep and affectionate sympathy for the friends and relatives of these lads who for the rest of their lives shall mourn them, though with a touch of pride, we know why we do not go away from this occasion cast down, but with our heads lifted and our eyes on the future of this country, with absolute confidence of how it will be worked out. Not only upon the mere vague future of this country, but upon the immediate future. We have gone down to Mexico to serve mankind if we can find out the way. We do not want to fight the Mexicans. We want to serve the Mexicans if we can, because we know how we would like to be free, and how we would like to be served if there were friends standing by in such case ready to serve us. A war of aggression is not a war in which it is a proud thing to die, but a war of service is a thing in which it is a proud thing to die.

Notice how truly these men were of our blood. I mean of our American blood, which is not drawn from any one country, which is not drawn from any one stock, which is not drawn from any one language of the modern world; but free men everywhere have sent their sons and their brothers and their daughters to this country in order to make that great compounded nation which consists of all the sturdy elements and of all the best elements of the whole globe. I listened again to this list of the dead with a profound interest because of the mixture of the names, for the names bear the marks of the several national stocks from which these men came. But they are not Irishmen or Germans or Frenchmen or Hebrews or Italians any more. They were not when they went to Veracruz; they were Americans, every one of them, and with no difference in their Americanism because of the stock from which they came. They were in a peculiar sense of our blood, and they proved it by showing that they were of our spirit—that no matter what their derivation, no matter where their people came from, they thought and wished and did the things that were American; and the flag under which they served was a flag in which all the blood of mankind is united to make a free nation.

War, gentlemen, is only a sort of dramatic representation, a sort of dramatic symbol, of a thousand forms of duty. I never went into battle; I never was under fire; but I fancy that there are some things just as hard to do as to go under fire. I fancy that it is just as hard to do your duty when men are sneering at you as when they are shooting at you. When they shoot at you, they can only take your natural life; when they sneer at you, they can wound your living heart, and men who are brave enough, steadfast enough, steady in their principles enough, to go about their duty with regard to their fellow men, no matter whether there are hisses or cheers, men who can do what Rudyard Kipling in one of his poems wrote, "Meet with triumph and disaster and treat those two impostors just the same," are men for a nation to be proud of. Morally speaking, disaster and triumph are impostors. The cheers of the moment are not what a man ought to think about, but the verdict of his conscience and of the consciences of mankind.

When I look at you, I feel as if I also and we all were enlisted men. Not enlisted in your particular branch of the service, but enlisted to serve the country, no matter what may come, even though we may sacrifice our lives in the arduous endeavor. We are expected to put the utmost energy of every power that we have into the service of our fellow men, never sparing ourselves, not condescending to think of what is going to happen to ourselves, but ready, if need be, to go to the utter length of complete self-sacrifice.

As I stand and look at you today and think of these spirits that have gone from us, I know that the road is clearer for the future. These boys have shown us the way, and it is easier to walk on it because they have gone before and shown us how. May God grant to all of us that vision of patriotic service which here in solemnity and grief and pride is borne in upon our hearts and consciences![2]

Printed in *Address of President Wilson at the Brooklyn Navy Yard* . . . (Washington, 1914).

[1] Wilson spoke at a memorial service at the Brooklyn Navy Yard for the nineteen sailors and marines killed in the attack on Veracruz. Secretary of the Navy Josephus Daniels presided. For a detailed account of the event, see the *New York Times*, May 12, 1914.

[2] There is a WWT outline, dated May 10, 1914, and a WWsh outline, dated May 11, 1914, of this address in WP, DLC; and a CLST copy, with WWhw emendations, in the C. L. Swem Coll., NjP.

From William Bauchop Wilson

My dear Mr. President: Washington May 11, 1914.

In response to your letter of the 7th instant, enclosing telegram received from a number of coal operators of Colorado,[1] sent to you in order that you might be more fully informed with reference to their position respecting the so-called United Mine Workers of America, I have the honor to submit the following comment:

The position taken by the operators in this telegram, defending their refusal to have business dealings with the United Mine Workers of America, is based upon the assumption that the United Mine Workers of America is a lawless organization; that its officers, leaders and members have encouraged intimidation, assaults, arson, murder, armed resistance to organized government, and anarchy in general. If this arraignment were true, the operators would be amply justified in refusing to deal with such an organization or with such men. The United Mine Workers of America is an organization composed exclusively of men employed in and about the coal mines of the United States and Canada. It has approximately 430,000 members in the United States. There are approximately 750,000 coal-mine workers in this country. It establishes no qualification for membership except that the member must be or have been employed as a miner or mine laborer, on the theory that, if the employer finds it necessary to employ him, it is just as necessary that the union should have him associated with his fellow-workers. Since 1897 it has annually, biennially and triennially, as the circumstances warranted, been making wage contracts with all the employers in Ohio, Indiana, Illinois, Iowa, Missouri, Kansas, Arkansas and Texas, and with a part of the operators of Pennsylvania, Kentucky, Tennessee and Alabama. Later it has been making wage contracts with the operators of West Virginia, Wyoming and Washington. Wherever it has entered into contractual relations with employers it has built up a reputation for fair dealing and strict adherence to the terms of its contracts. Its officers and leaders, who are responsible for its policies as an organization, command the respect of these employers even when they widely differ with them as to the terms of wage contracts under consideration for adoption.

During strike periods it has been the universal policy of the officers of the organization to use their influence to have the strikers conduct themselves in a peaceful and law-abiding man-

[1] This telegram is printed at May 5, 1914, Vol. 29.

ner. This of course does not always apply to local leaders, who are more apt to be influenced by the inflamed sentiment of their respective communities. The charge that the United Mine Workers of America is a lawless organization whose officers promote violence would have greater force if it came from men who themselves have been conservators of the peace, but these companies have not been. They have maintained for years an armed guard ostensibly to protect their property, but which has been used to intimidate the workmen and others. I have in mind a number of instances where organizers of the mine workers have been waylaid on the highway or attacked while sitting peacefully in their seats on passenger trains and hammered into insensibility by those guards with guns in their hands. In the present dispute the first person killed was an organizer of the United Mine Workers by the name of Lippiat, who was shot to death by a Baldwin-Felts guard named Belcher on the streets of Trinidad, on the day preceding the holding of the convention which was to determine whether or not a strike should be called.

Albert C. Felts, representative of the Baldwin-Felts Detective Agency, testified before the Committee on Mines and Mining that his firm had been employed by the Colorado Coal Operators Association to furnish guards in Colorado for a number of years past, and that after the strike began they imported guns and ammunition, among which were three or four machine guns which had been used against the strikers on a number of occasions.

I have cited these matters not for the purpose of palliating any offences which have been committed by the strikers, but for the purpose of showing that the operators themselves have been responsible for the commission of acts which are similar in their nature to the offences committed by mine workers, which are held by the operators to constitute reasons why they should not do business with the representatives of the United Mine Workers. The telegram states: "In the present issue we are not opposing or waging war against organized labor as such. We are, however, unalterably of the conviction that we can never recognize nor have any dealings of any kind with the organization purporting to be a labor union and calling itself the United Mine Workers of America." The strike was inaugurated on September 23, 1913, by a convention of mine workers held in Trinidad. Several weeks prior to the holding of the convention this Department was notified by Vice President Frank J. Hayes of the National Organization of Mine Workers that a strike was imminent unless the operators would meet representatives of the workmen for the purpose of discussing and adjusting the grievances complained

of. On September 5th I detailed Mr. Ethelbert Stewart, Chief
Clerk of the Bureau of Labor Statistics, to act as a conciliator.
He proceeded to New York to consult the various interests there
and was informed by them that they would not interfere in the
Colorado situation unless requested to do so by their representatives in Colorado. He then proceeded to Colorado, reaching
Denver on the night preceding the inauguration of the strike. He
met the representatives of both sides, and among other things
proposed (1) "that the managers of the mining properties
involved in this dispute hold a formal, official conference with the
officials of the miners' organization at any place the operators
might suggest," (2) "that the managers meet the Governor and
these men named as individuals not as union officials, together
with myself in the Governor's office, in a purely informal way to
talk the matter over, such meeting to be unofficial, not to commit anyone to any policy but simply to try in a gentlemen's meeting to induce each side to consider the claims put forth by the
other," and (3) "that the mine managers deliver to me any counter proposition they might have to offer for me to submit to the
miners." The operators refused both of the first two propositions
and declined to submit any counter propositions. When you take
into consideration the fact that these propositions were made before the acts of violence complained of were committed, one is
led to the conclusion that the opposition was to any organization of workmen rather than to the particular organization called
United Mine Workers of America. Again I quote from the telegram: "The official membership roll of this organization in District 15, of which Colorado is a part, at that time contained the
names of 2,048 out of a total of 23,000 men employed in the
coal mining industry in that district. The agitators mentioned
and certain delegates of their selection met in the convention
at Trinidad in September, 1913, and called a strike of our workmen. By threats and intimidation, by incendiary and anarchistic
speeches, and through fear of bodily injury or death many of our
employes were induced to go on strike. This strike was in its inception, and always has been, a strike for union recognition only."
That is scarcely a correct statement of the fact. District 15 is composed of Colorado, New Mexico and Utah. The total number of
miners in the three states is approximately 23,000. Of that number 13,000 are located in Colorado. There are no members of
the union in Utah, and only one small local union in New Mexico.
I do not know what the official membership roll was at that
time, but whatever it was it represented the membership in
Colorado, with the exception of the few members located in New

Mexico. When a convention of the mine workers is held, each local union selects its delegate by ballot, and the testimony before the Committee on Mines and Mining indicates that practically every mining camp in Colorado was represented at the Trinidad convention. I am informed that none of the officers or organizers participated in the discussion of the resolution proposing to strike, and that notwithstanding that fact the vote was unanimous in favor of striking. That would not seem to indicate that the men in the mines who had selected these delegates were contented as stated in the telegram. If these men were contented, it would be difficult to imagine a force of six or seven organizers going in amongst them, with all the machinery of government under the control of coal operators, and intimidating 13,000 men into a strike against their will. In the inception of the strike the miners insisted upon recognition of the union. But during my visit to Denver in November I suggested to them that they withdraw from that position, which they agreed to do provided some means was devised by which committees of the workmen would be received by the representatives of the coal companies for the purpose of presenting such grievances as might from time to time arise.

Again I quote from telegram: "Our statutes are enforceable and have been and are being enforced." That statement is incorrect. The statutes have not been enforced in the past and some of them are of such nature that they cannot be enforced except through the collective action of the miners. I have particular reference to a checkweigh law. No individual workman can select and pay for a checkweighman. If he is paid for at all, it must be through the collective contributions of the workmen. As long as you prevent the miners from acting collectively at any mine, you thereby prevent them from enforcing the statute relative to the weighing of coal.

That insurrection and anarchy have prevailed for some time in the coal regions of Colorado is admitted, but that the mine workers are solely responsible for that condition may well be questioned; nor does the solution of the problem lie in the suggestion that "if the 2,000 members of this organization now militant in this state do not care to work in our mines, it is their privilege to decline to do so and go elsewhere." That theory might have worked well enough prior to the development of modern industry with its hundreds or thousands of employes of one corporation, or may work very well in our agricultural communities where the number of employers and employes are more equally balanced, but it does not solve the problem in our industrial centres. The history of mining in Colorado itself demonstrates that. They had a general strike there in 1894, another in 1903, and the present one started in 1913. The strike breakers of 1894 became the strikers of 1903, and the strike breakers of 1903 became the strikers of 1913, and if the present strike ends as the others did in the complete defeat of the strikers, the strike breakers of today will be the strikers of some years hence.

That their present employes may be satisfied is possible, but the probabilities are that the great bulk of them are workmen whose necessities compel them to find some immediate means of subsistence and they have accepted employment for that reason rather than that they are satisfied with the conditions.

Faithfully yours,   W B Wilson

TLS (WP, DLC).

From Scott Ferris

My dear Mr. President: Washington, D. C. May 11, 1914.

I hope you will pardon me for calling your attention to what might well be termed the Administration Conservation Program that has eminated from the Public Lands Committees of the House and Senate respectively.

As you are aware, all platforms of all political parties assert their willingness and readiness to enact legislation on conservation. I may be over-zealous in the matter, but I feel that it would not be over-stating it to say that this is one of the great issues in the country today. Our 700,000,000 acres of public domain in continental United States and Alaska, holding within its depths and beneath its surface minerals of all sorts and values, is a question so multitudinous and so colossal that I feel that we all might well pause and give it consideration. The preceding administrations have done this and this only, to-wit: they have withdrawn from any sort of entry or use the minerals and public lands of the West, including oil, gas, coal, phosphate, potash and sodium and power sites. That, you will observe, Mr. President, does not solve in any sense the conservation question. It merely makes it possible for those who follow to solve the question.

I hope you will not let Congress adjourn until some action is taken on the following bills, copies of each of which I am inclosing herewith:

1st. The Alaskan Leasing Bill, it being H.R. 14233.

2d. The General Leasing Bill, providing for the leasing of the oil, gas, coal, phosphate, potassium and sodium lands, it being H.R. 16136.

3d. The Water-Power Bill, it being H.R. 14893.

If this conservation program could go through, Mr. President, I think it will merit the approval of all parties and of all thinking men. I cannot but feel that it is essentially necessary that it be done before this Congress adjourns.

The only possible way to accomplish this, Mr. President, and to have it receive consideration, due to the congested condition of the calendars, is for you sometime tomorrow to telephone or communicate with Mr. Underwood and ask him to include them or make it possible for their consideration at the House Caucus Tuesday night, May 12, 1914.

I have long hesitated to annoy you with this, coupled with your other multitudinous tasks, but our pledge to the people was so positive and Secretary Lane's untiring efforts in its behalf are so refreshing and so unusual that I would feel it was short of my duty if I did not urge the necessity of this legislation.

With great respect, I am

Very sincerely yours,   Scott Ferris

TLS (WP, DLC).

From the Diary of Colonel House

May 11, 1914.

I went to the Pennsylvania Station at 7.30. The President was at breakfast. I joined him and we discussed the advisability of his taking part in the parade.[1] He said he had no fear, that he did not believe anyone would make an attempt on his life. The fact that the papers had stated the Mayor had dissuaded him from going would in itself determine the matter. He believed the I.W.W.'s were good sports and would not try to do anything of that sort. I replied that he, himself, was something of a sport to insist upon going through with the program as planned.

We fell to talking of his speech. He had not prepared anything, but he would think it out en route from the Battery to the Navy Yard. It is his way of doing. Sometime he will make a serious blunder. It is an occasion for something great, and he may or may not rise to the occasion.

We discussed Mexico, Villa, Huerta and the Mediation Board. He told me Justice Lamar was an old boyhood friend, and they used to play together and fight roosters. He was full of Lamar and his early boyhood days.

At 8.30 they left the car. I did not go with them for I did not care to have the reporters see me. We arranged for him to lunch and dine with me and I suggested that we go to the Piping Rock Club this afternoon. When I asked if he would like someone to dine with us, he replied no, for he wished to talk with me concerning the Federal Reserve Board and other matters.

The President returned to our apartment about noon. There was a great crowd in front of the house. He changed his clothes and we talked of various matters before luncheon. Dr. Grayson lunched with us. After lunch we drove to the Piping Rock Club on Long Island. The President dozed most of the way. He often does this when motoring. I noticed he was more absent-minded than usual. At luncheon he told me something he had told me at breakfast. He also spoke of the fact that he was getting distressingly absent-minded.

Four automobiles followed us to Piping Rock. One contained Secret Service men, who refused to let any car pass ours, so we were free from dust. There were three cars filled with newspaper men. These hover around the President like birds of prey. They are there to be ready in the event of an accident or something untoward occurring.

We had tea at the Club, walked over the golf course and then returned to New York. After crossing the bridge at 59th Street we had a wild and exciting drive down Second Avenue. It had begun to rain and the motor cyple [cycle] man was clearing our passage, and between the roar of the Elevated, the patter of the rain, and the hooting of the horns, the ride did not lack excitement.

No one dined with us excepting Grayson and after dinner he left us. The President read poems to me for nearly an hour. It was Wordsworth, Matthew Arnold, Edward Sill and Keats. What he particularly liked was "A Fool's Prayer" by Sill, and "A Conservative" by Gilman.[2] When he finished reading I took out my budget.

I spoke first of the proposed visit of Queen Eleanora of Bulgaria which I had discussed with the State Department, and I told him she had been advised it would be best to postpone her visit.

Governor Osborne, First Assist. Secretary of State, has indicated his intention of resigning and I thought it wise to have a man ready for the place. I suggested Phillips, which met with the President's approval. I thought we could pick a man for Phillips' place easier than we could one for First Secretary.

In the event of war with Mexico, I asked him to give Major [General] Joseph Wheeler a regiment, and gave my reasons for thinking it would be a good thing to do.

I discussed with him the tentative proposal of the Progressives to fuse the election of delegates to the Constitutional Convention.[3] We went into this at considerable length. I also suggested the advisability of sending an invitation to one of the de Lesseps to take part as a guest of our Government in the opening of the Panama Canal.

My next item was, should intervention occur, to invite the A.B.C. Powers to join.

Then came McReynolds, and the trusts and the Colorado situation. The President thought the labor clause in the trust measure now pending could be gotten through, provided he read the riot act to the labor leaders and told them they must stand up to their first agreement or he would fight it out with them. Next on the list was a letter from Walter Page which we read and which concerned my visit to the Kaiser. I asked the President to write me a letter of farewell and put in it something which would give me an excuse to show it to the Kaiser without having "to drag it in by the heels." This, I explained, was merely to show our relationship. He wished to know if I desired him to say something of the object of my mission. I did not, and he too, thought that was best. He made a memorandum in shorthand to send such a letter as I desired. He said his heart misgave him to think I was going so soon, but he added, "it is worth while for you go upon a great mission."

I explained the New Haven-Folk-Department of Justice situation.[4] After that we discussed the Federal Reserve Board appointments. I called up Warburg while he was here. Warburg had been trying to get me during the day and I thought perhaps he had something of importance which the President should know. This I found was true.

I told the President that Tumulty had said that within the next six months he thought he would resign. I believed he was sincere, but he had some purpose in giving me this information which he wished me to impart to him. He seemed upset over the idea of losing Tumulty. Dr. Grayson came in at this point and we made ready to go to the train where I left him.

[1] Wilson had been advised by Tumulty, William J. Flynn, chief of the Secret Service, and others not to participate in the procession through New York in honor of the men who died at Veracruz. However, after an announcement on the previous day that Wilson would not take part, he did in fact take his place in the line of carriages which followed the horse-drawn caissons bearing the dead from the Battery up Broadway to City Hall Plaza, and thence across Manhattan Bridge to the Brooklyn Navy Yard, where the main ceremonies took place. *New York Times*, May 12, 1914.

[2] Charlotte Perkins Gilman, author, lecturer and feminist. The brief poem, "A Conservative," described a quondam caterpillar so unhappy over its transformation into a butterfly that it climbed back into its chrysalis.

[3] House referred to a plan approved by a conference of New York Progressive leaders on May 5 to begin a movement to have delegates elected to the forth-

coming New York State Constitutional Convention on a nonpartisan basis. This would enable Progressives, progressive Republicans, and anti-Tammany Democrats to unite behind single candidates. *New York Times*, May 6, 1914. As it turned out, the movement failed, and the delegates were chosen on a partisan basis.

⁴ Joseph Wingate Folk was at this time the chief counsel of the Interstate Commerce Commission. In that capacity, he had, on April 29, begun hearings in the commission's third investigation of the affairs of the New Haven Railroad. When Folk and other members of the investigating team proposed to hear testimony from Charles S. Mellen, ex-president of the New Haven, and other high officials of the railroad, McReynolds strongly objected on the ground that their testifying before the commission would give them immunity from any criminal prosecution which the Justice Department might later institute. The dispute culminated in an angry confrontation in McReynold's office on May 13. With the strong support of Senator George W. Norris, who had instigated the new investigation, Folk and his colleagues decided to ignore McReynolds's objection, and Mellen and other railroad officials testified as scheduled. See the *New York Times*, May 12 and 14, 1914, and Louis G. Geiger, *Joseph W. Folk of Missouri*, University of Missouri Studies, xxv (Columbia, Mo., 1953), 156-57.

To Carter Glass

My dear Mr. Glass: [The White House] May 12, 1914

After our conference of this morning, I feel that it is really my duty to tell you how deeply and sincerely I feel that the Government should not itself be drawn into the legislation for credits based on farm mortgages. I think that the bill as it has been outlined would be very serviceable indeed without this feature and that the drawing of the Government into the purchase of land mortgages would launch us upon a course of experimentation in which we should have no guidance from experience either in this country or elsewhere because of the fundamental dissimilarity of conditions here and abroad. Moreover, I have a very deep conviction that it is unwise and unjustifiable to extend the credit of the Government to a single class of the community.

Since I have learned that my convictions in this matter are not shared by a considerable number of the gentlemen who have given some attention to this matter in the House and in the Senate, I have felt it my duty to consider the matter very deliberately and very carefully and you can rest assured that I would not express to you the conviction I have just avowed if I did not feel it my conscientious duty to do so and if I did not feel privileged to do so because of a study of the conditions and consequences of such legislation. You can see, moreover, how the very fact that this conviction has come to me, as it were, out of fire fixes it very clearly and permanently.

Cordially and sincerely yours,   Woodrow Wilson

TLS (Letterpress Books, WP, DLC).

To William Jennings Bryan, with Enclosure

My dear Mr. Secretary: The White House May 12, 1914

Thank you sincerely for having let me see the enclosed letter from our Minister at Athens. It has interested me very much indeed, particularly what he says about Villa and the land system. It is all very interesting how views seem at last to be clearing up.
    Always
        Cordially and faithfully yours,   Woodrow Wilson

TLS (W. J. Bryan Papers, DNA).

E N C L O S U R E

George Fred Williams to William Jennings Bryan

My dear Mr. Secretary,   Athens April 22, 1914.

I am watching with vital interest the Mexican situation, and am tempted to telegraph today "Do not fire a gun: blockade & starve Huerta."

I dread the use of force, & see a great lesson to be taught the nations in the use of the Army & Navy to cut off means of sustenance, comfort & income, without firing a gun. The cessation of commerce will arouse the trading interests of Mexico & the world to overthrow Huerta.

I have the right to an opinion concerning the Mexican policy, because I am heavily interested in mining & smelting there. I am president of a company operating in the State of Mexico, fifty miles Southwest of Toluca, the capital. We have given to a Scotch Company an option to purchase, but cannot deliver peaceable possession.

Now I want to impress upon you one point. Villa is a godsend to Mexico. He is doing that which alone can save Mexico, viz. confiscating the great stolen holdings & driving out the Spanish, who have cursed the country. Had we the responsibility we could not take such a course: therefore blockade, & let Villa do the rest. I am sure my properties will never be secure until the people get their rights to the soil. Around our properties one man claimed nearly all the land for miles. He has fled, & it is found that his titles rested mainly on forcible possession, backed by Diaz.

The registration system was a plan of land robbing, & revolutions will continue till justice is done. Madero promised justice, but he did not sweep the robber class out of the parliament as Villa will do: hence this class was able to overthrow him. Count me as a property holder, who insists upon justice to the people, however drastic: we have honest titles & do not fear a real patriot in control.

The philosophy of it all is that the administration's policy of watchful waiting will enable Villa to free his country, & that is what we should aid. But if we begin to use cannon & slaughter men, the policy of peace will be broken, & I hope it may not be. I wish Lind could whisper to Villa that he may become a Washington or a Bolivar, & to make this his aim.

Yours most sincerely   Geo. Fred Williams

ALS (W. J. Bryan Papers, DNA).

From Josephus Daniels

Dear Mr. President: Washington. May 12th, 1914

Adding to my statement to-day with reference to the forces the Navy could land in Mexico, I give you below the figures:

In addition to the nearly 3,000 marines now on shore at Vera Cruz, we can land 1,168 more marines from ship detachments. We can land 8,358 sailors, making a total of 9,526 we can land any day. They will be armed with rifles and machine guns and three inch field artillery. Added to marines now on shore, the Navy could therefore, place about 12,000 men in Vera Cruz, in addition to the 5,000 soldiers at Vera Cruz, making now in and near Vera Cruz 17,000 trained and armed men, ready for any emergency.

On the West coast, we have an organized marine brigade of 1,150 men, and can land from our ships 199 marines, 2,748 sailors, making a total of 4,097 well equipped and well armed sailors and marines.

When you reflect that within a few hours the Army and Navy could send 17,000 into the interior of Mexico if necessary, I think you will not be troubled by fear that we lack sufficient force to meet any emergency.

We could land all these men and still leave on the ships at Vera Cruz enough men to man the ships and use the guns to fully protect Vera Cruz. A study of these figures convinces me that there is no need for further movements and I thought they would reassure you.

Sincerely yours,   Josephus Daniels

ALS (WP, DLC).

To Josephus Daniels

Dear Daniels   The White House [May 12, 1914]
    Thank you with all my heart for the reassuring figures!
                            Woodrow Wilson

ALS (J. Daniels Papers, DLC).

From Edward Mandell House

Dear Governor: New York City. May 12th, 1914.
    I had a long talk with McAdoo today over the telephone.
    After explaining that Hamlin was eliminated and after telling him what Williams thought of Simmons, he seemed to be reconciled.
    I told him you had under consideration at the moment, Russell,[1] Hershey and Simmons. He thought with Warburg, whose letter I enclose,[2] that a Chicago man should be given a place.
    If Wheeler declines then a good combination would be Hershey and some Chicago or Northwest banker or business man that was big enough to be Governor of the Board.
    I am having one or two looked up to submit to you before I leave.   Your affectionate,   E. M. House

TLS (WP, DLC).
    [1] Probably Joseph Ballister Russell, real estate developer and financier of Boston. Wilson had met and played golf with him in Bermuda in 1910 (see WW to EAW, Feb. 20, 1910, n. 2, Vol. 20). Wilson had nominated him for Collector of the Port of Boston on May 29, 1913, but was forced to withdraw the nomination when Russell refused to accept the appointment for reasons of health and business.
    [2] It is missing.

To Scott Ferris

My dear Mr. Ferris: [The White House] May 13, 1914
    I feel just as strongly as you do the importance of the Alaskan Coal Leasing Bill, of the General Mineral Leasing Bill, and of the Water Power Bill, but I did not see when the House leaders conferred with me just how it was possible to put these bills on a programme which represented the effort of the party to carry out its platform obligations. Pray rest assured that I am deeply interested in the passage of these bills. I think that nothing could do us more good with the country in showing our interest in genuine conservation not only, but our knowledge of how to

handle conservation matters intelligently and sufficiently, than these bills. I am doing what I can to see that they are given a chance to get their fair showing.

> Cordially and sincerely yours,   Woodrow Wilson

TLS (Letterpress Books, WP, DLC).

To Franklin Potts Glass

My dear Glass: [The White House] May 13, 1914

Thank you for your letter of May ninth.[1] As I was saying to one of the Senators last night, I feel as if I ought, amidst my present perplexities and the unconscionable pressure of such a fluid matter as the Mexican situation, to put up in the office the sign that was put up on the organ loft of a country church for the defense of the organist. On it was written, "Don't shoot; he is doing his damnedest."

I dare say that your criticism of my acting too quickly and without hearing enough of what might be said is justly taken, and yet it is hard to know just what to do. When there is delay, there is a tremendous collision of opinions and a great contest sets in. When the appointment is promptly made there is a great chance for error, but there is the compensation of preventing a contest.

> In haste
> Cordially and faithfully yours,   Woodrow Wilson

TLS (Letterpress Books, WP, DLC).
  [1] F. P. Glass to WW, May 9, 1914, TLS (WP, DLC), implying that Wilson had been too hasty in his decision to appoint Congressman Henry D. Clayton to a federal district judgeship in Alabama.

To Lindley Miller Garrison

My dear Mr. Secretary: [The White House] May 13, 1914

Here is reassurance: There are at Vera Cruz 1,168 marines on the ships (that is, additional to those already on shore) and 8,358 sailors armed with rifles and machine guns and three-inch field artillery. The 8,358 sailors could be landed and yet leave men enough on board the ships to work the ships and the ships' guns and take care of all the approaches to Vera Cruz. We have, therefore, in fact, besides the men now on shore under Funston's command, 9,526 men who could be used as a really effective force.   Cordially and faithfully yours,   Woodrow Wilson

TLS (Letterpress Books, WP, DLC).

To William Bauchop Wilson

My dear Mr. Secretary: [The White House] May 13, 1914

Thank you sincerely for your very careful review in your letter of May eleventh of the statements made by the Colorado mine operators. They assist me very materially in understanding the situation.   Faithfully yours,   Woodrow Wilson

TLS (Letterpress Books, WP, DLC).

Sir Cecil Arthur Spring Rice to Sir Edward Grey

(No. 178. Confidential.)   Washington, May 13, 1914.

Representatives of oil interests were received by the President to-day, and tell me that he expressed entire confidence in Villa, who, he was sure, would allow no outrage on life or property.[1]

They are in possession of affidavits showing that Villa held many persons to ransom after the capture of Monterey and confiscated property on a large scale, and are convinced that he would do the same in the oil district when he obtained control. My Spanish colleague has similar evidence.

They fear that the President's language means that the United States Government is either ignorant or indifferent, and take a grave view of the situation. He is stated to have been quite inaccessible to argument. The United States consul who accompanies Villa[2] is, they say, agent for the sale of his stolen goods.

T telegram (FO 371/2028, No. 21537, PRO).
  [1] For another account of this meeting, see E. Grey to C. Barclay, July 2, 1914.
  [2] George C. Carothers.

From William Jennings Bryan

My Dear Mr President   [Washington, c. May 14, 1914]

The Columbia treaty is here but I assume you do not want it presented to the Senate until next week & *after* the tolls question is settled.

Can I promise Nicaraugua to present her treaty also as soon as the tolls question is settled? They are in desperate condition.

The Japan question is, according to promise, to go before the Senate immidiately after tolls question out of the way.

With assurances etc   Yours truly   W. J. Bryan

ALS (WP, DLC).

From Edward Mandell House

Dear Governor: New York City. May 14th, 1914.

I am enclosing you a letter from Mr. Warburg in which he makes a suggestion that seems to me good,[1] because of the fact that there will probably now be no one on the Board conspicuously prominent in the public mind as being suited to the place.

McAdoo is coming down tonight to be with me tomorrow for a last word about this and other matters.

I never hated to leave you so much as I do now, but I have the supremest confidence in the final outcome of all the difficulties which beset you. My thoughts will follow you day by day and I shall be glad when my face is turned westward again.

With a heart full of love for you and yours, I am,

Your affectionate friend,   E. M. House

P.S. We sail on the Imperator, Saturday at ten o'clock. My address will be, care, Brown, Shipley & Co. 123 Pall Mall, London. My cable address is, "Emhouse, care Shiprah, London."

TLS (WP, DLC).

[1] P. M. Warburg to EMH, May 12, 1914, TLS (WP, DLC), urging the importance of having someone from Chicago on the Federal Reserve Board, and suggesting that W. P. G. Harding would be a good choice for the governorship, even though the appointment would probably not arouse much enthusiasm in the beginning.

To Edward Mandell House

My dear Friend: The White House May 15, 1914

It is hard to say good-bye, but knowing what I do it is delightful to think of what awaits you on the other side, and it is particularly heartening to me to know that I have such a friend and spokesman.

Mrs. Wilson and my daughters join with me in most affectionate messages and in the hope that you will both find your trip refreshing and stimulating in every way.

Your affectionate and grateful friend,

Woodrow Wilson

TLS (E. M. House Papers, CtY).

To Charles Richard Crane

My dear Friend: [The White House] May 15, 1914

I ought not to delay longer my decision as to the Embassy at St. Petersburg. Do you still feel that it is impossible for you to release yourself from your engagements in this country and go? You know with what reluctance I have contemplated that decision, but whatever my personal feelings in the matter I must take the second best course if I cannot take the best.

With the warmest regard,

Cordially and faithfully yours,   Woodrow Wilson

TLS (Letterpress Books, WP, DLC).

To John Worth Kern

My dear Senator: [The White House] May 15, 1914

There are five bills which are of so great consequence both to the country and to the party that I venture to ask what their present status and prospects are on the calendar of the Senate. Their passage would show the country, and particularly the western part of the country, that for the first time there is a party in power which knows how to act constructively upon great matters about which there has been infinite debate but no intelligent action. The bills are:

S.4425, the Alaska leasing bill, now on the Senate calendar.

S.4898, the general leasing bill for coal, oil, phosphate and other lands, in committee on Public Lands, in charge of the sub-committee consisting of Senators Robinson, Pittman and Smoot.

S.4405, the radium bill, on Senate calendar. This bill has been held up for several months, during which time more than five hundred radium land claims have been filed.

S.4318, the Alaska Development Board bill, in Committee on Territories.

S.4373, Senator Smoot's mining commission bill.

I feel that you will consider them as important as I do.

Cordially and faithfully yours,   Woodrow Wilson

TLS (Letterpress Books, WP, DLC).

To William Allen White

My dear Mr. White: The White House May 15, 1914

Amidst the rush of my confusing days I do not often see editorials but my attention has been brought to your exceedingly generous recent tribute to myself.[1] I did not deserve it. I am only an ordinary chap spending his whole energy in trying to do his best, but that does not prevent my being deeply grateful even for praise that I do not deserve. I want you to know that it went to the quick when I read it and will henceforth constitute an additional stimulus to try to do difficult things in the right and conscientious way. Such utterances mean a vast deal to men in the midst of perplexities, and I am sincerely grateful.

Very cordially yours,   Woodrow Wilson

TLS (W. A. White Papers, DLC).
[1] He referred to "Our President," *Emporia, Kan., Gazette*, April 20, 1914. "How well he seems to have managed it—this whole sordid business of going to war"; it began, "how fair he has been; how patient, how dignified, how infinitely gentle and kind. No bluster, no threats, no snicker of anticipation, no licking of the nation's chops—just a simple-souled, brave, soft-hearted, hard-headed man. It is sad enough to go into war of any kind at any time; but it is less sad to go knowing that every honorable means has been taken to keep away from war. And this consolation President Wilson has given us by his wise, forbearing, Christian attitude before the provocation of a foe mad and desperate and foolish. The good God, who knows all and watches over all, and sees all, and directs all, was in our hearts deeper than we knew when as a Nation we choose this great, serene soul to lead us."

To Joseph Rucker Lamar and Frederick William Lehmann

Gentlemen: The White House May 15, 1914.

May I not express my sincere appreciation of your willingness to act as special commissioners of the President of the United States near the mediators who are to discuss a settlement of the difficult Mexican situation, and also my lively hope for the best possible outcome of the conference?

This letter is handed you to serve as your credentials in acting in this high capacity. I should like it known to all who may read this letter that you are authorized to take part in this conference as the special representatives of the President of the United States and that you are to be regarded as in every way speaking at his request and as enjoying his entire confidence.

Cordially and sincerely yours,   Woodrow Wilson

TLS (F. W. Lehmann Papers, MoSW).

From Edward Mandell House

Dear Governor: New York City. May 15th, 1914.

I had a long conference with McAdoo today. He is very earnest in his view that it would be risking a great deal to get a Board unfriendly to the spirit and purpose of the Act.

He thinks perhaps that Simmons of Saint Louis and A. C. Bartlett[1] of Chicago might be the best available timber, though he would like to look into Bartlett further and then report to you.

Charles R. Crane was with me this morning. He recommends Bartlett as being the best man available in Chicago. Bartlett is a retired hardware merchant, a man of philanthropic purposes and was on the original list that I gave you.

I hope you will talk to McAdoo freely before making an appointment for he has a fine conception of the purposes and scope of the measure.

Your affectionate friend,   E. M. House

Your letter of yesterday has just come. It touches me more deeply than you can ever know. Good-bye and more, and may God sustain you.

TLS (WP, DLC).
 [1] Adolphus Clay Bartlett.

Sir Cecil Arthur Spring Rice to Sir Edward Grey

CONFIDENTIAL.   Washington, May 15, 1914.

The Secretary of State told me yesterday that all is ready for sending adequate reinforcements if it becomes absolutely necessary, but that the President is absolutely convinced that active measures would only increase the danger of foreigners, and force us to await orders at Galveston. Assuming that all preparations are made, this would delay the expedition, if ordered, about a week. In the meantime the United States Government is taking measures to impress on Villa, and even Zapata (with whom they are trying to communicate), that they will incur the greatest personal danger if outrages on foreigners are permitted. Villa is believed to understand that the United States Government is ready and able to carry out this threat.

The attitude of the Secretary of State seems to have changed in the last few days, which is ascribed to the President's belief in mediation, by which he hopes that a settlement will be secured, including land and other reforms and the retirement of Huerta.

(Sent to Mexico.)

Printed telegram (FO 371/2028, No. 21922, PRO).

An Address on Commodore John Barry[1]

[May 16, 1914]

Mr. Secretary, ladies, and gentlemen: I esteem it a privilege to be present on this interesting occasion, and I am very much tempted to anticipate some part of what the orators of the day will say about the character of the great man whose memory we today celebrate. If I were to attempt an historical address, I might, however, be led too far afield. I am going to take the liberty, therefore, of drawing a few inferences from the significance of this occasion.

I think that we can never be present at a ceremony of this kind, which carries our thought back to the great Revolution, by means of which our government was set up, without feeling that it is an occasion of reminder, of renewal, of refreshment, when we turn our thoughts again to the great issues which were presented to the little nation which then asserted its independence to the world; to which it spoke both in eloquent representations of its cause and in the sound of arms, and ask ourselves what it was that these men fought for. No one can turn to the career of Commodore Barry without feeling a touch of the enthusiasm with which he devoted an originating mind to the great cause which he intended to serve, and it behooves us, living in this age, when no man can question the power of the nation, when no man would dare to doubt its power and its determination to act for itself, to ask what it was that filled the hearts of these men when they set the nation up.

For patriotism, ladies and gentlemen, is in my mind not merely a sentiment. There is a certain effervescence, I suppose, which ought to be permitted to those who allow their hearts to speak in the celebration of the glory and majesty of their country, but the country can have no glory or majesty unless there be a deep principle and conviction back of the enthusiasm. Patriotism is a principle, not a mere sentiment. No man can be a true patriot who does not feel himself shot through and through with a deep ardor for what his country stands for, what its existence means, what its purpose is declared to be in its history and in its policy. I recall those solemn lines of the poet Tennyson, in which he tries to give voice to his conception of what it is that stirs within a nation: "Some sense of duty, something of a faith, some reverence for the laws ourselves have made, some patient force to change them when we will, some civic manhood firm against

[1] At the unveiling of a statue in his memory in Franklin Park in Washington. Josephus Daniels presided at the affair.

the crowd"; steadfastness, clearness of purpose, courage, persistency, and that uprightness which comes from the clear thinking of men who wish to serve not themselves but their fellow men.

What does the United States stand for, then, that our hearts should be stirred by the memory of the men who set her Constitution up? John Barry fought, like every other man in the Revolution, in order that America might be free to make her own life without interruption or disturbance from any other quarter. You can sum the whole thing up in that—that America had a right to her own self-determined life. And what are our corollaries from that? You do not have to go back to stir your thoughts again with the issues of the Revolution. Some of the issues of the Revolution were not the cause of it, but merely the occasion for it. There are just as vital things stirring now that concern the existence of the nation as were stirring then, and every man who worthily stands in this presence should examine himself and see whether he has the full conception of what it means that America shall live her own life. Washington saw it when he wrote his Farewell Address. It was not merely because of passing and transient circumstances that Washington said that we must keep free from entangling alliances. It was because he saw that no country had yet set its face in the same direction in which America had set her face. We cannot form alliances with those who are not going our way; and in our might and majesty and in the certainty of our own purpose we need not and we should not form alliances with any nation in the world. Those who are right, those who study their consciences in determining their policies, those who hold their honor higher than their advantage, do not need alliances. You need alliances when you are not strong, and you are weak only when you are not true to yourself. You are weak only when you are in the wrong; you are weak only when you are afraid to do the right; you are weak only when you doubt your cause and the majesty of a nation's might asserted.

There is another corollary. John Barry was an Irishman, but his heart crossed the Atlantic with him. He did not leave it in Ireland. And the test of all of us—for all of us had our origins on the other side of the sea—is whether we will assist in enabling America to live her separate and independent life, retaining our ancient affections, but determining everything that we do by the interests that exist on this side of the sea. Some Americans need hyphens in their names, because only part of them have come over; but when the whole man has come over, heart and thought and all, the hyphen drops of its own weight out of his name. This man was not an Irish-American; he was an Irishman who became an American. I venture to say if he voted he voted with regard to the questions as they looked on this side of the water and not on the other side; and that is my infallible test of a genuine American—that when he votes or when he acts or when he fights, his heart and his thought are nowhere but in the center of the emotions and the purposes and the policies of the United States.

This man illustrates for me all the splendid strength which we brought into this country by the magnet of freedom. Men have been drawn to this country by the same thing that has made us love this country—by the opportunity to live their own lives and to think their own thoughts and to let their whole natures expand with the expansion of a free and mighty nation. We have brought out of the stocks of all the world all the best impulses and have appropriated them and Americanized them and translated them into the glory and majesty of a great country.

So, ladies and gentlemen, when we go out from this presence we ought to take this idea with us—that we, too, are devoted to the purpose of enabling America to live her own life, to be the justest, the most progressive, the most honorable, the most enlightened nation in the world. Any man that touches our honor is our enemy. Any man who stands in the way of the kind of progress which makes for human freedom cannot call himself our friend. Any man who does not feel behind him the whole push and rush and compulsion that filled men's hearts in the time of the Revolution is no American. No man who thinks first of himself and afterwards of his country can call himself an American. America must be enriched by us. We must not live upon her; she must live by means of us.

I come, for one, to this shrine to renew the impulses of American democracy. I would be ashamed of myself if I went away from this place without realizing again that every bit of selfishness must be purged from our policy, that every bit of self-seeking must be purged from our individual consciences, and that we must be great, if we would be great at all, in the light and illumination of the example of men who gave everything that they were and everything that they had to the glory and honor of America.[2]

Printed in *Address of President Wilson at the Unveiling of the Statue to the Memory of Commodore John Barry* (Washington, 1914), with corrections from the full texts in the *New York Times* and *New York Herald*, May 17, 1914.
    [2] There is a WWT outline of this address, dated May 16, 1914, in WP, DLC.

To Elias Milton Ammons

[The White House] May 16, 1914

Am disturbed to hear of the probability of the adjournment of your legislature and feel bound to remind you that my constitutional obligations with regard to the maintenance of order in Colorado are not to be indefinitely continued by the inaction of the state legislature. The federal forces are there only until the state of Colorado has time and opportunity to resume complete sovereignty and control in the matter. I can not conceive that the state is willing to forego her sovereignty or to throw herself entirely upon the Government of the United States and I am quite clear that she has no constitutional right to do so when it is within the power of her legislature to take effective action. Woodrow Wilson.

T telegram (Letterpress Books, WP, DLC).

To Josephus Daniels

My dear Mr. Secretary: The White House May 16, 1914

I understand that you are to speak on Monday at my old Alma Mater, Davidson College. Will you not be kind enough to convey my cordial greetings and to say with how sincere an interest and affection I remember the college and wish it the best possible enlarging fortunes?

Cordially and sincerely yours, Woodrow Wilson

TLS (NcDaD).

From Elias Milton Ammons

Denver, Colo., May 16, 1914.

I regret exceedingly that you have been misinformed. The legislature has just passed an act which I have approved providing for a bond issue of one million dollars for the purpose of paying the indebtedness which has been incurred and which may be incurred in suppressing insurrection and defending the State. As soon as these bonds can be issued these funds will be available and this State can and will control the situation. This is the only constitutional method of raising funds in immediate future. In addition to this act the legislature has enacted a law permitting the governor to close saloons in times of disorder and also a law prohibiting the carrying and disposition of firearms in times of disorder, moreover a committee on mediation on the present strike has been provided for and appointed.

E. M. Ammons.

T telegram (WP, DLC).

Benjamin Barr Lindsey to Joseph Patrick Tumulty

Personal

My dear Mr. Tumulty: Denver May 16, 1914.

I have been importuned by some of our citizens to come to Washington for a personal interview with President Wilson over the strike situation here. Truly, my dear Mr. Tumulty, the situation is serious, and I think almost hopelessly desperate unless President Wilson can bring about a settlement. If the federal troops are withdrawn, there is not the slightest question, in my mind, that there will be bloodshed and disorder of the most serious kind and a terrific loss of property and human life. I believe that President Wilson can solve the whole situation and that public sentiment will be strong enough to back him up and approve a plan some of us have to propose. In general, it would involve keeping the militia here and closing down the mines and calling on the two contending parties to submit to arbitration before a board to be appointed by the President that would be acceptable to both sides or to which they could find no objection. Somehow, I believe that Mr. Rockefeller and his interests would welcome this solution, and I have also reason to believe that the labor people would, though of course I do not speak with any authority or assurance from either. It is my surmise and opinion from what I know of the situation. I feel quite confident that it would bring about a prompt and complete settlement of the entire matter, and result in the saving of millions of money and undoubtedly many human lives. The legislature has been a grievous disappointment in many ways. It will undoubtedly adjourn today, with the situation just about as bad, if not worse than ever.

Would I be asking too much to ask you to wire me on receipt of this letter if President Wilson could see me for a brief half hour sometime Saturday, May 23rd? I figure that I can leave here Wednesday morning and get to Washington Friday evening or Saturday morning. I will wire you just when I shall arrive. My plan is also to attempt to see Mr. Rockefeller, Jr., in person. I want to try and present the matter to him from a different angle and in a different light from that in which he views it as a member of his company, and see if he will not take the position that if the President feels that it is necessary to appoint such a commission as a military necessity and in the interests of peace, that he will not object to it at least, and agree to co-operate in such a settlement. I think it would give him the chance to get out from under the difficulty he is now in, which, in my judgment, comes from listening to bad advice.

I am figuring that you will get this letter by Tuesday afternoon, and if you could send me a night wire I would receive it Wednesday morning.[1]   Sincerely yours,   Ben B Lindsey

TLS (WP, DLC).
[1] Lindsey's well publicized trip to Washington and New York was inspired and financed by the journalist George Creel and the muckraking novelist Upton Sinclair, both of whom were active in the miners' cause in Colorado at this time. Lindsey left Denver on May 17 with a party which included three women and two children who had survived the Ludlow Massacre. One of the women, Mary Petrucci, had lost three children at Ludlow. Wilson received the group at the White House on May 21, listened sympathetically to their harrowing stories, and expressed his deep concern over the situation in Colorado. John D. Rockefeller, Jr., refused to see Lindsey or his party. See the *New York Times*, May 18 and 22, 1914, and George S. McGovern and Leonard F. Guttridge, *The Great Coalfield War* (Boston, 1972), pp. 276-78.

A News Report[1]

[*May 18, 1914*]
WILSON TELLS U.S. ENVOYS ARMY WILL STAY IN MEXICO UNTIL PEACE IS GUARANTEED

WASHINGTON, May 18.—President Wilson spent an hour this afternoon in final conference with the American Commissioners to the mediation conference at Niagara Falls—Justice Lamar of the Supreme Court and former Solicitor-General Frederick W. Lehmann, with H. Perceval Dodge, their secretary.

The President told the commissioners that the settlement of the entire Mexican problem in some definite form must come before our forces are recalled from Vera Cruz.

This settlement, the President said, seemed to him to necessitate the elimination of Huerta's government and the establishment in its place of a provisional administration that can conduct an election giving fair treatment to all factions and guaranteeing a solution of the internal problems that have bred revolution for the last three years.

The economic system for which Zapata has been fighting in the south, as well as Carranza and Villa in the north, is to be included in the scheme of settlement, the President said, and at the same time it must embrace the rightful interests of the people in the territory still controlled by Huerta. This exends it, of course, to the trouble-breeding agrarian problem, but it goes beyond that.

Mr. Wilson spoke hopefully of mediation. He declared his earnest desire that it should succeed, and broadly intimated that every legitimate influence at the disposal of the Washington Government would be exerted to insure its success.

He laid emphasis upon his conception of the United States' duty to seek unselfishly to assist Mexico to set up a government which could be accorded recognition by the world because of its capacity, not alone to maintain peace at home but to observe its international obligations. . . .

President Wilson is forming a Mexican policy to which he will pledge the Government of the United States when Gen. Huerta is finally eliminated as dictator and hostilities in Mexico have ceased.

This policy has for its foundation the breaking up of the Cientifico or landed party, the splitting up of the great estates and their disposition so that the peons, who compose about 85 per cent of the population, may obtain them.

Whoever succeeds to the Presidency of Mexico must guarantee the acceptance of this new policy of the American Government as a precedent condition to his recognition by the United States.

Moral support of this policy the President hopes to obtain from the nations of the world. He has discussed phases of it with the Ambassadors and Ministers of the principal nations here and is of the opinion that he will have the moral support of the world.

It must be given, many of the President's advisers believe, to make the policy successful. By keeping the Monroe Doctrine alive and strong the President can force this moral support, they think.

A high official of the Administration said to The World representative to-night that money would be the power which would force any new government of Mexico to an acceptance of the policy and the giving force to a guarantee that it will be carried out to the letter.

Whoever becomes head of the Mexican government will need funds. The nation will have to borrow a great amount to even begin a restoration of order. While the United States Government under its constitution cannot loan Mexico any money, there are many American bankers ready to advance vast sums when the United States is willing to approve the loans and guarantee the payment of principal and interest.

Thus an acceptance of the President's new policy would open the vaults of American banks to the Mexican Government.

The World's informant cited this extract from a speech of Tiberius Gracchus, made about 133 B.C., as describing conditions in Mexico and as the reason why the President will demand a guarantee that his policy will be carried out by the Government of that country:

> The wild beasts of Italy have their caves to retire to, but the brave men who spill their blood in her cause have nothing left but air and light.

> Without houses, without settled habitations, they wander from place to place with their wives and children, and their generals do but mock them when at the head of their armies, they exhort their men to fight for their sepulchres and the gods of their hearths, for among such numbers perhaps there is not one Roman who has an altar that has belonged to his ancestors or a sepulchre in which their ashes rest.

> The private soldiers fight and die to advance the wealth and luxury of the great, and they are called masters of the world without having a sod to call their own.

The President has had ever before him this condition. In the beginning, when he asserted he would not recognize Gen. Huerta, he made the pledge to himself he would do his utmost to force Huerta's successor to a realization of this situation, and that there must be a change. The President and his advisers believe the Mexican Constitution broad enough to make such an achievement not only possible but a reality.

It is intended to make the Mexican constitution a living one, and give to the peons those rights which are theirs under the Constitution, but which they always have been denied.

But present day conditions alone have not persuaded the President. He has studied the Mexican situation of the past also, and studied its social and economic history.

It is not Huerta alone, either, who caused the President's determination, but it is what Huerta represents and what every Mexican when he gets into office represents—power and the landed gentry. It was this condition which forced Zapata to revolt, that drove Madero to revolution and later caused his overthrow.

All of this was in the President's head when he sent instructions to Fletcher at Vera Cruz to stop the shipment of arms and ammunition to Huerta. It was there when he accepted the offer of Argentina, Brazil and Chili for mediation.

That the mediators will be successful in inducing Huerta to

eliminate himself is the President's hope. If they do not his plans will not be altered, for when Huerta is driven into flight the President will begin his negotiations with the revolutionists for the carrying out of his plans.

He expects aid from Carranza and Villa, for they have told him through representatives that they are fighting only for the liberation of the peons from slavery.

Printed in the New York *World*, May 19, 1914.
[1] The following exclusive report was obviously based upon a conversation with Wilson.

To Walter Hines Page

My dear Page: The White House May 18, 1914

First, let me tell you that the pending Consular and Diplomatic Appropriation Bill carries an item of $15,000 for the payment of the rentals at London.

And, second, as to the attitude of mind on that side of the water toward the Constitutionalists, it is based upon prejudices which cannot be sustained by the facts. I am enclosing a copy of an interview by a Mr. Reid[1] which appeared in one of the afternoon papers recently and which sums up as well as they could be summed up my own conclusions with regard to the issues and the personnel of the pending contest in Mexico. I can verify it from a hundred different sources, most of them sources not in the least touched by predilections for such men as our friends in London have supposed Carranza and Villa to be.

These hasty notes of mine to you carry a real freight of deep regard and gratitude to you for all that you are doing. Your letters illuminate what they touch and are of immense service to me. I wish I had the time and the spirits for such letters such as I would love to write to you. I must merely dash these things off as the moment offers. I hope that you are getting now something like systematic information. I have tried to arrange for it in the department.

In haste
        Cordially and faithfully yours,   Woodrow Wilson

TLS (W. H. Page Papers, MH).
[1] Wilson referred to John Reid [Reed], "The Causes Behind Mexico Revolution," *New York Times*, April 27, 1914. Reed argued that the revolution in Mexico was basically a movement by the masses of peons to regain lands taken away from them by the great landowners during the Díaz era. An interest in democratic government had arisen only later and secondarily among the peons as a result of their participation in the revolution. Reed praised Zapata and Villa for their support of the cause of the masses but asserted that Car-

ranza had no real interest in restoring the land to the people. He concluded his statement with a bitter denunciation of the occupation of Veracruz by the United States. Reed is identified in n. 1 to W. Phillips to JPT, June 6, 1914.

To Andrew Carnegie[1]

My dear Mr. Carnegie: The White House May 18, 1914

The very generous way in which you responded to my little note of a few weeks ago about Berea College and the Southern mountaineers makes me bold to write you another letter about that subject, because my own interest is very deep and of long standing in this matter. My former letter was too brief and hasty to make clear the things I feel you will wish to know.

There is really an extraordinary condition in the Southern mountains with which the general public is by no means acquainted. My own early experiences in visiting the mountains and my later studies have put me in possession of some very significant facts.

Our Southern mountain region is vast and its people have been more isolated than any other white people in the world. They need very special educational treatment,—prompt aid and aid of the right kind.

They are the very stuff out of which America was made, capable, good-intentioned, vigorous and prolific. The educational aid they get or fail to get in the next few years will greatly affect the question of *what elements shall dominate in the future of America.*

We must, of course, do our best for the South Europeans who come and for the colored people already here, but I feel that it is hazardous and heartless longer to neglect this great mass of people of our own stock and traditions.

The case is made urgent[2] by the present invasion into the mountain regions of mining camps and commercial interests. These promise ultimate good, but they will demoralize and spoil the simple mountaineers unless they can be quickly furnished with some education of the right sort.

It seems to me that the wise plan is to give the mountaineers one well-equipped institution which can produce patterns and[3] leaders and do for them what Hampton is doing so effectively for the colored people. All who know this mountain field feel this deeply,—the need of a Hampton for the mountains.

Berea stands ready and suited to be developed into such a school. It is the oldest, largest and best adapted of all existing institutions of that kind. It has experience, devotion, proved ability, and already possesses the confidence of the mountain and the Southern people.

But the means are insufficient. Two million dollars ought to be raised by the friends of Southern education for this purpose, and I feel great confidence in appealing to you to give your serious attention to this large enterprise.

I should not write in behalf of any ordinary institution; but this is a cause of general concern, long neglected, and in danger of being pushed aside until it is too late to save this precious American element. The conference for education in the South just held at Louisville brought forward no problem to compare in importance than[4] this one.

I feel that you have a right to lasting satisfaction in the immense service to the Nation you have rendered in the line of negro education, and it seems only the natural corollary that you should do for this three million white population something commensurate with their particular need. The South and the Nation would certainly appreciate such action.

I know that many others will support my judgment in this important matter.

Wishing you a pleasant and refreshing summer and a happy return,

> Cordially and sincerely yours,   Woodrow Wilson

TLS (A. Carnegie Papers, DLC).
    [1] Wilson dictated this letter after a conference with William G. Frost at the White House at 12:45 P.M. on May 18.
    [2] Wilson dictated "apparent" to Swem.
    [3] Wilson dictated "potential" instead of "patterns and."
    [4] Wilson dictated "to."

To Henry De Lamar Clayton

My dear Judge: [The White House] May 18, 1914

May I not say that you take with you in the assumption of your new duties as Judge my most cordial good wishes?

It is a happy circumstance that the work I was counting upon you to assist in, namely, the maturing of the legislation with regard to the trusts, has been practically completed. Only the guidance of the matter for the committee on the floor of the House remains, and you are surrounded by men in your committee highly qualified for that task.

May I not thank you for your unremitting attention to this great subject and express the satisfaction that I have had in working with you and in bringing this important matter so near completion?

> Cordially and sincerely yours,   Woodrow Wilson

TLS (Letterpress Books, WP, DLC).

From William Jennings Bryan

My Dear Mr President,   [Washington] May 18 [1914]

The Sec of the Treasury of Liberia—a colored man[1]—is here on business. Mr. Phillips thinks it might be well to show him some attention and suggests that he give him a dinner or luncheon—inviting just a few. I do not think any thing is absolutely necessary though he would, of course, appreciate it. Remembering the fuss raised by the Booker Washington incident I thought I had better get your opinion before approving of Mr Phillips plan.[2]

Mr Swarez intimated that while he thought the Mexican delegates would agree to the necessary reforms and agree to having the provisional gov't issue the necessary decrees for the reforms he thought it would be necessary to have Caranza sacrifice his ambitions. I told him I thought that would depend upon whether the reforms were *sufficiently satisfactory* and were secured *before* the election. I think the personel of the government may be harder to agree upon than the principles.

With assurances of esteem I am my dear Mr President
                    Very truly yours   W. J. Bryan

ALS (WP, DLC).
  [1] John L. Morris.
  [2] Wilson did not reply in writing.

From Elias Milton Ammons

Sir: Denver May Eighteen Nineteen Fourteen.

Supplementing my telegram of Saturday with reference to the strike situation in this state, I desire to assure you the state authorities will proceed as rapidly as may be to prepare and dispose of our bonds, as authorized by the extraordinary session of the legislature just closed, in order to be in a position to take care of the situation in this state. In the meantime the joint committee appointed by the General Assembly will make an earnest effort to bring about a termination of the strike. In everything the authorities here wish to act in entire harmony with the wishes of yourself and the national administration. Without the help of the federal government I fear it will be exceedingly difficult to bring about a settlement. This unfortunate industrial dispute is not a local affair and is controlled by forces from beyond our boundaries. We have exhausted every means suggested to secure an agreement here. Being an interstate issue I fear we will not be able to succeed without assistance from the national administration.

The public mind here and elsewhere has been so inflamed through exaggerated and untruthful representations of what has occurred in the strike district, and the contending forces have become so bitter against each other that I believe it would be much better in the interest of the protection of both life and property if the Federal troops can be kept in the field for some time. They would probably make conditions much easier for accomplishing a settlement.

If there is any information you desire please command me. I assure you the people of the state appreciate your assistance in this emergency.

Regretting exceedingly that it has seemed necessary to trouble you with our local affairs at a time when the Mexican situation must demand all your time and attention, I am

Sincerely yours,   E M Ammons.

TLS (WP, DLC).

From Charles Richard Crane

Dear Mr President   Chicago May 18, 1914

I am very unhappy to be obliged to write you that I do not see any hope of being able to serve you at St. Petersburg within any reasonable length of time. I have tried hard to arrange my affairs so as to take part in your great work and am entirely discouraged at the result. If you find an ambassador satisfactory to you, please appoint him and I shall do everything in my power to aid him. You have been very good to think of me in this way and also to be so patient about it.

Yours always faithfully   Charles R. Crane

ALS (WP, DLC).

From John Philip White

Fort Smith, Ark., May 18, 1914.

Colorado Legislature adjourned, having done nothing except appropriate money to pay debts of militia who murdered our men, women and children at Ludlow, and other places. Acting upon request of our Colorado officials we recommend that federal troops be not withdrawn at this time for if militia returns they fear repetition of Ludlow outrages. We further recommend that steps be taken to close down those mines.

John P. White.

T telegram (WP, DLC).

From William Jennings Bryan

My Dear Mr President,   [Washington May 19, 1914]

Gov Lind wants to go home for awhile but I am inclined to think he had better stay for awhile—we do not know when we may need him. What do you think?

2nd Mr Hall[1] thinks Mr Martinez[2] the Zapata envoy, ought to be here to represent Zapata's views on the agrarian question[.] Hall claims that Zapata represents more people than Caranza.[3] This may be an exageration but we need all the light we can get and I see no objection to Martinez being here. He will leave some one through whom Hall can keep in touch with Zapata. What do you think?

3d The Chilian minister, Mr. Swarez, reports (confidentially) that Mexican delegates are in a favorable mood. He thinks they will agree to the things necessary.

4th Do you think it would be worth while to encourage an agreement by which the Constitutionalists would agree to suspend hostili[ti]es during mediation on condition that Federal forces be withdrawn from Saltillo, San Louis Potosi & all territory north of Tampico. We need to have the Constitutionalists in the conference to be sure of a satisfactory settlement. Lind thinks they would not agree to anything but he expects them to be in capital within a month.

With assurances etc I am

Very truly yours   W. J. Bryan

ALS (WP, DLC).

[1] Hubert L. Hall, born in the United States but a long-time resident of Cuernavaca, Morelos, Mexico, and a strong supporter of Emiliano Zapata and his agrarian revolution. He had come to Washington in April to seek aid for the *Zapatistas*. See Larry D. Hill, *Emissaries to a Revolution: Woodrow Wilson's Executive Agents in Mexico* (Baton Rouge, La., 1973), pp. 245-49, and John Womack, Jr., *Zapata and the Mexican Revolution* (New York, 1969), pp. 236-37.

[2] Jacobo Ramos Martinez. He was later exposed as an extortionist, whose claims to represent Zapata were false. See Hill, *op. cit.*, pp. 247-51.

[3] In H. L. Hall to W. J. Bryan, May 14, 1914, TLS (WP, DLC), which Bryan enclosed with his letter.

To William Jennings Bryan

My dear Mr. Secretary,   [The White House] 19 May, 1914.

I think I have already explained that this little machine is my pen, and that when you see this type you may know that I am writing with my own hand, and not by dictation.

This is to answer your note of this evening,—at least handed me this evening.

First. I quite agree that we cannot spare Lind while these mediation negotiations are in progress, though it is probably hard on him to keep him.

2nd. It is a very good idea to have Mr. Martinez, or some other confidential friend of Zapata's, here while this business is under settlement.

3rd. The Chilean Minister's information is most gratifying. All the signs seem for the present good.

4th. I do not think it worth while to try for a cessation of arms between Huerta and the Carranzistas. We could not get it; and it may be useful to have the Mexican delegates feel that things will settle themselves if they do not promptly come to terms.

Faithfully and heartily,   Woodrow Wilson

WWTLS (W. J. Bryan Papers, DNA).

To Elias Milton Ammons

My dear Governor Ammons: [The White House] May 20, 1914

Thank you for your telegram in reply to my own. I hope sincerely that you will turn out to be right in thinking that the Legislature has taken adequate measures to meet the present extraordinary conditions in the State.

I hope, however, that you will pardon me if I say that I was not entirely reassured by what you told me of the measures adopted by the Legislature:

As I understand that action, it provided some $300,000 over and above the amount already expended for the maintenance of the National Guard of the State in active service; gave you authority to take necessary precautions, such as closing the saloons, etc., in time of disorder; and authorized the appointment by you of a board of conciliation.

But the serious part of the situation, so far as I am informed, is that *any* action by the military forces of the State is apt to kindle the flame again into its old violence. What is your own judgment and expectation? Will the operators consent to enter into negotiations which will cover the whole matter in controversy? If they will not, what course do you think it will be feasible for you to pursue?

I ask these questions because of my very serious doubt whether it is my constitutional privilege to remain in the State very much longer in the absence of assurance that the State is permanently unable to handle these serious affairs, an assurance which, of course, I know that the Legislature of the great State of Colorado would not think of giving. It is in the light of this doubt and difficulty that I feel I ought to ask what the programme immediately ahead of you is, what steps you expect to take, and what prospect of success you think lies ahead of you.

I know that you will understand and sympathize with the motives which lead me to make these earnest inquiries.

Cordially and sincerely yours,   Woodrow Wilson

TLS (Letterpress Books, WP, DLC).

To Lindley Miller Garrison

My dear Garrison: [The White House] May 20, 1914

Will you not be kind enough to have the men on the ground there ascertain for me, if they can, the present strength of the National Guard of Colorado and the probabilities as to its recruitment and capacity, so far as strength is concerned, to handle the situation out there in the near future? I dare say they can find this out better than we could through the extraordinary Adjutant General of the State[1] if we were to apply to him.

Faithfully yours,   Woodrow Wilson

TLS (Letterpress Books, WP, DLC).
[1] John Chase, ophthalmologist of Denver and brigadier general in command of the Colorado National Guard. He was militantly anti-union and a leader in the efforts to suppress the strike of the Colorado coal miners. See McGovern and Guttridge, *Great Coalfield War, passim.*

From William Jennings Bryan, with Enclosure

My Dear Mr President   [Washington, May 20, 1914]

I have tried to embody your instructions in a telegram. If you will make such changes as you like I will have Mr Davis put it in cipher & send it from White House

With assurances etc   Yours truly   W. J. Bryan

ALS (SDR, RG 59, 812.00/23452b, DNA).

ENCLOSURE

American Commissioners   [Washington, D. C., May 20, 1914]

From reports which have reached us from entirely reliable sources we learn that Mexican delegates are ready to agree to Huerta's elimination and the establishment of a provisional government made up of men favorable to agrarian reform. You are therefore justified in urging that those members of the provisional government selected from territ[or]y controlled by Huerta shall be in sympathy with policy of dividing up large landed estates. They will doubtless object to Caranza being one of provisional government but he should be free to run as a candidate. The reforms agreed upon should be put into operation by decree before the election and all candidicates should be pledged to the support of the decree.   Bryan[1]

WJBhw telegram (SDR, RG 59, 812.00/23452b, DNA).
[1] Swem made a typed draft without any changes by Wilson, except to correct Bryan's misspellings. The CLST telegram sent is SDR, RG 59, 812.00/23452b, DNA.

From William Gibbs McAdoo

Dear Governor: Windsor, Vermont. May 20th, 1914.

We are having such a wonderful time of rest and peace in this paradise, that I have been unwilling to get back to the World, even with a business letter until I had to, so you must forgive me for not having written to you sooner about the Federal Reserve Board. Again I thought it possible that I might return to Washington by this time, but I learn through telephone communications with Washington that the Tolls fight is in good shape, and that affairs in the Department are going smoothly. So we have decided to stay until June first, unless some exigency arises.

I enclose two significant Editorials from the New York Sun,[1] one of the most subservient champions of the Money Trust and interests. They protest against a regulation of the Organization Committee, concerning Election of Directors of the Reserve Banks. The Organization Committee is in sympathy with the purpose and spirit of the Federal Reserve Act. The rulings have, therefore, favored always the carrying out of the Act in accordance with one of the objects of its creation, viz. to deprive the "Money Trust" of the arbitrary power and unfair advantage it has exercised so long under the present system.

Had the Organization Committee been out of sympathy with the Act and hostile to the Administration, its rulings on this question would, undoubtedly have favored the Wall Street view as expressed by the Sun.

I mention this because it emphasizes the point I have made with you several times, viz. that it is most important, in fact, to my mind, *vitally important*, that at least four members of the Federal Reserve Board should be men of known sympathy with

[1] The enclosures are missing, but they were "Another Attack on the Banking Centres," New York *Sun*, May 14, 1914, and "The Election of Reserve Bank Directors," *ibid.*, May 18, 1914.

the spirit and purposes of the Federal Reserve Act and of undoubted loyalty to the Administration.

A meeting of the "Big Banks" of New York (composing the
largest in capital of the three groups into which the Banks have
been classified by the Organization Committee) was held in New
York City yesterday. A Committee was appointed to confer with
similar committees of the other two groups with a view to an
agreement on the six Directors who are to represent the banks on
the Board of the Federal Reserve Bank. Mr. Hepburn made a
speech in which he said "Bankers are not politicians; they can
and will work harmoniously." This indicates what may be expected throughout the Country, viz. A *solid* banker front in the
Reserve banks, making it absolutely necessary that a majority,
at least, of the Reserve Board shall be independent of the Bankers
influence and loyal to the administration in the critical and
formative period of the Federal Reserve System.

There are many questions of administration and interpretation to be decided by this Board during these next two years. The
definite character and form of the System will be shaped by this
Board. I do not want to tire you with an enumeration of the many
important points that the Reserve Board must determine, but I
shall mention one merely by way of illustration: Section 16 of the
Act provides among other things, "that the Federal Reserve Board
may, at its *discretion*, exercise the functions of a clearing house
for such Federal Reserve Banks, or *may* designate a Federal
Reserve Bank to exercise such functions, and *may* also require
each such bank, to exercise the functions of a clearing house for
its member banks."

The purpose of this provision was to do away with or to destroy
the power of the existing privately owned and despotically controlled Clearing Houses, in the different cities, through which the
money power has been able to tighten its hold on the finances of
the country.

The Federal Reserve Board is not *compelled* to make the Federal Reserve Banks exercise these clearing house functions. Warburg has already said to me that he thinks it wise to defer action
in this particular. Involved in this, is the question of the substitution of a system of check clearances for the present slow, cumber-
some and expensive system of check collections. This will be
revolutionary, but of enormous advantage to the business of
the Country. My judgement is that these reforms should be effected as quickly as possible. Bankers will, I believe, generally oppose them as long as possible.

All Government Directors of the Federal Reserve Banks are

chosen by the Federal Reserve Board and it alone has the power of removal.

Now if four members of the Federal Reserve Board happen to have the view of the reactionaries and hide-bound bankers of the Country, the clearing house and check clearance system may be long deferred. Directors for the Government, may be unsympathetic with the Act, and the power of removal may not be exercised in the public interest.

Moreover, experience will demonstrate, beyond doubt, that some ammendments and changes in the Act are needed. Suppose a majority of the Board recommend to Congress, changes that the Administration does not favor? It would precipitate an awkward fight. I should not be afraid of a *minority* recommendation. The recommendations of this Board are going to have weight with the Country and with Congress.

There are many other important powers which the Board is to exercise. A subservient majority of this Board could give the Money Trust great comfort.

We have fought a great fight to win what we have got. Your administration is likely to be judged more by the success of the Federal Reserve System than by any other single act because it is bound to have a profound effect upon the economic future of the Country.

We have the selfish interests in our control if we do not now, from over confidence or to take, as you have expressed it a "sporting chance," put that control in jeopardy.

No one likes better than I do, to take a sporting chance—but is it wise or reasonable to do it *unnecessarily* in a matter of such grave importance? Where the vital interests of the Country are at stake, I believe in playing safe. Especially when it can be done, as in this case, with such good reason and justification.

Please don't think me unduly fearful of the "Money Trust." I am not. I simply know, after a year's experience in the Treasury, that it is not a fiction, but a real thing and I want to keep the upper hand for the people while we have it.

Of the three men who have accepted, I think Miller is absolutely sympathetic with the Act, and the Administration; Harding being a Democrat, would naturally incline that way politically. I do not know where he will stand on the Act itself. He has been a Banker, always, having close affiliations with New York and he may take the Bankers view on important questions. I should consider him doubtful. Warburg is, as is well known, one of the Chief Champions of the Central Bank idea. His leanings will probably always color his rulings and judgments in favor of the Wall Street view. Already he has told me that he thought the Organization of the Reserve Banks should be delayed until the decision of the Organization Committee can be reviewed by the Reserve Board; also that he thinks the twelve units of the System should be grouped in to three or four and so administered as to practically make three or four Reserve Banks, out of the twelve. This idea he strove hard to have incorporated in the Bill, but I successfully opposed it.

If you would, therefore, appoint one more man upon whose cooperation Miller, Williams and I could count, we could depend upon an interpertation of the Federal Reserve Act and an administration of the Federal Reserve System in the interest of *all* the people, and not of any particular class. This, to my mind, is the paramount consideration.

Of all the men I know or who have been mentioned, Hamlin is the ideal one for the two year term. I fully appreciate the force of the objections you have raised to him, but after all, are they not out weighed by the manifest advantages of his appointment? He has unusual qualifications for this position. His long experience in finance, Law and economics—his valuable work in the Treasury Department, and his loyalty to the Administration argue strongly in his favor. I am sure the Country would approve. Politically I think it would be wise. I wish very much that you would ask Mr. Olneys opinion of Mr. Hamlin, and get his judgement as to the wisdom of his appointment before you act.

If, however, you are decided against him, then my next choice would be George W. Norris, of Philadelphia—but not for the two year term. I think the man who is made Governor should have the two year term. Norris is a progressive Democrat, a high minded citizen, and has your ideals. He has had a banking experience and is a man of high character and ability.

If you appoint Norris, you could offer the two year term to Simmons of St. Louis. He has a great business reputation and I think too that he would pull with us. The only difficulty about this is that Simmons is probably a Democrat, and this would leave but one Republican, (Warburg) on the Board. Probably Simmons could qualify, as a Republican! Many democrats have voted that way, during the past ten years.

If you don't take Norris, then Simmons being given the two year term, Bartlett could be given the long term. I understand that Bartlett is a Republican. This would complete your Board, but we would be able to count absolutely on only *three*.

If you should decide, on Simmons, please see Houston and let him tell you how to go about securing Simmon's acceptance, otherwise you may not get him. Houston knows just what must be done.

I do not think well of the Hershey suggestion. He is, I understand, a good Lawyer, but I am sure that his appointment would be a mistake. Already the Baltimore District is represented on the Board by Comptroller Williams. This District is not important enough to justify dual representation in the Board. I do hope you won't make the Hershey appointment. I think Colonel House agrees with me about this, since I gave him my reasons.

To sum up: I respectfully urge:

1 Hamlin as first choice for the two year term.
2 Simmons as second choice for the two year term.
3 Norris for the long term if Simmons should be chosen.
4 Bartlett for the long term if Hamlin is chosen.
5 If neither Hamlin nor Norris is chosen then I suggest Simmons for the short term and Bartlett for the long term.
6 If the Board should consist of Hamlin, Warburg, Bartlett, Harding and Miller, I should make Hamlin Governor and Harding Deputy Governor.
7 If the Board consists of Simmons, Bartlett, Warburg, Harding and Miller, I should make Simmons Governor and Harding Deputy Governor.
8 If the Board consists of Norris, Bartlett, Warburg, Harding and Miller, I should make Harding Governor and Bartlett, Deputy Governor. It would hardly do to make Bartlett Governor, as I think it better to name a Democrat for this position.
9 If the Board consists of Norris, Simmons, Warburg, Harding and Miller, I should make Simmons Governor and Harding Deputy Governor.

I should like to impress upon you another reason for having at least *four* men on the Board who will act in harmony. The Secretary of the Treasury has such large powers under the Act, and his cooperation is so essential to the success of the System that it would be most unfortuanate and harmful to the Administration, if he should find himself in a minority on this Board, and be forced to act independently. I do hope that this may not happen. After two years it won't make so much difference because by that time the System will have been well established.

I need not tell you how relieved I should be and how secure I should feel about the Federal Reserve System during this crucial period, if my argument should convince you of the advisability of appointing Hamlin. I do not want to urge it against your settled convictions and you know, dear Governor, that I shall accept cheefully your judgement whatever it may be. I think

the Board should be completed without further delay, and I
hope that these suggestions may be of service to you.

If you should prefer to confer with me personally about this
matter, before you act, please telegraph me, and I shall be
glad to return immediately. I shall really feel better if you will
send for me, if you want me.

It seems almost brutal to inflict you with such a long letter
and I should spare you the punishment, but for the great importance of this matter.

Nell is looking splendidly and we are having a surpremely
happy vacation. We hope that you keep well, and that you and
all of you may soon be able to come here for a long delightful
rest.

The real truth is that since you have given me this glorious
girl, I don't care very much what you do with the Federal Reserve
Board!

With love for you all,

Devotedly yours,   W G McAdoo

P.S. I have a very poor "typist" so please excuse errors!

TLS (WP, DLC).

The Special Commissioners
to William Jennings Bryan

RECEIVED AND DECIPHERED
AT THE WHITE HOUSE.

Niagara Falls, New York, May 20, 1914.

We met mediators 9:30 this evening and they brought
forward as a plan of their own suggestion and which they
believed was feasible and could be made acceptable that General Huerta should appoint as Minister for Foreign Affairs a
man of standing and character and of Constitutionalist principles
who would be satisfactory to the Constitutionalists, neutrals, and
to the United States and then he should himself resign, the
person appointed as Minister for Foreign Affairs thereupon succeeding under the constitution of Mexico as provisional President and thereupon steps would be taken to carry out a constructive program, that is the election of a President and Congress
under the Constitution and with provision for the reforms
deemed to be essential to permanent results. That upon the retirement of General Huerta and the accession to the presidency of
the person appointed as Minister for Foreign Affairs as before
stated there should be an end of all hostilities and a general

amnesty, and for the purpose of making an end of hostilities if there should be any attempt to continue them, that there be an embargo upon the importation of arms and ammunition; the embargo to take effect upon the retirement of General Huerta and the succession to the provisional presidency of the Constitutionalists provided for in the manner stated. As one man who might well be considered for the provisional presidency the mediators mentioned Senor [Pedro] Lascurain, who was Minister for Foreign Affairs appointed by Francisco Madero and who upon the death of Madero would and should have succeeded to the provisional presidency if he had not been forced to resign by General Huerta and who might therefore be considered to be the Constitutional and Constitutionalist successor to Francisco Madero. But the mediators stated that there might be other persons chosen who would be entirely satisfactory.

While the mediators had had a conference with the Mexican representatives during the day the proposition was not made as coming from the Mexicans, but was suggested on the part of the mediators themselves as their own plans and coupled with the statement that they believed that it would be acceptable [to] Mexican representatives. And plan of course was predicated upon the assumption that General Huerta would resign and as to this they seemed to be very sanguine. The argument was that arms ought no longer to be imported when there was no occasion for further war, Huerta having been eliminated. They also seemed to assume that in the election that would be held the Constitutionalists would inevitably be successful, having the prestige of victors in the field.

We stated to the mediators that we could not at present give them an answer and might not be able to do so in the morning when they are to have a formal conference with the Mexican representatives.   Commissioners.

T telegram (WP, DLC).

To the Special Commissioners[1]

[The White House] May 21, 1914

We are pleased and encouraged by the character of the proposal contained in your telegram of last evening. It will be necessary for us to ascertain the actual attitude and environment of Lascurain before forming a judgment and we would appreciate it very much if other names were suggested of men whose connections and sympathies we could at once look up. Meantime, we hope that this alternative plan may be frankly discussed, namely, the appointment of such a man as Lascurain and the association with him of someone actually chosen by the now victorious party, and of a third man chosen by the two in order to get away from the apparent succession to Huerta and set up an authority free from former cabinet influences and exceptional enough in the very circumstances of their authority to undertake with a free hand the formulation of the decrees of reform to be ratified by the Congress in due time elected. Is it too early to obtain opinions with regard to the scope and character of the agrarian reforms which would be involved?

T telegram (WP, DLC).
[1] There is a WWsh draft of this telegram in WP, DLC.

The Special Commissioners to William Jennings Bryan

RECEIVED AND DECIPHERED
AT THE WHITE HOUSE.

Niagara Falls, New York, May 21, 1914.

On receipt of your wire at once met mediators and found them in no sense opposed to the alternative plan suggested in your telegram of today, one preferring it, the others not objecting but thinking their original suggestion was more in consonance with constitutional form. In addition to the name mentioned last night, they suggested General Rafael Angeles, Chief of Artillery, Constitutionalist Army, Luis Cabrerra, Ernesto Madero and Bonilla,[1] a member of Carranza's Cabinet, and stated they would make inquiries of Mexican delegates as to whether they thought these names would be satisfactory to all concerned, and would ask delegates for other names. They were unable to give the present whereabouts of several of the persons named. As to the reforms, they expressed themselves as willing to go as far as might be thought proper, having in mind that this remains the peculiar work of Mexican people and government, but that the provisional government remains pledged to an immediate effort to solve the question desired, the guarantee of good faith solely to be found in the personnel of the provisional government. The mediators seemed very anxious as to embargo and amnesty, expressing the belief that the mediation will be weakened as the Constitutionalist Army advances on Mexico City.

Commissioners.

T telegram (WP, DLC).
[1] The aforementioned were Felipe Angeles, Luis Cabrera, adviser to Car-

ranza, Ernesto Madero, uncle of Francisco I. Madero, who had served as minister of finance in President Madero's administration, and Ignacio Bonillas, minister of communications and development in Carranza's cabinet.

To the Special Commissioners

[The White House] May 21, 1914

In view of the commanding position the constitutionalists have secured in Mexico and the necessity of considering the views of those whom they represent the President suggests that you ask the mediators whether they do not consider it advisable to renew the invitation to the constitutionalists to send commissioners without attempting to define the scope of what is to be discussed and without reference to the suspension of hostilities. It is likely to involve many delays and uncertainties if the discussion is conducted without them and it is extremely difficult to confer with them satisfactorily by indirect ways such as are open to us here.

Bryan.

WWT telegram (SDR, RG 59, 812.00/23452c, DNA).

To Charles Richard Crane

Personal and Private.

My dear Friend: [The White House] May 21, 1914

It is cheering to be associated with anybody as disinterested as you are. I value your letter of the eighteenth very highly. It fills me with admiration at the same time that it brings me a great disappointment. I cannot find a real substitute but I will look around and see what the field affords.

In haste, with the warmest regard,

Faithfully yours,   Woodrow Wilson

TLS (Letterpress Books, WP, DLC).

From Sir Cecil Arthur Spring Rice, with Enclosures

Dear Mr President   Washington. May 21 1914

I have the honour to enclose paraphrase of a cypher telegram which I have received via London from Mexico in which Carden describes the result of an interview which he had with Huerta on Tuesday night with the object of persuading him not to allow his personal claims to stand in the way of any settlement which the mediators might see fit to recommend.

I have also the honour to enclose paraphrase of a telegram from Sir Edward Grey on the subject of the Mexican situation in which he expresses his confidence that your government will exercise a salutary influence over the Constitutionalist leaders.

I have already spoken in this sense to the Secretary of State and informed him that I would send you copies for your convenience.

I sincerely hope that Mrs Wilson is making good progress.

I have the honour to remain dear Mr President, with the highest respect   Yours very sincerely   Cecil Spring Rice

ALS (WP, DLC).

E N C L O S U R E   I

Washington.

Sir Lionel Carden reported on May 20 that at an interview with him General Huerta had promised to instruct his representatives at Niagara Falls to announce his intention to cooperate loyally with the mediators, and to add that he himself would not be an obstacle to any settlement which the mediators may recommend in order to provide Mexico with a guarantee for peace and order.

E N C L O S U R E   I I

Telegram from Sir Edward Grey to Sir Cecil Spring Rice, dated May 20, 1914.

The previous record of the troops employed by the Constitutionalist party justifies apprehension, although their behaviour at Tampico shows that such apprehension is not always justified. I agree with the Secretary of State that further advance of the troops of the United States might precipitate further disorder and anti-foreign violence and I do not urge the use of force. But I am confident that the United States Government will continue to exercise the influence which they have over Villa personally in order to ensure innocent persons from violence and to prevent outrages on life and property.

T MSS (WP, DLC).

From Lindley Miller Garrison

My dear Mr. President: Washington. May 21, 1914.

In further response to your letter of May 20th about the Colorado National Guard.

At the last inspection, about a year ago, of the National Guard of Colorado, it mustered 137 officers and 1309 men, of which approximately one thousand were infantry, and the rest were cavalry, artillery and auxiliary troops.

Curiously enough, the Assistant Adjutant General of Colorado and one of the Majors of the Guard[1] came in to see me today, and I took occasion to examine them to ascertain the situation, with the following result: They think that at the present time they could not at the outside get more than 800 infantry and, say, 400 cavalry, artillery and auxiliary troops; they doubt whether they could get this many. They say that they doubt if they could get any new enlistments for strike duty. They further say that among the men that were on guard in the strike districts not more than twenty-five had previously been mine guards. They also say that some of the men who were in the militia served as mine guards at times when the militia was not in the field; they place this number at about twenty-five also. They have recruited a new company at Walsenburg and Trinidad, which is right in the heart of the biggest strike district. This company consists of 150 men, all of whom have been connected in some capacity with the mining industry, and probably many of them, if not all, still are so connected.

This answers all of your questions, excepting as to their "capacity, so far as strength is concerned, to handle the situation out there in the near future." With regard to this, these two officers were of exactly opposite opinions. The Assistant Adjutant General felt that if the State Troops were put into the field again now, the chances were that the old bitter resentment on the part of the strikers against the State Troops would lead to conflict; the younger man, the Major, seemed to feel that they could handle the situation without serious consequences.

All of our officers in the field have reported to me that the feeling against the State Troops is very bitter, and that, in their judgment, if the State Troops were returned to the strike districts, there would undoubtedly be trouble.

The Assistant Adjutant General of the State told me that the Governor's state of mind concerning this matter was as follows: That if the United States Troops were withdrawn upon the assumption that peace had been restored, he would consider that matters were in a state of quietude and would not send troops into the districts until after outbreaks had indicated the necessity therefor.   Sincerely yours,   Lindley M. Garrison

TLS (WP, DLC).
    1 The Assistant Adjutant General of Colorado cannot be identified. The major was almost certainly Edward J. Boughton, major of the Colorado National Guard and lawyer of Denver, who had been sent to the East Coast by the Governor and Adjutant General of Colorado to publicize the state's version of the story of the coal strike. See McGovern and Guttridge, *Great Coalfield War*, pp. 280-84.

Two Letters from Andrew Carnegie

My Dear Friend   New York May 21st, 1914

I leave for the Moors Saturday morning feeling that you are in grave danger—& of course our Country. Your interview in Philada's Saturday Post[1] if correctly reported commits you to the task of righting Mexicos wrongs altho your first words are a challenge to prove that liber[t]y was ever handed down from *above*. You assert it is always attained by the forces working from below by great movement of the people.

Yet you promise it from above. The more Civilized Nation is to begin Civilization in Mexico. If you succeed it will be proof against your challenge. If not, history is to vindicate your Contention.

Knowing the Sister Republics well, I tremble, seeing you as it were on the brink of a precipice where one mistep brings such disaster to our Country as the Civil War alone entailed

My hope is that you will soon see that our departure from Mexico,—having tried our best to promote peace by friendly counsel *but not by War*,—is our duty,—for it is true that real progress in Civilization comes from the abused Masses below, as you state, not from the Rulers of Foreign Countries possessors of higher Civilization.

The presuming Civilized Nation determined to interfere and Coerce his less advanced nabor deserves repulse and usually gets it

I would give millions this moment to see my Country, after having exhausted friendly Kindly, heartfelt advice to our poor & troubled sister Republic,—peaceably recalling it's forces.

Numerous Engagements, freedom of Two Cities—Speech National Liberal Club (note Wales now free from a foreign Religious Hierarchy)[2] & several others. These call me abroad but my thoughts will be in Washington hoping that the kind fates will open the path of withdrawal for you, in peace.

Nothing will justify War. Poor distracted Mexico against our gigantic resources, what a sad page in history this would be. With every good wish, I am your deeply concerned friend

                                    Andrew Carnegie

ALS (WP, DLC).

[1] Printed at April 27, 1914, Vol. 29.

[2] A bill providing for the disestablishment of the Church of England in Wales passed in the House of Commons on May 19 for the third consecutive session, thus insuring its enactment despite the opposition of the House of Lords. See Kenneth O. Morgan, *Wales in British Politics, 1868-1922*, rev. edn. (Cardiff, 1970), pp. 259-71.

My dear Mr President: New York, May 21 1914

I am in receipt of your very interesting letter regarding Berea College and the possibilities of its work. Your letter reaches me only two days before sailing for Skibo, and too late for me to go into an immediate enquiry concerning the scope of the Institution.

I believe, however, that the following method would not only meet your views but would in the end be of great service to the Institution itself. There is, I believe, quite a general feeling among those familiar with education that some form of industrial training is the most necessary education for the Southern mountain whites. I think, however, there is considerable dout among those acquainted with the conditions in this region as to whether one such institution as Berea can reach the three or four millions of people in these remote mountains. It may perhaps be wiser to develop several such institutions on a more modest scale. For example, I have been urged to help the Lincoln Memorial University at Cumberland Gap, on the ground that it could serve this same population.

The best plan to pursue in attempting to assist in the development of this mountain people can perhaps only be determined by a thorogoing examination of the work at Berea, which would indicate fairly whether its work is mainly local or whether it can serve to advantage in an educational way this large area.

I will call on the Carnegie Foundation to have such an examination made during the Autumn, and when the results are brot together I will endeavor to giv assistance to whatever plan seems in the judgment of those who know the conditions, to promis the best results.

You may be sure that your recommendation of the greatness of this cause gives it high importance in my eyes, not only because it is from the President of the United States, but because it comes from one who has an expert knowledge of education. In addition, my sympathy is drawn to this body of Scotch-Irish Americans who have so long been isolated from the great mass of our citizens, and I would esteem it a privilege to be connected with a cause which effectively helped toward development and particularly to a closer communion with their fellow citizens, upon which advanced civilization depends.

Ever Yours   Andrew Carnegie

TLS (WP, DLC).

From William Goodell Frost

My Dear President: New York, May 21st, 1914.

Your letter did its work. Dr. Pritchett is to be sent down to see the mountains in October, and assures me that "a million, or more if needed" will be forthcoming for sound plans for effective educational work adapted to the conditions.

And he conspires with me to draw other capitalists into the project.

You did two great things on the 18th of May, 1914—arranged the Niagara Mediation and started this higher conservation for our native stock.

I am glad to be your contemporary and your agent.

Sincerely,   Wm Goodell Frost

ALS (WP, DLC).

To Andrew Carnegie

Personal

My dear Mr. Carnegie: The White House May 22, 1914

Allow me to acknowledge the receipt of your two letters, and to express my pleasure in learning that you are to have an exhaustive survey made of the Berea College situation.

I note what you say of the Mexican situation, and assure you that the matter of effecting a peaceful solution is very near to my heart.   Sincerely yours,   Woodrow Wilson

TLS (A. Carnegie Papers, DLC).

To William Goodell Frost

My dear Doctor Frost: The White House May 22, 1914

Thank you for your letter of May 21st. I am delighted to hear the result of your mission, and congratulate you heartily on what I feel sure will be a successful outcome.

Cordially and faithfully yours,   Woodrow Wilson

TLS (W. G. Frost Papers, KyBB).

The Special Commissioners to William Jennings Bryan

RECEIVED AND DECIPHERED
AT THE WHITE HOUSE.

Niagara Falls, New York, May 22, 1914.

Acting upon your telegram of 21st we made an appointment with the mediators for 1:45 p.m. today and at that time as requested by you inquired whether they would not consider it advisable to renew the invitation to the Constitutionalists to send Commissioners without attempting to define the scope of what was to be discussed and without reference to suspension of hostilities. After extended discussion the mediators answered individually and as a body that as the Constitutionalists had definitely declined the invitation personally extended to them and had declined to recognize anything except the issues between General Huerta and the United States as appropriate to the mediation, all questions relative to reforms to be for the Constitutionalists themselves to determine, it would not be consistent with the honor of the Nations represented by the mediators nor with the dignity or prestige of the mediation itself to renew the invitation.

Commissioners.

T telegram (WP, DLC).

Lincoln Steffens to Joseph Patrick Tumulty

Dear Mr. Tumulty: New York City, May 22, 1914.

Frank Walsh came back yesterday from Washington, and told me that the President said that he had not said to me what Mr. Walsh quoted me as saying about the pardoning of labor leaders. The President is quite right. Mr. Walsh didn't quote me with the precision of a reporter. Good citizens aren't as accurate as we newspaper men are.

But Mr. Walsh's conclusion from his interview with the President is alarming to me. He is inclined to drop the whole matter. I do not think the President means to have it dropped, and I wish you could find an opportunity, when he is not too preoccupied, to set me right on it.

You remember the business. I spoke to the President about it before his inauguration, and again about two months ago. At that time, I told you also about it. And, in brief, it is a proposition to the President and to the governors of states to declare a sort of general amnesty in the labor war by pardoning certain individuals who are serving sentences for distinctly labor crimes; and the purpose of it would be to turn, if possible, attention from prosecution and aggressive fighting to a reasonable inquiry into the labor problems which the Committee of Industrial Relations is making.

If there is any doubt about it, do let me come down to Washington next week some day to see you and, if possible, the President.

Please let me add that, while I do not think my thing is the most important thing in the world, and I realize to the full all the many more important subjects, I do think this matter of dealing generously and even beautifully with the labor problem is worth the few minutes time I am asking. Just to show you how the thing goes when properly presented, I may tell you that Governor Glynn of New York told me he would do his part in such a general action and do it gladly. He is the only governor I have spoken to so far, but I stand ready to go to California to see Governor Johnson, who would have the most serious cases to deal with; and others.

With my compliments to the President, I remain,

Yours very sincerely,   Lincoln Steffens

TLS (WP, DLC).

To Theodore Roosevelt

[The White House] May 23, 1914.

Glad to learn you are to be in Washington on the twenty-sixth. Will you not give me the pleasure of lunching with me at one on that day.[1]   Woodrow Wilson.

T telegram (Letterpress Books, WP, DLC).

[1] Roosevelt was coming to lecture to the National Geographic Society on his recent experiences in South America and to confer with members of Congress and officials of the Progressive party. He did not come to lunch at the White House on May 26, but he did visit with Wilson for twenty-five minutes in the late afternoon. The *New York Times*, May 27, 1914, reported that the two discussed "travel and books, the visit being entirely social." It also noted that they "told stories" and that "all controversial subjects were avoided."

Three Telegrams from the Special Commissioners
to William Jennings Bryan

Niagara Falls, N. Y. May 23, 1914.

The mediators requested that we meet them at twelve and thereupon stated that the situation in Mexico City was very urgent owing to the fact that the report of General Huerta's possible resignation was constantly weakening his position, both in the city and in the country at large with the result that there was a constantly increasing danger of mob rule and anarchy; that while it was possible for him to withdraw with his army to Pueblo [Puebla], where there was a much stronger military defensive position, such withdrawal would not only leave Mexico City exposed to anarchy, but would lead to a prolongation of the war. Besides this the mediation was operating harmfully to the weaker party and to the benefit of the stronger so long as arms could be obtained by Carranza and not by Huerta.

They further state that when they made their first suggestion as to the plan at the first conference they had only stated that they believed it to be feasible and practicable but had since learned definitely that the Mexican representatives had plenary power and would be [prepared] to have him resign and a provisional government or provisional junta appointed by him or in some method satisfactory to the American government, provided only that coincident with such resignation and the appointment of the provisional government or junta, an armistice should be arranged, or if Carranza would not consent to an armistice that then a general embargo be imposed. Such an embargo they regarded as equivalent to an armistice.

Their information being that the failure to advance is largely due to the lack of ammunition.

The immediate appointment of the provisional government or provisional junta they consider of prime importance to the protection of life and property and while they are willing to have such appointment coupled with decrees on the subject of land reform they thought that discussion of that subject might well be somewhat deferred in order to secure a[s] satisfactory plan as possible.

This outline is sent in order that you may have the substance of the proposition before you in replying to the inquiry contained in the telegram of last night as to which the Mediators asked this morning if we had an answer. This dispatch will be followed by one which will [present] more at length the views and arguments advanced by the Mediators at the conference held this morning. We are likely to adjourn to attend a meeting at six this afternoon when the Mexican representatives will also be present.

Commissioners.

Received and translated at
The White House, May 23, 1914.

Niagara Falls, N. Y., May 23, 1914.

The views of the Mediators expressed with great earnestness are as follows:

Mediation between the parties in Mexico is practically impossible while active hostilities are continued. A cessation of hostilities is therefore imperative, and this may be obtained either by an armistice agreed to by the parties or by a general embargo against munitions of war which would have the same practical effect.

General Huerta is represented before the mediators and the understanding is general that he will resign. His authority is weakened thereby, while General Carranza is strengthening day by day. The restraint of the mediation proceedings is operative only upon the weaker party.

There is grave danger of anarchy in Mexico City as a consequence of the existing situation, which should be promptly met.

General Huerta will give way to a Provisional president or junta, but there must be coincident with this an armistice or embargo to insure respect for the provisional government. For General Huerta to to [sic] resign without a provisional government to succeed at once, with moral support of armistice or embargo, is to incur the danger of anarchy.

That settlement is impossible if General Carranza is to continue operations in the field, unreserved in any way and not committed to and even in advance repudiating any adjustment reached by the mediation.

The provisional government whether a president or a junta of three or five should be attained by pursuing constitutional forms as far as possible and so not be a government imposed by strangers.

Above all things a truce of some kind is imperative. From now on every success gained and every advance toward Mexico City made by Gen. Carranza impairs the work of mediation and his arrival in Mexico City before the work of mediation is accomplished means the end of it.

In connection with the first step, the establishment of a provisional government, there must be an armistice or what is equivalent thereto. Work of a permanent nature may then be taken up and carried as far as deemed appropriate.

Commissioners.

RECEIVED AND DECIPHERED
AT THE WHITE HOUSE.   Niagara Falls, N. Y., May 23, 1914.

At six o'clock the conference was opened with a statement by the Ambassador of Brazil that it had been called at the request of the Mexican delegates. Thereupon Senor Rabasa[1] said that they had been instructed to state at the first meeting where it could be done that General Huerta's sole idea was the good of Mexico and that he was willing to resign if that would contribute to such an end, but that his resignation could only be upon the fixed condition that it would contribute to the establishment of firm government. The American representatives expressed satisfaction at what had been stated by Senor Rabasa and inquired as to whether he was prepared at that time to discuss what he conceived to be the conditions which would establish a firm government, to which reply was made that the Mexican representatives heartily approved of their method of private conference with the mediators and preferred to adopt that method of expressing their views upon that subject and having them communicated to the American representatives. The American representatives then inquired as to whether there would be a public statement of General Huerta's willingness to resign or whether it was desired by the Mexican representatives that the communication should be treated as confidential. With great earnestness they insisted that they regarded it as of great importance that the matter should be treated as confidential. The meeting adjourned and the mediators requested us to meet them again and the time was fixed for tonight at ten.   Commissioners.

T telegrams (WP, DLC).
[1] Emilio Rabasa, one of Huerta's delegates.

Notes for a Telegram to the Special Commissioners

[May 24, 1914]

Embargo proposed would, if effectual, be intervention: that is, it would inevitably lead to armed control of the movements of the constitutionalists and to direct administrative control at Mexico City, with the support of arms.

We wish (and, without intervention, can) only to set the stage for a settlement and receive guarantees that a settlement will be effected. Seeking to make use of us to prevent a standpat cataclysm,—to head off the Revolution; whereas we must see the Revolution through, while seeking to moderate its processes as much as possible. To that end, conditions sine quibus non: Huerta's withdrawal (already inevitable);

A provisional authority to effect the transition;

A pledge from that authority that the necessary reforms will be effected.

We are inclined to believe that it would be unwise to attempt to work out the details of the reforms anywhere but at Mexico City and through the provisional government.

Before we insist on *any*thing from the constitutionalists we must know what it is that we are to insist that they accept.

For the whole thing depends, if there is to be no force used by the U. S., on acceptance of the programme by the Carranzistas.

Our weapon: RECOGNITION.

WWT and WWsh MS (WP, DLC).

A Draft of a Telegram

[May 24, 1914]

Mexico[1]

We cannot refrain in response from expressing our grave concern at the plan disclosed. To encourage or even to countenance any interference in the internal affairs of an independent country with which we are at peace, when that plan plainly involves the possible use of armed force, would be a manifest violation of our sacred obligations to the entire world. We feel it to be our plain duty to see that no plans for controlling the politics or government of Mexico should emanate from or be guided, directed, or assisted from the United States or by any of its citizens. With every effort to bring peace and orderly government, with liberty, to that distressed country every thoughtful American must of course sympathize, but ⟨Americans⟩ citizens of the United States are not at liberty to take any part in such efforts, either directly or indirectly, beyond the limits of the moral power of public opinion.

1) Can deal only with the facts as they are.
2) Must deal with them if possible without any use of armed force on our part.
3) The removal of Huerta by one process or another is inevitable and the only question remaining being how he will be eliminated.
4) The present object is to find a method by which the inevitable can be accomplished ⟨peacefully⟩ without further bloodshed. By the inevitable we mean the transfer of political power from Huerta to those who represent the interests and aspirations of the people.
5) To attempt to put a stop to the present processes of revolution before we have a peaceful method to suggest would be impracticable and futile because based upon no fixed program.
6) See notes. The use of force by the United States against the *Carrancistas* can be justified only by the rejection ⟨of definite⟩ of terms ⟨which they⟩ of such a character ⟨that they could not afford to reject them⟩ that refusal on their part to accept them would be clearly indefensible ⟨in the view of the whole world⟩.

T Transcript (WC, NjP) of WWsh (WP, DLC).
[1] Words in angle brackets crossed out by Wilson.

To the Special Commissioners

[The White House] May 24, 1914

The President directs me to say:[1]

CONFIDENTIAL. It is clear to us that the representatives from Mexico are keenly aware that General Huerta no longer has the force or standing to insist on anything; and they of course cannot expect us to supply him with the force or influence he lacks. We get the impression that the Mexican representatives are chiefly anxious that we should by some means intervene to prevent the complete success of the revolution now in progress. We on our part cannot afford in right or conscience to do that and can only act in the spirit and for the purposes expressed in the propositions I shall presently state. We are encouraged by your despatches to believe that the mediators realize the situation in all its elements as fully as we do, as shown by their willingness that a representative of the constitutionalist cause should exercise the powers of the provisional presidency and that a constitutionalist should be chosen president at the elections which would follow. We appreciate this very much and see in it a great hope for a logical and complete settlement.

Please present to the mediators as you have occasion and in the way you think best the following considerations and conclusions by which we feel that we must be guided:

First, we can deal only with the facts in Mexico as they now stand. Concerning them it is too late to exercise any choice or effect any change.

Second, We must deal with those facts, if possible and get our solution out of them without the use of the armed force of the United States.

Third, the elimination of Huerta by one process or another is now clearly inevitable, the only question remaining being the method, the occasion and the circumstances of his elimination.

Fourth, the object of our conferences now is to find a method by which the inevitable can be accomplished without further bloodshed. By the inevitable we mean not only the elimination of Huerta but the completion of the revolution by the transfer of political power from Huerta to those who represent the interests and aspirations of the people whose forces are now in the ascendency.

Fifth, to attempt to put a stop to the present processes of revolution before we have a peaceful method to suggest would be impracticable and futile because based upon no definite programme. It would, moreover, in all probability, very soon force active intervention upon us and delay and confuse all we have hoped for.

Sixth, we can at the present stage of things do little more than set the stage for a settlement and demand guarantees that a settlement will be effected. Before we can insist on the acceptance of anything by the constitutionalists, even the cessation of arms, we must know what it is that we are to insist that they accept. The whole settlement obviously depends, if there is to be no force used by the United States, on the acceptance of the programme by the Carranzistas. The use of force by the United States against them could be justified only by their rejection of terms of such a character that refusal on their part to acc[e]pt them would be clearly indefensible, terms which meant the full attainment of the just objects of the revolution without further bloodshed.

Seventh, we are inclined to believe that it would be unwise to attempt to work out the details of the reforms involved anywhere but at Mexico City and through the proposed provisional government.

We suggest that a prompt agreement upon a clear programme which the constitutionalists can accept is the best and only way to stop the process of arms.   Bryan

WWT telegram (SDR, RG 59, 812.00/23452d, DNA).
    1 WJBhw. Hereafter such insubstantial insertions by Bryan and others will not be noted.

Two Letters to Mary Allen Hulbert

Dearest Friend,   The White House 24 May, 1914.

I have sent you two letters addressed to Sandanwede, without knowing for certain that you were there, because, when you last wrote you were on the point of leaving for Nantucket. I am sending another letter there to-day, which I am anxious to have you receive on your birthday. This is only a line, written on the chance that you are still in Boston, and to let you know where my letters have been going.

With most affectionate messages from all,
                    Your devoted friend,   Woodrow Wilson

My dearest Friend,   The White House 24 May, 1914.

This letter is timed to reach you on the twenty-sixth, and to wish you many, many happy returns of the day. I wish I knew just how to say the interesting things that are in my mind when I think of your birthday. The thoughts are interesting because *you* are so interesting. A birthday chronicles more in the case of a person so *vital* and quick with everything that life contains and suggests than it can mean in the case of any other sort. I never knew anyone who had contributed more to those with whom she was thrown than you have; and a life that scatters life wherever it goes counts double, treble, quadruple. I have so often noticed how each circle you joined brightened, how each person you spoke to seemed awakened and put at his best, as if challenged by the life in you. It is wonderful. You give out so much, indeed, that you do not always keep enough for yourself to live on, worse luck, and are sapped and tired, and feel yourself "no good" merely because you have given out all the good to others in extraordinary largess. So that in wishing you many happy returns I am really wishing the rest of the world the happiness: though you yourself could not escape your large share of it if you only realized what you do for others. I know that I myself am more deeply in your debt than I can ever hope to pay. It quickens and helps my dull faculties even to think of you! Write, please, and tell me how and what fares with you. I am well, much as I feel the loss of my two sweet daughters from out the house. Most of what you read in the papers about me is false, invented; but I am managing to see a little light in the Mexican matter and to make a slowly increasing number of other people see it; and the load of other things is not yet, I am surprised to find, intolerable, though I sometimes *think* it so. Do you remember how I predicted once in Bermuda that the presidency would probably kill me? Well I think so still; but somehow the catastrophe does not come off!

    With affectionate best wishes from all,

Your devoted friend   Woodrow Wilson

WWTLS (WP, DLC).

To Joseph Patrick Tumulty

Dear Tumulty: [The White House, c. May 25, 1914]

    I would be very much obliged if you would say to Mr. Steffens that attractive as I found his idea (and my thought has so often returned to it that he may rest assured that no further presentation of it is necessary) the more I thought about it the more unwise I deemed it to act upon it.

    Please impress on Mr. Steffens my warm appreciation and the genuine consideration I have given to this matter.

The President.

TL (WP, DLC).

To Charles William Eliot

My dear Doctor Eliot: The White House May 25, 1914

    I certainly owe you an apology for not having acknowledged sooner your letter of May seventh, to which your letter of May twenty-first[1] again calls my attention. I need not tell you that I read your earlier letter with the greatest interest and appreciated the friendly purpose which led you to put such things into my mind for my guidance.

    I, of course, do not know exactly what dispatches were in the hands of the lecturer at the meeting to which you refer, but there was evidently one misapprehension as to the facts. Martial law was not declared at Vera Cruz. What happened was this, that when, after earnest solicitation, we found that the Mexican officials were unwilling to resume their authority and administer the city, we were obliged to furnish administrative officers ourselves from the Army and Navy. This is government by military persons but it is not military government, inasmuch as we are seeking in every respect to administer Mexican law, not our own.

Cordially and sincerely yours,   Woodrow Wilson

TLS (photostat in RSB Coll., DLC).
  [1] C. W. Eliot to WW, May 21, 1914, TLS (WP, DLC).

To James Woodrow, with Enclosure

My dear James: [The White House] May 25, 1914

At last I have been able to complete an inscription for my dear father's tombstone. I enclose it herewith. I hope that it is not too long to fit the stone that is prepared.

There is one point I shall have to get you to verify for me. The Southern and Northern branches of the Presbyterian Church have almost exactly the same names. One is the General Assembly of the Presbyterian Church in the United States; the other is the General Assembly of the Presbyterian Church in the United States *of America*. I think that the Southern Assembly has the shorter title as I have used it in the inscription, but I shall have to ask you to make sure of that.

All unite in sending most affectionate messages to you all.

Faithfully yours,   Woodrow Wilson

TLS (Letterpress Books, WP, DLC).

E N C L O S U R E

JOSEPH RUGGLES WILSON

Son of James and Anne Adams Wilson
Born at Steubenville, Ohio, 28 February, 1822
Died at Princeton, New Jersey, 21 January, 1903.

Pastor, teacher, ecclesiastical leader
For thirty-four years Stated Clerk of the General
Assembly of the Presbyterian Church in the United States

Steadfast, brilliant, devoted, loving and beloved.
A master of serious eloquence, a thinker of singular
power and penetration, a thoughtful student of life
and of God's purpose, a lover and servant of his
fellow men, a man of God.[1]

T MS (WP, DLC).
¹ This is the epitaph on Dr. Wilson's tombstone in the cemetery of the First Presbyterian Church in Columbia, S. C. There is a WWT draft of the epitaph in WP, DLC.

An Estimate of His Father

[c. May 25, 1914]¹

Joseph R. Wilson

I remember my father as essentially humble and devout before God, spirited and confident before men. A natural leader, with a singular gift of clear, eloquent, convincing speech. Generous, playful, full of high spirits, and yet given to most laborious industry, alike in the use of books and in the administration of church affairs. A man who believed much more in the efficacy of Christian simple and pure living than in dogmatic advice or spiritual conversation,—a robust Christian.

The description I naturally associate with his name would be something like this:

Generous, high-spirited, thoughtful, studious, a master of men and of thought, who sought the life of dogma in conduct and preferred a pure life to a pious profession.

Transcript (WC, NjP) of WWsh (WP, DLC).
¹ The date ascribed to this document is purely arbitrary.

The Special Commissioners to William Jennings Bryan¹

RECEIVED AND DECIPHERED
AT THE WHITE HOUSE.

Niagara Falls, New York, May 25, 1915 [1914].

In your telegram of the 24th you suggested that we submit to the mediators, in the manner we thought best, the points therein mentioned. After discussing it among ourselves and in view of matters hereafter to be stated we deemed it advisable not to read to the mediators either the telegram or extracts from it but arranged for a meeting at ten p.m. We then stated to the mediators that because of the consequences to which it might lead and the responsibilities that might be involved the President could not accede to their plan of securing an armistice or forcing an embargo, but that he recognized that their suggestion for the withdrawal of Huerta and the appointment of a provisional government composed of Constitutionalists contained the germ of a plan that should be successful where all were interested in the speedy cessation of arms.

We further stated that we did not desire to invade the province of the mediators and would not at this time undertake to outline any plan unless they themselves desired that we should do so. After considerable discussion among themselves they requested that we should make any suggestions as a basis for discussion in which each one could frankly and without being committed feel at liberty to propose whatever might occur to him. Though they did not express themselves they were evidently disappointed at the failure to secure an armistice. That fact coupled with statements of previous meetings as to the serious personal and official embarrassment in which they felt themselves to be placed as mediators induced us to say as little as possible about the matters contained in items four and six. For while we construed six to contemplate a plan which though acceptable to the United States *might* be rejected by Carranza, and while item four did not exclude the idea of provisional government, yet we feared that the mediators would raise serious personal and official objections if they construed the proposal as a whole to contemplate *a direct transfer of government from Huerta to Carranza.* Our apprehension was based on their previous expressions of what they conceived to be the function of mediation and their personal and official obligation to the parties before them. Having this in mind therefore, we only stated generally that the President considered that nothing could be done until some specific plan had been agreed upon and that therefore the first and necessary step was to formulate that which was not only acceptable to the parties to the mediation, but so just that the Constitutionalists might be invited to accept its definite terms. In answer to their inquiry as to how such plan would be carried into effect and what would follow if Carranza rejected it, we stated that those were matters beyond the present scope of the mediation and that the method of enforcement was a matter for Executive determination and action. *Qus.*[2] This brought on a general discussion during which they asked if the *status quo* would be maintained? *Yes.*[3] If the embargo against shipments of arms across the Texas border would continue? *Yes*[4] If it would be a violation of the truce if beyond the limits of the port of Vera Cruz Huerta gunboats should undertake to stop ships carrying arms to Carranza? If they might assume that representatives of all Mexican parties would be appointed in the provisional government?

We replied that while nothing had been (said) upon the subject, we assumed that the status quo would be maintained pending negotiations but could not answer as to the gunboats and made no assumption as to the personnel of the Provisional

Government further than that inasmuch as all persons named by them in previous conference had been Constitutionalists, although they had not excluded others, we had assumed that they would assent to the establishment of a government composed exclusively of Constitutionalists. With this they seemed much disappointed and suggested that in the correspondence leading up to the acceptance of mediation, it had been assumed that all elements of the Mexican people would be taken into account. Notwithstanding their disappointment they agreed that we might give to the Press a statement that they had heretofore made suggestions as to a plan of adjustment but that we, after conference with Washington, had made other suggestions and that the matter was hopeful and proceeding favorably. They then proposed that we should meet the next day at three for the purpose of beginning the formulation of a plan. During the writing of this dispatch we have a message from them stating that they are in the midst of what promises to be a lengthy conference with the Mexican representatives and requesting us to postpone our meeting until tomorrow.

We beg to call to your attention that in the minutes prepared by their secretaries of the meeting of the full conference, which means the mediators, the Mexican representatives and ourselves, they uniformly speak of the Mexican representatives as the *representatives of the Mexican Government*. It was provided in the order of proceedings of the mediation conferences that the minutes of the meetings of the full conference shall be attested by the secretaries of all the parties, and while we had so far not signed these minutes nor raised any question nor thought it wise to raise any question as to the designation of the Mexican representatives, we deem it proper to submit this matter for your consideration.   Commissioners.

T telegram (WP, DLC).
  1 Italicization by Wilson.
  2 WWhw in margin.
  3 *Ibid.*
  4 *Ibid.*

Sir Cecil Arthur Spring Rice to Sir Edward Grey

Sir   Washington May 25 1914

It will no doubt have struck you, Sir, as a somewhat remarkable fact that the President has recently issued an authoritative statement as to his policy in Mexico in which he lays it down as essential that the land laws should be reformed and the peons emancipated and that even if Huerta retires that will not end the question.[1] On the contrary the President seems to believe that it is his duty to insist that, before any other steps are taken, the party of oppression should be eliminated and the party of freedom and emancipation take its place. Thus the question of the flag incident and even the question of Huerta's personality sinks into the background and the foremost duty of the United States is declared to be,—the internal reform of this unhappy neighbour. Since the days of the Holy Alliance it is doubtful if any government has thus declared its mission to reform the moral shortcomings of foreign nations, and this declaration is likely to cause some anxiety among the nations of this continent. I need not say that it is extremely embarrassing to the mediators who are now in the position of prescribing internal legislation for an American state at the instance of the President of the United States. I can well believe that all over this continent the declaration has been received with surprise and alarm.

I have the honour to be with the highest respect, Sir, your most obedient humble servant   Cecil Spring Rice

TLS (FO 371/2029, No. 24538, PRO).
    [1] Wilson's interview on Mexico, printed at April 27, 1914, Vol. 29, had just appeared in *The Saturday Evening Post*.

Sir Cecil Arthur Spring Rice to Sir Edward Grey, with Enclosure

Sir: Washington, May 25, 1914.

With reference to my despatch No. 154 of the 11th instant, I have the honour to report the following summary of events arising out of the Mexican crisis during the fortnight ending this day.

On May 11, I heard that the Brazilian Ambassador had the day before called upon the President to complain of the non-representation of the Constitutionalists in the mediation proceedings and that he had been told by Mr. Wilson that the United States representatives would represent them. Monsieur da Gama, it appears, also complained of the alleged breach of armistice by the United States in dispatching troops to Vera Cruz. The President told him that he would resist as long as possible pressure being brought to bear upon him by the War Department for that purpose.

On the 12th the mediators informed the Secretary of State that President Huerta considered the seizure of Lobos Island[1] as

    [1] Located seventy miles south, southeast of Tampico. There was a lighthouse on it.

an act of war, and that he demanded the retirement of the American forces from that island on the ground that the United States had violated the armistice. Mr. Bryan replied that the United States did not consider the seizure as an act of war, and that whatever General Huerta considered it, the American forces would not be withdrawn. The next day he announced that if the Mexicans undertook to keep the lights burning there, the American force would be withdrawn.

On the 13th the rebels entered Tampico. The question at once presented itself as to the course the United States Government would adopt—namely, whether they would prevent arms reaching the rebels by Tampico, or, if they did not, whether this action might not be construed as active assistance to the rebels, leading to their ultimate recognition as belligerents. The Government decided not to allow an embargo to be imposed on Tampico by the Federal vessels, but they have not so far recognised the Constitutionalists as belligerents, nor have arms been imported, so far at least as is known.

On the 14th, in order to prevent a repetition of the arrest of newspaper correspondents the Secretary of War telegraphed to General Funston at Vera Cruz strict orders to command them not to leave his jurisdiction.

On the 15th the mediators were received in audience by the President, who gave them his assurances of warm sympathy and support.

On the 16th the Mexican representatives, who had landed at Key West two days before, arrived in Washington and were entertained at dinner together with the United States Representatives and the mediators by the Spanish Ambassador. After dinner His Excellency made a short speech merely welcoming the delegates and expressing confidence in the success of the mediation.

On the evening of the 14th, upon the receipt of Sir L. Carden's telegram No. 138, stating that he had strong reason for believing that nearly all the supporters of President Huerta and the whole Mexican Cabinet fully realised the hopelessness of the situation and were pinning their faith on the action of the mediators as affording the only means of restoring order in the country and also that he thought that President Huerta would be prepared to retire, not at the dictation of the United States, but at the suggestion of the mediators, I thought is advisable to communicate that information to the mediators. They at once expressed the opinion that it would greatly strengthen their hands in appealing to the United States to restrain the Constitutionalists from any further advance, if General Huerta could empower his representatives to announce at the very first meeting at Niagara that he wished to eliminate his own person from the discussion, leaving absolute freedom to the mediators to recommend their own proposals for a settlement. They said that they would without delay instruct the Brazilian Minister in Mexico City, their only representative there, to endeavour to persuade General Huerta to give the necessary instructions to his delegates, but at the same time they requested me to telegraph in the same sense to Sir. L. Carden, saying that they knew that his words would have much greater weight than those of Monsieur Oliveira, who is not a strong man.

On the 19th Sir L. Carden reported that President Huerta had promised him to instruct his representatives at Niagara to announce his intention to cooperate loyally with the mediators and to add that he himself would not be an obstacle to any settlement which the mediators might recommend to provide Mexico with a guaranteee for peace and order.

On May 13 I spoke to the Counsellor of the State Department about the impending fall of Tampico and of the fear expressed on all sides lest outrages should be committed upon the person and property of foreigners. I asked him if I was right in assuming that the United States Government were doing all they could to restrain the Constitutionalists from offences against person and property. He agreed with me when I said that his Government would, under existing circumstances, be held to incur at least moral responsibility for what might happen. I understood that the French Ambassador had the day before used similar language when speaking to Mr. Bryan.

The latter told me on the 15th that he was taking steps to impress on Villa and Zapata the great danger which they would run personally should outrages on foreigners be committed. He also said that the President was convinced that the danger to foreigners would only be increased if more active measures were taken by the United States. All arrangements however had been made to send an adequate force to the front should it become absolutely necessary to do so.

In the course of subsequent conversations I had with the Secretary of State and the Secretary of War on the 21st instant, I communicated to them the fears expressed by Sir L. Carden in his telegram No. 145 of May 20 as to the grave dangers to which all in Mexico City would be exposed not only from Villa when he captured the town, but also from other bands of bandits. Both Mr. Bryan and Mr. Garrison thought that it would be some time before Mexico City fell, in the meantime Villa's conduct seemed to be improving, and they were convinced he understood the necessity in his own interest of sparing foreigners and preventing riot. They were "continually and contin[u]ously" urging moderation, and they believed with success, upon the Constitutionalist leaders. I also took the opportunity to tell Mr. Garrison that while abstaining from using force ourselves, or from advising the United States to do so, we held them to some extent morally responsible for the conduct of that party with which they were on friendly terms. Mr. Garrison having replied that he thought the United States Government should be warned beforehand of what Europe believed their obligation to be, and having suggested that I should communicate with the President direct, I took the opportunity, in sending Mr. Wilson a short paraphrase of Sir L. Carden's telegram No. 146 of May 20 describing the result of his interview with President Huerta on that day, to enclose a paraphrase of your telegram No. 188 of the same day, in which you expressed your confidence that the United States Government will continue to exercise the wholesome influence which they have over Villa personally. To this communication I received on the next day a reply from Mr. Wilson stating that whilst slow to anticipate things that have not happened, events seemed in the past few days to indicate a possible settlement in Mexico more hopefully than at any time hitherto. Copies of my letter to the President with its enclosures, and of his reply, are enclosed herewith.[2]

I regret that I am unable to supply you with authentic news as to the proceedings at Niagara. The United States delegates are in close touch with the White House and receive instructions direct from the President who allows nothing to transpire. From my conversations with the Secretary of State I gather that the President and he are greatly in favour of the mediation of the three South American Powers and inclined to make the best use possible of it in the interests of peace. President Huerta seems to take the same view of the activities of the mediators. On the other hand General Carranza and his advisers (possibly his North American advisers) are anxious that hostilities should be pressed and the capital occupied as soon as possible and without conditions. Their point of view is that the main object is to obtain entire control of the Government and the Treasury, and that they are entitled by their military successes to obtain this control. To be arrested in their victorious progress by any sort of

[2] C. A. Spring Rice to WW, May 21, 1914, TCL, enclosing a paraphrase of a telegram from Carden to Spring Rice and E. Grey to C. A. Spring Rice, May 20, 1914, both TC.

diplomatic drag is highly disagreeable to them, and believing as they do that the United States Government does not intend to use force they are not inclined to pay too much attention to their protests, which, I may add, some people believe to be only half-hearted.

In the meantime the President has allowed an interview to be published (copy enclosed) in which he is described as saying that the United States Government must insist on the entire elimination of the reactionary and capitalistic party which has for so long ruled Mexico, and on the triumph of the "new order" —that is the party of land reform and the emancipation of the poorer classes. In this interview he also asserts that "Villa's men are endeavouring to live up to the rules of civilised warfare"— an assertion which was published almost simultaneously with well authenticated accounts of the massacre by the Constitutionalists of the entire garrison of Tepic and of the execution, by Villa's order, of a Federal General and his staff in the neighbourhood of Saltillo.

I have the honour to be with the highest respect, Sir, your most obedient, humble servant,   Cecil Spring Rice

TLS (FO 371/2029, No. 24531, PRO).

ENCLOSURE

My dear Mr. Ambassador: The White House, 22 May, 1914.

I am warmly obliged to you for your kindness in sending me a paraphrase of the telegram from Sir Edward Grey and the report of Sir Lionel Carden's interview with Huerta which you were so thoughtful as to send me yesterday. Both are reassuring.

I am slow to anticipate things that have not happened, but I must say that events have seemed during the past few days to indicate a possible settlement in Mexico more hopefully than at any time hitherto. The mediators seem fully alive to all the conditions to be considered and the news from Niagara brings many indications of thoroughly sensible, and, I hope and believe, practicable proposals.

With warm regard,

Sincerely yours,   Woodrow Wilson.

TCL (FO 371/2029, No. 24531, PRO).

To the Special Commissioners

[The White House] May 26, 1914.

Replying to your telegram of the twenty-fifth, please say to the mediators in answer to their questions that it is the intention of this government to maintain the *status quo* between this government and General Huerta in every possible particular and that the embargo against shipments of arms across the Texas border will be continued throughout the negotiations, but that we should deprecate any interference with the trade of the Port of Tampico as involving questions of search and seizure likely to create serious international complications.

By way of comment upon several passages in your telegram and for the purpose of clearing as many points as possible, the President directs me to make the following statements:

We have not proposed or contemplated a direct transfer of government from Huerta to Carranza. On the contrary, we think a provisional government necessary, at the same time it is evident to us that the preponderate influence in such a government would of necessity, in the circumstances, be with the Constitutionalists. Perhaps a single provisional president is preferable to a commission, in which case the single man would of necessity be a Constitutionalist as we view the present conditions. What influences our thought and our preferences in this matter is entirely the state of the facts and the method of dealing with them in such a way as to carry out a programme of peace and accommodation. Events have moved very fast and very far since mediation was agreed upon and we are endeavoring to interpret those events and to adjust each step to a programme of peace rather than of coercion, feeling that a programme which necessitated intervention and coercion would involve the interests, the welfare, and the pride of the Mexican people much more deeply than an accommodation with the Constitutionalists carried out upon equitable terms. Even the occupation of Vera Cruz seemed for a little while to bring the danger of war with a whole people. The scope of the present negotiations has broadened in the view of the whole world and with the approbation of all who are concerned for the most permanent interests of America. We believe that this is the spirit and point of view in which the mediators are handling the matter.

Request a correction of the minutes to read "Mexican representatives" or some equivalent phrase instead of "representatives of the Mexican Government." We do not feel that we would be justified even in this indirect way in being drawn into an apparent recognition of the government at Mexico City.

CLST telegram (WP, DLC).

Two Letters from William Gibbs McAdoo

Dear Governor,   Cornish N. H. May 26 '14

We shall see you some time next Saturday afternoon. *My "Scotch conscience"* has been worrying me for some time and I am glad you, at last, pointed the way.

You need read only the headlines of the enclosed[1] to see how the big banks of New York are already trying to nullify the plain provisions of the Federal Reserve act in reference to the election of Class A & B Directors. I think we have thwarted them but it may be necessary to declare the election invalid, if the law and the Organization Committee's regulations are disregarded. This development simply confirms the prediction and the position outlined in my long letter to you a few days ago.

Nell is looking splendidly and grows more lovely each day. We both send best love to you all.

Devotedly yours   W G McAdoo

[1] It is missing.

Dear Governor,   Cornish May 26, '14

Here is a short editorial in a recent issue of the Springfield Republican that shows understanding about Wall St & is very gratifying to me[1]—so I wanted you to see it.

Affectionately yrs   W G McAdoo

ALS (WP, DLC).
[1] An untitled editorial in the *Springfield*, Mass., *Republican*, May 7, 1914. "In all of the criticism which the new banking and currency system has encountered from its inception to the present day," it began, "nothing has seemed more entirely without foundation than the personal attacks upon Secretary McAdoo and John Skelton Williams. . . . The country was blessed in having such sound and able men in high financial position under a democratic administration instead of some windy and visionary populistic financiers of the greenback school from the South or West." McAdoo, it added, was "a high-grade business man of great achievement whose chief field of activity had been New York itself." "Their real crime," it concluded, "has been complete independence of the financial overlordship of Wall Street but the country as a whole will never think the worse of them on that account."

From Richard Olney

PRIVATE & CONFIDENTIAL

My dear Mr. President,   Boston, 26 May, 1914

I am sure you will give me credit for having been careful not to obtrude upon you suggestions or views upon various public questions you have had to consider and in which I could not help taking a lively interest. I have purposely so refrained from fear of adding to your weighty burdens and wasting your valuable time and because of my implicit confidence both in your purposes and in your wise choice of ways and means.

I wish to be pardoned if I break over my rule to say something about the New England railroad situation in which of course I am greatly interested. The union of the New Haven and Boston & Maine systems under one management making one continuous trunk line of road from New York to the Provinces has always seemed to me to be in the public interest—to make for efficiency —to serve the populous communities on the route better than they could be served in any other way—to violate no law of Congress— but to be in harmony with the general policy of Congress as respects connecting and continuous roads. I had hoped that that union might be preserved at the same time that trolley lines and outside steamship lines and other excrescences were lopped off from the New Haven. The Attorney-General and the New Haven management, however, decided otherwise, and in substance agreed that a decree for the separation of the two corporations should be entered in a suit to be brought by the United States, and should be carried out by a sale of the New Haven's interest as a majority stockholder of the B. & M. In order that the New Haven's interest might not be sacrificed by a forced sale in bad times, a transfer of its shares of the Boston Railroad Holding Co. stock is to be made to Trustees who are to operate the B. & M. pending such sale. Governor Walsh, who entered upon his office early in January, was at first disposed to the view that Massachusetts had nothing to do with the matter and so expressed himself in various public utterances. As he was obviously in error, I wrote him a note calling attention to the reserved rights of the Commonwealth and to the fact that the Boston Railroad Holding Co's stock could not be transferred or sold except by consent of the Commonwealth. I also suggested that time was of importance and that, as negotiations were proceeding for the choice of Trustees and the proposed stock transfer, the Commonwealth should define its position without delay. Thus far, however, nothing official of any consequence has been done in that direction. Unofficially, however, there has been so much criticism of the Trustees agreed upon by the government and the New Haven, that one of them has resigned and another has gone off the Board of the Elevated Railway Co.

It has seemed to me from the start that, in so far as the consent decree called for a Board of Trustees to be chosen by the government and the New Haven, it would be found troublesome and unwise. It has already proved so as shown above. It is likely to prove even more troublesome if an agreement in that form is presented for action to the Massachusetts Legislature. Even if the other features of the agreement are acquiesced in, the personnel of the Board of Trustees is tolerably sure to excite criticism and opposition. It would not be strange if differences over the composition of the Board defeated the legislation altogether.

What I want to suggest, therefore, is this: That it be suggested to Governor Walsh—and I understand he goes to Washington at once for a conference on the subject—to send a message to the Legislature recommending that it approve the proposed consent decree and authorize the transfer of the Holding Co's stock on the condition that the Court in which the consent decree is entered name and appoint the Trustees, fix the time and terms of sale, and conduct all the proceedings incident to the trust. All wrangling over the persons to be Trustees would thus be avoided and a Board thus appointed would command universal confidence. The government would lose nothing—in all probability the persons it has already approved would be re-named by the Court unless new and decisive objections appeared. The Governor's recommendation, if it were understood that Washington was back of him, would pretty surely be adopted—with the result of added prestige for both the national administration and himself. Further, much time would probably be saved—and how seriously all efforts at reorganization, financial and otherwise, are prejudiced by suspense and delay, only those immediately concerned can realize.

Again apologizing for writing you on this subject at all and especially apologizing that it has seemed necessary to do so at such length—

I am—with sincerest regards

Very truly yours,　Richard Olney

N.B. Whomever the parties may agree upon as Trustees, the Court in which the decree is entered must confirm them and undoubtedly will hear any party in interest who alleges that one or more is unfit. The foregoing suggestions, therefore, simply make the Court consider who shall be Trustees in the first instance rather than later.   R.O.

TLS (WP, DLC).

The Special Commissioners to William Jennings Bryan[1]

Received and translated
at the White House.   Niagara Falls, N. Y., May 26, 1914.

At the meeting this morning, the mediators submitted as a basis of discussion, the following propositions:

1) In order to conform as far as possible to the existing constitution, General Huerta should appoint a person as Minister for Foreign Relations, submit his resignation to the Congress and
2) turn over the reins of the Government to the Minister of Foreign Relations who would appoint a cabinet of four to constitute Board of Provisional Government. This Board to be composed of one Huertista, one Constitutionalist, two Neutrals. From the neutrals the provisional Government was to be chosen. A general, absolute amnesty to be declared. The board promptly to call an election for president and congress in accordance with the existing constitution, the election to be held under the Act of May 1912, of which they are informed was adopted at the instance of the Maderista and head of the government with the selection of electors and provides for direct vote for president. Board to be
3) *requested* to devote special attention to the *agrarian question, electoral legislation, compulsory primary and agricultural education, organization of schools and experimental institutions* and would be also requested to institute steps for the creation of international commissions looking to the settlement of claims of for-
4) eigners for damages due to military acts or the acts of national authorities. Settlement of the claims of Mexicans, United States
5) to agree not to present claims for war indemnity. Provisional government to be recognized by us and A.B.C. countries. American forces to withdraw within fifteen days after the Board gives notice of its organization, the evacuation to be completed within thirty days unless the provisional government consents to an extension.

Discussion principally devoted to the first two propositions, they urging that the provisional government remains composed of all elements and we insisting that the value of that fair proposition depended upon whether it would be acceptable to the Constitutionalists who must now be recognized as the victorious force. They evidently objected to a transfer to a person recognized as the representative of Carranza.

One of them stating that while it was not inconsistent with mediation to adopt a plan based on the recognition of all the contending revolutionary forces, yet to consent to a transfer to a representative of Carranza might appear to be an encouragement to revolution and he himself might feel bound to inquire of his own government whether he could consent to such a plan. In any event he stated that it would require serious consideration as to whether the transfer to Carranzista[s] was within the spirit of the original proposal by them and accepted by Huerta and the United States.

In the informal discussion we urged that the urgent demands of the situation to prevent bloodshed as well as the permanent peace of Mexico might be better served by transferring the government to a provisional president instead of a board with divided responsibility and weaker executive action. They urged that this provisional government was only to be in power for a short time and was appointed more in the nature of satisfying all parties than with a view of anything it could do in the short period of its existence. In answer to which we urged that under the most favorable conditions the situation required a man of great ability to maintain order and deal with the problems incident to the transfer of authority, to say nothing of the difficulties incident to the disbandment of troops and return to their vocations. There was a lengthy exchange of views, but on these points we made little progress, the discussion in every instance returning to the matter of names and to which they made no suggestions beyond those previously mentioned. We adjourned to continue the discussion tomorrow, notwithstanding the engagement at Toronto.[2]

We think it possible differences as to mediators first and second propositions may be adjusted by agreement as to the personnel of provisional government without attempt to classify according to parties. The same man or men might be acceptable to all elements.

At the hour of this telegram we received yours which has been deciphered.   Commissioners.

T telegram (WP, DLC).
  [1] Numbers and italicization in the following telegram by Wilson.
  [2] To attend a garden party given by the Governor General of Canada, Arthur William Patrick Albert, Duke of Connaught and Strathearn.

An Address at the Opening of The American University[1]

May 27, 1914

Bishop Cranston, ladies and gentlemen: The distinguished gentlemen who arranged the program of the afternoon have been gracious enough to excuse me from making an address. They have permitted me to say the few and simple words, which I can say with so much depth of feeling, which will welcome into the world of American scholarship this new university.

There is a sort of imaginative excitement about witnessing the inauguration of a great adventure of the mind, an adventure of the immortal part of us, which, if it do its work as it should be done, may leave its mark upon mankind for all time. Universities may outlast nations, and their history is not marked by the movements of parties or the changes of politics.

I do not know of any fight which is more heartening than fighting for the ideals of scholarship. I have never pretended, of course, that in a college you could make a scholar in four years. A Yale friend of mine said that, after teaching for twenty years, he had come to the conclusion that the human mind possessed infinite resources for resisting the introduction of knowledge; and it takes considerably more than four years to break down the defenses and begin the high enterprise of scholarship. But I have at least fought to have the opportunity to begin it and to awaken the mind to the seriousness of the undertaking.

Scholarship is the mastery, the exact mastery and comprehension, of great bodies of knowledge; and the comprehension is more difficult than the mastery. It is much easier to know than it is to understand. It is much easier to acquire than it is to interpret. And yet all knowledge is dead which is not interpreted. The vision of the scholar is worth more to the world than his industry.

It is appropriate that a university should be set upon a hill. It must be a place of outlook, and there must be eyes in it that can comprehend the things that are seen, even the things distant and vague upon the horizon. For the object of scholarship is not to please the scholar, is not to amuse the leisure of inquisitive minds, but to be put forth to release the human spirit from every kind of thralldom, particularly from the thralldom of darkness, from the thralldom of not knowing the path and not being able to see the way as it treads it. It is knowledge properly interpreted, seen with a vision of insight, that is uniting the spirits of the world. Charles Lamb made a remark once which seems to me to go pretty deep as a human remark. He was speaking very ill of some man not present in the little company in which he was talking, and one of his friends said, "Why, Charles, I didn't know that you knew him." He said, "I-I-I don't; I-I can't h-hate a man I-I-I know." How profound and how human that is! There are races whom we despise, and it generally turns out that we despise them because we do not know them. We have not found the common footing of humanity with which to touch them and deal with them. I have sometimes, when sitting in the company of particularly ably dressed people who were interested in philanthropy, wondered whether they knew how to be philanthropic. Philanthropy does not consist in giving your money to pay for what somebody else will do for mankind. It consists, at the fountainhead, of putting yourself on the same level of life and comprehension with the persons whom you wish to help and letting your heart beat in tune with their heart so that you will understand.

The object of scholarship, the object of all knowledge, whether you call it by the large name of scholarship or not, is to understand, is to comprehend, is to know what the need of mankind is; and to find that need in yourself, so that you can interpret it without going to the books,—merely by looking in your own heart and listening to your own understanding. That is the reason, ladies and gentlemen, why scholarship has usually been most fruitful when associated with religion; and scholarship has never, so far as I can at this moment recollect, been associated with any religion except the religion of Jesus Christ. The religion of humanity and the comprehension of humanity are of the same breed and kind; they go together. It is very proper, therefore, that under Christian auspices a great adventure of the mind, a great enterprise of the spirit, should be entered upon.

There is no particular propriety in my being present to open a university merely because I am President of the United States. Nobody is president of any part of the human mind. The mind is free. It owes subservience and allegiance to nobody under God. The only thing that one can do in opening a university is to say we wish to add one more means of emancipating the human mind, emancipating it from fear, from misunderstanding,—emancipating it from the dark and leading it into the light.

I hope there may be lecturers in this university who can interpret life. I have not met many, but I hope you will catch some of them. Carlyle had a fancy once of an old professor who was the Professor of Things in General; and I do not see how anybody can be a successful professor of anything in particular unless he is a professor also in some degree of things in general; because unless he knows, and knows with real vision, how that particular thing is related to all the rest, he does not know anything about it. I have often used this illustration: A man loses his way in a desert, and we say he has lost himself. If you will reflect for a moment, that is the only thing he has not lost. He is there; but he has lost all the rest of the world. He does not know where any other fixed thing in the world is. If he did, he could steer by it and get home, or get out of the desert, at any rate. His whole validity as a man depends upon his knowledge of the points of the compass and where everything else in the world is. He will run his head against a stone wall if he does not know where the stone wall is; and after he has run his head against the stone wall his identity is of no particular importance. He has lost his identity. He has lost his life, not by not knowing himself, but by not knowing where the stone wall was. That is what the German scholar has in his mind when he speaks of orienting ourselves,—knowing where the East is. We will not have to go East, but if we know where the East is we can steer for any part of the compass by relating ourselves properly to the East.

So we are here setting up on this hill as upon a high pedestal once more the compass of human life with its great needle pointing steadily at the lodestar of the human spirit. Let men who wish to know come and look upon this compass and thereafter determine which way they will go![2]

T MS (C. L. Swem Coll., NjP), with WWhw emendations.
[1] The Rev. Dr. Earl Cranston, resident Bishop of the Methodist Episcopal Church in Washington, presided at the ceremonies. William Jennings Bryan and Josephus Daniels also spoke.
[2] There is a WWT outline of this address, dated May 27, 1914, in WP, DLC.

To the Special Commissioners

[The White House] May 27, 1914

The President directs me to say that we are seriously disappointed by the character of the proposals outlined in your despatch of the twenty-sixth. We have reason to believe that the acceptance by Huerta of such a plan as that proposed could have been secured by this government some months ago.

The most serious and pressing question with regard to any plan, the question by which it must, whatever our preference, be tested, is this, Who would put it into operation if the victorious party refused to accept it? We are of necessity seeking a solution which is practicable as well as just and likely to yield the results we have all along had in mind. Our object is the pacification of

Mexico by reforms and changes instituted by her own leaders and accepted by her own people. A provisional arrangement established by force, especially if established by the force of the United States, would inevitably be temporary at best and the prelude to other revolutions. Certain things are clearly inevitable in Mexico as things now stand, whether we act or not. One of these is the elimination of Huerta. Another is resistance, and successful resistance, to any arrangement which can be made to seem to be a continuation of the Huerta regime.

It would, in our judgment be futile to set up a provisional authority which would be neutral. It must, to be successful, be actually, avowedly, and sincerely in favour of the necessary agrarian and political reforms, and it must be pledged to their immediate formulation, not merely "requested to devote special attention" to them.

And it will be impossible for the United States to withdraw her hand until this government is finally and fully satisfied that the programme contemplated will be carried out in all respects.

We are putting these conclusions bluntly, not in the form, of course, in which we wish you to present them to the mediators, but flatly for the sake of clearness.

The case lies in our mind thus: the success of the Constitutionalists is now inevitable. The only question we can now answer without armed intervention on the part of the United States is this, Can the result be moderated, how can it be brought about without further bloodshed, what provisional arrangement can be made which will temper the whole process and lead to the elections in a way that will be hopeful of peace and permanent accommodation? If we do not successfully answer these questions, then the settlement must come by arms, either ours or those of the Constitutionalists.

Every plan suggested must, therefore, of necessity be subjected to the test of these questions. We will not make war on the Mexican people to force upon them a plan of our own based upon a futile effort to give a defeated party equality with a victorious party. The whole present hopeful effort for peace would fall to pieces were we to attempt it.

Confidentially, we suggest that the Mexican representatives, being Cientificos, are making a last desperate attempt to save their privileges from the reforms which the Carranzistas would certainly insist on. It is too late to save that regime. If we went in ourselves we would not try to save it. It seems plain to us that their real interest lies in as early a settlement as possible and at our hands rather than at the hands of Carranza. Delay is likely to be fatal to them. It may be worth considering whether Huerta's pride might be saved by resigning in favour of his present foreign minister and letting him do the rest.   Bryan[1]

CLST telegram (SDR, RG 59, 812.00/23445, DNA).
[1] There is a WWT virtually indentical draft of this telegram in WP, DLC.

From Juliet Barrett Rublee

My dear Mr. President: [Washington] May 27, 1914.

Please forgive my writing to you but I am afraid I talked very stupidly this afternoon and I want to *add* a word of explanation. I have seen Mr. Foruseth[1] only twice, but was impressed by his earnestness, intelligence & disinterestedness & by his great desire to get better men—men of real efficiency & skill—to go to sea. He says the safety of the passengers in times of danger, depends upon having trained men & enough of them, and seats for all in the life boats, and that the right kind of men will not go to sea until sailors are made free and are paid better wages. In some countries they get only $15.00 a month and Lascars can be hired for $8.00 a month. The sailors, it seems, are now the only working men who are not free to stop work if they choose, but are liable to arrest for so doing and can be taken back to the boat and forced to work against their will—though this is no longer true of American sailors. It seemed rather terrible that such a condition should exist—in this age of freedom.

However, the thing I care most about and really wanted to ask you about, I did not mention! It is that I cannot help hoping that some day you will establish a National Health Department. If we could make health in this country a matter of study and National concern as did the Ancient Greeks, we might in time rival or even surpass some of their achievements!

If ever we do see you in Cornish perhaps some time you will tell me what you think about it.
          Sincerely yours,   Juliet Barrett Rublee

ALS (WP, DLC).
[1] That is, Andrew Furuseth.

A News Report

[*May 28, 1914*]

WILSON REFUSES PLEA OF BUSINESS

WASHINGTON, May 28.—President Wilson today, in a brief address at the White House to representatives of Western commercial bodies, put an end to all hope that anti-trust legislation might be limited at this session of Congress to the enactment of a trade commission bill. The President admitted the existence of a temporary depression of trade, but said that there was abundant evidence that the depression was only "psychological" and that there was nothing substantial to prevent prosperous and expanding conditions. . . .

The President's callers were not quite certain as to the full significance of his remarks. The prevailing impression was that the President, in a friendly way, meant to indicate his willingness to leave business in quiet after certain necessary reforms had been accomplished. It was not understood that he meant that to threaten opposition to his programme now would drive him to harsher recommendations next year.

This encouraging interpretation of the President's remarks on anti-trust legislation seemed to be borne out by what he said to another delegation that called on him, one from the National Foreign Trade Convention, now holding sessions in Washington. To these delegates he expressed the warmest interest in the development of the country's industries, foreign trade, and merchant marine. He told his callers that only the influence of his parents had kept him from going to sea as a lad, and that the impulse that impelled him then had remained with him ever since.

The President's remarks on anti-trust legislation were in answer to a petition for the curtailment of the anti-trust programme presented personally by representatives of three large manufacturing associations. The importance of these associations and the frequency with which reports emanating apparently from the Capitol had circulated lately, indicating that the President might soften his plans for this year's legislation, added to the finality of his reply.

Officers of the National Implement and Vehicle Manufacturers' Association, the Ohio Manufacturers' Association, and the Illinois Manufacturers' Association comprise[d] the delegation. Senator Pomerene accompanied them.

The petition presented to the President stated that "business is hesitating," that "the unemployed are numbered in the hundreds of thousands," and that "abundant capital awaits investment." It was declared that thoroughly digested legislation affecting the business world would doubtless remedy that condition. The petitioners stated they represented 33,107 factories, with 1,084,- 000 employes, and an investment of $782,000,000, and added:

"We favor an interstate trade commission, properly regulated, but we are opposed to all legislation which is discriminatory, and we ask that all other business legislation be deferred until the business men of the United States can become acquainted with the proposed laws, of which they are now entirely ignorant."

The White House gave out this statement:

The President said in reply to the Illinois delegation that, in his judgment, nothing was more dangerous for business than uncertainty; that it had become evident through a long series of years that a policy such as the Democratic party was now pursuing was absolutely necessary to satisfy the conscience of the country and its perception of the prevailing conditions of business; and that it was a great deal better to do the thing moderately and soberly now than to wait until more radical forces had accumulated and it was necessary to go much further.

The President also said that, while he was aware of the present depression of business, there was abundant evidence that it was merely psychological, that there is no material condition or substantial reason why the business of the country should not be in the most prosperous and expanding condition. He urged upon his hearers the necessity of patriotic co-operation on the part of the business men of the country in order rather to support than oppose the moderate processes of reform and help guide them by their own intimate knowledge of business conditions and processes.

He told his visitors that it was his earnest desire to serve and not to hinder or injure the business of the country in any way, and that he believed that upon reflection they would see that the course he was urging would in the long run not only, but in the short run, also, be the wise and serviceable course.[1]

To the delegation from the Foreign Trade Convention the President said:

I had hoped that Secretary Redfield would put into my ear what I should say to you, for I cannot claim to be an expert in subjects you are discussing. I am sure he expressed the feeling which I would wish to express, which is the feeling of encouragement that is given by the gathering of a body like this for such a purpose. There is nothing in which I am more interested than the fullest development of the trade of this country and its righteous conquest of foreign markets.

I think that you will realize from what Mr. Redfield has said to you that it is one of the things that we hold nearest to our heart that the Government and you should co-operate in the most intimate manner in accomplishing our common object.

One of your members just now said something in my ear about the merchant marine, and I am sure I speak the conviction of all of you when I say that all our country needs is to have a merchant marine, because if we have to deliver our goods in other people's delivery wagons their goods are delivered first and our goods are delivered incidentally on their routes.

This is a matter I have had near my own heart for a great many years. It was only by authority of my parents that I was prevented from going to sea, and I only hope that it is not a universal regret that I did not.

I hope this is only the first of a series of conferences of this sort with you gentlemen, and I thank you for this opportunity.

Printed in the *New York Times*, May 29, 1914.
    [1] There is an undated CLST press release of the foregoing three paragraphs in the C. L. Swem Coll., NjP.

To David Ignatius Walsh

My dear Governor Walsh,   The White House 28 May, 1914

In view of your having been prevented from coming down to see me, I am asking Dudley Malone to go up to Boston to discuss with you the New Haven matter. It will admit of no further delay, and is of such vital importance not only to New England but to the whole business situation of the country, that I feel justified in pressing it upon your attention in the most direct and earnest manner.

Cordially and sincerely yours,   Woodrow Wilson

TCL (RSB Coll., DLC).

The Special Commissioners to William Jennings Bryan

Received and translated at
The White House.   Niagara Falls, N. Y., May 28, 1914.

We had not received your telegram of the 27th when we had the conference in Toronto on yesterday. We then called attention to the many and serious objections to the appointment of a Provisional Government the majority of whose names are neutrals, urging that the Huertista approval of such a plan would be the same at the expense of the hostility of the Constitutionalists who claimed that their success (entitle?) them to the sole power and who in justice were certainly entitled to the preponderance of authority. They stated that we had misunderstood their proposals numbered two and three as would be demonstrated by analyzing the political complexion of the names they had previously proposed, one of whom, Lascurain, was a constitutionalist and by virtue of his position as Foreign Relation minister was now in law entitled to be Provisional President, General Angeles was now in the Constitutionalist army, Rivero[1] was an appointee of Madero as minister to Argentine who resigned when Huerta came into power and ought to be acceptable to the Constitutionalists. Carbejal[2] appointed president of the Supreme Court by Diaz, they understand, was in sentiment a neutral, and they thought ought to be acceptable to all parties. They had been informed that Delama,[3] the only Huertista, was a moderate who earnestly favored settlement of the present problems. They argued that it was not necessary in making the appointment to designate the names of the factions to which the men had belonged if they were of a character that would tend to secure the desired end and were otherwise satisfactory to the parties to the mediation. We incline to think that the men to constitute the Provisional Government might be agreed upon if we disregarded classification and division among various elements and undertook to select individuals to constitute it. Would any of the five names suggested be satisfactory? If not what names could we suggest? The discussion on the subject above indicated continued until we were obliged to adjourn in order to attend the official receptions which had carried us to Toronto.

In view of previous conversations with the Mediators individually and in conference we hope to be able to substitute "pledged" for "requested."

When the mediators suggested evacuation at the end of fifteen days we at once urged that this would leave only a paper plan with nothing to guarantee its enforcements and exposing the country to the turmoils attendant upon the transfer to the Provisional Government whose ability to preserve peace and conduct the elections safely depended solely upon the willingness of the Mexican people to have the plan of pacification carried into effect. The interest of all concerned therefore demanded that the evacuation should not be made until after the election had been held and the regular government was in operation. They thought this objection was answered by the provision that the withdrawal should be within the forty-five days unless the Provisional Government consented to an extension of time and that extension definite or indefinite might be left to the decision of the Provisional Government which they assume to be in sympathy with the fundamental idea and disposed to act in accordance with the best interests of the Mexican people. That feature not having been discussed by us with you in Washington and not knowing the President's wishes in the matter we were not in a position to do more than to suggest general consideration of international difficulties having regard to the desire of the United States to secure the interest of the people of Mexico without intervention. In our next discussion on that point, shall we suggest that this feature be eliminated altogether from the plan or that it be left for settlement by the United States and the Provisional Government or by the United States and the Government established after the election?

While this telegram is being put in code we have a visit from the Ambassador of Brazil who states that in view of the intense partisan feeling now existing in Mexico, it might be ruinous to the reputation and standing of any man with his party if it were known that his name was under consideration for membership on a board of Provisional Government intended to bring about pacification. The mediators therefore begged that the names mentioned by them in this and our previous telegram to you remain kept strictly confidential. He further suggests that as it (has) not been decided whether the Provisional board should consist of three or four or any other definite number it might be advisable to request both the Huertista and Carranzaistas to designate names fitted in character and ability for appointment on such a board, the mediators to select the third, or third and fourth man, as the case might be, so as to give the preponderance to the Constitutionalists.   Commissioners.

T telegram (WP, DLC).
 1 Don D. Ignacio Rivero.
 2 Francisco S. Carbajal, a Constitutionalist sympathizer.
 3 Adolfo de la Lama, sometime Minister of Finance in Huerta's cabinet.

From Sir Cecil Arthur Spring Rice

Dear Mr President   Washington. 28 May 1914

I propose to leave here on the evening of the 3rd and shall be in London on the 9th when I shall see Sir Edward Grey. I should be very grateful if you could accord me an audience before leaving in case you have any message for my government.

I have the honour to be with the highest respect
                    Yours very sincerely   Cecil Spring Rice

ALS (WP, DLC).

To the Special Commissioners[1]

[The White House] May 29, 1914

The President directs me to say[:] In reply to your despatch of the twenty-eighth, we call attention to the letter sent today by special messenger to the mediators by the authority of Carranza asking that the Constitutionalists be admitted to representation in the conference.[2] Time will be gained by waiting to arrange this and all the processes of the mediation will be facilitated by the admission of representatives of Carranza. We assume that they will of course be admitted.

In the meantime, we suggest that the appointment of a foreign minister by Huerta to succeed him might raise questions very embarrassing to this government as it would also certainly meet with strong objection from the Constitutionalists. It is doubtful whether it would be wise for this government to recognize the legal right of Huerta in this or any other detail or particular of the plan to be agreed upon. Another process would answer the same purpose. Huerta and his present foreign minister could resign by agreement and Lascurain could succeed him as if by right, he having last year foregone the succession under duress when Madero was displaced, and it could be agreed upon and stipulated that Lascurain should then appoint as minister of foreign affairs and immediately give way to a person agreed upon between this government and the mediators who should then be supported as constitutional president *ad interim*, administer the government and formulate and promulgate the reforms pending the election. The more we consider this difficult matter the more clear the difficulty grows of finding men for a board or commission among whom the intimate relations of mutual confidence and cheerful cooperation could be successfully established which will be necessary for their task. But it might be wise to associate with the provisional president a board of three persons to be agreed upon who would have charge and superintendence of the elections but not be permitted to share the powers of the presidency. You will see that the perplexities of the situation have turned our thoughts back to the idea of the mediators that there should be a single provisional president and to our preference for a provisional government disconnected from both the Huerta regime and the previous regime.

We agree with you that the most practical course is to select persons and not attempt to define the factions they represent or even go on the theory that they do represent factions. We will give our immediate and careful attention to the discussion of names and hope that the mediators will be patient of apparent delay and great deliberation in this matter, perhaps the most critical of all. It should be agreed and stipulated that neither the provisional president nor any member of the provisional government should be a candidate at the elections.

As we said in our last, it seems to us absolutely essential that the provisional government should be explicitly pledged and bound to undertake the reforms without which no settlement can last six months.

The question of our evacuation should be left to be discussed and agreed upon between this government and the government to be created at Mexico City, whether the provisional government, which might need our support and be conscious that it needed it, or the regularly constituted government which would succeed it after the elections.   Bryan

CLST telegram (SDR, RG 59, 812.00/23446, DNA).
   1 There is a partial WWsh draft and two WWT drafts of the following telegram in WP, DLC.
   2 Rafael Zubáran Capmany to the Mediators, May 28, 1914, printed in FR 1914, p. 519.

The Special Commissioners to William Jennings Bryan

Niagara Falls, New York, May 29, 1914.

Your telegram states that time will be gained by waiting to arrange for the admission of the Constitutionalists. In view of that statement we would be glad to know whether you desire us to have a conference with the Mediators to-day and discuss the other matters referred to in your telegram or to postpone further meetings until after the messenger has arrived.

Commissioners.

T telegram (WP, DLC).

To the Special Commissioners[1]

Enciphered at
The White House.   The White House, May 29, 1914.

Have reported telephone conversations and President approves of position taken by you and of advice given you. Please insist most earnestly to mediators that a peaceful settlement is the supreme object of our efforts and that no formalities or technicalities should be permitted to interfere. We are not dealing with ideal conditions but with conditions as they are and no progress can be made toward a peaceful settlement of the Mexican situation without considering the opinions and wishes of the Constitutionalists. If they are not there to speak for themselves the burden of conferring with them is thrown upon us with consequrnt delay in addition to feeling which refusal of representation is sure to arouse. You will therefore urge representation of Constitutionalists even though they insist upon conditions which may seem unreasonable. When they become acquainted with the mediators and see with what patriotism, patience and unselfishness they are working they will catch the spirit and grow more trustful and accommodating. Assure the mediators of the President's profound appreciation of their labors and say that he advises them freely because of his desire to render them every possible assistance.   · Bryan.

CLST telegram (WP, DLC).
  1 There is a WJBhw draft of this telegram in SDR, RG 59, 812.00/23452g, DNA. Wilson either dictated it to Bryan, or the two collaborated in writing it.

The Special Commissioners to William Jennings Bryan

Received and translated at
The White House.   Niagara Falls, N. Y., May 29, 1914.

After telephoning the substance of our conversation with the Ambassador of Brazil this morning, a member of the press stated to us that a Carranzaista messenger[1] had arrived and told him that he was to have a meeting with the mediators at five, but that the messenger thought that they would decline to accept the letter.[2] This we thought would be most unfortunate and give Carranza an opportunity to say that his letter had not been even opened. The effect on the public would have been most unfortunate, to say nothing of the added difficulty of getting Carranza to assent to any plan proposed by the mediators.

We therefore visited the mediators at once and have just returned from a lengthy conference. We found them very much disposed not to receive the letter, as they considered it most improper that a communication intended for them should first have been published in the papers[3] and if, as the messenger stated, the newspaper report was correct, they considered the letter was in the nature of a protest against the scope of the mediation. We urged that the message may not have been intentionally given out but may have been caught on the wire. That it was not to assume that the letter offered was the same as the press telegram, and in any event it was unwise   (omission)   to until the letter was actually opened. They answered that the messenger himself had stated that the letter was the same as the telegram and they therefore felt called upon to act in the light of such information. It is impracticable to state all of the discussion which involved their unwillingness to receive the letter or to answer it if received. It was suggested that the question as to the answer should be determined by the character and contents of letter and at most, we urged, that the interest of the mediation was such that the failure to answer would certainly be better than the failure to receive it. Their unwillingness to accept the communication seemed to be based on the idea that the new representative might not come in a proper spirit for a mediation in conference but with a view of injecting nuisances and irritating features and cause a delay in the completion of the plan on the theory that delay was to the interest of the Constitutionalists. To this we replied that the United States was above all others concerned in having a representative of the proper character and if we were satisfied on that question it might be sufficient evidence that he was such and properly accredited. That if he took an improper part in the conference his action need not interfere with the proper and prompt action of the mediators and in any event it was to the highest interests of the Mexican people and to the results intended that the Constitutionalists should be represented for they would certainly be more bound if they had a representative than they are at present even though they may object to the plan finally agreed on. Without stating the arguments pro and con it is sufficient to say that they decided to receive the communication but do not intend to reply to it if it is of character indicated by the newspapers account of its contents.

We anticipate difficulty on the subject of evacuation because of the expressions of the mediators indicating their unwillingness to do anything inconsistent with the sovereignty of Mexico by consenting to the United States army remaining in the country. It was for this reason we asked whether the plan should be silent on that subject or whether the matter should be left open for future adjustment between the United States and the provisional or permanent government. Either plan must necessarily give rise to serious problems. While silence will leave the subject in the control of the United States, such silence would occasion comment and leave the matter at large. If left to adjustment after the election the permanent government would be greatly embarrassed at home if it failed to insist upon immediate withdrawal. On the other hand, a provision that the withdrawal should be determined by the members of the Provisional Government and the United States would leave the question undecided and shift without removing the difficulty.

The episode of messenger made it impossible to continue the discussion on this and the other matters mentioned in your telegram of this morning. Commissioners.

T telegram (WP, DLC).

1 Don Juan Urquidi, of the Constitutionalist agency in Washington.

2 R. Zubáran Capmany, representing Gen. Carranza, to the Mediators, May 28, 1914, printed in FR 1914, p. 519. In this letter, Carranza, after reviewing his earlier correspondence with the mediators, declared that they had not defined the scope of the mediation and that he had been notified that the mediators would withdraw their invitation if he did suspend hostilities. Carranza added that he regretted that the mediation was continuing without representation by the Constitutionalists who now controlled substantial and important areas of the country. The civil war in Mexico, he concluded, should not be the subject of continued negotiations without the presence of representatives of the First Chief of the Constitutionalist Army.

3 A text of the letter had been released in Durango, Mexico, on May 29. See the New York Times, May 30, 1914.

Remarks to the Princeton Alumni Association of the District of Columbia[1]

Mr. Toastmaster and Gentlemen: May 29, 1914

I am tempted as I see these men around me to tell some of the things I know about them; and yet I have learned since I moved to this town to be so discreet that I think perhaps I will observe silence out of respect for them. I could tell things, for example, about the new member of the Commerce Commission,[2] who not only has been associated with me for a long time at the university, but for a long time in the complicated politics of New Jersey and is now associated with me in the very simple and lucid politics of the United States. For there are lucid intervals in the politics of the United States!

When Mahlon Pitney came to see me to invite me to this feast, I tried to beg off, because I realized that I had only just finished my freshman year in office and that it was unusual to call upon a sophomore to make a speech, particularly when that sophomore was raising Cain, according to the true and immemorial traditions of his class. But Mahlon would not let me off. I suppose he remembered an episode of an evening of a few weeks ago when we were both dining in the house of a friend. I forgot (there are happy intervals when I do forget) that I was President of the United States, and I forgot that Mahlon was a justice of the Supreme Court of the United States, and I made a remark to him which I had to explain to the company. We were talking about a very singular character in New Jersey, an old man named Crandall,[3] and Mahlon was setting the stage for an incident in his dealings with Crandall and was expressing—I don't know whether sincerely or not—the fear that he had entertained that the Court of Errors and Appeals, of which Mahlon was then a member, might have to throw the old man out on a technical error in the pleadings; and with the true spirit of a reformer I said, "Mahlon Pitney, do you mean to say that you would have thrown that man out of court on a mere technical error?" Mahlon, with the countenance of a justice, said, "Of course; we had to." "No," I said, "if you had been big and righteous men you wouldn't have had to," and then I realized that there was a chill upon his countenance. He thought it was a great indiscretion that the President should talk in that most extraordinary fashion to a justice of the Supreme Court. I turned at once to our friends and said, "I beg that you will remember, or will let me tell you, that Mahlon Pitney and I were classmates at college, and I can say anything I please to him!"

Crandall was a great character, and no doubt he did make technical errors in pleadings; because one day, when he was leaving the court, he was mumbling to himself, having lost the case, "It has cost my clients a lot of money to teach me law."

As I look at this company, gentlemen, my thoughts are carried back to the old university, and it is very hard for me to speak of the university without deep emotion; because I devoted what I believe to have been, on the whole, the best years of my life to the service of Princeton, with a passionate longing to do something that would elevate her above all other universities by seeming to give her some clear vision of what it is possible for a university to do for a great nation. I think I am not more sensible now than I was then of the extraordinary need of this nation, and, I dare say, of all modern nations, for men who have taken pains to comprehend and to get their brains in such shape that they can put them to the service of any undertaking, great or small. The peculiarity of the modern world is this: The circumstances of industry are constantly changing. If a man learns to do one thing, and only one thing, he may find himself suddenly put entirely out of the running because that thing, that particular thing, may be no longer necessary to do; that process may have been passed in the development of industry, and he thrown aside as the machinery which he knew how to manipulate is thrown aside. So also with the changing aspects of the social life of the nation and of the world. There never was a time when so many changes occurred within a single century as the time in which we live. This nation, every nation, needs intellectual athletes.

I have often argued this with the people who insisted upon the university's giving vocational training. There is an imperative need for vocational training—we haven't half enough vocational schools—but not all our educational institutions ought to do the same thing. There is room for a larger thing than the vocational school, namely, the university and the college of liberal arts, and I have always illustrated the use of it this way: Men have said, "I don't want to study this particular thing because it is of no practical use and significance to me." You might say the same thing of the dumbbells or the trapeze in the gymnasium. I do not suppose that any man ever expects to do the double trapeze with his partner in business; a man has not got this apparatus rigged up in his office. He goes into the gymnasium, not because he expects to gyrate through life, but because he wants to have his muscles and his veins and arteries in such shape that he can endure any strain the modern world may put upon him. That is the use of the gymnasium. Now, the college of liberal arts is the intellectual gymnasium. You want to get your brain in such shape that the modern world cannot take it by surprise and cannot overcome it and bear it down by the burdens it puts upon it— so that there will be a quick response to every challenge.

When I see youngsters in college apparently getting no idea of what they are there for my heart burns within me. It is as if men were declining distinction. I remember once going to a preparatory school[4] which I was told contained chiefly, if not only, the sons of very rich men—so that there was a very small proportion of men there who would ever have to work to earn their living— and I said to them that I looked upon them with compassion as a body of men probably foredoomed to obscurity; that they probably never would "hump" themselves; that in the modern world it was no distinction to be rich—it was only a temptation; that there were too many rich men now for riches to be any longer a distinction in America; that they would have to do something else; and if they had loafed their way through school and college they would find that they did not know how to do anything else, and therefore would join the ranks of the commonplace and obscure.

It is a pretty serious business to see youngsters thinking that they get sufficient distinction in being captain of a football team. I would like to be captain of a football team myself; I would like the physical zest of it and the proof of prowess attendant upon

it. I am not depreciating those things; but I would also like to
know when I was captain of the football team that after I graduated I would know how to do something else, and do it just as
well as I knew how to captain a football team. But that does
not dawn upon the average undergraduate until too late, and
the world is full of college men who are kicking themselves all
around the block because they did not have sense enough when
they were in college to know what it was all about. That is rather
a pitiful situation—the number of regrets that follow college life.
It ought not not to be so, and there is only one way, it seems to me,
of preventing it.

As I look back on my boyhood, it seems to me that all the sense
I got, I got by association with my father. He was good fun; he
was a good comrade; and the experience he had had put a lot of
sense in him that I had not been endowed with by birth, at any
rate; and by constant association with him, I saw the world and
the tasks of the world through his eyes, and because I believed
in him I aspired to do and be the thing that he believed in. We
are carried forward, gentlemen, by our association with men of
deeper and wider experience than ourselves. It is a peculiarity
of human beings that they long for something bigger than they
have yet been able to get. I suppose that it is the instinct of travel
that leads us to read books of travel; that it is the sense of con-
finement in the little round of our own day that leads us to
study things that our daily life has nothing to do with. You will
find that a man like Joseph Jefferson, for example, who was a
consummate actor, was very anxious that the world should know
him rather as a landscape painter. He painted some good pictures, but not quite as good as he thought they were. Dr. Weir
Mitchell greatly preferred, in spite of his extraordinary distinction in the world of medicine, to be known as an author of successful novels. Every man feels that he is a little smaller than his
genius would enable him to be if he only had the chance. So the
whole impulse of expansion in us is touching the things that
are larger than ourselves and the experiences that attract us, because they show us a bigger world; they open windows to us upon
scenes that we had never dreamed of, and experiences that have
not been reckoned with in our philosophy. The companionship
of older men, if they are worth being companions, with younger
men must create the feeling that a college is not a place for play,
except play as a relief from work and an enrichment of work:
that the zest of play is to know that during the rest of the twenty-
four hours you are doing something which may turn out to be

useful; to know that you are part of the action and thought of the world.

But I would get very didactic and go on all night if I kept this up. All I started out to say, before I was tempted, was that these are the things that are most in my heart with regard to the university. I believe that every body of alumni should think of their university not merely as a delightful place to go back to—for that it is, of course—not as a place which they visit to renew their youth, but as a place to which they must contribute the impulse of their own thought and experience by converse with the men who are running it and frequenting it and letting the vision of the world as we have seen it play upon the place. We want our mother, who is immortal, to be as young as the age in which she lives, as fresh as the year of grace in which we visit her, as new as all the forces that are blowing across the face of the world—younger and fresher and fuller of initiative than all her sisters. We want her to be running ahead of us and showing us and all mankind the way, with the light lifted high which shows the path shining on the way ahead.

Her immortality is in her spirit, not in her architecture, exquisite as that is. The singular fact that men would rather live their physical life than be immortal is very interesting and very extraordinary. Sometimes the only way to be immortal is to die. Who would ever have heard of young Poinsett[5] if he had not been at the halyards that were to lift the first flag of the United States that was hoisted at Veracruz and been shot? The bullet brought him immortality; and he is immortal because we remember the simplicity, the matter-of-course way with which he did his duty, a perilous duty. He is not dead; his spirit lives. It is worthwhile to live a short physical life if you may live a long spiritual life. The only thing that lifts the world from century to century is the accumulating power and purity of the human spirit; and the university is a place in which spirits are bred, in which ideals are formed, in which dreams are dreamed—not dreams that go to the ceiling as the smoke out of our pipes, but dreams in which one sees mankind serving and being served in all the great tasks of enlightenment which ought to be understood by the rulers and the graduates of a university better than by any other body of men in the world.

There is a great deal of cant talked nowadays about service. Service is not merely getting out and talking and being busy and butting into other people's affairs, and giving gratuitous advice. Service also and chiefly consists in comprehension. You cannot serve your friend unless you know what your friend's needs are, and you cannot know what his needs are unless you know him inside and out. Philanthropists whose philanthropy consists in giving money, so that somebody else who understands what they do not understand can spend it, are not the real philanthropists. I cannot do the least good turn to a man upon whom I look down. If I want to serve the lowest of human beings I have got at least to put myself, imaginatively, in his place and see the world as he sees it. I have got to give him a boost, not take him by the hair of the head and yank him up and say, "My dear fellow, come to my high level." You do not want to mortify people if you would try to help them. You ought to say, "Don't you see that you have got just exactly the same spark in you that I have and just as much of it if you will let it burn and kindle, will give it a little inflammable material upon which to spread its flame?" So the university ought to know mankind, ought to know the unfortunate man, ought to help him and bless him; and every youngster that goes into a university ought from the time he begins his freshman year to be associated with older men who can say to him, "You have been drawn into a company of privileged workers and students from which you cannot go out without a baptism of increased vision and power."

T MS (WP, DLC).
  [1] At the annual dinner held at the Chevy Chase Club in Washington. Mahlon Pitney presided. For a brief report of the affair, see *Princeton Alumni Weekly*, XIV (June 10, 1914), 713-14.
  [2] Winthrop More Daniels.
  [3] John J. Crandall, lawyer of Atlantic City, well-known for his unorthodox courtroom procedures.
  [4] See the news report of an anniversary address printed at June 3, 1909, Vol. 19.
  [5] George Poinsett of Philadelphia, seaman, the first American serviceman killed at Veracruz.

From Edward Mandell House

Dear Governor,   Berlin, May 29. 1914.

When Germany was reached I was fairly well informed as to the situation here. Prince Münster[1] and the Count von Moltke[2] were fellow passengers, and I came to know von Moltke well. Münster is what we would call a reactionary, and I let him do all the talking. Von Moltke, on the contrary, is, perhaps, the only noble in Germany who has a detached point of view and sees the situation as we do. He gave me valuable information which merely tended to confirm the opinion as to the nearly impossible chance of bettering conditions. I have not seen the Kaiser, but have been invited to lunch at Potsdam on Monday. Just what opportunity there may be to talk with him is an uncertainty, for nothing has been well managed here. I have had long talks with [Gottlieb] von Jagow, Minister for Foreign Affairs, and Admiral von Tirpitz.[3] Jagow is a clever diplomat without much personality. Von Tirpitz is the father of the greater navy, and is forceful and aggressive. Neither have ability of the highest order. I was told not to talk to von Tirpitz because of his well known opposition to such views as we hold, but finding that he is the most forceful man in Germany, excepting the Kaiser, I concluded to go at him. We had an extremely interesting hour together, and I believe I made a dent—not a big one, but sufficient at least to start a discussion in London. I am careful always not to involve you. Opinions and purposes I give as my own, and you come in no further than what may be assumed because of our relations. The situation is extraordinary. It is jingoism run stark mad. Unless some one acting for you can bring about an understanding, there is some day to be an awful cataclysm. No one in Europe can do it. There is too much hatred, too many jealousies. Whenever England consents, France and Russia will close in on Germany and Austria. England does not want Germany wholly crushed, for she would then have to reckon alone with her ancient enemy, Russia, but if Germany insists upon an ever increasing navy— then England will have no choice. The best chance for peace is an understanding between England and Germany in regard to naval armaments, and yet there is some disadvantage to us by these two getting too close. It is an absorbing problem and one of tremendous consequence. I wish it might be solved and to the everlasting glory of your administration and our American civilization.

Your faithful and affectionate,   E. M. House

We go to Paris on June 2nd and to London June 13th.

ALS (WP, DLC).
  [1] Alexander, Prince Münster von Derneburg.
  [2] Helmuth, Count von Moltke (1876-1939), nephew of Helmuth Johannes Ludwig von Moltke, Chief of the General Staff; grand nephew of Field Marshal Helmuth Karl Bernhard, Count von Moltke; and father of Helmuth James von Moltke, a leader of the German resistance movement against Adolf Hitler. Helmuth James von Moltke was executed by the Nazis.
  [3] Grand Admiral Alfred von Tirpitz, Secretary of State for the Imperial Navy Department, father of the modern German navy.

From Henry French Hollis

Dear Mr. President: [Washington] May 29, 1914

I have been in close touch lately with Congressman Stevens of New Hampshire, Louis D. Brandeis and George Rublee, sincere and high-minded men, who are experts on the pending trust legislation.

It has been my fear that the Democratic Administration might apply the soft pedal on trust legislation, making a practical surrender to the demands of big business. I was stoutly opposed to such surrender.

I am now satisfied, however, that the only trust measures which are ripe for immediate legislative action are the Trade Commission Bill and the Railroad Securities Bill. I believe it is far better not to insist upon action on the other measures until we are all better informed as to the exact shape that legislation should assume.

I have talked freely with democratic Senators, and they agree to my conclusion, naturally for varying reasons. Standpat democrats wish to help big business. The radical democrats do not feel sure of their ground, and are afraid to enact ill considered legislation, which may prove hurtful to the Party. Perhaps all of them are influenced somewhat by the desire to get away from Washington speedily. All agree that the Party chances will improve if there is an early adjournment.

I send you this information so that you may know that one radical, at least, who has feared until now the application of the soft pedal, has changed his mind, and believes that the whole trust program should not be carried out at this session.

Sincerely yours,   Henry F. Hollis

TLS (WP, DLC).

A Memorial Address[1]

[May 30, 1914]

Ladies and Gentlemen: I have not come here today with a prepared address. The committee in charge of the exercises of the day have graciously excused me on the grounds of public obligations from preparing such an address, but I will not deny myself the privilege of joining with you in an expression of gratitude and admiration for the men who perished for the sake of the Union. They do not need our praise. They do not need that our admiration should sustain them. There is no immortality that is safer than theirs. We come not for their sakes, but for our own, in order that we may drink at the same springs of inspiration from which they themselves drank.

A peculiar privilege came to the men who fought for the Union. There is no other civil war in history, ladies and gentlemen, the stings of which were removed before the men who did the fighting passed from the stage of life. So that we owe these men something more than a legal re-establishment of the Union. We owe them the spiritual re-establishment of the Union as well; for they not only reunited states, they reunited the spirits of men. That is their unique achievement, unexampled anywhere else in the annals of mankind, that the very men whom they overcame in battle join in praise and gratitude that the Union was saved.

There is something peculiarly beautiful and peculiarly touching about that. Whenever a man who is still trying to devote himself to the service of the nation comes into a presence like this, or into a place like this, his spirit must be peculiarly moved. A mandate is laid upon him which seems to speak from the very graves themselves. Those who serve this nation, whether in peace or in war, should serve it without thought of themselves. I can never speak in praise of war, ladies and gentlemen. You would not desire me to do so. But there is this peculiar distinction belonging to the soldier, that he goes into an enterprise out of which he himself cannot get anything at all. He is giving everything that he hath, even his life, in order that others may live, not in order that he himself may obtain gain and prosperity. And just so soon as the tasks of peace are performed in the same spirit of self-sacrifice and devotion, peace societies will not be necessary. The very organization and spirit of society will be a guarantee of peace.

Therefore, this peculiar thing comes about, that we can stand here and praise the memory of these soldiers in the interest of peace. They set us the example of self-sacrifice, which, if followed in peace, will make it unnecessary that men should follow war any more.

We are reputed to be somewhat careless in our discrimination between words in the use of the English language, and yet it is interesting to note that there are some words about which we are very careful. We bestow the adjective "great" somewhat indiscriminately. A man who has made conquest of his fellow men for his own gain may display such genius in war, such uncommon qualities of organization and leadership, that we may call him "great," but there is a word which we reserve for men of another kind, and about which we are very careful. That is the word "noble." We never call a man "noble" who serves only himself; and if you will look about through all the nations of the world upon the statues that men have erected—upon the inscribed tablets where they have wished to keep alive the memory of the citizens whom they desire most to honor—you will find that almost without exception they have erected the statue to those who had a splendid surplus of energy and devotion to spend upon their fellow men. Nobility exists in America without patent. We have no House of Lords, but we have a house of fame to which we elevate those who are the noble men of our race, who, forgetful of themselves, study and serve the public interest, who have the courage to face any number and any kind of adversary, to speak what in their hearts they believe to be the truth.

We admire physical courage, but we admire above all things else moral courage. I believe that soldiers will bear me out in saying that both come in time of battle. I take it that moral courage comes in going in the battle, and the physical courage in staying in. There are battles which are just as hard to go into and just as hard to stay in as the battles of arms, and if the man will but stay and think never of himself, there will come a time of grateful recollection, when men will speak of him not only with admiration but with that which goes deeper, with affection and with reverence.

So that this flag calls upon us daily for service, and the more quiet and self-denying the service the greater the glory of the flag. We are dedicated to freedom, and that freedom means the freedom of the human spirit. All free spirits ought to congregate on an occasion like this to do homage to the greatness of America as illustrated by the greatness of her sons.

It has been a privilege, ladies and gentlemen, to come and say these simple words, which I am sure are merely putting your thought into language. I thank you for the opportunity to lay this little wreath of mine upon these consecrated graves.[2]

T MS (C. L. Swem Coll., NjP), with WWhw emendations.
   [1] Delivered at Arlington National Cemetery under the auspices of the Grand Army of the Republic, Department of the Potomac. James Knox Polk Gleeson, M.D., commander of the department, presided. Champ Clark and Senator Reed Smoot of Utah also spoke. Wilson had first declined the invitation to speak and then changed his mind, thus causing some criticism. See the *New York Times*, May 31, 1914, II, 15.
   [2] There is a WWT outline of this address, dated May 30, 1914, in WP, DLC.

From William Jennings Bryan, with Enclosure

My Dear Mr President,   [Washington, c. May 30, 1914]

I enclose two written reports[1] rec'd from Niagara. They cover matters already discussed in communications we have had with them by wire or over the telephone. The only thing that has not been answered is the reference to the minutes. I am not sure that the reservation which they propose is sufficient. The fact that the Huerta delegates are described as representatives of the United Mexican States possibly explains the disinclination to receive Caranza's representatives. Am not sure but we should insist upon a designation that would not raise the question of recognition—as, for instance "Gen Huerta's representatives" or "Representatives of Gen Huerta's government." What do you think?

We have said all we can in regard to the importance of receiving Caranza's representatives. If in spite of our urging they refuse, they take the responsibility and give us an excuse for insisting upon things satisfactory to the Constitutionalists.

Their (the mediators') disinclination to consider details of necessary legislation not only relieves you of embarassment but enable[s] you to *require* the selection of the right men if they are to take upon themselves the great responsibility of securing the reforms needed.

The first proposal in regard to personel of govt contemplates the selection of a *neutral* president and two *neutral* members of the Cabinet of four. Only one Caranza man! In a fight for reforms every *neutral* can be counted as opposed.

I sent you yesterday a letter from Gov Lind.[2] It is a strong argument *against* having Huerta appoint his successor but weak, I think, in the argument in support of Caranza's right to succeed as the "First Chief."

I think you will be interested in Mr Halls letter,[3] also enclosed. They have made more progress than I had supposed in devising a plan for agrarian reform. I am asking for copies of the "decatmen" and "solicitude" to which Mr Hall refers.

With assurances of esteem I am my dear Mr President
                    Yours truly   W. J. Bryan

P.S. Am *very* glad you went to Arlington. Your speech is in striking contrast with the other speech reported.[4] Have seen Seldomridge.[5] He will favor the bill[6] as you desire it. Have also seen Weaver[7] & think he will do same—although not certain. Hollis will be away until June 8. I have written him.

ALS (WP, DLC).

1 The other written report is missing, but it was a memorandum submitted by the mediators to the special commissioners on May 26 as a basis of discussion and is summarized in the Special Commissioners to WJB, May 26, 1914. See H. P. Dodge to WJB, May 29, 1914, TLS (WP, DLC), the covering letter.

2 J. Lind to WJB, May 29, 1914, CCL (W. J. Bryan Papers, DLC). As Bryan suggests above, Lind devoted much of his letter to a demonstration that Huerta had no valid claim to be president *ad interim de jure* and hence could not constitutionally pass the office on to any successor. As for Carranza, Lind argued that anyone who took control of Mexico City would have to act as a dictator until a new election could be held; Carranza had the best claim to that position since he had been the first to take up arms against Huerta. Lind also concluded that the ABC mediation had no chance of success since there was really nothing to mediate. The quarrel between the United States and Huerta was "a question of national honor and dignity," which could not be arbitrated. Moreover, the mediators could not settle the "purely domestic conflict" within Mexico.

3 H. L. Hall to WJB, May 21, 1914, TLS (WP, DLC). Hall discussed the abortive plans for agrarian reform in Mexico during Madero's presidency, emphasizing especially one in which distribution of land to the landless would be carried out as a private enterprise backed by government loans. Hall himself had been involved in this scheme, and he offered to send Bryan copies of the *solicitud* (petition) which his organization had made to the government and the *dictamen* (opinion) of the government in response.

4 The "other speech reported" on Memorial Day at Arlington National Cemetery was by Speaker Clark. The news reports printed in the *New York Times* and the *New York Herald*, May 31, 1914, indicate that it was longer and much more bellicose than Wilson's.

5 Harry Hunter Seldomridge, Democratic congressman from Colorado and a member of the House Banking and Currency Committee.

6 The rural credits bill.

7 Claude Weaver, Democratic congressman from Oklahoma and a member of the House Banking and Currency Committee.

ENCLOSURE

The Special Commissioners to William Jennings Bryan

Sir: Niagara Falls, N. Y., May 29, 1914.

The episode of the messenger with the letter from Carranza, which had apparently been previously given to the press, created great embarrassment because the Mediators considered such a course to be discourteous to them. It seemed likely for a time to precipitate a crisis, for such we think it would have been had they definitely refused to receive the letter. The situation, however, has been met for the present, as stated to you over the telephone. The discussion, however, has made it manifest that difficulties will present themselves if the contents of that letter were correctly reported in the newspapers.

According to that report, Carranza objects to mediation in anything except the Tampico incident and objects as unwarranted interference with the internal affairs of Mexico any propositions related in any way or to any extent with agrarian and educational reforms. This position will make it all the more difficult to secure the approval of the Mediators to a plan of turning over the provisional government to Carranzistas, when they are informed in advance that such a government would antagonize the larger purpose and prevent a settlement of existing troubles upon a durable basis. The participation of the Constitutionalists in the mediation has seemed to us necessary to its success and, as far as we could, we endeavored to get the Mediators to invite them to participate, and hope that if they should come in they will not antagonize the President's purpose of securing a stable government founded on a plan of justice to the Mexican people by attempting to restrict mediation to the narrow scope indicated by the newspaper reports.

The fact that the special messenger is returning and can carry a written communication gives us the opportunity to state by letter the situation as we have found it more fully than could have been done by telegraph or telephone.

Some embarrassment has been found to result from the fact that in the beginning the Mediators tende[re]d their good offices for the settlement of the difficulties existing between the United States and Mexico and in the communications since they have recognized Senor Rabasa and his associates as Representatives of the United Mexican States. When the first protocol was presented outlining the method of procedure and referring to the Representatives of Mexico, we called attention to the fact that this language was inconsistent with the position of our Government which did not acknowledge that there was any difficulty with the people of Mexico and did not acknowledge that Huerta was the President of Mexico or that his Representatives were the Representatives of Mexico or of the Mexican people, though he was in possession of certain powers. They appeared to assent to our proposed amendment and used some such expression as that the American and Mexican Representatives were present, and we had hoped that similar language would be used in the minutes of subsequent meetings. In this we have been disappointed because the minutes of the first full conference refers to the Representatives of the United States of America and the Representatives of the United Mexican States. We have not signed these minutes and we had hoped that it would not be necessary to reopen the matter with a risk of friction and it has occurred to us that it might be advisable to submit once for all a note substantially as follows to the Mediators:

"In the minutes of the first meeting Messrs. Emilio Rabasa, Augustin Rodriguez, Luis Elguero and Rafael Elguero, Secretary, are described as the Representatives of the United Mexican States.

"The Government which we represent has not recognized as the Government of Mexico the authorities by whom the gentlemen named have been accredited to this Conference and while pleased and ready at all times to meet them as Representatives of those whose credentials they bear, we cannot consistently with the attitude maintained by our Government, accept them as the Representatives of the United Mexican States. With this reservation and explanation, we are prepared to sign the protocol."

In the light of our formal conferences and private interviews with the Mediators we have been impressed with the fact that the formation of the Provisional Government presents a problem that is essentially personal. Can the man or men be found who have the confidence of the great body of Mexican people in the measure necessary to enable them to carry out the delicate and difficult work which must be done to secure a just and lasting peace? And if so, how is this to be done?

At first it was suggested that the transfer to Lascurain had the double advantage of securing a man satisfactory to the Constitutionalists and at the same time entitled to the office under the constitution. But since then the Mediators seem to be more disposed to the appointment of a Board which would represent the two factions, although giving the preponderance to Carranza and in their discussions have indicated that they considered that the spirit of mediation did not contemplate the exclusive recognition of one party. They urge that it is inconsistent with the spirit of impartiality due from them in their position as Mediators.

They have manifested a high appreciation of the spirit and purpose of the United States in dealing with the difficulties of the situation, but at the same time maintain that they have tendered their friendly offices to all parties. They recognize and all the parties admit the necessity of reform, especially of land reform, as a condition of permanent pacification. As to the principle, scope and methods of these reforms there is a disagreement between the Mexican parties and no doubt within the several parties themselves, arising out of the fact that what might be suited for the tropical lands in South Mexico would be unsuited for those near the Texas border, and that what would be equitable in land capable of irrigation would be utterly inadequate in the mountainous and more arid portions of the country. The Mediators have therefore indicated that in their view the determination of these differences, both in principal and detail, is for the Mexican Government, when constitutionally reestablished.

We think we may say that while not in terms conceded by all

parties, it is in fact taken for granted by all parties that the election will result in the success of the Constitutionalists and that therefore the new government will be of that type and interested in the reforms of the land and educational law. Some doubt has been suggested as to the wisdom of excluding any person, qualified under the constitution, from candidacy at the election, it being suggested that no restraint from the outside should be imposed upon the absolute right of choice by the Mexican people.

The Mediators, while impressed with the high purpose of the United States, are concerned at stipulating for any provision that would appear to impair autonomy and sovereignty of Mexico, in the imposition of terms and conditions relating to the internal policies of the Government, fearing that suggestion of what was good might itself be used as an argument against its adoption because proposed by outsiders, even though these were acting from the highest motives. They therefore seem to hesitate to propose anything more than the most general recommendations. The task of carrying out the various reforms they conceived to be the right and duty of the Mexican people, working through a government established with the forms and provisions of the Mexican constitution. The Mediators seem to be loathe to approve anything which, peace restored and constitutional government established, would impair the autonomy of the Mexican states.

We have the honor to be, Sir,
　　　　Your obedient servants,　J. R. Lamar
　　　　　　　　　　　　　　　F. W. Lehmann
　　　　　　　　　　　　　　　Special Commissioners.

TLS (WP, DLC).

The Special Commissioners to William Jennings Bryan

Received and translated at
The White House.　　　　　Niagara Falls, N. Y., May 30, 1914.

We have learned from the mediators that the Mexican delegates have a telegram, date not designated, urging that a protocol be completed and signed as soon as possible, because of the danger from the advancing Constitutionalists. The mediators themselves insist, however, that Carranza's present willingness to come into the conference is because of his want of ammunition which they say is the reason why he has not followed up his advantage by marching toward Mexico City. At the same time they urge that his purpose in coming into the conference is to secure delay. From the morning paper we infer that in addition to matters of form mentioned in our telegram of yesterday, they will object to the admission of a Carranza representative unless there is during the mediation a cessation of arms. This was one of the points incidentally discussed when last week we urged them to renew the invi[t]ation. They then insisted that they did not see how they could undertake to mediate when one of the parties refused an armistice and continued active hostilities.   Commissioners.

T telegram (WP, DLC).

From William Jennings Bryan, with Enclosure

My Dear Mr. President: Washington May 30, 1914

Here is a suggestion. If you think it wise to give some such advice as this please make such changes in the wording as you think best.

I have just talked with Justice Lamar by telephone. Carranza's representative[1] had a talk with the mediators and at the time Justice Lamar was telephoning the Carranza representative was conferring with Mr. Lehmann. Justice Lamar asked whether there was any objection to your commissioners conferring with Carranza's representative and I told him there was no objection to their talking with him unofficially and that I did not think the mediators could object. If this was not the proper advice to be given it might be well to correct it in this proposed message.

Governor Lind and Judge Douglas think it would make it much easier for the Carranza representatives[2] if Huerta would turn the government over to somebody—they care not to whom—and get out of the country. That is why I suggested the second paragraph of the dispatch.

With renewed assurances, I am, my dear Mr. President,
                              Very truly yours,   W. J. Bryan

TLS (WP, DLC).
[1] Rafael Zubáran Capmany.
[2] Carranza's other representative was Luis Cabrera.

ENCLOSURE

William Jennings Bryan to the Special Commissioners

[Washington] May 30, 1914.

If mediators insist upon armistice as a condition—which you think possible—call their attention to the fact that the convention signed at the Hague in nineteen hundred seven, a copy of which I sent to Rose, specifically states that mediation does not suspend hostilities unless suspension is provided for by special agreement. This can only be construed as meaning that the suspension of hostilities ought not to be insisted upon. It is all right where both parties are willing but a demand for an armistice should not be permitted to prevent mediation.

Referring to the request of the Mexican representatives for an early signing of a protocol it might be well to remind them that it is impossible to agree upon a protocol until the mediators have arrived at a plan which promises to restore permanent peace. If Huerta is willing to retire now there is no objection to his doing so. He can turn the government over to anyone whom he pleases and leave the country. The mediation can then proceed, Huerta's appointee surrendering to the man selected by the mediators when mediation is completed.   Bryan

This has my entire approval. Thank you.   W.W.

CLST telegram (SDR, RG 59, 812.00/23452h, DNA).

From John R. Mott

Mr President   Montclair, New Jersey May 30th, 1914

I improve this first opportunity since my return from Boston to express to you my deepest gratitude for the personal message you so kindly sent to me at the time of the Dinner of the Congregational Club.[1] The fact that in the midst of your great responsibilities you should take time to remember me in this way touched me very much and came as a means of the greatest encouragement and inspiration. I shall strive more earnestly than ever to prove myself worthy of such confidence.

I cannot close this note without expressing again to you, as I so constantly do in my contact with others, my profound appreciation of the remarkable way in which you are bringing to bear the principles of righteousness and unselfishness in all your relations to national and international affairs. My world-wide travels have enabled me to see that you are lifting our nation into a high and large place in the thought of those whose opinion we most value.

　　With renewed expression of gratitude and highest regard

　　　　　　　　　Very sincerely yours　　John R. Mott

ALS (WP, DLC).

¹ John R. Mott spoke to the Boston Congregational Club on May 25, 1914, his forty-ninth birthday. On April 25, Thomas Weston, Jr., secretary of the Boston Congregational Club, wrote to Wilson, requesting him to send a word of congratulation on the occasion. Wilson did so in WW to J. R. Mott, April 28, 1914, TLS (Letterpress Books, WP, DLC): "May I not wish you many, many happy returns of the day? I think you know with what deep sympathy and admiration I have followed the great work you have been carrying on here in America and throughout the world, and I am sure that my prayers are joined with those of vast numbers of Christians everywhere that you should be spared for many years of increasing usefulness and service. I am sure that in wishing you these things I am also wishing you happiness of the deepest kind."

To the Special Commissioners¹

　　　　　　　　[The White House] May 31, 1914

　　This government is seriously disturbed by the attitude of the mediators with regard to admitting representatives of the constitutionalists to the conference, and it wishes in particular most respectfully but most earnestly to protest against the apparent willingness of the mediators to base their conclusion in this extremely important matter on newspaper articles or upon impressions derived from unauthoritative sources which they suspect to be inspired. Nothing could be so unsafe or so full of serious risk as that. Representation of the constitutionalists in the conference is not only desirable, it seems to us all but essential to the success of the conference. The pacification of Mexico cannot be hoped for or secured unless the leaders of the revolution assent to the plan suggested by the mediators. The mere fact that General Carranza has now sent an agent to Niagara Falls seeking admission to the conference,² in spite of his earlier refusal to do so, seems to us to show very clearly that he did not at first realize the scope that was to be given to the discussion and to the plan to be proposed, and that it is just because that scope is so inclusive of everything he is interested in that he wishes admission. It is evidence of good faith, for if he participates he will be under the stronger compulsion before all the world to accept the results. Nothing that has come to our knowledge either directly or indirectly would justify the suspicions or the distrust which seems to have taken such deep root in the minds of the mediators. If the representative of the constitutionalists is not admitted to the conference we shall have to constitute ourselves judges of what would be just to them and reasonable to expect them to accept without any adequate means of forming the judgment. They might insist upon less, if consulted directly by the mediators, than we would in the present circumstances think it fair to insist upon for them. We do not mean to say that the continued refusal of the mediators to receive the representative of the constitutionalists would necessarily render the conclusions of the conference impracticable and futile; but it would certainly deprive the mediators of the approval and support of public opinion in this country, which they now enjoy in so gratifying a degree and would darken the whole outcome with doubt and ·searching criticism. We would deeply deplore any conclusion which might even seem to throw the least doubt upon the impartiality of the mediators by any circumstance which we could not heartily justify or successfully explain away.

Upon another matter. It is clear to this government that its representatives would not be justified in signing minutes which described the present Mexican delegates as representatives of the United Mexican States or of the Mexican government, though we should be quite willing to have them spoken of as the representatives of General Huerta or of the government of General Huerta or of the government at Mexico City, or by some equivalent description. We do not see how it would be consistent with the present attitude of the governments of Brazil, Argentina, and Chile towards the de facto govebnment at Mexico City, to go any further, inasmuch as their attitude is exactly the same as that of the government of the United States, to our great gratification, a circumstance which happily made it possible for us to accept their gracious offer of mediation.   Bryan

CLST telegram (SDR, RG 59, 812.00/23451, DNA).
  ¹ There is a WWT draft of this telegram in WP, DLC.
  ² That is, Zubáran.

A Memorandum for the President

The President: The White House, May 31, 1914.
Memorandum by telephone From Mr. Bryan.

Have had a conversation with Judge Lamar this morning over telephone. He says that the mediators seem to be resolute in their objection to receiving the Carranza representatives unless they agree to an armistice as well as to the consideration of all the questions involved in the Mexican controversy. I reported to him the conversation which I had with the mediators when their letter was sent to Carranza withdrawing the request for representatives.[1] I reported to you at the time and am sending a telegram of which the following is a copy * * * confirming what I said by telephone so that he can have the facts before him. The mediators are putting a telegraphic report of some length in cipher. It will probably not reach here until six or seven o'clock. I told him to make a brief abstract to send in advance so that you can have it as early as possible.

I am going out in country for a few hours but have left with the White House operator my telephone number so that I can come in at any time. It would take me about an hour to get in after hearing from you. If I do not hear from you I will be back to my house about 5:30.

I think the affairs are at a crisis at Niagara Falls and that we ought to send a message early this evening if possible.

Bryan.

T MS (WP, DLC).
    [1] The mediators to General Carranza, May 3, 1914; printed in *FR 1914*, pp. 518-19.

William Jennings Bryan to the Special Commissioners

The White House, May 31, 1914.

Confirming what I said by telephone I repeat that the Mediators read me their communication to Carranza. I called attention to the sentence in regard to an armistice and expressed the fear that it might be misunderstood by Carranza and regarded as a condition precedent to mediation. They replied that it would not be misunderstood in the Spanish and called my attention to the fact that they did not say that an armistice would be indispensable to mediation but only indispensable to the best results. They explained that what they meant to say, and they were sure that Carranza would understand it as expressed in the Spanish language, was that they would have to withdraw the request for representatives unless Carranza was willing that the whole question concerning Mexico's difficulties was to be considered. I am not quoting the exact words but that is the substance as you will see by examining the communication to which I am referring.

Bryan.

T telegram (WP, DLC).

Thomas Watt Gregory[1] to Joseph Patrick Tumulty

Confidential

Dear Mr. Tumulty: [Washington] May 31/14. 11 a.m.

Have *just* had talk with Mr. Malone in Boston. He reports that message will surely go in Monday or Tuesday[2] & that everything is all right. He urges absolute secrecy as to his mission to Boston & that nothing whatever be given out as to communications between Governor & White House—says the publication of such information would spoil everything.

He will watch situation carefully & "keep on the job." He asks me to report this to the President. Will you kindly do this & say I will be glad to report details of telephone conversation if the President wishes me to do so?

Will rely on your seeing that nothing gets out in so far as you can control. Situation seems to me to be getting in good shape.

Yours Truly T. W. Gregory

ALS (WP, DLC).
  [1] At this time special assistant attorney general of the United States in charge of the New Haven suit.
  [2] That is, Governor Walsh's special message to the Massachusetts legislature on the New Haven settlement. He sent it to the legislature on June 1.

The Special Commissioners to William Jennings Bryan

Received in cipher and
translated at the White House.

Niagara Falls, N. Y., May 31, 1914.

We have just returned from a very lengthy conference with mediators where we failed to obtain their consent to the admission of the Constitutionalists representative except on the terms stated in the correspondence between the mediators and Carranza. Every suggestion and argument we made was met by the mediators with the statement that they had undertaken the mediation of all existing conditions, whether internal or international and on the express condition that an armistice should be declared. They say that the original scope of the mediation was broadened at the suggestion of the United States so as to take in all subjects, and that it would be inconsistent with the position the mediators had assumed to admit one party on terms which were different from those proposed by them and accepted by the United States and by Huerta, both of whom had declared an armistice. Indeed they seemed to consider that the consent of their governments for them to act as mediators had been given on this understanding.

They recognized the rule of the Hague, but insist that it has no application where the terms of the mediation were stated in advance and form a special rule for this special case. They also insist that the consent to the armistice is particularly essential as an evidence of the good faith of party who now asks to come into the mediation. The importance of this guarantee they say has been increased by the fact that while the letter addressed to them is silent on the subject, they read in the morning paper a statement that Carranza will only come into the mediation on the understanding that the mediators shall deal with the Tampico incident and one or two closely related matters enumerated in an article in the New York TIMES of the 30th instant which they consider to have been prepared by an authorized representative of Carranza. This view they say has been confirmed from sources which they consider reliable, and their position is that they cannot accept a representative who comes with the protest and distinct statement that he will not consent to the mediation of other than the matter which he points out. They claim that this amounts to advance notice that the Constitutionalists will not feel bound by any decision that may be made, and while the mediators say they are willing and anxious for the Constitutionalists to become parties, they are not willing to have them as parties occupying a different position from those already in the conference.

We urged all of the arguments stated in your telegrams and pressed the importance to the United States of having Carranza before the mediation in any capacity, urging that even if he did attempt to limit the scope of the discussion and plan he would be in a sense bound by the decision, notwithstanding his protests. We urged that a mediation plan without Carranza would only half settle the question and impose upon the United States the burden of securing his assent and with the risk of forcing upon the United States the very intervention it was endeavoring to avoid. They answered that the mediation had begun without his presence and that he could become a party on the same terms as others. They felt sure that as soon as a plan was agreed upon and approved by the United States Carranza would be obliged to yield, since he could not afford to attack a provisional government which had the moral support of this country. That he could not make a permanent success without the recognition of the United States nor afford to resist the provisional government set up as the result of mediation to which he had been invited to become a party which invitation he had accepted and then in effect declined by his construction of the office of the mediators and his attempt to limit the scope of their work.

At the outset they were very reticent and for a while made no answer to our earnest request to waive irregularities and conditions beyond the statement of their position. Later they expressed themselves more freely, replying to our arguments however by reiterating the statement that they desired Carranza to come in provided he did so on the same terms as the others. We expressed earnestly and as strongly as we could the wish of the President in the matter and the many and weighty reasons which made him desire that the Carranzaistas should be permitted to become parties, even though they did not consent to the same terms as had been accepted by Huerta and the United States.

At the close of the lengthy discussion, however, we had not succeeded in getting them to recede in the slightest from the position taken at the outset that their duty to themselves and to their governments would not permit the admission of the Carranza representative except on the terms stated in the original correspondence, and as illustrating the fixedness of their views, they stated at first that even if both parties to the present conference should join in a request to have the Carranza representative admitted without terms they would feel bound to decline. Later it was suggested that such a condition would call for future consideration. They showed us a copy of the letter from Zubaron, which proved to be most courteous and which we understand the mediators will answer.[1]

While declining our request to admit the Constitutionalists without condition they urged upon us the desirability of continuing our negotiations and not to allow the incident of the letter, and the question to which it had given rise, to interrupt the progress of the plan which they thought should be agreed upon as soon as possible, with the statement that in their opinion that if the plan was approved Carranza would likewise approve of it when he saw that the mediation had accomplished the work of the Constitutionalists party insofar as that could be done by eliminating Huerta and establishing a provisional government in which the Constitutionalists would be predominant and which was pledged to the reforms which had been proclaimed as the purpose of the revolution.

It is rumored here that the Mexicans propose to take no part in the question as to the conditions on which the Constitutionalists may come in, expressing themselves as willing to allow that matter to be determined by the mediators. Our next meeting with the mediators has been fixed by them for Monday at eleven o'clock, they appearing to be disinclined to meet us before then, possibly on account of the desire to consult.

Finding we were able to do so before five o'clock we have sent the whole telegram instead of the abstract.

Commissioners.

T telegram (WP, DLC).
   [1] The mediators to R. Zubáran Capmany, June 2, 1914, printed in FR *1914*, pp. 529-30.

Remarks at a Press Conference

June 1, 1914

Adjournment?

> I didn't know there was going to be any.

There is an effort to present a conservation bill at this session, Mr. President. Have you any attitude as to that?

> Why, I am deeply interested in that group of five bills, all of which I heartily support and was fearing that they could not be considered at this session because they need careful consideration, and yet hoped that they might be. That was my attitude. You see, they were completed after the program of the session was also completed, and I didn't feel at liberty to urge that they put them in the way of the program, but I am just as interested in them as I was in the program itself. . . .

Mr. President, what do you hear about the future of the seamen's bill?

> I have been so much engrossed in other matters, I hadn't heard anything about it. I hadn't asked about it, to tell the truth.

Mr. President, the amendment to the Clayton bill, defining the status of labor under the Sherman law, that amendment is said to have been agreed to by you and representatives of the House. I wondered whether that agreement in any way involved any compromise with your position when you accepted that rider to the sundry civil bill, in which you said you would not favor any measure that would limit the opportunity or the power of the Department of Justice to prosecute under the Sherman law?

> No, sir. I consider it perfectly consistent. You see, ever since the antitrust legislation, ever since the Sherman Act was passed, it has been understood that the meaning of the Act was not that labor organizations were themselves illegal. They have been complaining, and I think their complaint

was not clearly sustained by the decisions of the Supreme Court, but it might be implied from them, that they existed by the suffrance of the Department of Justice. Now, that clearly was not intended.

I think the whole country approves of the right of laboring men to organize and to present their claims for just treatment by means of organization. And it was in order to remove all doubt as to whether they were in themselves illegal under the Sherman Act, that clause number seven, I think it was, was put in, and the amendment added for perfect clarity.

Doesn't paragraph number eighteen go farther than that, however? Wouldn't it make it open for reconstruction—for legalizing the secondary boycott?

I think paragraph eighteen was very carefully drawn as part of the anti-injunction bill and has been recognized as practically the legislation that had already been passed by one or the other of the two houses, but not at the same time with regard to injunctions. You will notice that the acts are very carefully specified in that bill and cover those things which have generally been recognized to be the legitimate means of insisting upon the rights of labor. That was the intention, at any rate.

Then does the amendment confer any right upon labor under the Sherman law that it does not already possess?

I don't think that it does, but some of the decisions of the Supreme Court would leave that open to doubt. At any rate, it is open to doubt in some minds.

The purpose of the amendment, then, is to remove that doubt?

The purpose of the whole legislation is to remove all doubt as to whether these are legitimate organizations, whether they are disobeying the laws of the United States in carrying out their legitimate objects. That is the way I understand it. I think the justice of that is manifest.

Without any specific wording, the same law, then, would permit businessmen or employers to organize under similar conditions, would it not, although they are specific amendments?

I haven't thought of that. I don't know. I suppose so. You see, clause number seven describes these organizations. They are organizations for mutual aid, not joint stock organizations and not for profit.

I had in mind, for instance, chambers of commerce, boards of trade, or the Hardware Manufacturers' Association. They have occupied so high a social plane that their existence has never been challenged. The law would permit them to do anything that would be illegal for other organizations.

I don't understand that it would, no.

If they transgressed the law, they would be liable just the same?

Yes. That is understood all around.

Mr. President, in your conversation with the Ohio manufacturers and the Illinois manufacturers, you said in the statement that was given out, you were quoted as saying that you were as aware of the depression of business as we had been. So that if you can tell us what does—if you can tell us what are the causes, as your correspondence reports them to you?

I am afraid that is too large an order. I should say that the depression was confined. These are merely impressions. They need to be very carefully confirmed. I wouldn't like them quoted as my views because they are merely impressions. My impression is that there is no depression in business in what might be called the business of the country. For example, you take wholesale houses—houses that send their salesmen out for miscellaneous sales of all sorts of goods throughout the country—they are not finding the depression. The average purchases of the country, the ordinary purchases of the country, are going on just as usual.

There is a depression which seems to radiate from the railroad offices. I am not saying that in criticism at all, but merely to mention this. Of course, a great part of the steel industry depends upon the extent of the purchases made by the railroads. If the railroads feel themselves embarrassed and don't place their orders, there is a considerable contraction in the steel business, and that affects all the allied or related manufacturers—all the makers of all the things that are related to the general steel and iron industry of the country; and that, in turn, has its effect upon the credit market—I mean, the market of lenders—because they are a little afraid that business is not quite good enough to put their money out, and they are timid.

Yet, in spite of that, you will notice that Mr. Gary and somebody else—Mr. Farrell[1]—have stated that the outlook in the steel industry is excellent, which means that in other fields, then—the railroad field—the country is going forward and has full heart in its business.

So that, in spite of the fact that on the face of it the steel business is affected by the prosperity of the railroads and there is depression, there is not depression in the steel industry. Taken as a whole, now, I construe that to be a very interesting and, indeed, a remarkable circumstance which is quite reassuring. What I said to those gentlemen meant this: If they believed that prosperity was coming, it would come, and come with a jump. That is the reason I said it was psychological. They are in a state of mind. And as long as you are in that state of mind, you don't undertake very much.

Has the tariff very much to do or anything to do with it?

I don't think the tariff has anything to do with it. As a matter of fact, I recently had a long conversation with the Secretary of Commerce, who said that our exports were increasing more rapidly than our imports, which would show that the tariff certainly hadn't had a depressing influence on our [business].

Mr. President, has the Secretary given you any information showing these conditions are more or less world-wide?

He has spoken of that, but that is very well known, that the business depression is world-wide. That is a well known fact. The interesting part of it is that the depression is less felt in the United States than anywhere else. That also is clearly established.

Mr. President, is it your impression that if the rates are advanced with the rate advance for the railroads, business would improve immediately?

I have explained that I don't feel I have any right to comment about a pending decision of the Interstate Commerce Commission.

Mr. President, what has been your attitude toward the investigation of the New Haven going on by the Interstate Commerce Commission?

I haven't had any other attitude than that of the interested public.

Can you tell about the Reserve Board yet, Mr. President?

I am waiting for the Secretary of the Treasury to come back. He ran away with somebody's daughter. I want to have a final conversation with him. He will be back some time this week.

Mr. President, any comments to make on Colonel Roosevelt's remarks?[2]

Oh, no.

Mr. President, do you feel that these investigations against the railroads have in any way affected their business?

I don't learn that they have.

Mr. President, have you any comment to make on the suggestion of curtailing the Senate on the interstate trade bill, to let Congress go home earlier?

> Perhaps you don't know that the Senate interstate trade commission bill has all the rest of the program in it. Perhaps you don't know that it is loaded to the gunnels. It was, when I saw it. I handled it very gingerly.

It differs slightly from the House bill?

> Yes, it does, in a number of particulars. What I meant was, it covers the subject matter.

JRT transcript (WC, NjP) of CLSsh (C. L. Swem Coll., NjP).

¹ James Augustine Farrell, president of United States Steel.

² Just before sailing for Europe on May 31, Roosevelt gave out a statement briefly setting forth his current position vis-à-vis New York politics. However, he also devoted a paragraph to national politics. It said that the Wilson administration had failed to solve the economic problems of the country and that the only solution lay in implementing the tariff and trust provisions of the Progressive platform of 1912.

To Walter Hines Page

My dear Page: The White House June 1, 1914

Please never apologize for your letters. They are most serviceable to me not only but I enjoy them and find myself guided by them. I thank you for them most heartily.

It seems to me that you are handling our critics, one by one, most admirably. I wish that the restrictions of your office permitted you to handle them collectively in some public way, but, after all, what you are doing will, I am convinced, percolate very far.

The fundamental thing is that they are all radically mistaken. There has been less disorder and less danger to life where the Constitutionalists have gained control than there has been where Huerta is in control. I should think that if they are getting correct advices from Tampico, people in England would be very much enlightened by what has happened there. Before the Constitutionalists took the place there was constant danger to the oil properties and to foreign residents. Now there is no danger and the men who felt obliged to leave the oil wells to their Mexican employees are returning, to find, by the way, that their Mexican employees guarded them most faithfully without wages, and in some instances almost without food. I am told that the Constitutionalists cheered the American flag when they entered Tampico.

I believe that Mexico City will be much quieter and a much safer place to live in after the Constitutionalists get there than it is now. The men who are approaching and are sure to reach it are much less savage and much more capable of government than Huerta.

These, I need not tell you, are not fancies of mine but conclusions I have drawn from facts which are at last becoming very plain and palpable, at least to us on this side of the water. If they are not becoming plain in Great Britain, it is because their papers are not serving them with the truth. Our own papers were prejudiced enough in all conscience against Villa and Carranza and everything that was happening in the north of Mexico, but at last the light is dawning on them in spite of them and they are beginning to see things as they really are. I would be as nervous and impatient as your friends in London are if I feared the same things that they fear, but I do not. I am convinced that even Zapata would restrain his follow[er]s and leave, at any rate, all foreigners and all foreign property untouched if he were the first to enter Mexico City.

The mediation is by no means to be laughed at, as you yourself see. We are dealing with men perhaps too touchy and punctilious and they are, I am afraid, very much more likely to be influenced by the cientifico point of view than by the point of view from which we would like to have them view the whole matter, but we are in real communication with our Commissioners by wire and hope to be able to guide the whole matter to a successful issue.

In the meantime, thank you again for your letters. I am every day pleased to think that you are there.

Cordially and faithfully yours,   Woodrow Wilson

TLS (W. H. Page Papers, MH).

To George Lawrence Record

Personal.

My dear Mr. Record: [The White House] June 1, 1914

I have read with real interest your letter of May twenty-sixth.[1] It makes me wish that we were going to have a more intimate part in the settlement of the land question in Mexico than it is possible for us to have. The principle that I am going on is that we ought studiously to seek to leave the settlement in their hands and that our only part is to see that they get a chance to make it. I am very hopeful that we can, though things are going slowly and a little too punctiliously, perhaps, at Niagara Falls.

Cordially and sincerely yours,   Woodrow Wilson

TLS (Letterpress Books, WP, DLC).
[1] G. L. Record to WW, May 26, 1914, TLS (WP, DLC), saying that the wise solution of the land problem in Mexico lay in imposing the single tax.

The Special Commissioners to William Jennings Bryan

RECEIVED AND DECIPHERED
AT THE WHITE HOUSE.   Niagara Falls, N. Y., June 1, 1914.

We have just returned from a meeting and while we can report some change in the position of the mediators, we do not know that it means any lessening of the practical difficulty.

We pressed with earnestness the views expressed in your telegram and the danger of mistake in construing Carranza's letter by newspaper articles. They replied that their construction was borne out by the words of the Zubaron letter itself to which we replied that we found in it no protest. That the American Government construed the letter as indicating Carranza's willingness to come into the mediation because it was so inclusive of everything in which he was interested and considered the fact that he wished admission to be an evidence of his good faith. They replied that if there was any doubt as to what the letter meant, the doubt could easily be removed by an explicit statement. We urged that they must bear in mind Carranza's position as a leader of a revolutionary army, and that they could not expect him to make a statement that would seriously weaken him at home and that the mediators had resolved the doubt against Carranza and had indicated an unwillingness to answer his letter or to give him an opportunity to say what it meant. One of them suggested that a reply might be written stating that his letter had been received and found to be susceptible of different constructions and inquiring how they were to understand it, and if he was willing to have all matters mediated. This led up to the meaning of their original letter and to their conversation with you in which they said that an armistice was essential to best results but not essential to mediation. They agreed to your recollection of the conversation, but said that since the mediation began there had been such a change in affairs as to make an armistice now essential by all the parties to the mediation and that they could not undertake mediation with its consequent delay while Carranza was advancing on one of the parties who had agreed to an armistice. They claimed that the mediation would not only be futile, but that they would be put in a ridiculous position if Carranza should take Mexico City while the mediation was in progress and be a party to it. One of them suggested that the difficulty arising out of delay might be met if Carranza assented to the scope of the mediation and came in with the understanding that it should be completed within a given number of days during which time an armistice should be declared. They stated that they desired to be explicitly understood as being willing and anxious to have Carranza a party to the mediation if he would assent to the conditions above referred to.

We said that the American Government was urging the vital importance of having Carranza a party in order to secure the pacification of Mexico; that it considered his presence was so essential to success of mediation that it could consistently and earnestly ask the mediators to be astute in removing obstacles and devising methods by which Carranza be brought in as a party and thus be bound by the plan that might ultimately be adopted.

The mediators constantly urged the serious consequences that might arise from delay, and urged that they fear the inevitable result of Carranza being admitted will bring about delay and they expressed the constant fear that unless matters are speeded that Carranza will be in Mexico City before the mediation is completed. Prompt progress in agreeing upon terms of the mediation may have the advantage of aiding us to secure now assent to terms which would not be acceptable after Carranza had come in. It is possible that it might be advisable to us to agree now on as many details as possible because Carranza and Huerta might themselves object to some conditions which the United States may regard as essential.

In the light of our meeting this morning we are disposed to think the next step might be to ask the mediators to promptly write a letter to Zubaron who could then reply in the light of the facts we have reported.   Commissioners.

T telegram (WP, DLC).

Sir Cecil Arthur Spring Rice to Sir Edward Grey

CONFIDENTIAL.   Washington, June 1, 1914.

Mediators are unwilling to admit Constitutionalist representation unless they agree to armistice. This the latter refuse to do. United States Government is trying to induce mediators to submit their plan to Constitutionalists. Huerta appears to have refused to retire unless he has a voice in the new arrangements, and Constitutionalists will not accept any plan originated by Huerta. There is thus a deadlock.

President told me to-day that Constitutionalists cannot accept armistice because their army would disband, and that United States Government cannot force them to change their attitude except by threat of war, which he is unwilling to make. He is convinced that United States Government can put such pressure on them as practically to make certain that foreigners will be respected, but he cannot make them stop their advance nor accept terms which they think unacceptable. He hopes that mediators may be induced to suggest someone acceptable to both United States and Constitutionalists as provisional President, who could take on the government when Huerta retired. He spoke in high terms of Huerta's patriotism, and said that he hoped to find a solution of the difficulty honourable to Huerta, and that Huerta would understand that what United States Government in their own interest desired was restoration of peace without United States intervention. He felt that it was impossible to prevent advance of Constitutionalists, and that the best thing for all parties would be a quick and quiet transfer of power.

It seems plain from what President says that he regards the occupation of the Central Government by the Constitutionalists as inevitable, and I fear that plan described in Sir L. Carden's telegram No. 155 of 1st June to you (sent after I had seen President) would be regarded as an attempt to prevent their further advance.

T telegram (FO 371/2029, No. 24419, PRO).

To Henry French Hollis

My dear Senator: [The White House] June 2, 1914

Thank you sincerely for your frank letter of May twenty-ninth. I agree with you, and I disagree with you. I believe that we can by a combination of the measures now pending accomplish what it is necessary to accomplish at this session. What I have in mind is a little too intricate to be put into a hastily dictated letter, but conference will easily bring it out as we progress.

I think you will agree with me that we cannot now, as we could not at any former stage, afford to show the least hesitation or lack of courage on this point which is going to be the point of attack during the campaign, as Mr. Roosevelt has kindly apprised us. The men you speak of,—Representative Stevens, Mr. Brandeis, and Mr. Rublee,—have themselves suggested, I hope, a better way of dealing with the only really debatable part of the Clayton Bill. The rest of it seems to me rather plain sailing.

Cordially and sincerely yours,   Woodrow Wilson

TLS (Letterpress Books, WP, DLC).

To Juliet Barrett Rublee

My dear Mrs. Rublee: [The White House] June 2, 1914

Thank you for your letter of May twenty-seventh. I think I understood entirely.

I want to say that I am deeply interested in the question of a health department.

In haste   Sincerely yours,   Woodrow Wilson

TLS (Letterpress Books, WP, DLC).

To George Canada Taylor[1]

My dear Mr. Taylor: [The White House] June 2, 1914

It is with deep and genuine regret that I find myself prevented by public duties here from attending the celebration of the centennial of New Harmony. Everything that I know about that interesting and remarkable community and its unusual history of progress and enlightenment has made me desirous of taking part in a celebration which will illustrate so many of the most interesting features of American life. The history of New Harmony is in a way a type of what America has afforded men of high ideals and steadfast purpose an opportunity to do. The people she has bred, the men she has sent out from her public service, all attest ideals and achievements which I would fain believe to be peculiarly characteristic of the great country we love when seen at its best.

Cordially and sincerely yours,   Woodrow Wilson

TLS (Letterpress Books, WP, DLC).
[1] Native and resident of New Harmony, Ind. He was a lawyer, real estate executive, and secretary of the New Harmony Centennial Commission.

To the Special Commissioners

The White House, June 2, 1914.

The President will send you as early tomorrow as possible a plan to submit to the mediators for discussion in connection with their plan. If the letter has not already been sent to Carranza[1] please try to remove the ambiguity which there still seems to be. It was the mediators letter[2] which Carranza construed to mean that an armistice was necessary. We are afraid that he will construe this letter in the same way. The President is not willing to stand for such a demand. He believes that the presence of Carranza representatives is necessary if the best results are to be secured, and that an armistice should not be made a necessary condition.   Bryan.

T telegram (SDR, RG 59, 812.00/23453a, DNA).
  1 That is, the Mediators to Señor Zubáran, June 2, 1914.
  2 That is, the Mediators to General Carranza, May 3, 1914.

The Special Commissioners to William Jennings Bryan

RECEIVED AND DECIPHERED   Niagara Falls, New York.
AT THE WHITE HOUSE.   8:30 p.m. June 2, 1914.

We have just returned from a conference where we expressed the hope that the mediators would as soon as possible reply to the Zubaron communication. After some talk in which we urged the importance of this course the mediators stated that they had already drafted such a letter which they then read to us. We found it to be couched in the most courteous terms and stating in effect that the Zubaron letter had been construed a different way and they therefore wrote to inquire whether they were to understand that the chief of the Constitutionalist Army desired to have a representative in the conference on terms stated in the original correspondence and asking that if such was his intention that he appoint delegates as soon as possible.

We expressed our gratification that so courteous a letter had been written and after some further conversation on that subject the Brazilian Ambassador inquired if we were willing to continue the discussion of the written plan by the mediators. We expressed a willingness to have the discussion proceed and there was more or less informal talk about the different items listed by them. It was finally agreed that we should put their plan in one column and our modifications, suggestions or substitutes in another as a working basis for future discussion so that any progress made to [be] presented in writing and not left to the memory of the various members of the conference.

All of the items have been so far discussed that we have their general view. They also have ours, but under this suggestion of the double column it will be necessary for us to prepare something definite and concrete. For this reason we should be glad for you to have the double column prepared as we do not consider that our instructions warrant us in making even a tentative proposition in writing on any one of the items. We think it would be undesirable for us to submit to them any written statement even for discussion in which we might not accurately express the wishes of the President.   Commissioners.

T telegram (WP, DLC).

To the Special Commissioners

[The White House] June 3, 1914

While the mediators are debating the admission of a representative of the revolutionists we take the opportunity of setting the whole matter under discussion at Niagara in its full light as it appears to this government, a light which to us grows clearer every day. The attitude of the mediators towards the revolutionists seems to us to indicate as nothing else has their point of view and the radical error of that point of view. They seem to have conceived their outlined plan and to have conducted their discussions with you on the theory that it is the constitutionalists who must be made to yield to the arrangement agreed upon, whereas it is obviously Huerta and the whole body of persons who in any degree support or sympathize with him who must be made to yield. The discussion does not now turn upon terms of accommodation between the United States and Huerta. At the very outset it was understood and it is now obvious to the whole world that Huerta must be eliminated and with him his whole regime. The problem is how peace is to be secured for Mexico, and that means simply this, How is the triumph of the constitutionalist party, which is now clearly triumphant, to be accepted and established without further bloodshed; or, to put it differently, How are representatives of that party to be placed in control of the government under conditions which can be approved and assented to and earnestly pressed for acceptance by the government of the United States. We are not seeking a plan which we would be willing to enforce by arms but a plan which will promptly bring peace and a government which we can recognize and deal with. Recognition or non-recognition is the only means of compulsion we have in mind. A plan which would require the backing of force would if acted on do Mexico more harm than good and would postpone peace indefinitely, not secure it. With these thoughts and conclusions constantly in view, which we have urged repeatedly and from the first, we feel obliged to say that we could not consider the recognition of a provisional government made up in any part of neutrals. There can be no such persons in Mexico among men of force and character. All men of real stuff must have taken sides in one way or another and those who call themselves neutrals are quite certainly partisans of the kind of order and supremacy which Huerta tried to establish whether they adhere to Huerta personally or not. We are convinced that peace can be secured only by facing the inevitable and facing it promptly and with the utmost frankness. The plan, therefore, should be of this sort: an avowed constitutionalist of undoubted character and ability, other than Carranza or Villa, should be made provisional president and should be personally charged with the formulation and promulgation of the necessary and inevitable reforms as a duty to which he would be definitely pledged beforehand, and a board of three persons acceptable to the revolutionists, but one of whom should be a conservative not actively identified with the revolution, should be associated with him to arrange for and have complete charge of the conduct and oversight of the elections which should be planned for to occur not immediately but at a definite future date to be proclaimed by them in consultation with the provisional president. We should in no circumstances outline or even suggest the detail of the reforms. The provisional president would of course consult with whom he pleased in formulating them and their success is entirely dependent upon their being of domestic origin and in no respect dictated by the United States or any other outside government. Both the provisional president and the members of the election board should be pledged not to be candidates at the elections. There should, of course, if we can bring it about, be a general amnesty. This is a very simple plan. The Mexican representatives will, we fear, quite certainly protest against it and the mediators may be very reluctant to accept it until convinced by patient argument on the general lines indicated above that that is all that this government can consider consistently with its avowed policy, but it seems to us in substance inevitable, the only sort of plan that would have the least prospect of producing the settlement and the peace we desire. You will know how to present and urge it. We are delighted to feel that we have spokesmen whose force and method in handling this tedious and difficult but still hopeful business need no direction or improvement[1] from Washington. Following your request as to the parallel columns and using the numbers of the paragraphs used in the statement of the plan proposed by the mediators as set forth in your memorandum sent by mail,[2] we suggest opposite paragraph one: the withdrawal of Huerta and the recognition at Mexico City of an avowed constitutionalist other than Carranza or Villa as provisional president by any process that may prove practicable in the circumstances. A constitutional process is impossible. There is no congress in existence except that which Huerta caused to be chosen in contempt and violation of the constitution. Paragraph second, a board of two constitutionalists and one man associated with those who have refrained from active participation but have liberal sympathies;

that board not to be associated with the provisional president in any administrative matter, but to be constituted a board invested with complete authority to arrange for and conduct the elections. Neither the members of this board nor the provisional president to be a candidate for office at the elections. Paragraph third, a general amnesty to all Mexicans for all political offences. Fourth, elections within a reasonable time after the organization of the provisional government and the promulgation of the reforms to which it should be pledged, the election law of May, 1912, to control. Fifth, the provisional president to be pledged to formulate and promulgate at the earliest possible time such agrarian political and electoral reforms as are necessary to quiet the present revolutionary agitations of the Republic. Sixth, as proposed by the mediators except that the provisional president should be substituted for the board of government. Seven, recognition so soon as it is made evident that the plan is to be carried out as agreed upon. Eight, the time and manner of evacuation by the forces of the United States in Mexico to be matter of agreement between the United States and the provisional government. It ought to be conclusive even with the Mexican representatives that unless the United States is to intervene with arms and practically conquer Mexico, which nobody desires, the only alternative to such a plan as we propose is the armed entrance of Carranza into Mexico City and the assumption of the provisional presidency by Carranza himself.   Bryan

CLST telegram (SDR, RG 59, 812.00/23455a, DNA).
   1 Wilson wrote "prompting" in his shorthand draft (WP, DLC). He misread his shorthand when he made his WWT draft (WP, DLC), and Swem of course followed Wilson's copy.
   2 This memorandum is missing. See WJB to WW, May 30, 1914, "I enclose two written reports . . . ," n. 1. However, the mediators' plan, to which Wilson responded, is reproduced in Secretary Dodge to the Secretary of State, June 17, 1914, *FR 1914*, pp. 539-41.

From Edward Mandell House

My dear Friend: Paris, France. June 3rd, 1914.

   We came from Berlin yesterday. Since writing you I have seen everyone that was worth while excepting the Chancellor. His wife died a few days before our arrival consequently he was not in evidence.

   I was at Potsdam from eleven o'clock until three and talked with the Kaiser for a half hour alone. I am glad to tell you that I have been as successful as anticipated and have ample material to open negociations at London.

I told the Kaiser that you thought perhaps an American could compose this situation better than a European. He concurred in this view and seemed pleased that I had undertaken to start the work. He understands that I am to take the matter up with the British Government, and it was arranged between us to keep him informed in the event results were accomplished. It is my purpose not to write him anything concerning what is said there without first giving the official who makes the statement an opportunity of verifying the correctness of what was said.

The Kaiser concurred also in my suggestion that whatever program America, England & Germany agreed to would be successful. I made it plain, however, that it was the policy of our Government to have no alliances of any character, but we were more than willing to do our share towards promoting international peace.

I find that both England & Germany have one feeling in common and that is fear of one another. Neither wants to be the first to propose negociations, but both are agreed that it should be brought about, though neither desires to make the necessary concessions.

Outside of the Kaiser I had long talks with the Minister for War[1] and Herr Zimmerman[2] Under Sec'y for Foreign Affairs who is much more sympathetic with our purposes than von Jagow. The Minister for War is one of the ablest men that I met. He is a General of much distinction and has been drafted for this place by the Kaiser because of his ability.

I also arranged to keep in touch with Zimmerman. So altogether I am very happy over what has been accomplished and I am eager to get to London to see what can be done there. I have a feeling that the soil will be much more fallow.

If my plans follow completely it is my plan to get Sir Edward Grey to go with me to Kiel at the end of this month ostensibly for the purpose of attending the regatta,[3] but really for the purpose of the three of us getting together, so there may be no go-betweens or misunderstandings.

I am trying to work rapidly as I hope to return by the middle or end of July.

You can never know how I have wished for the benefit of your counsel.   Your faithful and affectionate,   E. M. House

T and HwLS (WP, DLC).
[1] Erich von Falkenhayn.
[2] Arthur Zimmermann.
[3] Which the Kaiser was to attend.

Sir Cecil Spring Rice to Sir Edward Grey

Sir,   Washington, June 3, 1914.

I have the honour to state that the President spoke to me on the 1st instant on the subject of the tolls question. He said that it was unfortunately the case that the democratic majority in the Senate had not an idea of the proper management of business and that as there were no rules a debate could be prolonged indefinitely. This was the more unnecessary that it was known that there was a majority of at least nine in favour of repeal. He added that the question was not regarded as being of great importance in the country, certainly not from the point of view of foreign relations, although the Irish societies had been mobilized against the bill with some success. He did not think that it would play a great part in the November elections. In any case it was beginning to be understood that the only people who would benefit from exemption would be the small body who controlled the coast-wise shipping who already enjoyed a complete monopoly and now desired to add to their advantageous position by getting a subsidy at the expense of the public. . . .

I have the honour to be with the highest respect Sir
    your most obedient humble servant   Cecil Spring Rice

TLS (FO 371/2057, No. 26761, PRO).

A Memorial Address[1]

[June 4, 1914]

Mr. Chairman,[2] Mrs. McLaurin Stevens,[3] ladies and gentlemen:

I assure you that I am profoundly aware of the solemn significance of the thing that has now taken place. The Daughters of the Confederacy have presented a memorial of their dead to the Government of the United States. I hope that you have noted the history of the conception of this idea. It was proposed by a President of the United States who had himself been a distinguished officer in the Union Army. It was authorized by an act of Congress of the United States. The cornerstone of the monument was laid by a President of the United States elevated to his position by the votes of the party which had chiefly prided itself upon sustaining the war for the Union, and who, while Secretary of War, had himself given authority to erect it. And, now, it has fallen to my lot to accept in the name of the great government, which I am privileged for the time to represent, this emblem of a reunited people.

I am not so much happy as proud to participate in this capacity on such an occasion—proud that I should represent such a people. Am I mistaken, ladies and gentlemen, in supposing that nothing of this sort could have occurred in anything but a democracy? The people of a democracy are not related to their rulers as subjects are related to a government. They are themselves the sovereign authority, and, as they are neighbors of each other, quickened by the same influences and moved by the same motives, they can understand each other. They are shot through with some of the deepest and profoundest instincts of human sympathy. They choose their governments; they select their rulers; they live their own life, and they will not have that life disturbed and discolored by fraternal misunderstandings. I know that a reuniting of spirits like this can take place more quickly in our time than in any other because men are now united by an easier transmission of those influences which make up the foundations of peace and of mutual understanding, but no process can work these effects unless there is a conducting medium. The conducting medium in this instance is the united heart of a great people.

I am not going to detain you by trying to repeat any of the eloquent thoughts which have moved us this afternoon, for I rejoice in the simplicity of the task which is assigned to me. My task is this, ladies and gentlemen: This chapter in the history of the United States is now closed, and I can bid you turn with me with your faces to the future, quickened by the memories of the past, but with nothing to do with the contests of the past, knowing, as we have shed our blood upon opposite sides, we now face and admire one another. I do not know how many years ago it was that the Century Dictionary was published, but I remember one day in the Century Cyclopedia of Names I had occasion to turn to the name of Robert E. Lee, and I found him there in that book, published in New York City, simply described as a great American general. The generosity of our judgments did not begin today. The generosity of our judgments was made up soon after this great struggle was over. Men came and sat together again in the Congress and united in all the efforts of peace and of government, and our solemn duty is to see that each one of us is in his own consciousness and in his own conduct a replica of this great reunited people. It is our duty and our privilege to be like the country we represent and, speaking no word of malice, no word of criticism, even, stand shoulder to shoulder to lift the burdens of mankind in the future and show the paths of freedom to all the world.[4]

T transcript (WC, NjP) of CLSsh (C. L. Swem Coll., NjP).

¹ At the unveiling of a monument to the dead soldiers of the Confederacy, erected by the United Daughters of the Confederacy at the Arlington National Cemetery. General Bennett H. Young, commander in chief of the United Confederate Veterans, and General Washington Gardner, commander in chief of the Grand Army of the Republic, also spoke.

² Hilary A. Herbert, chairman of the Arlington Confederate Memorial Association, former congressman from Alabama; Secretary of the Navy during the second Cleveland administration.

³ Daisy McLaurin (Mrs. William Forrest) Stevens, President General of the United Daughters of the Confederacy.

⁴ There is a WWT outline of this address, dated June 4, 1914, in WP, DLC.

To Walter Hines Page

My dear Page: The White House June 4, 1914

I am very grateful to you for your letter of May twenty-first.¹ By reproducing for me the life of those among whom you move and the talk that goes on, you give me something like the inside view and the vivid personal impressions which you yourself get, and I am genuinely grateful. It helps me immensely, at the same time that it interests me most deeply.

The thing which seems to me most important now with regard to the Mexican business is that the people over there should get a more just and correct view of Villa. Carranza I believe to be an honest but a very narrow and rather dull person whom it is extremely difficult to deal with but who can be counted upon no doubt to try to do the right thing by those who are now centering their hopes in him for working out a decent solution of the economic problem which underlies the situation in Mexico just as much as the land question underlay the settlement of affairs in Ireland. A landless people will always furnish the inflammable material for a revolution.

There is an article on Villa, under the title "The Man of the Hour in Mexico," appearing in this week's number of the (American) Outlook,² which, so far as I can judge by the hasty examination I have so far been able to give it, contains an intimate estimate of Villa which I think it would be worth your while to look up and to filter into London society.

With warmest regard and abiding appreciation,
                    Faithfully yours,   Woodrow Wilson

TLS (W. H. Page Papers, MH).

¹ WHP to WW, May 21, 1914, ALS (WP, DLC), describing a dinner given for King Christian X of Denmark at Buckingham Palace.

² He referred to Gregory Mason, "The Mexican Man of the Hour," *The Outlook*, cvii (June 6, 1914), 292-306. After studying Villa at close hand, Mason reported that he was "the right man in the right place," "the only Mexican strong enough to save Mexico from herself." Although cruel and uneducated, he possessed "natural shrewdness" and had "developed under growing responsibility." Villa, moreover, was the only Constitutionalist officer in favor of peace

with the United States, and he had won the others over "by sheer force of personality." At a dinner given to Villa by the war correspondents, Mason said that Villa had exhorted his followers and Americans to practice mutual forbearance and to stand together for the elimination of Huerta. As he spoke, he looked "not so much like a great general whose name spells terror to his enemies as like a big, earnest boy—the captain of a football team, if you will —urging his companions to fight harder."

To Stephen Samuel Wise

My dear Friend: The White House June 4, 1914

I thank you for your letter of June second[1] and for the enclosure from Mr. David Stern,[2] which I herewith return.

I am very much distressed that the friends in North Carolina, with whom you spoke, should have got the impression they have got. I do not blame them in the least, but there are many circumstances upon which I do not think they reflect. In the first place, I am bound by the old practice and expectation of everybody as opinion is organized here in Washington to respect and accept the recommendations of Congressmen and Senators, if they recommend men unexceptionable in character and ability. I have again and again turned away from recommendations made me because I wished to recognize the men closely associated with what I had striven for, but I have had no means of getting advice on that head except from individuals, and very often the individuals who offered their advice were interested parties. It is a thorny and difficult matter altogether in which I have not satisfied myself and in which I am grieved to learn I have not satisfied my friends.

Cordially and sincerely yours,   Woodrow Wilson

TLS (S. S. Wise Papers, American Jewish Archives).
  [1] S. S. Wise to JPT, June 2, 1914, CCL (S. S. Wise Papers, American Jewish Historical Society).
  [2] A young lawyer of Greensboro, N. C.

To Lindley Miller Garrison

My dear Mr. Secretary: [The White House] June 4, 1914

I saw Mr. Jones, of the House of Representatives, yesterday, who discussed with me the bill with regard to the government of the Philippine Islands which the Democrats on his committee have agreed to. He told me that he had been in conference with General McIntyre. I am wondering whether you, yourself, went over the provisions of the bill or are familiar with them.

In haste   Faithfully yours,   Woodrow Wilson

TLS (Letterpress Books, WP, DLC).

A Commencement Address[1]

[[June 5, 1914]]

Mr. Superintendent,[2] young gentlemen, ladies and gentlemen:

During the greater part of my life I have been associated with young men, and on occasions, it seems to me without number, have faced bodies of youngsters going out to take part in the activities of the world, but I have a consciousness of a different significance in this occasion from that which I have felt on other similar occasions. When I have faced the graduating classes at universities, I have felt that I was facing a great conjecture. They were going out into all sorts of pursuits and with every degree of preparation for the particular thing they were expecting to do; some without any preparation at all, for they did not know what they expected to do. But in facing you I am facing men who are trained for a special thing. You know what you are going to do, and you are under the eye of the whole nation in doing it. For you, gentlemen, are to be part of the power of the Government of the United States. There is a very deep and solemn significance in that fact, and I am sure that every one of you feels it. The moral is perfectly obvious. Be ready and fit for anything that you have to do. And keep ready and fit. Do not grow slack. Do not suppose that your education is over because you have received your diplomas from the academy. Your education has just begun. Moreover, you are to have a very peculiar privilege which not many of your predecessors have had. You are yourselves going to become teachers.[3] You are going to teach those 50,000 fellow countrymen of yours who are the enlisted men of the navy. You are going to make them fitter to obey your orders and to serve the country. You are going to make them fitter to see what the orders mean in their outlook upon life and upon the service; and that is a great privilege, for out of you is going the energy and intelligence which are going to quicken the whole body of the United States Navy.

I congratulate you upon that prospect, but I want to ask you not to get the professional point of view. I would ask it of you if you were lawyers; I would ask it of you if you were merchants; I would ask it of you whatever you expected to be. Do not get the professional point of view. There is nothing narrower or more unserviceable than the professional point of view—to have the attitude toward life that it centers in your profession. It does not. Your profession is only one of the many activities which are meant to keep the world straight, and to keep the energy in its blood and in its muscle. We are all of us in this world, as I understand it, to set forward the affairs of the whole world, though we play a special part in that great function. The navy goes all over the world, and I think it is to be congratulated upon having that sort of illustration of what the world is and what it contains; and inasmuch as you are going all over the world you ought to be the better able to see the relation that your country bears to the rest of the world.

It ought to be one of your thoughts all the time that you are sample Americans—not merely sample navy men, not merely sample soldiers, but sample Americans—and that you have the point of view of America with regard to her navy and her army; that she is using them as the instruments of civilization, not as the instruments of aggression. The idea of America is to serve humanity, and every time you let the Stars and Stripes free to the wind you ought to realize that that is in itself a message that you are on an errand which other navies have sometimes forgotten; not an errand of conquest, but an errand of service. I always have the same thought when I look at the flag of the United States, for I know something of the history of the struggle of mankind for liberty. When I look at that flag it seems to me as if the white stripes were stripes of parchment upon which are written the rights of man, and the red stripes the streams of blood by which those rights have been made good. Then in the little blue firmament in the corner have swung out the stars of the states of the American Union. So, it is, as it were, a sort of floating charter that has come down to us from Runnymede, when men said, "We will not have masters; we will be a people, and we will seek our own liberty."

You are not serving a government, gentlemen; you are serving a people. For we who for the time being constitute the government are merely instruments for a little while in the hands of a great nation which chooses whom it will to carry out its decrees and who invariably rejects the man who forgets the ideals which it intended him to serve. So that I hope that wherever you go you will have a generous, comprehending love of the people you come into contact with, and will come back and tell us, if you can, what service the United States can render to the remotest parts of the world; tell us where you see men suffering; tell us where you think advice will lift them up; tell us where you think that the counsel of statesmen may better the fortunes of unfortunate men; always having it in mind that you are champions of what is right and fair all 'round for the public welfare, no matter where you are, and that it is that you are ready to fight for and not merely on the drop of a hat or upon some slight punctillio, but that you are champions of your fellow men, particularly of that great body one hundred million strong whom you represent in the United States.

What do you think is the most lasting impression that those boys down at Veracruz are going to leave? They have had to use some force—I pray God it may not be necessary for them to use any more—but do you think that the way they fought is going to be the most lasting impression? Have men not fought ever since the world began? Is there anything new in using force? The new things in the world are the things that are divorced from force. The things that show the moral compulsions of the human conscience, those are the things by which we have been building up civilization, not by force. And the lasting impression that those boys are going to leave is this, that they exercise self-control; that they are ready and diligent to make the place where they went fitter to live in than they found it; that they regarded other people's rights; that they did not strut and bluster, but went quietly, like self-respecting gentlemen, about their legitimate work. And the people of Veracruz, who feared the Americans and despised the Americans, are going to get a very different taste in their mouths about the whole thing when the boys of the navy and the army come away. Is that not something to be proud of, that you know how to use force like men of conscience and like gentlemen, serving your fellow men and not trying to overcome them? Like that gallant gentleman who has so long borne the heats and perplexities and distresses of the situation in Veracruz—Admiral Fletcher. I mention him, because his service there has been longer, and so much of the early perplexities fell upon him. I have been in almost daily communication with Admiral Fletcher, and I have tested his temper. I have tested his discretion. I know that he is a man with a touch of statesmanship about him, and he has grown bigger in my eye each day as I have read his dispatches, for he has sought always to serve the thing he was trying to do in the temper that we all recognize and love to believe is typically American.

I challenge you youngsters to go out with these conceptions, knowing that you are part of the government and force of the United States and that men will judge us by you. I am not afraid of the verdict. I cannot look in your faces and doubt what it will be, but I want you to take these great engines of force out onto the seas like adventurers enlisted for the elevation of the spirit of the human race. For that is the only distinction that America has. Other nations have been strong, other nations have piled wealth as high as the sky, but they have come into disgrace because they used their force and their wealth for the oppression of mankind and their own aggrandizement; and America will not bring glory to herself, but disgrace, by following the beaten paths of history. We must strike out upon new paths, and we must count upon you gentlemen to be the explorers who will carry this spirit and spread this message all over the seas and in every port of the civilized world.

You see, therefore, why I said that when I faced you I felt there was a special significance. I am not present on an occasion when you are about to scatter on various errands. You are all going on the same errand, and I like to feel bound with you in one common organ for the glory of America. And her glory goes deeper than all the tinsel, goes deeper than the sound of guns and the clash of sabers; it goes down to the very foundation of those things that have made the spirit of men free and happy and content.[4]

Printed in *Address of President Wilson to the Graduating Class of the United States Naval Academy* (Washington, 1918).
    [1] At the United States Naval Academy. Congressman Lemuel Phillips Padgett of Tennessee, chairman of the House Committee on Naval Affairs, also spoke.
    [2] Captain William Freeland Fullam, superintendent since February 7, 1914.
    [3] A reference to Secretary Daniels' General Order 53, issued October 1, 1913. It provided for a system of continuing education, to be conducted by officers, on every ship in the navy. See Josephus Daniels, *The Wilson Era—Years of Peace, 1910-1917* (Chapel Hill, N. C., 1944), pp. 253-56.
    [4] There is a WWT outline of this address, dated June 5, 1914, in WP, DLC.

To William Jennings Bryan

My dear Mr. Secretary: The White House June 5, 1914

I return the enclosed papers.[1] I have already told you, I believe, what is my judgment in the matter of Carothers' retaining his connection with the government while serving as superintendent of a plantation.

With regard to Canova,[2] I would be very much obliged if you would act upon my suggestion of the other day by bringing him into touch with General Scott and obtaining General Scott's impression of his fitness for the delicate duty we have thought of assigning him to.

                    Faithfully yours,   Woodrow Wilson

TLS (SDR, RG 59, 812.00/12344, DNA).
    [1] B. W. Long to WJB, June 2, 1914, TLS (SDR, RG 59, 812.00/12343, DNA), enclosing G. C. Carothers to B. W. Long, May 27, 1914, TLS, same file number.
    [2] B. W. Long to WJB, June 1, 1914, TLS (SDR, RG 59, 812.00/12342, DNA), with numerous enclosures, suggesting that Leon Joseph Canova be sent to General Carranza as a special agent of the State Department. Canova was a native Floridian, businessman, and journalist. He sympathized with the Cubans

in their war for independence from Spain. After the war, in 1898, he went to Havana and engaged in the real estate business. For five years, he edited *La Lucha,* one of Cuba's leading newspers. From 1909 until 1913, he served as chief of the Cuban Bureau of Information.

To Thomas Davies Jones

My dear Friend, The White House 5 June, 1914.

I am going to take the liberty of asking you a very intimate question: If I were to nominate you as a member of the Federal Reserve Board under the new banking and currency law, could you and would you accept?

I need not tell you what deep gratification it would give me to have you say Yes to that question. What I need here more than anything else, and desire more deeply than I know the right way to say, is the presence of men about me whom I know and have seen tested and can feel absolute confidence in at every turn of the difficult business of the government.

I am writing this letter with my own hand (this machine is my pen); so that the question and answer are just between ourselves.

With warmest regard,

Faithfully Yours, Woodrow Wilson

WWTLS (Mineral Point, Wisc., Public Library).

From Walter Hines Page

Dear Mr. President: London. June 5. 1914

I have been here a year and I have spent of my own money somewhat more than $30,000, and for a part of this I have been obliged to go into debt. The pending appropriation bill, of which you were kind enough to write me, will add $8,000 a year to the allowance of $7,000 hitherto made for all the business expenses of the embassy—clerk-hire, rent, telegrams etc. etc. The offices have for 30 years cost $1,500 a year rent, but they will henceforth cost $5,000. There will, therefore, be left out of the $15,000, only $4,500 to apply to the rent of the ambassador's residence. In other words, my deficit (say) of $30,500 will be reduced to $26,000 a year. This is so much more than I can afford that I wrote you a letter on Sunday giving my resignation and asking you to have a letter of recall sent to me. But I have decided first to send you this tiresome letter instead—to see, since you are kind enough to wish me to remain here and since I have just reached a place in my adjustment to this task that

will, I hope, enable me to be of some real service in the future
—to see if some way cannot be found for you to have at least
one representative in a great capital who need not be a rich man.

At the risk of wearying you (rather, it is a dead certainty that
I will weary you) I will try to explain the whole situation. For,
looked at from the United States, it seems preposterous that an
American ambassador in London must have from $45,000 to
$50,000 a year properly to do his task. But this is the centre of the
world, and the American ambassador has by far more duties laid
on him than all the rest of the ambassadors here put together.
Ambassadors are given precedence over all but royal persons, and
this preëminence carries very costly obligations. Everybody in
official and in social life offers him entertainment, and some
of these entertainments must of course be returned. I have returned perhaps one in five—not more. This is necessary, if for no
other reason, to prevent hindering criticism. Every Thursday
afternoon—Mrs. Page's day at home—from 100 to 250 people
call, besides large numbers on other days. These callers are persons in official life, the ruling class in English society, and Americans. A record of them must be kept & calls must be returned.
This all means servants, tea, sandwiches, a secretary for Mrs.
Page, a motor-car, and visiting cards by the thousand. Then there
are invitations to dinner, to luncheon, to country houses, palace-
functions—all mean expense; and every member of the diplomatic
corps accepts them in the regular pursuit of his business. In
addition to all these the American ambassador is asked sooner
or later to all the cities where the Lord-Mayors and councils
entertain him; learned societies and all other sorts of organizations invite him. All these cost. Not a day passes but I am making speeches or taking journeys, short or long, by rail or by
motor, trying to interpret our institutions and our life. All these
activities are essential, being part & parcel of the better understanding of the two peoples and warp & woof of our international
friendliness. There is no other way to give expression to these
close relations.

Then there are thousands of Americans who come here. Presently, for example, the training ships from Annapolis will come
to the coast. The commanding officer will call on me. I must
go to his ship in return. We must exchange dinners, I inviting
certain English admirals to meet him. We may dispense with
these things in the U. S. If we omitted them here, we shd. start
unfriendly gossip throughout Europe. Again on any nation's
natal day, the London ambassador opens his house to his com-
patriots. A few hundred call on the other ambassadors. On the

American from 3,000 to 4,000 call. I have to hire a hotel—
$1500! I have thought of omitting it, but everybody warns me
not to do so. There surely wd. be a howl if I did. The ambassador
is the visible symbol of the U. S. to these folk.

Now such activities as these are not merely the fashion. They
have become fixed by long use and habit. Things of mere fashion
I have persistently omitted and disregarded. In other words, a
man who is going to be the American ambassador in London has
got to do these and such things. Else he wd. not represent the
U. S. to these people at all. He could be a clerk and transmit
and carry messages to the Foreign Secretary. But he could have
no influence on public opinion—could not be a personage in any
sense; he could not know the English people, he would not be
highly regarded by them, nor could he ever hear or find out such
things as I have sometimes written you in my letters.

Of course I have thought all this out. I have thought of omitting most of these things and of taking a small house on a side
street and living within my salary. That's possible, and, seen from
the U. S., it seemed practicable. But it isn't practicable, without
utterly changing the nature of the task and omitting the most
important parts of it. As it is, the U. S. Government (God knows)
is held in contempt enough for not providing its ambassador with
a home. This omission has been flung in my face, I am sure,
every day that I have been here. Even in official circles, it is
continually held against us. This British Government has a house
in Washington, it makes its ambassador an allowance for various
expenses and pays him a salary of $50,000 a year. It is regarded
as a poor return compliment that our Gov't has no home here
and skimps our ambassador or sends a rich man who makes a
merely gorgeous display of wealth. They don't like it. Every
other country that has an ambassador here (except the Turkish)
owns a house or has a house and a long lease; it has furnished
it well; it allows a fund for entertainment. Everybody knows
that my house (much the shabbiest of all the embassies) is hired
by me from year to year, and is not properly furnished but has a
sort of respectable-boardinghouse appearance, as furnished-
houses-to-let generally have.* The absence of an embassy here
has become a public scandal. As I think of this criminal omission
all these years while every town of any size in the U. S. has got
its big post-office building, I feel an almost irresistible impulse to
send my letter of resignation without more ado. For men and

* I have just come from dining with the Swedish Minister. His house in its
furnishing and dignity puts mine to shame—Sweden, if you please—about as
big as New Jersey!

governments do not waste their money in these ways. And here, in the principal capital of Europe, while France, Germany, Austria, Italy, Spain, Japan all have proper homes, costing each from $250,000 to $500,000, we have—nothing; and yet the American ambassador has to bear this burden and disgrace and to do more duties than all the others put together and—to pay his own bills!

The offices have remained the same for about 30 years. In that time the whole street where they are has become a cheap shopping street—as if they were between two stores down on Pennsylvania Ave. in Washington. The stores have caused an increase in rental value and made the place less desirable for our uses. The entrance is the same as to the cheap flats above. A little while ago, a woman who lives in one of these flats made a sensation in the courts; and once in a while I have met immodest-looking women in the hall. I have always wished to move these offices. But these offices have been the one stable thing about our establishment in London. So long as there was hope that a house might be leased for a term of years for the Ambassador, it seemed best to let the offices remain till such a house could be taken and then move them (the offices) also—but not to move them twice.

During the last 15 or 20 years living conditions (and the duties laid on the American ambassador) have greatly changed. In Lowell's day, a man, [(]under Queen Victoria's simple reign) could live and do his duty on $20,000 to $25,000 a year. But even then Lowell went home poor, and Phelps, I have heard, was literally a bankrupt. Hay was a rich man. Choate (so I have heard since I came here) spent at least $65,000 a year. Of course Mr. Reid did the harmful absurdity of spending several hundred of thousands. Old Henry James, who often comes to my house, the other day told an American lady—in a complimentary way to me—that I was "doing-er the task-er just—just right"—in one of his endless sentences—"no Dorchester house vulgarity and no third-story-room back." Not a man in any big capital in Europe, as our ambassador, gets off, I hear, with less than $50,000, and I suspect that every one spends more. Herrick in Paris spends more than $100,000 a year. Not an ambassador in London (again excepting the Turk, who doesn't count) gets off with $50,000 if his house-rent were reckoned in. We had as well say, then, that the American ambassador here—necessarily the most costly of all the diplomatic posts—so long as he has to pay his house-rent and all his official entertainment bills, must have at least $50,000, if he do his task creditably.

There has been a curious reversion from a fair start. Isn't it true that Dr. Benj.' Franklin, in France, received $17,000 a year— a great deal more than $17,000 a year now—a grant for official entertaining and a coach and pair? That was before the day of the backwoods Congressman and the professional Irish politician. And to give the ambassador here and in Madrid & in Mexico the same salary is a ridiculous absurdity. No other Government does such a thing.

As matters now stand, I have as salary $17,000; for rent of a residence (out of the pending $15,000 appropriation) $4,500— total $21,500. I have an income of about $19,000 a year (I have already spent it, however, for this year and next) but counting this, the deficit still is $18,500—reckoning total cost at $50,000. I have this year spent several thousand more.

I have varying moods. As I write this, I feel as I felt last Sunday when I wrote out my resignation—that's the wisest way out of the difficulty: give it up and tell the public the whole truth, that we can have only rich men for ambassadors—swallow my loss, forget it, and go back to my work and earn my living. Then I have another mood—that it is exceedingly unfortunate to change ambassadors so often, that I owe it to you to make every even desperate effort not to have to give up for sheer financial reasons. Moreover, I believe, at least in my vainer moments, that I have now made such an adjustment of myself to this task as to warrant the hope of doing it with some credit the next two or three years: I have made most of the inevitable mistakes and outlived them, and I have made the acquaintance of the people. The following plans have suggested themselves to me—whether they are practicable, I do not know and I do not presume to say:

An old acquaintance of mine, as I wrote you, has offerred me $10,000 a year as long as I stay here. *I* can't accept it; but could the Department accept it and pay it to me, as the Agricultural Department, for example, accepts money from the General Education Board and pays it to government employes?

Could the general contingency fund be made to yield any additional sum? say for purely official entertainments, automobile keep etc?

Of course, hiring a furnished house, year by year, is the most costly way to live. I have even thought of trying to raise a fund of $200,000, more or less, among my friends to take a long lease on a house and to furnish it properly (for residence and offices) trusting to the Government to take it off my (their) hands. But I am hindered from that by the fact that I personally shd. profit by that: I can't ask men to put up money for me—personally.

Besides, God knows whether the Government wd. ever take it over.

For we have gone on in this shabby fashion so long that perhaps no conceivable Congress can be made to understand what an embassy is—or ought to be. We have gone on making them the social happy-hunting-grounds of rich men and continually lowering our standing in English eyes at least; and this is one reason why our Government is held in contempt here, cordially as they regard our people and our nation.

As soon as Parliament adjourns and the Court functions are over, which an ambassador must in proper courtesy attend, I am going 25 miles out of London where I have hired a tiny cottage for three months; I shall dismiss most of my servants and close up this house. I can live for this vacation time much more cheaply. But the question of the future is urgent. In less than a month I must say whether I want this house for another year. As matters stand now, I must say 'No' and must prepare to go home in October.

I fear I must take some blame on myself for getting into this box at all; for, if I had know[n] what the real task is and that the obligatory cost is so great, of course I should not have dared to come. But nobody was frank with me about this aspect of the post —neither Mr. Choate nor Mr. White. In fact nobody (but you and me) seems ever to be quite frank about our relations to Great Britain. Consequently the public here, both official and private, construes our lack of an embassy as proof of our fear of the Irish and of the yellow press. They assume that these determine our policy; and this assumption fits practically every fact and every occurrence for the last decade or two, except only your Message asking for the repeal of the discriminating tolls-clause in the Panama act. And when an ambassador talks about a really satisfactory mutual understanding and trust, the man who sits next him says when he sits down: "It's a real pity that your great government can't have an embassy in London." Merely as a diplomatic asset, a good house here would be worth to us a thousand times what it wd. cost. The lack of it plays so import[ant] a part in British public opinion that I have had moods when it seemed to me hardly worth any man's while to keep going night and day to try to counteract the effect of this omission. It is often said here by men who are kind enough to like me that I am the only entirely frank and friendly ambassador that has been here since Lowell—the only one that frankly recognizes our English background. The others seemed to leave the impression that the Irish, the Italians, the Jews, the Lithuanians etc. etc.

have become so numerous and important that English is spoken by perhaps only a small majority of our people. I don't believe that this is a fair criticism or that it reflects the opinion of any considerable number of people here; but it is only an exaggeration of a feeling that has a wide existence

I pray you pardon all this, my dear Mr. President. It is an unpardonably long explanation of an unfortunate situation. I imagine after all that the best way out of it is for you to relieve me of further duties that I cannot pay for, find a man of fortune for this post, too, and let my resignation help, if it can be made to help, towards an understanding of the whole diplomatic problem. Perhaps that's the best service I can render, after all. But I shouldn't be candid if I didn't express a profound regret, for I am eager now, since I have begun to learn how, to serve you and to do what I can to build up a right understanding of us & of our Government abroad. The first step in building up such a right understanding here must be a home for our ambassador. If I go away, however, because I can't afford it and my successor has to pay for his own house—that'll not be a flattering or helpful condition for him to begin his labour under. If I thought it defensible from any point of view to go further into debt, I should have done so & never written this letter; for it's surely a bad predicament.

Yours most heartily,   Walter H. Page

ALS (WP, DLC).

From Lindley Miller Garrison

My dear Mr. President: Washington. June 5, 1914.

I received your letter of June 4th, in which you refer to your conferences with Mr. Jones and query whether I have gone over the provisions of his bill and am familiar with them.

I have never seen the bill that Mr. Jones showed you; however, I have from time to time been familiar with many of the details. Mr. Jones very frequently comes to the Department and goes over different features of the matter with General McIntyre, who then comes in at times when he can get me disengaged, and goes over the matters with me, so that I have had a general running knowledge of what was being formulated.

Today I have taken up the matter in detail, and hope, by the first of the week, to furnish you with a written commentary on the subject. Later, and after you have read that, I, of course, will be delighted to take the matter up with you in a personal interview at any time fixed by you.

I have thought well to cable to the Philippines a skeleton of the Jones Bill—that is enough to indicate to our Commissioners there the essential features to be considered. I have asked each of the four to give us their views upon the general subject and such details as are essential in their nature. I did this, first, because I wished to do them the courtesy which I felt was necessary and proper, and, second, because their views will, in my judgment, be valuable as an aid to us.

Sincerely yours,   Lindley M. Garrison

TLS (WP, DLC).

From John Grier Hibben

My dear Mr. President   Princeton, New Jersey June 6/1914

I have had several interviews with Mr. Wilder and Mr. Bridges concerning your proposed visit to Princeton on Saturday next; but inasmuch as my information as to your plans comes indirectly through these gentlemen, I am writing to learn from you yourself in what way the University may best meet your wishes in this matter. I would assure you that we shall be pleased to do anything which lies in our power to add to the enjoyment of your visit, and particularly we should be honored if your plans permit your staying with us at Prospect.

Sincerely yours   John Grier Hibben

ALS (WP, DLC).

William Phillips to Joseph Patrick Tumulty, with Enclosure

Dear Mr. Tumulty: Washington. June 6, 1914.

I have received the enclosed letter from Mr. John Reed,[1] a well known newspaper correspondent, who has been publishing articles on Carranza and Villa in the Metropolitan and Cosmopolitan magazines. I saw him recently in Washington at the President's request, and he was full of interesting information relative to the conditions in northern Mexico. He now seeks an interview with the President, and I shall be glad to have you advise me in the matter.

Sincerely yours,   William Phillips

Okeh, if you think other newspaper men will not follow his example in too great numbers.   W.W.

---

[1] John [Silas] Reed, born 1887, Harvard 1910, poet, journalist, and socialist.

ENCLOSURE

John Reed to William Phillips

Dear Mr. Phillipps: Provincetown Mass. June 4, 1914.

I intend to publish my articles on Mexico in a book the first part of September.[1] I am going to try and just present pictures of the struggle down there as I saw it, keeping as far as possible my own opinions and deductions in the background. But I think that possibly I can have an opportunity to put over the Administration's point of view in an introductory chapter.

I should like to have an interview with President Wilson if possible inside of two weeks. It begins to look as if his policy with regard to Mexico were going to be magnificently successful. I should like to present that policy and have him tell me what he thinks will be its effect upon the relations between the United States and the other American Republics, upon the relations of the Great Powers and the subordinate nations, and generally its effect upon the foreign policy of the United States. I want him to give me his intimate personal notions about why peace is more desirable than war, and why the social and economic freedom of a people is more important than property. I want him to tell me the inside story of the non-recognition of Huerta and the occupation of Vera Cruz, and to indicate, if possible, in what way our Mexican policy has been consistent from first to last. I would like to know as much as he can tell me of the history of the secret pressure brought to bear upon him by foreign nations whose citizens were heavily interested in the Republic.

I do not think the various moves of the Administration with regard to Mexico are at all understood, even in the United States. The newspapers favorable to the President's policy have, in their bewilderment, failed to convey anything but the impression that the whole business is a series of lucky blunders based on an unworldly idealism. I have an idea that it is a pretty careful, well-thought-out plan. It seems to me that it would be of value to present the whole thing to the world. I would like, before putting it in my book, to publish it in magazines both here and abroad.

Will you try and arrange an interview, please, and let me know at Provincetown?   Yours sincerely,   John Reed

TLS (WP, DLC).
1 It appeared as *Insurgent Mexico* (New York and London, 1914).

To Mary Allen Hulbert

My dearest Friend,   The White House 7 June, 1914.

I cannot tell you how it startled me to get a letter from you from a hospital, and learn that you had been there for two weeks to be treated and observed! I am taking you at your word and assuming that you will be back at Nantucket by the time this gets there, carrying my messages of affectionate sympathy and concern. Please tell me just what the doctors did and said, and whether they think that you should soon have an operation on your neck. We shall all worry until we know just what and how much is the matter. I was touched by your suggestion about giving a haven and rest at Nantucket to some tired old lady in need of what the big house, with its empty rooms, and the wholesome sea, with its free airs, and the gracious lady whose presence makes the place so full of warm human sympathies, could give, and you may be sure I shall keep the thing in mind, both for your sake and for hers.

I am very, very blue and out of heart to-day. My dear one absolutely wore herself out last winter and this spring and has not even started to come up hill again yet. She can eat and retain almost nothing, and grows weaker and weaker, with a pathetic patience and sweetness all the while which make it all the more nearly heart-breaking for those of us who love her. There is nothing at all the matter with her organically: it is altogether functional; and the doctors assure us that all with care will come out right. But a nervous break down is no light matter and my heart is very heavy. I am, therefore, unfit to write you a cheerful letter, such as you need and I would so love to write. I can only tell you how we are all thinking of you with genuine affection and sympathy and solicitude. I am well, despite the accumulated strain of things. I seem to have powers of endurance I never suspected. And no amount of business or strain of anxiety can even weaken my consciousness of dear friends or long interrupt my eager thought of them. Welcome back to your garden and your little domain by the sea!
          Your devoted friend,   Woodrow Wilson

WWTLS (WP, DLC).

Remarks at a Press Conference

June 8, 1914

Gentlemen, I will have to tell you, for your information, confidentially—though this is a rather large group—I say confidentially, because it hasn't come very directly or directly from this government, that we have learned that General Huerta has suspended his order for a blockade of Tampico. What is on your minds this morning?

Mr. President, have you ever expressed any disapproval at any time of the so-called Norris amendment?[1]

> I haven't been given an opportunity to express a favorable or unfavorable opinion.

Mr. President, when you asked for the repeal of the exemption, you said something to the effect that you hoped it would be given in such ungrudging measure to enable you to meet without embarrassment certain other questions. Will the amended repeal bill with the amendment fail to meet that hope?

> No, it does not. It does not alter the repeal in the least degree. Of course, as you understand, and as I interpret the whole matter, it is quite unnecessary. Legislation doesn't waive treaty rights and can't conceivably waive treaty rights, so that it doesn't alter the character of the legislation at all.

It doesn't really raise the question, then, of whether we are right or wrong, which you hope will be avoided?

> It doesn't necessarily raise it at all. It is a strong intimation that, at any rate, some of the gentlemen who voted for the repeal don't wish to be understood as settling the question of right or wrong by their vote. That is the point, I understand, it is intended to mean. And of course, any one of them could have done that by a personal statement on the floor.

You won't object, Mr. President, to its going through? You have no particular objection to it?

> Well, I'm not saying.

Mr. President, can you tell us anything with regard to the form that the Philippine legislation is expected to take?

> The form—you mean the character of it? No, I can't. Mr. Jones has a bill which I understand he is about to introduce, which he was kind enough to bring to me, and I have been reading it over very carefully and am just now consulting with the men in the War Department who have been most familiar with Philippine affairs, to see what details of the matter need to be re-studied, so that it is now just in that shape when I am forming an opinion about it.

Do you expect any action on that by either House or Senate, or both, at this session?

> Action on anything additional is of course problematical to, of course, the state of business in the Senate.

Is there anything about the conservation program, Mr. President, in the House?

> I understand from one conference which I held that there is a very good prospect of the conservation bills passing the House. I sincerely hope so.

Is that the old Jones bill?

> No. It is an entirely different bill.

Has it been introduced so that you could—

> It hasn't been introduced yet, and I don't feel at liberty to discuss the features of it yet. It may be modified before it is introduced.

Mr. President, is there anything you can tell us about the Colorado situation? Is there any change? Are the troops to be left there?

> The troops are to remain there for the present, pending developments, which I think are hopeful. That is why there are some rifts in the clouds that hang over the attempt at a settlement by conference. And I am waiting to see how that develops—I mean a conference between the operators and the miners.

How about the Federal Reserve Board, Mr. President?

> I hope I shall be ready in a day or two to announce my nominations.

The ratification of the Colombian treaty—is it urged at this session?

> That is a matter upon which I haven't talked with the Secretary of State recently, and I can't say. He is in conference with the Foreign Relations Committee and will know better than I whether they will be ready to take it up or not.

JRT transcript (WC, NjP) of CLSsh (C. L. Swem Coll., NjP).

[1] The Norris-Simmons amendment to the Sims bill. Introduced by Senator Furnifold M. Simmons on June 6, it reserved all American rights under the Hay-Pauncefote Treaty. It represented a compromise of the amendment originally introduced by Senator George W. Norris on April 1, affirming the right of the United States to exempt its coastwise traffic from the payment of tolls. The Senate passed the Sims bill with the Norris-Simmons amendment on June 11, 1914.

To William Atkinson Jones

My dear Mr. Jones: [The White House] June 8, 1914

The night of the day you handed me your Philippine Bill I read it very carefully and the next morning got into conference with the Secretary of War to see if he had been in touch with General McIntyre and had anything to suggest. He has been actively preparing to advise me in the matter and has promised to do so the early part of this week. I write you these things as a report of progress.

Cordially and sincerely yours,   Woodrow Wilson

TLS (Letterpress Books, WP, DLC).

From Norman Hapgood, with Enclosure

Dear Mr. President: New York June 8, 1914

I am sending along a letter from Charles McCarthy. Please do not trouble to return it. He has had a large share in the creative forward movement in Wisconsin, and his devotion to you is very genuine. I do not think I have ever known any one whose interest in his own career bore a smaller proportion to his desire to get the right thing done.

Yours sincerely,   Norman Hapgood

E N C L O S U R E

Charles McCarthy to Norman Hapgood

Dear Mr. Hapgood: Madison [Wisc.] June 3, 1914.

I want to thank you for Julian Mason's great article.[1] It was good stuff, and is exciting the right kind of attention in our state. Anything I can do to help you at any time, please let me know.

I suppose you are now in touch with Mr. Rublee, in Washington. Am sorry the Clayton bill is going so far, as I regard it as an entirely vicious bill. I think Mr. Brandeis is of the same opinion, as he expressed it to the President and to me. It may be that we can fix something up in the Senate. If I can do anything to help this matter along, please let me know.

The Industrial Relations Commission is doing magnificent work, and is going to put out a grand plan for social justice. It will give you great opportunity to get behind it. I worked hard for the Commission last week. They have offered me the position as managing expert, but, unfortunately, while I am helping the Democratic program, and the great Democratic President, the Democrats in Wisconsin are trying to get rid of me, and I must stay here and fight my own battles. I am willing to do anything I can to help this program, and am not afraid of the consequences. It may be that some plan can be evolved whereby I can work part time for the Industrial Relations Commission and for the State of Wisconsin. Of course, if President Wilson should request it, it would put some of the Stalwart Democrats here in the hole, and at the same time give me a chance to build up this great program. Command me at any time.

As ever, yours very truly,   C McCarthy

TLS (WP, DLC).
¹ "Wisconsin Faces Reaction," *Harper's Weekly*, LVIII (May 30, 1914), 9-11.

To Norman Hapgood

My dear Mr. Hapgood: [The White House] June 9, 1914

I thank you for your letter of June 8th, enclosing one from Mr. Charles McCarthy which I have carefully noted.

Sincerely yours,   Woodrow Wilson

TLS (Letterpress Books, WP, DLC).

To Sam Taliaferro Rayburn¹

My dear Mr. Rayburn: [The White House] June 9, 1914

We have all looked on with admiration and genuine appreciation as your stock and bond bill has been put through the House.² It seems to me you deserve a great deal of praise for your part in the matter and I want to make my humble contribution to the congratulations which I am sure you must be receiving.   Cordially and sincerely yours,   Woodrow Wilson

TLS (Letterpress Books, WP, DLC).
¹ Freshman Democratic representative from Texas.
² The Rayburn bill, which gave the Interstate Commerce Commission far-reaching authority over the issuance of new railroad securities, was an outgrowth of the New Haven scandal. It passed the House on June 5 but later died in the Senate.

To Herman Bernstein

My dear Mr. Bernstein: [The White House] June 9, 1914

I am sorry that there should have been any unfair implication in what I said at the opening of the American University last week.¹ You may be sure that there was nothing of the kind in my mind, for there certainly is nothing in my thought that would discriminate in the important matter you speak of against Judaism.

I find that one of the risks and penalties of extemporaneous speaking is that you do not stop to consider the whole field but address yourself merely to the matter directly in hand.

With sincere respect and appreciation,

Cordially yours,   Woodrow Wilson

TLS (Letterpress Books, WP, DLC).
¹ Bernstein's letter is missing.

To David Ignatius Walsh

My dear Governor Walsh: [The White House] June 9, 1914

May I not give myself the pleasure of expressing my sincere appreciation of the service you have rendered the Government and also the people of New England in the public-spirited and statesmanlike part you have played in effecting a settlement of the New Haven difficulties?¹ It has been an undertaking full of perplexities and involving complications which it was very difficult to unravel, and what gratifies me most about the outcome is the way in which the forces we had a right to count upon have worked together.

Cordially and sincerely yours,   Woodrow Wilson

TLS (Letterpress Books, WP, DLC).
¹ In a message to the legislature on June 1, Governor Walsh recommended legislation which would enable the voters of Massachusetts to decide whether or not the state should purchase the Boston and Maine stock held for the New Haven by the Boston Railroad Holding Co.

After debating various proposals for a month, the legislature passed an act enabling the sale of the stock which did not include a referendum on its purchase by the state but did include a provision reserving to the state the right to purchase the stock at any time. *New York Times*, June 1, July 1, July 8, 1914. For the dénouement of this legislation and the New Haven situation, see WW to J. C. McReynolds, July 21, 1914, and n. 3 thereto.

To John Grier Hibben

My dear Mr. President: [The White House] June 9, 1914

I appreciate your thoughtful kindness in thinking of my pleasure while in Princeton. My best enjoyment would come if everybody would forget during my visit to Princeton that I am President of the United States and let me conduct myself throughout the day as any other member of the class of '79 would conduct himself. I am expecting to reach Princeton between twelve and one o'clock on Saturday and shall be obliged to start home again at midnight of that day, lunching and dining, in the meantime, with my class, marching with them in the parade before the game, and sitting with them at the game.

This programme not only satisfies me, but delights me, and I am begging everybody to let me conform to it, while, at the same time, I, of course, deeply appreciate the desire which has been expressed to honor me in some way while I am there.

Sincerely yours,   Woodrow Wilson

TLS (Letterpress Books, WP, DLC).

From Thomas Davies Jones

My dear Mr. President: Chicago June 9, 1914.

Your note of the 5th instant did not reach me until yesterday. I have been greatly perplexed to know just what answer I ought to give. I have concluded to say yes, and have sent that answer to you by telegram today.

It is useless to bother you with my own perplexities, except in one particular. I think that you know that for the past five years I have been a director of the International Harvester Company. Though I have owned but one share of stock (qualifying share) in that Company, and have had no other financial interest in it, I am just as responsible for the conduct of the Company during that period as if I owned a controlling interest in its stock. I have not the slightest inclination to shirk that responsibility. The Company has unfortunately become something of an issue in politics. If my appointment should increase your political difficulties I would be deeply sorry, but that is a question I must leave with you. A fight upon my nomination—even the rejection of it—would not disturb me personally in the least. If I were nominated and confirmed I would of course expect to sever at once that and all other similar connections.

I need not add, but I want to add that whether nominated or not, it will always be a source of deep gratification to me that you should have thought me worthy of consideration in connection with so high a position.

Faithfully yours,   Thomas D. Jones

TLS (WP, DLC).

To William Jennings Bryan, with Enclosure

My dear Mr. Secretary: [The White House] June 10, 1914

This letter from Vick shows a distressing state of affairs, but I am sincerely obliged to you for having let me see it.

I am very much obliged to you for letting me see also the letter from Mr. Harper.[1]   Faithfully yours,   Woodrow Wilson

TLS (Letterpress Books, WP, DLC).
¹ Not found.

ENCLOSURE

Walker Whiting Vick to William Jennings Bryan

My dear Mr. Secretary: Santo Domingo May 30, 1914.

I do not desire to trouble you further in connection with Legation matters here, but in view of my confidential letter to you of April 14th in which I stated "I did not desire to inject myself into Legation matters either personally or officially," I think you should know that on yesterday the American Minister here, Honorable James M. Sullivan, stated to Mr. A. M. Archer, that his action in demanding that the Banco Nacional be given the depositary,¹ etc., was upon the direct instructions of Secretary Bryan.

Judging from other statements that Minister Sullivan quoted to Mr. Archer, it seems certain that some one has sent him a copy of my confidential communication of April 14th, written at your request.

Captain John T. Vance, the Deputy General Receiver of Dominican Customs, is now in Washington on official business, and should you desire, he can doubtless inform you of a great deal concerning Dominican affairs, which will be of interest.

Chaos is prevalent everywhere, and there is practically a reign of anarchy. Customs revenues are decreasing at an alarming rate, and the Receivership finds itself unable to administer its affairs within the five per cent. The blockading of the ports is principally responsible for the larger proportion of customs losses. The responsibility for these losses should be placed squarely upon the shoulders of the Dominican Government, and it seems reasonable that they should pay the cost of administration over the five per cent. Such a thing as an election which would be anything but local here, as well as farcical in its military tyranny, is impossible. Seemingly, the only solution is that the American Government actually supervise an election which will provide freedom of ballot and insure an honest count, and then insist upon the Government being upheld for its constitutional term. The situation is certainly most distressing for Americans really desiring to do something of constructive value in official life.

With expressions of my esteem, I am, with best wishes,
Very sincerely yours,   Walker W. Vick

TLS (SDR, RG 59, 123 Su51/64, DNA).

¹ About this matter and the subsequent scandal involving Sullivan, see Link, *The New Freedom*, pp. 108-10, and Dana G. Munro, *Intervention and Dollar Diplomacy in the Caribbean, 1900-1921* (Princeton, N.J., 1964), pp. 275-301.

From the White House Staff

The White House
Memorandum for the President: June 10, 1914.

Mr. Brandeis dictated the following over the telephone:

"I wish to report to the President on my talk with Senator Saulsbury. I saw the Senator who stated that he was inclined to agree with the Stevens amendment to the Trade Commission bill;¹ that he had been disinclined to agree that the thing to do was to amend it in committee; that he was more inclined to amend it in the House. He seemed quite set on the method of procedure; was not very well content with the Chairman's management of the proposition; but said that he had been gradually overcoming his objection to the amendment *as such*. I asked him whether he thought it advisable for me to talk with Senator Pomerene, who was the other objector, and he said that on the whole he thought I had better not until he (Saulsbury) had first considered the matter and could let me know. I agreed not to do anything until I heard from him. My general impression was that he was a little set on a mere matter of procedure.

"Also say to the President that I saw Senator Newlands before I saw Senator Saulsbury, and I reported to Senator Newlands the substance of our conversation with the President today.² I still think it would be very desirable if the President could get word in some appropriate way to Senator Saulsbury and Senator Pomerene, but I am pretty sure that Senator Saulsbury has no objection to the amendment *as such* upon which he would insist."

T MS (WP, DLC).

¹ About the Stevens amendment, or bill, see N. Hapgood to WW, April 21, 1914, and the notes thereto, Vol. 29.

² Wilson called Brandeis, Representative Stevens, Senator Hollis, and George Rublee to the White House on June 10 and told them that he had decided to incorporate the Stevens bill as an amendment to the Covington bill. Link, *The New Freedom*, p. 438.

From William Jennings Bryan, with Enclosure

My Dear Mr President,   [Washington, c. June 10, 1914]

I am sending you an estimate of the character of Gen Caranza prepared by Mr Silliman¹ at my request. Gov Lind thinks Silliman would be a good man to have at Saltillo, through whom to make representations to Caranza who will make Saltillo his capital for the present[.] I agree with Gov Lind. There is one objection but I think it can be overcome. The Federalists presented charges against him and he was released on condition that he leave the country. I think these charges would be withdrawn if we requested it. It is quite certain too that at our request he would be released from the agreement not to return to Mexico. Would you think it worth while to make the request? And do you approve of sending him back if these matters can be cleared up?

With assurances of regard I am my dear Mr President

Very truly yours   W. J. Bryan

ALS (WP, DLC).
¹ John Reid Silliman, Wilson's classmate at Princeton. He had been farming in Mexico since 1897 and was appointed vice and deputy consul at Saltillo in 1907. For an account of his tribulations with the Federalists, see Hill, *Emissaries to a Revolution*, pp. 210-213.

E N C L O S U R E

John Reid Silliman to William Jennings Bryan

Sir: [Washington] June 8, 1914.

In compliance with the request that I furnish the Department with such information and impressions as I may have regarding Governor Venustiano Carranza, I have the honor to submit the following:

My personal acquaintance with Governor Carranza dates from the year 1909. During that year he was, for a time, Acting Governor of the State of Coahuila in the absence of Governor Miguel Cardenas from Saltillo. I had occasion to see him at different times on official business for the Consulate and found him uniformly considerate, courteous and obliging. He appeared to me to be a well informed man and of considerable culture. I found that he had visited the United States frequently and, if I remember correctly, he told me that his children had been to school in the United States. He understood English so as to read it fairly well but he preferred not to try to speak it. He has a tall and well built figure and in appearance, address and manner seemed to me to fit in very well with the office he was called upon to fill temporarily. He comes from a family that has lived in the State of Coahuila for several generations and is a native of the town of Cuatro Cienegas, west of Monclova, where he owns considerable property, principally grazing and agricultural lands. He is not what might be termed narrow or provincial and for years before Governor Cardenas had him appointed Acting Governor he had represented his district in the Federal Congress at Mexico City. He was a boyhood friend and long political associate of Governor Cardenas, though Governor Cardenas did not agree with him in his support of Madero.

I came to know Governor Carranza much better after his election to the office of Governor under the Madero Administration. During this period he manifested especial interest in public education and he continued the improvements and the general progressive policy undertaken by his predecessor, Governor Cardenas. The aristocracy and the monied class were not in sympathy with the Madero revolution and Governor Carranza did not get the hearty support of these people either in Saltillo, the Capital, or in other parts of the State. It has been said that Governor Carranza resented the social coolness which he found in Saltillo.

In previous despatches the Department has been informed of the immediate refusal of Governor Carranza to acknowledge the Government of General Huerta. The Department is aware that the present revolution began in Saltillo, and the Department has been furnished with Governor Carranza's proclamation in behalf of the State of Coahuila giving reasons why the Government of General Huerta should not and could not be accepted and calling upon other Governors and other States to support the State of Coahuila in this stand. . . .

I have noticed that Governor Carranza does not reach his conclusions quickly. Having once come to a decision he is slow to change it. I do not believe him, as has been published, to be in the least personally timid or cowardly. I have seen him in the saddle roughing it like his men. I am quite sure that no man of ordinary moral or physical force would have made the stand for a moral principle that Carranza has made with such odds against him and, at one time, such an uncertain future. I do not believe him to be personally corrupt and I do not think he could be influenced by flattery or vanity. He is what might be termed a serious, reflective man. He is a very patriotic Mexican and I think he would be extremely zealous in any point that he might consider as involving any concession of what the Mexicans are fond of calling their national dignity and honor. Governor Carranza is not what might be termed an easy, approachable man, or one who might inspire any considerable devotion or personal loyalty. I would consider it quite uncertain as to whether he is strong enough to maintain cohesion and order among all those who may pretend to be his followers.

Governor Carranza has always appeared quite cordial and friendly with me. I believe that I have his confidence and his regard. On that account I have felt that I might possibly be able to be of some service to the Department in communicating with him upon his return to Saltillo, if it should be deemed expedient.

I have the honor to be, Sir

Your obedient servant,   John R. Silliman

TLS (SDR, RG 59, 812.44/C23/1, DNA).

Baron Takaaki Katō[1] to Viscount Sutemi Chinda

[Tokyo, June 10, 1914]

Among the more important pending questions that confronted me when I assumed charge of this Department, was the issue resulting from the enactment last year of the Legislature of California respecting alien real property ownership. The measure, as you are aware, undertook in effect to draw a distinction in the matter of such ownership between aliens belonging to different races. The avowed purpose of the law was, on the one hand, to annul the then existing right of ownership so far as Japanese subjects were concerned and, on the other, to continue the right in favor of aliens of the white and black races.

I have given the subject my most serious consideration and am consequently well satisfied that the enactment in question is not only in disregard of the letter and spirit of the existing treaty between Japan and the United States of America, but is essentially unfair and invidiously discriminatory against my countrymen and inconsistent as well with the sentiment of amity and good neighborhood which has always presided over the relations between the two countries. Nor can I escape the conviction that the said enactment which was intended to have international effect is also in excess of the authority of the State of California for the reason, that the separate States of the United States are, internationally speaking, wholly unknown and entirely without responsibility. In any case, the Imperial Government are confident that such action as complained of stands without historical parallel, and they are happy to believe that the legislation in question forms no part of the general policy of the Federal Government but is the outcome of unfortunate local conditions. I therefore fully concur in the views which you, in pursuance of instructions from my predecessor, presented to the Honorable the Secretary of State on the subject.

I also cordially appreciate the motives which in the interest of international conciliation and good-will induced Baron Makino to give favorable consideration to the idea of concluding a convention regarding the matter. But the project as it stands at the present time, instead of composing existing misunderstandings, would, I fear, tend to create new difficulties. Accordingly, you are instructed to inform Mr. Bryan that the Imperial Government are disinclined to continue the negotiations looking to the conclusion of a convention on the lines of the project which has been under discussion, but that they prefer to recur to the correspondences which were interrupted by the ineffective negotiations and that they will now look for an answer to the Note which you handed to Mr. Bryan on the 26th. August last, hoping that in a renewal of the study of the case a fundamental solution of the question at issue may happily be found.

The negotiations looking to an adjustment of the matter in dispute by means of a convention having failed, the advantage of still withholding from the public the correspondences that have passed between the two Governments on the subject is no longer apparent. You are consequently also instructed to announce to the Secretary of State that the Imperial Government desire to make public the correspondences in question, believing that fuller and more accurate information regarding the matter will contribute to the final settlement of the controversy.

You are authorized in carrying out the above instructions to hand a copy of this Note to Mr. Bryan.

T MS (SDR, RG 59, 811.52/292, DNA).
[1] He had just succeeded Baron Makino as Japanese Foreign Minister.

From William Jennings Bryan

My dear Mr. President: Washington June 10, 1914.
. . . I have just rec'd note from Japanese Ambassador saying that his *gov't withdraws suggestion as to treaty* and desires to renew correspondence & asks answer to note of last August   I don't like the tone. They also want to publish correspondence

I think I had better have a few minutes with you in regard to this subject

TLS with Hw P.S. (WP, DLC).

Remarks at a Press Conference

June 11, 1914

Mr. President, I think you saw Mr. Raymond Stevens of New Hampshire yesterday with relation to his amendment to the interstate trade commission bill. Is there anything you can tell us about that?

No. That was merely for the purpose of discussing and getting thoroughly acquainted with what his proposals were —just the rough [outlines].

Mr. President, we were told that you approved his proposals as embodied in section eleven of the bill he introduced some time ago.

I approved his bringing it to the attention of the Senate committee and leaving it to their action. . . .

Mr. President, have you made any plans yet for participating in any of the state campaigns—Pennsylvania, Iowa, and so forth?

No, sir. . . .

Mr. President, have you been consulted by the House Committee on Merchant Marine and Fisheries with regard to changes in the seamen's bill?

No, sir. I saw a committee of gentlemen this morning headed by Mr. Furuseth,[1] but it was only—

That was not a congressional committee?

Just a committee of seamen.

Mr. President, last Monday you expressed some hope that there might be a settlement in the coal strike situation. Has that gotten any further?

I don't know whether to say yes or no. The little news I have had since Monday continues to be encouraging; that is to say, continues to indicate that there was a possibility.

Mr. President, do you know that the sundry civil bill carries the same exemption of labor unions that it carried last year?

The same special exemption?

Yes.

No, I didn't.

JRT transcript (WC, NjP) of CLSsh (C. L. Swem Coll., NjP).
[1] Wilson had received Andrew Furuseth and a delegation from the International Seamen's Union, which presented him with a memorial in favor of the seamen's bill.

To William Jennings Bryan

My dear Mr. Secretary: The White House June 11, 1914

Thank you sincerely for having let me see the enclosed most interesting paper from Silliman.

Cordially and sincerely yours,   Woodrow Wilson

TLS (W. J. Bryan Papers, DNA).

To William Atkinson Jones

My dear Mr. Jones: [The White House] June 11, 1914

I laid the bill you were kind enough to show me the other day before the Secretary of War and asked him for his comments. I have from him yesterday the enclosed very interesting paper[1] which seems to me thoughtful and liberal in every way.

I would be very much obliged to you if you would give it your careful consideration.

I have not yet digested all of the suggestions but I feel pretty clear that his suggestion, or, rather, Mr. Quezon's, about the veto power would be a very decided improvement over the corresponding provision in the bill. This is the item which I have been thinking most about.

Cordially and sincerely yours,   Woodrow Wilson

TLS (Letterpress Books, WP, DLC).
[1] Not found.

To James Clark McReynolds

[The White House]

My dear Mr. Attorney General: June 12, 1914

I have been a good deal disturbed from time to time about the question of the proper recognition of the women in such states as California. There is a Mrs. Adams there,[1] for example, whom Mr. Preston[2] desires as one of the Assistant District Attorneys at San Francisco. She has extraordinary endorsements and seems to be in every way an admirable woman. My own judgment is that it would be a great mistake to turn from her and not recognize her ability as it is recognized at home.

I have had this matter in mind for some time but have forgotten or neglected to speak to you about it, notwithstanding the fact that I feel very earnestly concerning it.

Cordially and faithfully yours,   Woodrow Wilson

TLS (Letterpress Books, WP, DLC).
[1] Annette Abbott (Mrs. Martin H.) Adams, J.D., University of California, 1912. She was principal of Modoc County High School, 1907-1910, admitted to the California bar in 1912, and the next year began private practice in partnership with Marguerite Ogden. She served as Assistant United States Attorney for the District of Northern California, 1914-18; as the first woman United States district attorney from 1918 to 1920; and, from 1920 to 1921, as the first woman Assistant Attorney General of the United States.
[2] John White Preston, United States Attorney for the District of Northern California.

To Joseph Patrick Tumulty

Dear T.   [The White House, c. June 12, 1914]

Here is some capital material.[1] What do you think is the best use to put it to. Cong. Record along with an effective speech, myself mention it to newspaper men, or what?[2]   W.W.

Johnson of S. C. received it.

WWhwLI (WP, DLC).

[1] There were four enclosures: a T circular letter from William Paul Ahnelt, president of the *Pictorial Review*, dated May 1, 1914; two undated enclosures to the circular letter, and a printed circular letter from the Simmons Hardware Co., dated June 9, 1914. The Ahnelt circular letter asked the recipient to send appeals to the President, Congress, and members of the Interstate Commerce Commission, urging that action on antitrust legislation be delayed. A sample letter asked: "Why subject business to any experimental legislation NOW, when it is not prosperous?" It declared that the "continual senseless attacks by governmental bodies upon merchants, by impending assaults upon railroad, industrial and mercantile corporations, revision of the tariff, and currency reform have resulted in sinking business to such an extent that it has thrown hundreds of thousands out of employment, reduced wages, and decreased values in railroad industries and mercantile corporations." A sample telegram suggested that "in view of unsettled business conditions," Congress should "postpone new legislation affecting business world until next regular session in December." The letter from the Simmons Hardware Co. stated that Congress should "adjourn and go home" because the country was "absolutely tired and surfeited with political agitation" which was "exceedingly injurious" and would retard an improvement in business. The letter urged the public to send protests along these lines to Congress.

[2] Wilson released the materials described in n. 1 for publication on June 15. See the remarks at a press conference printed at that date. They were printed, e.g., in the *New York Times*, June 16, 1914.

To Thomas Davies Jones

My dear Friend: The White House June 12, 1914

Your telegram and letter gave me deep and genuine pleasure. I knew I could count upon you if it was possible for you to consent.

There may be criticism and objection when the nomination comes up but I have every confidence that it can be overcome when the real facts are known, and I shall look forward with more pleasure than I can say to being associated with you here.

In haste, with warmest regard to all,

Cordially and faithfully yours,   Woodrow Wilson

TLS (Mineral Point, Wisc., Public Library).

From Joseph Patrick Tumulty

The White House,
Memorandum for the President: June 12, 1914.

Senator Saulsbury telephoned to ask that the President be advised that the Stevens amendment was put in the Trades Commission bill this morning.

Senator Saulsbury said that Senator Myers proposed an amendment to authorize the Commission to exempt combinations in the foreign trade. Senator Saulsbury offered a substitute to investigate that subject and report to Congress.

The Senator said he thought he would oppose any other amendments to the bill.

T MS (WP, DLC).

From Edward Mandell House

London, June 12, 1914.

Congratulations, felicitations and love.[1]

Edward House.

T telegram (WP, DLC).
[1] The Senate had approved the Sims bill repealing tolls exemption on June 11 by a vote of fifty to thirty-five.

From William Jennings Bryan

My dear Mr. President: Washington June 12, 1914.

I am enclosing some comments made by Mr. Lansing on the proposed Nicarauguan treaty, and the objections that are likely to be made.[1] You will notice that these objections are not presented with a view of preventing the submission of the treaty, but merely to indicate the line of argument that we are likely to meet. The objections have all been considered, and I take it for granted that you have not changed your views in regard to the wisdom of pushing this treaty. The Nicaraguan people are desperately in need of the money, and I think the option on the canal and the naval base in Fonseca Bay are of the highest importance. While the Platt amendment provision is asked for by the Nicaraguan government, and is intended for the benefit of that government, still I think that it is of advantage to us, in that it will give us the right to do that which we might be called upon to do anyhow. We cannot escape the responsibilities of our position, and this is an opportune time for us to secure the necessary treaty provision, as we can secure it at their request.

I have promised to present this treaty next Wednesday, that being the first committee meeting after the passage of the Tolls bill.

You will be interested to know that an examination of the record in regard to the Colombian treaty, abundantly justifies us in the offer of twenty-five millions. We could not have reasonably offered less, in view of the expectations that were aroused. While this sum was not offered by the Taft administration, it was so nearly offered that it amounts to the same thing, and the regular Republicans ought to assist us in ratifying the treaty. The only people who can oppose it for *party* reasons are the Progressives, and I hope that we may have the support of some of them. I think I ought to present this also on next Wednesday, as it has already been ratified by the Colombian government.

With assurances of high esteem, I am, my dear Mr. President,
Very sincerely yours,   W. J. Bryan

TLS (WP, DLC).
[1] R. Lansing, "PROPOSED NICARAGUAN TREATY," TS memorandum dated June 12, 1914 (SDR, RG 59, 817.812/168, DNA).

To William Jennings Bryan

My dear Mr. Secretary: The White House June 13, 1914

I return herewith the papers you were kind enough to send me about the Nicaraguan treaty.

I take it for granted that Mr. Lansing's suggestions about reports from the Navy Department and the Department of Commerce will be acted upon.[1] They seem to me sensible and important if the treaty is to be fully sustained in argument.

But, of course, I have not at all changed my attitude with regard to the treaty itself. I think with Mr. Lansing that we perhaps give more than we get and yet in spite of its generous character I think it a wise and indeed, in the circumstances, necessary agreement.

Cordially and faithfully yours,   Woodrow Wilson

TLS (SDR, RG 59, 817.812/168, DNA).
[1] W. C. Redfield to WJB, June 16, 1914, TLS (SDR, RG 59, 817.812/169, DNA), and T. Washington to WJB, June 23, 1914, TS memorandum (SDR, RG 59, 817.812/170, DNA).

To Furnifold McLendel Simmons

My dear Senator: [The White House] June 13, 1914

The great fight[1] is ended and I want you to know how I have followed from day to day with the greatest admiration and appreciation the part you have played in bringing about the final result. I think the whole country feels that result to be very decisive. Your work in behalf of this just end has been untiring and brilliant and I thank you for it with all my heart.

Cordially and sincerely yours,   [Woodrow Wilson]

CCL (WP, DLC).
  [1] That is, for tolls repeal.

Remarks to the Class of 1879[1]

June 13, 1914

Halsey and fellows: I know it is because of your generous desire to show your affection for me and your pleasure in the honors that have come to me that has led Halsey to speak of me more than once tonight as *President* Wilson; but I came here with the earnest wish that you might for the day forget that. Not that it is possible for me to forget it with the responsibilities that pursue me no matter how I try to get away from them; but it is a delight to get as far as possible away from them and come and spend the day with you in these places where I should love to spend it as often as the years come around.

I have no speech to make tonight. As I have told you almost every time I have stood up before you, I have never been able to make a speech to Seventy-nine. You know, in order to make a perfectly succcessful speech, it has to consist in part of bluff, and I cannot put up a bluff before you fellows. There has to be a certain attitude of confidence and of knowing what you are talking about—a disguise which you could easily penetrate, and, therefore, I am not going to put it on.

I have had some things very much in my mind during the day. I do not want to be too serious, and yet I think as we grow older there is a sort of pleasure and refreshment in seeing what the lessons are that we draw from our experience and our relations with one another. There is one fortunate circumstance in life: comradeship does not have to depend always upon intimacy or upon perfect confidence. There are some pretty grim things I have learned in life. For one thing, I hope never again to be fool enough to make believe that a man is my friend who I know to be my enemy. That is merely sensible conduct. But it is Christian conduct to treat him exactly as if you did think he was your friend; and the pleasure of reunions of all sorts, after you have seen men tested out, is to be privileged to lay aside the wisdom of the world and come down to the simplicity of the heart.

And yet we ought not to deceive ourselves. Men are tested. They do make their records. Their records are to be read. If a man has proved himself a coward, he is a coward. If he has proved himself unfaithful, he is unfaithful; and in performing public duties you should not associate yourself with him. The great malady of public life is cowardice. Most men are not untrue, but they are afraid. Most of the errors of public life, if my observation is to be trusted, come, not because men are morally bad, but because they are afraid of somebody. God knows why they should be: it is generally shadows they are afraid of. It is generally something they would only have to face to find it disappear.

There is nothing that succeeds in life like boldness, provided you believe you are on the right side. Boldness is mere bluff if you know you are on the wrong side.

When I come back here to gatherings of this sort, it is like coming out of a world of tempest, full of the queries of life, where at every turn you have to ask, "Is this man to be trusted? Can I say what I really think to that man?" Open all the windows again, and be in that unquestioning frame of mind we enjoyed when we were undergraduates, when one man was like another to us, except that some attracted us more than others, and we opened our hearts and minds to everybody. That is the kind of pleasure I have had today.

You see, I taught here for a good while, and a lot of the men who p-raded today were pupils of mine. I knew the sheep from the goats, but I like the goats just about as much as I do the sheep. I did not have the slightest feeling of distaste toward the fellows who I knew were no sort of good whatever. There were such men in the P-rade; and some of them were not as young as others were. Some were mature, and they have come to that goathood which precedes dissolution. They always were goats; they are goats now; and will—I will not make any prediction except to remind you that there will be an arrangement for goats in the next world.

So the human side, the natural brotherliness of men, is what is uppermost in one's thoughts on occasions like this; and that, if I may speak in small letters and not in capitals, is the real idea of democracy—that you do not distinguish between men because of their differences of gift or their differences of character in your general love of the great human element that unites us all together. The great error of classes of society is that they set up artificial barriers between people who have an equal humanity, though they may not have an equal chance or an equal place in the world. It is ridiculous to see some men set themselves apart, because they are trained, from other men. The others may be just as good as they are, though they have not their cultivation. I would a great deal rather associate with the men at whom I can get direct, whether they are cultivated or uncultivated. The great charm of the uncultivated man is that there is no palaver necessary as a preliminary to getting next to him and finding out what is in his mind.

The older I get the simpler I get—in one way, I mean—the more I get to love those things where the garb is stripped off and men really get down to direct, unaffected contact with one another. That is the exhilaration, the only exhilaration, that I have found in public life. It is the sense of contact with millions of men of all sorts.

I suppose you fellows can hardly have any conception of how many impressions from scores and hundreds and thousands of quarters, coming in through the mails and through personal visits and through casual clippings from the newspapers, pour into an office like that of the President of the United States. It is like a sort of clearinghouse for the needs and opinions of all sorts and conditions of men. And there is an exhilaration in that; there is an education that cannot be described. It makes it ridiculous to read the newspapers. I have stopped reading the newspapers, not because I would not need to if what they said was so, but because it isn't. If it were true, I would read them every day. With regard to the things that I am informed about, the newspapers are untrue in what they say; and so I have concluded that it is also a waste of time to read about things I do not know anything about in the newspapers, because the chances are that what the newspapers say about them is not true. In a great public office, the sources of information are so many and press upon you so insistently that you do not have to read the newspapers to find out the truth.

The truth comes to you in a very singular way. The voices and messages that come to you are contradictory, as a rule, but if you wait long enough with regard to any one subject there seems to be a sort of medium result which is obviously the fact. That was true with regard to Mexico. For months I was wondering what was the true situation in Mexico. All sorts of men came to me who said they had lived in Mexico all their lives and knew all about it.

I assumed from the first that if they said so it was not so, because no man knows all about anything, and if he has lived long enough in a place he has gained such prejudices that it is impossible for him to understand things to the bottom. And yet if you listen to enough of these men, and listen to them long enough, there begins to be a sort of residuum, something that runs through all that they tell you, and you presently begin to see that that must be the fundamental fact. So also with regard to a score of other things. If enough men come to you and tell you different stories you will presently be struck by the resemblance in the different stories. A man cannot lie, for example, elaborately without bringing in some of the truth, because his invention does not go far enough; and if enough men come in and lie to you on the same subject, since the truth always corresponds with the truth, you will find a large body of truth in their stories. It is a process I never dreamed of before I got into public office, and it is the most instructive process that I know of, this absolute self-consistency of truth. Wherever it comes in it matches with what the other liar told you, and the pattern begins to fill itself out; and if you wait long enough you will know something about some subject, though you never will know enough to be perfectly sure you are right about anything.

The greatest satisfaction in all the things that one tries to do comes from those persons whom you have tested and about whom you do not have to sit up nights and wonder what they are going to do. For example, I have asked, as the newspapers have reported on a surmise, at least, one man to be a member of the Federal Reserve Board of the new banking system whom I have seen tested by fire—Thomas D. Jones—and if he can make it possible to come to Washington, and I hope he can, there will be another man added to those whom I will not have to think about again, except pleasantly. It is just like putting a fellow on guard and then going off yourself and going to sleep. You do not have to bother yourself again. But those men are not numerous enough to allow you to go to sleep, and there are posts which are unguarded.

But I am simply wandering from point to point. What I really wanted to say to you men was that the day has refreshed me and cheered and rested me, and has enabled me to renew those delightful impressions of the heart which, after all, are the sources of life—the sources of physical life and the sources of spiritual life. It is a privilege to forget, and it is a privilege to remember. It is a privilege to blot out the years that have intervened since we graduated and to see the masks fall from your faces as they do so readily if I look long enough and see the boys behind the present mature faces. And it is also a pleasure to remember the things that have intervened, the honorable careers you have made for yourselves, the fine way in which the class has faced and promoted life, the way in which so many men have shown that they were bred in a common school of honor and of public spirit. And so both to remember and to forget is delightful.

T MS (C. L. Swem Coll., NjP), with WWhw and editors' emendations.
    [1] At a reunion banquet which was part of the annual Princeton commencement festivities. The dinner followed the traditional alumni luncheon, parade, and a baseball game. Wilson arrived shortly after noon, was greeted by a contingent from the Class of 1879, led by its president, the Rev. Dr. Abram Woodruff Halsey, and then walked to class headquarters at Seventy-Nine Hall. President Hibben stopped by the Hall to greet his former colleague. Wilson lunched there with his classmates, and then marched, amidst cheering crowds, with the other alumni in the reunion parade to University Field, where Wilson watched Princeton lose to Yale, 3-0. After the game, the class adjourned to the tower room of Seventy-Nine Hall, where dinner was served and Wilson was presented with bronze replicas of the tigers placed by the Class of 1879 on the steps of Nassau Hall. *New York Times*, June 14, 1914; *Daily Princetonian*, June 14, 1914 and June 14, 1914, extra; *Princeton Alumni Weekly*, xiv (June 17, 1914), 725-26, 746-48.

From William Jennings Bryan

My dear Mr. President: Washington June 13, 1914.

    I am enclosing a letter which I have just received from General Scott.[1] You will see that he speaks highly of Conova, and commends him if he is to work with Carothers, which is our idea. Carothers cannot be everywhere, and I believe that Conova would be a good man to have with Carothers and acting under his instructions. He could send him where he could not himself go, and we ought to have someone with every General who is in charge of a campaign. For instance, it would be well to have Conova, after meeting Villa and Carranza, go with instructions from Carothers, to Natera,[2] who is in charge of the attack against Zacatecas. After getting instructions from Carothers he could keep in touch with Natera, and urge respect for the rules of war and advise against harshness and cruelty. Governor Lind was also favorably impressed with Conova, and Mr. Lansing and Mr. Long have also a good opinion of him. Please let me know what your wishes are in the matter.

    With assurances of high esteem, I am, my dear Mr. President,
                              Sincerely yours,   W. J. Bryan

TLS (EBR, RG 130, DNA).
    [1] H. L. Scott to WJB, June 9, 1914, ALS (W. J. Bryan Papers, DNA).
    [2] General Pánfilo Natera.

From Henry French Hollis

Dear Mr. President: [Washington] June 13, 1914.

We were able to get all the Democratic members of the Senate Interstate Commerce Committee in line for the Stevens amendment. Senator Brandegee[1] was the only one who voted against it. The amendment was reported to the Senate this morning, and it seems likely that the Trades Commission Bill in its present shape may be put through the Senate without great delay. I certainly hope so.

It seems to me the sentiment is growing in the Senate in favor of passing the Trades Commission Bill and the Railroad Securities Bill, and permitting the Clayton Bill to go over until next winter.

Sincerely yours,   Henry F. Hollis

TLS (WP, DLC).
[1] Frank Bosworth Brandegee, Republican of Connecticut.

To Francis Griffith Newlands

My dear Senator: [The White House] June 15, 1914.

I am very much obliged to you for your kindness in sending me the Senate substitute for the Trade Commission bill. I shall examine it with care.

Cordially and sincerely yours,   Woodrow Wilson

TLS (Letterpress Books, WP, DLC).

Remarks at a Press Conference

June 15, 1914

Mr. President, have you selected the Reserve Board governor yet?
    I would never select the governor at the time of the nominations. I designate him subsequently.
Have you reached any decision?
    Yes. The names will go in today.[1] The blanks aren't quite ready. I make it rather a point of courtesy not to announce before the Senate is apprised. But that will be some time today.
We will know, then, who is to be the governor?
    No. Not until the board is confirmed.
Mr. President, has there been any opposition raised to the appointment of Mr. Jones?
    No. I haven't heard anything. Apropos of the question as to whether the President would present his psychology all

along, I am going to let you gentlemen see copies of correspondence that have come into my notice, showing you how the psychology is created. So if later in the morning you will inquire for these copies, you will be supplied an interesting and elaborate process.

Are you going to add anything of your own to these?

No. I don't think it is necessary.

These copies show where the psychology comes from?

In this case, from a publication called *The Pictorial Review*.

I don't know anything about it.

Mr. President, have you attempted in any way to trace the boom for immediate adjournment of Congress? There seems to be a piling up of letters. They have a similar ring. They all ring in the same tone.

That is part of that. That is part of the campaign. It won't have to be faced. You will just have to expose its face.

It commenced about two weeks ago in the Senate.

It may possibly be. If so, it escaped my notice.

Mr. President, have you gone behind the actual publications? You say this was from *The Pictorial Review*. Have you gone further back than that?

No.

Mr. President, businessmen whom I talked with say that the condition is this—that autumn business is good, but there is no new business. The real trouble is in the matter of new business. Is that your understanding?

No. Broadly, there is the normal amount of new business, and in some lines of business more than the normal amount of new business—just what might be called the normal growth, something more—

Mr. President, has there been some suggestion, after reporting these [appropriations] bills out of the committee in the Senate, and reporting out the trust bills, then to adjourn, with an agreement with the Republicans to take a vote in December?

I had not heard that. I had not heard that that has ever been suggested. I couldn't think of that. That is one I had not heard of.

The only suggestion we need pay much attention to is that we remain in session until the trust program is passed?

I think that is the thinking of the men who have considered the matter most thoroughly—that we ought to seek to adjourn as soon as possible, but not before we finish the business.

Don't they think they can get fairly quick action?

I think they do. I have to think of only one or two that have expressed an opinion on that subject. I don't see any reason why they should not. The minute it is known that we are going to finish the program, everybody will be interested to finish it.

Do you think, Mr. President, that there has been a good deal of unnecessary delay up to the point where they realize it?

It is perfectly obvious to the whole country that there was unnecessary delay on the tolls bill.

Mr. President, the impression has been pretty general that some influence here is going to try to hold up the trust legislation. They have been suggesting that all along the line. I thought you might say something a little emphatic that might convince us if that is true. I talked with a gentleman in Chicago yesterday, and he said throughout the country there was the idea [that] . . . if they can get a little cheerful word from you at this time, it will be helpful.

I think the prospects of the business being finished is much more cheerful than the prospect of its being left unfinished. And I think it is much more sensible. I would think the worst thing that can happen to business is to be in doubt, for another six to eight months, as to what the legislation of Congress is going to be; and that is the worst possible thing for business.

It is quite reasonable to assume that you will continue to press a little bit earnestly for trust legislation?

It is more than reasonable. It is certain. Just so far as my influence goes, it will be for completion of the program.

Mr. President, is there any further so-called business legislation in contemplation when the trust bill is out of the way?

Not that I know of. There is nothing pending, unless those conservation bills are business. They can hardly fall under that class.

Mr. President, in that connection, the Chamber of Commerce announced last night that it sent a protest to you against the Clayton bill and the sundry civil bill. Have you received those?

Yes.

Will you make any comment on the sundry civil bill, particularly?

No.

JRT transcript (WC, NjP) of CLSsh (C. L. Swem Coll., NjP).
  1 He nominated P. M. Warburg, T. D. Jones, C. S. Hamlin, W. P. G. Harding, and Adolph C. Miller.

A Flag Day Address[1]

[June 15, 1914]

I esteem it a privilege to be present on an occasion like this and to try to interpret for you the significance of this beautiful flag that floats before us. This flag is, of course, not a mere piece of bunting. It is much older than we are. The ideas which it symbolizes dominate us. We are true or we are untrue to it. It speaks a language which we must understand and which, understanding, we must obey. I am going to try, therefore, in a very few sentences to interpret for you the historical significance of the flag of the United States. I do not mean that I am going to try to tell you the history of the flag itself, but try to indicate to you the kind of history it stands for in the human race.

First of all, as everybody knows, this flag stood for independence. It stood for the right of a people with a life and ideals of its own to choose and establish their own polity, to govern their own affairs, and to choose their own rulers, without let or interference from any other peoples of the world. We were perhaps nearly half a century in convincing a skeptical world that we were able to do this great thing—to establish a nation without the aid of kings, without the aid of privileged classes, without any of those adventitious institutions which had grown up here and there throughout the world elsewhere—that by nothing but the united counsel of average men we could build and maintain and strengthen a nation. We had several times to meet the skepticism of the world in a way that called for the exercise of force. We had to speak to it for a little—happily, only for a little while—in the only language which up to that time had been understood—the language of physical power. But in the course of time our independence became unquestioned; and the next query that the world put to us was this, "Yes, on your separated continent you can hold us at arms length and do what you please with your own affairs, but do you know what to do with them? We have built up great civilizations; you are young, you are boastful, you are adventurous, you are ambitious to undertake things never undertaken before. Can you do it?" And then, not with haste, but with the steady exercise of self-directed intelligence, we built our nation up along lines of progress that the world had never surpassed before and had seldom equaled before, progress which in many respects was purged as progress never had been purged before of some of the more debased and selfish elements of human ambition; and, presently, by the mid-century of the last hundred years, we had shown that we knew how to make the same sort of progress that other nations had made, and to make it with fewer mistakes, with fewer of those elements which bore with injustice upon the average man and forbade the average man to enter into the gates of legitimate ambition. Then came one of the most searching tests that a nation has ever stood—the test of the Civil War. The country was not the same throughout its borders, either in its political ideals or in its social structure. It was not the same in its economic structure. It was trying to live a common life in two disparate and unlike sections. Here was something that went to the very root of things.

We were not able to settle that great matter as we had settled the initial questions of our national life with regard to the form of our government. You remember the fine thing that De Tocqueville said about us in regard to our change from the old Confederation to the modern Union. He remarked with unconcealed admiration upon the self-possession of a people which can look its own affairs over, see what is the matter with them, and fundamentally alter them, without, in his fine phrase, "having drawn either a single tear or a single drop of blood from mankind." But here at the time of the Civil War was something too deep for that. Tears had to be drawn; blood had to be shed; and tragedy had to be enacted; and the world looked on and said, "At last the catastrophe has come which is to pull this great structure down." But it did not. We worked almost blindly with tears and passion in our eyes through those dark years into a new light that dawned upon us, the light of a long day of peace and unquestioned stability—making errors, committing the mistakes of passion, but, nevertheless, moved and guided by the pure ambition of reuniting the spirits of a divided nation and making over again the thing which had been threatened with disruption. That was accomplished, and now more than ever this is the flag of the Union.

That chapter is closed. Our spirits as well as our states are reunited. Now we have to ask ourselves, "What does the flag stand for for the future?" Nobody questions our independence. Nobody questions our ability to push forward our economic affairs upon lines of unparalleled success and prosperity. Nobody denies our power to settle the most fundamental questions of our national life, though they involve tragedy, without breaking any of the essential principles or disturbing any of the essential foundations of our life. I sometimes wonder why men even now take this flag and flaunt it. If I am respected, I do not have to demand respect. If I am feared, I do not have to ask for fear. If my power is known, I do not have to proclaim it. I do not understand the temper, neither does this great nation understand the temper, of men who use this flag boastfully. You remember the touching reply of the old minister, a true servant of God, in whose presence some youngsters were telling of their spiritual experiences. He was silent, and they turned to him and said, "Have you had no spiritual experiences?" and he replied, "None to boast of." We have had the deepest experiences that a race could have. Do we boast of this majority and purity of our spirit? This flag for the future is meant to stand for the just use of undisputed national power. No nation is ever going to doubt our power to assert its rights; and we should lay it to heart that no nation shall ever henceforth doubt our purpose to put it to the highest uses to which a great emblem of justice and government can be put. It is henceforth to stand for self-possession, for dignity, for the assertion of the right of one nation to serve the other nations of the world—an emblem that will not condescend to be used for purposes of aggression and self-aggrandizement; that is too great to be debased by selfishness; that has vindicated its right to be honored by all the nations of the world and feared by none who do righteousness.

Is it not a proud thing to stand under such an emblem? Would it not be a pitiful thing ever to have to make apology and explanation of anything that we ever did under the leadership of this flag carried in the van? Is it not a solemn responsibility laid upon us to lay aside bluster and assume that much greater thing —the quietude of genuine power. The little engine makes a noise; the big engine makes none. And yet how fine the big engine grinds. The Corliss engine is not half as noisy as the smallest automobile, and, without any exertion, apparently without breath of life, it achieves the most delicate and difficult tasks of the mechanical world. So it seems to me that it is my privilege and right as the temporary representative of a great nation that does what it pleases with its own affairs to say that we please to do justice and assert the rights of mankind wherever this flag is unfurled.[2]

T MS (WP, DLC).
 [1] Before a public gathering assembled in front of the State, War, and Navy Building. Secretaries Bryan and Daniels also spoke.
 [2] There is a WWT outline of this address, dated June 15, 1914, in WP, DLC.

From John Reed

Union Station midnight
Dear Mr. President: Monday [June] fifteenth [1914]
    I forgot, when I was with you, to ask if you would allow me to write my own Interpretation of your Mexican policy in an article. It would, of course, be entirely mine; but I should write it in the

light of what you told me, and would not say or imply that you
had told me anything.

In addition, I should be glad to submit it to you before publication, if you would like to see it.

Of course I was disappointed not to be able to publish, or
even tell, the fine things you told me. But I think even yet that
people don't know what you're doing, or why, and that it would
help things immensely if I could write my Interpretation. Will you
have somebody drop me a line?

Yours sincerely   John Reed

ALS (WP, DLC).

To Henry French Hollis

My dear Senator: [The White House] June 16, 1914

Thank you warmly for your letter of June thirteenth and for
the part you have played in getting the Stevens amendment into
the Senate Interstate Trade Commission bill.

I had a long talk last evening with the members of the Steering
Committee and the chairmen of the Interstate Commerce Committee and the Judiciary Committee and think, after the conference, that the prospects for action on all the essential parts of
the trust programme are very much brighter than I supposed
they were. I want to have a talk with you about the whole matter at a very early date.

Cordially and faithfully yours,   Woodrow Wilson

TLS (Letterpress Books, WP, DLC).

To Edward Mandell House

My dear Friend: The White House June 16, 1914

Your letter from Paris, written just after coming from Berlin,
gives me a thrill of deep pleasure. You have, I hope and believe,
begun a great thing and I rejoice with all my heart. You are
doing it, too, in just the right way with your characteristic tact
and quietness and I wish you Godspeed in what follows. I could
not have done the thing nearly so well.

I have had a little glimpse of your movements in a letter from
Page[1] and wish very much that our means of following our
friends' movements were better than the occasional letter affords,
for my thought follows you constantly.

In haste, with sincere affection,

Faithfully yours,   Woodrow Wilson

TLS (E. M. House Papers, CtY).
    ¹ WHP to WW, June 9, 1914, ALS (WP, DLC).

To William Jennings Bryan

My dear Mr. Secretary: The White House June 16, 1914

I have already answered your note of June thirteenth about Mr. Canova over the telephone.¹ I now return General Scott's letter with thanks.

Faithfully yours,   Woodrow Wilson

TLS (W. J. Bryan Papers, DNA).
    ¹ Wilson approved Bryan's suggestion.

From Charles Sumner Hamlin

Dear Mr. President: Washington June 16, 1914

I can not tell you how much I appreciate the great honor you have conferred upon me in appointing me a member of the Federal Reserve Board. It will be my constant effort to justify the confidence you have reposed in me, and I can not tell you how proud I am to be identified with your administration in the important work of the Reserve Board.

With again my most grateful thanks, believe me,

Very sincerely yours,   Charles S. Hamlin

ALS (WP, DLC).

To Thetus Willrette Sims

My dear Mr. Sims: [The White House] June 17, 1914

If I have been a long time about it, you may be sure that it has not been because I had forgotten to express my very sincere admiration for and appreciation of the part that you played in the contest which led to the repeal of the tolls exemption. I want you to know how much I respect and honor you for the position which you took and how much I value the aid you rendered.

Cordially and sincerely yours,   Woodrow Wilson

TLS (Letterpress Books, WP, DLC).

To Cleveland Hoadley Dodge

My dear Cleve: The White House June 17, 1914

Your note, dated Sunday morning off Saybrook on board the Corona,[1] brought instantly to my mind the delightful time of your former visit to that part of the Sound when you came up to see us at Lyme and of all the delightful associations I have with the Corona, and it was perfectly delightful to get such a note from you. You always know, my dear fellow, how to say the things that it most cheers a friend to hear.

I perfectly understood your absence from the reunion and must admit that it cost me a great deal to be there myself. Fortunately, the thing was so arranged as not to bring me into contact with men whom it would be embarrassing for me to meet, and the day went off as delightful as it could, with Parker Handy coming up to me as often as he could and calling me Woodrow. The boys were, most of them, splendid, and the day was marred only by our loss of the game to Yale.

Mrs. Wilson is slowly, very slowly I am sorry to say, getting her strength back. She had evidently quite overtaxed herself, but she is coming uphill and a long period of rest ought to bring her back to her old form.

She and all my household join me in warmest and most affectionate messages to you all.

Your devoted friend,   Woodrow Wilson

TLS (WC, NjP).
[1] C. H. Dodge to WW, June 14, 1914, ALS (WP, DLC).

To John Reed

My dear Mr. Reed: The White House June 17, 1914

I am perfectly willing that you should use our interview of the other day in the way you suggest for an article of your own written in the light of what I told you but not bringing me in at all, and I want to say how warmly I appreciate your desire to help and your whole spirit in this matter.

Cordially and sincerely yours,   Woodrow Wilson

TLS (J. Reed Papers, MH).

From Edward Mandell House

Dear Governor,   [London] June 17, 1914.

Sir Edward Grey, Tyrrell and I have just lunched with Page and have had a two hours talk. I am quite satisfied with the beginning made. I found Sir Edward a willing listener and very frank and sympathetic. I am to stay the week end with Tyrrell, and lunch with Sir Edward next Wednesday. In the mean time he will doubtless discuss the matter with his colleagues. Page writes so well that I have asked him to send you a more detailed account. I find here everything cluttered up with social affairs, and it is impossible to work quickly. Here they have their thoughts on Ascot, garden parties etc etc. In Germany their one thought is to advance industrially and to glorify war. In France I did not find the war spirit dominant. Their statesmen dream no longer of revenge and the recovering of Alsace and Lorraine. The people do, but those that govern and know, hope only that France may continue as now. Germany already exceeds her in population by nearly fifty per cent, and the disparity increases year by year. It is this new spirit in France which fills me with hope, and which I used today to some advantage. France, I am sure, will welcome our efforts for peace.

Your faithful and affectionate   E. M. House

ALS (WP, DLC).

Remarks at a Press Conference

June 18, 1914.

Have you any plan yet as to any speaking tour this fall?
No.
Have you any further information about business conditions?
Nothing except this, that evidences abound in my mail of improving conditions. I suppose you saw, for example, the statement the other day of James J. Hill with regard to it. I do not know why some of the newspapers did not carry that statement. Mr. Hill is certainly informed of conditions over a large part of the country; and men who are in a position themselves to collect information write to me and say I am entirely right about the position I have taken. I want you gentlemen to understand what apparently was not quite clearly understood the other day. I gave out that letter of *The Pictorial Review* as a very interesting example as to the way in which the psychology was made up. I do not care how it was made up provided the country knows how it was made up. Everybody has a right to his opinion. I have no quarrel about that.
Did that letter have the desired effect?
What was the desired effect?

I suppose that is more definitely defined—

The desired effect was exactly what I intimated—to let the people know that the impression was being systematically worked up. It is being put into the mind not only, but in the correspondence of persons who otherwise would not have the thought.

I rather take it that the effect was designed to reach Congress.

No, I can reach Congress myself.

I thought it was an indirect way.

I thought it would be useful to everybody concerned to know what was going on. I do not mind anything that everybody knows about. That is my position about all public affairs. If everybody understands how the game is being played, I am satisfied.

Is there any change as to the Colorado situation?

No, I wish there were. I continue to hear hopes expressed that the way is opening for the arbitration or settlement by understanding, but I have not, I am sorry to say, anything definite in the way of things accomplished.

T MS (C. L. Swem Coll., NjP).

To Robert Latham Owen

My dear Senator: [The White House] June 18, 1914

I am afraid that Mr. Thomas D. Jones is the man about whom the committee will have the least information, and I venture to write you this letter to tell you what I know, and fortunately I can say that I do really know it.[1]

I have been associated with Mr. Jones in various ways for more than fifteen years and have seen him tried by fire in causes which were like the very causes we are fighting for now. He has always stood for the rights of the people against the rights of privilege, and he has won a place of esteem and confidence by his quiet power and unquestionable integrity in the City of Chicago which I think is very enviable indeed.

His connection with the Harvester Company is this: He owns one share, and only one share, of stock in the company which he purchased to qualify as a director. He went into the board of the Harvester Company for the purpose of assisting to withdraw it from the control which had led it into the acts and practices which have brought it under the criticism of the law officers of the Government and has been very effective in that capacity. His connection with those acts and practices is absolutely nil. His connection with it was a public service, not a private interest, and he has won additional credit and admiration for his courage in that matter.

He is a lawyer by profession but he has devoted his attention to special aspects of the law and has been very little in the courts, I believe. My close association with him was in the Board of Trustees of Princeton University, where he stood by me with wonderful address and courage in trying to bring the University to true standards of democracy by which it would serve not special classes but the general body of our youth. He graduated from Princeton University in 1876. He is of Welsh extraction, possibly of Welsh birth, though I am not certain on that point, and is a man whom I can absolutely guarantee in every respect to the committee. He is the one man of the whole number who was in a peculiar sense my personal choice.

　　　　　Cordially and sincerely yours,　　Woodrow Wilson

TLS (Letterpress Books, WP, DLC).

[1] Insurgent Democrats and progressive Republicans had already begun a heavy fire against Jones and Warburg. For an account of the bitter controversy over their confirmation, see Link, *The New Freedom*, pp. 452-57.

From John Reed

Dear Mr. President:　　　　　Provincetown Mass. June 18, 1914.

Just before I got on the train at Washington, I sat down and wrote you a little note upon the advice of one of your secretaries, asking permission, if you did not want me to use the interview, to write an article interpreting your Mexican policy in the light of what you told me. You said when I left that this was for me to think about. And I have thought about it.

When I left you, I went right back to the hotel, and wrote down my impressions of you and what you had told me, as nearly as I could remember it. I send the report[1] that I made to you in this envelope. And, in addition to my former request, I want to ask you if you will look through this and tell me whether some parts of it, at least, cannot be printed.

In the "English Review" for June I came across an article about you by Sydney Brooks[2] in which he says this:

"The country has never quite understood, and has therefore never quite subscribed to, the principles which have guided Mr. Wilson throughout the Mexican entanglement or the end he has been pursuing. It sincerely shares his abhorrence of intervention on a big scale and its aftermath of huge responsibilities. It has trusted, perhaps, too implicitly in his capacity to find a peaceable way out, and it now finds itself face to face with a situation, largely of the President's own creation, and full of unattractive possibilities that cannot well be shirked. It confronts that situation without enthusiasm and with an exasperated feeling that, under better management, it might have been avoided. Criticism in such circumstances is inevitable, and proofs have not been lacking that the extraordinary loyalty and patience with which his countrymen have watched the President's dealing with General Huerta are being mingled with the suspicion that he has bungled the whole business. * * *

"His whole Mexican policy, indeed—the problem of how such a man could act in such a way—only becomes comprehensible when the guess is hazarded that his conscience rather than his intellect dictated it."

Everybody I have talked to seems hopelessly at sea, both as to what was meant by the occupation of Vera Cruz, and the consistent policy which I see clearly now you have always maintained in the Mexican question. Nobody knows anything about it, Mr. President.

If you allow this to be made public, I think that a child might understand the developments which may come hereafter. And it seems to me that by taking the country into your confidence on a question like this a blow could be dealt the "secret diplomacy" of the world's governments, and an easy way opened for the coming of international peace.

All I want to do in this is to spread broadcast, and in a form which cannot be misunderstood, the principles which have guided you in your dealings with Mexico.

Yours sincerely,   John Reed

TLS (WP, DLC).
  1 It was the unrevised version of the article described in n. 1 to J. Reed to JPT, June 30, 1914.
  2 Sydney Brooks, "President Wilson," *English Review*, XVII (June, 1914), 372-84. Reed was quoting from pp. 381 and 383.

George C. Carothers to William Jennings Bryan

El Paso, Texas, June 18, 1914.

Arrived here five p.m., to-day delayed thirty hours account washouts. Preferred coming here to telegraph as service is most uncertain and unsatisfactory in Mexico at present, due to improper censorship. It was impossible to prevent rupture between Carranza and Villa,[1] but Villa's plan if carried out will not interfere with progress of revolution. His troops have left Torreon for Zacet[e]cas[2] and will push forward toward Mexico [City] rapidly.

Whenever he encounters other revolutionary leaders he will give them option of fighting under him or of going to some other division, to Gonzales or Obregon. When they reach Mexico Villa says he will bend to will of all the generals, and deliver the presidency to whoever they select in a council of generals, even if it be Carranza. He does not intend hostilities toward Carranza, but says he will still receive orders from him when they do not interfere with his military operations. I have read Cobb's relegrams [telegrams] June 16, 12:00 afternoon, June 17, 12:00 Forenoon, June 17, 11:00 afternoon,[3] and information therein stated is complete and strictly correct.

Villa is not only a general but has keen political perceptions. He is anxious for United States not to misinterpret his actions. I believe he can carry out his present plan without armed conflict with Carranza. I asked him his position as to mediation and he replied that should the United States recommend a certain course to him it would receive profound consideration as he knew the friendship that exists towards Mexico and that the United States would recommend nothing that would not be beneficial to country. Will remain here pending instructions from you. I did not bring out my family. Will telegraph about other matters tomorrow.   Carrothers.

T telegram (WP, DLC).
[1] For the background of the break between Carranza and Villa, see Charles C. Cumberland, *Mexican Revolution, The Constitutionalist Years* (Austin, Tex. and London, 1972), pp. 127-36; Hill, *Emissaries to a Revolution*, pp. 191-94; Robert E. Quirk, *The Mexican Revolution, 1914-1915, The Convention of Aguascalientes* (Bloomington, Ind., 1960), pp. 26-34; and Arthur S. Link, *Wilson: The Struggle for Neutrality* (Princeton, N. J., 1960), pp. 232-36.
[2] The immediate issue was the plan of attack against Zacatecas. Carranza had given command of the operation to General Natera and had ordered Villa to reinforce Natera's troops. Villa, refusing to cooperate on Carranza's terms, resigned his command. However, Villa's generals refused to accept his resignation, whereupon Villa, in defiance of Carranza, captured Zacatecas himself on June 23.
[3] Z. L. Cobb to WJB, June 16, 1914, 12 midnight; Cobb to WJB, June 17, 1914, 10 P.M.; and Cobb to WJB, June 17, 1914, 11 P.M., T telegrams, all in WP, DLC.

To Charles Allen Culberson

My dear Senator: [The White House] June 19, 1914

Here is a memorandum which the Secretary of Commerce prepared for me about the anti-trust legislation while it was pending in the House.[1] The second, third, and fourth sections being omitted, the letter has not just the bearing now that it had at that time, but I send it in the hope that it may be of some slight service to you in the discussion.
                    Cordially and sincerely yours,   Woodrow Wilson

TLS (Letterpress Books, WP, DLC).
¹ W. C. Redfield to WW, April 15, 1914, Vol. 29.

To Walter Hines Page

My dear Page: The White House June 19, 1914

Just a line to be followed later by particulars.

Please do not hesitate to engage the house for next year. I feel confident I can make arrangements. I could not in any circumstances think of losing you at that all-important post.

In haste   Faithfully yours,   Woodrow Wilson

TLS (W. H. Page Papers, MH).

From James Viscount Bryce

My dear President   [London] June 19th, 1914

Let me congratulate you heartily on the great victory you have won, in the passing of the Canal Tolls Exemption repeal bill, over the combined forces of monopolists seeking their own gain and mischief makers trying to create ill feeling between nations. Such a victory has a moral value reaching far beyond the particular case and is the more valuable because the worst elements in the press seem to have exerted themselves more virulently than ever before.

Eighteen months ago I told my Government at home that I believed you could carry this, because the best sentiment of the Nation would respond to an appeal coming from you as its head: it is a satisfaction to me who loves your people to see that this has happened.

I trust you will soon have a good long summer rest; you must need it after the strain of the last seventeenth months. Our warmest regards to Mrs. Wilson and your daughter.

Always sincerely yours   James Bryce

ALS (WP, DLC).

From William Graves Sharp

Dear Mr President: Elyria, Ohio, June 20, 1914.

I wish to express to you my most sincere thanks, as well as those of Mrs Sharp,¹ for the very great honor you have bestowed on me in naming me as Ambassador to France. If I am to judge from the many messages of congratulations coming to me the past week, I could well imagine that those who sent them are as deeply grateful as we are and share with us the pleasure which your action brings.

Let me assure you that it shall be my aim to the best of my ability to so discharge the duties of that high office as to reflect credit upon your administration. In this purpose I feel that I shall find great strength in the high esteem and confidence in which that administration is justly held abroad as well as at home.

During the past week I have been stopping at Cambridge Springs, Pa. with Mrs Sharp, whose health I am glad to say is fast improving. I expect, however, to return to Washington next week, when I shall be pleased to thank you in person.

With kindest personal regards, I am,

Most sincerely,   Wm. G. Sharp.

TLS (WP, DLC).
  [1] Hallie Clough Sharp.

To Mary Allen Hulbert

My dearest Friend,   The White House 21 June, 1914.

I have been waiting with not a little uneasiness to hear whether or not you had actually got back to Nantucket. The last letter you wrote was from the hospital and said that you were *expecting* to go back to Sandanwede at once, but I have not heard that you actually did and so do not know whether they let you leave the hospital or not. Please write and tell me. I have been hoping, as you know, very fervently that they would conclude to operate on your neck, for I know the operation to be easy and practically always successful, and it would be so delightful to see you free to be *perfectly* well!

The dear lady here is at last beginning to come up hill, and my reassurance lightens my heart immeasurably. For some time I was almost without hope: I thought, with leaden heart, that she was going to be an invalid, another victim of the too great burden that must be carried by the lady of the White House; but that fear, thank God, is past and she is coming along slowly but surely!

I myself seem too tough to damage, to my unaffected astonishment. The burden I have to carry seems to grow heavier rather than lighter, the perplexities more rather than less confusing; but I am schooling myself gradually to the strain, learning to live each day as it comes without the vain endeavour to see just what it is all leading to; and so am making shift reasonably well. Did you ever imagine anything the elements in which changed their values and their relations to one another as the elements in the Mexican situation do? There one *must* live from day to day and be confident about no to-morrow. Fortunately there are signs, not so many as I could wish, but some, that the people of the country are beginning to catch my point of view and understand what I am after; and when once they are behind me I can get everything in hand.

All join me in affectionate messages and in the hope that we may get news very, very soon.

Your devoted friend,   Woodrow Wilson

WWTLS (WP, DLC).

Rómulo Sebastian Naón to the Minister of Foreign Affairs

TELEGRAMA CIFRADO NO. 329   Niágara Falls, junio 21 de 1914.

Acabo de llegar de Washington después de haber conferenciado ayer tarde por más de dos horas y media con el secretario de Estado y anoche por cerca de dos horas con el Presidente Wilson. Discutimos la situación ampliamente exponiéndole de mi parte en la forma más clara posible recalcando sobre todo, sobre la inconveniencia que entrañaba la intervención directa y parcial de la delegación americana en favor de uno de los bandos en lucha y sobre el desprestigio que este hecho producía aun para la mediación misma. Recordé al Presidente su manifestación al despedirnos en Washington cuando nos expresó el pensamiento de su gobierno en estas palabras: "Solución mexicana del problema mexicano" para establecer la contradicción que importaba la actitud actual. No puedo entrar en todos los detalles de estas conferencias porque sería excesivo y me bastará anunciar a V. E. como resultado primero, que el Presidente aceptó la propiedad de que la formación del Gobierno provisorio fuese el resultado de un arreglo entre las facciones huertista y constitucionalista de acuerdo con mi sugestión para lo cual la mediación teniendo en cuenta que Carranza lo había aceptado en principio y ya que no podía asistir a la conferencia por falta del armisticio, podía sin embargo en su anhelo de conseguir un arreglo pacífico invitarlo a que sus representantes se entrevistaran con los de Huerta para discutir y convenir la organización de aquel gobierno provisorio con sus prerrogativas de elementos extraños. Por su parte el gobierno norteamericano protocolizaría ante la mediación todo aquello que se relacionara con aspecto internacional de la cuestión sometiendo su cumplimiento a la formación del gobierno provisorio que terminara la guerra y conviniese por consiguiente la evacuación del territorio por las fuerzas americanas. El Presidente convino en todo esto, manifestándome que la razón para discutir este punto, había sido sólo el temor de que no aceptándose el gobierno que se organizase por los carrancistas, continuara la guerra, pero que su gobierno vería con satisfacción la solución interna y reconocería el resultado de ella aceptando también las otras sugestiones relativas a la protocolización de lo relacionado con aspecto internacional, Por su parte los carrancistas, convenido el arreglo, se presentarían a la mediación ya con el armisticio y subscribirían con los huertistas, americanos y la mediación el protocolo definitivo de paz. Antes de ofrecer esta solución conversé ampliamente con el representante carrancista en Washington que me aseguró que acudirían a la invitación que le hiciéramos para conferenciar con los huertistas, ya estaba seguro de que arribarían a un arreglo.

Los colegas han recibido con júbilo esta solución lo mismo que los delegados mexicanos y norteamericanos y la prensa qué hasta ayer se mostraba absolutamente sin esperanzas parece hoy optimista. Mis conferencias con el secretario de Estado y el Presidente se han desenvuelto en una atmósfera de absoluta cordialidad sin que haya ello sido óbice para que expresase nuestro pensamiento con la claridad y la firmeza que imponían las circunstancias al discutirse los aspectos diversos de la difícil situación a que se había llegado.   Naón

TC telegram (Argentine Foreign Ministry Archives).

T R A N S L A T I O N

Coded telegram no. 329   Niagara Falls, June 21, 1914

I have just returned from Washington where, yesterday afternoon, I conferred for more than two hours and a half with the Secretary of State and, last night, for almost two hours with President Wilson. We went over the situation very thoroughly, and I stated my point of view as clearly as possible, emphasizing the impropriety involved in the direct and partisan intervention of the American delegation in favor of one of the two contending factions and the consequent discredit even for the mediating body. I reminded President Wilson that when he said goodby to us in Washington he expressed the position of his government in these words: "A Mexican solution of the Mexican problem" in order that he might realize the contradiction implicit in the present attitude.

I cannot enter into all the details of these conferences because it would be excessive to do so, and it will suffice to announce to Your Excellency, as the first result, that the President accepted as proper the idea that the setting up of a provisional government should be the result of an agreement between the *Huertistas* and the *Constitucionalistas* in accordance with my own suggestion. To this end, the mediators, since Carranza had accepted, but is unable to attend because there is no armistice, could, in their great desire to reach a peaceful solution, take advantage of their prerogatives as neutrals and invite Carranza to appoint representatives to meet those sent by Huerta for the purpose of discussing and agreeing upon the organization of a provisional government. The Government of the United States would make available to the mediators all protocols bearing on the international aspect of the question and would submit them for implementation upon the establishment of a provisional government that would end the war and consequently arrange for the evacuation of the territory of Mexico by the forces of the United States.

The President agreed to this plan, explaining that the reason why this point had to be discussed was the fear that if the government to be set up should be unacceptable to the *Carrancistas*, the war would continue. But his government would be pleased with an internal solution and would accept its results as well as the suggestion regarding the protocolization pertaining to the international aspect of the problem.

As to the *Carrancistas*, once an agreement should be reached, they would appear before the mediators, taking advantage of an armistice and, jointly with the *Huertistas*, Americans, and mediators would subscribe to the definitive protocol of peace.

Before suggesting this solution, I discussed it fully with Carranza's representative in Washington, who assured me that the *Carrancistas* would accept the invitation to confer with the *Huertistas*, expressing confidence that an agreement would be reached.

My colleagues have received this solution with the greatest pleasure. The same can be said of the Mexican and American delegates. The press, which up to yesterday had expressed hopelessness, today seems optimistic.

My conferences with the Secretary of State and with the President have taken place in an atmosphere of absolute friendliness, which has not prevented us from expressing our thoughts clearly and with the firmness required by the circumstances, when we considered the various aspects of the difficult situation that has developed. Naón

To William Jennings Bryan, with Enclosure

My dear Mr. Secretary: The White House June 22, 1914

Here is a letter from Mr. House which I am sure you will be glad to read. I did not know that the French had made any definite proposals for a revision of their commercial treaty with us. It certainly would be to our advantage to push the matter promptly.
          Cordially and faithfully yours,   Woodrow Wilson

TLS (W. J. Bryan Papers, DNA).

E N C L O S U R E

From Edward Mandell House

My dear Friend: London, England. June 11th, 1914.

Herrick told me in Paris that he considered it very important that the French proposal for a revision of the commercial treaty between France and the United States should be accepted at once. He wrote to Mr. Bryan two months ago, but he says nothing has been done.

I learn not only from Herrick but from other sources that the United States is being badly discriminated against. Even Germany has better terms given her than to us and we are on a level with the Congo States and Haiti.

Herrick has spent a great deal of time in trying to bring about a proposal from France looking to a revision of the treaty and it seems a pity not to push the matter through. He thinks great care should be given to the selection of a commission, and he suggests among others, Mr. Mason, our former Consul at Paris,[1] Mr. Benet[2] and John Bassett Moore.

It is the general impression that our Ambassadors are more or less ornaments, and that they accomplish but little of value, but now and then you find one that is doing effective work and Herrick is among these.

Gerard also shows remar[k]able diligence in looking after our commercial interests in Germany. He has no vision, but I doubt if you could have sent a man there who would be as persistently active in the direction indicated as he is. His mind seems to run in that direction.

I have just arrived here and have only had one talk with Page. I am to lunch with Sir Edward Grey early next week.

There is one thing I tried to do in Germany and that was to give the Kaiser and his official family a proper estimate of you and your purposes. I have had no difficulty as yet in making your

Mexican policy understood and appreciated. It seems so easy to do that I wonder they have not thought of it themselves.

I also let them know that Bismark himself had no more iron courage or inflexible will than you. I feel sure that my visit has not been without good results.

Your faithful and affectionate,   E. M. House

TLS (W. J. Bryan Papers, DNA).
    [1] Frank Holcomb Mason, consul general since 1905 and special commercial expert attaché of the Embassy, 1908-14.
    [2] Hiram D. Bennett, an American dentist practicing in Nantes since 1870. He was vice consul at Nantes, 1870-1876, was re-appointed in 1885, and was still serving in that capacity in 1914.

To Edward Mandell House

My dear Friend: The White House June 22, 1914

I have your letter of June eleventh from London about the French proposal for a revision of the commercial treaty between France and the United States. I will take the matter up with Mr. Bryan at once.

I can not tell you how constantly my thoughts follow you and how deeply interested I am and thankful besides to have a friend who so thoroughly understands me to interpret me to those whom it is most important we should inform and enlighten with regard to what we are really seeking to accomplish. It is a great source of strength and relief to me and I thank you from the bottom of my heart.

The mediation is going slowly here and with many variations of aspect, but I think at last we see a reasonable prospect of success, at any rate, of the success that will be incident to making the whole situation throughly understood and putting the responsibility where it belongs.

Give my warmest regard to Mrs. House and to the Pages and remember that I always think of you with deep gratitude and affection.   Affectionately yours,   Woodrow Wilson

TLS (E. M. House Papers, CtY).

To Robert Latham Owen

My dear Senator: [The White House] June 22, 1914

I have been looking over my files and find that the situation with regard to the nominees is just what I indicated to you when you mentioned it to me at the White House the other day. The whole board was selected by inquiry on my part, not a single member because of applications or recommendations filed with me as a candidate. The consequence is that I have only reports sent me by friends whom I asked to inquire into the character and standing of these several gentlemen, and in a majority of cases the reports were made to me orally.

I regret this very much if it is to inconvenience the committee, but I would be pleased to tell them anything that I, myself, know which they stand in need of by way of information about any one of these candidates. The one that I personally know and personally selected, as I said the other day, is Mr. Thomas D. Jones, but any inquiry made in Chicago would show his extraordinary standing there.

Cordially and sincerely yours,   Woodrow Wilson

TLS (Letterpress Books, WP, DLC).

From Joseph Patrick Tumulty

Memorandum: The White House. June 22, 1914.

Secretary Tumulty would like to talk with the President concerning Mr. Reed's article before the President approves it.

It contains various statements which might prove very embarrassing and which should be eliminated.

T MS (WP, DLC).

To John Worth Kern

My dear Senator: [The White House] June 23, 1914

Rather than trouble you to come to the office when I know that you are so busy, I am going to ask permission to send you a line about a matter Senator Owen presented to me very earnestly the other day, namely, his bill to amend the present Corrupt Practices Act with regard to campaign contributions. At present it is possible for our opponents to spend any amount of money they choose to spend against us, and there is no legal check upon anybody. It seems to me a very important bill and I am writing to ask if you think there is any chance of finding an interval of business in which it could be put through. I am assuming that it will provoke very little debate or opposition.

Cordially and sincerely yours,   Woodrow Wilson

TLS (Letterpress Books, WP, DLC).

To Robert Latham Owen

My dear Senator: [The White House] June 23, 1914

I am sending you a copy of a letter which has just been handed me by the Attorney General.[1] May I ask that you consider this letter confidential except, of course, so far as the members of your committee are concerned? It is part of the records of the Attorney General's Office. Mr. Grosvenor, who signs the letter, was employed by the department to take the proof in the Harvester case.

Cordially and sincerely yours,   Woodrow Wilson

TLS (Letterpress Books, WP, DLC).
[1] E. P. Grosvenor to G. C. Todd, June 22, 1914, TCL (WP, DLC), saying that, although Thomas D. Jones had been a director of International Harvester since 1909, he had no part whatever in the formation of the company in 1902, and that it would be unfair to use his directorship as an argument to deny his confirmation.

From William Jennings Bryan, with Enclosure

My Dear Mr President   [Washington, June 23, 1914]

I [am] enclosing a despatch to the Commissioners. I do not see that any change is necessary in the language of the amendments which they propose. Please pass judgment and send.

Query. In view of reported attacks on churches and crue[l]ty to priests do you think it necessary or advisable to add a paragraph about guaranty of religious liberty?

The Associated press report that Villa has told one of their representatives confidentially that he was ready to do any thing the U. S. wanted—that the people were worn out with fighting and that a peaceful settlement ought to be secured. This is encouraging.

With assurances of esteem I am, my dear Mr President,
Very truly yours   W J Bryan

P.S. I enclose copy of Dominican agreement.[1] It was *ratified by the Senate*.

ALS (WP, DLC).
[1] The American-Dominican Convention of 1907.

ENCLOSURE

William Jennings Bryan to the Special Commissioners

Enciphered & sent from The White House
June 23, 1914   [Washington] June 23, 1914

The President approves of including in the protocol the subjects covered by your amendments which read as follows: quote

AMERICAN AMENDMENTS:

2. The provisional Government mentioned in the foregoing paragraph is that which it is contemplated will be constituted by agreement of the delegations representing the two great parties between which the internal struggle in Mexico is taking place.
3. The provisional Government being contemplated and recognized, the international matters shall be settled upon these terms:

1. The provisional Government shall proclaim an absolute amnesty to all foreigners for any any [sic] and all political offenses committed during the period of civil war in Mexico.

2. The provisional Government shall provide for international commissions for the settlement of the claims of foreigners on account of damages sustained during the period of civil war as a consequence of military acts or the acts (of) national authorities.

3. The Government of the United States of America will not in any form whatsoever claim a war indemnity or other international satisfaction.

4. The Government of the United States of America agrees to evacuate the territory of the United Mexican States, now occupied by her military and naval forces within the time and under the conditions to be agreed upon with the Provisional Government.

end of quote

If the mediators fail to secure the consent of the Mexican delegates to the last provision leaving the question of evacuation to be arranged with the provisional government you will please to have that subject passed for the present. The President is not willing to fix a definite time for evacuation   Bryan

WJBhw and T telegram (SDR, RG 59, 812.00/23486a, DNA).

From Alfred Henry Mulliken and Elliot Hersey Goodwin[1]

Sir: Washington, D. C. June 23, 1914.

The Chamber of Commerce of the United States of America, representing five hundred and eighty-five associations, whose membership exceeds two hundred and fifty thousand individuals and concerns, respectfully draws your attention to a situation which we regard as most serious.

The Chamber of Commerce from the beginning of your administration has in every recommendation submitted to its constituent members endeavored to present fairly the constructive policies of your administration and to create public sentiment in favor of all policies which seemed to it likely to contribute to the general welfare.

This attitude of the Chamber was notable in connection with the Federal Reserve Act, contrary to the opposition and criticism freely expressed in other quarters. Its suggestions were constructive and were recognized as aiding substantially in the perfection of the bill.

In the Trust program it has assumed a like attitude, studying the question through a Special Committee, sitting in Washington in the atmosphere of legislation. The recommendations of this Special Committee disapproved only those things which could not agree with knowledge and experience. The Chamber's recommendations have not contemplated the abandonment of legislation, but have endeavored so to assist in its formation as to promote the general prosperity.

On the question, however, upon which we now appear, involved in Sections 7 and 18 of the Clayton Bill,[2] the Chamber has stood always unalterably opposed to what in its judgment, and the judgment of its constituent members, is utterly wrong. It considers this a time for plain speaking in that regard.

In nineteen hundred and thirteen, your attention was called by the Chamber to the danger that would arise from the signing of the Sundry Civil Appropriation Bill with the objectionable rider attached.[3] While the rider simply dealt with certain appropriated funds, it constituted what we believed would be an entering wedge for additional demands upon the part of the interests desiring exemption, which would be driven in further during the coming session and would re-act unfavorably not only upon general interests, but ultimately upon the interests asking for the exemption; and would be in conflict with your own expressed opinion at the time of the signing of this bill.

The apprehensions of the Chamber appear to have been fulfilled not only in the fact that there is a repetition in the present Sundry Civil Appropriation Bill, despite your objection above mentioned, of exactly the same exemption as in the bill of nineteen hundred and thirteen, but also in the fact that there has been carried into Sections 7 and 18 of the Clayton Bill a definite exemption of certain classes in a manner which we believe to be clearly contrary to right principles. Those sections embody class legislation in its worst form.

We are here to protest against such legislation and request that you protect the people, whose President you are, and not permit a discrimination between classes of the people in respect of organizations or purposes or actions of similar character and effect.

We are here to ask you to veto any bills passed by Congress that may embody any provisions of the effect incorporated in Sections 7 and 18 of the Clayton Bill and any appropriation bill carrying a rider prohibiting the use of such appropriations in the prosecution of any class of offenders.

We are here for this purpose for the reason that this legislation threatens the welfare of the country. It is not too much to say, from what has come to us, that this particular legislation has aroused a wave of protest and indignation beyond any other proposed legislation of which we have knowledge.

It is submitted that if organizations "instituted for the purpose of mutual help, and not having capital stock or conducted for profit" are to be exempted from the Sherman Act, *all* organizations of that nature (and not merely "fraternal, labor, consumers, agricultural or horticultural" organizations) should be exempted. Any distinction between such organizations is arbitrary, with no fair reason to sustain it; and the same observations apply to the provisions of Section 18 of the Clayton Bill, which limit the injunctive process of the courts as between employers and employees as compared with the power of the court in a controversy between two or more employers or other individuals.

We believe it to be self-evident that all persons should stand and be treated alike before the law and under the processes of the court by which the law is enforced.

Moreover, it is claimed that under Section 7 of the Clayton Bill any association organized for "mutual help" is declared to be legal and beyond the hand of the law, even though its by-laws and regulations may provide for secondary boycotts and other now illegal actions. It need not, we think, be urged that the introduction of such an ambiguity into an act, whose purpose it is to make clearer the law, would be wholly unjustifiable aside from all other considerations.

In conclusion we invoke your thoughtful attention to this subject, with a view to the prevention of what we believe would be a lamentable and disastrous error, if the provisions in question were for the first time spread upon the statute books of the Federal Government.

Very respectfully yours,

Chamber of Commerce of the
United States of America.

Elliot H. Goodwin   by   A. H. Mulliken
Secretary.   Acting President.

TLS (WP, DLC).

[1] Mulliken, a Chicago businessman, was president of Pettibone Mulliken Co., manufacturers of railroad frogs, switches, crossings and guard rails; Goodwin had been general secretary of the Chamber of Commerce of the United States since 1912.

[2] That is, the provisions relating to labor unions and farm organizations.

[3] E. H. Goodwin to WW, June 16, 1913, Vol. 27.

From William Jennings Bryan

My Dear Mr President   Washington June 24 1914

Mrs Bryan joins me in most cordial congratulations to you and Mrs Wilson on this your 29th wedding anniversary.

The kind Providence that brought your hearts together and blended your lives into one has graciously smiled upon the union and blessed it to the nation as well as to the family circle.

May you be spared to each other and to your ever increasing host of friends for many, many years, is the sincere wish of two, my wife and myself, who have greatly enjoyed your companionship.

With assurances of esteem I am, my dear Mr President,

Very truly yours   W. J. Bryan

ALS (WP, DLC).

The Special Commissioners to William Jennings Bryan

RECEIVED IN CIPHER AND   Niagara Falls, N. Y.,
TRANSLATED AT THE WHITE HOUSE.   June 24, 1914.

The mediators were furnished last night with a copy of the items of the plan you are willing to protocolize. They requested us to meet them at three-thirty today, and submitted their draft covering the same points. After discussion it was amended so as to read as follows:

"One. The Provisional Government referred to in the last protocol shall be constituted by agreement of the delegates representing the parties between which the internal struggle in Mexico is taking place.

"Two. A. Upon the constitution of the Provisional Government in the City of Mexico, the Government of the United States of America will recognize it immediately, and diplomatic relations between the two countries will then be restored.

B. The Government of the United States of America will not in any form whatsoever claim a war indemnity or other international satisfaction.

C. The Provisional Government will proclaim an absolute amnesty to all foreigners for any and all political offenses committed during the period of civil war in Mexico.

D. The Provisional Government will negotiate for the constitution of international commission for the settlement of the claims of foreigners on account of damages sustained during the period of civil war as a consequence of military acts or the acts of national authorities."

They pressed for protocolization at six o'clock p.m. We stated that we could not do so until after the matter had been referred to Washington. They then asked that we communicate and let them know the result as soon as possible and expressed their earnest desire that we could protocolize at ten tonight.

In answer to our inquiry as to whether they had any information as to when the Constitutionalists would be here to confer with the Huertistas, they stated that they had no official reply to their official invitation, but read to us a private letter from Cabrera to Naon, which was very vague, containing no distinct promise to be here, but stated that they had had no reply from their chief and expressed the opinion that domestic affairs—(probably differences between Carranza and Villa)—had caused delay. The letter while vague was courteous and expressed the hope of a satisfactory adjustment.   Commissioners.

T telegram (WP, DLC).

Remarks at a Press Conference

June 25, 1914

Mr. President, it is being said that you would like far-reaching legislation at this session—that the Jones bill be acted on at this session of Congress?

> Well, I haven't consulted with the leaders of the House about it, no. I have been consulting with Mr. Jones about the bill, which he was kind enough to bring to me, and which I think is being gotten up in fine shape.

He also said that you rather hoped for legislation along that line at this session?

> Of course, with the program that is now before the Senate, I am rather modest about hoping for anything in addition, but I don't know, of course, what will be the decision of the leaders.

Mr. President, did you read this morning the remarks of Colonel Roosevelt on the Colombian treaty?

> I never have time to read the morning papers until evening.

He claims that this payment of $25,000,000 is merely blackmail.[1] Anything you would care to say?

> No. I have no comment. . . .

Mr. President, can you say anything about your conference today with Mr. Fuller?

> Mr. Fuller called. It appears that Mr. Fuller is unusually well acquainted with the leading people and with conditions in general in Central America. He very generously called to tell me very many interesting things he knew about the attitude of individuals there, the general impressions obtained in South America about questions of policy. He didn't call on any special errand.

He didn't call representing the bankers?

> No, sir, he didn't call representing the bankers.

Mr. President, have you heard from either the governments of France or Germany about the reports on the certain indebtedness that Haiti owes?

> Not a word.

There is a persistent rumor that they are going to take some steps.

> That was, I think, just a rumor.

It has been published very broadly in the German newspapers.

> Yes. I dare say they [have] rumors as well as we do.

JRT transcript (WC, NjP) of CLSsh (C. L. Swem Coll., NjP).

[1] Roosevelt defended his actions in Panama by saying, "As President I declined to allow Uncle Sam to be blackmailed. President Wilson now desires the blackmail to be paid." "If this proposed treaty . . . is right," he went on, "then our presence on the Isthmus is wrong. In such case Panama should at once be restored to Colombia, and we should stop work on the canal. . . . If we as a nation have been guilty of theft we should restore the stolen goods." The Colombian treaty capped the climax of a foreign policy by Wilson and Bryan "which has been such as to make the United States a figure of fun in the international world." These comments were highlights of a long, rambling explanation of his administration's policy and actions regarding Colombia, Panama, and the canal. New York *World*, June 25, 1914.

Remarks on the Business Outlook[1]

June 25, 1914

Mr. Cook, Mr. Carlin:[2] I think it is appropriate, ladies and gentlemen, in receiving you to say just a word or two in assistance of your judgment about the existing conditions. You are largely responsible for the state of public opinion. You furnish the public with information, and in your editorials you furnish it with the interpretation of that information. We are in the presence of a business situation which is variously interpreted. Here in Washington, through the Bureau of Commerce and other instrumentalities that are at our disposal and through correspondence which comes in to us from all parts of the nation, we are perhaps in a position to judge of the actual condition of business better than those can judge who are at any other single point in the country; and I want to say to you that, as a matter of fact, the signs of a very strong business revival are becoming more and more evident from day to day.

I want to suggest this to you: Business has been in a feverish and apprehensive condition in this country for more than ten years. I will not stop to point out the time at which it began to be apprehensive, but during more than ten years business has been the object of sharp criticism in the United States, a criticism growing in volume and growing in particularity; and as a natural consequence, as the volume of criticism has increased, business has grown more and more anxious. Businessmen have acted as some men do who fear they will have to undergo an operation, and who are not sure that when they get on the table the operation will not be a capital operation. As a matter of fact, as the diagnosis has progressed, it has become more and more evident that no capital operation was necessary; that at the most a minor operation was necessary to remove admitted distempers and evils. The treatment is to be constitutional rather than surgical, affecting habits of life and action which have been hurtful. For on all hands it is admitted that there are processes of business, or have been processes of business, in this country which ought to be corrected; but the correction has been postponed, and, in proportion to the postponement, the fever has increased—the fever of apprehension.

There is nothing more fatal to business than to be kept guessing from month to month and from year to year whether something serious is going to happen to it or not and what in particular is going to happen to it, if anything does. It is impossible to forecast the prospects of any line of business unless you know what

the year is going to bring forth. Nothing is more unfair, nothing
has been declared by businessmen to be more harmful, than to
keep them guessing.

The guessing went on, the air was full of interrogation points,
for ten years and more. Then came an administration which
for the first time had a definite program of constructive correction; not of destructive correction, but of a constructive correction of admitted evil—a very clear program, disclosed, so far as
possible in a general program, in its particulars as well as in its
general features. And the administration proceeded to carry out
this program.

First, there was the tariff, and business shivered. "We don't
like to go in; the water looks cold"; but when the tariff had been
passed it was found that the readjustment was possible without
any serious disturbance whatever. So that men said with a sense
of relief, "Well, we are glad to get that behind us, and it wasn't
bad after all."

Then came the currency reform. You remember with what
resistance, with what criticism, with what systematic holding
back, a large body of bankers in this country met the proposals
of that reform, and you know how, immediately after its passage,
they recognized its benefit and its beneficence, and how, ever
since the passage of that reform, bankers throughout the United
States have been congratulating themselves that it was possible
to carry out this great reform upon sensible and solid lines.

Then we advanced to the trust program, and again the same
dread, the same hesitation, the same urgency that the thing
should be postponed. It will not be postponed; and it will not be
postponed because we are the friends of business. We know what
we are doing; we purpose to do it under the advice—for we have
been fortunate enough to obtain the advice—of men who understand the business of the country; and we know that the effect is
going to be exactly what the effect of the currency reform was—
a sense of relief and of security.

Because when the program is finished, it is finished; the interrogation points are rubbed off the slate; business is given its constitution of freedom and is bidden go forward under that constitution. And just so soon as it gets that leave and freedom there
will be a boom of business in this country such as we have never
witnessed in the United States.

I, as a friend of business and a servant of the country, would
not dare stop in this program and bring on another long period
of agitation. Agitation longer continued would be fatal to the
business of this country, and if this program is delayed there will

come agitation with every letter in the word a capital letter. The choice is a sober and sensible program, now completed, or months upon months of additional conjecture and danger. I, for one, could not ask this country to excuse a policy which subjected business to longer continued agitation and uncertainty; and, therefore, I am sure that it is beginning to be evident to the whole press of this country, and, by the same token, to the people, that a constructive program is at last not only to be proposed but completed, and that, when it is completed, business can get and will get what it can get in no other way—rest, recuperation, and successful adjustment. I cannot get rest if you send me to bed wondering what is going to happen to me in the morning; but if you send me to bed knowing what the course of business is to be tomorrow morning, I can rest. How much better is *certain* justice to the men engaged in business!

It is a matter of conscience, as well as a matter of large public policy, to do what this Congress I am now certain is going to do— finish the program. And I do not think that it is going to take a very long time. I believe that the temper of those engaged in this great thing is admirable, that the various elements some- times in antagonism in the Congress of the United States are drawing together, and that we shall witness an early statesman- like result for which we shall all have abundant reason to be thankful.[3]

T MS (WP, DLC).
  [1] Delivered in the East Room of the White House before 125 members of the Virginia Press Association.
  [2] Charles Berkley Cooke of Richmond, owner and publisher of the Richmond *Evening Journal*; Representative Charles Creighton Carlin of Virginia.
  [3] There is a WWT outline of these remarks, dated June 25, 1914, in WP, DLC.

Two Letters to William Jennings Bryan

My dear Mr. Secretary: The White House June 25, 1914

Mrs. Wilson and I were not only deeply pleased, we were greatly touched, by your message on our anniversary. We have learned to have a real affection for Mrs. Bryan and you, adding to the admiration we already so sincerely entertained. She joins me in the most cordial messages to you both and in the most heartfelt thanks for your generous thought of us.

          Cordially and faithfully yours,   Woodrow Wilson

TLS (W. J. Bryan Papers, DLC).

My dear Mr. Secretary: The White House June 25, 1914

I return the copy you were kind enough to send me of the Convention for the Dominican Republic. The general administrative arrangement is no doubt such as we could enter into with Haiti. I suggest that with the aid of memoranda from our representatives in Haiti we attempt a similar statement of the circumstances and have a convention tentatively drawn up along the same lines.

Always

Cordially and faithfully yours,   Woodrow Wilson

TLS (W. J. Bryan Papers, DNA).

To William Atkinson Jones

My dear Mr. Jones: [The White House] June 25, 1914

May I ask what the present status and prospects of the Porto Rican bill are? I have lost track of the bill, notwithstanding my deep interest in it.

I am sincerely glad to hear from the Secretary of War of the very interesting and, I hope, helpful consultations that you have had with him on the Philippine bill.

Cordially and sincerely yours,   Woodrow Wilson

TLS (Letterpress Books, WP, DLC).

To John Pierpont Morgan, Jr.

My dear Mr. Morgan: [The White House] June 25, 1914

I owe you an apology for not having replied sooner to your letter asking for an opportunity to talk with me,[1] but I am sure you will accept the reason as a good one. I have simply not been able to tell thirty-six hours in advance what the demands would be on my time and what time I would have free.

I am still in the same quandary but cannot wait longer to indicate to you the pleasure it would give me to see you and suggest that if you see an opportunity to come down and will let me have twenty-four or thirty-six hours notice, I shall do my best to arrange for it. It would, of course, be better still if I could have longer notice.

Cordially and sincerely yours,   Woodrow Wilson

TLS (Letterpress Books, WP, DLC).
[1] This letter is missing.

To Edward Mandell House

Dear Friend: The White House June 26, 1914

Your letters give me a peculiar pleasure whenever they come. They bring with them an air of sincere thought and constant endeavor for the right thing, which is just what I need to sustain the energies in me. I thank you with all my heart for your report of your meeting with Sir Edward Grey with regard to the matter we have so much at heart, and your plan to meet Tyrrell and Sir Edward again interests me as deeply as I am sure you knew it would.

I hope you are getting a lot of fun and pleasure out of these things, and all my little circle here join me in the warmest messages to both of you. Take care of yourself, and think of me always as   Your devoted friend,   Woodrow Wilson

TLS (E. M. House Papers, CtY).

From Edward Mandell House

My dear Friend: London, England. June 26th, 1914.

I had a very interesting luncheon with Sir Edward Grey Wednesday. The other guests were the Lord Chancellor, the Earl of Crewe[1] and Sir William Tyrrell. Page had to go to Oxford to take his degree and cound [could] not be with us.

I did not go into the details of my trip to Germany again, for I took it for granted that Sir Edward had given them to both Haldane and Crewe.

I gave it as my opinion that international matters could be worked out to advantage in much the same way as individuals would and I thought that most of the misunderstandings were brought about by false reports and mischief makers and if the principals knew of the facts, what appeared to be a difficult situation became easy of solution.

I illustrated this by mentioning the service Sir William Tyrrell performed in America last Autumn, and the consequent cordial relations between our two countries.

The conversation lasted two hours and it was agreed that it should be renewed at a later date. In the meantime, the general idea was accepted, that is, that a frank and open policy should be pursued between all the parties at interest.

They told me that there was no written agreement between England, France and Russia and their understanding was one merely of sympathy and the determination to conserve the interests of one another.

When Haldane and Crewe left, Sir Edward asked me something of Mexico and what you had in mind. He seemed entirely satisfied with my explanation. The only question he raised was that in the event Villa should become President, it would be difficult for his Government to handle the situation without in some way making a demand for an inquiry into the Benton murder. I told him we would not cross that bridge until we reached it, that Villa had expressly stated that, under no circumstances, would be [he] become a candidate or accept the Presidency, but should he change his mind, there would doubtless be some way found to satisfy the British public so that the Government might not be embarrassed.

Sir Edward was in a most delightful mood and paid you a splendid tribute. At our last meeting, he said it was his purpose, at the proper time in the House of Commons, to say publicly what he thought you had done for international morals.

I breakfasted with Lloyd George yesterday and had a most interesting conversation with him. I found him peculiarly ill informed regarding America and its institutions. I will tell you more of this when we meet.

I am lunching with the Prime Minister on Thursday of next week, and I will write you again when anything further of importance follows.

We are sailing for Boston on the Franconia, July 21st. I feel I have already done all that can be accomplished in the matter we have in hand for the present and that a long stride has been made in the direction of international amity.

Your faithful and affectionate,   E. M. House

TLS (WP, DLC).
¹ Robert Offley Ashburton Crewe-Milnes, 1st Marquis of Crewe and Earl of Madeley, at this time Secretary of State for India. The Lord Chancellor, Lord Haldane, is identified in Vol. 28.

From William Atkinson Jones

My dear Mr. President: Washington. June 26, 1914.

In response to your letter just received, requesting that I give you "the present status and prospects of the Porto Rican bill," I beg to be permitted to inform you that this bill, having received the unanimous favorable indorsement of the Committee on Insular Affairs, was reported to the House on March 26, 1914, and is now on the Union Calendar. If an opportunity to consider this bill in the House can be secured, there will be, in my judgment, little opposition to its passage. Gov. Yager thinks this bill should be enacted into law at the earliest possible moment, and I may add that it has the approval of Secretary Garrison, who also thinks early action very desirable.

I have read very carefully, and with much interest, the comments made by Secretary Garrison upon the Philippine bill which I had the honor of submitting to you. A number of his suggestions appear to me to be entirely meritorious, and I shall most willingly adopt them. There are others, however, which for one reason or another I have serious doubts in regard to, and I shall be much gratified if you will be good enough to give me an opportunity to present my views to you in relation thereto. Your suggestion that the Governor-General should be given only a qualified veto power and that the right to exercise absolute veto power be conferred upon the President is, in my judgment, a decided improvement over the provision at present incorporated in the bill.

Hoping that you may find it convenient to accord me an interview in order that I may personally be able to present my views to you in regard to the suggestions made by the Secretary of War,[1] I am, with sentiments of highest respect,

Sincerely yours,   W. A. Jones

TLS (WP, DLC).
[1] "Please assign Mr. Jones the first *hour* available on my calendar. W.W." WWhw undated MS (WP, DLC). They conferred on July 6.

From Lindley Miller Garrison

My dear Mr. President: Washington. June 26, 1914.

I spent three hours with Senator Hitchcock last evening on Philippine matters, and left with him all the data necessary to bring him up to date. I found that he had not thought about the matter much and would like some little time to acquaint himself with the conditions and propositions.

Might I suggest the advisability of our refraining from any commitment about new legislation until after I have heard again from Senator Hitchcock? The reason is obvious, but I might add that I fear that if we should commit ourselves to anything while he is still considering the subject matter, he might well wash his hands of the whole question and become disgruntled. Since he is the Chairman of the Committee in the Senate that handles the legislation, this, of course, would be almost disastrous to any legislation we might desire to have enacted.

Sincerely yours,   Lindley M. Garrison

TLS (WP, DLC).

From William Kent[1]

My dear Mr. President: Washington, D. C. June 27, 1914.

I am greatly disturbed over the Adamson water power bill,[2] and especially because it has been stated by Mr. Underwood that you were in favor of the measure, and that he proposed to use your endorsement to aid in its passage on the floor of the House.

I feel sure that you are not aware of what the bill contains. *Section 17* repeals all existing legislation in connection with dams built through Act of Congress, and throws them all under this Act. This, for example, would repeal all the clauses that were put into the Hetch Hetchy bill for the public benefit. How many other bills and outstanding contracts would be affected I have no means of knowing, but imagine that this clause might interfere seriously with many irrigation projects, as well as with grants made under conditions more favorable to the public than would be called for by this bill.

Inasmuch as almost every considerable stream in this country is at some point or other navigable, this bill would apparently transfer to the War Department *all jurisdiction now held by the Interior and Agricultural Departments* in the public domain and the forest reserves as affects any contracts that involve a dam, whether for dam itself, or other privilege in connection therewith. This change of jurisdiction is further evidenced by a clause which permits the taking of such public land as is needed in connection with dams, by payment of a rental of five per cent of its value.

You will note that the *50 year period is utterly indefinite*, because that period begins to run *after the "completion" of the work*. Without any sinister motive, and merely for the purpose of permitting the process of orderly development, it is doubtful whether these projects will ever be completed, so that no one can tell when the term actually begins to run. The correct practice of installing water power must be based upon the amount of current needed, instead of upon the full amount that could be developed. It would be a hardship on investor and consumer alike if completion should involve an unnecessary immediate immediate [*sic*] expense of installation in excess of demand.

You will note that, under this bill, the terms are fixed at the beginning, and that there is no right to repeal or amend except for violation of contract. To quote the words on page 13, section 13, additional to the ordinary repeal clause we find, "whenever Congress determines that the conditions of consent have been violated." This is in contradiction to the entire policy of the Gov-

1)

2)

3)

4)
Repeal

ernment, which has wisely insisted upon having a repeal and amendment clause in all such grants. The most expensive bridges that have been built by private persons across navigable waterways are all subject to this simple repeal provision.

5)   The public is not protected against having to repay community-created values for land, rights of way, and water-rights if, at the time of the expiration of the grant, the Government should desire to take over the property or lease it to another person.

These matters have all been handled with the utmost care in the Ferris bill, which, originally drafted by Secretary Lane, was carefully worked over for weeks in the Public Lands Committee, with all consideration of the best and most expert information available. The two bills are diametrically opposed to each other in policy.

In the Ferris bill, we acted on the supposition that it is our duty to use the leverage of Government ownership of land, and power of control over it, so as to protect the public to the last degree. We cast aside the theory that we would be doing our full duty if we merely obtained a pitiful revenue on present value of Government property, which latter thought is frankly embodied in the Adamson bill. Revenue may or may not be an important item, but the right to exact it gives real control. I consider the Adamson bill the worst piece of legislation that has come before the House, and believe it should not be permitted to become law in anything resembling its present form.

A careful comparison of this bill with the Ferris bill is all that is needed to show the two separate and distinct points of view.

It is very simple to state that the Government is not in any way interested in the development of power on navigable waterways, but should confine its functions solely to questions of navigation. The Adamson bill clearly nullifies this contention in a remarkable way.

After the Chandler-Dunbar decision, which showed the full sovereignty over navigable waterways to rest in the Government for all purposes,[3] it would seem to me a betrayal of trust for us to accept the narrower view, and to permit practically uncontrolled grants, and grants unlimited as to time, to be made under the guise of aiding navigation.

The water power question will before long be vastly more important to the people of this country than will navigation on the rivers and streams.

This letter is written you in sincere hope that it may be of service. I believe the passage of the Adamson bill will be considered as the most radically anti-conservation act that could possibly be committed. You have but to realize who the men are in the House who feel under obligation to fight it. You will find a splendid lot of Democrats lined up, all the Progressives, and practically all the Republicans. The best and most thoughtful men in the minority will make the fight on principle. The rest of them will take a hand in the scrap. We must radically amend this bill, or we must beat it.

Yours truly,   William Kent

TLS (WP, DLC).

[1] The numbers and the word in the margin and the italicizations in the following letter are Wilson's.

[2] For summaries of the Adamson bill and of the Ferris bill, mentioned later in this letter, see Link, *The New Freedom*, p. 129.

[3] The Supreme Court had ruled on May 26, 1913, that the federal government was not required to compensate the Chandler-Dunbar Water Power Co. of Michigan for water power rights appurtenant to land condemned for construction of additional locks and canals on St. Mary's River. The flow of the river, the Court declared, was in no sense the property of the owner of adjacent land or of the owner of the riverbed. Rather, control over all navigable rivers was vested in Congress, whose power in this case was "unfettered" and "great and absolute" because derived from the interstate commerce clause of the Constitution. 229 U.S. 53. As may be inferred from Kent's remark, conservationists hailed it as a landmark decision.

From Francis Griffith Newlands

My dear Mr. President: [Washington] June 27th, 1914.

I send you herewith extracts from the Congressional Record containing my opening speech on the interstate trade commission bill, and also the report of the Committee on Interstate Commerce upon the bill. I would be glad to confer with you, at an early day, concerning the trust legislation. It will take some time, and as my day is occupied with committee meetings and the debate, I would suggest the evening, if that is agreeable to you.

Very sincerely yours,   Francis G. Newlands.

TLS (WP, DLC).

From John Reed

Dear Mr. President: Provincetown Mass June 27, 1914

I enclose herewith the manuscript of the little article I wrote about your Mexican policy in accordance with the permission given me in your letter.[1]

I realize that it is a rather youthful piece of work, but I hope that you will think it comes closely enough to what you think as to be available for publication.

The Metropolitan Magazine wants to print it on the editorial page of their August number, and must go to press Tuesday morning next, the thirtieth of June.

Of course I don't want to publish it unless I know that it is in line with your real thoughts about Mexico. You know, of course, that I am in no way violating your confidence, and that no mention will be made of my talk with you, or any inference that these are your sentiments,—if they are,—expressed in a talk to me.

Unless I hear from you, by wire, Monday, however, I must let the article go as it is. I am sorry this is on such short notice, but I completed the article last night and heard from the Metropolitan people today.   Yours truly   John Reed

TLS (WP, DLC).
¹ An untitled T MS. It is in WP, DLC, and is described in J. Reed to JPT, June 30, 1914, n. 1.

Lázaro de la Garza¹ to Felix A. Sommerfeld²

El Paso, Texas, June 27, 1914.

General Villa wishes that you personally see General Scott in his name making following declaration, in order that he may communicate it confidentially to President Wilson.

"After taking of Zacatecas I intended to continue immediately the advance towards the interior of the Republic to the City of Mexico, but unfortunately the occurrences of the last hour have obliged me to act in a different way; and I have resolved, in accord with all the Chiefs of the Division of the North, which I command, to return to the North, leaving my forces stationed in the cities on the Central Railroad from Torreon to Juarez and leaving the City and State of Zacatecas in the hands of General Natera. This movement to the rear, seemingly inexplicable, is caused by the following motives: 1.   The evasive policy of General Pablo Gonzalez, Chief of the Division of the Northeast, in advancing southwardly against the City of San Luis Potosi simultaneously with the column under my orders which will cause the concentration of many more elements of the enemy in my route; 2. The determined attitude of Mr. Carranza not to supply this division with the necessary coal for the movement of our trains, although in the coal mines of Coahuila are enormous quantities of this fuel so indispensable for our movement, and without which it will be almost impossible to mobilize our troops; 3. The firm conviction we have that Mr. Carranza will not let this division have the ammunition necessary to advance in a strong and secure manner towards the interior of the country, as he is the only one who can import ammunition through the Port of Tampico, which is in the hands of forces personally addicted to him and which will obey his orders blindly.

"All these motives which I am pointing out have demonstrated to me in a clear and precise manner that Mr. Carranza is trying to obstruct and put the greatest possible number of obstacles in the way of the advance of this division towards the interior of the country, which obstacles and difficulties only have as origin a very unhealthy feeling of envy and jealousy towards this division, which to a great extent has had the good fortune to distinguish itself. Without these enumerated elements, and especially the ammunition which will become exhausted in the next fight, if we advance towards the south the moment necessarily must come in which we find ourselves without this indispensable war material and at the mercy of the huertista enemy, or possibly at the mercy of Mr. Carranza, who would try to impose his will using this power and our weakness.

"I am making the foregoing representations to General Scott, in order that he may kindly transmit them to Mr. President Wilson, in order that they may know the motives which have caused our return to the north and the temporary cessation of our fight against the usurping government, which fight will not be renewed until we have come to an arrangement with Mr. Carranza not to prevent the elements we need coming into our possession, or until the American government allows the importation of war material through the Custom Houses, which are under the control of our forces in the State of Chihuahua.

"For my part I protest in the most solemn manner that no personal ambition influences me in this fight. I am fighting for the good of my country and am now and always shall be disposed to bow to the popular will.

"I protest likewise that we have no intention to fight with the forces addicted to Mr. Carranza which are fighting for our same ideals and aspirations. We shall only defend ourselves in case we are attacked.

"However, I am afraid that we shall not travel united to the City of Mexico, where Mr. Carranza, as well as myself and the other revolutionary chiefs will respect and cause to be respected the will of the Mexican people."   L. de la Garza.

T telegram (WP, DLC).
  [1] A trusted friend of Villa.
  [2] Villa's principal financial agent in the United States. He was primarily responsible for purchasing guns, ammunition, and supplies of all kinds.

From Frederic Courtland Penfield

Vienna, June 28, 1914.

Regret advise assassination today at Sarajevo, Capitol Province of Bosnia, of Archduke Franz Ferdinand, heir thrones Austria Hungary, and wife Duchess Hohenberg by pistol shots fired by student. Archduke and wife were attending function and bomb thrown at them killed and wounded bystanders. They went inquire condition of wounded and were shot while returning.

Penfield.

T telegram (WP, DLC).

To Francis Joseph I

[Washington, June 28, 1914]

Deeply shocked at the atrocious murder of His Imperial and Royal Highness Archduke Francis Ferdinand and Consort at an assassin's hands, I extend to Your Majesty, to the Royal Family, and to the Government of Austria-Hungary the sincere condolences of the Government and people of the United States and an expression of my own profound sympathy.

Woodrow Wilson.

TC telegram (WP, DLC).

Remarks at a Press Conference

June 29, 1914

Mr. President, there are two or three conservation bills up there. Each claims presidential favor.

> That is a definite characterization of the bills. Of course I am very much interested in them, and I have had several conferences about them. Was there something special about them you had in mind?

There is some supposed conflict between the Adamson bill and the bill prepared by Secretary Lane—and the preserving of power and our public land.

> So I learned last week. I am going to try to bring about a conference on the subject between the two committees and the two departments which will eliminate any disharmony, if there is any. I am not perfectly clear, yet, that there is any.

They have been lining up in the House, getting ready for getting legislative committees as between the two bills.

> I learned that on Saturday.

The Adamson bill is opposed by the conservation organizations.

I think that may be due to a misunderstanding. At any rate, whatever it is, it will have to be cleared up. . . .

Mr. President, do you know whether there is any chance for safety-at-sea legislation in the House before adjournment?

I don't—I think there is.

Special rule?

I suppose it would have to be, but I just had a word with Judge Alexander the other day, in which he handed me some memorandum,[1] which I haven't had time to look at, except to glance at, but I understand that it is not beyond hoping for.

Mr. President, have you had any further assurances concerning the work of Democrats in the Senate on trust legislation? Some time ago, you were talking about getting together.

I don't know anything to the contrary. The last I heard, the two parties were working in the committee with a very fine spirit of cooperation.

JRT transcript (WC, NjP) of CLSsh (C. L. Swem Coll., NjP).
[1] It is missing, but it probably concerned the substitute for the original seamen's bill, largely drafted by Congressman Joshua W. Alexander, which was reported out by the House Committee on Merchant Marine and Fisheries on June 19, 1914. See Hyman Weintraub *Andrew Furuseth: Emancipator of the Seamen* (Berkeley and Los Angeles, 1959), pp. 127-28.

To Joseph Patrick Tumulty

Dear Tumulty: [The White House, June 29, 1914]

I have read Mr. Reed's article. I admire the man and the work he has done, but clearly it would not be possible for me to authorize the publication of the article he has sent us. I opened my mind to him completely and with the understanding that he was not to quote me.

If he were to recast the article so as to leave out all quotes or all intimation of directly echoing what I had said and confine himself to his own impressions received from the interview, I think it would be possible to authorize its publication. He could begin by saying something like this: "Talking with so frank a man, it was possible to get very clear impressions of what his attitude was in regard to the important matters we discussed. I got the impression, for example, that with regard to * * * he would be pretty certain to decide that, etc."[1]

The President.

TL (WP, DLC).
[1] JPT to J. Reed, June 29, 1914, CCL (WP, DLC), is a paraphrase of W's letter.

To William Kent

My dear Mr. Kent: The White House June 29, 1914

Thank you sincerely for your letter of Saturday. I yesterday had a long talk with Judge Adamson which makes me hope that some of the matters about which you have entertained an apprehension in regard to his bill may upon conference be cleared up. I am very much concerned that nothing such as you fear should happen and your letter made me fear that I had not given the bill as careful study as I should have given it, or, rather, that I had not had the necessary information in mind when I read it. I am going to try today to arrange for a conference between the Secretary of War, the Secretary of the Interior, and Mr. Ferris and Judge Adamson, in the hope that the policies of the two departments and the two committees may be brought into entire harmony.[1]

Cordially and sincerely yours,   Woodrow Wilson

TLS (W. Kent Papers, CtY).

[1] Wilson did call a conference at the White House on July 1, with Secretaries Garrison and Lane, Congressmen Adamson, Ferris, Lenroot, and Frederick C. Stevens, and Edward C. Finney, an Interior Department attorney. From this and subsequent conferences with the President and among themselves, there eventually emerged agreement between the Departments of War and the Interior as to jurisdiction over navigable rivers and between the committees on interstate commerce and on public lands as to the provisions of the Adamson and Ferris bills. The revised Adamson bill passed the House on August 4, 1914, by a vote of 191 to 47, but foundered in the Senate, despite presidential backing, in the face of strong opposition from a coalition of southern and western senators representing power interests. For the background of the formulation and passage of the Adamson bill and for the fate in the Senate of the administration's water power policies, and for numerous citations to the pertinent Wilson correspondence and other documentation, see Link, *The New Freedom*, pp. 129-32.

To Francis Griffith Newlands

My dear Senator: [The White House] June 29, 1914

I have your letter of June twenty-seventh with its enclosures, for which I sincerely thank you. I hope that it will be convenient for you to see me on Wednesday evening at 8:15, at the office which I find cooler in the evenings than the house is.

In haste

Cordially and sincerely yours,   Woodrow Wilson

TLS (Letterpress Books, WP, DLC).

To Lindley Miller Garrison

My dear Mr. Secretary: [The White House] June 29, 1914

Thank you for your note of June twenty-sixth about your conference with Senator Hitchcock. I find that I am going to see him today and will no doubt get from him an expression of his wishes in the matter.

In haste   Faithfully yours,   Woodrow Wilson

TLS (Letterpress Books, WP, DLC).

From John Randolph Thornton

Washington, D. C. 29 June 1914

Senator Thornton presents his compliments to the President with the earnest hope that he may sleep well this night in order to have steady nerves tomorrow to meet the feminine (?) onslaught that will be directed against him from which he trusts the President may emerge sound in both mind and body.

Not R.S.V.P.

AL (WP, DLC).

The Special Commissioners to William Jennings Bryan

RECEIVED IN CIPHER
AND TRANSLATED AT
THE WHITE HOUSE.   Niagara Falls, N. Y., June 29, 1914.

Referring to and repeating our conversation over the long distance telephone this afternoon:

The mediation was offered to settle the conflict between the United States and Mexico. The delegates who were here claimed to represent the United States of Mexico and are so referred to in the minutes. We however filed a protest, stating that we could not recognize them as representing the United States of Mexico, and all the minutes are signed subject to that protest.

In view of that protest and the four protocols agreed to last week, we are, however, in the position of having made a settlement of the international matters between the United States and Mexico when there is no representative of Mexico before the mediators.

The mediators have asked us to sign these last four protocols, and we do not see how we can refuse, but cannot refrain from calling attention to the apparent incongruity of making an agree-

ment as to international affairs when we ourselves claim that
there is no representative of Mexico before the mediation. These
minutes contain a statement that these protocols are signed on
the supposition that internal matters would be adjusted between
the representatives of the Mexican factions, but if, unfortunately,
that expectation was not realized, then the protocols could be
reconsidered, if necessary.

Of course this incongruity was originally occasioned by our
expectations that the Constitutionalists would either become
a party to the mediation or accept its decision, and the technical
difficulty will still be removed if the Constitutionalists do enter
into negotiations as to internal affairs with the representatives
who are now here.

In view of the fact that the mediators are very earnest in their
desire to have the minutes signed, and our promise to give it immediate attention, we should be glad to hear from you as soon
as convenient.   Commissioners.

5:53 p.m.

T telegram (SDR, RG 59, 812.00/23490, DNA).

Remarks to a Woman Suffrage Delegation[1]

June 30, 1914.

Upon being asked as an individual whether he would use his
influence to have the Bristow-Mondell Resolution[2] put through
Congress at this session, the President replied:

Mrs. Wiley,[3] and Ladies: No one could fail to be impressed
by this great company of thoughtful women, and I want to assure
you that it is to me most impressive. I have stated once before
the position which as the leader of a party I feel obliged to take,
and I am sure that you will not wish me to state it again. Perhaps
it would be more serviceable if I ventured upon the confident
conjecture that the Baltimore convention did not embody this
very important question in the platform which it adopted because
of its conviction that the principles of the Constitution, which al-
lotted these questions to the states, were well-considered principles from which they did not wish to depart. You have asked
me to state my personal position with regard to the pending
measure. It is my conviction that this is a matter for settlement
by the states and not by the federal government, and, therefore, that being my personal conviction and it being obvious that
there is no ground on your part for discouragement in the

progress you are making, and my passion being for local self-government and the determination by the great communities into which this nation is organized of their own polity and life, I can only say that since you turned away from me as a leader of a party and asked me my position as a man, I am obliged to state it very frankly, and I believe that in stating it I am probably in agreement with those who framed the platform to which allusion has been made.

I think that very few persons, perhaps, realize the difficulty of the dual duty that must be exercised, whether he will or not, by a President of the United States. He is President of the United States as an executive charged with the administration of the law, but he is the choice of a party as a leader in policy. The policy is determined by the party, or else upon unusual and new circumstances by the determination of those who lead the party. This is my situation as an individual. I have told you that I believed that the best way of settling this thing and the best-considered principles of the Constitution with regard to it is that it should be settled by the states. I am very much obliged to you.

Mrs. Dorr:[4] May I ask you this question? Is it not a fact that we have very good precedents existing for altering the electorate by the Constitution of the United States?

The President: I do not think that that has anything to do with my conviction as to the best way that it can be done.

Mrs. Dorr: It does not, but it leaves room for the women of the country to say what they want through the Constitution of the United States.

The President: Certainly it does. There is good room, but I have stated my conviction, and I have no right to criticise the opinions of others who have different convictions, and I certainly would not wish to do so.

Mrs. Wiley: Granted it is a state matter, would it not give this great movement a mighty impetus if the resolution now pending before Congress were passed?

The President: But that resolution is for an amendment to the Constitution.

Mrs. Wiley: The states would have to pass upon it before it became an amendment. Would it not be a state matter then?

The President: Yes, but by a very different process, for by that process it would be forced upon the minority; they would have to accept it.

Mrs. Dorr: They could reject it if they wished to; three fourths of the states would have to pass it.

The President: Yes, but the other fourth could not reject it.

Mrs. Dorr: Mr. President, don't you think that when the Constitution was made it was agreed that when three fourths of the states wanted a reform that the other fourth would receive it also?

The President: I cannot say what was agreed upon. I can only say that I have tried to answer your question, and I do not think it is quite proper that I submit myself to cross-examination.

Mrs. Wiley: Thank you, Mr. President, for the courtesy.

The President: I am very much obliged to you. It has been a pleasant occasion.[5]

T MS (WP, DLC).

[1] More than 500 women suffragists, representing organized clubwomen of nearly every state, and headed by leaders from the Congressional Union for Woman Suffrage, marched to the White House, and presented Wilson with an engraved copy of the suffrage resolution adopted by the Federation of Women's Clubs.

[2] Senate Joint Resolution 130, introduced by Joseph L. Bristow on March 20, 1914, and House Resolution 514, calling for consideration of House Joint Resolution 1, introduced by Frank Wheeler Mondell on May 13, 1914. They proposed an amendment to the Constitution extending the suffrage to women. *Cong. Record*, 63d Cong., 2d sess., pp. 5165, 8541.

[3] Anna Kelton (Mrs. Harvey Washington) Wiley of Washington, president of the city's Consumer's League, 1911-12, and of the Housekeepers' Alliance, 1912-14.

[4] Rheta Louise Childe (Mrs. John Pixley) Dorr, noted journalist who had worked in factories, mills, and department stores in order to study the labor conditions and social needs of women workers, author of *What Eight Million Women Want* (Boston, 1910). In 1914 she became the editor of *The Suffragist*, the official organ of the Congressional Union for Woman Suffrage.

[5] Wilson's departure was accompanied by hisses, for, in the crowded room, most women heard only his refusal to be further questioned, and missed his last statement. *New York Times*, July 1, 1914.

To the Special Commissioners

Washington, June 30, 1914

Have conferred with the President in regard to your telegram of last night. He desires me to present his views as follows: First, the time has not arrived for discussion of the question of evacuation. It becomes more and more evident that Huerta's representatives can speak for only a minority of the people and only for a government that is going out of power. To make an agreement with them in regard to matters with which the provisional government alone can deal would not only be premature but would be resented by the Constitutionalists whose influence in the provisional government must predominate. In arranging for withdrawal provision will have to be made for the protection of those who have paid duties during American occupancy and this can only be done with a new government.

Second, In signing the minutes it was sufficient to protest against the language describing Huerta's representatives as representatives of Mexico or of the Mexican government, but signing a protocol with them might not only be regarded as recognition of Huerta's claims but would be signing an agreement which they are not in a position to carry out. The protocol, for instance, provides for the appointment of commissioners to settle claims for damages. These commissioners would be appointed by the provisional government which has yet to be created and in which the Constitutionalists, not now represented in the Conference, will exert a controlling influence. The President understands that as the terms of the protocol are tentative and conditioned upon an agreement between the contending elements in Mexico, they should not be signed until the provisional government is agreed upon. This government has done everything that can be done now and is ready to take the further steps necessary so soon as such steps can be taken but it does not desire to put itself in the position of completing an agreement with the Huertistas until the provisional government is organized and ready to take charge of affairs in Mexico.

You will notice upon examining the various provisions of the protocol that this government has made all of the concessions and it is in a position to live up to its agreements. The representatives of General Huerta are not in a position to give any assurances on any subject. They have refused to consider the persons mentioned by us and have failed to name anyone who would be acceptable to the Constitutionalists. As we have reached a tentative agreement excepting withdrawal from Vera Cruz and the personnel of the provisional government, this agreement should stand until they are prepared to do their part.

As to the third matter the President is in favor of a recess rather than an adjournment but does not wish to have the question of recess considered except as an alternative to adjournment. If any steps are taken either toward recess or adjournment let them be taken by the Mediators or the representatives of General Huerta and you will agree to the proposition only when nothing better can be secured. Ours is the part of patience, toleration and perseverance. If adjournment is urged, propose recess instead of adjournment but advise waiting for the Constitutionalists as long as there is any possibility of the two elements getting together. Carranza's position that he should have the approval of his Generals is a reasonable one and we are urging action upon him.   Bryan.

CLST telegram with WWhw emendations (SDR, RG 59, 812.00/23490, DNA).

To William Kent

My dear Mr. Kent: The White House June 30, 1914

Our minds certainly do move in the same channel. I had come to entertain the same sort of uneasiness about Mr. Leon[1] as I read the various messages from him which you have been kind enough to send me.[2] I have learned to be very cautious (I hope not too suspicious) in accepting opinions, or even information, coming from persons who have in any way been close to Mexican politics.

I share your view of Villa,[3] and deeper than everything else in my mind lies the passionate desire to see something come out of this struggle which will redound to the permanent benefit of at least partial emancipation of the great body of the Mexican people. We can start out with the presumption that those who are trying to exploit Mexico have no interest or sympathy in this cause. Honest men though they may be, their point of view is not ours and everything that they think or suggest is approached from their point of view. Men generally see what they are looking for.

I shall be very glad indeed to have a talk with you about the Niagara conference. It would be simple enough if it were not for the complications in Northern Mexico.

Cordially and sincerely yours,   Woodrow Wilson

TLS (W. Kent Papers, CtY).
    [1] René León, a *Carrancista* sympathizer who was reporting to Kent from El Paso. Kent speculated that León may have been representing French corporate interests. W. Kent to WW, June 29, 1914, TLS (WP, DLC). Both René León, and his brother Maurice León, were writing to Kent, probably in an effort to discredit George C. Carothers, who favored the *Villistas*. About this, see Hill, *Emissaries to a Revolution*, pp. 196-97, and Clarence E. Clendenen, *The United States and Pancho Villa*, (Ithaca, N. Y., 1961), p. 204.
    [2] W. Kent to WW, June 10, 1914, TLS (W. J. Bryan Papers, DNA), and W. Kent to WW, June 11, 17, 18, 19, 27, 29, 1914, TLS (WP, DLC).
    [3] "It is my belief that Villa, a crude and cruel barbarian in many ways, is playing square, and is the only man in this troubled situation that is looking out for the welfare of his country. I believe the time will come when he will be considered the greatest Mexican in his generation." W. Kent to WW, June 29, 1914.

From Lindley Miller Garrison

My dear Mr. President: Washington June 30, 1914.

In your letter to me of the 29th, you stated that you were going to see Senator Hitchcock that day, and that he undoubtedly would give you his views on the Philippine situation. May I ask whether you did see him, and whether, under the circumstances, we shall go ahead along the lines that we have been working on?

Sincerely yours,   Lindley M. Garrison

TLS (WP, DLC).

John Reed to Joseph Patrick Tumulty

Provincetown, Mass., June 30, 1914.

Your letter received. Pay no attention to article mailed Saturday. Have stopped publication. Will write another according to lines laid down by you and submit to you before publication.

John Reed.

T telegram (WP, DLC).

John Reed to Joseph Patrick Tumulty, with Enclosure

Dear Mr. Tumulty: Provincetown Mass June 30 1914

Here is the final draft of the article,—somewhat reconstructed, according to the plan you suggested,[1]—which I hope can be authorized for publication.

I am extremely desirous of neither violating the President's confidence in any particular, nor of bothering him or you. But I thought what he said was so valuable, that it would do great good to get it out some way. How, I did not presume to dictate. I just wanted to do it the way it would suit him best, and that was the reason for all these letters and requests of mine

Would it be too much to wire me here collect, "Yes" or "No,"— so that I could get it in print as soon as possible, if it were authorized?[2] And does authorization mean any general endorsement by the President?   Yours sincerely,   John Reed

TLS (WP, DLC).
  [1] Reed substituted paraphrases for a few quotations attributed to Wilson in his first draft and added the first six paragraphs. Otherwise, the two drafts were similar.
  [2] Tumulty must have wired in the negative. The revised article was never published. There is a copy in the J. Reed Papers, MH.

ENCLOSURE

I had always got the impression that the President was a trifle cold and a trifle pedantic. Well, he isn't. He doesn't even choose his words when he is talking to you, and yet everything he says is sharply, definitively said,—often with the easy simplicity of Lincoln's talk. He seems animated by extremely simple ideals,— Christianity, Liberty, and Fair Play. His seems, at first, a mind so simple as to be naive. Presently you discover that this simplicity is the result of passing through an enormous complexity. He has every appearance of frankness with you; he answers your questions straight. I remember that there were many things that I wanted to ask him, and I thought I had asked and been answered them all. But after I had left the Executive Office, I suddenly realized that he had answered only what he had wanted to answer, and that some of the questions I thought had been answered had not been. I don't know yet how it happened.

He is very American. I think it grows upon those who have talked with Mr. Wilson that he almost perfectly expresses the American theory of government at the point at which it has arrived in the feelings of the great mass of our people. His conception of the New Freedom, which has governed all his acts in office, really means the actual attitude toward our government which the vast majority holds. We have discovered that there are serious evils in our national life: political corruption, wasteful strife between the three "check and balance" branches of our government, and an emphasis upon keeping a party in power rather than shaping a policy for the nation while that party is in power. The Democratic party does not in itself seem to Mr. Wilson to be the Word of God; there is nothing sacred about Democracy unless it expresses the will of the people. I think it is the first time in at least ten administrations that the President has been more interested in principles than in policies. That is why the politicians don't understand him.

President Wilson, as do most Americans, believes still in the fundamental principles upon which this government was founded; and in the power of the people peaceably to remedy evils by their common will. Yet he talked of "industrial tyrannies" which have grown out of our civilization, and which oppress so many thousands of workers. Most politicians take the soundness of our institutions for granted. Mr. Wilson seems to have survived doubts about them; to have found, after searching thought, a deep faith in our fundamental political genius.

I never met a man who gave such an impression of quietness inside. Deep within him is a principle, or a religion, or something, upon which his whole life rests. Roosevelt never had it, nor Taft. Wilson's power emanates from it. Roosevelt's sprang from an abounding vitality. Taft had none in this sense.

They told me in the State Department that I had better be on hand at the hour of my appointment, because everything now in the White House occurs on the exact minute of schedule time. Mr. Wilson was dressed all in white flannel, sitting at his desk alone in the middle of the great, round Executive Chamber. Three tall French windows looked out upon the fresh trees and lawns of the White House grounds. Several doors opened from the room to other offices, and rarely men passed through the Chamber without an appearance of haste carrying bundles of papers. There was none of that violent slamming of doors, clamor of voices, secretaries rushing to and fro, and the sense of vast national issues being settled in the antechamber that characterized Mr. Roosevelt's term in the White House. One heard scarcely a sound in the room. The window-curtains swayed slowly in a warm breeze; things were unhurried; yet the feeling in that room was of powerful organization, as if no moment were wasted, —as if an immense amount of work was being done. Somehow I never could feel that in Roosevelt's office.

I once talked with Roosevelt and noticed how he dominated and paled his surroundings. Wilson did not dominate this grey, harmonious room. He rose and came forward to meet me with a friendly smile, shaking hands as a friend shakes hands (so that you don't remember the hand-shake, but you *do* remember the warmth it gave you) and I found myself very remarkably at ease at once. The President's face was ruddy, his eyes tired-looking, and his mobile lips trembled and smiled and set as he talked, changing with every changing thought. It was his mouth that made him seem so human. He spoke without gestures, and almost without raising or lowering his voice, which made everything he said seem tremendously important.

It occurred to me, as I sat listening to him, that whenever a representative of the people comes along with a perfectly simple policy, based only on common-sense and on the principles of American democracy which everybody admits, he is often misunderstood by the politicians and the press,—and it follows, of course, by the public.

The startling thing about President Wilson's Mexican policy is that it is so obvious. It is neither "sentimental" nor "narrowly Presbyterian." There is nothing particularly secret about it. He has expressed it scores of times, and the political diagnosticians have refused to accept his words at their face value. They have all missed the point.

It is quite in character that Mr. Wilson, in the Government's foreign policy, returns to the attitude that this nation once took toward the world. We boast still that the Revolution of 1775 gave impetus and encouragement to revolutionary democracy all over Europe. We are proud that this nation was dedicated as a refuge for the oppressed of the world; that American sympathy has always been on the side of a people in revolt,—the Poles, the French, the Russians. We like to remember that the United States government allied itself with the struggling French Republic, although it was born in blood, and that we went to war with

Spain to set free the half-Indian population of a small island. At least, that is what the great mass of the people thought we went to war with Spain for.

But how far we have actually drifted from that attitude is illustrated by the way President Roosevelt's Administration supported the bloody dictatorship of Diaz in Mexico and handed over to execution hundreds of political refugees who had sought safety in the United States. An article in the New York Times the other day upon the recent abortive Italian revolution mentioned satirically that the people were trying to set up a "Republic"; they printed the word "Republic" in quotation marks, as if it were a new and obnoxious form of government.

The dominant note of the President's words,—the point to which he returned again and again, was that as long as he was there the United States government would not give its support to tyrannies. That sounds harmless,—as harmless as any platitude spoken by any statesman. But if a platitude is translated literally into terms of action, it becomes a startling thing. I think it means simply this: that it is none of our concern what government the people of any country elect to set up; but it is of very grave concern to us, as citizens of a country founded on the principle of self-government, that the people of that country be allowed to set it up. If Mr. Wilson refused to recognize the Huerta government primarily because it was a government founded upon assassination, that was a very inadequate reason indeed. But he did not. That it was a government founded upon assassination was secondary; the important thing was that it was not a government by the people.

I got a very clear impression that the President was emphatically opposed to interfering in the internal affairs of Mexico, and as he spoke I realized that he had not interfered, paradoxical as it may seem. That he has appeared to do so is due to the very interests that have tried to force upon us the conquest of Mexico.

It is important to bear in mind the closeness of the relationship of the United States to the Latin-American countries. No revolution down there has ever got anywhere without the sympathy of the United States, and the financial interests who back such outbreaks for their own purposes know that perfectly well. At the time of the last election, however, it was reported to the State Department that many such revolutions were being planned,—on the basis that the Democratic Party was loose and irresponsible, and that the "lid was off" as far as the foreign operations of big capital were concerned. Shortly after the President's election, he made a public statement that the United States would not countenance any "personal revolutions" in Latin America. What he meant is perfectly plain. The United States did not intend to lend its support, directly or indirectly, to the looting of the people of Central and South America.

As I understand it, Huerta came within the scope of this declaration, although he was already in power. A great part of the press combined in referring to our occupation of Vera Cruz as "Intervention in Mexico." That is a serious mistake. The occupation of Vera Cruz was not "interference in the internal affairs of Mexico."

President Wilson did not send the army and navy to Vera Cruz to force Huerta from the dictatorship. He sent them to prevent war, as he tried to explain many times. For a long time it was known that Huerta was deliberately trying to create irritation between the Mexican people and the American people so that he might unite the Mexicans behind him. If he could, by successfully abusing the patience of this country, bring about an act of retaliation, he might become what he was not,—the representative of a united people. He had not yet accomplished his purpose. He had not yet united the Mexicans. But the President saw what he was trying to do and called his bluff before he was ready to be called.

If the insult to the American flag at Tampico had been the reason for occupying Vera Cruz, it would have been a pretext unworthy of any great Power. But it was not. The fact that the United States, in the Protocol signed at Niagara Falls, abandoned without a struggle its demands for redress on that score, shows how small an element it was in the sending of armed forces to Mexico. As the President pointed out, it was merely one of a long series of like incidents which would have ended in some conspicuous offense against the United States or its people which might have caused great loss of life and would certainly have hurled us, on a wave of popular emotion, into a bloody war. The Tampico incident was the President's opportunity to check this tendency without harm to the Mexican people and with comparatively little bloodshed, coolly instead of by means of force.

With the press and the army clamoring to know why we didn't march upon Mexico City, the President acted strictly in accordance with his policy of non-interf[e]rence. If Huerta had agreed to salute the flag, it would have accomplished the same purpose.

Talking to so frank a man, it was possible to get a very clear idea of what his attitude had been toward Huerta at this time. As a matter of fact, Non-Recognition was the only weapon President Wilson used against Huerta. It is nominally a negative weapon. That is to say, this government merely refuses to support as a

Constitutional nation a nation which is ruled without the consent of its people. Actually, however, Non-Recognition is a very positive weapon. In the relation of States such as that which exists between the United States and Mexico, refusal of recognition by the greater power means bankruptcy to the smaller. In Mexico now they know that: Blanquet, who was planning a counter-revolution, saw its futility as soon as he found out that the United States would not recognize him.

It is a powerful weapon and a new one in the hands of the world's great States for International Peace. President Wilson is one of the new generation of Peace Advocates,—the kind that believes that war is objectionable not primarily because it is bloody or cruel, but because it no longer accomplishes its purpose. He thinks, with Mr. Norman Angell, that the whole fabric of civilization rests, not upon force, but upon the convention between human beings that they shall appeal to reason and not to coercion for the settlement of their differences. That is why we have courts and policemen. We have agreed, in theory at least, that in a difference between two men the stronger shall not be allowed to get a club and beat the weaker to death; and we have created impartial tribunals to settle the case according to its merits. There is no difference between men and nations. The honor, interest and beliefs of two men are just as sacred as those of two nations. The President did not use the army and navy to coerce Huerta. He used them as policemen, to neutralize the force which Huerta was generating in this country to wreck the Mexican Republic.

After Mr. Wilson's declaration of his interest in the land problem in Mexico, it seemed to be the general opinion that he intended to interfere in the distribution of the great estates to the peons. I have got an entirely different impression. His policy of non-interference still holds good. As far as this government is concerned the Mexicans can restore the land as they see fit. If they want to confiscate the great estates, that is their business; but it is in accordance with the President's belief in Law and Government, that he should prefer to see the Mexican government buy the lands back rather than take them,—pay their owners compensation with respect only to the fairness of their titles, and not to their political opinions at all. I do not believe, however, that the President will dictate any such course of action.

Nor did anything the President said indicate that the United States would restrict the kind of man selected by the Mexican people for President, so long as the people select him. If he were a bandit or a bull-fighter it would make no difference so long as he represents the Mexican people. Only if mediation is to prove successful in settling the Civil War, the man to be temporarily placed at the head of Mexico until a constitutional election can be held must, of course, be acceptable to both factions.

We had some talk about the Mediation Conference at Niagara Falls, whose double object is, first, to compose the differences between the United States and Huerta; and, second, to attempt to stop the wasteful civil war in Mexico by the agreement of both factions to submit their differences to a popular election. Nor is this in any sense of the word intervention. No pressure has been brought upon the Constitutionalists to force them to join this Conference; and up to date they have refused to do so. Still, I think the President is bringing no pressure to bear upon them on that account. If the Constitutionalist chiefs still refuse to abandon their campaign against Huerta, there is no reason to believe that they will be forced to by the Washington government. That part of the program, which is nothing more than the President's aversion to the needless use of force, will fail. The submitting of plans, and of the names of presidential candidates to the Conference, by the United States government, was strictly on the invitation of the Mexican delegates themselves, and carries no persuasion.

It is clearly the President's purpose that no one shall take advantage of Mexico,—in any way; neither military dictators, citizens of this country, citizens of foreign countries, nor foreign governments. It is because of this that the United States has interposed itself between Mexico and the nations of the world in the present crisis, but the situation is full of dangerous possibilities. The President has already pointed out that even the Monroe doctrine does not give this country any more right to protect Mexico in her foreign relations, than it does to interfere in her internal affairs. That is why he earnestly hopes that the new Mexican government will not begin the wholesale confiscation of foreign concessions. Many concessions were given to foreigners in Mexico in strict accordance with Mexican law; and throughout the civilized world it has been shown that it is practically impossible under any circumstances to deprive a man of his lawful property, no matter what his political offences have been. Besides these, however, many of the great concessions granted by President Diaz and his officers were illegal. But even they are now more or less valid,—under whatever Statute of Limitations is in force in Mexico. The principle of Quieting of Title is a very widespread one in law. Moreover, there are certain concessions,—such as Lord Cowdray's oil holdings, which are practically the British navy's only supply of oil,—that would be insisted upon by foreign governments without respect as to whether they were right or wrong. As to Huerta, however, shortly after his dissolution of Congress President Wilson served notice on the world that from that date no concessions or contracts would be recognized by this government.

This extraordinarily simple and direct policy toward Mexico, though it has not been recognized by the American people, has been pretty thoroughly accepted in the Chancelleries of Europe. It is a novelty in world politics, and its effect is bound to be tremendous in its effect on the dealing of nations with one another. For example, it is interesting to speculate what will be the attitude of the powers toward China in the next two or three years. The Chinese Republic has fallen; Yuan Shi Kai is nothing more or less than a Dictator of Huerta's stamp. As a matter of fact, the United States is not bound at this moment to recognize the Chinese government since the Republic has not continued according to the agreements contained in the notes exchanged between China and this country at the foundation of the Republic. In a short time the Chinese Revolution will break out again, and Yuan will probably make use of similar tactics to Huerta's. Will President Wilson be able to maintain his Mexican policy in the case of China?

I gained a sense of the question's being complicated by the President's realization of the limitation of his powers. The power to destroy what any people have consented to is linited [limited]. It is limited by organic law, and by the interests of other people and other nations. The relations which we have with other governments whose connection with China is closer than ours, and whose course of action might be different, might prevent us from acting independently of them.

According to the evidence of his words and acts, the President is fighting everywhere the small predatory minorities which balk the People's struggle for intelligence and life. But often the very conditions which gave rise to these minorities were established peaceably, with the consent of the people they oppress; and in that case if possible the conditions must be changed by the people peaceably, for upon the principle of government without coercion rests our civilization.

So the President seemed to fear that the Mexican Revolution might not be able to destroy by force the network of foreign exploitation that is choking the people.

T MS (WP, DLC).

Joseph Rucker Lamar to William Jennings Bryan

RECEIVED AND TRANSLATED
AT THE WHITE HOUSE.   Niagara Falls, N. Y., June 30, 1914.

We called you up tonight at the point where in deciphering your telegram it was stated that the minutes were not to be signed because at that time we were informed that Dr. Naon was greatly offended at the delay in signing the minutes containing the protocols, claiming that it was a discourtesy to him in person, and a refusal to sign what had actually been agreed upon in a full conference.

I am afraid that my telegram of day before yesterday in reference to the signing of the protocols has created an embarrassment that I did not intend. I said that I did not see how we could refuse to sign, but my purpose was to call attention to the fact that we were making an agreement as to the International affairs of Mexico when we ourselves had protested that the representatives here were not the representatives of Mexico. I supposed that if that defect was not cured by the statement that the protocols were conditional, it could be cured by some additional provision that signing the protocol should not be considered as a recognition of Huerta's government.

Your telegram shows that the objection to the signature is not only on the ground that signing the protocol might amount to a recognition of Huerta, but on the ground that, being tentative, they should not be signed until a Provisional Government had been established.

In the telephone conversation, we called attention to the fact that the protocols were in fact adopted last Friday and published in the newspapers, and that signing the minutes is not the adoption but the attestation of what has already been adopted, the signatures being affixed in accordance with the rules adopted at the first meeting that the minutes should be signed by the mediators and representatives of both parties.

The mediators invited us to take lunch with them tomorrow at one and have announced their intention to take a recess, leaving here tomorrow night.

If they are all as offended as Dr. Naon they may adjourn. They called twice during the day to ask that the minutes should be signed but I was out, and on meeting Mr. Lehmann tonight, made the statement as to discourtesy above referred to.

As stated in the conversation, we will make an abstract of the telegram, giving reasons why the minutes cannot be signed at this time, and submit it to the mediators tomorrow, if they make another request for our signature.

If I had realized when these protocols were first discussed, that the effect now under discussion would be involved in their adoption, attention would of course have been called to it, but this did not occur to either of us until after the protocols had been submitted by the mediators, transmitted to Washington, amended and adopted at a full conference. Then it did occur to me that we were making an International agreement with no person recognized by us as representing Mexico before the mediators. When that view presented itself we were obliged to call your attention to it, thinking that in addition to providing that the protocols were conditional we might in signing the minutes further provide that in adopting them we did not intend to recognize that General Huerta represented Mexico as might have otherwise been inferred. The additional ground of objections mentioned in your telegram had not been thought of by us.

We have neglected to say that the protocols are a part of the minutes and are only signed in so far as the minutes are signed.

Lamar for Commissioners.

T telegram (WP, DLC).

To John Randolph Thornton

My dear Senator: [The White House] July 1, 1914

I came through the ordeal yesterday intact, I believe. It was very delightful to have your little note and to know that you were thinking of me.

Cordially and sincerely yours,   Woodrow Wilson

TLS (Letterpress Books, WP, DLC).

To Leonard Wood

My dear General: The White House July 1, 1914

I do not want to let you leave the position of Chief of Staff without sending you a word of very warm and genuine congratulation on the admirable service you have rendered the Army and the country. I am sorry that your connection with the General Staff should be severed and I hope that you will enjoy your new assignment as at least a relief from the responsibilities which you have carried here.

Cordially and sincerely yours,   Woodrow Wilson

TLS (L. Wood Papers, DLC).

To William Jennings Bryan

My dear Mr. Secretary: [The White House] July 1, 1914

I return herewith the proposed Haytian Convention.[1] I have made one or two slight verbal alterations, as, for example, in the first line of Section nine, but have not changed the meaning of the document at all.

Cordially and sincerely yours,   Woodrow Wilson

TLS (Letterpress Books, WP, DLC).
[1] "OUTLINE OF A DRAFT OF A CONVENTION BETWEEN THE UNITED STATES AND THE REPUBLIC OF HAITI," T MS (SDR, RG 59, 838.51/341a, DNA).

From the White House Staff, with Enclosure

The White House,
Memorandum for the President: July 1, 1914.

Secretary Bryan has just talked over the telephone with Judge Lamar, who called his attention to this telegram and asked for instructions at once so that he would be prepared to answer the Mediators.

Secretary Bryan will be glad to talk with the President over the telephone.

T MS (WP, DLC).

ENCLOSURE

Joseph Rucker Lamar to William Jennings Bryan

RECEIVED IN CIPHER AND   Niagara Falls, N. Y.,
TRANSLATED AT THE WHITE HOUSE.   July 1, 1914.

On receipt of your telegram I at once went to see Naon and explained to him our cordial and friendly appreciation for his work in the mediation and the utter absence of any intent to reflect upon him personally. He accepted the explanation most cordially and the visit was entirely satisfactory when I explained that the delay had been occasioned by an investigation into the question as to whether signing the minutes containing these protocols might not be construed into a recognition of the Huerta Government, notwithstanding the previous protest, he at once and before I made any reference to a stipulation like that contained in your telegram said that if there was room for doubt it was entirely proper to remove it and that possibility of misconstruction could be avoided by making a stipulation which was almost identical with that contained in your telegram.

At my request he then saw the other mediators, explained to them situation and they came in and heartily assented to our making a stipulation before signing.

I also stated to Naon that you had expressed the hope that he might visit Washington before taking a recess but he and the mediators said that it had already been decided to take a recess.

Since returning we have heard that the mediators have changed their plans and instead of leaving tonight it is likely that Naon will go direct to Washington, Da Gama will remain here to-day and tomorrow, and Suarez had not expected to leave until Thursday. We hear also that the Mexicans do not expect to leave until the end of the week and one of them has expressed a desire that other delegates should be selected for the purpose of negotiating with the Constitutionalists in the event that the latter decide to send representatives. Under the circumstances we will not leave tonight and will keep you advised as to the situation with a view of deciding how long we shall remain.

                              Lamar for Commissioners.

T telegram (WP, DLC).

From Edward Mandell House

My dear Friend: [London] July 1st, 1914.

Your letters of June 16th and 22nd have come to me within the past few days and I want you to know that I feel deeply grateful and encouraged.

It makes me more content to desert you during the hot months if I can feel I am doing something for you that is worth while on this side, and there is so much to be done.

You have more than fullfilled expectations at home, great as they were, and I have a keen desire for you to become the world figure of your time. Never again can the old order of statesman hold sway, and you are and will continue to be the prophet of a new day.   Your faithful and affectionate,   E. M. House

TLS (WP, DLC).

From Francis Griffith Newlands

My dear Mr President,   Washington, D. C. July 1st, 1914.

Preliminary to our meeting this evening, I am sending you Senator Borah's speech, which thus far is the strongest presented against the Bill. I have marked certain interruptions of mine covering the questions of Court review, and the transfer of the duty of enforcing the Sherman law from the Attorney General to the Commission. I am more convinced than ever that the latter thing should be done, and that the opinion of the Senate is ripening in this direction, but I have not urged this view in Committee because I realized that you were desirous of proceeding with caution.

Very sincerely yours   Francis G. Newlands

ALS (WP, DLC).

Remarks at a Press Conference

July 2, 1914

Can you tell us something about Mr. Morgan's visit?[1]

I can tell you anything that there is to tell. Mr. Morgan just came down on a visit of courtesy. I have known Mr. Morgan for a good many years; and his visit was lengthened out chiefly by my provocation, I imagine. Just a general talk about things that were transpiring.

Mr. President, what did he say about the conditions of business in the country?

I didn't go into that. Not that I felt that I knew as much about it as he did, but the talk didn't lean in that direction. It was one of those discussions that just drifted of its own volition. It wasn't about anything in particular, in short.

Is this to be the forerunner, Mr. President, of a series of talks with men high in the world of finance?

No, there is no plan about it. I am hoping I may have a visit from Mr. Ford,[2] but that is the only one in prospect. No, I believe there is a committee that wishes to see me, the Chicago Chamber of Commerce, next Wednesday.

Mr. President, do you find more acquiescence of spirit among the businessmen in the country in the trust program?

Yes, I do. I think they feel the force of what has been urged as to relieving business of its uncertainty and getting through with a well-known program. Because, of course, there is nothing new in this program. It is what has been implicit in practically every party platform for two or three campaigns.

In so far as that matter stands, the objections and suggestions looking to an adjournment of Congress—on the ground that the trust program would influence the business of the country—in any of your correspondence, was there any specific explanation given as to how the trust bills, and what provisions of the trust bills, would influence the business of the country?

> No, that is the peculiarity of it. It has been fairly—what preceded the currency bill—the objections have all been general. None of them has been specific. I can only conjecture the same thing is happening now that was happening then. They haven't read the bill.

I have some letters from a Cincinnati merchant where the objections were all too general.

> That has been true all through our correspondence.

Did Mr. Morgan express any opinion on business conditions, Mr. President?

> No, he did not. Our talk was partly reminiscent of the warm friendship we had had, and our summer meetings.

He didn't happen to mention the Claflin failure?[3]

> No, not at all.

The talk next week with Mr. Ford will relate to business conditions, will it not?

> I suppose so. There is no specific plan about it.

Mr. President, properly connecting these Ford visits and the Chicago Chamber of Commerce you were mentioning to us just now—

> They have absolutely nothing to do with one another. . . .

Mr. President, can you tell us anything about Haiti?

> No, chiefly because of my ignorance. It is a very conflicting situation, and I haven't been able to catch up with it in the last three weeks.

Do you think that there is a danger of our being compelled to intervene down there in some way?

> Oh, I don't think that there is any danger of our intervening in the literal sense of the word. Of course, we are trying to exercise such influence as we can now, to quiet things and accommodate things down there.

Has there been any suggestion about taking charge of customhouses?

> That is always suggested, but that has not taken any concrete form. . . .

Do you understand, Mr. President, the amended detailed bill—the Adamson bill? Is it satisfactory to the administration?

> We had a conference last week that I think resulted very satisfactorily to everybody.

You don't expect any difficulty in agreement on those amendments in the House?

No. The Republicans in the House who were present—
and three or four of them were present—didn't intimate that
there would be any difficulty at all.

Did they represent both sides?

Yes. There was the chairman of each committee, Mr.
Adamson and Mr. Ferris, and their Republican colleagues,
Mr. Stevens[4] and Mr. Lenroot. We all feel, of course, that
it is not a partisan matter at all.

JRT transcript (WC, NjP) of CLSsh (C. L. Swem Coll., NjP).

[1] Wilson met J. P. Morgan, Jr. at 12:30 that day in the White House.
When Morgan emerged from the conference, he was besieged by reporters but
refused to discuss the meeting, saying only, "My visit with the President was
very cordial. You will have to ask him what we talked about." *New York Times*,
July 3, 1914.

[2] Henry Ford, the automobile manufacturer.

[3] H. B. Claflin Co. of New York, the great dry goods concern, which was
also a holding company for retail stores in various parts of the country, was
put into the hands of receivers on June 25 because it was unable to meet the
maturing notes of its subsidiaries.

[4] Frederick Clement Stevens of Minnesota.

To Lindley Miller Garrison

My dear Mr. Secretary: [The White House] July 2, 1914

I am ashamed to say that it did not occur to me to mention
the subject of the Philippines to Senator Hitchcock the other
day. We were discussing the very difficult and disagreeable matter of appointment to office and everything else went out of my
head.   Faithfully yours, Woodrow Wilson

TLS (Letterpress Books, WP, DLC).

Sir Edward Grey to Colville Barclay

(No. 377. Confidential.) No. 1.

Sir,   Foreign Office, July 2, 1914.

Lord Cowdray called at this Office on the 23rd ultimo and
introduced Mr. Furber,[1] an Englishman, who has lived in Mexico
for a considerable time, and who is understood to be the manager
of a United States oil company in that country.

Mr. Furber's remarks on the Mexican question were in substance those contained in a letter which he had written to a
personal friend of President Wilson, with a view to its being
shown to the President. A copy of the letter, as communicated
by Mr. Furber, is enclosed for your information.

From what Mr. Furber said it appeared that his friend was

advised not to show the letter to the President, in view of the attitude adopted by the latter in regard to the Mexican question. Mr. Furber said that if the President expected the present disturbances in Mexico to end with the removal of General Huerta, he was much mistaken, as only then would the real trouble begin, since Villa, Zapata, and other chiefs would fight amongst themselves. General Carranza, in Mr. Furber's opinion, counted for nothing.

Mr. Furber added that there already existed to his knowledge a strong organisation, with financial support in Paris, to oppose Villa should he try to make himself President of Mexico.

I am, &c.   E. Grey.

Enclosure in No. 1.

Copy of Letter communicated by Mr. Furber.

My dear——,   New York, May 14, 1914.

As you know, I was named one of the Committee to present a petition to President Wilson on behalf of the oil interests in Mexico. President Wilson received us yesterday, and gave us a very nice reception.[2] After listening to what we had to say, he told us the facts we had laid before him did not add any new data to the information he had already received; that he fully realised the magnitude of the oil interests and the danger they were now in, and assured us that the matter was constantly in his mind, and that whenever the right time arrived he would do whatever was in his power to enable our men to get back to the properties and resume work. The President then told us that, from advices just received, he expected Tampico would fall into the hands of the Constitutionalists, and, judging from the morning papers, this has actually happened, and Tampico is now in their hands. He then referred to Villa, and judging, not only from the President's actual words, but his whole manner, it was clear to all of us that he had formed a very high opinion of Villa, and expected him to "make good." If it had not been agreed upon by the members of the committee that we would leave all remarks to be made by Mr. Kellogg,[3] whom we had nominated as our spokesman, I should certainly have commented upon this part of the President's statement. It was not merely what he said, but it was his whole manner that struck me so forcibly. I was sitting exactly opposite to him when he was making the remarks, and it was very evident to me that he was thoroughly sincere when he gave us to understand that Villa was a wonderful man, and that the way he had conducted himself was such as to to [*sic*] give President Wilson great hopes for the future. . . .[4]

Printed telegram (FO 371/2029, No. 29368, PRO).

[1] Percy Norman Furber, president of the Oil Fields of Mexico Co., New York.

[2] Furber's memoirs record that representatives from the Texas, Gulf, Sinclair, Standard of New Jersey, and Mexican Eagle oil companies met with Wilson for more than a half hour. Their spokesman, Frederic R. Kellogg, a lawyer, spoke and presented a petition asking for co-operation between the oil companies and the administration in solving the oil companies' difficulties in Mexico. Percy Norman Furber, *I Took Chances, From Windjammers to Jets* (Leicester, Eng., 1954), pp. 174-75.

[3] Frederic Rogers Kellogg, corporation lawyer of New York who represented many firms having interests in Mexico, most notably the Standard Oil Co. of New Jersey.

[4] The balance of this letter was devoted to Furber's personal observations on Villa and the Mexican situation.

From Edward Mandell House

My dear Friend: London. July 3rd, 1914.

I had a most interesting conversation with Mr. Asquith yesterday at luncheon.

Much of it was about Mexico. He said Mrs. Asquith had a few Mexican bonds and that she had just been notified that the interest would not be paid. He said these Mexican securities were widely scattered throughout Europe, and that was one reason why the public mind over here was so largely fixed upon that country.

I undertook to explain your position and your policy, and when I had finished he expressed himself as being satisfied that you were right. He was good enough to tell Spring-Rice afterwards that I had "explained the matter to him in the fewest possible words which a busy man always appreciated."

During the conversation, he said "As a sincere friend of America, I am glad that the President has not been induced to intervene. We did it in South Africa, only to regret it always."

We talked also of your remarkable success with your legislative program, which he thought was wonderful under our system of government.

He has a very keen and incisive mind and is one of the biggest men I have met on this side.

He expressed a desire to have a further talk with me and we are to meet again on Tuesday at dinner at Page's.

Tyrrell brought word to me today that Sir Edward Grey would like me to convey to the Kaiser the impressions I have obtained from my several discussions with this Government in regard to a better understanding between the Nations of Europe, and to try and get a reply before I leave. Sir Edward said he did not wish to send anything official, or in writing, for fear of offending French and Russian sensibilities, in the event it should become known. He thought it was one of those things that had best be done informally and unofficially.

He also told Page that he had a long talk with the German Ambassador here in regard to the matter, and that he had sent messages by him directly to the Kaiser.

So you see things are moving in the right direction as rapidly as we could hope.

Your faithful and affectionate,   E. M. House[1]

TLS (WP, DLC).
  [1] House enclosed tear sheets from the House of Commons debates, June 29, 1914, printing Grey's response to a question concerning the settlement of the tolls dispute. Grey praised Wilson, saying that his actions were not the result of a bargain or "diplomatic pressure" by Great Britain, that Wilson was not motivated specially by a desire to please Britain, but, rather, that he had been impelled by "a much greater motive and feeling that any Government . . . which is going to use its influence . . . between all the great civilised and peaceful countries of the world . . . must never, when the occasion arises, flinch or quail from interpreting Treaty rights . . . in a strictly fair spirit." *Parliamentary Debates,* 5th Series, Vol. LXIV, cols. 106-107.

A Fourth of July Address[1]

[[July 4, 1914]]

Mr. Chairman and fellow citizens: We are assembled to-day to celebrate the one hundred and thirty-eighth anniversary of the birth of the United States. I suppose that we can more vividly realize the circumstances of that birth standing on this historic spot than it would be possible to realize them anywhere else. The Declaration of Independence was written in Philadelphia; it was adopted in this historic building by which we stand. I have just had the privilege of sitting in the chair of the great man who presided over the deliberations of those who gave the Declaration to the world. My hand rests at this moment upon the table upon which the Declaration was signed. We can feel that we are almost in the visible and tangible presence of a great historic transaction.

Have you ever read the Declaration of Independence or attended with close comprehension to the real character of it when you have heard it read? If you have, you will know that it is not a Fourth of July oration. The Declaration of Independence was a document preliminary to war. It was a vital piece of practical business, not a piece of rhetoric; and if you will pass beyond those preliminary passages, which we are accustomed to quote about the rights of men, and read into the heart of the document you will see that it is very express and detailed, that it consists of a series of definite specifications concerning actual public business of the day. Not the business of our day, for the matter with which it deals is past, but the business of that first revolution by which the nation was set up, the business of 1776. Its general statements, its general declarations, cannot mean anything to us unless we append to it a similar specific body of particulars as to what we consider the essential business of our own day.

Liberty does not consist, my fellow citizens, in mere general declarations of the rights of man. It consists in the translation of those declarations into definite action. Therefore, standing here, where the declaration was adopted, reading its businesslike sentences, we ought to ask ourselves what there is in it for us. There is nothing in it for us unless we can translate it into the terms of our own conditions and of our own lives. We must reduce it to what the lawyers call a bill of particulars. It contains a bill of particulars, but the bill of particulars of 1776. If we would keep it alive, we must fill it with a bill of particulars of the year 1914.

The task to which we have constantly to readdress ourselves is the task of proving that we are worthy of the men who drew this great Declaration and know what they would have done in our circumstances. Patriotism consists in some very practical things—practical in that they belong to the life of every day, that they wear no extraordinary distinction about them, that they are connected with commonplace duty. The way to be patriotic in America is not only to love America but to love the duty that lies nearest to our hand and know that, in performing it, we are serving our country. There are some gentlemen in Washington, for example, at this very moment who are showing themselves very patriotic in a way which does not attract wide attention but seems to belong to mere everyday obligations. The members of the House and Senate who stay in hot Washington to maintain a quorum of the houses and transact the all-important business of the nation are doing an act of patriotism. I honor them for it, and I am glad to stay there and stick by them until the work is done.

It is patriotic, also, to learn what the facts of our national life are and to face them with candor. I have heard a great many facts stated about the present business condition of this country, for example—a great many allegations of fact, at any rate—but the allegations do not tally with one another. And yet I know that truth always matches with truth; and when I find some insisting that everything is going wrong and others insisting that everything is going right, and when I know from a wide observation of the general circumstances of the country, taken as a whole, that things are going extremely well, I wonder what those who are crying out that things are wrong are trying to do. Are they trying to serve the country, or are they trying to serve something smaller than the country? Are they trying to put hope into the hearts of the men who work and toil every day, or are they trying to plant discouragement and despair in those hearts? And why do they cry that everything is wrong and yet do nothing to set it right? If they love America and anything is wrong amongst us, it is their business to put their hand with ours to the task of setting it right. When the facts are known and acknowledged, the duty of all patriotic men is to accept them in candor and to address themselves hopefully and confidently to the common counsel which is necessary to act upon them wisely and in universal concert.

I have had some experiences in the last fourteen months which have not been entirely reassuring. It was universally admitted, for example, my fellow citizens, that the banking system of this country needed reorganization. We set the best minds that we could find to the task of discovering the best method of reorganization. But we met with hardly anything but criticism from the bankers of the country; we met with hardly anything but resistance from the majority of those, at least, who spoke at all concerning the matter. And yet so soon as that act was passed there was a universal chorus of applause, and the very men who had opposed the measure joined in that applause. If it was wrong the day before it was passed, why was it right the day after it was passed? Where had been the candor of criticism not only, but the concert of counsel which makes legislative action vigorous and safe and successful?

It is not patriotic to concert measures against one another; it is patriotic to concert measures for one another.

In one sense, the Declaration of Independence has lost its significance. It has lost its significance as a declaration of national independence. Nobody outside of America believed when it was uttered that we could make good our independence; now nobody anywhere would dare to doubt that we are independent and can maintain our independence. As a declaration of independence, therefore, it is a mere historic document. Our independence is a fact so stupendous that it can be measured only by the size and energy and variety and wealth and power of one of the greatest nations in the world. But it is one thing to be independent, and it is another thing to know what to do with your independence. It is one thing to come to your majority and another thing to know what you are going to do with your life and your energies. And one of the most serious questions for sober-minded men to address themselves to in the United States is this: What are we going to do with the influence and power of this great nation? Are we going to play the old role of using that power for our aggrandizement and material benefit only? You know what that may mean. It may upon occasion mean that we shall use it to make the peoples of other nations suffer in the way in which we said it was intolerable to suffer when we uttered our Declaration of Independence.

The Department of State at Washington is constantly called upon to back up the commercial enterprises and the industrial enterprises of the United States in foreign countries, and it at one time went so far in that direction that all its diplomacy came to be designated as "dollar diplomacy." It was called upon to support every man who wanted to earn anything anywhere if he was an American. But there ought to be a limit to that. There is no man who is more interested than I am in carrying the enterprise of American businessmen to every quarter of the globe. I was interested in it long before I was suspected of being a politician. I have been preaching it year after year as the great thing that lay in the future for the United States—to show her wit and skill and enterprise and influence in every country in the world. But observe the limit to all that which is laid upon us, perhaps more than upon any other nation in the world. We set this nation up, at any rate we professed to set it up, to vindicate the rights of man. We did not name any differences between one race and another. We did not set up any barriers against any particular people. We opened our gates to all the world and said, "Let all men who wish to be free come to us, and they will be welcome." We said, "This independence of ours is not a selfish thing for our own exclusive private use. It is for everybody to whom we can find the means of extending it." We cannot, with that oath taken in our youth, we cannot, with that great ideal set before us when we were a young people and numbered only a scant 3,000,000, take upon ourselves, now that we are 100,000,000 strong, any other conception of duty than we then entertained. If American enterprise in foreign countries, particularly in those foreign countries which are not strong enough to resist us, takes the shape of imposing upon and exploiting the mass of the people of that country, it ought to be checked and not encouraged. I am willing to get anything for an American that money and enterprise can obtain, except the suppression of the rights of other men. I will not help any man buy a power which he ought not to exercise over his fellow beings.

You know, my fellow countrymen, what a big question there is in Mexico. Eighty-five per cent of the Mexican people have never been allowed to have any genuine participation in their own government or to exercise any substantial rights with regard to the very land they live upon. All the rights that men most desire have been exercised by the other 15 per cent. Do you suppose that that circumstance is not sometimes in my thought? I know that the American people have a heart that will beat just as strong for those millions in Mexico as it will beat, or has beaten, for any other millions elsewhere in the world, and that, when once they conceive what is at stake in Mexico, they will know what ought to be done in Mexico. I hear a great deal said about the loss of property in Mexico and the loss of the lives of foreigners, and I deplore these things with all my heart. Undoubtedly, upon the conclusion of the present disturbed conditions in Mexico, those who have been unjustly deprived of their property or in any wise unjustly put upon ought to be compensated. Men's individual rights have no doubt been invaded, and the invasion of those rights has been attended by many deplorable circumstances which ought sometime, in the proper way, to be accounted for. But back of it all is the struggle of a people to come into its own, and, while we look upon the incidents in the foreground, let us not forget the great tragic reality in the background which towers above the whole picture.

A patriotic American is a man who is not niggardly and selfish in the things that he enjoys that make for human liberty and the rights of man. He wants to share them with the whole world, and he is never so proud of the great flag under which he lives as when it comes to mean to other people, as well as to himself, a symbol of hope and liberty. I would be ashamed of this flag if it ever did anything outside America that we would not permit it to do inside of America.

The world is becoming more complicated every day, my fellow citizens. No man ought to be foolish enough to think that he understands it all. And, therefore, I am glad that there are some simple things in the world. One of the simple things is principle. Honesty is a perfectly simple thing. It is hard for me to believe that in most circumstances, when a man has a choice of ways, he does not know which is the right way and which is the wrong way. No man who has chosen the wrong way ought even to come into Independence Square; it is holy ground which he ought not to tread upon. He ought not to come where immortal voices have uttered the great sentences of such a document as this Declaration of Independence, upon which rests the liberty of a whole nation.

And so I say that it is patriotic sometimes to prefer the honor of the country to its material interest. Would you rather be deemed by all the nations of the world incapable of keeping your treaty obligations in order that you might have free tolls for American ships? The treaty under which we gave up that right may have been a mistaken treaty, but there was no mistake about its meaning.

When I have made a promise as a man, I try to keep it, and I know of no other rule permissible to a nation. The most distinguished nation in the world is the nation that can and will keep its promises even to its own hurt. And I want to say parenthetically that I do not think anybody was hurt. I cannot be enthusiastic for subsidies to a monopoly, but let those who are enthusiastic for subsidies ask themselves whether they prefer subsidies to unsullied honor.

The most patriotic man, ladies and gentlemen, is sometimes the man who goes in the direction that he thinks right even when he sees half the world against him. It is the dictate of patriotism to sacrifice yourself if you think that that is the path of honor and of duty. Do not blame others if they do not agree with you. Do not die with bitterness in your heart because you did not convince the rest of the world, but die happy because you believe that you tried to serve your country by not selling your soul. Those were grim days, the days of 1776. Those gentlemen did not attach their names to the Declaration of Independence on this table expecting a holiday on the next day, and that Fourth of July was not itself a holiday. They attached their signatures to that significant document knowing that if they failed it was certain that every one of them would hang for the failure. They were committing treason in the interest of the liberty of 3,000,000 people in America. All the rest of the world was against them and smiled with cynical incredulity at the audacious undertaking. Do you think that if they could see this great nation now they would regret anything that they then did to draw the gaze of a hostile world upon them? Every idea must be started by somebody, and it is a lonely thing to start anything. Yet if it is in you, you must start it if you have a man's blood in you and if you love the country that you profess to be working for.

I am sometimes very much interested when I see gentlemen

supposing that popularity is the way to success in America. The way to success in this great country, with its fair judgments, is to show that you are not afraid of anybody except God and His final verdict. If I did not believe that, I would not believe in democracy. If I did not believe that, I would not believe that people can govern themselves. If I did not believe that the moral judgment would be the last judgment, the final judgment, in the minds of men as well as the tribunal of God, I could not believe in popular government. But I do believe these things, and, therefore, I earnestly believe in the democracy, not only of America, but of every awakened people that wishes and intends to govern and control its own affairs.

It is very inspiring, my friends, to come to this that may be called the original fountain of independence and liberty in America and here drink drafts of patriotic feeling which seem to renew the very blood in one's veins. Down in Washington, sometimes when the days are hot and the business presses intolerably, and there are so many things to do that it does not seem possible to do anything in the way it ought to be done, it is always possible to lift one's thought above the task of the moment and, as it were, to realize that great thing of which we are all parts—the great body of American feeling and American principle. No man could do the work that has to be done in Washington if he allowed himself to be separated from that body of principle. He must make himself feel that he is a part of the people of the United States, that he is trying to think not only for them, but with them, and then he cannot feel lonely. He not only cannot feel lonely, but he cannot feel afraid of anything.

My dream is that, as the years go on and the world knows more and more of America, it will also drink at these fountains of youth and renewal; that it also will turn to America for those moral inspirations which lie at the basis of all freedom; that the world will never fear America unless it feels that it is engaged in some enterprise which is inconsistent with the rights of humanity; and that America will come into the full light of the day when all shall know that she puts human rights above all other rights, and that her flag is the flag, not only of America, but of humanity.

What other great people has devoted itself to this exalted ideal? To what other nation in the world can all eyes look for an instant sympathy that thrills the whole body politic when men anywhere are fighting for their rights? I do not know that there will ever be a declaration of independence and of grievances for mankind, but I believe that if any such document is ever drawn it will be drawn in the spirit of the American Declaration of Independence, and that America has lifted high the light which will shine unto all generations and guide the feet of mankind to the goal of justice and liberty and peace.[2]

Printed in *Address of President Wilson at Independence Hall.* . . . (Washington, 1917).

[1] Delivered before an enormous crowd gathered at Independence Square in Philadelphia. Wilson spoke from a temporary stand set up in the shadow of Independence Hall. During the opening ceremonies, he occupied a chair used by John Hancock, while before him was the table on which the Declaration of Independence was signed. After the speech, Wilson unveiled a tablet marking the spot from which the Declaration was read to the people on July 8, 1776. John H. Baizley, chairman of the Philadelphia Common Council's committee on the ceremony, presided.

[2] There is a WWsh outline, dated July 4, 1914, of this address in the C. L. Swem Coll., NjP; a WWT outline, dated July 4, 1914, in WP, DLC; and two CLST transcripts, dated July 4, 1914, in the Swem Coll. A comparison of the above text with Swem's shorthand notes of it and other contemporary texts reveals that Wilson, at some time before its publication, edited it to improve its literary form. However, he made no substantive changes.

From Edward Mandell House, with Enclosure

My dear Friend: London, England. July 4th, 1914.

I am enclosing you a copy of a letter which I wrote you on the 26th by hand, but which I am not altogether sure was not destroyed before mailing. I had made a penciled memorandum of it and I am afraid I destroyed the original instead of the latter which I find before me.[1]

In furtherance of this idea, Sir Cecil Spring-Rice, Sir William Tyrrell and Walter and Thos. Nelson Page,[2] who is now here, took lunch with me yesterday to go into a more detailed discussion of it.

Tyrrell told me that Sir Edward Grey was deeply interested and approved entirely its general purpose, and that you could count upon this Government's cooperation.

It was the general concensus of opinion that a great deal of friction in the future would be obviated if some such understanding could be brought about in this direction, and that it would do as much as any other one thing to insure international peace.

The idea, of course, is based entirely upon your Mobile speech, and it is merely that we are trying to mold something concrete from what you have already announced in general as your policy. I suggested that it would be well to keep the matter absolutely confidential until after I had talked it out with you, and you had decided how best to bring all the other governments into agreement, if at all. I do not think it wise to have it known that England was the first to accept the proposal.

Tyrrell thought that after we had worked out a plan here which was acceptable to this Government, I could take it to you for your approval and further suggestion. You could then, if your judgment approved, take it to the other governments through Jusserand; ostensibly because he is the Dean of the Diplomatic Corps at Washington, but really because the Central and South American Republics would feel more kindly towards a proposal coming from a Latin Nation.

Tyrrell, Spring-Rice and I meet again on Wednesday to bring the matter into final form. Page may or may not be present. I think perhaps he had better not be, for the reason that it would lend something of an official character to it which we wish to avoid.

I touched lightly upon this subject to the Kaiser and I feel sure he, too, will approve. This was fortunate for the reason that it can be said it was brought to his attention first.

Your faithful and affectionate,   E. M. House

As Page puts it this is a concrete example of what may be accomplished if a better international understanding can be brought about.

TLS (WP, DLC).
    [1] He had indeed destroyed the original.
    [2] United States Ambassador to Italy.

E   N   C   L   O   S   U   R   E

Dear Governor: London. June 26th, 1914.

There is another matter which I have taken up which I hope may have your approval. I have suggested that America, England, France and Germany and the other money lending and developing nations, have some sort of tentative understanding among themselves for the purpose of establishing some plan by which investors on the one hand, may be encouraged to lend money at reasonable rates and to develop, upon favorable terms, the waste places of the earth, and on the other hand, to bring about conditions by which such loans may be reasonably safe.

I suggested that each country should warn its people that in the future, usurious interest and concessions which involve the undoing of weak and debt involved countries, would no longer be countenanced. That the same rate must hereafter prevail in such investments as is now maintained in all civilized lands in regard to private loans.

I brought this matter up at luncheon on Wednesday and Grey,

Haldane and Crewe were equally cordial in their discussion of it. I told them I wanted to get their views so that they might be laid before you when I returned.

If this can be brought about, it will not only do away with much of the international friction which such things cause, but it will be a step forward towards bringing about a stable and healthful condition in those unhappy countries which are now misgoverned and exploited both at home and abroad.

Your faithful and devoted,   [E. M. House]

TCL (WP, DLC).

From Josephine Marshall Jewell Dodge[1]

Dear Sir: New York City July 4, 1914.

Will you allow me to express to you the thanks of the organization opposed to woman suffrage which I represent, for your judicial attitude on the occasion of your reception of the delegation of advocates of woman suffrage, on Tuesday, June thirtieth.

I wish also to express our regret that any body of women should have so presumed on your courtesy in receiving them as to subject you to personal questions.

Very truly yours,   Josephine Dodge

TLS (WP, DLC).
[1] President of the National Association Opposed to Woman Suffrage. She was a leader in the movement for daytime nurseries for the care of children of working women and widow of the philanthropist, Arthur Murray Dodge.

From Walter Hines Page

Dear Mr. President: London. July 5. 1914.

I heartily thank you for your kind letter instructing me to renew the lease of my house, wh. I have done for one year with the option of one-and-a-half years more—wh. makes 4 years in all, if I shd. take this option. I am very sorry that I was obliged to trouble you with such a matter at all. It's a most embarrassing business; but, having committed (I trust) all the natural and inevitable mistakes and having learned something at least of the task this year, I can do better, both by omission and by commission, the next year—perhaps, on less money than the appalling sum that this year has cost me. And I'm very glad that you will make it possible for me to go on. I shall move the offices to more dignified quarters.

Laughlin

I take the liberty to bring up a subject that is (properly) none of my business—only on the chance that I may possibly serve you; and you must consider it, if you consider it at all, only if it may aid you. If the Greek Mission be vacant, as this morning's London papers say, Laughlin wd., in my judgment, make an admirable Minister. He has served at Athens, as at most other capitals; we have no man in the service, so far as I know, who has had more experience or who is more careful or prudent. I do not wish to lose him here: indeed, he wd. be, I fear, an embarrassing loss to me. But he deserves promotion; of his success I shd. have not a shadow of doubt. It is of him & of the service that I am thinking & of you—in case you have any doubt whom to send. On the other hand, he can wait, and he is, I am sure, quite content here; and, of course, he knows nothing about this word from me. So far as I'm concerned, I don't want him to leave this Embassy so long as I am here.

House and his Mission

House has, I am sure, written you of his success and of the letter he is writing to the German Emperor. He has something to write and I regard it as a very substantial triumph. His most excellent work leaves the situation the best possible in this way: the future negotiations of almost every sort whatsoever between Germany and England and between our country and either of them or both can proceed on the very friendly understanding that has been reached. This Government has met the whole idea not only sympathetically but with an undercurrent of genuine gratitude to us. The whole effort has turned out remarkably well. Of course I needn't tell you that they are all charmed with House— Sir Edw. Grey, the Prime Minister, Tyrrell, Haldane. An enormous amount of constructive work can be done along the way that he has opened.

I hope that you'll be able soon to get away from Washington. Spring-Rice said to me with great emphasis the other day that he hoped you wd. I'm going in a fortnight to a pretty little country house, 20+ miles out of London for the vacation months—not on a vacation, however, but within an hour of the embassy. I'll spend the quiet months there, and quiet months will be heartily welcome.   Yours very gratefully   Walter H. Page

ALS (WP, DLC).

Henry Prather Fletcher to William Jennings Bryan

Santiago, Chile, July 5, 1914.

Minister for Foreign Affairs has received telegram from Huerta expressing gratification of his government for services rendered by Chile in the mediation. I venture to suggest that a similar telegram from President Wilson to the President of Chile would be appreciated very much and have a very good effect.

Fletcher.

T telegram (SDR, RG 59, 812.00/12399, DNA).

Remarks at a Press Conference

July 6, 1914

Mr. President, as a step toward the continuing independence of the Philippines, has there been substantial agreement on the bill which will make for an elective Senate?

> There has been a substantial agreement. More than a substantial, entire agreement in the House committee on a bill framed by Mr. Jones and modified by consultation; but, so far, the Senate committee has not taken the matter up at all and, therefore, it is only half in shape so far as the Congress is concerned.

Well, does that meet with your general idea on the subject?

> Yes, sir, that bill does.

Does your program go any further than that?

> Well, of course, I don't suppose you have seen the bill, have you? I would rather wait until the bill is published so all features can be discussed together.

It is maybe regarded as the administration's views on the subject?

> Yes, sir. I want you gentlemen to understand, if you please, that when I say that with regard to a House bill, I don't mean to be understood as attempting to preclude any consideration of the details that will be undertaken in the Senate. I mean, I don't want it to look that I am trying to ram it down the Senate's throat, because I have no such attitude towards it at all.

What do you think the chances are this session?

> I hardly think it is possible that it will pass the two houses this session. . . .

Have you any definite information, Mr. President, as to the plans of General Huerta personally?

> No. I am not his confidante. You remember Mr. Dooley's remark? He said "It was understood."

I see nothing on Santo Domingo?

 Nothing that I know of.

Mr. President, have you been informed as to the position of the Senate Committee on the confirmation of Mr. Jones, as to what they intend to do?

 I don't think that that is serious.

JRT transcript (WC, NjP) of CLSsh (C. L. Swem Coll., NjP).

To James Viscount Bryce

My dear Viscount Bryce: The White House July 6, 1914

 Pray pardon a simple democrat for not knowing how to address you.[1] I think when addressing you only of our long friendship which has been so gratifying and enjoyable to me.

 Your letter of June nineteenth gave me deep pleasure. I realized the political risks in undertaking to obtain a repeal of the tolls exemption, but I do not know of anything I ever undertook with more willingness or zest and I think that we have reason to be proud of the way in which public opinion of the United States responded to the challenge. My own feeling is that the whole country is heartened and reassured by the repeal. I am not so much proud of it as deeply grateful that the country I love should be set in the right light, in the light of its real principles and opinion.

 Thank you with all my heart for your generous words of encouragement. They have done me a lot of good.

 Mrs. Wilson and my daughters join me in warmest regards to you both.

                    Cordially and sincerely yours,   Woodrow Wilson

TLS (J. Bryce Papers, Bodleian Library).
 [1] Bryce had been ennobled on January 1, 1914.

To Joseph Swagar Sherley

My dear Mr. Sherley: [The White House] July 6, 1914

 I have been very slow in learning of your illness and have now learned of it with the deepest regret. I fear that your strenuous work in behalf of the repeal of the Panama Canal tolls exemption may have played an important part in bringing on your illness, and, therefore, I feel as if I were myself in some part responsible. But there is this consolation and fine side to it, that if that cause did play a part it merely illustrated the fine way in which you devoted yourself to a great public duty. This letter gives me an opportunity to express my very deep and lasting appreciation of what you did in that fight, as well as for sending you my most sincere and earnest sympathy and expressing the hope that you may soon feel like yourself again.

Cordially and sincerely yours,   Woodrow Wilson

TLS (Letterpress Books, WP, DLC).

From Francis Griffith Newlands

My dear Mr. President: [Washington] June [July] 6, 1914.

I am informed by Senator Ashurst, who warmly favors the Trade Commission bill, that most of the members of his Committee (the Judiciary Committee) are opposed to it. In my conversations with members of that Committee I have not been able to ascertain decisively their views either upon the Trade Commission bill or upon the various provisions of the Clayton bill. Their views still seem to be in process of incubation, though Senator Hoke Smith informed me that whilst at first opposed, he is now inclined to favor the Trade Commission bill. I think the opposition is mainly confined to the Judiciary Committee. I know of no Democrats outside of that Committee who are opposed to it, except Senators Bankhead and Lane; but I am not a very good hand at canvassing votes.

I hope you will read the speeches of Senators Borah and Cummins, the former against, the latter for the bill. Both speeches cover several days, but they are published in their entirety, Borah's in the CONGRESSIONAL RECORD of June 30th and Cummins' in that of July 2nd, 1914. The most of my running debate was locked up in these speeches and did not appear in the current RECORD. This debate gives some idea of the crucial points of criticism and attack.

I regard Senator Cummins' speech, though long, as a very clear, just, and temperate treatment of the subject. I entirely agree with him as to the importance of the independence of the Commission. If I had my full way, I would turn over the entire enforcement of the Sherman Anti-Trust Law to this tribunal. The law alone should be its guide. It should be kept by the courts within the line of its authority and constitutional power; but it should receive no suggestion or direction from any political official or body. I presume, however, that it will be necessary to wait until the slow process of legislative evolution accomplishes this result.

I call your attention also to Senator Sutherland's criticism in the RECORD of July 3rd.

Whilst I am hopeful of bringing the bill to a vote within a few days, I am told by several Senators of excellent judgment that this will be impossible; that there is a strong disposition to delay final action until the report of the Judiciary Committee on the Clayton bill comes in. I am aware that this is an embarrassing feature in the early disposition of the Trade Commission bill.

With congratulations upon your admirable address at Philadelphia, I remain,

Very sincerely yours,   Francis G. Newlands

TLS (WP, DLC).

To William Jennings Bryan, with Enclosure

My dear Mr. Secretary: The White House July 7, 1914

Thank you for letting me see Fletcher's telegram from Chile. I have prepared the enclosed. If you like it, I would be very glad indeed to have you send it to each of the three Presidents.

Faithfully yours,   Woodrow Wilson

TLS (SDR, RG 59, 812.00/12430, DNA).

ENCLOSURE

The President of the United States desires me to express to the President of _____ the deep appreciation of this Government of the friendly services rendered by the Government of _____ to the Government and people of the United States in offering its good offices to accommodate the differences which have, unhappily, arisen between the Government of the United States and the *de facto* authorities at Mexico City; its admiration for the ability, the patience, and the gratifying success with which the distinguished representative of the Government of _____ in association with the other mediators conducted the conference at Niagara Falls; and its great satisfaction that so much has already been accomplished by the mediation in the interest of the peace of America.   Bryan[1]

CLST MS (SDR, RG 59, 812.00/12430, DNA).
[1] This telegram was sent, *mutatis mutandis*, to the Presidents of Argentina, Brazil, and Chile on July 7, 1914 (SDR, RG 59, 812.00/12430, DNA). A WWsh draft of the telegram is in WP, DLC.

A Statement on the Warburg and Jones
Nominations

[July 8, 1914]

When asked to comment on Mr. Warburg's desire to withdraw
his name,[1] the President said that he earnestly hoped that
Mr. Warburg would reconsider his decision and that he was
urging him to do so. He expressed confidence that the nomination of Mr. Jones would be confirmed and said:

"It would be particularly unfair to the Democratic party and
to the Senate itself to regard it as the enemy of business, big or
little. I am sure that it does not regard a man as an object of
suspicion merely because he has been connected with great business enterprises. It knows that the business of the country has
been chiefly promoted in recent years by enterprises organized on
a great scale and that the vast majority of the men connected
with what we have come to call big business are honest, incor-
ruptible and patriotic. The country may be certain that it is clear
to members of the Senate, as it is clear to all thoughtful men,
that those who have tried to make big business what it ought
to be are the men to be encouraged and honored whenever they
respond without reserve to the call of public service.

"I predict with the greatest confidence that nothing done by
the Democratic majority of the Senate of the United States will
be of a sort to throw suspicion upon such men. Mr. Jones and
Mr. Warburg, in manifesting their willingness to make personal
sacrifices and put their great experience and ability at the service
of the government, without thought of personal advantage, in the
organization of a great reform which promises to be so serviceable to the nation, are setting an example of patriotism and
of public spirit which the whole country admires. It is the obvious
business of statesmanship at this turning point in our development to recognize ability and character wherever it has been
displayed and unite every force for the upbuilding of legitimate
business along the new lines which are now clearly indicated
for the future."[2]

T MS (WP, DLC).
  [1] Warburg had refused to appear before the Senate Banking and Currency
Committee and, on July 3, had asked Wilson to withdraw his nomination.
  [2] There is an undated WWsh draft of this press release in WP, DLC, and
a CLST draft, with many WWhw emendations, in the C. L. Swem Coll., NjP.

To Samuel Gompers, with Enclosure

My dear Mr. Gompers: The White House July 9, 1914

You must have wondered what had become of the request contained in your letter of June fifth[1] that I send a message to be published in the Federationist on Labor Day. I had not forgotten it and am taking sincere pleasure in enclosing with this a brief message which I hope you will regard as acceptable.

Sincerely yours,   Woodrow Wilson

TLS (photostat in RSB Coll., DLC).
[1] S. Gompers to WW, June 5, 1914, TLS (WP, DLC).

E N C L O S U R E

To the Editor of the American Federationist:

I feel that I can in good conscience and with a heart full of deep confidence send a word of cheer, as you suggest, to the workers of America on this Labor Day of the interesting year 1914. No one can look about him with frank eyes, either in our beloved country or in any of the great nations of our time which have civilization in their hands, without feeling that there is a steady movement both of purpose and of action towards justice and a fuller comprehension and realization of the essential rights and liberties of men. The movement may be slow, may at times seem distressingly and discouragingly slow, but it is unmistakable; and all that we have to do to set it forward with ever increasing momentum is to think justly, purpose the things that are right, and be afraid of nothing except to be unfair and selfish and hasty when interests as great as the country itself are involved.[1]

T MS (photostat in RSB Coll., DLC).
[1] There is an undated WWsh draft of this message in WP, DLC.

To Edward Mandell House

My dear Friend: The White House July 9, 1914

I have just received and read yours of June twenty-sixth and hurry this note off to send you affectionate messages not only but renewed congratulations on the way you are serving the country we love and the peace of the world. It is perfectly delightful to read your letters and to realize what you are accomplishing. I have no comments except praise and self-congratulation that I have such a friend.

We shall very eagerly look for your return to this side of the water. All join me in warmest regards to Mrs. House and yourself.
Affectionately yours,   Woodrow Wilson

TLS (E. M. House Papers, CtY).

From Edward Mandell House, with Enclosures

My dear Friend: London. July 9th, 1914.

I am enclosing you copies of letters which I have written to the Kaiser and to Herr Zimmermann which will explain themselves.

I submitted them to Page before sending, and I hope they may have your approval.

I have a letter from Gerard this morning saying that when he dined with the Emperor at Kiel, he spoke of me most pleasantly and that von Tirpitz had thanked him for bringing us together.
Your faithful and affectionate,   E. M. House

I am told that it is absolutely safe to write anything one may desire to the Kaiser, if sent through the Foreign Office.

TLS (WP, DLC).

E N C L O S U R E   I

Edward Mandell House to Arthur Zimmermann

My dear Herr Zimmermann: London, England. July 8th, 1914.

When His Majesty did me the honor to invite me to Potsdam I expressed a wish to inform him concerning certain matters in connection with my visit to England.

His Majesty was good enough to consent, and I was instructed to send any communication through you and the Foreign Office.

I shall greatly appreciate your forwarding to His Majesty the enclosed letter.

In the event it should please His Majesty to communicate with me, I shall be in London until July 21st. After that time I may always be reached in care of The White House, Washington.

With assurances of my very high regard, and with thanks for your many courtesies while at Potsdam, I am, my dear Herr Zimmermann,   Sincerely yours,   Edward M. House.

ENCLOSURE II

Edward Mandell House to William II

Sir: London, England. July 8th, 1914.

Your Imperial Majesty will doubtless recall our conversation at Potsdam, and that with the President's consent and approval I came to Europe for the purpose of ascertaining whether or not it was possible to bring about a better understanding between the great powers, to the end that there might be a continuation of peace, and later a beneficent economic readjustment which a lessening of armaments would insure.

Because of the commanding position Your Majesty occupies, and because of your well known desire to maintain peace, I came, as Your Majesty knows, directly to Berlin.

I can never forget the gracious acceptance of the general purposes of my mission, the masterly exposition of the world wide political conditions as they exist today and the prophetic forecast as to the future which Your Majesty then made.

I received every reasonable assurance of Your Majesty's cordial approval of the President's purpose, and I left Germany happy in the belief that Your Majesty's great influence would be thrown in behalf of peace and the broadening of the World's Commerce.

In France I tried to reach the thoughts of her people in regard to Germany and to find what hopes she nursed. My conclusion upon leaving was that her Statesmen have given over all thought of revenge, or of recovery of the two lost provinces. Her people in general still have hopes in both directions, but her better informed rulers would be quite content if France could be sure of her autonomy as it now exists.

It was then, Sir, that I came to England and with high hopes, in which I have not been disappointed.

I first approached Sir Edward Grey, and I found him sympathetic to the last degree. After a two hours conference, we parted with an understanding that we should meet again within a few days. This I inferred to mean that he wished to consult with the Prime Minister and his Colleagues.

At our next conference, which again lasted for two hours, he had to meet me, the Lord Chancellor, Earl Crewe and Sir William Tyrrell.

Since then I have met the Prime Minister and practically every important member of the British Government, and I am convinced that they desire such an understanding as will lay the foundation for permanent peace and security.

England must necessarily move cautiously lest she offend the

sensibilities of France and Russia, but with the changing sentiment in France there should be a gradual improvement of relations between Germany and that country which England will now
be glad to foster.

While much has been accomplished, yet there is something
still to be desired in order that there may be a better medium
created for an easy and frank exchange of thoughts and purposes. No one knows better than Your Majesty of the unusual
ferment that is now going on throughout the world, and no one
is in so fortunate a position to bring about a sane and reasonable understanding among the statesmen of the Western Peoples,
to the end that our civilization may continue uninterrupted.

While this communication is, as Your Majesty knows, quite unofficial, yet it is written in sympathy with the well known views
of the President, and, I am given to understand, with the hope
from His Britannic Majesty's Government that it may bring a
response from Your Majesty which may permit another step
forward.

Permit me, Sir, to conclude by quoting a sentence from a letter which has come to me from the President:

"Your letter from Paris, written just after coming from Berlin,
gives me a thrill of deep pleasure. You have, I hope and believe,
begun a great thing and I rejoice with all my heart."

I have the honor to be, Sir, with the greatest respect, Your
Majesty's   Very Obedient Servant,   Edward M. House.

TCL (WP, DLC).

Remarks at a Press Conference

July 9, 1914

Can you tell us anything about your talk with Mr. Ford today,
Mr. President?

It was just a pleasant get-acquainted and an exchange of
general impressions about the business of calming the attitude of businessmen, and so forth. It was, to me, a very
reassuring conversation. Mr. Ford himself is in a very happy
frame of mind.

Mr. President, may the same be said with regard to your conversation with the gentlemen from Illinois?[1]

Yes, though that conference has a more business-like aspect.
They had come down to say that they were not at all opposed

[1] A special committee of the Chicago Chamber of Commerce who had come
to ask for the adoption of legislation establishing a strong trade commission.

to the general character of the legislation we were contemplating on pending trust legislation, but wanted to point out certain features which they thought would be better modified. And I think that, after I explained some of the changes that were in contemplation, they felt that their points were, most of them, met. At any rate, it was a cooperative thing and not a critical thing. They did not come down here to criticize but to cooperate.

Mr. President, can you tell us briefly what some of these contemplated changes are?

Well, nothing that I think you don't know already. You knew all along that the uneasiness of the businessmen has been about attempting to express the definitions that would be reached, that might cover more than we intended to cover in the prohibitions of the law. Everybody sees that the most difficult thing to do is to make a definition which will cover just what you want it to cover, not more, not less. What they were pleading for was some method of adaptation to the varying circumstances of a different case, which we all desire, and I furnished it, I think in what is now, I believe, the fifth section of the trade commission bill of the Newlands bill, which makes illegal unfair practices in trade and gives the commission the right to check those practices where they regard them as unfair.[2]

Will any change of phraseology in the paragraph define the rights of labor resulting from this conference?

Well, they didn't speak of that. I mean, they didn't speak in any way that would suggest a change. They simply referred to it as one of the debatable parts of the measure, but what they said didn't go beyond that.

If that measure means what you explained to them that it does mean, I suppose they are fully satisfied?

They are fully satisfied.

It is only the other interpretation?

It is only the other interpretation, which I don't think in the least is there.

Mr. President, in the defining paragraph, will not that make it more indefinite about unfair competition?

It will, in a way. You see, this is a very close analogy. The law forbids fraud, but nobody can define fraud. No lawyer has ever attempted to define fraud, and when in that vague field of fraud the court undertakes in specific instances, where fraud is alleged, to determine whether there was any

[2] About this section, see n. 1 to F. K. Lane to WW, July 10, 1914.

fraud or not, fraud is found elusive, a thing that may be committed in a myriad different ways. Some things may bear the appearance of fraud which, upon examination, don't turn out to be such at all. So there are certain competitive practices which in some circumstances are restrictive of competition and in others are not—the very same practices. I can give an illustration. Take the exclusive agency forbidding anyone to deal with an agent that had handled the goods of competitors. In certain rural districts, that might shut out competition altogether because there are only one or two men with whom he could make the exclusive arrangement. But in a big city, making an exclusive arrangement with a dealer doesn't seriously interfere with competition, if it interferes with it at all, so that the very same kind of contract of the exclusive agency would, in one neighborhood and in one set of circumstances, constitute restraint of competition in another town.

I don't know of any means in a law of foreseeing or discriminating between those cases. . . .

Mr. President, is it that the businessmen are trying to make sure that the trade commission will be a sort of clearinghouse for those problems; that is, they will have somebody to whom to go to resolve the doubt whether a certain practice is fraudulent?

A great many of them do. It is that part of the legislation, as it stands, that does not put the commission in quite that position. It puts it in the same position that the Interstate Commerce Commission is in, of checking certain practices, but not of okaying them before they have occurred, yes.

Do any of them suggest they have somebody to go to with a certain business problem, to find out whether it is illegal?

Yes, some of them want immunity powers beforehand.

That is at the bottom of their uncertainty, as to what is fraud and what is not fraud, and that is all you are trying to clear up?

Yes, but of course there are two methods of clearing it up—one after a practice has been entered into and one before it is entered into—and I don't think it is safe to say beforehand whether a practice is going to be good, bad, or indifferent. You don't know until the effects are clear.

The idea is to have the same effect as the Interstate Commerce Commission hearing on complaints?

As the bill stands, there is no provision for complaint. You can readily understand how, in the business world, a great many men might deliberately make trouble by constantly lodging complaints, provided the law said that the complaint had to be acted on. . . .

Mr. President, as a result of this conference, can you say that it might change your attitude as to having legislation at this time?

No, I wouldn't say that they have changed our attitude. I will say that I know more about their attitude than I knew before, and their attitude is not hostile to having legislation at this time, and that the average businessman of the country appreciates having things done upon a definite plan.

Mr. President, have you been given any information as to when the Interstate Commerce Commission will face the rate case?

No, none whatever.

Do you still get information from various parts of the country that that is holding up—

Yes, and I think we also get information that the railroads are going ahead with their necessary expansions and taking on their men again.

Has Mr. Warburg requested to have his name withdrawn?

Not yet. No, sir. I am hoping he will not.

You haven't heard from him?

I have heard from him,[3] but I won't accept it as a final answer. I think the whole country approves of his appointment and desires his confirmation. That is enough for me.

The statement given out by the Committee on Banking and Currency dealing with the testimony of Mr. Jones[4]—does that in any way shake your conviction as to the accuracy of your own characterizations of his purposes in joining the harvester trust company?

No, sir. It shakes my faith in the accuracy of the statement given out for the committee. I mean that if it conveyed any impression contrary to the estimate I put upon it, it was inadvertent and was not essentially contradictory at all.

I think the statement of the committee rather made it appear that Mr. Jones is in sympathy with the purposes of the harvester company as at present constituted.

Well, if it did, why of course it was an imperfect statement.

[3] P. M. Warburg to WW, July 8, 1914, T telegram (WP, DLC).

[4] Following Jones' appearance before the committee on July 6, Senator Hitchcock released a summary of his testimony to the press. Jones was reported to have said that he had become a director of the International Harvester Co. only to oblige his life-long friend, Cyrus H. McCormick, and that he "fully approved all acts of the company since he became a director in 1909, believing them proper and within the law." He also revealed that he and his brother, David B. Jones, were among the principal stockholders in the New Jersey Zinc Company, popularly known as the zinc trust. See the *New York Times*, July 7, 1914, and Link, *The New Freedom*, p. 454.

The fact is that Mr. Jones said that in his opinion the actions of the company since he had been connected with it were legal and proper, and I think that is true, from all I can learn. You see, there are some companies—I don't know enough about the harvester company to know whether it is one of them—but there are some companies which, though they may have been organized in contravention of the law, have not used their organization in a way to contravene the law, or that, although their very organization may be, in itself, tainted with illegality, their operations have been legitimate.

They have the power for evil without using it.

Exactly. The Supreme Court has said, as I understand it, that the Sherman law forbids businessmen putting themselves in a position where they can monopolize the market, whether they do so or not. So it may be that the initial step was illegal.

Mr. President, do you know whether Mr. Jones was opposed to voluntary dissolution in the suggested—

I don't know anything about that.

It was said by a member of the committee that he said that.

I simply know that I would rather trust Mr. Jones' judgment than mine. I have been associated with him for twenty years. There have been occasions when I would have made mistakes if I had not had Mr. Jones by. I don't mean since I got into politics, but before. He is one of the sort of men that doesn't offer his advice. He is one of the best persons that I know. He is not trying to run things.

JRT transcript (WC, NjP) of CLSsh (C. L. Swem Coll., NjP).

From Edward Mandell House

My dear Friend: London. July 9th, 1914.

Sir Cecil Spring-Rice, Page and I met yesterday morning as planned, in order to discuss the matter about which I wrote you last.

It was decided that nothing further be done until I report to you. That I was to give you the assurances of this Government, that it would follow your lead in any way which seemed to you best.

It was the concensus of opinion that you would perhaps want to talk to the A.B.C. Powers, and broach it to them as an original proposition looking to the welfare of the two Americas. Afterward, if you thought best and they approved, you might discuss the matter with Jusserand, and later take some proper occasion to further elaborate on your Mobile speech.

It would be then that England would come to the front and give her hearty approval, and lend all her influence towards bringing the other European Powers to your support.

In the meantime, it was decided for all of us to forget it, and even that any conversation had been passed, so whatever is finally done will originate with you.

Your faithful and affectionate,   E. M. House

TLS (WP, DLC).

From Charles Richard Van Hise

My dear Mr. President: Castine, Maine, July 9th., 1914.

Several times I have written you regarding the Interstate Trade Commission Bill. It seems presumptious for me to further write you concerning Trust Legislation. Nevertheless the Clayton Bill appears to me so defective that I am impelled to make certain suggestions concerning this Bill.

It seems to me that this Bill is inexpedient, in that it deals with classes and special cases rather than in accordance with a principle. What I mean is best illustrated by the clause relating to farmers' and laborers' organization. It seems to me there can be no possible defense for one law for merchants and manufacturers and another law for farmers and laborers.

All that is proposed to accomplish by the Clayton Bill and a great deal more can, it seems to me, be done, by adding a simple ammendment to the first section of the Sherman Act. The idea may be expressed as follows:

The restraint of trade or Commerce meant by this section is that restraint which is detrimental to the public welfare; and the presumption is that any restraint of trade is thus detrimental.

If the Interstate Trade Commission were given the power of advice, suggested in your message and the Sherman Act were thus ammended, there would be no necessity for special Legislation such as the proposed exemptions of laborers and farmers. The labor organizations would be free to co-operate in all legitimate ways; and they should ask no more than this. The farmers could go forward with their co-operative movement along all desireable lines. Finally bankers, merchants and manufacturers would be restrained w[h]ere restraint is needed, but could co-operate w[h]ere such co-operation is fair to the public.

In all cases, the public would be protected because each organization, that wished in any way to co-operate would be compelled to prove that such co-operation was not detrimental to the public welfare.

In trying to state the case concisely, I am aware that it has a certain tinge of dogmatism; but I am sure you will believe this is not intended.

With high regard, I remain

Very respectfully yours,   Charles R Van Hise

TLS (WP, DLC).

To William Jennings Bryan, with Enclosure

My dear Mr. Secretary: The White House July 10, 1914

Thank you sincerely for letting me see the enclosed and for the steps you are taking to set the matter right.[1]

Cordially and faithfully yours,   Woodrow Wilson

TLS (SDR, RG 59, 811.52/293, DNA).

[1] The *New York Times*, July 10, 1914, reported that conferences were in progress between Bryan and Viscount Chinda regarding proposed new immigration legislation on which Representative John Edward Raker of California was working. "The Raker bill," it continued, "would exclude all Asiatic laborers and an effort is being made . . . that it be amended so as to exempt laborers whose immigration into the United States is regulated by existing agreements as to passports."

The nature of Raker's proposed bill is made clear by his earlier attempt to amend the pending general immigration bill introduced by Representative John Lawson Burnett of Alabama in June 1913 (about which see Link, *The New Freedom*, pp. 274-76). On February 3, 1914, Raker offered an amendment which prohibited the immigration of "all Asiatic laborers" and specifically defined an Asiatic laborer as "a native of any country or district or island adjacent thereto situate east of a line composed of the Red Sea, the Mediterranean Sea, the Aegean Sea, the Sea of Marmora, the Black Sea, the Caucasus Mountains, the Caspian Sea, the Ural River and the Ural Mountains, with the exception of Turkey in Asia" (*Cong. Record*, 63d Cong., 2d sess., p. 2818). After a brief debate, in which Burnett opposed the amendment and several California congressmen made clear their determination to exclude "Asiatic laborers" by one means or another, Raker's amendment was defeated by a vote of 182 to 6 (*ibid.*, p. 2825). On January 16, 1915, Raker introduced a separate bill "to prohibit the coming of Asiatic laborers into the United States"; it was referred to the Committee on Immigration and Naturalization and was never heard of again (*ibid.*, 63d Cong., 3d sess., p. 1734). Hence, it appears that Bryan did manage to "set the matter right" by forestalling legislative exclusion on a geographical basis.

ENCLOSURE

TELEGRAPHIC INSTRUCTIONS FROM BARON KATO.

Imperial Japanese Embassy Washington July 7, 1914.

With reference to your telegram * * *, the bill under contemplation proposes to exclude, as a matter of principle, Japanese subjects with the rest of the Asiatic peoples on the basis of geographical demarkation, and is consequently in direct contravention of Article I of the Treaty of 1911 between Japan and the United States. Moreover, it constitutes an entirely new departure which will not fail to serve most unfortunately as precedent for future legislation of a similar nature.

Viewing the matter in the above light, the Imperial Government feel constrained to raise fundamental objection against the proposed measure, even if it contain such exception clauses as mentioned in your telegram.

You are therefore instructed to clearly represent to the Secretary of State that, in case the geographical demarkation should ever be adopted as a basis of exclusion, Japan should be excepted specifically from within the limits of such demarkation, in due regard to the express provision in the treaty as well as in consideration of the relations of good neighborhood between the two countries.

T MS (SDR, RG 59, 811.52/293, DNA).

From Franklin Knight Lane

My dear Mr. President: Washington July 10, 1914.

I inclose herewith a memorandum prepared by Mr. Rublee concerning Section 5 of the bill to create a Federal Trade Commission.[1] I have looked over this memorandum, and it seems to contain the answer to most, if not all, of the objections that have been raised to this provision of the bill, and have thought it might be helpful to you.   Faithfully yours,   Franklin K Lane

TLS (WP, DLC).
    [1] In this twenty-two page "Memorandum Concerning Section 5 of the Bill to Create a Federal Trade Commission" (T MS, WP, DLC), Rublee quoted the provisions of Section 5, described how they would correct the evils of unfair competition, and sought to answer several criticisms of the section.
    Section 5, Rublee said, declared unfair competition to be unlawful and empowered the commission to investigate and prevent or halt such competition by cease and desist orders which would be enforced by federal district courts.
    The Sherman Act applied only to restraint of trade by a combination and to monopolization of commerce. Unfair competition, to be sure, was a means of restraining or monopolizing commerce; however, there was some doubt whether the mere use of an unfair method by a small corporation fell under the ban of the Sherman Act. In any event, the Department of Justice had brought suits under the Sherman Act only in cases of "great magnitude involving clear violations of the Act." In such suits, he continued, "the Attorney General usually alleges the use of unfair competitive practices in support of his main contention that a monopoly exists which ought to be dissolved. The injunction against the future use of such practices is only an incidental part of the decree. Countless competitors succumb before relief is finally obtained." In contrast, the trade commission under Section 5 would "prevent not only the infliction of harm, but also the monopoly to which that harm would have led." "If a trade commission armed with the power to prevent unfair competition had existed when the

founders of the tobacco trust began to carry out their calculated policy of exterminating competitors, that astoundingly successful attempt to monopolize could have been frustrated."

Rublee then addressed himself to what he claimed were the weaknesses in those sections of the Clayton bill which sought to define specific monopolistic practices and made each a criminal offense. It was an impossible task, he said, because there was no way to frame a set of definitions that would embrace all unfair practices. Nor would an apparently complete list suffice for long, because "the number and variety of unfair practices is as unlimited and inexhaustible as the wit of man." In addition, it would be difficult to use language in framing definitions that would not present problems of construction to the courts. Attempts by the courts to qualify the language of decrees so as to give them a universal application would only give rise to lengthy litigation and result in obscuring instead of clarifying the law. Definitions, Rublee observed, once put into statutory form, could not be modified to meet other situations, whereas orders of a commission issued under Section 5 would remain flexible and might be modified or even set aside; meanwhile the courts would retain jurisdiction over the commission's decrees, modifying them when appropriate.

No one defended unfair competition, Rublee said. The only question was how best to prevent it with the least risk to legitimate business operations. That the procedures available under Section 5 were a desirable method had been recognized even by the directors of the United States Chamber of Commerce, which had sent to its members a special bulletin outlining the merits of the section. Surely, Rublee insisted, the process to be followed by the commission in any particular case would be acknowledged as fair by all businessmen not engaged in creating monopolies because it provided ample protection against arbitrary or unjust action. First, informal discussions would accompany the commission's initial investigations. Second, if the issue proceeded further, there would be full hearings before the commission. Third, the corporation under investigation would always have its day in court should it decide to defy a cease and desist decree. Small businesses would find the procedures especially advantageous, for they would have on their side the "strong arm of the government" to fend off the great corporations and would be relieved of the expense of long-drawn-out legal proceedings.

Among the criticisms which Rublee sought to counter was the charge that Section 5 was unconstitutional because it involved a delegation of legislative power to a quasi-executive body. Not so, replied Rublee, for the commission, in carrying out the legislative will of Congress, would simply be exercising delegated administrative powers such as did the Interstate Commerce Commission in administering the Commerce Act of 1887. In the case of the trade commission, it would also achieve legislative objectives by administrative means. The constitutionality of such administrative commissions and agencies had been firmly established in court decisions in numerous cases.

To the accusation that the term "unfair competition" was too vague and had no definite meaning in law, Rublee replied that a precise definition was unnecessary; furthermore, in many significant cases the courts had had no difficulty in identifying what constituted unfair competition. For examples of practices which the courts had so defined, Rublee pointed to the long list of decrees issued in cases under the Sherman Act and to numerous published authorities on antitrust law.

Finally, Rublee sought to allay the fears of those, such as Senator Borah, who thought that defendants under indictment for violating the Sherman Act might use the trade commission's decisions as shelters from prosecution under the Act. Such fears were unfounded, Rublee said, because the commission would have no power to authorize the use of a method of competition as fair, or to give immunity from the Sherman law. "The only orders the Commission can issue are orders prohibiting the use of unfair methods of competition. It is not possible to weaken the Sherman law in that way." "Unfair competition," Rublee concluded, "is the most effective weapon of monopoly. Prevention of unfair competition, instead of putting business in a straight-jacket, will liberate business. Fair, free and open competition is the object which the Sherman Act, no less than this bill seeks to promote. The two laws will be in perfect harmony."

To Franklin Knight Lane

My dear Mr. Secretary: [The White House] July 10, 1914.

I have received your letter of July 10th, and thank you very much for sending me the memorandum prepared by Mr. Rublee. I shall examine it with the greatest care.

Cordially and sincerely yours,   Woodrow Wilson

TLS (Letterpress Books, WP, DLC).

To Mary Allen Hulbert

Dearest Friend,   The White House 12 July, 1914.

It distressed us all very deeply to learn, by your letter to Helen, that you were unwell again, and, I gather, a bit discouraged about yourself. Our thoughts turn to you again and again, with deep sympathy and solicitude. I wish the messages could be as frequent as the thoughts! I never dreamed of being so driven on from one thing to another in hurried and uninterrupted sequence as I am here. I did not know before that a man could stand up and be well under this kind of thing. I often think, with a sort of pensive amusement, of how hard I used to think I was working and striving when I was president of the University! Looked back upon now, those seem to me almost days of leisure,—at any rate of leisure of spirit. It is the constant presence and pressure of great responsibility that tells, rather than the constant call of work,—the questions to be decided that involve our own dear country and often other peoples as well. What interests me is how the individual life keeps on in its own channels and retains its separateness and distinctness the while; and the old thoughts of friends and loved ones and all the little sometimes only half remembered things that make up the intimate experiences of life. If you counted the letters you would have no idea of the number of times we think of you. It *must* be thinking without speaking: there is no time to speak. The flood of tasks and duties, never ceasing, never slackening, sweeps on and there is no pause in which you can *do* what you please; but your mind is a domain of which you do not lose the mastery. There your friends live. You are conscious of their presence with a constand delight, all the more vivid because of the crowd of strangers and of those indifferent to you by which you are constantly surrounded. I wonder if there will be any more leisure when Congress is not sitting? You know it convened within a month after my inauguration and has been sitting ever since. Perhaps the President has breathing intervals occasionally when the session is over! And, since one cannot write to one's friends and tell them what is happening (since there would hardly be time to describe these crowded days unless one were to spend almost as much time in the writing as in the living of them), how are one's friends to know the simple fact of what is happening to him? They certainly cannot know from the newspapers. A few, like the New York World, for example, or the Springfield Republican, give the real facts, in their editorials if not in their news columns; but the rest are a tissue of inventions and speculations and of versions of what they would like to believe to be true. I never imagined anything like it. And most of the newspapers are owned or controlled by men who fear and would discredit the present administration! *Please* believe only so much of what you read in the newspapers about me as you can know is true from what you certainly and without conjecture know of *me*[.] But I know that I can trust you to do that.

I am well, absolutely well (a marvel though that be). Ellen is slowly (ah, how slowly!) coming to her strength again. We see our dear baby, Mrs. McAdoo (!) every day and are made happy by her radiant happiness. Jessie is at Cornish, very well and happy. God is very good to us. But we yearn for the friends we cannot see and hope (ah, how we do hope!) that everything that is good and fraught with happiness may come to them. Please, if you would make our hearts light, write to us that you are better, much better! All send affectionate messages.

Your devoted friend,   Woodrow Wilson

WWTLS (WP, DLC).

To Cleveland Hoadley Dodge

My dear Cleve,   The White House 12 July, 1914.

Something you once, in your great generosity, offered to do for me when I wanted Harry Fine to accept the post of Ambassador to Germany, emboldens me to turn to you in a great difficulty with which I find myself brought face to face. Walter Page is obliged to spend twenty-five thousand a year more than the government allows him or he has to spend. He must come home unless I can find the money for him from some source that will put him under no obligations which will in any way touch him in the performance of his duties. He has learned his job,—learned it admirably: speaks my mind and my point of view to the ministers over there as I am sure no one else could speak them; has got a real hold, socially *and* politically; is, if I know one when

I see him, for the present at any rate, an indispensable man in the right management of our foreign relations. I would not know what to do if I were obliged to part with him. My relations with him are intimate, and he has furnished me with more light on difficult foreign matters than all my other informants and advisers put together. I have, therefore, bidden him engage his present house for another year and count on me to do something to help him.

Will you forgive me and understand me, if I turn to you? I know that you will, and that you will come to my aid if you can. I know of no other friend like you, and of no other friend to whom I could afford to turn in such a matter and with such a request. You will tell me if you cannot do it; and if you can, it will be help that I can afford, in honour and with unmeasured confidence, to acc[e]pt. Thank God that it is so, and that there is room somewhere for perfect trust!

Mrs. Wilson gains slowly (ah, how slowly!) but I believe surely, and my heart grows lighter because of it even amidst this daily and hourly struggle here. She would send her warmest greetings, if she knew I was writing.

Your devoted friend,   Woodrow Wilson

WWTLS (WC, NjP).

From Cyrus McCormick, Jr.[1]

Dear Mr. President,   Oxford. July 12, 1914.

It is never my desire to go back on what I have said so I shall give myself the pleasure of repeating the congratulations I had the honor of sending you on the occasion of your election to the presidency. But I am unable to remain silent on the subject of the letter you recently addressed to Senator Owen on the subject of Mr. Thomas D. Jones' nomination to the Federal Reserve Board.

Were it not for the unanimity of the various clippings that have reached me describing it, I should hope that there had been some mistake, that you had been misquoted—my admiration for you leads me still to hope that such may be the case. To say that Mr. Jones "went into the board of the Harvester company for the purpose of assisting to withdraw it from the control which had led it into the acts and practices which have brought it under the criticism of the law officers of the government" is a statement which infringes closely upon the precincts of campaign hyperbole and savors, to my mind of a misguided desire to shield a fine man from the attacks of those against whom he is well able to defend himself. And in so doing you bring a direct and unwarranted attack against my father who always has considered himself one of your friends and still does so as far as I know. Is this fair? Entirely neglecting the fact that your communication drags into unfavorable criticism a corporation whose affairs are sub judice, I fail to see how your information can be of such a meager nature.

My father does not know that I am writing this letter, would doubtless disapprove of my doing so if he knew. But I find that it is impossible for me to remain silent. I have always endeavored to support you in such small ways as I could, on paper and by word of mouth, and I trust that future developements will permit me to continue to do so. But for the present you will, I hope, pardon me if I speak with some feeling, for such an attack on my father is a matter which touches me very nearly.

Very respectfully yours,   Cyrus McCormick Jr.

ALS (WP, DLC).

1 Princeton 1912, at this time a student \at Balliol College. He did not have his father's middle name.

Remarks at a Press Conference

July 13, 1914

Mr. President, have you any comments on the Warburg situation so far as the White House is concerned?

> No. I would like to say this, gentlemen. The newspapers have apparently got the impression that there is some kind of contest on between me and the Senate. I am not aware of any contest at all. On the contrary, I am acting in complete harmony with the Democratic majority in the Senate, perhaps with one or two exceptions. But I have been in conference with the members of the Senate, and there is absolutely no difference between us in the way in which we think this thing should be handled and considered. I hope you will get rid of the impression that there is some kind of contest on, because there isn't.

Are Senator Hitchcock and Senator Reed making trouble over there?

> No. I don't comment on individuals. . . .

Mr. President, these conferences that you have had with the Democratic members of the Senate on the Warburg-Jones nominations—do you believe that they will be confirmed without much division in the majority?

> Why, yes. I have definite assurances with regard to Mr. Jones who is—that is, the only one who has been acted on in

the committee. The action of the committee would of course have something to do with the other case and the way in which the committee felt they ought to handle the matter. I don't think it is respectful to the Senate to go too fast in matters of that sort and run ahead of what the constituted authorities of the Senate put on the boards. The only case ready, as I understand it, is the case of Mr. Jones.

The action of the committee on it—

It is the fact that the action of the committee on Mr. Warburg is not final so far as the committee is concerned. They have not acted.

They have decided to postpone action indefinitely?

Pending his attitude, as I take it, with regard to coming down and meeting the committee. That is the way I interpret it.

Mr. President, do you know whether he is coming down to meet them at the conferences?

I haven't heard in two or three days what his present thought was.

It has been suggested that there should be a compromise that would serve the purpose of a hearing and not be an inquisition.

Personally, I feel that the Senate committee would of course accord him the most courteous treatment. No one has a right to doubt that. . . .

Have you taken up the question of Mr. Justice Lurton's successor?[1]

No, sir, I haven't. Some of the newspapers reminded me of the widow who was proposed to just as soon as she reached the house, after attending her husband's funeral, and she said she was sorry but a man had proposed at the grave. They reported the very next morning my having certain persons in mind. I had been too genuinely distressed to have anybody in mind, and haven't been going very fast in the matter. It appears that he was an old friend of my father's,[2] and one of the justices whom I personally knew well.

JRT transcript (WC, NjP) of CLSsh (C. L. Swem Coll., NjP).
  [1] Associate Justice Horace Harmon Lurton had died of a heart attack in Atlantic City on July 12.
  [2] Lurton had lived in Clarksville, Tenn., when Dr. Wilson taught there.

To William Jennings Bryan

My dear Mr. Secretary: The White House July 13, 1914

I enclose the memorandum about the Seamen's Bill.[1]

It seems to me a very dignified document whose arguments carry great weight. I would be very much obliged if you would take it up with the Secretary of Labor and through him with the gentlemen who are handling this important matter in Congress. It seems to me that we ought to see to it that these arguments have due and immediate consideration.

Always

Cordially and faithfully yours,   Woodrow Wilson

TLS (W. J. Bryan Papers, DNA).
1 British Embassy to the Secretary of State, July 10, 1914, T memorandum (SDR, RG 59, 196/8, DNA). It objected to several provisions of the seamen's bill then before the House on the general ground that they would lead to a "most unfair discrimination" against British commerce vis-à-vis its principal competitors such as Germany and France, because of their differing treaty arrangements with the United States.

To Charles Richard Van Hise

My dear President Van Hise: The White House July 13, 1914

Pray never apologize for writing to me. Your letters are always welcome.

I have your letter of June ninth and believe that much of the criticism which it embodies with regard to the Clayton Bill will be offset by changes which are being made in the bill in the Senate. The modified bill is, I believe, to be reported today.

The so-called labor exemption does not seem to me to do more than exclude the possibility of labor and similar organizations being dissolved as in themselves combinations in restraint of trade. We are laboring over the whole matter here with the most earnest desire to do the right thing.

Cordially and sincerely yours,   Woodrow Wilson

TLS (Presidents' Files, WU).

From Cleveland Hoadley Dodge

My dear President   [Riverdale, N.Y.] July 13th 1914

Your beautiful letter of 12th inst off that dear old typewriter is well worth the whole price of admission and I thank you from the bottom of my heart for this new mark of your confidence.

It is needless to say that I fully understand & appreciate the situation & consider it a great joy to be able & privileged to help you & the whole country in the way which you suggest.

Fortunately I have no longer any burdens connected with Princeton, & moreover your much abused friend "Psychology" is so greatly improved in health, that I can attend to this little matter without embarrassment & will gladly provide the whole sum which is needed to retain Mr P., at the rate of $25000.00 per annum, until he leaves his present post. I will not mention the matter to a soul, except my wife, who in case of my illness or death will see that my promise is kept.

As to the best way of carrying out your idea, I should think it would be just as well not to have my name appear in any way, or have the money go through your hands if it can be avoided. How would it do to confide in Bob Bridges or Sheldon & let one of them act as an intermediary. All such details I will of course leave to your judgment & when you have decided what to do, I shall be glad to know how much will be needed at once & how much for the balance of this year. I expect to be here, with a few days off, for the rest of July, but shall be away most of August.

My heart has gone out to you constantly during the past months as I have thought of all the burdens you are carrying, & especially that hardest of all, in connection with Mrs Wilson's health, and I am devoutly thankful that you are at last more relieved & encouraged about her & sincerely trust that she may speedily recover.

The Warburg Jones affair is very interesting & exciting but oh how profoundly sad & ridiculous. Jones is superb & I only wish that Warburg had a little more fighting blood in him. When Jones was here last week I took him in to see Warburg & we had a most interesting talk which I hope did good. I trust that some way may be found out of the present impasse & that after the Senators have blown off enough hot air, you may win out with both men

Your interviews with "business" have had a wonderful effect & I am rejoiced over the good prospects of your bills and the better outlook in Mexico. May everything work out soon as you desire so that you may get your much needed rest is the earnest prayer of one who will always be glad to do anything in his power to help you carry your burdens   Yr's affly   C H Dodge

ALS (WC, NjP).

From William Bauchop Wilson

My dear Mr. President,   Washington July 13, 1914.

I would be extremely well pleased if Mr. Frederick C. Howe,[1] President of the Peoples' Institute of New York, could be named as Commissioner of Immigration at the Port of New York. He is a man of the type I have continuously had in mind for that position.[2]

If he could be selected it would be a happy solution to the problem.   Faithfully yours,   W B Wilson

TLS (WP, DLC).

[1] Frederic Clemson Howe, lawyer and municipal reformer, who had been a member of the Cleveland law firm of Garfield, Garfield and Howe until 1910, when he moved to New York. He was an expert on taxation and urban problems and had published several books on these subjects. He had known Wilson while studying for the Ph.D. at The Johns Hopkins University, 1889-1892.

[2] He was appointed on August 19.

To William Jennings Bryan

My dear Mr. Secretary: The White House July 14, 1914

Thank you for having let me see the enclosed.[1] I have read it with deep interest and a good deal of concern.

Some of the details I seriously doubt but probably the thing may be true in bulk.

    Always

        Faithfully and cordially yours,   Woodrow Wilson

TLS (W. J. Bryan Papers, DNA).

[1] L. J. Canova to WJB, July 8, 1914, TLS (SDR, RG 59, 812.00/14805, DNA). Canova reported that William Randolph Hearst was attempting to embarrass the Wilson administration and bring about American intervention in Mexico by fomenting conflict within the Constitutionalist ranks. He was doing this, Canova claimed, through his newspaper agents based in El Paso.

To William Bauchop Wilson

My dear Mr. Secretary: [The White House] July 14, 1914

Thank you for your letter about Mr. Frederick C. Howe. Would it be possible for you to ascertain whether Mr. Howe would be willing to consider the position, and would you be kind enough, if you found that Mr. Howe was willing, to suggest the appointment to Senator O'Gorman as one which I desire to make and ascertain his attitude towards it?

        Cordially and faithfully yours,   Woodrow Wilson

TLS (Letterpress Books, WP, DLC).

From Alfred Henry Mulliken

Sir: Washington, D. C. July 14, 1914.

The Senate having adopted the labor and agricultural exemption clause in the Sundry Civil Appropriation Bill in the same form that it passed the House, it is now clear that in the near future it will be presented to you for your action in the identical language in which it came before you last year. At that time it met with your publicly expressed and emphatic condemnation although you felt it necessary, under existing circumstances, to sign the appropriation bill.

On June 24 I had the honor to call upon you with Mr. Charles F. Mathewson of our Committee on Trust Legislation and to hand you a memorial upon this very subject of labor and agricultural exemption from law adopted at a special meeting of the Board of Directors of this Chamber, held in Washington the day before for the sole purpose of considering the situation created by these legislative proposals to discriminate between classes,—against business and in favor of labor and agriculture.

All our action in this matter is based upon the opinion of the business men of this country submitted through their commercials organizations in a referendum conducted last year, in which the vote was 669 against exemption to 9 in favor.

On this same authority, I now address you, asking on behalf of the Chamber of Commerce of the United States, representing 586 commercial organizations in every State of the nation except one that you will veto the bill. Your action of last year has not prevented the legislation, to which you took such strong and just exception, from being presented in the same form and under like circumstances to you again and this may be expected to be continued annually with probably an extension of the prohibition to other appropriations unless action more definitive is taken.

We are aware of the gravity of a veto of the Sundry Civil Bill but in so far as delay in enactment involves hardship, it is operating now through failure to pass the bill before July 1. A further delay with consequent extension of last year's appropriations for such time as is necessary to pass the bill without the objectionable clause cannot involve very serious additional hardship.

Very respectfully yours,   A. H. Mulliken
Acting President.

TLS (WP, DLC).

To James Hamilton Lewis

My dear Senator: [The White House] July 15, 1914

I understand that the International Convention on Safety at Sea is to come up before the Committee on Foreign Relations today. I know how much interested you are in the Convention and write to ask if there is any way in which I can be of assistance in securing its adoption by the Senate.

Cordially and sincerely yours,   Woodrow Wilson

TLS (Letterpress Books, WP, DLC).

From Edward Mandell House

My dear Friend: London, England. July 15th, 1914.

In the last day or two I have seen both Norman Hapgood and Charles Grasty and they fell to talking about the Kansas City postmastership. They each expressed a hope that you would select a high class progressive democrat, and not let the place fall into the hands of the spoilsmen.

Grasty thought it would be an excellent political move to ask Colonel Nelson to suggest one or two such men. I concur in this opinion. If you do this, I would suggest that you write Nelson such a letter that he might publish, for it would have a far reaching effect.

I know of no newspaper that influences a wider audience than the Kansas City Star.

I am sorry to hear of Justice Lurton's death. I hope you may not change your decision as to McReynolds and Gregory,[1] for that seems to be the wise solution.

We are sailing next Tuesday, the 21st and this will probably be my last letter from here. We should arrive in Boston, July 29th and my address will be, Prides Crossing, Massachusetts.

Your faithful and affectionate,   E. M. House

TLS (WP, DLC).
[1] That is, to elevate McReynolds to the Supreme Court and appoint Gregory as Attorney General.

To Leon Joseph Canova

Washington, July 16, 1914. 6 pm

Answering your July 14th, 11 pm.[1] You will please join Villa as suggested by Carranza, and go south with him, keeping in touch of course with Carothers wherever you have an opportunity. Urge two things upon Carranza, Villa and other Constitutionalists with whom you have occasion to talk, namely: First, to avoid revenges. There should be no execution of those who surrender. The Constitutionalists are now approaching a complete national victory,[2] and when successful will come into diplomatic relations with the outside world. It is important that they should cultivate the good opinion of the nations with whom they will then have to deal, and a display of cruelty or revenge will be embarrassing to them. The second thing to urge upon them is respect for the person and property of those engaged in religious work, both in the church and in the school. Protection should be given to all churches and all denominations. We are just informed of the killing of two brothers of the Christian school at Zacatecas, and the imprisonment of eleven others. We are endeavoring to secure the release of those imprisoned. You cannot too strongly advise against any acts that would seem to indicate antagonism to those engaged in religious work. In conferring with Villa, commend the patriotism that has lead [led] him to harmonize his differences with Carranza, and point out to him that the securing of reforms which will bring justice and prosperity to the people of Mexico will be a reward for such sacrifices as he may have made. No personal differences or antagonisms should be permitted to prevent the restoration of peace in Mexico.   Bryan

T telegram (SDR, RG 59, 812.00/12501, DNA).
¹ L. J. Canova to WJB, July 14, 1914, T telegram (WP, DLC). Canova reported that Carranza was about to attack San Luis Potosí and Querétaro, preparatory to a march on Mexico City. The First Chief suggested that Canova go to see Villa, returning in a few days to join Carranza in the advance southward. Canova asked for instructions on this point. Canova continued: "At our interview I was assured Villa difficulty has been settled definitely so far as he [Carranza] is concerned. If it should be opened again it will be through some act of Villa. He [Carranza] declares that he has no personal ambition; that he is sustaining the armed protest as matter of principle that equal justice and liberty might triumph. He declares that after he had accomplished the overthrow of the usurping Government and prepared the country for free and honest elections his work would be done and he would gladly return to his home in Coahu[i]la. He spoke with conviction."
² Huerta had abdicated on July 15, leaving his government in the hands of Francisco S. Carbajal, a Constitutionalist sympathizer.

From James Hamilton Lewis

My dear Mr. President: Washington, D.C. July 16, '14.

I acknowledge your kind note in respect to the Safety at Sea Conference. I thank you for your offer of assistance. I understand that our friend, Senator John Sharp Williams has some opposition. He is the only one of our people who I hear proposes opposition. I shall confer with you upon this subject at a time I shall take up other matters with you very shortly.

I have the Honor to be,
          Your very obedient servant,   Jas. Hamilton Lewis

TLS (WP, DLC).

From William Charles Adamson

Dear Mr. President: Washington, D. C. July 16th, 1914.

I cannot refrain from expressing my gratification at your unbounded and unparalelled success in the Mexican situation. I think your wisdom and forbearance followed by your grand triumph will give you the lofty place which you deserve in the estimation of your contemporaries and posterity.

It now appears that your success is complete. Of course the world accepts success as the test of merit. I realize your merit in the performance, even if it were not crowned with complete success, but the apparently complete success of your enterprise will certainly give you the first place in history. Almost any other public man in your stead would have involved our country in a disastrous and bloody war costing us hundre[d]s of thousands of lives and untold millions of money, would have involved the destruction of our sister republic, the enmity of all Central and South American countries and involved us in interm[i]nable broils financial and diplomatic with all of the nations of the world, whose people could conjure up anything on which to base a claim on account of our interferrence with Mexico. But I didn't intend to write you such a long letter, but merely to express my own gratification and congratulate you and your country on the complete vindication of your wise policy.

Yours truly,   W. C. Adamson

TLS (WP, DLC).

From Edward Mandell House

Dear Governor: London, England. July 17th, 1914.

When I came to London, Sir Horace Plunkett was one of the first men I talked to concerning your Mexican policy. I straightened him out in short order, and he advised me to take hold of Sidney Brooks and put him right.

This I did in several conversations and you will see the result by the enclosed clippings from The Times of today.[1] I am also sending you what their Washington correspondent has to say, showing hostility to your policy.[2]

The papers in Europe have generally been favorable to Huerta, and I have done what I could to give the real facts so your purposes might be understood.

The Times is still the most powerful organ in Europe towards influencing public opinion, and to get them right, is to turn the tide in the proper direction. Everyone has been telling me for a year or more that you could not do what you have done, and that you could never compose the situation without war, and I have been set down time and again as a very partial friend because of my insistence to the contrary.

You do not know how happy I am that you have succeeded in

the first great step, and I hope and pray that the Constitutionalists may listen to your counsel and bring confusion to your critics. They all admit that if you succeed in composing Mexico without war, you will have done the greatest conceivable act of statesmanship.

I am so eager for this culmination that I can scarcely maintain myself, for it means so much to your prestige and place in history.

Your faithful and affectionate,   E. M. House

TLS (WP, DLC).
[1] An editorial, "Exit President Huerta," and an article, "President Wilson's Methods." The latter was declared to be a statement to a representative of the *Times* by "a prominent American politician who is in close touch and sympathy with President Wilson's Administration."
[2] "End of the Huerta Regime."

To Cleveland Hoadley Dodge

Dear Cleve.,   The White House 19 July, 1914.

Certainly God has blessed me with one of the truest and most generous friends a man ever had. Friendship such as yours, coming by fresh froof [proof] to me here in the midst of business at every turn of which it is necessary, in common caution, to scrutinize motives and reckon with what may be covertly involved, is like God's pure air to a man stifled and breathing hard to keep his lungs going. I am deeply grateful and happy whenever I think of you. May God bless you as he has blessed me *in* you!

I shall wait until House comes back to determine how the thing is to be managed.[1] He will be our best counselor, fresh from the scene. He sails on the twenty-first and should be here before the end of the month.

We are having a desperate (and, I fear, losing) struggle for the confirmation of Jones for the Reserve Board. The Harvester combine is so thoroughly hated by the farmers that the senators from agricultural States are genuinely trembling at the idea of being obliged to vote for one of its directors. I shall not know for a day or two yet what to count on; but just at this writing it looks like a defeat by about one or two votes, the Republicans being solidly lined up, for party advantage, or spite, as you may choose to look at it, and Messrs. O'Gorman, Reed, and Hitchcock having worked on the fears I have mentioned with malevolent ardour, to strike at me. Warburg's case seems quite hopeless.

My dear lady grows slowly better, and sends her warmest greetings to you both.

Your grateful and devoted friend,   Woodrow Wilson

WWTLS (WC, NjP).
    ¹ As it turned out, House relayed the payments from Dodge to Arthur Wilson Page, the ambassador's son.

From Walter Hines Page

                                              Beaminster, Dorset. England.
Dear Mr. President: Sunday, July 19. 1914

   Just this line of jubilant congratulations on the course of events in Mexico. Of course the big constructive job is yet to be done, and of course there are grave difficulties. But this is an eight-league step forward—Huerta's quiet going. With the A.B.C. Governments sufficiently in the job to feel a certain responsibility and with the demonstration of the rightness of your vision and method, all the quiet great forces in the world must now come to your side.

   I am everywhere talking a right explanation of it, in surroundings that are yet incredulous but that are now at least eager to listen. They see slowly, but they'll now begin to see.

   For the moment the English press is very dense on the subject; but events are very convincing things.

   I send you my heartiest congratulations.

                          Very faithfully yours,   Walter H. Page

ALS (WP, DLC).

To William Charles Adamson

My dear Judge: [The White House] July 20, 1914

   That was an extremely generous letter you wrote me on July sixteenth about the outcome in Mexico and I thank you for it from the bottom of my heart. Such approbation from a man whose judgment I so highly esteem goes very deep.

   The final working out of the situation in Mexico is still a little blind, but we have certainly cleared the stage and made a beginning and with the support of thoughtful men it should be possible to hold things steady until the process is finally complete.

   With warm appreciation,

                      Cordially and sincerely yours,   Woodrow Wilson

TLS (Letterpress Books, WP, DLC).

To Zach Lamar Cobb[1]

Washington, July 20, 1914.

Please see that the following telegram gets to Carothers or to Villa if Villa is at Juarez: Quote.

Please see Villa at once and impress upon him the patriotic duty of using his influence to prevent discord among Constitutionalists. It is of vital importance that they do not allow personal feelings or personal quarrels to jeopardize the victory which they have won. Huerta has gone and the transfer of the government can now be secured without further bloodshed. The outlook is bright for peace and prosperity in Mexico and the President is very anxious that nothing shall occur to delay the forms needed to restore justice to the people. Villa has played an important part in winning the victory and the President feels sure that he will use his influence on the side of harmony and cooperation among the constitutionalists.   Bryan.

T telegram (SDR, RG 59, 812.00/12552, DNA).
[1] Collector of Customs at El Paso.

To the American Consulate in Monterey, Mexico

Washington, July 20, 1914.

Have asked Brazilian Minister[1] to inform acting President Carbajal of Carranza's willingness to meet his representatives at Saltillo. We hope that this will result in a meeting of the representatives of Carbajal and Carranza. We have promised to use the influence of this government to secure promise of amnesty and such other guarantees as would accompany transfer.

Please say to General Carranza that the President is much gratified at his willingness to suspend military operations and receive representatives of Carbajal. Impress upon General Carranza the important fact that the approval of the outside world which becomes more and more necessary as he approaches authority will be dependent upon the extent to which amnesty is granted. The President is anxious that the success of the Constitutionalists shall result in the permanent peace and prosperity of Mexico.   Bryan.

T telegram (SDR, RG 59, 812.00/12552, DNA).
[1] José Manuel Cardoso de Oliveira, who represented United States interests after the landing at Veracruz.

To José Manuel Cardoso de Oliveira

Washington, July 20, 1914.

We have just learned that Carranza is willing to appoint representatives to confer with representatives appointed by acting President Carbajal at Saltillo. He suggests that they come north by way of San Luis Potosi. He will provide for their protection when he is informed their names and of their departure from Mexico City. He takes it for granted that they will be duly accredited and fully authorized to agree upon the form of the unconditional delivery of the government at Mexico City to him as first chief of the Constitutionalists. Carranza will agree to temporary suspension of military operations during conference. This government will use its influence to secure promise of amnesty and such other guarantees as would properly accompany a transfer of authority.   W. J. Bryan.

T telegram (SDR, RG 59, 812.00/12552, DNA).

Two Letters from Thomas Davies Jones

My dear Mr. President: Chicago July 20, 1914.

I have reached a definite conviction that it is my duty to ask you to withdraw my nomination as a member of the Federal Reserve Board. You are aware that I was in no sense whatever an applicant for the office. It was with the gravest reluctance that I agreed to accept the honorable but heavy burdens of that office in case my nomination were sent to the Senate and confirmed by it. I did not then anticipate a protracted and bitter contest. At the invitation of the Committee on Banking and Currency I willingly appeared before it to answer any questions which they might desire to ask of me, and I endeavored to answer with entire frankness all the questions that were asked, and my testimony was made public at my request.

It is not for me to surmise motives or to complain of results. That my nomination and the controversy that has arisen over it in the Committee on Banking and Currency is seriously embarrassing your administration and is causing injury to the party of which you are the leader is too clear to admit of any doubt. And in view of the character of the report made by the majority of the Committee on Banking and Currency, a majority composed of six Republicans and two Democrats—much of it based on distortion of facts and perversion of truth—I feel convinced that

such opposition has developed to the confirmation of my appointment and such criticism has been made of my nomination that
even if the nomination were confirmed by the Senate my usefulness as a member of the Federal Reserve Board would be seriously
impaired.

I am not willing longer to remain the cause of embarrassment to you and to your administration, and in view of the considerations above stated I now ask that you withdraw my name
from consideration.

Faithfully yours,   Thomas D. Jones.

My dear Mr. President: Chicago July 20, 1914.

Referring to the letter to you which is enclosed herewith, I want
to say that I have thought it good policy to make it studiously
quiet. In that respect my judgment has differed from that of some
of my friends. There are one or two phrases in it which even as
it stands I was tempted to eliminate.

I cannot let the matter go without a personal word, which I
deemed inappropriate to be inserted in that letter. I confess that
the opportunity to be associated with you, even in a minor way,
in the actual creative work of government took strong hold upon
my imagination. It served to overbear doubts of the wisdom of
my undertaking the task presented, growing mainly out of considerations of health. I doubt whether I could have stood the
work long, but I was prepared to devote the last ounce of strength
there was in me to the work which your proposal seemed to bring
to me.

Now that the vision is passed my preponderant feeling is that
of profound relief. I had come to feel that I was in some way
the occasion of getting you into inextricable difficulties, and that
those difficulties might easily lead to disaster. I am sure that
my withdrawal is wise.

I hardly dare trust myself to say how deeply I prize the confidence you have shown in me and your endeavors to carry the
matter through. It will always be a matter of real and deep pride
to me.

With light apparently ahead in Mexico, and with achievements
already accomplished which even the most sanguine could not
have anticipated a year and a half ago, you can afford to face
minor irritations with entire equanimity. If from now on you are
to be beset with controversy and difficulties you can in my opinion
rely with entire confidence upon the fact that your past achieve-

ments will rank among the highest achievements of the holders of your great office.

Ever faithfully yours,   Thomas D. Jones.

TLS (WP, DLC).

To James Clark McReynolds

[The White House]

My dear Mr. Attorney General: July 21, 1914.

I have your letter of today,[1] enclosing a copy of your letter of July 9 to Mr. J. H. Hustis, President of the New York, New Haven and Hartford Railroad Company,[2] which together disclose the failure of the directors of the New York, New Haven and Hartford Railroad Company to comply with the terms of the settlement proposed by them and accepted by us in the matter of their railroad holdings.[3] Their final decision in this matter causes me the deepest surprise and regret. Their failure, upon so slight a pretext, to carry out an agreement deliberately and solemnly entered into and which was manifestly in the common interest, is to me inexplicable and entirely without justification.

You have been kind enough to keep me fully informed of every step the Department took in this matter and the action of the Department has throughout met with my entire approval. It was just, reasonable and efficient. It should have resulted in avoiding what must now be done.

In the circumstances the course you propose is the only one the Government can pursue. I therefore request and direct that a proceeding in equity be filed, seeking the dissolution of the unlawful monopoly of transportation facilities in New England now sought to be maintained by the New York, New Haven and Hartford Railroad Company; and that the criminal aspects of the case be laid before a grand jury.

With much regard,

Sincerely yours,   Woodrow Wilson[4]

TLS (Letterpress Books, WP, DLC).
  [1] J. C. McReynolds to WW, July 21, 1914, TLS (WP, DLC).
  [2] J. C. McReynolds to J. H. Hustis, July 9, 1914, TCL (WP, DLC).
  [3] The New Haven directors had refused to sell their stock in the Boston and Maine Railroad, arguing that a provision of the enabling act recently passed by the Massachusetts legislature, reserving to the state the right to purchase the stock at any time thereafter, made the stock unsaleable at a fair price. See the letter cited in n. 2 above.
  [4] There is an undated WWsh draft of this letter in WP, DLC.

To Alfred Henry Mulliken

My dear Sir: [The White House] July 22, 1914

I have your letter of July fourteenth and must apologize for not having answered it sooner. The delay has been due to a brief indisposition.

I feel just as I felt a year ago about the embodiment of the restriction you speak of in one of the items of the Sundry Civil Bill, but I also feel as I did then that I should not be justified in vetoing the bill because of the presence of the restriction in that item. The Department of Justice is not in any way hampered by that particular restriction in the matter of prosecuting any offence against the laws of the United States. The fund provided in that particular item is a fund for a special purpose. It is a comparatively small sum and its embodiment in the form in which it is appropriated does not in any way limit the activities or the discretion of the department.

Much as I regret the embodiment of restrictions of that sort in an appropriation bill, I feel that my duty in the matter is made sufficiently clear by the considerations I have already stated.

                      Sincerely yours,   Woodrow Wilson

TLS (Letterpress Books, WP, DLC).

A Telegram and a Letter from Henry Lee Higginson

                    Boston, Massachusetts, July 22, 1914.

I respectfully ask you to delay action about New Haven Railroad one day. A letter follows my request.

                          Henry L. Higginson.

T telegram (WP, DLC).

Dear Sir: Boston July 22, 1914.

I believe that the action of the New Haven directors is misunderstood by the United States Government and I know that these directors sincerely wish to follow the orders of the United States Attorney General.

These directors have offered to give to the Massachusetts authorities an irrevocable power of attorney for the control of its Boston & Maine shares until the next session of the Massachusetts Legislature, and they have offered to give up at once control of the trolleys and of the Boston & Maine Railroad and to confine themselves to the business of their own road. What greater earnest of their good faith and their obedience to the law can they give?

They wish to sell the outside securities of their corporation at as good a price as possible for the benefit of their shareholders. The State of Massachusetts is thwarting their action; the State of Massachusetts has attached such a condition to the sale of the Boston & Maine shares as to make them almost, if not entirely, unmarketable. It is the buyer and not the seller of these shares who can settle this point, and with this imposed restriction I assert that the shares can only be thrown away. A buyer must consider that they may be assessed, they may prove valueless, or he, the buyer, may spend much money in making them valuable and then lose it, or, in any case, lose all his labor.

Shares once stamped are not marketable except at a concession, and will not pass in the markets without an explanation. This is not an opinion, but a matter of fact.

The United States orders the sale of these shares and Massachusetts almost forbids the sale. Who is it that is thwarting the United States order? At best, it would be a sale at a ruinous price. In truth, only two buyers of these Boston & Maine shares are in sight, namely, the Delaware & Hudson or the Canadian Pacific, and of course they would not touch the shares if any conditions were attached to them. Still further, the State of Massachusetts would not sell the shares to these corporations or either of them. By order of the Attorney General the Boston & Maine shares may not be sold to the New Haven shareholders.

May I add that neither I nor my firm own any New Haven or Boston & Maine shares, and I make this statement to you for the sake of the New Haven shareholders and as a citizen of the United States who wishes to see the truth and to have justice done.

I repeat that, knowing the officers of the New Haven Railroad, more especially Mr. Howard Elliott, I am sure they wish to obey the laws of the United States, and as promptly as possible.

I am, with great respect,

Very truly yours,   Henry L. Higginson

TLS (WP, DLC).

From Francis Griffith Newlands

My dear Mr. President: [Washington] July 22d, 1914.

I send you herewith a copy of the last draft of the railway securities bill. It will be reported tomorrow. We have been delayed somewhat by the consideration of certain objections of Messrs

Brandeis and Rublee, who proposed notification and publicity in place of the control of security issues.

The committee has concluded to abide by the recommendation of the Interstate Commerce Commission, which calls for control over security issues. We feel that it is time to absolutely check the scandalous system of over-issue of stocks and bonds, and that it will not do to wait until the railway valuation is completed before this is accomplished.

We will now press vigorously the whole trust program and hope to bring it to a speedy conclusion, although there are indications of a disposition to filibuster and protract the session.

Very sincerely yours,   Francis G. Newlands

TLS (WP, DLC).

Remarks at a Press Conference

July 23, 1914

Mr. President, can you tell us something about the government's attitude in the Haitian situation? I refer particularly to the fact that announcement was made by the War and Navy Departments that several marines were going to be sent to Guantánamo, to be held in readiness there for eventualities in Haiti and Santo Domingo, although we understood that Haiti was meant particularly. That indicates that the administration certainly has some policy in view that might involve the use of force.

> No. It indicates only that the administration has some anxiety with regard to the case. It is one of those situations that is just bristling with interrogation points. I don't know what is going to happen from day to day. We didn't feel at liberty to be so far away that if it should appear with regard to saving lives, for example, or interests that ought to be protected, then we could not act, but it doesn't in any way seem plain.

Could you say, Mr. President, whether any negotiations are afoot now for taking over the customs revenues of Haiti under the—

> No, sir. There are no negotiations.

Mr. President, has this government sent anything to the government of Haiti and Santo Domingo about the necessity of restoring order?

> Yes, sir. We have been very eloquent on that.

Do the representations approach an ultimatum?

> We can't get the audience to sit still long enough to hear us, like some other audiences that I have addressed.

Could you tell us, when you catch them, what you are going to say to them?

No, that's too conjectural.

JRT transcript (WC, NjP) of CLSsh (C. L. Swem Coll., NjP).

To George C. Carothers and John Reid Silliman[1]

To Carrothers Torreon for Villa
and to Silliman, Tampico
for Caranza   [Washington] July 23 [1914], 5 pm

By direction of the President I send the following to be com-municated by you to——at once.

"Not only the United States, but all the world, will watch with the greatest interest and concern the course now to be pursued by the leaders of the Constitutionalist cause in effecting a trans-fer of power at Mexico City. This government feels that the critical time has come when the choice which is now to be made by the Constitutionalist leaders will practically determine the success or failure of the government they mean to set up and the reforms they hope to effect.

We venture to say this because of our earnest sympathy with the main purposes of the Constitutionalists and our desire to be of permanent service to them in bringing Mexico out of her troubles. We have been forced by circumstances into a position in which we must practically speak for the rest of the world. It is evident that the United States is the only first-class power that can be expected to take the initiative in recognizing the new government. It will in effect act as the representative of the other powers of the world in this matter and will unquestionably be held responsible by them for the consequences. Every step taken by the Constitutionalist leaders from this moment on and every-thing which indicates the spirit in which they mean to proceed and to consummate their triumph must of necessity, therefore, play a very important part in determining whether it will be pos-sible for the United States to recognize the government now being planned for.

In the most earnest spirit of friendship, therefore, this govern-ment wishes to call attention to the following matters of critical consequence:

First, the treatment of foreigners, foreign lives, foreign prop-erty, foreign rights, and particularly the delicate matter of the financial obligations, the legitimate financial obligations, of the government now superseded. Unless the utmost care, fairness and liberality are shown in these matters the most dangerous complications may arise.

Second, the treatment of political and military opponents. Unless there is to be a most generous amnesty it is certain that the sympathy of the whole world, including the people of the United States, now the real friends of the Constitutionalists, will be hopelessly alienated and the situation become impossible.

Third, the treatment of the Roman Catholic Church and of those who represent it. Nothing will shock the civilized world more than punitive or vindictive action towards priests or ministers of any church, whether Catholic or Protestant; and the Government of the United States ventures most respectfully but most earnestly to caution the leaders of the Mexican people on this delicate and vital matter. The treatment already said to have been accorded priests has had a most unfortunate effect upon opinion outside of Mexico.

You cannot too earnestly urge these matters upon the attention of those now in the counsels of the Constitutionalists. It is obvious to us that the whole future of what the Constitutionalists are attempting will depend upon the way and the spirit in which they deal with these questions. Nothing ought to be overlooked or dealt with hastily which may result in our being obliged to withhold the recognition of this government from the new government to be created at Mexico City as we withheld it from General Huerta. Our ability or inability to serve them they must now determine. *quote*   *Bryan*[2]

CLST telegram (SDR, RG 59, 812.00/14052a, DNA).
  [1] The words in italics in the following dispatch are WJBhw.
  [2] There is a WWsh draft of this telegram, dated July 23, 1914, in WP, DLC.

Two Letters to Thomas Davies Jones

My dear Friend: The White House July 23, 1914.

Your letter of the twentieth of July brings to me, I think, more kinds of regret than any other letter I ever received: regret, first of all, that the country should lose the invaluable services of such a man as I, and all fair-minded men who know you at all, know you to be; regret that I should have brought upon you so unpleasant an experience in which you were treated with gross and manifest injustice; regret that such circumstances should seem even for the moment to be associated with appointment to high office under the great government of the United States, representing a generous, fair, and honorable people; regret that the organization of a great banking system should be so embarrassed and obstructed.

The Rev. Dr. Isaac Stockton Keith Axson

The Rev. Dr. Joseph Ruggles Wilson

William Ewart Gladstone

Prospect Gate

Prospect Gardens

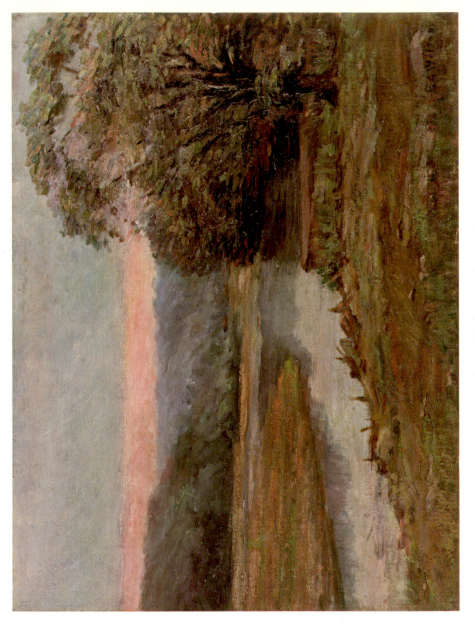

Scene Near Old Lyme, Connecticut

"Autumn," 1910

Pastoral

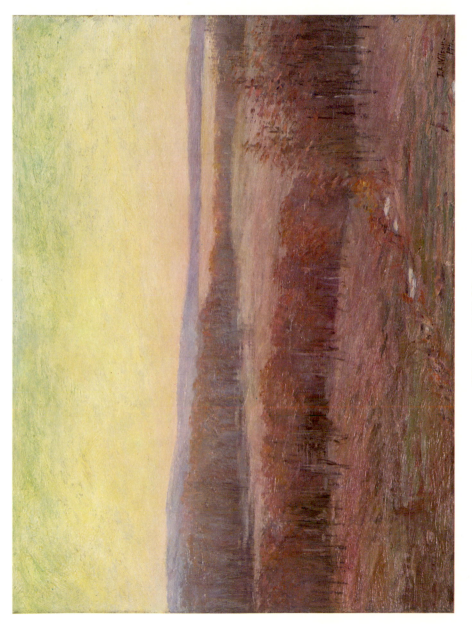

Woods and Fields, 1911

Apple Orchard

Moonlight Scene

Landscapes

You need not think that anything in the present circumstances has embarrassed me in the least. It causes me not the slightest embarrassment. I have no moment of hesitation or flagging enthusiasm, in standing by men whom I honor and believe in. It gives me nothing but pleasure and exhilaration to stand by them at any time and to any extent. You may leave my feelings (my feelings for myself) out of the reckoning.

The aspect of this matter which seems to me of gravest concern and consequence is that the choice of members of the Federal Reserve Board of the new banking system should have been made an occasion of partisan alignment and action. The adverse report on your nomination, to which you justly refer as unfair and untrue is, of course, not to be charged to the feeling or action of the Senate of the United States or to anything for which that great body as a whole can be held responsible. The report is signed only by the minority members of the committee[1] and by two members of the majority who have usually acted with them.[2] There is no reason to believe that either in its temper or in its conclusions that report represents the attitude of the Senate itself. I wish most heartily that the inauguration of the new national banking system, a system conceived and enacted with no element of partisanship in its objects or provisions, might have been free from this unfortunate and ominous incident.

I believe that the judgment and desire of the whole country cry out for a new temper in affairs. The time has come when discriminations against particular classes of men should be absolutely laid aside and discarded as unworthy of the counsels of a great people. The effort for genuine social justice, for peace, the peace which is founded in common understandings, and for prosperity, the prosperity of cooperation and mutual trust and confidence, should be a united effort without partisan prejudice or class antagonism. It is only of such just and noble elements that the welfare of a great country can be compounded. We have breathed already too long the air of suspicion and distrust. The progress of reform is not retarded by generosity and fairness.

Your action in requesting that your name be withdrawn displays your usual sensitive regard for considerations other than your own personal interest and sincerely as I regret it I can not but honor you for the action you have taken. I have no right to ask, much less to urge, that you continue to allow yourself to be made the football of the sort of contest which has sprung up over this nomination. It is a matter of genuine sorrow to me that a man like you should be excluded from the public service upon great occasion. But neither of us is responsible for these extraordinary circumstances. We must both accept them. I can not ask you to undergo more than you have undergone. I can only hope that better, cooler, wiser counsels may presently prevail.

Moreover, a great programme of corrective and constructive legislation is upon the eve of completion and I am sure that you would not wish, as I do not wish, anything of a personal character to stand, even temporarily, in its way, to delay or in any respect divert it. It is already clear that the country comprehends and will itself redress the injustice which has been done you.

With warmest regard,

Cordially and faithfully yours,   Woodrow Wilson[3]

[1] Joseph L. Bristow of Kansas, Coe I. Crawford of South Dakota, George P. McLean of Connecticut, Knute Nelson of Minnesota, and John W. Weeks of Massachusetts.

[2] Gilbert M. Hitchcock of Nebraska and James A. Reed of Missouri.

[3] There is an undated WWsh draft of this letter in WP, DLC. The exchange thus far was printed, e.g., in the *New York Times*, July 24, 1914.

My dear Friend: The White House July 23, 1914.

I cannot let this letter go without a supplement addressed to your private ear. I cannot say when I have had a disappointment which cut me more keenly than this of turning away from the possibility of having you as my colleague down here in the great work we are attempting for the government and the people. I rejoiced in an opportunity to show my confidence in you. Allow me now to express also my admiration and affection, and to say that I am facing this outcome of the matter with the keenest personal sorrow.

Cordially and sincerely yours,   Woodrow Wilson

TLS (Mineral Point, Wisc., Public Library).

To Francis Griffith Newlands

My dear Senator: [The White House] July 23, 1914

Thank you sincerely for your courtesy in sending me a copy of the last draft of the railways and securities bill. I have read it with attention and hope that it affords a solution of a very difficult matter. I am sincerely glad to know that the measure is complete and will be introduced at once.

Cordially and sincerely yours,   Woodrow Wilson

TLS (Letterpress Books, WP, DLC).

To Cyrus McCormick, Jr.

My dear Mr. McCormick: [The White House] July 23, 1914

I have not at present the text of the letter before me but I think the quotation you make from my letter about Mr. Jones is correct.

But you have put an entirely wrong construction on it. There is no man whom I respect or in whom I have a more complete and unwavering belief, as well as affection, than your father. I knew that Mr. Jones had gone into the directorate of the corporation at your father's request and that every purpose he had was also your father's purpose. I have been most unfortunate if I have conveyed any other implication. I wish now that I had made the statement differently. I was making it with all this in my mind and I am sure if you will recall the circumstances you will see that what I meant was true.

Hoping that you are enjoying your experiences at Oxford,
Sincerely yours,   Woodrow Wilson

TLS (Letterpress Books, WP, DLC).

To William Jennings Bryan

My dear Mr. Secretary: The White House July 23, 1914

Thank you sincerely for having let me see the enclosed.[1] I have read it with interest and the part you especially called my attention to with concern.[2]

Always
Cordially and faithfully yours,   Woodrow Wilson

TLS (W. J. Bryan Papers, DNA).
[1] G. C. Carothers to the Secretary of State, July 9, 1914, TLS (SDR, RG 59, 812.00/12717, DNA), enclosing a memorandum of agreement between certain *Carrancista* and *Villista* generals, T MS, *ibid.*, together with a handwritten translation of the memorandum, *ibid.* This agreement, signed at Torreón on July 8, stipulated that Villa's Division of the North recognized Carranza as First Chief of the Constitutionalist army, and that Villa would remain commander of the Division of the North. Carranza was to furnish Villa with all equipment and supplies necessary for the speedy and proper conduct of military operations. Villa was to have "freedom of action in administrative and military affairs," but was obliged to report his actions to Carranza for "rectification or ratification." The Divisions of the North and of the Northeast submitted a list of twelve men to Carranza "for him to choose from among them the members of his cabinet." Upon assuming the office of Provisional President of the Republic, Carranza was to call a convention made up of delegates from the Constitutionalist army to discuss the holding of national elections, the plan of government to be instituted, and "other topics of national interest." It was to be Carranza's "exclusive province" to appoint and remove governmental employees in the areas controlled by the Constitutionalists and to assign their jurisdictions, duties, and powers. Finally, the Divisions of the North and of the Northeast pledged themselves to fight on until the Federalist army had been completely vanquished, set up democratic institutions in the country, bring welfare to labor,

emancipate the peasants by equitable apportionment of land, and "correct, chastise and hold to their responsibilities" such members of the Roman Catholic clergy as had supported Huerta.

2 Bryan must have done this orally. Wilson undoubtedly referred to the provision promising punishment for certain Roman Catholic clergymen.

To Henry Lee Higginson

My dear Major Higginson: [The White House] July 24, 1914

Receipt of your telegram asking for a day's delay in the filing of the New Haven suit gave me hope that there might be daylight ahead. But when your letter came and I got into consultation with the Attorney General he informed me that, unfortunately, there was nothing in your letter that the department had not already considered. "Of course," he says in his letter to me, "there was a possibility that the Boston & Maine stock might be more advantageously marketed, if the Legislature of Massachusetts had not retained any rights in respect of it; but we have no power to control the action of that Commonwealth, and, if the New Haven people had accepted what was done, there would have been abundant time for them to return to the Legislature and ask for the removal of any restrictions too harsh practicably to be complied with."[1]

I feel that we have made the utmost effort on our part to arrange this matter in accordance with the law without suit and I regret more than I can say our failure.

Cordially and sincerely yours,   Woodrow Wilson

TLS (Letterpress Books, WP, DLC).
[1] Wilson was quoting from J. C. McReynolds to JPT, July 23, 1914, TLS (WP, DLC).

To Joseph R. Wilson Jr.

My dear Brother: The White House July 24, 1914

I thank you with all my heart for your letter of yesterday.[1] It has given me the deepest and most lasting sort of pleasure and has touched me very deeply.

Things go as usual with us. I wish Ellen were making more rapid progress, but I can't complain so long as she is making actual advance from day to day.

Please send our warmest love to your dear ones when you write.

In haste   Gratefully yours,   Woodrow Wilson

TLS (received from Sarah [Mrs. Jack B.] Harrie).
[1] J. R. Wilson, Jr. to WW, July 23, 1914, ALS (WP, DLC), praising Wilson's handling of the Mexican situation.

To William Jennings Bryan

My dear Mr. Secretary: The White House July 24, 1914

Thank you sincerely for having let me see the enclosed.[1] It is not only interesting but I think decidedly reassuring.

Cordially and sincerely yours,   Woodrow Wilson

TLS (W. J. Bryan Papers, DNA).

  [1] L. J. Canova to WJB, July 14, 1914, TLS (SDR, RG 59, 812.00/12564, DNA). Canova first reported on what he considered to be his successful efforts to persuade Carranza's advisers to take a more favorable view of Villa. He then discussed his interview with Carranza on July 14, for a summary of which see WJB to L. J. Canova, July 16, 1914, n. 1.

From Cleveland Hoadley Dodge

Confidential

My dear Mr President   New York July 24th 1914

Perkins told me on Sunday that the day before, when he was at Oyster Bay, the Colonel[1] suddenly remarked out of a clear sky, "Tell Cleve Dodge, when you see him, that Wilson loves him for his loyalty, but *I* love him for his many sins" (You can imagine the grin)   Which is the greater love, I do not know, but I am perfectly satisfied with your's, and your last expression of it, in your letter of 19th inst, has made me a very happy man.

I write now, not only to thank you heartily for all you say, and to express my thoro' approval of your plan to consult Col. House, but to tell you that I am obliged to leave here, the end of next week to be gone for about ten days. I have had no vacation yet, and I have to take the family up to Nonquit on Buzzards Bay where we have taken a cottage for August, and want to be with them there & on Corona for a few days, and do not expect to be back at my office, until August 11th & then only for a few days

If Col. House comes on a fast steamer & goes to Washington early next week, there would be ample time to make any necessary arrangement before I leave, early Friday afternoon, the 31st inst, but if there is no immediate hurry in the matter, it could wait. A line from him, telling me what to do will of course receive my prompt attention.

I have just written to Tom Jones, commiserating & congratulating him. How splendidly he has shown up. The letters which were in today's papers, were a credit to you both, & your noble tribute to him was beautiful. But, alas, the pity of it all!

I sincerely trust that you have entirely recovered your strength

& that the awful heat will not pull you down, & that Mrs Wilson may steadily gain

>With heartiest wishes for you all

>>Yours affectionately   C. H. Dodge

My heart is bubbling over with joy for you & the whole country, over the better outlook in Mexico

ALS (WP, DLC).
  [1] Theodore Roosevelt.

To Paul Moritz Warburg

My dear Mr. Warburg: [The White House] July 25, 1914

Of course, you have followed the recent developments here in connection with the nominations to the Federal Reserve Board, and I write to ask if you would be willing to reconsider your determination not to appear before the Senate Committee on Banking and Currency.

I hesitate to ask this question, because I know the position you have taken and the dignity and consistency with which you have maintained it, but, after all, the Senate Committee on Banking and Currency is doing nothing unprecedented in this matter. The Senate has always considered it a privilege of its committees to have personal interviews with men nominated for office and I feel that I could not in entire respect for the Senate request it to act upon your nomination in the present circumstances. It is rightly jealous of the prerogatives of its committees and I am sure that I have no desire to invade or deny those prerogatives in any way.

Of course, I am sincerely and deeply anxious to have you become a member of the Reserve Board. It is because of this desire on my part that I venture to put this question before you once again with the explanation I have made. May I not say that I hope that you will find it possible to appear before the committee and that your appearance there will enable me afterwards to have the genuine pleasure of urging your confirmation?[1]

I am sure that you will understand the circumstances and my motives in the matter and will not think that I am trying to force upon you anything that you may think inconsistent with your personal dignity.

>Cordially and sincerely yours,   Woodrow Wilson

TLS (Letterpress Books, WP, DLC).
  [1] Warburg swallowed his pride, appeared before the committee on August 1 and 3, and was confirmed on August 7.

From Charles William Eliot

Northeast Harbor, Maine, July 25, 1914.

Your New Haven letter shocks many friends and supporters because it attributes dishonorable conduct to honorable men, approves further attack on important railroad when public object[s] of original attacks have already been accomplished and calls trivial the Massachusetts proposal towards government ownership railroads cannot letter and suit be withdrawn or obliterated.   Charles W. Elliot.

T telegram (WP, DLC).

From William Lea Chambers[1]

Dear Mr. President: Chicago July 26, 1914.

I deeply regret the necessity of sending you this message, but a proper sense of my obligations to the public, my responsibilities in the execution of the law, and my duty to advise you in advance of conditions that may result in a national calamity, require it. On October tenth, 1913, the Brotherhood of Locomotive Engineers and the Brotherhood of Locomotive Enginemen and Firemen, acting in concert, served notice upon ninety-eight Railroad Companies operating 148,000 miles of track and including all that part of the country East of the territory traversed by the Illinois Central System, demanding improvements in conditions of service and increases in rates of pay. These demands were refused and on the same day the Railroad served notice abrogating all existing schedules throughout the territory and proposed the negotiation of an entirely new schedule of rules and rates, which the men refused. Lengthy correspondence and many conferences followed without reaching any conclusion. The contention grew severer and the parties drifted farther apart, until, in June a strike vote was taken, on all roads, and practically every one of the 56,000 engineers and firemen then in service voted to strike and notice to that effect was served on the Railway Companies on July 14th. On the 17th the Railroad[s] invoked the mediation services of the United States Board of Mediation and Conciliation after the employees had refused to join them in the request. The Board granted the request promptly and immediately tendered its services to the employees which they accepted, and Judge Knapp, Mr. Hanger[2] and I came at once to Chicago, as we regarded the situation grave enough to engage the best services of all the Mediation Officials. We arrived here last Monday morning and without delay began conferences with the parties, observing strictly our rule of meeting them separately in Executive Sessions, and from then until now day and night we have been employing our utmost endeavors to bring about an amicable settlement. Being convinced on Friday that mediation alone would not avail, we submitted to both parties a basis for arbitration as required by the Act of Congress, approved by you July 15, 1913, commonly known as the "Newlans' Law." Both parties declined the proposal. We held lengthy sessions with both parties yesterday (Saturday) and decided to re-submit our proposal accompanied with the *recommendation of the Board that it be accepted*. This has precipitated a very acute situation. The proposal is undoubtedly open to objections by either party, and neither of them has acted although in session until late last evening and have been in session all of this forenoon. The only encouraging feature of the situation is that our proposal has not been declined. It embodies what we believe to be the only basis of arbitration to which we see any chance of bringing the contestants. If both decline, then our efforts must end. If either declines we will continue our endeavors to avert the calamity. At the moment it appears as though one certainly, if not both, will decide to stand the consequences of a strike rather than yield.

The Railways are represented by a Conference Committee of managers composed of many able and long experienced officials. The employees are represented by their Executive Officials and ninety-eight general chairmen, one from each road. The meetings are held in separate halls in widely removed parts of the city, and the proceedings at each conference are conducted secretly, but so that everybody in the conference is kept fully informed.

I need not attempt to remind you of the dire and widespread effect of such a strike which would admittedly stop the movement of every train wheel in this vast territory. Mail train service would doubtless be resumed after some delay with irregularities, but all freight movement and much of the passenger service would be indefinitely suspended. The mining operations would stop at once, then the industries generally; all crop movements suddenly cease, 2,500,000 bushels of wheat, 750,000 bushels of corn, and a million bushels of other grains now being delivered daily at central distributing points; and then the insufferable conditions of the helpless millions of the people. With all the force at our command and with all the persuasiveness of our limited eloquence, we have depicted these possibilities. In view of the fact that the Government directly is so largely interested, and in a much broader sense, because of its obligations to the public, I have thought that you should be made fully acquainted with the situation. Such a strike as this one would be, will not only check the return of prosperity, of which there are unmistakable evidences on every hand, but would be most harmful to the policies of your administration. Coming just at this time it would be in full swing, or rather its ill effects would be most conspicuous at the time of the Fall elections. If there is a change in the situation to more favorable conditions it will give me much pleasure to advise you by wire.   Very respectfully,   W. L. Chambers

TLS (WP, DLC).
 1 Commissioner of the United States Board of Mediation and Conciliation.
 2 Martin Augustine Knapp, chairman of the U. S. Board of Mediation and Conciliation and also judge of the Circuit Court of Appeals of the 4th judicial circuit; Grossbrenner Wallace William Hanger, assistant commissioner of the U. S. Board of Mediation and Conciliation.

Portion of Remarks at a Press Conference

July 27, 1914

Mr. President, I don't know whether you deem it wise to say anything at all on the subject, but I would like to ask you whether the United States is in a position to maintain the peace of Europe at this time.

> Well, that is a matter which it would be, perhaps, unwise for me to say anything about. I can only say that the United States has never attempted to interfere in European affairs.

JRT transcript (WC, NjP) of CLSsh (C. L. Swem Coll., NjP).

To Various Dominican Leaders[1]

San Domingo. Proposed Memorandum.   [July 27, 1914]

The Government of the United States desires nothing for itself from the Dominican republic and no concessions or advantages for its citizens which are not accorded citizens of other countries. It desires only to prove its sincere and disinterested friendship for the republic and its people and to fulfill its responsibilities as the friend to whom in such crises as the present all the world looks to guide San Domingo out of its difficulties.

It, therefore, makes the following earnest representations not only to the existing *de facto* government of the Dominican republic, but also to all who are in any way responsible for the present posture of affairs there:

I. It warns everyone concerned that it is absolutely imperative

that the present hostilities should cease and that all who are concerned in them should disperse to their several homes, disband-
ing the existing armed forces and returning to the peaceful
occupations upon which the welfare of the people of the republic depends. This is necessary, and necessary at once. Nothing
can be successfully accomplished until this is done.

II. It is also necessary that there should be an immediate
reconstitution of political authority in the republic. To this end
the Government of the United States very solemnly advises all
concerned with the public affairs of the republic to adopt the
following plan:

(1) Let all those who have any pretensions to be chosen President of the republic and who can make any sufficient show of
exercising a recognized leadership and having an acknowledged
following agree upon some responsible and representative man
to act as provisional President of the republic, it being understood that Mr. Bordas will relinquish his present position and
authority. If these candidates can agree in this matter, the Government of the United States will recognize and support the man
of their choice as provisional President. If they cannot agree,
the Government of the United States will itself name a provisional President, sustain him in the assumption of office, and
support him in the exercise of his temporary authority. The
Provisional President will not be a candidate for President.[2]

(2) At the earliest feasible date after the establishment and
recognition of the provisional government thus established let
elections for a regular President and Congress be held under the
authority and direction of the provisional President, who will,
it must, of course, be understood, exercise during his tenure
of office the full powers of President of the republic; but let it
be understood that the Government of the United States will
send representatives of its own choosing to observe the election throughout the republic and that it will expect those
observers not only to be accorded a courteous welcome, but also
to be accorded the freest opportunities to observe the circumstances and processes of the election.

(3) Let it be understood that if the United States Government
is satisfied that these elections have been free and fair and carried
out under conditions which enable the people of the republic to
express their real choice, it will recognize the President and Congress thus chosen as the legitimate and constitutional government of the republic and will support them in the exercise of their
functions and authority in every way it can. If it should not be
satisfied that elections of the right kind have been held, let it be

understood that another election will be held at which the mistakes observed will be corrected.

III. A regular and constitutional government having thus been set up, the Government of the United States would feel at liberty thereafter to insist that revolutionary movements cease and that all subsequent changes in the government of the republic be effected by the peaceful processes provided in the Dominican constitution. By no other course can the Government of the United States fulfill its treaty obligations with San Domingo or its tacitly conceded obligations as the nearest friend of San Domingo in her relations with the rest of the world.[3]

CLST MS (SDR, RG 59, 839.00/1582, DNA).

[1] The following document was handed to John Franklin Fort, Charles Cogeswell Smith, and Minister James M. Sullivan, special commissioners to the Dominican Republic, on August 10. About the background and dénouement, see Arthur S. Link, *Wilson: The Struggle for Neutrality, 1914-1915* (Princeton, N. J., 1960), pp. 511-16.

[2] This sentence WJBhw.

[3] There is a WWsh draft of this document, dated July 27, 1914, in WP, DLC.

To Charles William Eliot

My dear Doctor Eliot: The White House July 27, 1914

I have read your telegram of July twenty-fifth with real concern. I was not aware that my letter attributed dishonorable conduct to anybody. It merely stated what I am sorry to say is my real opinion, that they were not justified for the reason they gave in receding from the understanding which had been arrived at with the Department of Justice. I think that their conduct was a very grave mistake not only, but without support of sufficient reason.

It always pains me to differ with you in opinion, but I have been over this matter so often and so carefully with the Attorney General that my views are very deeply rooted.

          Cordially and sincerely yours,   Woodrow Wilson

TLS (photostat in RSB Coll., DLC).

From Samuel Gompers

Sir: Washington, D. C., July 27, 1914

At the meeting of the Executive Council of the American Federation of Labor, the vacancy existing upon the Supreme Court bench became a subject of interesting discussion, and the question of the propriety of writing you in connection herewith, that is, in regard to the appointment to be made by you to fill that vacancy was also considered. Inasmuch as the matter is of such great moment, and that other bodies of citizens as well as citizens in their individual capacity have addressed former Presidents in like manner, the undersigned was directed to submit for your consideration the following:

It is not a reflection upon the character or honor of the distinguished men who have occupied the exalted position of Justices of the Supreme Court and other courts of our country, to say that often their concept of right and justice, their understanding of the newer ideas and ideals of social justice, have been absent from their trend of thought and decisions.

The members of the Executive Council find themselves in happy, mental and hearty accord with the declarations in your book, "The New Freedom," in which you say:

Yesterday, and ever since history began, men were related to one another as individuals. * * * To-day the every-day relationships of men are largely with great impersonal concerns, with organizations, not with other individual men.

Now this is nothing short of a new social age, a new era of human relationships, a new stage-setting for the drama of life.

There is no doubt in my mind and in the minds of my associates that the general trend of your activities is in exact line with this, your excellent expression of thought and purpose, and yet, it may not be amiss, although perhaps entirely unnecessary, to say that there are no men occupying positions as governmental agents so potent to give final expression to these thoughts as are the Justices of the great courts of our country.

We have no candidate to present, no name to suggest for your consideration, to be appointed as an Associate Justice of the United States Supreme Court, but we entertain the hope that the gentleman upon whom the great honor will be conferred will be one whose learning and whose sympathies will lean toward the newer concepts of the essentials of social justice.

As representatives of a great body of your fellow citizens, on behalf of the Executive Council of the American Federation of Labor, I have the honor respectfully to present these matters to your consideration.

I beg to remain,

Very respectfully yours,   Saml. Gompers.

TLS (WP, DLC).

From Thomas Davies Jones

My dear Mr President   Chicago July 27, 1914

Your private note accompanying your letter of the 23rd inst is in truth and soberness a precious possession. It gave and still gives me that choking sensation which assures me that I have not yet passed into the state or period of eternal cold.

I am sure that the appeal which you make for a "new temper in affairs" will meet with quick response. I enclose an editorial note from the Chicago Herald.[1]

I do hope Mrs. Wilson is getting to be herself again.

Ever Faithfully Yours   Thomas D Jones

ALS (WP, DLC).
[1] "The President's Appeal for 'A New Temper,'" *Chicago Herald*, July 25, 1914.

George C. Carothers to William Jennings Bryan

El Paso, Texas, July 27, 1914, 11 p.m.

Arrived Chihuahua Saturday night. I saw Villa on Sunday, returned here immediately to earnestly request come to Washington to personally confer with you. Villa claims Carranza has repudiated secret and other clauses Torreon agreement causing very critical situation which the President and you should clearly understand. Villa earnestly desired that I relate situation to you in person. He will make no move in the meantime. Please rush answer. Can leave Tuesday two thirty afternoon.

G. C. Carothers.

T telegram (WP, DLC).

To Walter Hines Page

The White House. July 28, 1914.

Is there in your opinion any likelihood that the good offices of the United States if offered under Article Three of the Hague convention would be acceptable or serve any high purpose in the present crisis?   Bryan.

T telegram (SDR, RG 59, 763.72119, DNA).

To Edward Parker Davis

My dear Davis: [The White House] July 28, 1914

Thank you warmly for your note of the other day about Jones.[1] It was a keen disappointment to me, but bringing me as it does such notes as yours there are compensations.

Mrs. Wilson's troubles are constantly taking on new forms and she seems, I must say, at present to be making little progress, and yet it still seems certain that there is nothing organic the matter and we are hoping and believing that it is only the weather that holds her back.

With warmest regard from us all,

Affectionately yours,   Woodrow Wilson

TLS (Letterpress Books, WP, DLC).
  [1] E. P. Davis to WW, July 25, 1914, ALS (WP, DLC).

From Robert Latham Owen

My dear Mr. President: [Washington] July 28, 1914.

I send you my report on the Stock Exchange Regulation Bill, and the Bill itself,[1] and I earnestly request you to give it your immediate attention.

No part of your trust program is more important than the control of the stock exchanges, where every panic has had its breeding place and where the enemies of fair play manipulate the markets, to the enormous loss of the people who are lured by the gambling spirit, by hope, and by "sure tips."

I wish to confer with you when you have read this report, if you will indicate the time it will suit your convenience.

Yours, faithfully   Robt L. Owen

TLS (WP, DLC).
  [1] Owen's bill to regulate stock exchanges was introduced in the Senate on January 12, 1914. It provided that all stock exchanges had to be incorporated in the states in which they were located and required full disclosure of the facts about the formation and management of every concern the securities of which were listed on the exchanges. The Postmaster General was charged with the enforcement of these and other provisions of the bill and was required to close the mails and telegraph and telephone lines to the transmission of quotations unless the exchanges had complied with all its requirements (New York *World*, Jan. 11, 1914). As early as January 22, Wilson let it be known that Owen's bill was not a part of the administration's antitrust program, on the ground that the Baltimore platform did not call for such legislation (*New York Times*, Jan. 23, 1914). The measure was reported from the banking and currency committee to the Senate on June 24 but was recommitted to the committee on June 26. It never re-emerged. For further details, see Cedric B. Cowing, *Populists, Plungers, and Progressives: A Social History of Stock and Commodity Speculation, 1890-1936* (Princeton, N. J., 1965), pp. 55-62.

Myron Timothy Herrick to William Jennings Bryan

Paris. July 28, 1914. Rec'd 7:30 P.M.

Confidential. To be communicated to the President:

Situation in Europe is regarded here as the gravest in history. It is apprehended that civilization is threatened by demoralization which would follow a general conflagration. Demonstrations made against war here last night by laboring classes; it is said to be the first instance of its kind in France. It is felt that if Germany once mobilizes no backward step will be taken. France has strong reliance on her army but it is not giving way to undue excitement. There is a faith and reliance on our high ideals and purposes so that I believe expression from our nation would have great weight in this crisis. My opinion is encouraged at reception given utterances of British Minister for Foreign Affairs. I believe that a strong plea for delay and moderation from the President of the United States would meet with the respect and approval of Europe and urge the prompt consideration of this question. This suggestion is consistent with our plea for arbitration treaties and attitude toward world affairs generally. I would not appear officious but deem it my duty to make this expression to you.

Herrick.

T telegram (WP, DLC).

To Samuel Gompers

My dear Mr. Gompers: [The White House] July 29, 1914

I have your letter of July twenty-seventh and have read it with attention and sympathy. I shall certainly try to select for the Supreme Court a man of adequate breadth of sympathy and perception.   Sincerely yours,   Woodrow Wilson

TLS (Letterpress Books, WP, DLC).

From Martin Augustine Knapp and Others

Chicago, Illinois, July 29, 1914.

It is greatly to be feared that a strike of the engineers and firemen on all the Western roads cannot be averted. On Friday last after five days and nights of repeated conferences we succeeded in getting both parties to withdraw what seemed to be the most objectionable of their demands, but we then became convinced and now regard it as certain that a peaceable solution of the dispute could be found only in an arbitration of the remaining demands of the employees, the other counter demands of the railroads to be withdrawn. We accordingly proposed this plan of arbitration and recommended to both parties its adoption. After two days of strenuous endeavor and with the aid of their leaders the men finally voted to accept our proposal but the railroad managers refuse to accept and will not consent to any arbitration which does not also include the submission of some of their own demands, this the employees absolutely reject. We have exhausted every effort to find some other basis of adjustment which both parties would accept but it appears now out of the question, neither side shows any disposition to yield. We deeply regret giving you this information but believe it our duty to do so.

Martin A. Knapp, W. L. Chambers, and G. W. Hanger.

T telegram (WP, DLC).

To Martin Augustine Knapp and Others

[The White House] July 29, 1914.

Before final adverse decision by either side I think it my duty to ask for a conference with representatives of both sides designated to confer with me. Please arrange such a conference. Mediation must not fail.[1]   Woodrow Wilson

T telegram (Letterpress Books, WP, DLC).
    [1] There is a WWhw draft of this telegram in WP, DLC.

From Walter Hines Page

Dear Mr. President: London July 29 1914

Yesterday before the news came that war had begun between Austria and Servia, yielding to the impulse that every American feels, I went to see Sir Edward Grey and told him that I had come on my own initiative informally to ask him if he saw any way in which the good offices of our Government cd. be used and that, if he did or should see any way, I prayed that he wd. inform me. He thanked me with feeling and said that he knew that the good influence of the United States cd. be counted on for peace and he promised to inform me if he shd. see anything that we cd. do. I reminded him again that I had no instructions, but I reminded him also of your wish (of wh. I felt sure) and of the feeling of the whole American people.

Then this morning came Mr. Bryan's telegram of inquiry

whether I saw a way for us to help. I immediately sent that to
Sir Edward with a reminder of our conversation. There the matter for the moment rests. I do not yet see any way in wh. we
could help, for England seems to me to be doing everything that
can be done—England, with more direct influence on the Continental Powers that we cd. have. There has been running
through my mind vaguely all day the query whether perhaps we
might not in some way add our voice to England's—the wisdom
or the uselessness of wh. you will have seen and decided before
you receive this—in case the danger of a general war continue.

I think that every Ambassador here saw Sir Edw. yesterday
and I purposely waited till late in the afternoon when they—all
the rest—had all gone. I think I shall never forget yesterday. There
sat this always solitary man—he and I, of course, in the room
alone, each, I am sure, giving the other his full confidence. He
looked 10 years older than he looked a month ago. He told me a
day or two after the murder of the heir to the Austrian throne
that he feared just what has happened and worse than has yet
happened. He is, I imagine, the foremost Forn. Sect'y in Europe.
He has held this office 8 years. He knows his European politics
as perhaps no other man knows it. He is a forward-looking
liberal-minded man—a sort of sad and wise idealist, restrained
and precise in speech and sparing in his use of words, a genuine,
clear-thinking man whose high hopes for mankind suffer sad
rebuffs but are never quenched—a grave philosopher who feels
the prodigious responsibility he carries. He had received Germany's refusal of his proposition of an Ambassadorial Conference. He was grieved but I think not surprised. He still had hope
that Russia and Austria wd. get together directly. "If Germany
wd. give the word," said he, "war wd. be averted." Throughout
his frank talk I felt the possibility of a sort of crack of doom for
Continental Europe.

This is the man who if the Liberals lose and win again in 10
years or if they hold on for a few years more, will be Prime Minister. Even the Conservative papers today, in spite of the intense
party feeling, praise him and call on the whole Nation to stand
behind him.

A few hours later I went to dinner at Lord Glenconner's whose
family are all especial friends of Sir Edw; and he was there. I
do not often meet him dining out. He spends his evenings in the
House and later at home with his dispatches and reports, and he
frequently does several hours' work in bed in the morning.
At dinner he was the same sad figure, saying little, absorbed,
waking up once in a while with a smile and then slipping back

into silence. After dinner there was music and he sat in a corner of the room—alone. He folded his arms and mechanically kept time with his foot, of course not hearing the music or anything else. The hostess sought him and marched him across the room, and he affected a certain gayety wh. fooled nobody, not even himself. Lady Glenconner told me that he spent Sunday at her country house. In the afternoon he and she took a long walk and he told the whole European-political story to her two or three times. After they came back to the house, he went off on a still longer walk alone.

All this is intensely interesting to me. Here is a great and sincere man working with a great government as his tool, working to save Europe from itself and (most likely) failing. Monarchy and privilege and pride will have it out before they die—at what cost! If they do have a general war they will so set back the march of progress in Europe as to set the day forward for American leadership. Men here see that clearly. Even in this Kingdom every ship is ready, every crew on duty and every officer of the Admiralty office in London sleeps with a telephone by his bed wh. he expects to ring and the telegraph men are at their instruments every minute. But of all men here the most impressive is the brooding, saddened, solitary Foreign Secretary, at whom men turn back and gaze as he drives along the street and for whose success every wise man in all Europe prays to-night. And he will tell me with a melancholy smile the next time I see him of his unfortunate fate that he cannot go fishing.

It's the Slav and the German. Each wants his day, and neither has got beyond the stage of tooth and claw. While I was talking to Sir Edw. Mrs. Page was talking to a brother of King Peter of Servia, a ferocious Slav who wishes to fight, who talks like a mediaeval man and so loves the blood of his enemies that, if he can first kill enough of them, he is willing to be whipped. He went home last night. Meantime the price of bread has risen even in England.

Again and ever I thank Heaven for the Atlantic ocean.

Very heartily yours,   Walter H. Page

ALS (WP, DLC).

Walter Hines Page to William Jennings Bryan

London, July 29, 1914, Rec'd. 11:10 A.M.

Your undated telegram received this morning. I informally requested Sir Edward Grey yesterday that if the good offices of the United States could at anytime or in any possible way be used please to inform me. He expressed his thanks and said he would do so. I am renewing the same suggestion today.

Page.

T telegram (WP, DLC).

Remarks at a Press Conference

July 30, 1914

Mr. President, have you taken any action at all on behalf of this government in connection with the war in Europe?

No, sir. . . .

Has there been any suggestion, Mr. President, from any of the governments of the world that we might offer our services?

None at all that have reached me.

Mr. President, have you considered offering such services on your own initiative?

I have practically answered that question. I don't see the key yet to the situation—what lock to insert it in. . . .

Mr. President, can you tell us what the status of Mr. Warburg's case is, as you understand it?

Well, I understand, just as I have seen it reported, that Mr. Warburg is coming down and will certainly meet with the Senate committee, as I understand it. His message to me[1] was practically the same that the papers contained this morning.

In merely having an informal conference with some of the senators preliminary to going before the committee?

I don't know about that. You see, I don't know what Senator Hitchcock or Senator O'Gorman may have said to him, or what expectations they led him to have about it.

Mr. President, in view of the expectation of the six weeks before adjournment, has there been any change in the attitude toward the Colombian and Nicaraguan treaties, or any treaty pending?

No, there has been no change of attitude on this end at all. I don't know of any on the other end.

Have you chosen a successor to Mr. Jones?

No. I hope to do that within a very short time.

Have you decided on the locality from which he will come?

I am trying to find a man from the same general region. . . .

Mr. President, it was announced yesterday that Judge Alexander of the Merchant Marine and Fisheries Committee would discuss with you certain features of the seamen's bill and the London Safety-at-Sea Convention.

That was to save time. I have received a number of letters from men who evidently knew what they were talking about, calling attention to the public oppression of some of the crews; and I had sent those letters to Judge Alexander, and he came in to discuss the question whether these gentlemen understood thoroughly the operation of the bill or not, just to clear up doubts about it.

Does it appear from yesterday's talk that the measure will be passed this session?

It wouldn't appear whether it would or not. Of course, it has no place on the agenda on the calendar. It may be it will be crowded out. I don't know. You see, questions of this sort arise: The bill provides that the crews of vessels shall be made up of men who can understand the orders of officers, as well as that they themselves understand and speak the same language, to that extent, at any rate; and that affects the shipping on this side of the continent in a different way from that which would affect the shipping on the Pacific coast. There are difficult questions of that sort which have to be canvassed.

Mr. President, have you gone at all into the probable effect of the European war on business conditions in this country?

Not at all yet. I have been hoping and praying there may not be any general European war.

Mr. President, have you made any plans for the fall campaign tour?

No, none at all. . . .

Mr. President, do you care to say what Mr. Chalmers[2] reported on conditions?

I am quite willing to say anything that I recall that was significant. Mr. Chalmers said that his business for the year had been better than in previous years. I am speaking—I don't remember how many years he said. At any rate, the business was everything he could desire, though he did say that during the last two months, I believe it was, there had been somewhat more than the seasonal falling off in sales—still leaving the average for the fiscal year, however, above previous years.

He explained to me that so soon after new models are announced, people are apt to stop buying, because they want to wait for the next year's models. That always happens, but it has gone a little further this year than previously. I think that was the sum and substance.

Did he support you in passing the legislation before the end of the session?

Very heartily. Strangely enough, although one was led to believe that the preference of the business community was the other way at one time, it seems unmistakably in that direction now. I think reflection has shown that it, incidentally, is just the very thing they want to get passed.

Mr. President, did you get that from the wholesalers[3] yesterday also?

Yes. They didn't come to offer the least objection to the legislation. On the contrary, they came to express some of that, but they came to offer details and express certain objections to the Clayton bill. I hope I was able to throw a little new light on the sections that they referred to.

Mr. President, did you take any definite action in Santo Domingo or Haiti?

That is not in a position lately to be discussed because it is in flux in both places.

Is there any prospect or has any progress been made in the efforts to send the—to send Americans to Haiti?

No.

Mr. President, a great deal has been published in the Philadelphia newspapers regarding—about your interest in the Pennsylvania state fight, and there has also been a good deal said about dissatisfaction in the Democratic party over there. Has that been discussed with you recently?

No, it has not. And I dare say the speculations are wide of the mark. I don't appear to see them.

JRT transcript (WC, NjP) of CLSsh (C. L. Swem Coll., NjP).

[1] P. M. Warburg to WW, July 29, 1914, T telegram (WP, DLC), and P. M. Warburg to WW, July 29, 1914, TLS (WP, DLC).

[2] Hugh Chalmers, an automobile manufacturer, visited Wilson at the White House on July 29.

[3] A delegation from the National Trade Association of Wholesalers visited the White House on July 29 to discuss the pending antitrust legislation and business conditions generally. They proposed some specific changes in the Clayton bill and the trade commission bill. Wilson agreed with some of the proposals but rejected others. His remarks were generally conciliatory, stressing that the administration and Congress were not "running amuck" but rather were seeking to put an end to an era of "ceaseless agitation about business" through constructive legislation. For a detailed report of this meeting, as well as that with Hugh Chalmers, see the *New York Times*, July 30, 1914.

To Charles Allen Culberson

My dear Senator: [The White House] July 30, 1914

It was very kind of you to send me a copy of the amendment to Section V of the Trades Commission Bill which you introduced yesterday. I venture to drop you this line to suggest my very grave doubt as to the advisability of attempting any definition whatever of unfair competition. It seems to me that we ought to leave it for the plotting out it will get by individual decisions with regard to particular cases and situations, just as we have been obliged to plot fraud out in the same way by the processes of experience and the examination of particular relationships. I think that what is most to be desired in the Legislation we are now contemplating is elasticity without real indefiniteness, so that we may adjust our regulation to actual conditions, local as well as national.

I hope that you will pardon this suggestion.

Cordially and sincerely yours, Woodrow Wilson

TLS (Letterpress Books, WP, DLC).

To Walter Hines Page

My dear Page: [The White House] July 30, 1914

This will introduce to you Mr. Samuel G. Blythe. It seems superfluous to introduce Mr. Blythe. Of course, you know him and, of course, you know his extraordinary gifts. Perhaps if you have not met him, you do not know how delightful a fellow he is. I am sure I shall be contributing to your pleasure by enabling you to know him personally.

Cordially and faithfully yours, Woodrow Wilson

TLS (Letterpress Books, WP, DLC).

From Joseph Edward Davies

My dear Mr. President: Washington July 30, 1914.

Pursuant to your suggestion, I have examined Section 4 and Section 9-b of the Clayton Bill, with reference to the leasing or selling of goods on condition that the purchaser or lessee shall not use or deal in the goods of a competitor, and find that your impression, as stated, is sustained by the language of the bill.

The Clayton Bill, considered alone, in Section 4, very evidently intends to *absolutely prohibit* such conditions in contracts for sale *under any and all circumstances*. There are no exceptions as to its enforcement provided for by statute. The words of Section 9-b are mandatory:

> Whenever the Commission * * * has reason to believe * * * that any corporation is violating any provisions of Section 4 * * * *it shall* issue and cause to be served a notice * * * upon such corporation, who shall thereupon be called upon * * * to appear and show cause why an order should not issue to restrain the *violation* charged.

It would appear conclusively therefore that the Commission's only duty would be to determine whether Section 4 had been violated, and then to enter a restraining order. In the face of such an express and definite prohibition as is contained in Section 4, the Commission, in case it decided that a particular contract of this kind was not inimical to the public welfare and was therefore not unfair by reason of certain conditions, would be placed in the position of making an exception to the law which Congress itself had refused to make and enact into law.

If we were to consider Section 5 of the Newlands Bill in conjunction with Section 4 and Section 9-b of the Clayton Bill, the same conclusion, I think, must be reached. The Newlands Bill simply contains a general prohibition of unfair competition. Section 4 of the Clayton Bill is specific in its terms, and I think that under the rules of construction the courts would undoubtedly hold that the general prohibition as to unfair competition would not permit the exercise of discretion on a set of facts where the prohibition was mandatory, as contained in Section 4 of the Clayton Bill.

Section 4, therefore, of the Clayton Bill, as it stands, is fixed and inelastic, and does not permit of the exercise of any discretion by the Commission, as to whether in a given instance such a conditional sale might be advantageous to the public welfare. If the conditional sale exists, it must be restrained, regardless of any possible salutary rather than inimical effect upon the public.   Faithfully yours,   Joseph E. Davies

TLS (WP, DLC).

To John Reid Silliman[1]

Washington, July 31, 1914, 12 m.

Our telegram of July twenty-third, five p.m., was not meant to imply the slightest lack of confidence in the first chief or in any of the leaders of the constitutionalist cause, but we deemed it imperatively necessary as an act of friendship to apprise General Carranza and his associates, now rather than later when it might be too late to serve them, of the circumstances upon which we know their success to depend. Excesses of any kind, even toward their own people, and especially extreme measures against political opponents or representatives of the church, if such excesses should occur in connection with their assumption of power at Mexico City, might make it morally impossible for the United States to recognize the new government. Without recognition that government could obtain no loans and must speedily break down. The existence of war in Europe would clearly make it impossible to obtain assistance anywhere on the other side of the water, even if such excesses as we have alluded to did not themselves make it impossible; and such excesses would be quite as certain to alienate sympathy in Europe as they would be to alienate sympathy in the United States. After the new government is established it can adopt such deliberate and well-considered policies toward its own people and its own domestic institutions as it deems best and can successfully and temperately work out; but vindictive and punitive measures adopted at the out-set and carried into effect by military force and authority are quite a different matter and might have the most far-reaching and disastrous results. This government would not be dealing frankly with General Carranza and his associates if it did not state these facts very plainly now, before it is too late; and it cannot state them too plainly. The success or failure of the constitutionalist cause is to be determined now at the out-set; it is to be judged by what happens now in connection with the transfer of power. The advice offered and everything stated in our telegram of the twenty-third cannot be abated or sub-tracted from in the least without deep and perhaps fatal harm to the prospects of the present revolution, which, if that advice is heeded, in the spirit in which it is given, may now be made completely and gloriously successful. This government is reluc-tant to contemplate the possible consequences to Mexico if it should be forced to withhold recognition from those who are now to succeed General Huerta. It is our plain duty as friends, therefore, to reiterate with deep earnestness all that we have said. Our recent messages have of course been most deliberately con-ceived, with a full consciousness of all they implied, and were sent with a very solemn feeling of our responsibility to Mexico, to ourselves, and to the world. Bring the foregoing to the atten-tion of General Carranza.[2]   Bryan.

T telegram (SDR, RG 59, 812.00/27481a, DNA).
    [1] There is a WWsh draft of this telegram, dated July 29, 1914, and a WWT draft, dated July 29, 1914, in WP, DLC.
    [2] This last sentence was added by someone in the State Department.

From Edward Mandell House

Dear Governor: Prides Crossing, Mass. July 31st, 1914.

When I was in Germany it seemed clear to me that the situation, as far as a continuation of peace was concerned, was in a very precarious state and you will recall my first letter to you telling of the high tension that Germany and Southeastern Europe were in.

I tried to convey this feeling to Sir Edward Grey and other members of the British Government, but they seemed astonished at my pessimistic view and thought that conditions were better than they had been for a long time.

While I shook their confidence, at the same time, I did not do it sufficiently to make them feel that quick action was necessary. Consequently they let matters drag until after the Kaiser had gone into Norwegian waters for his vacation before giving me any definite word to send to him.

It was my purpose to go back to Germany and see the Emperor, but the conservative delay of Sir Edward and his confreres made that impossible.

The night before I sailed Sir Edward sent me word that he was worried over conditions, but he anticipated nothing of what has followed.

I have a feeling that if a general war is finally averted it will be because of the better understanding that has been brought about between England and Germany. England is exercising a restraining hand upon France and, as far as possible, upon Russia, but her influence with the latter is slight.

If the matter could have been pushed a little further, Germany would have laid a heavy hand upon Austria and peace would have continued until a better understanding could have been brought about.

Russia thought, so I was told in England, that Germany was trying to project Austrian and German influence deep into the Balkan States in order to check her. She has evidently been preparing for some decisive action since the Kaiser threw several hundred thousand troops on his eastern frontier two years ago, compelling Russia to relinquish the demand that she had made in regard to a settlement of Balkan matters.

What I particularly want to say to you is that if either now or at any time soon you feel that you may be able to use me to advantage in this trouble, I shall be, as always, entirely at your command.

Both Germany and England know that I hold your confidence,

and I would perhaps understand better how to proceed than one new to the situation as I am in close touch with both Governments.

For the moment, I do not see what can be done, but if war comes, it will be swift and terrible and there may be a time soon when your services will be gladly accepted. It is then I would hope to be of use to you.

Your faithful and affectionate,   E. M. House

TLS (WP, DLC).

A News Report

[*July 31, 1914*]

PUT WORLD TRADE UNDER FLAG OF U. S.,
PRESIDENT'S PLAN

WASHINGTON, July 31.—With a general European war believed to be almost a certainty by the Administration, President Wilson to-day took steps toward developing the merchant marine of the United States so that ships flying the American flag may become the carriers of the world.

He summoned to a conference at the White House Senator Kern, the Democratic leader of the Senate; Senator Clarke, Chairman of the Committee on Commerce; Leader Underwood of the House and Chairman Adamson of the House Committee on Interstate and Foreign Commerce.

The object of this conference was to discuss ways and means to develop in a hurry the merchant marine. If necessary the President will ask Congress to amend the American ship registration laws so as to let in more foreign built ships.

The President had already taken up with Secretary Redfield the matter of a threatened world-wide blockade of the sea against the ships of most nations except those of the United States. A general tie-up of all the ships that fly the flags of the nations involved in the war in Europe, Mr. Redfield told the President, will paralyze international commerce.

The serious feature of this situation would be an almost certain paralysis of commerce, and without ships this country would be unable to ship its goods and its products abroad, where they would command high prices.

An instance at hand was the fact that in Chicago to-day the bears knocked wheat down 6 cents a bushel because of the threatened lack of vessels to carry the grain to Europe.

Representatives Underwood and Adamson, after the conference, began a search for information on the subject of the world's
merchant marine, the number of ships and officers, and clerks
were turned loose in the reference library to find all that has
been written on crises similar to the present one.

Printed in the New York *World*, Aug. 1, 1914.

Walter Hines Page to William Jennings Bryan

London. July 31, 1914. Rec'd 5:54 P.M.

I am just come from a talk with Sir Edward Grey. He again
expressed his great gratitude for the suggestion of offering the
good offices of the United States in case they could be used.
After the failure of his proposal of an ambassadorial conference
to prevent Austria from going to war with Servia he made
proposals looking to the localization of hostilities and he has yet
received no responses. Grey asked me if the United States has
offered its good offices at Vienna or Saint Petersburg or Berlin,
about which, of course, I have no information. Perhaps you will
inform me of proposals or other actions of our government if it
does anything.

There is great gloom here this afternoon. As Grey expressed
it, "it looks as if Europe were in the clutch of blind forces."

Page.

T telegram (WP, DLC).

A News Report

[*Aug. 1, 1914*]

NEW SHIPPING BILL
WILL BE PUSHED THROUGH MONDAY

WASHINGTON, Aug. 1.—Faced by the gravest international
situation in history, President Wilson, Democratic Leader Underwood and Representative Carter Glass, Chairman of the House
Banking and Currency Committee, to-day completed the plans
for legislation to furnish immediate relief to the American
business world. The House on Monday probably will pass the
Emergency Currency act,[1] already passed by the Senate, and
also with the greatest possible speed a bill written to-day by the
President and Representative Underwood, designed to admit
foreign ships to American registry.

The Merchant Marine bill was drafted in the White House after Mr. Underwood and the President had talked of the situation confronting the world. Mr. Underwood had with him information as to the carrying power of all the merchant vessels afloat, together with suggestions as to whether they would be able to be registered as American craft in view of the fact that many European ships will undoubtedly be grabbed by their own Governments for war purposes.

The President and Representative Underwood both realized that the situation regarding the scarcity of ships to carry American produce is one of gravity. The President was told that if all the nations of Europe become embroiled the ships of neutral countries now plying the Atlantic can handle but 17 per cent. of the normal American transatlantic freight. He was also shown that ships of British registry carry over 60 per cent. and German ships carry 18 per cent. The part that Canadian wheat and Canadian ships, both transatlantic and coastwise, could play in the world-problem of carrying American commerce abroad was seriously considered by the conferrees at the White House, but it is the belief that they will be of slight service inasmuch as they will probably be needed by England.

The bill amends the section of the Panama Canal act which specifies that foreign ships can be admitted to American registry five years after launching; lets down the bars in respect to surveying and measuring the ships and gives the President the authority to use his discretion in allowing foreign officers to command the ships that may come in under the American flag by the proposed act. . . .

The other relief measure, which is the bill to amend the currency law by modifying the clause compelling banks of national currency associations to have 40 per cent. of outstanding currency notes, would have been reported out by the Banking and Currency Committee of the House to-day had it been possible to obtain a quorum. Two attempts to gather more than nine members failed and the bill will be brought up in the House under suspension of the rules on Monday.

Printed in the New York *World*, Aug. 2, 1914.

[1] The act, passed by Congress on August 4 and signed by Wilson on the next day, permitted banks organized into "National Currency Associations" to receive at least an additional billion dollars in "emergency" currency beyond the $500,000,000 limit set by the Aldrich-Vreeland Act of 1908. See the *New York Times*, Aug. 4 and 5, 1914, and Link, *Struggle for Neutrality*, pp. 78-80.

From Edward Mandell House

Dear Governor: Prides Crossing, Mass. August 1st, 1914.

There are one or two things that would perhaps be of interest to you at this time which I shall tell you now and not wait until I see you.

Sir Edward Grey told me that England had no written agreement with either France or Russia or any formal alliance, that the situation was brought about by a mutual desire for protection and that they discussed international matters with one another with as much freedom as if they had an actual written alliance. Their agreement is therefore purely sympathetic.

It is evident that England is laying a restraining hand upon France and is urging Germany to do the same with Austria. I have a feeling that war may not come about for there is no question that they are all very much afraid of one another.

The great danger is that some overt act may occur which will get the situation out of control. Germany is exceedingly nervous and at high tension and she knows that her best chance of success is to strike quickly and hard, therefore her very alarm may cause her to precipitate action as a means of safety.

Please let me suggest that you do not let Mr. Bryan make any overtures to any of the powers involved. They look upon him as purely visionary and it would lessen the weight of your influence if you desired to use it yourself later. When you decide to do anything, it had best be done by you directly for they have the highest possible opinion and respect for you which Mr. Bryan unfortunately in no way shares.

If I thought I could live through the heat, I would go to Washington to see you, but I am afraid if I reached there I would be utterly helpless. I wish you could get time to take the Mayflower and cruise for a few days in these waters so that I might join you.

Your faithful and affectionate, E. M. House

TLS (WP, DLC).

To Mary Allen Hulbert

Dearest Friend, The White House 2 August, 1914.

How hard it was to read your little note and know that I must disappoint you. I cannot imagine how the papers got it that I was to be in New Bedford. I do not remember even being invited there; and certainly never had the least idea of going. I must train you literally to believe *nothing* that you see in the news-papers, particularly about the movements and intentions of W.W. About his intentions they know nothing; and they report that he is expected anywhere that he happens to have been invited, no matter what his answer to the invitations may have been!

And just now I am held in Washington by the most serious duties any President has had to perform since Lincoln. This incredible European catastrophe has wrought effects upon the business, and the public affairs, of this country which, for the time being at least, are of the most disturbing kind; and there is not a moment when we must not be watchfully on guard, to do what we can to guide and to help. I must be at my post every minute. Even to-day, Sunday, has been full of anxiety and of business.

And added to all the rest is the unspeakable distress that my dear one gets no better. She is struggling through deep waters of utter nervous prostration, the symptoms of which seem to change almost from day to day; and I carry lead at my heart all the time!

My vacation has evidently flown out at the window. If Europe should indeed be plunged into wars like those of the time of Napoleon, it will be as necessary for me to be steadily here "on the job" as if Congress were in session. There will be business of delicacy every day. I was evidently not meant for days of ease and quiet! Why was I so imprudent as to choose this particular term of office?

All join me in the most affectionate messages.

Your devoted friend,   Woodrow Wilson

WWTLS (WP, DLC).

To Arthur W. Trenholm[1]

My dear Sir: [The White House] August 2, 1914.

I greatly appreciated the opportunity to confer yesterday with you and the Committee of Managers associated with you, and with the representatives of the engineers and firemen employed on the western roads; and was very much gratified indeed by the frank spirit of cooperation with which I was met.

I am sure that you appreciated the extreme gravity of the situation into which the country and your roads would be plunged if the strike now threatened should unhappily occur. In view of world-wide conditions, unparalleled in recent history, which have arisen within the last few days, it is obvious that the suspension of business on roads serving more than half the territory of the United States would be a calamity of incalculable magnitude. The situation has reached a crisis which hardly permits a full consideration of the merits of the controversy, and I feel that in the circumstances I can appeal with confidence to your patriotism and to your regard for the public welfare to make whatever sacrifice is necessary to avert a National disaster. The mediators under the Newlands law were impelled to propose a certain plan of arbitration because they were fully convinced, as I am also convinced, that under existing conditions no other peaceful solution of the dispute is possible. For these reasons, I very earnestly urge your acceptance of that plan, even though you may regard it as in some respects unfair to the interests you represent; and I am certain that in so doing you will perform an invaluable public service which will be everywhere applauded and deeply appreciated.

Very sincerely yours,   Woodrow Wilson

TLS (Letterpress Books, WP, DLC).
¹ General Manager of the Chicago, St. Paul, Minneapolis & Omaha Railway.

A Message to Martin Augustine Knapp

[The White House, c. Aug. 2, 1914]

After the fullest and most earnest consideration of the matter, the President is convinced that the committee representing the men *cannot* change the conclusions of those whom they represent; that the representatives of the railroads *can* change their former conclusion; and that they *ought*, in the interest of the country and of the world, to accede to the proposals of the Mediators as they were acceded to by the men. They are now the only party free to act. The President earnestly and entirely concurs in the plan and terms of arbitration proposed by the Mediators.

W.W.

WWhw MS (WP, DLC).

From Walter Hines Page

Dear Mr. President,   London, Sunday night, Aug. 2, 1914.

It seems useless and almost silly to write by mail about this quickly changing drama, for whatever one might write will become obsolete before you get it. Yet the impulse to put down what one hears and fears is irresistible. I detect even in English opinion an acquiescence, almost a satisfaction, that war between England and Germany is certain. They feel that it must come some time—why not now and have it over? It is better to have it when Germany will have other enemies than England in the field than at some time when England might alone have to fight Germany—better, too, when the responsibility for starting it lies at Germany's door.

In one way at least race-hatred is at the bottom of it—the Slav against the Teuton. The time to have that fight out seems favourable to Russia—the old Austrian Emperor is in his last years, the Slav states of his Empire are restive, not to say rebellious, England may be drawn in now to help weaken Germany, Russia feels the need of a patriotic race-cry at this stage of her growth and the need of a war to cause forgetfulness of the Russian-Japanese disaster. I am told, too, that the Tsar—as, of course, most of his subjects—is really superstitious and that miracle-working priests—a sort of modern soothsayers—have a great influence over him; and of course the military party know how to use such machinery. We have to stop and think of such absurd things as this to realise the deplorable mediaevalism of a large part of Europe and to understand why the criminal folly and the economic suicide of war do not have more effect on them. Russians, Germans and even Frenchmen are, moreover, yet in that stage of evolution where the "glory" of war makes a strong appeal to them.

Already the foregoing is out of date. While I was writing the news came of Germany's declaration of war against Russia and of her marching into Luxemburg, which of course means that France and England must become involved: I can see no escape from that. The general conflag[r]ation has begun.

My thoughts run quickly to what *we* may do. On my own initiative I asked Sir Edward Grey nearly a week ago if he could use the good offices of the U. S. for peace. Sir Edward is very appreciative of our mood and willingness. But they don't want peace on the Continent—the ruling military classes do not. But they will want it presently and then our opportunity will come —*your* opportunity to play an important and historic part. Ours is the only great Government in the world that is not in some way entangled. (How wise our no-alliance policy is!) Of course I'll keep in daily touch with Sir Edward and with everybody who can and will keep me informed.

The imagination simply baulks at what may happen—at what *is* happening. The Embassy is already besieged by people who wish to go to the United States and can't, who have travellers' cheques for which they cannot get money, and who have other unexpected troubles. I hear of even worse confusion in Paris.

This island is even now practically cut off from the Continent. Three days ago we talked with Paris by telephone. Now it is impossible to get a private telegram through with any certainty and telephone communication is wholly cut off.

Our shipping and foreign commerce will gain immensely; our chance to help settle the quarrel will surely come—there was nothing that we could have done to prevent it; and our intimate and frank and confidential relations with this country are such that we will, I am sure, be called on as soon as they are willing to call on anybody to point the way back to reason.

Events here alone seem to me likely to make your Administration historic. Let's watch closely for chances to serve.

Yours—dazed—Walter H. Page

TLS (WP, DLC).

From Franklin Knight Lane

My dear Mr. President: Washington [Aug. 2, 1914]

I suppose you have thought of it but I will second the motion: Why not offer to all powers in Europe our good offices in a personal note from you addressed to the head of each country? It seems to me the one last chance (if it has not already been taken) to avert war.

Sincerely yours   Franklin K. Lane

ALS (WP, DLC).

Remarks at a Press Conference

August 3, 1914

Gentlemen, before you question me, I want to say this: I believe it is really unnecessary, but I always want to tell you what is in my mind. It is extremely necessary, it is manifestly necessary, in the present state of affairs on the other side of the water, that you should be extremely careful not to add in any way to the excitement. Of course, the European world is in a highly excited state of mind, but the excitement ought not to spread to the United States. So far as we are concerned, there is no cause for excitement. There is great inconvenience, for the time being, in the money market and in our exchanges and, temporarily, in the handling of our crops, but America is absolutely prepared to meet the financial situation and to straighten everything out without any material difficulty. The only thing that can possibly prevent it is unreasonable apprehension and excitement.

If I might make a suggestion to you gentlemen, therefore, I would urge you not to give currency to any unverified rumor or to anything that would tend to create or add to excitement. I think that you will agree that we must all at the present moment act together as Americans in seeing that America does not suffer any unnecessary distress from what is going on in the world at large. The situation in Europe is perhaps the gravest in its possibilities that has arisen in modern times, but it need not affect the United States unfavorably in the long run. Not that the United States has anything to take advantage of, but her own position is sound, and she owes it to mankind to remain in such a condition and in such a state of mind that she can help the rest of the world. I want to have the pride of feeling that America, if nobody else, has her self-possession and stands ready with calmness of thought and steadiness of purpose to help the rest of the world. And we can do it and reap a great permanent glory out of doing it, provided we all cooperate to see that nobody loses his head. I know from my conferences with the Secretary of the Treasury, who is in very close touch with the financial situation throughout the country, that there is no cause for alarm. There is cause for getting busy and doing the thing in the right way, but there is no element of unsoundness and there is no cause for alarm. The bankers and businessmen of the country are cooperating with the government with a zeal, intelligence, and spirit which make the outcome secure.[1]

Can you elaborate a little, Mr. President, on the subject of shipping, beyond the mere fact of the introduction of the bill?

Of course, so far as we are concerned, our national interest in the shipping is not merely to sell our crops—the surplus crops—but to be serviceable to Europe in getting foodstuffs to her in this emergency. We owe it not only to our own farmers, but we owe it to the world at large to release the surplus foodstuffs that is in sight in our present enormous crops; and we are going to do everything that is possible to

---

[1] Wilson permitted reporters to quote the foregoing paragraphs.

find ships and to get ships for that world purpose—for that purpose which is as much unselfish as selfish.

I am wondering, Mr. President, if you can say anything of the possibility of converting coastwise ships into trans-Atlantic carriers?

> I think from what I can learn that will be done to a very considerable extent. Of course, many of the coastwise ships are built for particular services which render them relatively unserviceable for grain shipments, without internal alterations or arrangements. So that how many of them —how many of the fruit ships, for example—could be used for that purpose, I am not yet informed.

Has there been any thought of using sailing ships?

> Yes, sailing ships will be used so far as available. I was going to say that, according to statistics, we have a larger proportion of sailing ships than other countries have. It just shows that we are behind the times, as a matter of fact; but as a matter of statistics, we have more sailing ships in proportion. I guess—for I have no means of knowing—that they consist largely of these large three and four masted schooners which are used for the most part in the coastwise trade, but they can be used for trans-Atlantic trade. They are absolutely seaworthy and, except for their slowness, will be available for that purpose.

Do you regard the rate decision[2] as being favorable to the domestic financial situation?

> I can only judge by what I saw in the papers this morning, which calculated that it would add to the income of the railroads to whom the advance was granted, some ten or fifteen million dollars—and, of course, that ought to be helpful. But I am speaking now at third hand. I haven't personally gained any knowledge of it.

Have you since your conference with the railroad men on Saturday heard anything further from them?

> No, but I have every reason to believe that the railroad managers will take a satisfactory course of action in the matter.

Can you say whether Germany or any other other nations have transferred their interests to our diplomatic representatives?

[2] The Interstate Commerce Commission on July 29 granted an increase of 5 per cent on freight rates for railroads operating in the so-called "central freight association territory," which included Illinois, Indiana, Michigan, Ohio, and parts of western Pennsylvania and New York. See the *New York Times*, Aug. 2, 1914.

No, I cannot. Mr. Bryan can give you that list. Of course, we are going to be in the very singular position of being one of the very few neutral powers to which the various governments can turn over their interests. We will, of course, be of any service that we can.

Do you expect to be able to complete the Reserve Board this week?

I hope so. So far as I am concerned, it will be completed this week.

Will the nominations go in today?

I am not sure. I am waiting to hear from one gentleman whom I wish to nominate.

Is it true, as reported, that the Queen of Holland invited the United States to join her in an attempt to avert the European situation?

Not so far as I know. That is the first I have heard of it.
I haven't seen anything about it.

Have you had any advices from Secretary McAdoo in respect to the New York situation?

Mr. McAdoo was on the phone just a little while ago—he had Mr. Tumulty on the phone. He was very much encouraged and felt that it would work out very successfully.

I understand some suggestion has been made that Mr. Carnegie is proposing a plan to the administration.

None has reached me.

How soon can the Federal Reserve System be in working order after the nominations are acted upon?

The time would be different in different parts of the country. There are several steps to be taken. You see, not all the regional banks have elected their directors. They elect their directors and then the Reserve Board completes the directorates; and then they have to establish their physical headquarters.

Do you feel that the quick organization of the Federal Reserve Board would help the situation.

Very much. The Federal Reserve Board by itself cannot perform its useful functions; it must perform its service through the regional banks. As soon as the regional banks are in operation, they can control the rates on call money and things of that sort and help govern the market.

Would the inauguration of the Federal Reserve System be complicated by the use of emergency currency?

No, not at all. If you look at this feature you will see that the emergency act is to serve until next June in order to give time for the organization, and therefore the Aldrich-Vreeland Act is really a part of this act, making this much more available. It is part of the intermediate machinery. The call of 3 per cent of the capital stocks the banks will have to pay will not tighten up the money market.

Have the shipowners or shipbuilders indicated their attitude toward the proposed legislation about ships?

I do not know whether they have or not; not to me.

Has this government taken any formal or informal action toward the offering of its good offices?

No, sir.

Will the European situation make it necessary for Congress to remain in session?

Oh, no. I do not see why it should alter their plans.

Do you think it advisable or necessary to act on the suggestion that ships be sent to bring Americans back?

Mr. Tumulty tells me that in a telephone conversation he had with Mr. McAdoo this morning, Mr. McAdoo said he had been consulted by the New York banks as to the means of assisting our people, our tourists, through their correspondents on the other side of the water, and that he thought it could be arranged. As for sending ships, this is easier said than done—where are the ships? Of course, we will do everything of any sort that is necessary. We are looking around now to see just what is at hand in the way of available means of getting them here.

Could transports be spared for that service?

Yes, they could; they are highly suitable.

Has the suggestion been taken up of neutralizing the liners held here?[3]

That does not appeal to us. The matter has been discussed, but no plan has been suggested. Neutralization has to be bona fide. It can not be make-believe; and it is a violation of the neutrality merely to hoist the American flag over the ship when she is not an American ship. There might conceivably be some understanding about it, but when the European governments are so much engaged, it will be hard to manage a detail of that sort; and we could not commandeer them.

Have any of the shipping interests suggested that they will purchase these foreign ships?

[3] That is, German liners in American ports.

I haven't heard of that suggestion, but I have very little doubt if American registration were open a great deal of that would be done. It would be profitable.

T MS (C. L. Swem Coll., NjP).

To Edward Mandell House

My dear Friend: The White House August 3, 1914

I must have seemed to you singularly indifferent to your return that I should have sent you no message before this, and yet I hope that I have not. The delight and comfort of having such a friend as you are is to be sure that he understands perfectly, and the pressure and anxiety of the last week have been the most nearly overwhelming that I have yet had to carry. I have not had a thought or a moment except for public business, but you may be sure that there was constantly in the front of my private thoughts a contentment that you should be back in this country and that I should presently have a chance to see you and confer with you as I am longing to do.

Your letters are invaluable to me. I know how deep a sorrow must have come to you out of this dreadful European conflict in view of what we had hoped the European world was going to turn to, but we must face the situation in the confidence that Providence has deeper plans than we could possibly have laid ourselves.

So soon as the programme in Congress is thoroughly well in hand, I shall think of some plan by which I can see you, though just at present Mrs. Wilson is so weak and is suffering so much that I cannot find it in my heart to be away over night. There are a thousand things I must discuss with you, some of them very pressing, but here again we must wait on what is possible.

With great affection and the warmest welcome home,
Faithfully yours,   Woodrow Wilson

TLS (E. M. House Papers, CtY).

To Franklin Knight Lane

My dear Lane: [The White House] August 3, 1914

Your message about offering our good offices to the European powers was very welcome. As a matter of fact, I had already done so, as far as I thought it prudent or possible, but things went so fast and so far there upon the very first rush that apparently there is at present, at any rate, no opening for us.

Cordially and faithfully yours, Woodrow Wilson

TLS (Letterpress Books, WP, DLC).

To John Joseph Fitzgerald

My dear Mr. Fitzgerald: [The White House] August 3, 1914

We are receiving so many messages showing the extreme distress of Americans in Europe and the immediate necessity of doing something for their assistance and relief that I am going to take the liberty of sending a message to Congress proposing some such action as would be embodied in a Joint Resolution of the following tenor:

"Resolved by the Senate and House of Representatives of the United States of America in Congress assembled, That for the relief, protection and transportation of American citizens, for personal services and for other expenses which may be incurred in connection with or growing out of the existing political disturbances in Europe, there is appropriated out of any money in the Treasury not otherwise appropriated the sum of $250,000 to be expended at the discretion of the President."

I have every confidence that we could manage this in such a way that the whole sum, or practically all of it, would eventually be paid back by the persons concerned, but it seems to me imperatively necessary that the Government should for the time being have funds at its command for these uses.

I sincerely hope I am acting in a way in this matter which you approve.

Cordially and sincerely yours, Woodrow Wilson[1]

TLS (Letterpress Books, WP, DLC).
[1] Wilson wrote this same letter, *mutatis mutandis*, to Thomas S. Martin, chairman of the Senate Appropriations Committee.

A Special Message to Congress

The White House,

To the Senate and House of Representatives: August 3, 1914.

The present disturbances in Europe, with the consequent interruption of transportation facilities, the increase in living expenses, coupled with the difficulty of obtaining money from this country, have placed a large number of American citizens, temporarily or permanently resident in Europe, in a serious situation and have made it necessary for the United States to provide relief and transportation to the United States or to places of safety.

The situation has also thrown upon our diplomatic and consular officers an enormous burden in caring for the interests of Americans in the disturbed areas and makes it necessary to provide for greatly increased expenses.

In view of the exigency of the situation as above outlined, I recommend the immediate passage by the Congress of an act appropriating $250,000, or so much thereof as may be necessary, to be placed at the disposal of the President, for the relief, protection, and transportation of American citizens, for personal services and for other expenses which may be incurred in connection with or growing out of the existing disturbance in Europe.[1]   Woodrow Wilson

Printed in *Cong. Record*, 63d Cong., 2d sess., p. 13142.
  [1] Both houses passed the requested bill on that day. At Wilson's request, Congress appropriated an additional $2,500,000 on August 5. *New York Times*, Aug. 6, 1914.

To Henry Lee Higginson

My dear Major Higginson: [The White House] August 3, 1914

I have your letter of July thirty-first[1] and sincerely appreciate its frank expressions of opinion.

I believe that Congress will promptly complete its business. The spirit of both parties in the matter is excellent and a common purpose seems to prevail. But I am sorry to say that I cannot agree with you that it would be wise to drop the programme, because that would leave the fatal question mark as to what was to be done at the next session of Congress, and I think that the country is now entitled to every element of certainty and definiteness. My whole endeavor shall be to bring as prompt action as possible.

I think that the Congress will act today in the matter of the shipping and the very best spirit of cooperation prevails with regard to anything that it may be necessary to do.

In haste with much appreciation,
                              Sincerely yours,   Woodrow Wilson

P.S. Your advice about the shipping is timely and admirable. We were already proceeding to act along that line when your letter of the thirtieth of July[2] came.

TLS (Letterpress Books, WP, DLC).
  [1] H. L. Higginson to WW, July 31, 1914, TLS (WP, DLC).
  [2] H. L. Higginson to WW, July 30, 1914, ALS (WP, DLC).

Two Letters from William Jennings Bryan

My dear Mr. President: Washington August 3, 1914.

I had a talk with Corrothers yesterday. I questioned him very frankly about his own matters and he denies positively, and with seeming truthfulness, that he has any business connections with Villa, denying specifically the charges that I heard. He says that he has no income aside from his salary, except that he collected one debt due him for work done prior to the Mexican trouble.

He says that Villa asked him to come to Washington and explain his position. He says that Villa insists upon the convention being held in the City of Mexico on the arrival of the Constitutionalists, in accordance with the agreement made at Torreon. This agreement was tacitly consented to by Carranza and was carried out as to some of its terms. One part of the agreement was that coal should be furnished to Villa's army, and that has been done. Another part of the agreement was that the persons imprisoned ar [at] Jaurez should be released, which was done, and also that between five and six million pesos, worth about twenty-five cents on the dollar of our money, should be turned over to Carranza; this was done.

The agreement was that the convention should be held in the City of Mexico, and that each one thousand soldiers should be represented by one delegate, and that this convention should select the man to be Provisional President to hold until the election should be held, which was to be called at once.

Villa is afraid that Carranza will refuse to live up to this agreement and will insist on holding the office himself and then use it to continue himself in power. Villa prefers Angeles and would really prefer a civilian, but thinks that some military experience would be necessary to begin with and regards Angeles as the best of all the Generals. Corrothers said that Villa will meet Carranza half way. Villa will not go to Mexico City with the army, but will remain in Chihauhau and will not make any effort to prevent Carranza getting into Mexico City, but, to all appearances, Villa is preparing for what he regards a probability, namely, that Carranza will not live up to the agreement and that when Carranza tries to hold himself in power there will be trouble. Villa is raising his army to 60,000, which will be about equal to both of the other divisions. That would give him half of the convention. He also claims a considerable following in the divisions of the Northeast and Northwest.

Villa also fears that Carranza will not carry out his promised agrarian legislation. Corrothers thinks that Villa is much more deeply interested in agrarian legislation than Carranza is, although Corrothers speaks highly of Carranza and says that, while the two men are very different, they have qualities that supplement each other and that they ought to act together. He says Carranza cannot be regarded as a rich man. He and two brothers own a ranch of grazing land of possible 250,000 acres, but that it is not valuable and that the income from it is small. He says that Carranza is well educated, and Carrothers seems anxious to hold the two together.

I questioned him about Villa. He says that he is a mixture of Spanish and Indian and that there may be some trace of African blood. He says he can barely write his name. If you will remind me when I see you I will tell you about his domestic relations. Corrothers says Villa has a great deal of natural sense and the elements of leadership. His soldiers idolize him and he claims to have no ambition whatever except to see these reforms carried out. He is a teetotaler and does not gamble except at cock-fights. He is very fond of cock fighting, and attends a cock-fight every Sunday when they have one and bets on his favorite rooster; but Corrothers says it is not for the purpose of winning so much as to help along the fight. The women members of his family are Catholics and attend church, but he does not attend. Corrothers says he has no hostility to the church except where he thinks the church officials are taking part in the politics of the country.

Villa likes Caldaron[1] and also Cabrera, but thinks that Zubaron has been the cause of discord.

Would you like to have a talk with Corrothers? I think it might be well for you to see him. It would give him more authority when he reports to Villa. I believe, from what he says, that we can have some influence with Villa, but he is anxious for us to exert an influence on Carranza also to keep him up to his agreements.

With assurances of my highest respect, I am, my dear Mr. President,   Very sincerely yours,   W. J. Bryan

[1] Fernando Iglesias Calderón, leader of the Mexican Liberal party and an adherent of Carranza. Wilson had conferred with him at the White House on July 21. See the *New York Times*, July 22, 1914.

My dear Mr. President: Washington August 3, 1914.

I have not had an opportunity to report on Blair Lee's visit to the Cardinal.[1] He was cordially received and the Cardinal heartily approved of the terms of the telegram and said it could not have been made better in any respect and appreciated highly that it was sent to him. He was also grateful for what you did in the matter of Venezuela.[2] He fully endorses the administration's position in regard to Colombia—proposed payment small to us but the attitude of fairness of great value. He heartily approved also of the Mediation. He says feeling in Europe is strongly against Carranza and Villa and will remain so until something is actually done by them to answer criticism. He is deeply interested in the attitude of the new Government toward the church officials. He said he would be pleased to call at the State Department whenever it was so desired. Lee undertook the matter very promptly and I think the suggestion that he should go was a wise one. I thought you might be interested in this report that Lee gave me of his visit.

With assurances of my highest regard, I am, my dear Mr. President,   Very truly yours,   W. J. Bryan

TLS (WP, DLC).

[1] On the occasion of his eightieth birthday on July 23, James Cardinal Gibbons gave an interview to the press in which he denounced Carranza and Villa for their treatment of the Mexican Roman Catholic clergy and said that the government of the United States should play a leading role in deciding whether the new Constitutionalist regime would receive international recognition. As a result of this interview, Wilson and Bryan decided to send Senator Lee of Maryland to call upon the Cardinal. At an interview on July 26, Lee gave Cardinal Gibbons a copy of Wilson's message for Carranza and Villa printed at July 23, 1914. "I expressed my gratification on reading the dispatch," the Cardinal wrote soon afterward, "but I remarked to Senator Lee and begged him to inform the President that Carranza's and Villa's records are so bad that their protestations of compliance with the President's communication will have little weight before the discerning public unless supplemented by deeds. I referred to the anxiety of the Bishops of Mexico and of the members of religious orders. I promised the Senator that I would see the Secretary of State as soon as I had anything to communicate." TC of memorandum dated July 27, 1914 (Archives of the Archdiocese of Baltimore).

[2] See FR 1914, pp. 1102-1103.

From Edward Mandell House

Dear Governor: Prides Crossing, Mass. August 3rd, 1914.

Our people are deeply shocked at the enormity of this general European war, and I see here and there regret that you did not use your good offices in behalf of peace.

If this grows into criticism so as to become noticeable, I believe everyone would be pleased and proud that you had anticipated this worldwide horror and had done all that was humanly possible to avert it.

The more terrible the war becomes the greater credit it will be that you saw the trend of events long before it was seen by other statesmen of the world.

Your faithful and affectionate,   E. M. House

P.S. The question might be asked why negociations were only with Germany and England and not with France and Russia. This, of course, was because it was thought that Germany would act for the Triple Alliance and England for the Triple Entente.

TLS (WP, DLC).

To Edward Mandell House

The White House [Aug.] 4 [1914]

Letter of third received   do you think I could and should act now[1] and if so how.   Woodrow Wilson

Hw telegram (E. M. House Papers, CtY).
[1] Senator McCumber had just introduced a resolution declaring that it was the Senate's judgment that the President should offer his good offices of mediation or arbitration. *Cong. Record*, 63d Cong., 2d sess., p. 13210.

A Press Release

[Aug. 4, 1914]

The President has sent the following message to the Emperor of Germany, the Czar of Russia, the Emperor of Austria-Hungary, the President of France, and the King of England:

As official head of one of the powers signatory to the Hague convention, I feel it to be my privilege and my duty under article three of that convention to say to you in a spirit of most earnest friendship that I should welcome an opportunity to act in the interest of European peace, either now or at any other time that might be thought more suitable, as an occasion to serve you and all concerned in a way that would afford me lasting cause for gratitude and happiness.

T MS (Letterpress Books, WP, DLC).

To William Jennings Bryan

My dear Mr. Secretary: The White House August 4, 1914

Thank you sincerely for your report of Senator Blair Lee's mission. It is most interesting and satisfactory.

Cordially and sincerely yours,   Woodrow Wilson

TLS (W. J. Bryan Papers, DNA).

To Charles Richard Crane

My dear Mr. Crane: [The White House] August 4, 1914

Thank you for your letter with the article by Professor Hart.[1] I have read it with genuine interest. The more I read about the conflict across the seas, the more open it seems to me to utter condemnation. The outcome no man can even conjecture.

It interests me very much that you are to go and see some of these things at close range. I hope that you will be careful not to go where you will be seriously inconvenienced.

With warmest best wishes to you both.

Cordially and faithfully yours,   Woodrow Wilson

P.S. Please thank Mrs. Crane for her telegrams.[2]

TLS (Letterpress Books, WP, DLC).
[1] C. R. Crane to WW, c. Aug. 3, 1914, ALS (WP, DLC). The article is missing but it was Albert Bushnell Hart, "Austrian Fear of Serb Empire is Real War Cause," *New York Times*, August 2, 1914, V, 1.
[2] Cornelia Smith (Mrs. C. R.) Crane to WW and EAW, Aug. 1 and 3, 1914, T telegrams (WP, DLC).

From Edward Mandell House

Prides, Massachusetts, August 4, 1914. 9:05 p.m.

Telegram received. Would advise doing nothing for the moment. Richard Olney lunches with me here tomorrow and with your permission I will confer with him and get his opinion. I am entirely satisfied of its value in this country.

Edward M. House.

T telegram (WP, DLC).

From William Lea Chambers

My dear Mr. President: Washington August 4, 1914.

I regret that an appointment at my office for a mediation conference involving a controversy on a West Virginia railroad prevented my calling with Judge Knapp this forenoon for the purpose not only of acquainting you with results but of expressing in person my high appreciation of your great help, without which the national calamity of a western strike would not have been averted. We took up negotiations directly with the Managers' Committee, and shortly after received from Mr. Tumulty copies of your correspondence with that Committee, and were delighted to find them agreeable to proceeding to a conclusion. The representatives of the employees were equally agreeable to this plan and the arbitration contract was signed, after much tedious work in conciliating both sides as to its details, at 2 o'clock this morning.

As it may be of interest to you, I beg to enclose one of the originals of the arbitration submission.[1]

Most respectfully yours,   W. L. Chambers

TLS (WP, DLC).
 [1] A typed document dated Aug. 3, 1914 (WP, DLC).

From Thomas Davies Jones

My dear Mr. President: Chicago August 4, 1914.

I have just telephoned Mr. Tumulty that Mr. Delano[1] will accept membership on the Federal Reserve Board if nominated and confirmed.

After giving the matter anxious consideration and discussing various persons with everybody who could throw light upon them, I believe that this is the best that can be done in this vicinity. He is a man of the highest character and is a man of ability. He will be giving up a salary of $25,000 a year as president of the Monon road, and as his outside means are not large the acceptance of the place will mean a real sacrifice to him. When I began negotiating with him I had rather faint hopes of his agreeing to accept, and his first answer was in the negative.

He tells me that he has never had any relations whatever with any concerns that could by any possibility be called trusts. He has been a railroad man all his life, first with the Burlington in a subordinate capacity, then as president of the Wabash, and now president of the Monon road. He does not hold any bank stock and I cannot imagine any reasonable objection that can be raised to the appointment.

He requested me to make a statement to you on his behalf of which I made a memorandum and read it to Secretary Tumulty this morning, as follows: "Mr. Delano feels that good faith toward the President requires that he advise the President before his nomination is determined upon that if the Senate Committee should require him to appear before it for examination he will refuse to do so. There is nothing in his record that he desires to conceal but he will not appear before the Committee."

Whether he is right or not in taking this stand, it is certainly right for him to apprise you of the fact before his nomination is determined upon.

I hope that the despatches are correct in reporting that Mr. Warburg will be confirmed by the Senate.

Faithfully yours,   Thomas D. Jones.

TLS (WP, DLC).
¹ Wilson and Jones had obviously been talking over the telephone about another appointee for the Federal Reserve Board, and Jones had recommended Frederic Adrian Delano of Chicago.

From Edward Mandell House

Dear Governor: Prides Crossing, Mass. August 4th, 1914.

Please be careful about that shipping bill. There are all sorts of possible future troubles lurking in it.

Feeling throughout Europe is at such high tension that it is exceedingly probable that foreign ships brought under the American Flag in the manner proposed, would be constantly intercepted and dealt with in a way that might hurt our national sensibilities. Even if care was used not to offend us for the moment, there would be a reckoning with us by the dominant nations after the war was over, just as we brought England to terms about the Alabama.

Your faithful and affectionate,   E. M. House

TLS (WP, DLC).

To Stockton Axson¹

[The White House] August 5, 1914.

Ellen is ser[i]ously ill. If you are free to leave hope you will come directly to Washington.   Woodrow Wilson.

T telegram (Letterpress Books, WP, DLC).
¹ Axson was teaching in the summer school of the University of Oregon.

To Edward Mandell House

My dear Friend: The White House August 5, 1914

Events moved so fast yesterday that I came to the conclusion that if you had known what I knew as soon as I knew it, the advice of your telegram would probably have been different.

At any rate, I took the risk and sent messages to the heads of the several countries. It can, at least, do no harm.

This is written in great haste, but also in great affection.

Affectionately yours,   Woodrow Wilson

TLS (E. M. House Papers, CtY).

To William Jennings Bryan, with Enclosure

My dear Mr. Secretary: The White House August 5, 1914

Mr. Browne,[1] who wrote the enclosed very interesting letter which I am returning, of course, does not know that he was speaking our own opinion in wishing that some man of first-rate capacity could be sent down to be present and exercise what influence he can during the present happenings in Mexico.

As you know, I have not thought Governor Lind the proper person in the circumstances because of the violent prejudice that has been formed against him by the representatives of the Roman Catholic Church, whom we are at present trying to protect in Mexico. I think, therefore, that his telegram should be answered to the effect that so far as we can now see we shall not immediately need to call upon him.

But it occurs to me that Mr. Paul Fuller, of the firm of Coudert Brothers,[2] whom there were reasons for not asking to go to San Domingo, would serve us admirably in this case if he were willing to go to Mexico. I formed a most delightful impression of Mr. Fuller. He is a Democrat, is in full sympathy with the purposes of the administration, and is accustomed by long habit to deal with our friends in Latin-America. I hope that this suggestion commends itself to you.

Always

Cordially and faithfully yours,   Woodrow Wilson

TLS (W. J. Bryan Papers, DNA).

[1] Herbert Janvrin Browne, journalist of Washington and Carranza's agent for the shipment of arms to Mexico.

[2] Prominent lawyer of New York. He specialized in international law, was a Roman Catholic, and spoke Spanish fluently.

E N C L O S U R E

Herbert Janvrin Browne to William Jennings Bryan

My dear Mr. Secretary: Washington, D. C. August 4, 1914.

Intimate observation of conditions in Northern Mexico during a period of nearly ten weeks just closing leads me to urge the need of a man of the first rank to aid the Administration's Peace Policy in that section. I know of no one whose qualifications will compare favorably with those of Hon. John Lind for that position.

The situation is delicate and difficult in the extreme. Gen. Carranza is sensitive, disposed to be somewhat critical in his attitude, and is not easily approached. I have, however, been in position to scrutinize his actions and his policy, to study the machinery of his administration, and have come to the conclusion that he can handle the situation in every direction save one with success. That one direction, which is extremely menacing, relates to the attitude of Gen. Villa in the State of Chihuahua, and the immediate region to the South. There Gen. Villa holds an imperium in imperio. He has installed his own officials and has by force thrown out the Carranzista occupants of office; he collects not only the State and Municipal revenues but also the Customs revenues at El Paso. He is a law unto himself. Through his agent, Felix Sommerfeld, and the instrumentality of Flint & Co., of New York, he is making extensive purchases of arms and ammunition, no small quantity of which is even now being openly directed to El Paso, in absolute confidence that it will find its way across the border. He is enlisting hundreds of peons in his division, notwithstanding the fact that there is no longer serious armed opposition to the Constitutionalist cause. This can have but a narrow interpretation,—armed opposition to the program of Gen. Carranza, which may flame out at any moment into a most serious counter-revolution.

Without embodying in this communication any reflections on U. S. Consul George C. Carrothers, it is quite plain that his close relations with and friendship for Gen. Villa have made him unavailable in dealing with the situation in connection with Gen. Carranza. Villa has great natural ability, but he is a man of equally marked limitations and is at this moment surrounded by and influenced by men whose motives are of the most questionable character and whose principals have sought, are still hoping for, and can only profit by, the armed intervention by the United States. Gen. Villa has certain just grievances in respect of the treatment which has been extended to him, largely in the direction of curtailing the overwhelming prestige due to his wonderful military successes. But the justification for that disposition to curb his growth is found in the fact that otherwise a new and most dangerous "man on horseback" would dominate Mexico in absolute disregard of every foreign interest save those which had secured his momentary ear and favor.

The presence in Northern Mexico in the immediate future of a man of Gov. Lind's known friendliness to the Constitutionalist cause, possessed of his patience and tact, of his homely closeness to the soil, of his wide democracy, will have a most beneficial and saving effect on the situation.

I therefore beg leave to suggest the advisability of directing a tactful inquiry to Gen. Carranza as to whether Gov. Lind's presence in Mexico at this time would be acceptable. Subject to superior information on the part of your Department and to Gov. Lind's own desires, I will take the liberty also of speaking in high terms of Mr. Leon J. Canova as being on excellent footing with Gen. Carranza and the other officials of the Constitutionalist Government, and on account of his thorough knowledge of Spanish and his intimate acquaintance with the Latin-American temperament and customs, possessing eminently the qualifications which would make him of great value to Gov. Lind as an interpreter, translator and secretary.

I shall ask the privilege of following this confidential communication in the immediate future with a detailed memorandum of my observations in respect of the administrative machinery of the Constitutionalist Government.

Very respectfully,   Herbert J. Browne.

TLS (W. J. Bryan Papers, DNA).

To William Charles Adamson

My dear Judge Adamson: [The White House] August 5, 1914

I understand that a vote is set for today on the Trade Commission bill in the Senate. It will, therefore, I suppose, go to conference tomorrow.

I have been meaning for some days to ask the pleasure of a conference with you about the bill, but these war matters and a score of others have come upon me in such a flood that apparently it is a matter of despair to set aside the half hour, or whatever it may be, that would be necessary. I am, therefore, going to ask you to forgive me if I take the liberty of sending you this note to express my deep interest in the retention in the bill in its integrity of Section V, the section about unfair competition.

It seems to me a feasible and very wise means of accomplishing the things that it seems impossible in the complicated circumstances of business to accomplish by any attempted definition. I have gone over the matter again and again in my conferences with the business men with whom I have been talking and I find them so much relieved that that kind of elasticity and exercise of judgment is going to be embodied in the bill that I feel we owe it to ourselves to take this step and to take it with decision.

It meets the difficulties of my thought admirably which were largely concerned with the effort to regulate competition without making terms with monopoly.

I hope that you will think that the circumstances warrant my taking this means of getting my views on this subject to your consideration.

Cordially and faithfully yours,   Woodrow Wilson

TLS (Letterpress Books, WP, DLC).

A Telegram and a Letter from Edward Mandell House

Beverly, Massachusetts, August 5, 1914.

Olney and I agree that in response to the Senate resolution it would be unwise to tender your good offices at this time. We believe it would lessen your influence when the proper moment arrives. He thinks it advisable that you make a direct or indirect statement to the effect that you have done what was humanly possible to compose the situation before this crisis had arrived. He thinks this would satisfy the Senate and the public. In view of your disinclination to act now upon the Senate resolution the story might be told to the correspondents at Washington and they might use the expression "We have it from high authority." He agrees to my suggestion that nothing further should be done now than to instruct our different ambassadors to inform the respective governments to whom they are accredited that you stand ready to tender your good offices whenever such an offer is desired. Olney also agrees with me that the shipping bill is full of lurking dangers.   E. M. House.

T telegram (WP, DLC).

Dear Governor: Prides Crossing, Mass. August 5th, 1914.

I am enclosing you a copy of a telegram which I have just sent you.

If a statement is made, let me suggest that you make it clear that what you have done was at your own instance. If the public either here or in Europe thought that Mr. Bryan instigated it, they would conclude it was done in an impractical way and was doomed to failure from the start.

I hate to harp upon Mr. Bryan, but you cannot know as I do how he is thought of in this connection. You and I understand better and know that the grossest sort of injustice is done him.

Nevertheless, just now it is impossible to make people think differently.

It may interest you to hear that Olney expressed regret that he did not accept your tender of the Ambassadorship to London. He said he had no idea it would mean anything more than social activity.

My heart is full of deep appreciation for your letter of August 3rd. I never worry when I do not hear from you. No human agency could make me doubt your friendship and affection. That my life is devoted entirely to your interests, I believe you know, and I never cease from trying to serve you.

Your faithful and affectionate,   E. M. House

I am terribly sorry to hear that Mrs. Wilson is still sick.

TLS (WP, DLC).

From Frederic Adrian Delano

My dear Mr. President: Chicago August 5th, 1914.

You have done me the great honor of appointing me a member of the Federal Reserve Board. As I explained to Mr. Thos. D. Jones, when he spoke to me about the matter, it was a position I did not covet and for which I did not feel that I had any special qualifications; but in view of the decision you had arrived at and of the apparent necessities of the situation, I felt that it was my duty to accept the post. You may rest assured, Mr. President, that I will do my utmost to merit the great confidence you have placed in me.

Several months ago you nominated me for a position on the Federal Commission on Industrial Relations, and I have been serving on that Commission,—in fact, giving a good deal of time to it. In view of my new duties, it seems that I must give up my position on the Industrial Commission. Indeed, as I was nominated as a representative of the employer class, I could no longer qualify if I entered the public service. I would, therefore, respectfully request that you accept this letter as notice of my desire to be relieved from service on the Federal Industrial Commission.   Faithfully yours,   Frederic A Delano

TLS (WP, DLC).

From William Charles Adamson

Dear Mr. President: Washington, D. C. August 5th, 1914.

I have your esteemed favor of this date by the hand of a special messenger, and I am subject to your command at any time for a conference about the Trade Commission Bill, or anything else.

You know, I cherish great deference for your opinions and wishes and I am anxious to co-operate with you to the end that your administration may be entirely successful.

I shall not undertake to reach any conclusion about the amendments to the Trade Commission Bill until I know definitely what they are, because the Senate is liable to make some changes in them, but when the Senate passes the bill and I see what they have finally determined upon then I will be glad to consider your views as to any issues in conference.

With high regards and best wishes, I remain,

Yours truly   W. C. Adamson

TLS (WP, DLC).

From Theodore Roosevelt

Oyster Bay, New York, August 5, 1914.

Very deep sympathy. Earnestly hope reports of Mrs. Wilson's condition are exaggerated.   Theodore Roosevelt.

T telegram (WP, DLC).

To Joseph R. Wilson, Jr.

My dear Brother: [The White House] August 6, 1914

Ellen's condition gives us a great deal of alarm but we have by no means lost hope and are fighting hard to bring her through. The trouble centers in the kidneys. I will, of course, let you know if any decided turn one way or the other takes place.

Thank you with all my heart for your letter.[1]

Your affectionate brother,   Woodrow Wilson

TLS (Letterpress Books, WP, DLC).
[1] It is missing.

To Theodore Roosevelt

My dear Colonel Roosevelt: [The White House] August 6, 1914

I deeply appreciate the telegram of sympathy you sent me yesterday. I am afraid I cannot say that the reports about Mrs.

Wilson's condition are exaggerated, but we have by no means given up hope and the indications are today a little encouraging.

With deep appreciation,

Sincerely yours,   Woodrow Wilson

TLS (Letterpress Books, WP, DLC).

To Edward Mandell House

My dear Friend: The White House August 6, 1914

Your warning about the shipping bill is quite justified but I think the bill is so phrased that we could control action under it pretty carefully. Of course, it would be our purpose to do so and I think we would have the means.

I hope you do not disapprove my little attempt at mediation. I have received no replies whatever yet from the governments concerned, but that is no matter. All I wanted to do was to let them know that I was at their service.

Mrs. Wilson's condition is giving me a great deal of anxiety, but we are still hoping and the doctors are doing noble work.

In haste   Affectionately yours,   Woodrow Wilson

TLS (E. M. House Papers, CtY).

To Lindley Miller Garrison

My dear Mr. Secretary: The White House August 6, 1914

I write to suggest that you request and advise all officers of the service, whether active or retired, to refrain from public comment of any kind upon the military or political situation on the other side of the water. I would be obliged if you would let them know that the request and advice comes from me. It seems to me highly unwise and improper that officers of the Army and Navy of the United States should make any public utterances to which any color of political or military criticism can be given where other nations are involved.

Cordially and faithfully yours,   Woodrow Wilson[1]

TLS (WDR, RG 94, AGO Doc. File 2194822, DNA).
[1] This order was aimed primarily at Admiral Alfred Thayer Mahan who, in a statement to the press on August 3, had been sharply critical of Austrian and German motives and ambitions. About this matter, see Link, *The Struggle for Neutrality*, p. 66.

To Thomas Davies Jones

My dear Friend: The White House August 6, 1914

Thank you warmly for your letter of August fourth. As you have probably seen in the newspapers, the names of both Mr. Warburg and Mr. Delano have been favorably reported by the committee. Alas that the report of your nomination did not come up a little later! The same thing would have happened. These men are now thoroughly frightened. But regrets are vain, and I am glad to say that they are a little relieved because I know so certainly that the whole country shares them.

You have been very generous in cooperating with us in looking for a right man and I hope with all my heart that we have found him in Mr. Delano.

With the warmest regard, in haste
                        Faithfully yours,   Woodrow Wilson

TLS (Mineral Point, Wisc., Public Library).

To Stockton Axson[1]

                  The White House Aug 6 1914 408 PM

Ellen died this afternoon quietly[2] and without pain at the last will telegraph arrangements later   Woodrow Wilson

T telegram (S. Axson Papers, TxHR).
 [1] This telegram was sent care Train No. 18, Union Pacific Railroad, enroute East, Pendleton, Ore.
 [2] According to the *New York Times*, Aug. 7, 1914, her last words to Dr. Grayson were: "Doctor, if I go away, promise me that you will take good care of my husband."

From Charles William Eliot

CONFIDENTIAL

Dear President Wilson: Asticou, Maine 6 August, 1914

Has not the United States an opportunity at this moment to propose a combination of the British Empire, the United States, France, Japan, Italy, and Russia in offensive and defensive alliance to rebuke and punish Austria-Hungary and Germany for the outrages they are now committing, by enforcing against those two countries non-intercourse with the rest of the world by land and sea? These two Powers have now shown that they are utterly untrustworthy neighbors, and military bullies of the worst sort,—Germany being far the worse of the two; because she has already violated neutral territory.

If they are allowed to succeed in their present enterprises, the fear of sudden invasion will constantly hang over all the other European peoples; and the increasing burdens of competitive armaments will have to be borne for another forty years. We shall inevitably share in these losses and miseries. The cost of maintaining immense armaments prevents all the great Powers from spending the money they ought to spend on improving the condition of the people, and promoting the progress of the world in health, human freedom, and industrial productiveness.

In this cause, and under the changed conditions, would not the people of the United States approve of the abandonment of Washington's advice that this country keep out of European complications?

A blockade of Germany and Austria-Hungary could not be enforced with completeness; but it could be enforced both by sea and by land to such a degree that the industries of both peoples would be seriously crippled in a short time by the stoppage of both their exports and their imports. Certain temporary commercial advantages would be gained by the blockading Nations,— a part of which might perhaps prove to be permanent.

This proposal would involve the taking part by our navy in the blockading process, and, therefore, might entail losses of both life and treasure; but the cause is worthy of heavy sacrifices; and I am inclined to believe that our people would support the Government in taking active part in such an effort to punish international crimes, and to promote future international peace.

Is it feasible to open *pourparlers* by cable on this subject? The United States is clearly the best country to initiate such a proposal. In so doing this country would be serving the general cause of peace, liberty, and good will among men.

This idea is not a wholly new one with me. The recent abominable acts of Austria-Hungary and Germany have brought to my mind again the passages on the Fear of Invasion, and the Exemption of Private Property from Capture at Sea, which I wrote a year ago in my report to the Carnegie Endowment for International Peace, entitled—*Some Roads Toward Peace*, pp. 16-17.[1] The outrageous actions of the last fortnight have re-enforced the statements I then made, and have suggested a new and graver application of the doctrines therein set forth.

I offer this suggestion in entire submission to your judgment as to its present feasibility and expediency. It seems to me an effective international police method, suited to the present crimes, and the probable issues of the future, and the more attractive because the European concert and the triple alliances have conspicuously failed. It, of course, involves the abandonment by all the European participants of every effort to extend national territory in Europe by force. The United States has recently abandoned that policy in America. It involves also the use of international force to overpower Austria-Hungary and Germany with all possible promptness and thoroughness; but this use of force is indispensable for the present protection of civilization against savagery, and for the future establishment and maintenance of federal relations and peace among the nations of Europe.

I am, with highest regard,
Sincerely yours,   Charles W. Eliot

TLS (WP, DLC).
1 *Some Roads Towards Peace: A Report to the Trustees of the Endowment on Observations Made in China and Japan in 1912* (Washington, 1914).

From William Jennings Bryan

My Dear Mr President   Washington Aug 6th 1914

Words are impotent to assuage a grief so great as that which has overwhelmed you, but I can not withhold from you this brief assurance of the deep sympathy which Mrs Bryan and I feel for you and your daughters. My heart has been heavy since I learned of the fatal character of Mrs Wilson's illness. Our wives were so much alike in helpfulness and in the spirit of comradship which has animated them that I can appreciate your lonliness. Allow me to extend such condolence as friend can speak to friend and command me if in this dark hour I can further testify to my affectionate regard. I am my dear Mr President
Yours most sincerely   William Jennings Bryan

ALS (WP, DLC).

From Thomas Riley Marshall

My dear Mr. Wilson,   Washington 6 Aug. 1914.

It is no time for idle words or high-sounding phrazes. This only, that you may be assured that every man, in all the land, who loves his wife reaches toward you an invisible hand bearing in its mystic touch the clasp of sympathy.

Neither Mrs. Marshall nor I would touch with impious hand the sacred Ark wherein you keep memory and misery, but we would have you know that there are few outside your chosen and sacred circle who more fully realized what She meant to you than do we. May the memory of the years gone by lighten a little the days to come.

Sorrowfully Yours,   Thos. R. Marshall

ALS (WP, DLC).

From Josephus Daniels

Dear Governor: The White House Aug. 6. 1914.

Except in your own home circle the sorrow that envelopes you can be felt no more deeply than in our home. My wife called with me and sends her love and tender sympathy. Her love for your good wife was deep and genuine. We both wish that we could comfort you or help you in the sadness and loneliness.

My regard was so great that I would feel it a privilege to come to the White House to-night if it should be desired.

With love and sympathy

Your faithful friend   Josephus Daniels

ALS (WP, DLC).

From William Cox Redfield

My dear Mr. President   Washington Aug. 6. 1914

One may not intrude into the sacred places even of those dear to them. Yet perhaps one who has passed through deep waters of pain and bereavement may say that there is light beyond them. Three of my own little ones await me on the farther side and dearly as I would love their continued presence here they give a living reality to the world beyond that is also precious

May the God of all comfort sustain, aye may he enrich you in this trying hour   Sincerely   William C Redfield

ALS (WP, DLC).

From James Viscount Bryce

My dear President   [London] August 6th 1914

My wife and I are deeply grieved at the news which has just reached us of your terrible bereavement. Such a sorrow, closing a happy wedded union, is the greatest that can befal any of us in this world of sorrows, and we feel all the more for you because we knew what help and comfort came in moments of anxiety from the constant counsel and sympathy of a pure soul, close to one's own.

May God help and strengthen you to bear such a loss. Our knowledge of her, of her sweetness and simple goodness, was enough to enable us to divine what she was to those who were nearest to her. Our thoughts are and will be with you and your children   Ever sincerely yours   James Bryce

Please do not think of answering this.

ALS (WP, DLC).

From Marcus Aurelius Smith

Dear Mr President   Washington, D. C. Aug 6th 1914

I wish I knew what I could say or do, that would take the least weight from you[r] overburdened heart. May I not hope that a mite of comfort will reach you in the assurance that I would, if I could take the burden from your heart and bear it myself through the fast closing days of my life. Is it a comfort to know that so many others would do the same for you? How hopeless is my wish to help you! How helpless the sympathy of all the world! Please try to find some solace in the profound sympathy of your countrymen
          Most sincerely yours,   Marcus A. Smith

ALS (WP, DLC).

To Mary Allen Hulbert

Dearest Friend,   The White House [Aug. 7, 1914]

Of course you know what has happend to me; but I wanted you to know direct from me. God has stricken me almost beyond what I can bear.   Your friend,   W.W.

WWTLI (WP, DLC).

From Mary Allen Hulbert

Nantucket Massachusetts
My dearest Friend: August 7th [1914]

It seems incredible that this terrible thing has come to you, *now*, now, when you need that sweet soul to help you in this terrible time. I know I can say nothing that can really help any of you, but just to take to yourself the comfort of remembering she had much, *much* that was beautiful in her life, much that makes life worth-while. Whatever comes, God is good I *know*.

When you can, write to this one of your legion of devoted friends. I am well, and am with you in thought and deepest sympathy every moment. In event of your hearing of Allens boat burning and his narrow escape with some burns & cuts, I was *not* with him, as the paper stated. God bless you all.

Your friend   Mary Allen Hulbert.

ALS (WP, DLC).

From Florence Stevens Hoyt

Dear Cousin Woodrow,   [Tamworth, N. H., c. Aug. 7, 1914]

It seems an intrusion. I am not sure that I have the right but I must reach out to you. I have seemed very far away. I wanted desperately to go to you to get closer but I was afraid that you dear people would have me on your mind.

I think there is no need for me to tell you that you are al-together filling my thoughts. I am so glad that she had you to the last! You have given her for all these years what, I think, no one else can ever have had so fully; and you have as your permanent possession that rarely fine, splendidly noble spirit that has been wholly yours. I cannot bear, though, to think of all the tangible loneliness for you. I who care so much know that even love cannot reach through to help. I suppose work is the only thing—even though that too is lonely. God help you! Is the thought that you help countless others any comfort?

You know a little of how I loved her. All that I read, think or see brings her to me. I feel that I have no right to look at my own pain. I can never be grateful enough for the intimacy she gave me. I might so easily have missed it! I treasure words that let me have glimpses of her wonderful noble nature—they make me feel close to all that is holy, to the vision. Even now in the midst of the hurt I know that I must try to be worthy of the gift of her love and help to keep alive on earth her unselfish courage.

But though her rich nature had love for us others, it was only you who had her completely. But words can't say what one wants said. Please forgive me for writing.

With great love,   Florence.

ALS (WP, DLC).

From Cleveland Hoadley Dodge

My dear Woodrow,   New York. Aug. 7th 1914

Our hearts literally ache for you and the dear girls

May the God of all comfort bless & keep you is the heartfelt prayer of your devoted friend   Cleve Dodge

ALS (WP, DLC).

From Edward Mandell House

My dear Friend,   Prides Crossing, Mass. August 7, 1914.

I never dreamed that Mrs. Wilson was so mortally ill, and her death leaves me unnerved and stunned. It only proves again how near to us the angel of death hovers. I know, as few do, how deeply you are stricken, but I thank God you have the fortitude to withstand the blow. My affection for you is such that your troubles must ever be my troubles, and your sorrows must be mine as well. It has fallen to your lot to bring a great nation through an epoch making time, and the noble, gentle soul that has gone would be the first to bid you bring to bear that splendid courage, which is yours and yours alone.

Your faithful and affectionate,   E. M. House

ALS (WP, DLC).

From Sir Edward Grey

London, Aug. 7, 1914.

Please accept the expression of my deep sympathy in your great bereavement.   Edward Grey

T telegram (WP, DLC).

From Edmund William Gosse[1]

Sir   London S. W. August 7 1914

At the recommendation of the Lord Chancellor (Viscount Haldane) I venture to send you a copy of the White Book just issued.[2]

It is on the basis of these documents that the English Government justifies its action in declaring war against Germany, and the favour of your consideration of them will be deeply appreciated.

Permit me to remain Sir

Your obedient Servant   Edmund Gosse

ALS (SDR, RG 59, 763.72/746, DNA).
¹ Poet, literary critic, and scholar, at this time librarian to the House of Lords.
² Great Britain, Foreign Office, *Correspondence Respecting the European Crisis* (London, 1914).

Lindley Miller Garrison to Joseph Patrick Tumulty

Dear Joe: Washington. August 7, 1914.

I hand you herewith an important cablegram from General Funston.¹ I do not know whether you are presenting any matters to the President, but if you are, I suggest that you show him this.

I will be at the Department in case you want to communicate with me about anything.

                              Sincerely yours,   Lindley M. Garrison

TLS (EBR, RG 130, DNA).
¹ F. Funston to Adjutant General, Aug. 7, 1914, T telegram (EBR, RG 130, DNA). It contained a translation of an undated intercepted telegram from Carranza to Carbajal, threatening him and his "civilian accomplices" with execution if they did not, in mustering out the Federal army, surrender all its arms and ammunition to a Constitutionalist general designated by Carranza.

Joseph Patrick Tumulty to Lindley Miller Garrison

Personal

Dear Mr. Secretary: [The White House] August 8, 1914

With reference to the despatch from General Funston which you sent over last evening, the President directs me to say that he takes it for granted that General Funston will act toward such news as if he were not in Mexico at all. Events must take their course.   Sincerely yours,   [J. P. Tumulty]

CCL (EBR, RG 130, DNA).

From Lindley Miller Garrison

My dear Mr. President: Washington. August 8, 1914.

I must let the gravity of the situation be my excuse for bringing up at this time a well-worn subject. I do feel the necessity of referring to it again so as to learn if your judgment is altered by the most recent developments.

It is known officially that Carranza has notified Carbajal that if the latter does not surrender arms, etc., he and those who have been serving in the Federal army will be considered as subject to the law which authorizes their execution as criminals, —the same law which was applied to Maximilian and his people.

It is also known officially that there is great apprehension in the City of Mexico, doubt as to the intentions of Carranza, despair on behalf of those who have adhered to the Federal cause, and fear that the defensive possibilities are slight. The number of those fleeing to Vera Cruz is constantly and largely increasing.

Carranza has not succeeded in making a satisfactory and thoroughly understood agreement with Zapata. Villa is really hostile to Carranza, and the designs and plans of Villa are undisclosed and unknown, excepting that he is gathering food, forage, horses and recruits, and is moving some of his troops southward.

The newspapers this morning state that the Carbajal Government in desperation has determined that its only recourse is to stand and fight.

When we talked on Wednesday last you felt that you could not agree with me in the necessity of strengthening our position at Vera Cruz by transportation, equipment and men, because of the disastrous effect which such a move might have upon the peace proceedings between the factions. I simply want to be sure now that you feel the same way. It appears to me that the situation has radically changed, because there seems to be no hope of a satisfactory settlement or agreement; and the leaders—on the revolutionary side at least—do not appear to be sympathetic with our desires in this respect.

Our forces, as you know, are absolutely tied to Vera Cruz for lack of land transportation equipment, and are of course inadequate in numbers to penetrate into the country.

I need hardly recall to your memory my long-settled conviction that prudence requires us to be ready with everything necessary for what may be reasonably foreseen and expected. I cannot escape from the feeling that in view of the attitude assumed by Carranza, the uncertainty of the attitude of Zapata and of Villa, and the implication of responsibility that rests upon us, we should strongly reenforce the Vera Cruz garrison and certainly send them sufficient land equipment to move to the interior if needed. In view of the attitude of the revolutionary leaders as now disclosed, it is apparent that this would not prejudicially interfere with the settlement by agreement, but, in my judgment, would rather tend to bring it about.

You must know how I shrink from intruding upon you now, but I feel that I must. Please let me know if you desire me to do anything under the circumstances.

Sincerely yours,   Lindley M. Garrison

TLS (EBR, RG 130, DNA).

To Lindley Miller Garrison

My dear Mr. Secretary: [The White House] August 8, 1914

I have your letter of this morning and understand perfectly the motives and the sense of duty which led you to write it.

But my judgment remains unaltered and I want you to know why.

We shall have no right at any time to intervene in Mexico to determine the way in which the Mexicans are to settle their own affairs. I feel sufficiently assured that the property and lives of foreigners will not suffer in the process of the settlement. The rest is political and Mexican. Many things may happen of which we do not approve and which could not happen in the United States, but I say very solemnly that that is no affair of ours. Our responsibility will come after the settlement and in the determination of the question whether the new government is to receive the recognition of the Government of the United States or not. There are in my judgment no conceivable circumstances which would make it right for us to direct by force or by threat of force the internal processes of what is a profound revolution, a revolution as profound as that which occurred in France. All the world has been shocked ever since the time of the revolution in France that Europe should have undertaken to nullify what was done there, no matter what the excesses then committed.

I speak very solemnly but with clear judgment in the matter, which I hope God will give me strength to act upon.

Faithfully yours,   Woodrow Wilson

TLS (Letterpress Books, WP, DLC).

From William Jennings Bryan

My dear Mr. President: Washington August 8, 1914.

I am enclosing a memorandum prepared by Counselor Lansing relating to the situation in the Far East.[1] You have doubtless read the telegram recently received to the effect that China would make the same proposition to Japan that she expects to make to us, namely, that good offices be used to prevent the extension of war into the Far East.[2]

Until the telegram from China is received, we cannot, of course, discuss its exact terms, but the memorandum presented by Counselor Lansing presents a course which you might have under consideration.

While I approve of his suggestions, I believe it might be well to go even further, that is, we might suggest in our representations (1) an agreement that hostilities *be not extended to the Far East*, and (2) if that is not agreeable to the contending powers, an agreement as to the neutralization of treaty ports, respect for Chinese neutrality and preservation of the status quo in China.

This is simply offered for your consideration in order to make easier the final decision when the message from the Chinese President arrives.

With assurances of my highest regard, I am, my dear Mr. President,   Very truly yours,   W. J. Bryan

P.S. I shall, in compliance with your request, bring Mr. Fuller to the White House at 2:30 tomorrow (Sunday).[3] Governor Fort has accepted a position on the Commission going to San Domingo. He looked upon it as a matter of duty and when I told him we wanted a Republican, he intimated that you had made it almost impossible for him to consider himself a Republican any longer. He will arrive here on Monday morning and will leave Monday afternoon with Sullivan and Smith. Do you desire to see Governor Fort during Monday forenoon? He will be at the Department as early as ten o'clock and I can communicate your wishes to him. Also let me know whether, if you want to see Governor Fort, I shall have Sullivan and Smith, the other members of the Commission, accompany him.

TLS (WP, DLC).
    [1] The enclosure is missing; however, it was "Memorandum by the Counselor . . ." and is printed in *FR-LP*, 1, 1-3.
    [2] It is described and quoted in *ibid.*
    [3] Fuller came to the White House on August 9 and left soon afterward on a special mission to Villa. No record of the Wilson-Fuller conversation is extant; however, Fuller's reports will make clear the nature of Wilson's instructions.

From Bliss Perry

My dear Wilson: Errol, N. H., Aug. 8 1914

I am in the woods, far from the railroad, and have only just now learned of Mrs. Wilson's death. You will let me tell you, I am sure, of the poignant sorrow which I feel, and give you my assurances of profoundest sympathy. My heart aches for you in your bereavement and I pray that you may have strength granted to you for a continuance of the heroic service which you are performing for the country. You must and will bear up, I know, and go straight forward, and I hope that it may be some measure of comfort to you to remember that all of your old friends cherish the most sacred and happy memories of your devoted wife. We can never forget her kindness to us in Princeton.

With deepest sorrow and all affectionate greetings, I am
                                    Faithfully yours   Bliss Perry

ALS (WP, DLC).

From George McLean Harper

Dear Wilson: Grasmere [Eng.] August 8, 1914

It is with a heavy heart that I think of your grief & loss. We heard the terrible news yesterday from Mr. Walmesley,[1] in Ambleside, just after Belle[2] had posted a letter to the dear one. There seemed to be a mute offer of sympathy from the trees, the hills, the lake, which have given you both such happiness.

Our sorrow is beyond expression. We are thinking of you & the girls both day & night, with the vain desire to help. Few can know as well as we know how that bright & ardent being was the centre of all your lives.

The thought of her will ever bring sunshine to my heart, notwithstanding present sorrow. I remember our first meeting & many a delightful hour scattered through the intervening twenty-four years, as veritable gleams of sunshine. And there was also the constant sense of her friendship, something to be proud of indeed.

God grant that in her name & under her sacred inspiration you may go bravely on, upholding peace & righteousness in the world. We, Belle & I, know how truly it has been not your work alone, but yours & hers together. For her sake you will not lose heart nor grow faint.

With love from us all,
                          Yours ever,   Geo Mc Harper

ALS (WP, DLC).
  [1] Unidentified.
  [2] His wife, Belle Dunton Westcott Harper.

From Henry van Dyke

                    •   The Hague.
My dear friend and President,   Sunday, August 9, 1914.

The news of your great sorrow reached me on Saturday night and gave me a deep shock of distress. I telegraphed at once to assure you of my sympathy from the bottom of my heart.

I know something of your dear wife's character and the wonderful love between you. Missing her presence you must suffer more than words can tell. There is no real consolation save in the love of the Eternal, and the precious promises of Jesus Christ our adorable Redeemer. These are yours, I know. And even the strongest man can rest and repose on those kind arms of everlasting love like a little child on his mother's breast. Do it, dear friend. Pray the prayer without words, which Christ so often heard and answered. But though there is no *consolation* elsewhere, there is a certain support and renewal of strength in the thought of duty done and yet to do. This also is yours.

I am proud every time I think of the great success of your administration. Nowhere is it more remarkable than in what you have done and what you have refused to do in regard to Mexico. That is a triumph of patience and firmness, won almost *contra mundum*. I know how your dear wife was with you in this. God preserve and strengthen you for what you have still to do for our country.

I want you to know that, though there is no precedent in the diplomatic instructions for it, I have put the flag at half mast on this Legation for three days. This morning at the English Church, we had special prayers for you, and at the close of service we all stood in silence while the funeral march was played on the organ. Many faces were wet with tears. Many of the Hague people have expressed their profound sympathy with you and with our country.

We are in the midst of dark days and nights, working here at the Legation sixteen hours a day, helping the distressed, trying to reunite families which have been separated by the state of war, relieving the needs of the destitute, sending our people home to America as fast as possible. Thanks to the fine arrangements which our Government and the Netherlands Government have made in response to my request, we have had no financial difficulties for Americans here in Holland. They have all been safe and reasonably comfortable. Pray God that the neutrality of Holland and America may be preserved.

It is a great happiness to serve under you. My head and heart are engaged.

The cause of Peace, alas, looks dim, but I believe that when this horrible war is over it will shine brighter and be nearer than ever before.

I close this Sunday night letter with a prayer for your comfort, your peace, your life, your strength, in God.

Ever Faithfully   Henry van Dyke

ALS (WP, DLC).

From Robert Bridges

Dear Tommy: New York Aug 9 1914

There is nothing to say in your sorrow except that your friends are thinking of you always; that they know what you suffer and know you will meet it, as you have met every crisis in your life.

All that she ever wished for you, you have achieved—and she has been a part of it in sympathy, counsel and unfailing affection. That is your imperishable remembrance.

Dear Tommy you have my deepest thought and sympathy always in the great burdens you must bear.

Affectionately Yours   Robert Bridges

ALS (WP, DLC).

From Walter Hines Page

Belated, I fear, beyond any value or interest.

Dear Mr. President: London, Sunday, August 9, 1914.

God save us! What a week it has been! Last Sunday (Aug. 2) I was down here at the cottage I have taken for the summer —an hour out of London—uneasy because of the apparent danger and of what Sir Edward Grey had told me. During the day people began to go to the Embassy but not in great numbers—merely to ask what they should do in case of war. The Secretary whom I had left in charge on Sunday telephoned me every few hours and laughingly told funny experiences with nervous women who came in and asked absurd questions. Of course, we all knew the grave danger that war might come, but nobody could, by the wildest imagination, guess at what awaited us. On Monday I was at the Embassy earlier than I think I had ever been there before, and every member of the staff was already on duty. Before breakfast-time the place was filled—packed like sardines. This was two days before war was declared. There was no chance to talk to individuals, such was the jam. I got on a chair and explained that I had already telegraphed to Washington—on Saturday— suggesting the sending of money and ships, and asking them to be patient. I made a speech to them several times during the day, and kept the Secretaries doing so at intervals. More than 2,000 Americans crowded into those offices (which are not large) that day. We were kept there till two o'clock in the morning. The Embassy has not been closed since.

Mr. Kent of the Bankers' Trust Co. in New York[1] volunteered to form an American Citizens' Relief Committee. He and other men of experience and influence organized themselves at the Savoy Hotel. The hotel gave the use of nearly a whole floor. They organized themselves quickly and admirably and got information about steamships and currency, etc. We began to send callers at the Embassy to this Committee for such information. The banks were all closed for four days. These men got money enough—put it up themselves and used their English banking friends for help—to relieve all cases of actual want of cash that came to them. Tuesday the crowd at the Embassy was still great but less. The big space at the Savoy Hotel gave them room to talk to one another and to get relief for immediate needs. By that time I had accepted the volunteer service of five or six men* to help us explain to the people—and they have all worked manfully day and night. We now have an orderly organization at four places—the Embassy, the Consul-General's Office, the Savoy, and The American Society in London, and everything is going well. We now have offices for inquiries & for disbursing agents also. Those two first days, there was, of course, great confusion. Crazy men and weeping women were imploring and cursing and demanding—God knows it was bedlam turned loose. I have been called a man of the greatest genius for an emergency by some, by others a d—d fool, by others every epithet between these extremes. Men shook English banknotes in my face and demanded U. S. money and swore our Government and its agents ought all to be shot. Women expected me to hand them steamship tickets home. When some found out they could not get tickets on the transports (which they assumed would sail the next day) they accused me of favoritism. European folk regard an Ambassador as a man who represents their government; Americans, as a personal servant to secure them state-rooms! These absurd experiences will give you a hint of the panic. But now it has worked out all right, thanks to the Savoy Committee and other helpers.

Meantime, of course, our telegrams and mail increased almost as much as our callers. I have filled the place with stenographers, I have got the Savoy people to answer certain classes of letters, and we have caught up. My own time and the time of two of the Secretaries has been almost wholly taken with governmental problems: hundreds of questions have come in from every quarter that were never asked before. But even with them we have now practically caught up—it has been a wonderful week!

* There are now, I think, 14 extra men at work, besides the relief-group of as many more.

Then the Austrian Ambassador[2] came to give us his Embassy —to take over his business. Every detail was arranged. The next morning I called on him to assume charge and to say good bye, when he told me that he was not yet going! That was a stroke of genius by Sir Edward Grey who informed him that Austria had not given England cause for war. That *may* work out, or it may not. Pray Heaven it may! Poor Mensdorff, the Austrian Ambassador, does not know where he is. He is practically shut up in his guarded Embassy, weeping and waiting the decree of fate.

Then came the declaration of war, most dramatically. Tuesday night five minutes after the ultimatum expired the Admiralty telegraphed to the fleet "Go." In a few minutes the answer came back "Off." Soldiers began to march through the city going to the railway stations. An indescribable crowd so blocked the streets about the Admiralty, the War Office, and the Foreign Office, that at one o'clock in the morning I had to drive in my car by other streets to get home.

The next day the German Embassy was turned over to me. I went to see the German Ambassador[3] at three o'clock in the afternoon. He came down in his pajamas—a crazy man. I feared he might literally go mad. He is of the anti-war party and he had done his best and utterly failed. This interview was one of the most pathetic experiences of my life. The poor man had not slept for several nights. Then came the crowds of frightened Germans, afraid that they would be arrested. They beseiged the German Embassy and our Embassy. A servant in the German Embassy who went over the house with one of our men came to the desk of Princess Lichnowsky, the Ambassador's wife. A photo. of the German Emperor lay on the desk, face down. The man said: "She threw it down and said: 'That is the swine that did this,'" and she drew a pig on the blotting pad, wh. is still there. I put one of our naval officers in the German Embassy, put the U. S. on the door to protect it, and we began business there, too. Our naval officer has moved in—sleeps there. He has an assistant, a stenographer, a messenger; and I gave him the German automobile and chauffeur and two English servants that were left there. He has the job well in hand now, under my and Laughlin's supervision. But this has brought still another new lot of diplomatic and governmental problems—a lot of them. Three enormous German banks in London have, of course, been closed. Their managers pray for my aid. Howling women come and say their innocent German husbands have been arrested as spies. English, Germans, Americans—everybody has daughters and wives and invalid grandmothers alone in Germany. In God's name, they ask, what can I do for them? Here come stacks of letters sent under the impression that I can send them to Germany. But the German business is already well in hand and I think that that will take little of my own time and will give little trouble. I shall send a report about it in detail to the Department the very first day I can find time to write it. In spite of the effort of the English Government to remain at peace with Austria, I fear I shall yet have the Austrian Embassy too. But I can attend to it.

Now, however, comes the financial job of wisely using the $300,000 which I shall have tomorrow. I am using Mr. Chandler Anderson[4] as counsel, of course. I have appointed a Committee— Skinner, the Consul-General,[5] Lieut. Commander McCrary of our Navy,[6] Kent of the Bankers' Trust Co., N. Y., and one other man yet to be chosen—to advise, after investigation, about every proposed expenditure. Anderson has been at work all day today drawing up proper forms etc. to fit the Department's very excellent instructions. I have the feeling that more of that money may be wisely spent in helping to get people off the continent (except in France, where they seem admirably to be managing it, under Herrick) than is immediately needed in England. All this merely to show you the diversity and multiplicity of the job.

I am having a card catalogue, each containing a sort of who's who, of all Americans in Europe of whom we hear. This will be ready by the time the Tennessee[7] comes. Fifty or more stranded Americans—men and women—are doing this work free. I have a member of Congress in the general reception room of the Embassy answering people's questions—three other volunteers as well.

We had a world of confusion for two or three days. But all this work is now well organized and it can be continued without confusion or cross-purposes. I meet committees and lay plans and read and write telegrams from the time I wake till I go to bed. But, since it is now all in order, it is easy. Of course I am running up the expenses of the Embassy—there is no help for that; but the bill will be really exceedingly small because of the volunteer work—for awhile. I have not and shall not consider the expense of whatever it seems absolutely necessary to do—of other things, I shall always consider the expense most critically. Everybody is working with everybody else in the finest possible spirit. I have made out a sort of military order to the Embassy staff, detailing one man with clerks for each night and forbidding the others to stay there till midnight. None of us slept more than a few hours last week. It was not the work that kept them after the first night or two, but the sheer excitement of this awful cataclysm. All London has been awake for a week. Soldiers are marching day and night; immense throngs block the streets about the government offices; thousands and thousands throng before the Palace every night till the King comes out on the balcony. But they are all very orderly. Every day Germans are arrested on suspicion; and several of them have committed suicide. Yesterday one poor American woman yielded to the excitement and cut her throat. I find it hard to get about much. People stop me on the street, follow me to luncheon, grab me as I come out of any committee meeting—to know my opinion of this or that—how can they get home? Will such-and-such a boat fly the American flag? Why did I take the German Embassy? I receive yet a great deal of criticism for having the German Embassy—from Americans chiefly. I have to fight my way about and rush to an automobile. I have had to buy me a second one to keep up the racket. Buy? no—only bargain for it, for I have not any money. But everybody is considerate, and that makes no matter for the moment. This little cottage in an out-of-the-way place 25 miles from London where I am trying to write and sleep has been found by people today, who come in automobiles to know how they may reach their sick kinspeople in Germany. I had not had a bath for three days: as soon as I got in the tub, the telephone rang an "urgent" call!

Upon my word, if one could forget the awful tragedy, all this experience would be worth a life-time of common-place. One surprise follows another so rapidly that one loses all sense of time: it seems an age since last Sunday.

I shall never forget Sir Edward Grey's telling me of the ultimatum—while he wept; nor the poor German Ambassador who has lost in his high game—almost a demented man; nor the King as he declaimed at me for half-an-hour and threw up his hands and said, "My God, Mr. Page, what else could we do?" Nor the Austrian Ambassador's wringing his hands and weeping and crying out "My dear Colleague, my dear colleague."

Along with all this tragedy come two reverend American peace-delegates who got out of Germany by the skin of their teeth and complain that they lost all the clothes they had except what they had on. "Don't complain," said I, "but thank God you saved your skins." Everybody has forgotten what war means—forgotten that folks get hurt. But they are coming around to it now. A U. S. Senator telegraphs me "Send my wife and daughter home on the first ship." Ladies and gentlemen filled the steerage of that ship, not a bunk left; and his wife and daughter are found three days later sitting in a swell hotel waiting for me to bring them state-room tickets on a silver tray! One of my young fellows in the Embassy rushes into my office saying that a man from Boston with letters of introduction from Senators and Governors and Secretaries et al. was demanding tickets of admission to a pic-ture-gallery, and a Secretary to escort him there. "What shall I do with him?" "Put his proposal to a vote of the 200 Americans in the room and see them draw and quarter him." I have not yet heard what happened. A woman writes me four pages to prove how dearly she loves my sister and invites me to her hotel —5 miles away—"please to tell her about the sailing of the steam-ships." Six American preachers pass a resolution unanimously "urging our Ambassador to telegraph our beloved, peace-loving President to stop this awful war"; and they come with simple solemnity to present their resolution. Lord save us, what a world!

And this awful tragedy moves on to—what? We do not know what is really happening, so strict is the censorship. But it seems inevitable to me that Germany will be beaten, after a long while, that the horrid period of alliances and armaments will not come again, that England will gain even more of the earth's surface, that Russia may next play the menace; that all Europe (so much as survives) will be bankrupt; that relatively *we* shall be im-mensely stronger financially and politically—there must surely come many great changes—very many, yet undreamed of. Be ready; for you will be called on to compose this huge quarrel. I thank Heaven for many things—first, the Atlantic Ocean; second, that you refrained from war in Mexico; third, that we kept our treaty—the canal tolls victory, I mean. Now, when all this half of the world will suffer the unspeakable brutalization of war, we shall preserve our moral strength, our political power, and our ideals.

God save us!   Yours faithfully   Walter H. Page

TLS (WP, DLC).
   1 Fred I. Kent, vice-president of the Bankers Trust Co. of New York.
   2 Albert, Count Mensdorff-Pouilly-Dietrichstein.
   3 That is, Prince Lichnowsky.
   4 Chandler Parsons Anderson, Counselor of the Department of State, 1910-1913, at this time serving unofficially as legal adviser to Page.
   5 Robert Peet Skinner.
   6 Frank Robert McCrary.
   7 Armored cruiser *U.S.S. Tennessee* sailed from New York for England on August 6 with a cargo of $5,867,000 in gold from the U. S. Treasury and New York banks for the relief of American tourists stranded in Europe. *New York Times*, Aug. 7, 1914.

From William Jennings Bryan

My Dear Mr. President: Washington August 10, 1914.

I beg to communicate to you an important matter which has come before the Department. Morgan Company of New York have asked whether there would be any objection to their making a loan to the French Government and also the Rothchilds—I suppose that is intended for the French Government. I have conferred with Mr. Lansing and he knows of no legal objection to financing this loan, but I have suggested to him the advisability of presenting to you an aspect of the case which is not legal but I believe to be consistent with our attitude in international matters. It is whether it would be advisable for this Government to take the position that it will not approve of any loan to a belligerent nation. The reasons that I would give in support of this proposition are:

First: Money is the worst of all contrabands because it commands everything else. The question of making loans contraband by international agreement has been discussed, but no action has been taken. I know of nothing that would do more to prevent war than an international agreement that neutral nations would not loan to belligerents. While such an agreement would be of great advantage, could we not by our example hasten the reaching of such an agreement? We are the one great nation which is not involved and our refusal to loan to any belligerent would naturally tend to hasten a conclusion of the war. We are responsible for the use of our influence through example and as we cannot tell what we can do until we try, the only way of testing our influence is to set the example and observe its effect. This is the fundamental reason in support of the suggestion submitted.

Second: There is a special and local reason, it seems to me, why this course would be advisable. Mr. Lansing observed in the discussion of the subject that a loan would be taken by those in synpathy with the country in whose behalf the loan was negotiated. If we approved of a loan to France we could not, of course, object to a loan to Great Britain, Germany, Russia, Austria or to any other country, and if loans were made to these countries our citizens would be divided into groups, each group loaning money to the country which it favors and this money could not be furnished without expressions of sympathy. These expressions of synpathy are disturbing enough when they do not rest upon pecuniary interests—they would be still more disturbing if each group was pecuniarily interested in the success of the nation to whom its members had loaned money.

Third: The powerful financial interests which would be connected with these loans would be tempted to use their influence through the newspapers to support the interests of the Government to which they had loaned because the value of the security would be directly affected by the result of the war. We would thus find our newspapers violently arrayed on one side or the other, each paper supporting a financial group and pecuniary interest. All of this influence would make it all the more difficult for us to maintain neutrality, as our action on various questions that would arise would affect one side or the other and powerful financial interests would be thrown into the balance.

I am to talk over the telephone with Mr. Davidson[1] of the Morgan Company at one o'clock, but I will have him delay final action until you have time to consider this question.

It grieves me to be compelled to intrude any question upon you at this time, but I am sure you will pardon me for submitting a matter of such great importance.

With assurances of high respect, I am, My dear Mr. President,

Yours very truly,   W. J. Bryan

P.S. Mr. Lansing calls attention to the fact that an American citizen who goes abroad and voluntarily enlists in the army of a belligerent nation loses the protection of his citizenship while so engaged, and asks why dollars, going abroad and enlisting in war, should be more protected. As we cannot prevent American citizens going abroad at their own risk, so we cannot prevent dollars going abroad at the risk of the owners, but the influence of the Government is used to prevent American citizens from doing this. Would the Government not be justified in using its influence against the enlistment of the nation's dollars in a foreign war?

The Morgans say the money would be expended *here* but it must be remembered that if foreign loans absorb our loanable money it might affect our getting government loans if we needed

TLS (WP, DLC).
[1] Henry Pomeroy Davison.

Joseph R. Wilson, Jr., to Kate Wilson and Alice Wilson

My precious Ones: Wednesday [Aug. 11, 1914] on the Train.

We are enroute home. As I wired last night, we had an uneventful trip to Rome. Rain had laid the dust and cooled the atmosphere, so we did not suffer much from the heat. Everything possible was done for the safety and comfort of the party. There were crowds at every station and marked evidences of sympathy. The casket rested in one end of the President's private car. Stockton Axson, Ed Wilson,[1] Geo. Howe and I had compartments with private washing arrangements, toilet etc. in the car next the President's. Stockton and I had our meals with the family. The entire populace had turned out at Rome. The town was draped in mourning. The services at the church where sister Ellie's father was pastor for over 16 years, were very simple. As we reached the grave a driving rain came up, but a large tent covered the grave so we did not get wet. The grave was securely bricked up. The casket was sealed in a steel casing and this arched over with brick.

Brother has held up *wonderfully* well as the other members of the family have. We will reach Wash. at 5 and I will go directly home. I inclose newspaper clippings giving full details better than I could in a letter.

I did not get up until 11 this a.m. I took a bath in the bowl and a shave, my first shave on a fast moving train although I did shave yesterday while the train was moving slowly. I got on nicely.

Geo. McMaster was at Rome enroute from Columbia to Fort Leavenworth, Kan. to which post he has been transferred.

My! the flowers. How elaborate and numerous the exquisite designs. A special baggage car was provided on the train for them.

Not a hitch has marred the splendid arrangements for the trip. Everything has passed off with a degree of accuracy that has given evidence of expert management. No one is allowed in Brother's car except members of the family unless sent for by him. The train is guarded in every way. Secret service men surround his car whenever we stop, but being a special we stop seldom. Jim Woodrow and Fitz[2] joined us in Atlanta, also four of the younger Axson generation whom I have not yet placed. McAdoo is the only Cabinet member with us, and only as a member of the family, Brother preferring that all remain on duty in Wash. All has been simplicity itself with no pomp. Strange that it rained as we went from the White House to the station, then stopped; and again at the grave, then stopped. The Heavens were weeping. Great crowds lined the Washington streets and thronged the station—everybody respectful and scores tearful. I rode in the auto with Brother to the train. He gave his personal attention to all details so as to see that everything was done as he wanted, but was always mindful of others. For instance, he said for me not to come if it would interfere with my business. Mr. Bland[3] said "certainly" for me to come. Bond[4] is back so I came. I have endeavored to keep you constantly posted by wire and by mail, so you would know all. Every one thinks it was wise for you not to come. It would have been so trying for you.

I have kept well but, of course, am tired.

I will mail this the first chance I get.

I do love you both *so* deeply. Many, *many* kisses.

Your own   Husband.

ALS (received from Alice Wilson McElroy).
  [1] He probably meant Dr. Grayson, who was on the train.
  [2] Fitz William McMaster Woodrow.
  [3] His superior, John Randolph Bland of Baltimore, president of the United States Fidelity and Guaranty Co.
  [4] Thomas Bond, head of the agency department.

From Mary Eloise Hoyt

My dearest Cousin,   [En route] August 11 [1914].

May I talk to you a little about Ellen? You see I am living with Bertha Rembaugh[1] who knew her too slightly to make me like to say very often, "Oh, yes when Ellen and I were together there, this is what she did and said." And I have a habit of waking very early and thinking about her for an hour or two before I need get up. Hundreds of dear, half-forgotten little speeches of hers crowd into my mind and I should like to write some of them to you. It eases my heart to talk about her and while she is so constantly with us, it is almost as if she were really here.

I have thought ever so often about what you said yesterday and I cannot think that your career killed her. In the first place, her family on both sides is rather short-lived. In the second place, wherever she had been placed, she would have found people to whom she would have given herself, and there is never a lack of people who are ready to take. Don't you remember how, when she was studying here at the Art League, she could not keep herself away from some kind of social work. "The need is so great," she said; and she would always have found the need great, wherever she was. And is it not a thing to be glad of that you did place her where everyone in this whole land has been able to feel her influence? I do not believe that there are any persons in America who have not, since last Thursday, felt with renewed force the sweetness of the natural human lover and realised that they could lift the life of the affections to the upper levels and could get all the joy one needs to live by if they just cared nobly enough for their own people. It may have been my fancy, but I thought the men on the cars were peculiarly gentle to their wives.

And a little speech of hers comes back to me that makes me think she did almost realise what she was to you; "Woodrow says," she told me one day, with that little half-sweet, half-mocking smile of hers "that, if he ever writes anything that has literary value, he will owe his fame to me." I suppose it is largely because of that little speech of hers that I so long to have you write some more things that have literary value. She cared so much for *P O P*,[2] you know.

I wish I could see you for it is easier to talk than to write, although I am still rather a crybaby and not quite sure that I can keep my voice steady. It was very good to be with you and to talk about her. I feel as if I had been standing close to the gate of heaven and I find coming back rather hard.

Of course I know you have no time to write, with all the country depending upon you. I am sending this by the girls. I wish you could get things in some other than an official manner. And I do hope I shall see you before very long. You were so dear to me, you and the girls. Marjorie Brown said I looked like another person after I had been with you.

With much love,   Your loving cousin,   Mary

ALS (WP, DLC).
[1] Bertha Rembaugh, Bryn Mawr '97, a lawyer of New York. She and Mary Hoyt had taught together at the Bryn Mawr School in Baltimore.
[2] Wilson's projected magnum opus, "The Philosophy of Politics."

Remarks to the Federal Reserve Board[1]

August 13, 1914.

This meeting affords me an opportunity to say, gentlemen, what I am sure the whole country feels, namely, that it is extremely fortunate that at last all reasons for delaying the organization of the Board are removed, and that the country can now proceed to the organization of a system which I am sure will relieve it and steady it and reassure it in many ways.

We have for a great many years been looking forward to an expansion of the industry, not only, but of the trade of the country, for which our banking system was not adequately prepared, for which it was not suited, indeed, and it is very fortunate that, along with the expanding trade of the country, should come provision for an elastic currency. The currency of the country has been based upon the needs of the government and not upon the needs of the commercial community, an arrangement manifestly open to all sorts of accidents of occasion.

Recently, in the extraordinary circumstances now existing in the world at large, we have been obliged to resort to legislation intended for unusual circumstances, a resort which would not have been necessary if we had had the organization which you are now about to consummate and put into operation. I think it is very fortunate, therefore, that just at this time the country should feel that it has the instrument by which to do everything that it is necessary to do for itself in the way of the activity of the banking community without resorting any further to extraordinary measures of any kind.

I look forward with the greatest confidence to the result because I believe we have devised a system which, though novel in some particulars, is clearly adjusted to the circumstances of American industrial and commercial life; that has an element of local self-government in it which is quite consistent with the analogies of our political life and the habits of our regional life. For we have developed by regions, and there is every reason why we should function by regions, if the regions are drawn together in a common organization and act with a common spirit and guidance. Therefore, to have just at this time of expanding life and of critical life an entirely suitable instrument will in itself be a reassurance; and not only a reassurance but a distinct and consciously felt benefit to the country.

I am, personally, very happy to have played a small part in bringing this plan to a consummation, and I am particularly happy that you gentlemen have consented to serve the country in this disinterested way and to afford a guidance to which I am sure it will respond with the greatest alacrity. I owe you personal thanks for consenting at my request to serve the country in this way. I know what sacrifices many of you have made, and, after all, that is not real service for which we do not pay some price. The very fact that personal sacrifice is involved is a guarantee to the country of what the results will be. We will not serve ourselves, but the country at large.

I thank you sincerely for giving me this opportunity of congratulating the country and the banking interests of the country for this happy beginning of what I believe will be a very great benefit to the whole community.

T MS (WP, DLC).
   1 Prior to their first formal session, the members of the Federal Reserve Board called at the White House and were introduced to Wilson by McAdoo.

To William Joel Stone

My dear Senator: [The White House] August 13, 1914

Now that the peace treaties are under actual consideration, may I not send just a line to say that I most earnestly hope that it may be possible to secure their ratification without any restriction as to their scope? They are intended to cover all questions in dispute of every character, so that no cause for war will be left uncovered. This is their peculiar characteristic and is what gives them a force and character which other treaties have not had. If we can have investigation of all questions not covered by other treaties, we will hold war at arms length in such a fashion as I believe to render it practically impossible. This is a time when such action on our part would make the deepest possible impression upon the world and I covet and pray for it on that account.

Cordially and faithfully yours,   Woodrow Wilson

TLS (Letterpress Books, WP, DLC).

To John Pierpont Morgan, Jr.

My dear Mr. Morgan: [The White House] August 13, 1914

I have received the message you sent asking for an interview with me while you were in Washington this week. I hope that you know that in ordinary circumstances I would be very glad to see you, but I find myself so out of spirits that I have for the moment only strength and initiative enough for the absolutely necessary duties of my official day.

I know that in view of all that has happened you will understand and excuse.   Sincerely yours,   Woodrow Wilson

TLS (Letterpress Books, WP, DLC).

Remarks to a Delegation of Businessmen[1]

August 14, 1914.

Gentlemen: I am very much obliged to you for paying me the compliment of calling upon me in this way, though interrupting the important work you are assembled to do; and I certainly shall not detain you from that work by any speech of any kind. But I cannot refrain from expressing my gratification at conferences of this sort, where the method by which the government in all its departments can cooperate with the business and life of the country can be shown more intimately than it has ever been shown before. If we get no other benefit out of the present trying circumstances in the world at large, we shall at least get this benefit: We shall enjoy a period when we meet each other, not as members of different parties, all our prejudices fallen away from us, coming together as Americans for a common object that is not touched with selfishness or personal ambition of any sort. Surely handsome results will come out of the spirit in which conferences of this kind are held.

I believe you will discover, those of you, who did not know it before, that this government has means, somewhat fully developed means, for assisting the commercial and industrial operations of the country; and that, therefore, it is worthwhile to maintain the kind of connection which is here momentarily established. We have been face to face with very critical circumstances. For my own part, I feel that the period of apprehension has passed and that the period of steady, sensible, concerted, constructive action has come, and that we are in the temper to bring that action about in the most effectual way. I am sure that all of us here wish to put ourselves at your disposal, as I am sure you would wish to put yourselves at our disposal, to work out a common means for a common end. Such a conference as this furnishes acceptable proof to the country that the antagonism between government and business has disappeared and that there has come upon business the spirit of generous rivalry and cooperation which is the essence of statesmanship.

I have no thought except the thought of self-gratulation in the matter, because, as I have said, this is not a selfish but a wholly public-spirited operation, a thing that we shall look back to with pride. We shall remember that America knew how to handle herself in such a way as not only to help herself, but also to serve the rest of the world.

T MS (WP, DLC).
    1 Businessmen, bankers, shipowners, and shippers met on August 14 with Secretary McAdoo and other officials to discuss plans for cooperation during the crisis. Wilson received the delegation after their morning session.

To Charles William Eliot

My dear Doctor Eliot: The White House August 14, 1914

It is a momentous proposal you make in your letter of the sixth of August. I have just had an opportunity to turn to it among the papers awaiting my attention on my return home from Georgia. You may be sure that it will receive my most thoughtful consideration.

I am afraid that its feasibility at present is very doubtful and it might be that it would add to the burden already put upon mankind by this terrible war if the only neutral nation should withdraw from the position of influence afforded her by her neutrality. But this is only my first thought about the matter. Thank you for your frankness in laying so important a suggestion before me.

May I not thank you most sincerely for your generous personal sympathy.[1]   Cordially yours,   Woodrow Wilson

TLS (photostat in RSB Coll., DLC).
  [1] In a letter only the last page of which is extant in WP, DLC.

From Willard Saulsbury

My dear Mr. President: [Washington] August 14, 1914.

I cannot think that your impressions of the Shipping Bill have been accurately stated to me, or if they have, I think you must have been misled because insufficient information has been furnished you regarding it. I feel myself that with no safeguards thrown around the granting of American registry to foreign vessels, we are extending a broad invitation to the nationals of belligerents who happen to be vessel-owners to embroil us in European contentions without any possible corresponding benefit.

Briefly, suppose to change the drift of public sentiment in this country, some German ship-owners take out a New Jersey charter, transfer a German ship to the New Jersey corporation, receiving the stock of the corporation except two or three shares in payment for the ship, registering her as an American vessel and sail her out under an American flag with an American cargo, to be at once seized by British or French war vessels. It will be a fraud on the other belligerents and I believe a prize court would at once condemn the vessel. Then the howl would go up from the German citizen that the American flag had been degraded, &c.

I think the present terms of the Shipping Bill, which Senator Pomerene, Senator Cummins and I had been striving to throw some guards around, form absolutely an invitation to international fraud.

The report of the Conference Committee in my judgment makes a useless, ill-considered and wholly unnecessary assault on existing American shipping owned by Americans and will benefit no American. I have for a long time been considering and intending to try to improve our navigation and shipping laws but the amendments reported by the Conference Committees of the Houses tears up the present coastwise shipping plan without any possible corresponding benefit.

The subject is too long to bother you with now but I feel very deeply this conference report should not be accepted. The condition has been brought about by the very foolish and ill-judged attempts of shipping interests and shipyard interests to extend the coastwise laws to the Pacific trade. I favor holding the coastwise trade down to what I consider the coastwise trade on each coast and allowing foreign-built American-registered ships to engage in voyages requiring passage through the Panama Canal and proceeding to reform our shipping and navigation laws without affecting injuriously the owner of every ship actually built in America.

I do not know whether you know how largely individuals are interested in coastwise shipping. The usual way in which the smaller vessels are built is that some sea-captain, having demonstrated his ability gets his friends to take proportionate interests in a ship. The ship is not owned by a corporation but is divided into 8'ths, 16'ths, 32'ds and even 64'ths and each person takes as much as he is able to. The best business man of those interested becomes the ship's husband and the captain sails out to get his cargoes.

This is the condition certainly from Maine to the Virginia Capes. Every man who has the real smell of the sea in his nostrils likes to be interested in vessels and enterprises of the kind I have described are not generally profitable but very frequently are engaged in through sentiment. Every one of these men will be hurt and will feel it. Our friend Senator Johnson of Maine will be politically murdered by this Bill.

I feel sure my views are right and think those who are pushing the Bill in its present form cannot understand the situation. Senator Pomerene, Senator Johnson and myself would be glad to prevent this unfortunate Bill from becoming a law and place ourselves at your disposal to present our views.

Yours very truly, Willard Saulsbury
I concur in above, Atlee Pomerene

TLS (WP, DLC).

James Watson Gerard to William Jennings Bryan

Berlin via Copenhagen. Aug, 14, 1914.
Recd August 15, 7:30 p.m.

The following was communicated personally to me by the Emperor in writing.[1]

PRIVATE AND CONFIDENTIAL. Quote.

For the President personally.

One. His Royal Highness Prince Henry was received by His Majesty King George V in London who empowered him to transmit to me verbally that England would remain neutral if war broke out on the continent involving Germany and France, Austria and Russia. This message was telegraphed to me by my brother from London after his conversation with His Majesty the King and repeated verbally on the twenty-ninth July.

Two. My Ambassador in London transmitted a message from Sir Edward Grey to Berlin saying that only in case France was likely to be crushed England would interfere.

Three. On the thirtieth my Ambassador in London reported that Sir Edward Grey in the course of a private (sic) conversation told him that if the conflict remained localized between Russia—not Servia—and Austria, England would not move but if we mixed in the fray she would take quick decisions and grave maneuvers; in other words if I left my ally Austria in the lurch to fight alone England would not touch me.

Four. This communication being directly counter to the King's message to me I telegraphed to His Majesty on the twenty-ninth or thirtieth thanking him for kind message through my brother and begging him to use all his power to keep France and Russia, his allies, from making any warlike preparations calculated to disturb my work on [of] mediation stating that I was in constant communication with His Majesty the Czar. In the evening the King kindly answered that he had ordered his Government to use every possible influence with his allies to repudiate [refrain from] taking any provocative military measures. At the same time His Majesty asked me I should transmit to Vienna the British proposal that Austria was to take Belgrade and a few other Servian towns and a strip of country as a mainmise (sic) to make sure that the Servian promises on paper should be fulfilled in reality. This proposal was in the same moment telegraphed to me from Vienna for London quite in conjunction with the British proposal; besides I had telegraphed to His Majesty the Czar the same as an idea of mine before I received the two communications from Vienna and London. As both were of the same opinion I immediately transmitted the telegrams vice versa to Vienna and London. I felt that I was able to tide the question over and was happy at the peaceful outlook.

Five. While I was preparing a note to His Majesty the Czar the next morning to inform him that Vienna, London and Berlin were agreed about the treatment of affairs I received the telephone message from His Excellency the Chancellor that in the night before The Czar had given the order to mobilize the whole of the Russian army which was of course also meant against Germany; whereas up till then the southern armies had been mobilized against Austria.

Six. In a telegram from London my Ambassador informed me he understood British Government would guarantee neutrality of France and wished to know whether Germany would refrain from attack. I telegraphed to His Majesty The King personally that, mobilization being already carried out could not be stopped, but if His Majesty could guarantee with his armed forces the neutrality of France I would refrain from attacking her, leave her alone and employ my forces elsewhere. His Majesty answered that he thought my offer was based on a misunderstanding and as far as I can make out Sir Edward Grey never took my offer into serious consideration. He never answered it. Instead he declared England had to defend Belgian neutrality, which had to be violated by Germany on strategical grounds news having been received that France was already preparing to enter Belgium and the King of the Belgians having refused my petition for a free passage under guarantee of his country's freedom. I am most grateful for the President's message. Wilhelm."   Gerard

T telegram (SDR, RG 59, 763.72/433, DNA).

1 The Kaiser wrote this message out in his own hand on large telegraph blanks and gave it to Gerard for direct transmission. Gerard later gave the handwritten copy to Wilson, and it is now in WP, DLC. About this matter, see James W. Gerard, *My Four Years in Germany* (New York, 1917), pp. 199-202, 433-438 (a photographic reproduction). The corrections in square brackets are from the Kaiser's copy. Words followed by "(sic)" were in quotation marks in his draft.

To the White House Staff

[The White House, Aug. 15, 1914]

Return to Secy' of State with my appreciative thanks.[1]

W.W.

ALI (WP, DLC).

¹ L. J. Canova to WJB, July 2, 1914, T telegram (SDR, RG 59, 812.00/12462, DNA); G. C. Carothers to WJB, July 5, 1914, TLS (SDR, RG 59, 812.00/12472, DNA); G. C. Carothers to WJB, July 5, 1914, TLS (SDR, RG 59, 812.00/12473, DNA); and L. J. Canova to WJB, July 8, 1914, TLS (SDR, RG, 812.00/12474, DNA). They described the Villa-Carranza break and the attempts to reconcile differences between both factions. Carothers and Canova recorded conversations which they had had with Carranza and Villa. Carranza complained bitterly about Villa's lack of restraint and inability to control his troops, while Villa claimed that Carranza was doing everything possible to minimize his, Villa's, victories. However, the agents reported that both Villa and Carranza realized the disastrous effect of a rupture and were hopeful about an amicable settlement. Carothers's second telegram of July 5 was devoted to a description of the battle of Zacatecas.

To Willard Saulsbury

My dear Saulsbury: [The White House] August 15, 1914

It disturbs me to differ with men like yourself and Senator Pomerene but I must say that I do not see how the conference report on the shipping bill differs in principle from the law as it stood already. That made it possible for ships not more than five years old to be purchased by American corporations without any stipulation as to the proportion of the stock held by Americans; and in any case stock can be temporarily assigned without great difficulty and whatever requirements we might put in might be nominally but really complied with.

It seems to me the whole question comes down to the proof of *bona fides* in the transaction. There must, of course, be *bona fides* and we could offer no reasonable objection to seizures of ships in the ownership of which *bona fides* could not be shown.

I think the whole thing can be divested of its risks by a wise and prudent administration of the law.

Cordially and sincerely yours,   Woodrow Wilson

TLS (Letterpress Books, WP, DLC).

From Jenny Davison Hibben

Personal

My dear Mr. Wilson   St. Moritz Engadine Aug. 15th [1914].

In this hour of grief & sadness for you, our minds, & hearts go out across the sea to you in deepest sympathy. All the years of sad estrangement grow dim & we remember only the days when we were young & happy in the almost ideal life we led together in Princeton. I see again Mrs. Wilson as I first knew her —so fair & sweet & eager for all things for you, & now that it is all over & her life ended here, I know with what passionate gratitude you will cherish all her great work of love & devotion for you. In your grief you must comfort yourself by remembering her pride & joy in you, which never failed & which to such a wonderful measure was realized in all that you have become. I recall with gratitude her sweet sympathy for me when my Father died & I ask you to accept now from me as the friend for so many, many years of you both my earnest wish that courage & comfort may come to you in this dark day of trial. Jack & Beth join with me in this hope.

Ever yours,   Jenny D. Hibben.

ALS (WP, DLC).

From Edward Mandell House, with Enclosure

Prides Crossing, Massachusetts.

Dear Governor: August 16th, 1914.

I am sending you a letter which I have just received from Norman Hapgood, and have marked something that Lord Brice said of you.

In my opinion, you have already written your name as high as any man America has yet produced, and I am convinced that when the story is told in the future, it will be first.

I am hoping every day to receive word that you have left Washington for this coast, in order that you may have a much needed rest. You owe it to the country to do this, and I trust you may find it possible to do so this week.

Our automobile can follow the Mayflower from place to place, so that you may have diversion both by land and sea.

Your faithful and affectionate,   E. M. House

TLS (WP, DLC).

E N C L O S U R E

Norman Hapgood to Edward Mandell House

Dear Col. House: Ockham, Surrey. Aug. 1st [1914]

I gave up going on the Cincinatti in order to wait another week to see how big the war is to be. If the great powers go in I shall have a hard time making up my mind about the best thing to do. I dislike to be away from domestic efforts, but it seems a pity not to be near the scene of so great a conflict.

James Bryce, whose opinion is certainly second in value to

none, said Mr. Wilson was doing better than any President since Lincoln, if not even further back than that!

Well, be good. I am sorry to miss this contemplated call on you. My best to Mrs. House.

Yours sincerely   Norman Hapgood

ALS (WP, DLC).

Colville Barclay to Sir Edward Grey

Sir: Washington, August 16, 1914.

With reference to my telegram No. 297 of to-day's date I have the honour to report that the following official statement was issued last night:

"Inquiry having been made as to the attitude of this Government in case of American bankers being asked to make loans to foreign Governments during the war in Europe the following announcement is made:

There is no reason why loans should not be made to the neutral Governments, but in the judgment of this Government, loans by American bankers to any foreign nation which is at war is inconsistent with the true spirit of neutrality."

This statement is in reply to a direct enquiry made by the Swiss Legation here. It was stated by the Swiss Chargé d'Affaires that the loan was not for the Swiss Government but merely a private banking transaction calculated to enable Swiss interests to have a deposit on this side of the Atlantic to insure payments of grain purchases to be made in this country.

It is also a reply to enquiries made by Messrs. J. P. Morgan and Co. who, it is understood, had been approached, through private sources, for a loan, rumored at £20,000,000, for the French Government.

The decision is stated to represent absolutely the harmonious views of the President and Mr. Bryan who regard it as necessary to the same ideals set forth by them in statements regarding the Administration's stand on matters of International finance, namely, the Six Powers' loans to China, and relations with Central and South American countries.

The Administration believe that the position thus adopted by them will indirectly curtail the duration of the war. It is a reversal of the policy hitherto followed in this country. During the Russo-Japanese war, for instance, millions of dollars worth of Japanese securities were floated in the United States.

The decision of the Government is chiefly due, I am assured

on excellent authority, to another reason, namely to avoid competition in the matter of loans between the various elements of the community, which would ultimately have drained the United States of all their gold, besides causing animosities which would probably have ended in open strife in many localities.

I have the honor to be, With the highest respect, Sir,

Your most obedient, humble Servant,

Colville Barclay.

TLS (FO 372/582, No. 44329, PRO).

Remarks at a Press Conference

August 17, 1914

Mr. President, there was a suggestion in the papers this morning that England is displeased at this legislation we are about to pass regarding shipping?

I don't know anything about that.

There has been nothing from any other government?

There has been nothing from any government that I know of.

Mr. President, will you discuss the Japanese ultimatum now in the Far East?[1]

There is nothing to discuss about it. I feel one of the duties of neutrality to be to have no opinion about what other governments are doing.

Will you say whether this government is satisfied with Japan's assurance of the eventual restoration of German possessions over there to China?

Well, I dare say she has made the same assurances everywhere. We are satisfied with her good faith, certainly.

With reference to the ship registry bill, Mr. President, there is an intimation that there is to be a conference today. We don't know what your attitude is.

My attitude was expressed in the original House bill. That was framed after a conference in which I was asked to participate, and I am entirely satisfied with it. It just happens that I have not had an opportunity to follow closely the subsequent changes.

Do you share the apprehension, Mr. President, that this legislation is destructive to American control of coastwise trade?

No, I don't share any apprehension.

Mr. President, does the administration contemplate any legislation looking toward the permanent upbuilding of the merchant marine?

> This registry bill is, of course, not a temporary measure, and one of the things that I have held as most important and have been talking about for fifteen years has been to find the right means for building up our merchant marine. I haven't any very great confidence in my own judgment as yet whether we can find the right way or not, but we shall certainly diligently seek it.

In that conference of the Secretary of the Treasury the other day with the sixty-two business men it was pointed out that the ships would go back to the flag from which they came as soon as the war was over, unless there was legislation tending to remove restrictions on the operation of American ships.

> That, of course, is a matter of opinion.

Mr. President, has any decision been reached as to the proper attitude of this government toward censoring cable messages?

> Not as yet. I am trying to discover what is very difficult to find, an absolutely impartial treatment of the subject. I am consulting now with international lawyers and the Department of Justice as to what the power of the administration in that matter is and hope in twenty-four hours or so to work out something that is really impartial.

You haven't any outline yet of the real powers of the United States?

> No; for the reason, as I understand it, the United States Government has the right to do anything that is necessary to enforce neutral action within its territory, but just what the detail of that would be—how far it can be carried—depends upon developed and partly upon undeveloped principles of international law; so that part of the field is new. We have to feel our way all along.

Would the strict censorship of the wireless depend upon our ability also to impose a strict censorship on the cable.

> I think so. That is just what we are trying to figure out, what kind of control, if any, of the cable is required of us in an impartial treatment of this matter. The difficulty is this: The cable cannot deliver any message this side of the other side of the water. The wireless can deliver messages at least half way across. I don't know whether this is scientifically true or not, but I am told that vessels cannot be reached with the apparatus that they have directly from either shore more than half way across, so that there is a very considerable difference between the cable in the

objective point of its communication and the wireless. How
far, if at all, that should differentiate the two in treatment,
we are just now trying to determine.

Would the ability to get uncensored messages over to Canada
have any bearing on that question?

I don't know whether it would or not. Of course, the only
means of communication with foreign shores is the cable
or the wireless whereas there are scores of means of communication in the territory, the ordinary telegraph, etc.,
and I should imagine that the practical difficulties there
-would be insuperable.

Mr. President, has any agreement been reached yet with regard
to the revenue measures to be proposed to Congress?

No, I am going to have a conference presently with Mr.
Underwood and Mr. Simmons.

Have you any suggestions in that regard that you could tell us
of?

No, I haven't. My mind is entirely to let on that subject.

Can you tell us as to when the law might go into effect?

I have been so interrupted in my duties that I have lost
track of it. I am going to take it up.

The Treasury could issue Panama Bonds for any early need.

It has the right now for a deficiency of the Treasury to
issue bonds. The Panama Canal leaves a large balance in
the Treasury.

Is that in contemplation at all?

No, not at present.

Mr. President, do you think Congress will adjourn during September?

I haven't stopped to think anything about it. It depends so
much upon the development of events. So far as the program, the old program we used to talk about, is concerned,
I think that will be finished tolerably soon.

Mr. President, referring to Mexico for a moment, now that
Carranza has taken hold of the new government there, have
any plans been made about Veracruz?

No, no plans as yet.

Mr. President, the trade commission bill is in conference now.
The Senate added the section about unfair competition to the
House bill; have you taken any stand as to whether that should
remain in the bill or not?

I am very much in favor of that.

That is, in favor of the definition?

No; I think the definition so difficult as to be undesirable.

T MS (C. L. Swem Coll., NjP).
  1 See the Enclosure printed with WJB to WW, Aug. 17, 1914.

To Edward Mandell House

My dear, dear Friend: The White House August 17, 1914

It seemed for a time as if I would never get my head above the flood that came upon me, but the absolutely imperative character of the duties I have to perform has been my salvation and I am at last able to speak with some degree of composure about the unspeakable loss I have suffered.

I have acknowledged many letters of condolence but I am writing today for the first time to those whose friendship is dearest to me because there is something deeper in that and it is harder to get one's self-possession in doing it.

I do not know of any letter which touched me more deeply than yours did and it has given me a real sense of comfort and reassurance. Such friendship so expressed could not but bring heart back into a man. For the present I can only thank you in words which are inadequate and, therefore, must seem almost empty, but which are in fact full of deep gratitude and affection. May God show me the way!

Affectionately yours,   Woodrow Wilson

TLS (E. M. House Papers, CtY).

From William Jennings Bryan, with Enclosure

My Dear Mr President,   Washington [c. Aug. 17, 1914]

The enclosed is an important document to keep. It contains a definite state[ment] of purpose and a disclaimer of value. I will talk with you over the private wire after you have had time to read it. With assurances of regard I am my dear Mr President   Very truly yours   W. J. Bryan

Japan wants us to act for her in Germany & Germany wants us to act for her in Japan[.] We are in demand. We have, of course, acceded to the request of both.

ALS (WP, DLC).

ENCLOSURE

Washington August 16, 1914.

A TELEGRAM RECEIVED FROM BARON KATO, HIS
MAJESTY'S MINISTER FOR FOREIGN AFFAIRS.

The Imperial Government, considering the actual situation, have decided, upon proposal by the Government of Great Britain, to take, in cooperation with the latter, the measures deemed necessary to maintain and consolidate the general peace in Eastern Asia, contemplated under the Agreement of Alliance between Japan and Great Britain. However, prior to taking such measures, the Imperial Government undertook to offer to the German Government on the 15th of August the following advice:

(1) To withdraw immediately from the Japanese and Chinese waters the German men-of-war and armed vessels of all kinds, and to disarm at once those which cannot be so withdrawn;

(2) To deliver on a date not later than September 15, 1914, to the Japanese authorities without condition or compensation the entire leased territory of Kiao-chow with a view to eventual restoration of the same to China.

The above was accompanied by a declaration that the Imperial Government will be compelled to resort to such action as they may deem necessary, should they fail to receive by the noon of August 23 (Sunday) a reply signifying unconditional acceptance of the advice.

In view of the difficulties in communication arising out of the present situation, an ample and liberal period has been allowed for reply, and it will be a matter of sincerest gratification to the Imperial Government, if the advice fortunately proves to be acceptable to the German Government. On the contrary, should it unfortunately be found unacceptable, the Imperial Government will be compelled, however against their inclination, to adopt means necessary to attain the end in view.

In deciding upon the above course, the Imperial Government are not seeking in any wise territorial aggrandizement or any other selfish end, but they are actuated entirely and solely by the aim to establish a status which will amply insure a lasting peace in Eastern Asia and thereby to safeguard the general interests, contemplated under the Anglo-Japanese Agreement of Alliance. Consequently, the Imperial Government are determined to exercise utmost care not to injure in any way the interests in Eastern Asia of the country to whose Government you are accredited or of any other third Power.

You are instructed to communicate the above to the United States Government, and, in doing so, to add that the Imperial Government confidently hope that the United States Government will not fail to appreciate the real motive of the Imperial Government and will find no occasion for any possible misapprehension regarding the same.

T MS (WP, DLC).

From John Sharp Williams

My dear Mr. President: [Washington] August 17, 1914.

Have you considered the fact that the Bureau of Insular Affairs is still apparently governing Porto Rico? Don't you think it is about time we were recognizing the fact that Porto Rico ought not to be governed by the *War* Department, as if there were still a military occupation of it and that it ought to be governed upon ordinary American territorial lines? There is no more need for the interference of the War Department in the affairs of Porto Rico, it seems to me, than there was in Oklahoma, New Mexico or Arizona while they were territories. The people are happy, contented, satisfied, except in so far as they are dissatisfied with the military rule and therefore the somewhat arbitrary character of the government. I say this because from what I can learn from Mississippians living in Porto Rico a vast troop of office-holders down there, who are outside of the civil service, are Republicans and apparently kept in upon "the military principle," which is right enough in military affairs. I just throw these out as inquiries and suggestions for your information. Please don't take the trouble to answer the letter.

I am, with every expression of regard,

Very truly yours,   John Sharp Williams

TLS (WP, DLC).

Paul Fuller to William Jennings Bryan

Campargo, Mexico[1] Undated
Recd. Aug. 17, 1914, 1 P.M.

Had an interview with General Villa this morning at Santa Rosalia. Gives assurances absolute personal disinterestedness, has also suggested elimination all military leaders from New government. Purpose of the revolution was to compel observance constitution in allowing the people to elect the President, thus ending usurpations entirely. Independently of him country will not accept General Carranza assumption of Presidency. Elections must be held and peoples' vote registered. Until election present revolutionary regime remains and General Villa pledges himself to preserve the peace throughout section under his command. Has promised me written statement. Has sent for General Angeles who comes tonight for further conference tomorrow. I have already seen him in Chihuahua; made a very favorable impression. Will telegraph and will leave tomorrow after their conference.   Fuller

This is the first from Fuller[2]

T telegram (WP, DLC).
 [1] Actually, Ciudad Camargo, also known as Santa Rosalia.
 [2] WJBhw.

An Appeal to the American People[1]

My fellow countrymen: [Aug. 18, 1914]

I suppose that every thoughtful man in America has asked himself during these last troubled weeks what influence the European war may exert upon the United States, and I take the liberty of addressing a few words to you in order to point out that it is entirely within our own choice what its effects upon us will be and to urge very earnestly upon you the sort of speech and conduct which will best safeguard the nation against distress and disaster.

The effect of the war upon the United States will depend upon what American citizens say and do. Every man who really loves America will act and speak in the true spirit of neutrality, which is the spirit of impartiality and fairness and friendliness to all concerned. The spirit of the nation in this critical matter will be determined largely by what individuals and societies and those gathered in public meetings do and say, upon what newspapers and magazines contain, upon what ministers utter in their pulpits, and men proclaim as their opinions on the street.

The people of the United States are drawn from many nations, and chiefly from the nations now at war. It is natural and inevitable that there should be the utmost variety of sympathy and desire among them with regard to the issues and circumstances of the conflict. Some will wish one nation, others another, to succeed in the momentous struggle. It will be easy to excite passion and difficult to allay it. Those responsible for exciting it will assume a heavy responsibility, responsibility for no less a thing than that the people of the United States, whose love of their country and whose loyalty to its government should unite them as Americans all, bound in honor and affection, to think first of her and her interests—may become divided in camps of hostile opinion, hot against each other, involved in the war itself in impulse and opinon, if not in action. Such divisions among us would be fatal to our peace of mind and might seriously stand in the way of the proper performance of our duty as the one great nation at peace, the one people holding itself ready to play a part of impartial mediation and speak the counsels of peace and accommodation, not as a partisan, but as a friend.

I venture, therefore, my fellow countrymen, to speak a solemn word of warning to you against that deepest, most subtle, most essential breach of neutrality which may spring out of partisanship, out of passionately taking sides. The United States must be neutral in fact as well as in name during these days that are to try men's souls. We must be impartial in thought as well as in action, must put a curb upon our sentiments as well as upon every transaction that might be construed as a preference of one party to the struggle before another.

My thought is of America. I am speaking, I feel sure, the earnest wish and purpose of every thoughtful American that this great country of ours, which is, of course, the first in our thoughts and in our hearts, should show herself in this time of peculiar trial a nation fit beyond others to exhibit the fine poise of undisturbed judgment, the dignity of self-control, the efficiency of dispassionate action; a nation that neither sits in judgment upon others nor is disturbed in her own counsels and which keeps herself fit and free to do what is necessary and disinterested and truly serviceable for the peace of the world.

Shall we not resolve to put upon ourselves the restraints which will bring to our people the happiness and the great and lasting influence for peace we covet for them?

T MS (WP, DLC), with editorial corrections from the CLSsh (C. L. Swem Coll., NjP).
    1 There is an undated WWsh draft of the following document in WP, DLC.

To Edward Mandell House

My dear Friend: The White House August 18, 1914

Others as well as yourself who are affectionately solicitous about my health have urged that I leave my desk here for a little while and seek rest, but I really am very well indeed and could not satisfy my conscience in the matter of a vacation because of the truly critical questions arising at every hour of the day.

As a matter of fact, I think the best thing possible for me is to stick at my task. The matters I have to consider are imperative. They compel my attention and my great safety lies in having my attention absolutely fixed elsewhere than upon myself. I believe that this is good "doctor" sense, as well as good reasoning about the public welfare.

Such things as Lord Bryce has said about me and you are generous enough to think about me and to say for my comfort and encouragement give me a very deep sense of encouragement, and yet I must say they make me feel very humble indeed, because I alone know the inside of me and how little these generous judgments are really deserved.

I simply must see you soon and am thinking every day how to manage it.   Affectionately yours,   Woodrow Wilson

TLS (E. M. House Papers, CtY).

To Wade Cothran Hoyt[1]

My dear Mr. Hoyt: The White House August 18, 1914

Mr. Brown has sent me your letter to him of August fourteenth[2] and I thank you sincerely for the suggestions it contains.

I particularly want to say how much I was moved and how deeply I was pleased by the way in which you and Ellen's other cousins served us at the funeral. It touched me very deeply and I want to thank you and through you the others who took part for what was really very comforting to me, to have the casket handled only by those who really cared. If I had been able to command myself that day, I should have taken occasion to thank you all in person.

Cordiall[y] and sincerely yours,   Woodrow Wilson

TLS (WC, NjP).
  [1] Secretary and treasurer of the Rome, Ga., Supply Co., plumbing, heating, roofing, metal work, and electrical contractors.
  [2] W. C. Hoyt to E. T. Brown, August 14, 1914, TLS (WP, DLC).

From William Jennings Bryan

[Washington, Aug. 18, 1914]

This telegram prepared by Mr Lansing[1] is submitted to the President for his opinion. Mr Bryan is in doubt whether any communication should be made at this time.

ALS (WP, DLC).

[1] It is printed as Secretary of State to Ambassador Guthrie, Aug. 19, 1914, *FR-WWS 1914*, p. 172. After noting with satisfaction the assurances given in Baron Katō's telegram of August 16, it added: "Should disturbances in the interior of China seem to the Japanese Government to require measures to be taken by Japan or other powers to restore order, the Imperial Japanese Government will no doubt desire to consult with the American Government before deciding upon a course of action. This would be in accordance with the agreement made in the exchange of notes on the 30th of November, 1908 by His Excellency, Baron Kogoro Takahira, then Japanese Ambassador to the United States, and Hon. Elihu Root, then American Secretary of State."

From Shailer Mathews[1] and Others

New York August 18, 1914.

Following resolutions were adopted by the Federal Council of Churches of Christ in America yesterday and ordered to be presented to you:

(1) That the Federal Council of the Churches of Christ in America hereby expresses to President Wilson its profound gratitude and appreciation of his action in offering the services of the United States in mediation between the European powers now at war and earnestly requests him to renew this offer on the first favorable occasion, either alone or jointly with other neutral nations signatory to the Hague Convention for the pacific settlement of international disputes.

(2) That the Federal Council of the Churches of Christ in America cordially endorses the position taken by Secretary Bryan disapproving of loans by American capitalists for belligerent purposes and earnestly hopes that this position will be maintained, since such loans would not only help prolong the war in Europe, but also impoverish and cripple our own innocent people by draining our land of its gold and causing the cost of living to advance to a war basis.

(3) That the Federal Council of the Churches of Christ in America appeals to President Wilson, asking him to issue identical notes to Great Britain, France, Germany, Austria, Servia, Russia and any other Nations involved calling attention to the dangers of a repetition of the Balkan atrocities, and suggesting that each Government take special steps in forbidding

its soldiers to resort to such crimes, and providing for summary punishment for the same.

(4) That the Federal Council of the Churches of Christ in America, on behalf of the Protestant Churches of America, appeal to the free church council of Great Britain, to the Protestant Churches of Scotland and Ireland, to the Established Church of England, to the Evangelical and Lutheran Churches of Germany, and to the Evangelical Church of France, to issue appeals in their church services and in their religious press urging all christian families having kindred in the armies to write them personal letters, exhorting them, whatever may be the provocation of the enemy to resist all temptations to savage practices. That steps be taken to secure similar action on the part of the Roman Catholic Churches of the United States, appealing to the Pope and also to the Roman Catholic Churches of England, Ireland, France, Germany, and Austria, to take similar steps in this matter. That the Greek Churches of Russia, Greece and the Balkan States be also appealed to in the same way to the same end.

(5) That the Federal Council of the Churches of Christ in America hereby endorses the general principle of the Bryan Peace Treaties, and, in view of the fresh evidence of the importance of providing adequate time for diplomatic investigation and conference, when international difficulties arise, the Federal Council of the Churches of Christ in America hereby suggests to President Wilson and Secretary Bryan that they take steps at an early date to urge upon the Governments of the World the need of a universal treaty providing:

(1) That some definite interval of time, to be mutually agreed upon, shall intervene between the declaration of war and the beginning of active hostilities.

(2) That in the interval a commission of the signatory powers shall make careful investigation and report their findings to the World.

(3) That the signatory powers agree to enforce the observance of the agreement upon the Nation that transgresses the treaty, by immediate military intervention.

(6) That the Federal Council of the Churches of Christ in America suggests to the President of the United States, in view of the attempts already made to induce this country to take sides in the present European conflict that he appeal to the people of the United States as lovers of their country and of humanity, that neither as individuals nor as groups do they take any action to destroy the complete and absolute neutrality of the United

States. We believe that he who would attempt to drag this country into the present war is not only a traitor to his country, but would destroy all hope of speedy peace. Only as this Nation remains strictly neutral can she offer mediation. If she becomes involved there is no impartial court left to which the Nations may appeal.

(7) That as this peace reverse must drive devout people to their knees, we venture to suggest that an early Sunday and the preceding Saturday be designated by the President of the United States as a day of united prayer in all places of public worship and in the homes of the people to ask the Supreme Ruler to intervene in such ways as His divine wisdom may approve so as to calm the hearts of those who are filled with passion for war, dispose their minds to listen to the counsels of humanity and accept overtures for peace, and bring speedily to their distracted and distressed peoples the blessings of peace.

By taking the actions here suggested the United States will in fact, create a new status in the relations of Nation to Nation, one that is the extreme opposite to "hostility" on the one hand, and more friendly than the negative position of "neutrality" on the other; a status of "reconciliation," that expresses active goodwill to the combatants and also the sincere purpose (to[o] often obscured by the customary methods and hesitancy of political diplomacy) to find common ground for the establishment of justice and peace between them, as well as in its own relations to them.

Very respectfully,

> Shailer Mathews, President;
> Albert G. Lawson, Chairman of the
> Administrative Committee;
> J. B. Remensnyder, Chairman of the
> Commission on Peace and Arbitration;
> Charles S. MacFarland, Secretary;
> H. K. Carroll, Associate Secretary;
> Sidney L. Gulick, Representing
> Commission on Japan.[2]

T telegram (WP, DLC).

[1] Dean of the Divinity School of the University of Chicago.

[2] "Will you not please acknowledge the receipt of this paper, saying that I have read it very carefully, recognize its importance and admire the spirit in which it was conceived; and that I will take its suggestions under very respectful consideration. The President." WW to JPT, c. Aug. 19, 1914, TL (WP, DLC).

From James Cardinal Gibbons, with Enclosure

My dear Mr. President: Baltimore. August the 18th, 1914.

Since my conversation some time ago with Senator Lee in regard to the situation in Mexico, I have been doing my utmost towards calming the feelings of the Catholics in Mexico. However, I regret to say, I am almost daily in receipt of letters complaining of the bitter persecution of the Church by the Constitutionalists. I am sending you, herewith enclosed, a latin letter,[1] with its english translation, which I have received yesterday from the Bishop of Zacatecas, at present residing at Villa Brackenridge in San Antonio, Texas. From it you will see that neither he nor any of his priests can return to their city from which they have been exiled. I feel quite sure that just one word from you to the Constitutionalist leaders would have a great effect and would relieve the sad conditions of affairs.

I would be exceedingly grateful to you if you would let me know if something could not be done in this matter.

Thanking you in advance, I beg to remain with sentiments of the highest esteem,

Most faithfully Yours in Xto.,
          J. Card. Gibbons
          Archbishop of Baltimore.

TLS (WP, DLC).
[1] This enclosure not printed.

ENCLOSURE

A Translation of a Letter from the Most Reverend Michael M. de la Mora to James Cardinal Gibbons

San Antonio, Texas.
Your Eminence: August the 14th, 1914.

The undersigned Bishop of Zacatecas, Mexico, on account of the civil war at present residing in San Antonio, begs to submit to Your Eminence the sad condition of affairs which has caused him great sorrow and anguish, in order to obtain consolation and if possible relief.

The City of Zacatecas for the past two months mourns the absence of its beloved exiled priests; all the churches are closed, and the dying are deprived of the last consolations of religion. In the midst of these trials it is impossible for me to return to my flock on account of the imminent danger threatened to Christian people, for the Revolutionists are casting Bishops into prison in order to extort as ransom large sums of money from the faithful; the priests cannot return, for if they do they will be condemned to death.

As Bishop therefore of this unhappy flock, I beg of Your Eminence's kindness and charity to make every effort, through the President of the United States, to see that permission be given to at least a few of the priests of Zacatecas to return to the abandoned city, and that this may be the more easily effected, it is well to note that neither I nor anyone of my priests have ever taken any part or ever committed any crime in the present civil disturbances.

Almighty God who has promised a reward to those who give even a cup of water in His name, will surely reward your charity in this matter.   (signed)   Michael M. de la Mora,
                                          Bishop of Zacatecas.

T MS (WP, DLC).

From William Adams Copeland[1]

Dear Mr. President: Boston, August 18, 1914.

To my surprise and disappointment the Senate on Monday voted to strike out section 4 of the Clayton bill as passed by the House.[2]

As I have previously stated to you, section 4 is the one hope and possibility of immediate relief for the independent manufacturers of shoe machinery.

I say immediate relief for I am not skeptical about the ultimate outcome of the government suit[3] but the inevitable postponement of that outcome and of final action by the trade commission subjected to review by the courts means the extinction of my business as well as that of the few other concerns who with mine have survived the preemption of the market by the monopoly.

Within the past ten days the United Company has confronted the Farmington Shoe Manufacturing Company of Dover, New Hampshire, with the alternative of ceasing the use of competing machines or paying as a penalty for the privilege of using such machines a sum such as to render the use of those machines prohibitive. This means that the concern mentioned must yield to the monopoly or go out of business.

Both the shoe manufacturer and the maker of the competitive machines are ready and anxious to vouch for the actual existence of this state of affairs, if their word is desired.

This statement of the facts is the strongest plea that I can make to you to induce you to consider the advisability of reinstating section 4.   Very truly yours,   W. A. Copeland.[4]

TLS (WP, DLC).
[1] President of the Boylston Manufacturing Co. of Boston, makers of shoe machinery.
[2] This was the "exclusive-sale" or tying contract section, which made it illegal for any person to make, lease, or sell any commodity, or fix a price charged therefore, or discount from, or rebate upon any such price, on the condition or understanding that the lessee or purchaser would not use or deal in the goods, wares, etc. of a competitor. The senators reasoned that the provision was unnecessary since the Federal Trade Commission would be responsible for defining specific illegal practices. *Cong. Record*, 63d Cong., 2d sess., pp. 9398, 13849.
[3] The government's suit against the United Shoe Machinery Co.
[4] "Please say that this has been brought to my attention; that I have read it with a great deal of interest, but believe that the two bills ought to be passed, and that taken together they will meet the objects intended to be met by Section 4 of the Clayton bill." WW to JPT, Aug. 21, 1914, TL (WP, DLC).

From Frederic Yates

Rydal, Ambleside, Eng

My dear Mr. President,   18th Aug 1914

I have not written you really feeling that it was better not, that you would so surely know how our thoughts go out to you every day, when, yesterday, Mrs. Harper called here with her two children, and told me not to hesitate to write you at once. "You do not know how often they have talked of you and how often Mrs. Wilson spoke of your Millet lecture at Princeton and how determined she was to get you to do it again." Yes that was a time that I love to remember. And now dear Friend I think of you standing erect & firm and alone—alone in a sense—"alone in the heart's deeps with your God." Mrs. Wilson asked me to write that line out once for her—"That is Woodrow" she said, and somehow it was the first thought that flashed into my mind when we knew your helpmate had gone.

I think I may see you before very long. Senator La Follette I think is going to be painted by me. I shall not hurry over, until we know the extent of our dangers here. It may be a long war. Our People are behaving well—steady—and with no low feelings of hatred towards the German People. Everyone realizes the fault lies with the Military Party. And the English newspapers are setting a good example (with one exception that lately got pulled up in the House of Commons.) I would like Senator La Follette to see the drawing that I made of you in 1908 at Rydal, when you were last here.

Our great big love to you.   Fred Yates

ALS (WP, DLC).

A Press Release by Joseph Patrick Tumulty

[Aug. 19, 1914]

The conference[1] was about the development and safeguarding of the Merchant Marine and every aspect of the question was gone over. It was recognized that the present emergency called for prompt action to relieve a situation which can be relieved if action is promptly taken. It was agreed that a bill should be introduced in Congress providing for the insurance of war risks by the Government.

In addition to the agreement of opinion as to the insurance bill, there was an extensive discussion of the best means of immediately providing ships to carry the goods now waiting for their markets. Several plans were proposed and it was finally agreed that a bill should be drawn and introduced at a very early date which should provide for the purchase of an adequate number of ships by the government and their operation through a corporation controlled by the government, as in the case of the Panama Railroad Company which now operates ships as well as the railroad itself and which is controlled by the government.

Those at the conference were Senator Clarke, Chairman of the Senate Committee on Commerce, Senator Simmons, Chairman Chairman [sic] of the Finance Committee of the Senate, Mr. Underwood, Chairman of the Ways and Means Committee of the House, Judge J. W. Alexander, Chairman of the House Committee on Merchant Marine and Fisheries, the Secretary of the Treasury, and the President.

T MS (C. L. Swem Coll., NjP).
¹ At the White House on August 19. See Link, *Struggle for Neutrality*, p. 87.

To William Jennings Bryan

My dear Mr. Secretary: The White House August 19, 1914

On the whole, I think it would be wise to send this telegram. At first I shared your own doubt about it, but, on the whole, I think it wise for us to be on the safe side in letting the Japanese Government know what our own understanding of the situation is.   Cordially and faithfully yours,   Woodrow Wilson

TLS (W. J. Bryan Papers, DNA).

To Sir Edward Grey

My dear Sir Edward: [The White House] August 19, 1914

It was very gracious indeed of you to think of me in my great personal sorrow at a time when you are, yourself, so overwhelmed with affairs with which the whole world is concerned, and I wish to express not only my sincere appreciation but my hope that you will regard me as your friend. I feel that we are bound together by common principle and purpose.

Cordially and sincerely yours,   Woodrow Wilson

TLS (Letterpress Books, WP, DLC).

To James Viscount Bryce

My dear Lord Bryce: The White House August 19, 1914

Your letter of August sixth reaches me like the voice of a friend and I want you to know how deeply and sincerely I appreciate your thought of me at this time of supreme trial when I am to discover whether I am master of myself or not. Your words of sympathy are also words which go far to interpret my own thought and feeling and I thank you for them with all my heart.

Cordially and sincerely yours,   Woodrow Wilson

TLS (J. Bryce Papers, Bodleian Library).

To Charles William Eliot

My dear Doctor Eliot: The White House August 19, 1914

Your letter of August sixth contained suggestions of so great importance that I have taken some time to turn them over in my mind. I have consulted with my colleagues also and you may be sure that we have given the most careful and deliberate consideration to the momentous thing you suggest.

On the whole, our judgment does not accept it. I believe that we should not have the support of our own public opinion in it and that lacking that we should lack the momentum to accomplish the object in view, even if the course itself were practicable.

I do not feel that I can venture upon it.

Cordially and sincerely yours,   Woodrow Wilson

TLS (photostat in RSB Coll., DLC).

From Jenny Davidson Hibben and John Grier Hibben

Berne, August 19, 1914.

Notre sympathie sincère   Jenny et John Hibben.

T telegram (WP, DLC).

Remarks at a Press Conference

Aug. 20, 1914

Mr. President, you saw Mr. Covington today, I believe?
Yes.
Did he give you any idea with regard to the passage of or getting the trust program out of the way?
No. Our conference was entirely confined to the trade commission bill. Mr. Covington sought the interview, in order merely to acquaint me with the questions that have been raised in the conference, and the progress being made. And I think that everything he told me was very encouraging.
The conference has been going slowly, but I understood that to be because there were a number of senators who wanted to have both the Clayton bill and the trade commission bill in the final shape that the Clayton bill was in before voting finally on the conference report.
Mr. President, have you any idea as to the probable time that you will get this law for the purchase of those ships?
No, I haven't, but I have heard such universal assent to the principle of it, from gentlemen on the hill whom I have talked to and heard from indirectly, that I should think it would be accomplished somewhat promptly.

JRT transcript (WC, NjP) of CLSsh (C. L. Swem Coll., NjP).

To William Jennings Bryan

My dear Mr. Secretary: [The White House] August 20, 1914

Mr. Davis was kind enough to send over to me yesterday a copy of the message which Secretary John Hay sent to Rome upon the occasion of the death of Pope Leo XIII. May I suggest just for your consideration the following as our message:

"The President desires me to express his sense of the great loss which the Christian world has sustained in the death of His Holiness Pius X.[1] By his pure and gentle character, his unaffected piety, and his broad and thoughtful sympathy with his fellow-men he adorned his exalted station and attracted to himself the affectionate regard of all who felt his world-wide influence."

Cordially yours, Woodrow Wilson

TLS (Letterpress Books, WP, DLC).
[1] At 1:20 A.M. on August 20.

To John Worth Kern

My dear Senator: [The White House] August 20, 1914

Do you not think it would be very wise to pass the Rucker bill concerning corrupt practices at this session of Congress? It might help very materially to prevent any of our people from being unfairly defeated. I dare say you will wish to see some modifications of the terms of the bill but, on the whole, it seems to me a very desirable measure.

Cordially and sincerely yours, Woodrow Wilson

TLS (Letterpress Books, WP, DLC).

To Thomas Davies Jones

My dear Friend: The White House August 20, 1914

Your letter of August sixteenth[1] has just been handed me and I want to tell you how deeply I appreciate it. I believe that it would be unwise for me to leave Washington just now. I find that the very pressure of things upon me here,—the constant interviews, the necessity of consulting and being consulted upon matters of capital importance,—is serving to steady me and to take me out of myself during the greater part of every twenty-four hours and that this is for the present my tonic and salvation. I do not want for the present to be quiet but busy. I cannot think of any place I would rather be than at Lake Forest, and at your and your brother's bidding, but for the present I must be wholly and only a public man and stick at the job in the most public place there is. I know that you will understand.

As I said to your brother in a recent letter,[2] it was a real comfort to me to feel that you and he were present at the services in the East Room. I fancied that I could feel that you were there, though I could not venture to look at anybody. Your friendship is very precious to me.

Cordially and sincerely yours, Woodrow Wilson

TLS (Mineral Point, Wisc., Public Library).
[1] T. D. Jones to WW, Aug. 16, 1914, ALS (WP, DLC).
[2] WW to D. B. Jones, Aug. 18, 1914, TLS (Mineral Point, Wisc., Public Library).

To Florence Stevens Hoyt

My dear Cousin Florence: The White House August 20, 1914

I am a bit dumb now with what has fallen upon me at least.[1]
I cannot speak yet with entire self-possession but I want to bless
you for the sweet note that you have sent about Ellen. You knew
her and know what I have lost.

I hope that you know how tenderly and truly she loved you.
Some day we will talk about that.

Affectionately yours,   Woodrow Wilson

TLS (WP, DLC).
[1] Swem's shorthand notes read "at last."

To Frederic Yates

My dear Friend: The White House August 20, 1914

Your telegram of sympathy[1] touched me very deeply. You knew
the dear lady and know better than most people what the loss
means that I have suffered. My thought turned instinctively to
you and your dear ones, for I knew that your hearts would
meet mine half way. I can now only send you a message of
deep affection and gratitude.

Cordially and sincerely yours,   Woodrow Wilson

TLS (F. Yates Coll., NjP).
[1] It is missing.

To Melancthon Williams Jacobus

My dear Friend: The White House August 20, 1914

You certainly know how to speak such comfort as it is possible
for me to have in the struggle through which I am now passing
to get and keep command of myself and serve as it should be
served the great country which has trusted me. Your letter[1] came
like a grasp of your hand. I know how true you are, for I have
seen you tested, and I want you to know that your letter brought
me real reassurance and strength.

Affectionately yours,   Woodrow Wilson

TLS (WP, DLC).
[1] M. W. Jacobus to WW, Aug. 16, 1914, ALS (WP, DLC).

To Lyman Abbott

My dear Doctor Abbott: [The White House] August 20, 1914

I think it must be to you that we owe the beautiful tribute to Mrs. Wilson in the current number of the Outlook.[1] No one could have written it who did not know her. I find that it is very difficult for me to speak as yet about my loss but I wanted to send you at least this line of gratitude for the editorial. It is a great comfort to me that within so short a time she should have been able to show her quality to the whole country.

Cordially and sincerely yours,   Woodrow Wilson

TLS (Letterpress Books, WP, DLC).

[1] "A Private Grief: A National Loss," *The Outlook*, CVII (Aug. 22, 1914), 953-54. It described Mrs. Wilson as the "social head" of the nation, who, with her husband, had been a "neighbor to the whole country." The editorial continued: "The graciousness and charm of her manner were rooted in the unselfishness of her spirit. It was characteristic of her that in her intervals of consciousness during her last hours her concern was for the betterment by Congressional action of the slums in Washington." The American people knew of these qualities, but they could not know of "her fine intelligence, her breadth of intellectual interests, the intimacy and completeness of her fellowship with her husband," and they could not measure "the greatness of the loss he has sustained in his public as well as in his personal life."

To Walter Hines Page

My dear Page: The White House August 20, 1914

It was fine of you to have thought of me and of my distress in the midst of all that you are now going through, but it was characteristic of you and I thank you with all my heart.[1] I cannot write more about it now, as you will, I am sure, understand. But I am going to write you a letter presently to tell you just how we have valued the services you have been rendering in this peculiar crisis to Americans of all sorts, as well as to the Government.

Faithfully yours,   Woodrow Wilson

TLS (W. H. Page Papers, MH).
[1] WHP to WW, Aug. 7, 1914, T telegram (WP, DLC).

From the White House Staff

The White House,

Memorandum for the President: August 20, 1914

Secretary Bryan 'phones to ask if the President sees any objection to allowing dispatches to be sent over the wireless provided they are censored so as to prevent anything unneutral going— the same privilege being allowed to all countries. This to stand until a decision is reached in regard to the wireless and cables.

Mr. Lansing and the Secretary think this would relieve the situation for the present.

T MS (WP, DLC).

From Paul Fuller[1]

Memorandum for the President.

On train from El Paso, 20th Aug. 1914.

I reached El Paso on the 12th of August at ten o'clock in the evening and at once put myself in communication with Mr. Z. L. Cobb, the Collector of Customs to whom Mr. Bryan had recommended me. I found Mr. Cobb very vigilant on the subject of Mexico and informed about all the rumors as well as facts. His impressions, gathered from the many sources available in El Paso, which is the headquarters or the refuge of partisans of Huerta and of Carranza and of Villa, as well as of the birds of prey who hope to profit by the distressing situation, only confirmed those I had already gathered in New York and Washington as to the mercenary character of a number of the men in the immediate service of the two leaders.

Inquiry as to Villa's whereabouts left the matter in doubt, —he was first reported at Chihuahua and then at Parral considerably farther south where he was supposed to be inspecting garrisons. Finally the Constitutionalist Agency at Juarez reported him as returning to Chihuahua and Mr. Cobb accompanied me there to get the needful safe conduct and other facilities for the journey. I found Mr. Parchos Enriquez[2] who performs the functions of Collector and Colonel Juan N. Medina, formerly General Villa's chief of staff and at present municipal President (or Mayor) of Juarez. They furnished me the safe conduct and a paper which would avoid me Customs House examinations and delays. After some moments conversation, Colonel Medina offered to put a special car on the train leaving the following morning at six thirty and to get leave to accompany me.

We left for Chihuahua the following morning, Friday, August 14th and I had full opportunity to talk matters over with him. He was in accord with the effort to avoid any break at this critical

---

[1] The following text was typed in the State Department from Fuller's handwritten original and is the one that Wilson read. Fuller's handwritten report is in the archives of Coudert Brothers of New York. There is also a typed copy, made from Fuller's handwritten report, in WP, DLC, and another typed copy of the original in the archives of Coudert Brothers. We have made a few corrections from Fuller's original version of typographical errors made by the typist in the State Department.

[2] [Ignacio] "Perches Enriquez" in the Fuller handwritten report.

moment and yet very anxious, in common with General Villa, that the new government should be a constitutional one, responsive and responsible to the people and not a mere military or revolutionary dictatorship. On arrival at Chihuahua we found that General Villa instead of returning there from Parral had proceeded further to Hieves,[3] a place difficult to reach. His Chief of Staff, Colonel Medina Abeity[4] at once telegraphed him and on the following morning wired two urgent reminders.

I utilized the delay, with the aid of Colonel Medina, to make acquaintance of Mr. Ornelas, Municipal President of Chihuahua, of General Fidel Avila Governor of Chihuahua and to call on and converse with General Felipe Angeles, who is a distinguished artillery officer. Notes of the impressions gathered are inserted below. In the afternoon of Saturday the 15th, I was called on by Mr. Santos Coy, one of the General's entourage, who told me he had telegraphed orders from the General to furnish me at once with a special train for Santa Rosalia, about six hours distant, where the General expected to be that night. He had given orders to stop the regular train and would attach a special car to it if I could go at once, which was done. Col. Medina accompanied me, having been commissioned at his own request to do so and to aid me in my endeavor to communicate freely with General Villa. We reached Santa Rosalia about eleven thirty p.m., where we were met by two aides and escorted to the hotel where rooms had been engaged. General Villa had just arrived. An appointment was made for Sunday morning at nine fifteen, of which an account below in the form of notes:

13th Aug. Colonel Medina—about Villa.

14th Aug. personally about Carranza—Villa's absence of self seeking—Trouble makers and small politicians around both chiefs,—Capmany, Pesquiera, Becera[5] and others. Willingness of Villa to eliminate possibility of any military element in new government; to make agrarian reforms in conformity with legal requirements etc. Greater probability of understanding if Villa and Carranza could come together alone.

14th Aug. General Angeles—Warm appreciation of President Wilson's attitude. Hopefulness that his ideas would cement North and South America and eliminate dictatorships. Views of Villa and Carranza. Villa—Still an "incomplete" man, but with ele-

---

[3] "Nieves" in Fuller's report. It was Las Nieves in the mountains of the State of Durango.

[4] Thus in Fuller's report. Actually, he was Manuel Medinaveitia.

[5] Thus in Fuller's text, Rafael Zubarán Capmany has been identified earlier in this series. The other two men mentioned were Roberto V. Pesqueira and Alfredo Breceda. All three were or had been in the United States as spokesmen for Carranza.

ments of such value that two or three years should make him a great man for the good of his country. Without early training or opportunities—his sudden rise when the occasion presented itself, and his great success are of necessity somewhat of a peril. His unusual hold upon the loyalty and devotion of his officers and men is only equalled by his fidelity to them and the strong sense of his responsibility towards them. Gives his confidence freely and cannot comprehend another's lack of confidence in him. It was the apparent suspicion of him manifested by Carranza in setting him aside to inactivity and appointing others to carry out his work that came upon him with a shock and so irritated and chagrined him that he tendered his resignation, deeming his usefulness impaired; it was at once accepted with the corollary that Villa's generals (6) should name a provisional Chief of Division to be superseded by Carranza's appointee later. The Generals virtually declined to name any successor to Villa except himself. The Zacatecas incident fully related. Villa has no political aspirations and is not personally ambitious,—would be willing to retire to private life if he had guarantees that his officers and men would receive proper treatment and the just recognition of their loyal service and sacrifices.

Angeles' differences with Carranza were fully explained. He was Carranza's Secretary of War, is Chief of Artillery. As Secretary he was kept continually close to Carranza and given nothing to do. The mention of his name as Provisional President was without his assent or even previous knowledge and was not due to Villa but it made a bad impression on Carranza who deduced from it a pernicious union between Angeles and Villa to supplant him. There is no foundation for the suspicion and Angeles believes that Carranza must now be convinced of this in view of Villa's announcement that no military man should be Provisional President nor occupy any post in the Civil Administration of the new government, which should be entrusted to civilians. The real cause of resentment is a letter which Angeles was impelled to write Carranza advising him that he was continually alienating the people with whom he dealt, leaving enemies in every section through which he passed thereby risking and endangering the Constitutionalist cause. He is arbitrary and suspicious in manner and in act. Dictatorial in character; and the dread of the Constitutionalists is that at great cost of life and treasure they have displaced one system of dictatorship to make way for another.

Examine plan of Guadalupe.
Examine Convention of Torreon.

Details of Zacatecas Episode.

16th Aug. 9:15 a.m. Sunday—Santa Rosalia. Personal conversation with Villa. Alone; as he requested all others to leave the room, after President Wilson's letter was presented to him and at his request interpreted to him by Colonel Medina. I explained the intense interest of the President in the preservation of peace in Mexico and the avoidance of any possible conflict among the Constitutionalists at the very threshold of the new government which this successful struggle had made possible. Villa is an usually quiet man, gentle in manner, low voiced, slow of speech, earnest and occasionally emotional in expression but always subdued, with an undercurrent of sadness. He has no outward manifestation of vanity or selfsufficiency, is conscious of his own shortcomings and his lack of preparation for the task of reorganization, and makes no other claim than a lifelong desire to see the people of his country raised from the condition of virtual serfdom in which they are kept, which he esteems can be done by a strict observance of the Constitution and the laws so as to put in operation a real democratic representative government, which will do away with privilege and insure equality of opportunity and the equal application of the laws to all. He made this statement in answer to my first remarks after first expressing his very cordial appreciation of the warm interest taken by the President in the welfare of Mexico and the generous attitude maintained by the United States towards his oppressed and struggling people.

He then expressed his dread that the struggle for Constitutional regeneration would end in disorder and in the substitution of one Master for those of the old regime who had been displaced at the cost of four years of conflict and bloodshed beginning with Madero's movement in 1910. All that he and the majority of the Constitutionalist party were insistent upon was that an election of Municipal, State and Federal officials, including the President, be proceeded with at once. The interim neither required nor justified the exercise of any other governmental functions than the preservation of internal order. Any attempt to exercise general governmental powers, of legislation, of appointments, of international obligations would tend to intrench the provisional holder of the chief office in his dangerous power, and to precipitate a new born usurpation which would again postpone the realization of the people's rights to select their own officials and hold them responsible for the proper administration of the laws.

This dread of Carranza's assumption of power, if he should

be encouraged by foreign recognition instead of being strictly held to the limitations of an interim government and compelled by proper pressure to proceed at once to the Constitutional election of permanent officials. Villa bases his observations upon the growing arbitrary tendencies which Carranza has displayed for a long time past.

"It is an old saying" added Villa, "that soiled linen should be washed at home, and for this reason I have made no revelation of the many things which indicate why Carranza has alienated the greater part of the Constitutionalist body." "I have" he continued "a stack of despatches which show the harmful blunders and interferences of which he has been guilty but I have not deemed it wise to make use of them. Unity and not division is what suffering Mexico needs."

"If recognition should be withheld, I asked him, you will be held responsible for the preservation of the peace throughout Northern Mexico,—will you give assurance of it?"

"I will pledge myself to preserve the peace throughout the district under my command," he answered, and then after a moment's hesitation he added:

"There is Sonora. I hear that trouble has broken out there—but if I go there I can stop the trouble." But said I, "it must not be done with bullets—Haven't you enough influence with Maytorena[6] to make him understand that he is imperilling all you have fought for by making trouble?" After a pause he answered "Yes, I think so, and I will get to work at once. Maytorena has great grievances. He was one of Carranza's earliest friends and gave him great assistance. Some time ago we intercepted despatches in cipher from Carranza to Calles (I believe it was Calles) ordering Calles to remove every officer who was not absolutely subservient to Carranza and to have Maytorena shot. Some ten[7] weeks later another despatch ordered Calles to suspend the execution of Maytorena."

"I am a man of no education" he continued "but I love my country and I can give it unstinted labor and devotion. I don't know why any one should be jealous of me, for I have nothing but my work and they must be jealous because I give it all to my country. I have no personal ambitions, I am not looking for any office. I have had some success, largely due to the able officers

6 That is, José María Maytorena, Governor of the State of Sonora, partisan of Villa, who maintained his own army in defiance of state forces and was constantly at odds with both General Obregón and Colonel Plutarco Elías Calles, Constitutionalist commander of the state.

7 Fuller wrote "two."

who have been with me,—without them I could have done nothing."

I mentioned to him a statement attributed to him and published in the El Paso TIMES of 14th August 1914, in which he said that no military man should take office in the new government, that the agrarian reforms should be brought on in consonance with the Constitution and the laws. He confirmed the accuracy of the statement and added "I want no office—If I am to be a cause of disturbance and an obstacle to the progress of my country, I prefer to leave it and find work in some other country."

I asked him if he would put these statements in writing, that they might be permanent evidence of his feelings and desires, and he promised me he would. This ended the conversation. During the course of it, however, Villa stated that he felt a responsibility for the officers and soldiers who had effectively carried through the campaign and who in their loyalty to him had been unswerving and looked to him for protection. He feared that if he were to leave them they would be disbanded and sent to their homes without resources and without opportunities for labor, to relapse into the miserable condition from which it was the purpose of the revolution to enable them to escape. He is anxious for some measure of governmental aid for these thousands of men, such as the allotment of land for cultivation under some proper system of safeguards which shall make the industrious cultivation a condition of permanent ownership, and thus while protecting the country from the evil of thousands of unemployed, unused during their long campaign to the daily routine of country labor, would begin at once the work of elevating the people and putting them into condition to become selfrespecting, independent, and selfsupporting citizens.

August. 17th. Monday. . . . Mr. Carothers arrived from El Paso in the same special train which had brought General Angeles from Chihuahua. . . . Mr. Carothers made an appointment with the General for 3 p.m., and I accompanied him. The General had not been well and was resting. He sent word that he was starting for Chihuahua at six p.m., and we could talk fully with him on the train. . . .

I had further conversation with Villa immediately on starting and at dinner. General Angeles, Medina, Benavides, Santos Chocano[8] and myself present.

8 Luis Aguirre Benavides, Villa's personal secretary, and José Santos Chocano, a poet and sometime friend of Villa.

Almost immediately after the train had started, General Villa came to the special car and invited us into his car where were General Angeles, Colonel Medina and Doctor Silva, who was brought into conference with the others in the preparation of the document which had been promised me: he was formerly Governor of Michosean.[9] General Villa took a seat with me apart from the others and a desultory conversation was started. I urged the need of patience at this critical time, in order not to imperil the fruits of the long struggle so far successfully carried out, to which he replied, "Patience is the essential always, patience and cheerfulness, impatience never accomplished anything." I begged him to remember that and to act accordingly; not to put himself in the wrong and to make sure if any break was to come, that it should not come through his action; that the issue concerned Mexico and not one or another man. He said, "That is one great trouble, there are too many nominalists, followers of this or that name, when they should be simply 'Constitutionalists' followers of the Constitution. If that is observed and enforced, no matter under whose leadership, the people will get their rights; arbitrary action, irresponsible government against which there is no redress will cease. We have no intention of despoiling; with strict observance of the law of the land grievances can be redressed; for years the largest landholders have be [by] concealment and misstatement evaded the payment of taxes and defrauded the Treasury. We will not confiscate; the government will take the lands for the public good and make just compensation; they will pay the owners their own valuation attested by them for the purposes of taxation; if they insist that the need[10] valuation they insist upon today is the true value, they may have the alternative of paying the arrears of taxes on the real value which they have hitherto concealed. The oppression of the worker by these wealthy landowners is inhuman. I have been in revolt against their oppression and the privileges and immunities they enjoy through government agencies for twenty-two years. When I was fourteen years and a half old one of these privileged rich attempted to ruin my sister and I shot him. From that day I have been under the ban of persecution, and from that day I have lost no opportunity to free my people from their lawless bondage and secure for them real equality under the administration of the law. The first step was to overthrow the power that governed without regard to law or to ordinary human rights. The next is to see that the new men whom we put in office shall not by any device secure the opportunity to exercise

---

9 Fuller wrote, correctly, "Michoacán."
10 Fuller wrote "newer."

similar power; that the safeguarding against such a relapse shall be made effective. This is a task that requires training, experience and education, which I lack. But I know the needs of the people for I have lived and worked among them. I am one of them. I know that Constitutional government was meant to assure to each one his rights, but the requirements of its administration demand expert knowledge as well as disinterested spirit."

Referring again to Carranza's attitude towards him he said "I can not understand the man's mistrust of me. I have always served the people faithfully; I have never betrayed any man's confidence. If he would only trust me. I have no ambition to be President nor any ambition than to help my country to be prosperous and to be honored. When I think upon our present situation I am filled with shame." At this point he manifested the only outward emotion I have seen; his eyes moistened and he paused. "What a spectacle we must be to other nations. Are these people children, they must ask, incapable of governing themselves and requiring aid from others to govern their country? And yet Mr. Wilson has stood by us, and he and your country have sympathized with us. What can we do to requite it? Mr. Wilson's stand that he will refuse recognition to those who hold by usurpation the power they should hold only by the free will of the people is the foundation for new hopes throughout the land. It is a noble acknowledgment of the people's rights and a great aid. Shall we profit by it? or will my country fall back under the old degrading despotism?" I told him not to give way to discouragement, that persistence in a patient course would bring the right solution. On a previous occasion he had suggested that pressure for a peaceable and unselfish solution was more needed on Carranza than on himself, that recognition of Carranza would unquestionably aggravate his already intolerant attitude towards him,—to such an extent as would force a breach or end his usefulness. I now asked him if he thought it would be of use that a special representative of the President should discuss the situation with Carranza and he said yes. I asked him if he thought Carranza would listen to such a representative, and he answered, "Oh yes, he will listen." Will he do any more? I then asked and he answered "I don't know, but in any event it is only fair that both sides should be seen. You have come here and seen me and my surroundings and discussed my views, and for an impartial judgment the same should be done with Carranza."

He then passed on to the subject of his soldiers and his idea of his duty to them and what could be done for them, having in view the best interests of the country. He said that he had a compact body of 27,000 fully armed and well di[s]ciplined soldiery. Seven thousand infantry and twenty thousand cavalry, nine million rounds of ammunition, a good number of field artillery and I believe seven rapid fire guns. To disband these men and set them adrift would be a cruelty to them and a disadvantage to the community. Most of them would find it difficult to get remunerative labor; in the best of times their wages were not sufficient even for the most frugal maintenance; unemployment would create distress, breed habits of indolence, and fritter away the high spirit of service and selfreliance which patriotic opportunity and strict military discipline had bred in them. His purpose is to form groups, or colonies of these soldiers and their families, giving each an allotment of land on some homestead principle which would require them to utilize it in order to acquire title,—or putting a price upon it payable by small yearly installments upon an amortization plan. For a time they would remain subject to military discipline, with a few hours of military drill and instruction each day, keeping up the spirit of obedience and of public service. This in time would form a useful body of militia and the nucleus of a self supporting and selfrespecting citizenship, contributing its production to the nation, conscious of its rights and its opportunities and with the reasonable ambition of growing betterment for each succeeding generation. . . .

We reached Chihuahua about 10:30 p.m. . . . One of the things General Villa is proud of is the orderly conduct of his soldiers. He asked me if in the garrisoned towns I had passed through Juarez—Chihuahua—Santa Rosalia—and the country I had travelled in, I had seen any instance of misconduct or disturbance. As a fact the whole place I found extremely orderly.

Once when Carothers was mentioned he said Carothers was an honest straightforward man who never hesitated to tell him what he had to say however it tended and he added "Some people have said that he was seeking to make money by some dealings with me. I challenge any man to show the slightest evidence of anything of the kind. He is a good man interested in doing his work and attentive to it. As to himself he said "I do not need anything, for I can work. I am accustomed to work. I am a poor man today. I have had to deal with the Treasury. I have handled large sums of money, but I have used them for the operations of the war and I can challenge any man to say that Francisco Villa has any money laid aside for his own use." While conversing at table, General Angeles sat beside him. I told him that I would take this last opportunity to say one or two things concerning the action of the new government when it should be happily installed. (1) There should be no vindictive treatment of the defeated—no revenge; many of those he fought were honest foes and all were Mexicans. Enough Mexican blood had been shed already, to which he answered that he wanted no more blood and that we could count upon everybody being treated fairly. (2) The Catholic Church, its priests and its property—the Institution should not be confounded with any individual delinquents. To this he answered that the higher clergy had made trouble in the country, they had meddled with its politics and that the Church had made a loan of 20,000,000 to sustain the infamous Huerta regime. I questioned the correctness of the information but he affirmed it to be true, and General Angeles who sat beside him and to whom I appealed, nodded assent. He then spoke of the clergy and paid a tribute to many of them, whom he said, he had not interfered with, but that many were not industrious nor useful to their flock but the reverse, and mostly the foreigners. At this juncture Benavides, the General's secretary handed me the promised paper and the letter to President Wilson[11] and with them the telegram from Mr. Bryan to Collector Cobb advising of the report of the arrest of the American Consul at Hermosillo. I opened it, and after looking it over, I said "I have just received this telegram from the Secretary of State which I will read you. It relates to affairs in Sonora about which we have been talking." When I read it to him he arose saying he would telegraph at once, and calling his secretary told him to prepare a telegram at once. I joined him in the next room and after reading in his presence the open letter he had handed me for President Wilson, I repeated to him how much the occurrence was to be regretted. Mr. Carothers was with us at the time. The General replied "If he is not released at once I will go down there with my troops and put an end to the situation within two days." He spoke with unaccustomed energy and exhibited great annoyance. I thanked him for his prompt and energetic response and bade him goodbye. As we passed through the anteroom, his secretary handed him the despatch already typewritten and he signed it. A few moments before the receipt of Mr. Bryan's despatch I had again called his attention to the disturbances in Sonora and he then told me he had received advices from General Carranza to hold himself in readiness to accompany General Obregon whom he was going to send to Sonora. I asked when Carranza was going to send Obregon, as time pressed and each

11 They are printed as Enclosures with WJB to WW, Aug. 24, 1914.

day's delay was likely to add complications. He answered that the dispatch did not indicate when Obregon was going,[12] and that he did not need Obregon but could do all that was needed in Sonora as well without him. If he goes to Sonora upon the suggestion of urgency in the Secretary of State's despatch, he may lay himself open to another charge of insubordination. Carranza being still "First Chief" of the revolutionists or Constitutionalists.

On arrival at El Paso, 19th August, Mr. Cobb, the Collector of Customs informs me that he is advised that in the evening of the 18th after the last conversation above reported, Villa had a prolonged telegraphic conference, over a leased wire, with his agents in New York. . . .

This ends the narrative of the several conversations had, to which is only to be added the sum of impressions received. The impression of frankness and sincerity of purpose remains, despite the rumors of personal graft and of the confiscation of bullion or other property immediately available for war purposes; the impression of power to deal with the situation so as to neutralize any effort of Carranza to control the vital sections of Northern Mexico; the impression of earnest gratitude to the United States and to the President and the determination to adopt every caution to avoid everything that can embroil them in any difference with this country; the impression of readiness to put the administration into civil hands and to remove for ever all temptation to the use of military prestige to override constitutional power; the impression of willingness and power to ensure order within his territory while the constitutional government is being installed. Among his advisers or rather his entourage of secretaries or adherents are several of whom little good is said, and this includes men in Washington. The same, moreover, is said of Carranza. But among these who are near to General Villa, there are three whom I should trust as friends of free government, and these are General Felipe Angeles, Dr. Silva and Col. Juan Medina. The latter has been commissioned to establish good relations between Governor Maytorena and Colonel Calles at Sonora.

Paul Fuller.

T MS (SDR, RG 59, 812.00/15013, DNA).
[12] Fuller wrote "coming."

From Charles William Eliot

Dear President Wilson: Asticou, Maine 20 August, 1914

In revising a letter I had written you on August 17th, amplifying the proposal contained in my letter of August 6th, I have come to the conclusion that it would not be desirable "to open *pourparlers* by cable on this subject" at the present moment, even if it were feasible. Two considerations have led me to this conclusion: (1) We apparently do not possess full information on the real purposes and objects of either Russia or Germany; at least the thinking American public does not possess this information, and therefore cannot justly fix on Germany the chief responsibility for the present cataclysm. The extreme rashness of Germany's action cannot but suggest that elements of the situation, still unknown to the rest of the world, were known to her. I do not feel the confidence I then felt in the information accessible when I wrote my letter to you of August 6th. (2) Communications between our Government and the Governments of France and Great Britain, which would necessarily be secret, are undesirable at the present stage of the conflict. Indeed secret diplomacy is always to be disliked, whether used by free governments or despotic. These are sufficient objections to the *pourparlers* I suggested.

I am inclined to give new weight to certain reasons for holding to our traditional policy of neutrality in conflicts between other nations: (1) It seems probable that Russia, Great Britain, and France together can inflict ultimate defeat on Germany and Austria-Hungary—the only tolerable result of this outrageous war. (2) It seems possible that the seven nations now at war can give the much-needed demonstration that the military machinery which the last half of the nineteenth century created all over Europe cannot be set in motion on a large scale without arresting production to a very dangerous degree and causing an intolerable amount of suffering and misery. The interruption of production and commerce which has already taken place since July 31st is unexampled in the history of the world; and yet the destruction of life and property has hardly begun. If seven nations can give this demonstration, the other nations had better keep out of the conflict.

On reflection, I have also come to think that much public discussion of the interest of free governments in the reformation of the military monarchies of Europe will be necessary before American public opinion will sanction forcible opposition to outrages committed by those monarchies on weaker and freer neighbors.

I remain of the opinion that, in the interests of civilization and peace, neither Germany nor Austria-Hungary should be allowed to succeed in its present undertakings.

Your address to your countrymen on the conditions of real neutrality is altogether admirable in both form and substance.

Sincerely yours,   Charles W. Eliot

TLS (WP, DLC).

From Henry Lee Higginson

Dear Mr. President: Boston. August 20, 1914.

The foreign exchange situation is a menace to the whole credit system of the United States, already under a very severe strain. Our municipalities, merchants, banks and others owe large sums in Europe, particularly in England. But for the extension of thirty days granted by the British Government, these debts would be daily maturing. This extension, unless renewed, expires September 3rd, and unless some means is immediately found of supplying American debtors with foreign exchange to pay their foreign debts, they will be forced for that purpose to buy gold wherever they can, with the result that that commodity will go to a premium,—a very dangerous thing at all times, and especially now.

There is plenty of gold in this country, but this gold is chiefly held by the Government and the Banks. Private bankers and merchants do not keep gold, nor should they. Gold belongs in the banks as a reserve. The country having been forced nearly to a paper basis, the banks are not compelled to part with their gold and will not do so in any considerable quantity. On the contrary, the Government is amply supplied, and willing and anxious to help the situation in every way possible.

Presently we shall ship great quantities of grain and food-stuffs to Europe; indeed, these provisions are already moving, but not in the volume they would were it not for a partial dead-lock between exporter and importer as to the payment of war risks, etc., and also partially due to the breakdown of credits. One very large shipper of provisions told us lately that he would not ship any produce until he was paid here. The foreigner will do this eventually, but in the meantime this means a change in machinery, consequent delay, and blocking the wheels of commerce, which reaches to the most distant farmer. The farmer and the planter must have payment for their crops, else they cannot pay their laborers. The delay is bad, and may lead to what I fear most,—a premium on gold, with its consequent disastrous effect on our entire internal affairs. Our nation has had that experience and paid heavily for it. Through that sad experience it lost its credit and standing with the world. Don't let's repeat it.

We know that Europe will come to us for our goods, and will therefore pay for them in gold or in our debts. If we have shown the willingness to put up this gold (which need not cross the water) Europe will presently be putting up gold here to pay for our provisions; in short, the turn will come promptly. At the present time we need, for the sake of our national credit and character, to show our courage and promptness exactly as England, in her great distress, has shown her courage and character in all financial matters, and also as she showed her generosity in 1907, when she lent us $100,000,000 of gold. I am not proposing that we shall lend England gold, but simply pay our just debts promptly.

The remedy I would suggest is that the Government should offer American bankers the gold necessary to pay American debts maturing in Europe. I have no knowledge of what this debt amounts to, nor can anybody give more than a guess. It has been estimated as high as $200,000,000, but I have no idea that anything like that amount of gold will be required. If England knew that the debt were really going to be paid in gold if necessary, a fraction of that amount (perhaps fifty or seven-five millions) should suffice, because there are offsets of one kind or another, and because nations, like people, are not so anxious to have what they know they can get as they are if they fear it will be refused to them. It is simply human nature.

England has been the exchange place of the world, because of living up to every engagement, and because the power grew with the business. Today we can take this place if we choose; but courage, willingness to part with what we don't need at once, real character, and the living up to all our debts promptly will give us this power; and nothing else will. I repeat that it is our chance to take the first place.

All these measures will not help unless we keep our stock exchanges closed, and I believe you may feel sure that the stock exchanges will be kept closed. I know the opinion and feeling in New York and here, and I have tried and shall try to the extent of my power to keep them closed. As an old member of both Exchanges, I may have a little influence.

With great respect Yours very truly,

Henry L. Higginson

P. S.,–Since writing the above, it is said that the United States Treasury is acting along these lines. The statement is that the

Treasury is going to deposit gold with the banks for the purpose of relieving the exchange market. This method will help if the banks will play fair, but it is to be remembered that the banks themselves owe considerable money in Europe, and may take care of themselves first. Neither the banks nor anybody else should have a preference over the business men of the country and the private people.

Yours very truly,   Henry L. Higginson

With a real market of exchange—operations with foreign nations at your elbow—you will have all that is needed—far better than from me.

I rely on my conviction that courage & promptness in payment of debts is intelligent & wise. It shows character & thought of the other fellow. I've noted this in you.

TLS (WP, DLC).

To Elias Milton Ammons[1]

[The White House]

My dear Governor Ammons: August 21, 1914

Among the multitude of questions which have arisen with regard to the part the federal government is playing in the strike situation in Colorado we are at last face to face with this question: September is the month when the snow storms begin and if the troops are to winter there we must set about to provide shelter for men and animals. This will entail upon the federal government not only a large additional expense but would also be practically an advertisement of our intention to make our occupation permanent.

I hesitate to do this. I cannot believe that the great state of Colorado will let the winter come without taking the steps necessary to obtain control of the situation. The federal troops were sent there under the impression on my part that they would be there only for a comparatively short time, and I am very doubtful of my Constitutional right to maintain them there indefinitely.

I would be very much obliged, therefore, my dear Governor, if you could give me some definite information as to the prospects of action by the state. I feel it my official duty to make this inquiry, and I am also deeply interested personally in the answer to it.

Cordially and sincerely yours,   Woodrow Wilson

TLS (Letterpress Books, WP, DLC).
[1] Wilson wrote the following letter after reading LMG to WW, Aug. 20, 1914,
TLS (WP, DLC).

Two Letters to Charles Allen Culberson

My dear Senator: [The White House] August 21, 1914

A matter has been brought to my attention recently which seems to me of considerable importance. Would it not be wise to make the estoppal clause in the Clayton bill explicitly prospective? The fear that it may be construed as retroactive is now, for example, seriously standing in the way, I am told, of the New Haven settlement. That settlement, by the way, would suggest the importance of considering whether consent decrees should not in any case be excepted from the estoppal principle, since they are often, if not always, in the nature of compromises and do not in any true sense record a full judicial process in the sifting of proof.

Begging that you will pardon me for intruding in this matter, but knowing that you realize my deep and sincere interest in the whole settlement,

       Cordially and faithfully yours,   Woodrow Wilson[1]

[1] The response of congressmen, senators, and the conference committees on the Clayton and Federal Trade Commission bills to Wilson's suggestions will be duly noted as the documents unfold.

My dear Senator: [The White House] August 21, 1914.

By way of supplementing my note of this morning, may I not hand you the enclosed very able memorandum from Mr. T. W. Gregory, now assisting the Attorney General. The memorandum was put in my hands this morning by Mr. McReynolds, the Attorney General. I feel the very great force of these representations and know that you will be willing to give them very serious consideration.

May I not call your attention to this possible effect of not excepting decrees entered by consent without the taking of testimony? It is feared by the Department of Justice that if such decrees are not excepted, the government will practically be obliged in every case to push its purposes through the full processes of trial and that decrees by consent, which accomplish all the purposes sought, will be past hoping for.

With warm regards,

       Cordially and faithfully yours,   Woodrow Wilson

TLS (Letterpress Books, WP, DLC).

To Francis Griffith Newlands

My dear Senator: [The White House] August 21, 1914

I have lost sight recently of the progress of your Trade Commission bill through the conference. I am so anxious to see the whole programme brought to a prompt consummation, so that we may go to the country with a clear record and a free conscience presently, that I venture to ask if it will be possible to speed the processes of the conference at all. I dare say you are already holding daily sessions of the conference, but just because I am so deeply interested I venture to make this inquiry. I know that you will not think this an unwarrantable intrusion.

   Cordially and sincerely yours, Woodrow Wilson

TLS (Letterpress Books, WP, DLC).

To James Cardinal Gibbons

Personal.

           The White House
My dear Cardinal Gibbons: August 21, 1914

I have your letter of August eighteenth. Alas, I am sorry to say that it is not true that "one word from me to the Constitutionalist leaders would have a great effect and would relieve the sad condition of affairs" in Mexico with regard to the treatment of the priests, for I have spoken that word again and again.

My influence will continue to be exerted in that direction and, I hope, with increasing effect. For the present, apparently, we shall have to await the subsidence of the passions which have been generated by the unhappy condition of the country.

   Cordially and sincerely yours, Woodrow Wilson

TLS (Archives of the Archdiocese of Baltimore).

To John Sharp Williams

My dear Senator: The White House August 21, 1914

I entirely agree with you about the status of Porto Rico. There is a bill pending which would do them full justice. I wish with all my heart it might be brought out and passed, but other things are for the present apparently crowding it to the wall.

   Cordially and faithfully yours, Woodrow Wilson

TLS (J. S. Williams Papers, DLC).

To Jessie Bones Brower

My dear, dear Cousin: [The White House] August 21, 1914

Bless you for your letter of sympathy![1] You know perhaps as vividly as anybody in the world just what Ellen meant to me and just what she was. My thought has gone back so often throughout our life together to the days in Rome when you took so much pleasure in bringing us together. You certainly brought an incomparable blessing into my life and now that she is gone your loving sympathy genuinely helps and comforts me.

Lovingly yours,   Woodrow Wilson

TLS (Letterpress Books, WP, DLC).
[1] Jessie B. Brower to WW, Aug. 6, 1914, ALS (WP, DLC).

To Margaret Randolph Axson Elliott

My dear Madge: The White House August 21, 1914

Your sweet note[1] really gave me a great deal of comfort. The thing has come as an overwhelming blow upon all of us and I have not yet begun to realize, I am sure, what it means and will increasingly mean.

You were right not to come. I sincerely rejoice in your improvement in health and beg that you will do nothing to set it back or check it.

Our thoughts turn lovingly in your direction many and many a time. Let us hear from you occasionally. We shall be anxious to know that you continue to improve.

Affectionately yours,   Woodrow Wilson

TLS (WC, NjP).
[1] Margaret R. A. Elliott to WW, Aug. 7, 1914, ALS (WP, DLC).

To Edith Gittings Reid

My dear, dear Friend: The White House August 21, 1914

Your little note of August eighth[1] has just reached me. I cannot thank you for it enough. I would have known how you felt even if you had not written, but it is very sweet indeed to have these spoken words of yours to help me in this time when I need the support and affection of every friend I have.

I am so glad that you knew her. I dare not let my thoughts go back very often these days and I dare not dictate more than a line or two, but you may be sure that they are freighted with gratitude and deep affection.

Your devoted friend,   Woodrow Wilson

TLS (WC, NjP).
¹ Edith G. Reid to WW, Aug. 8, 1914, ALS (WP, DLC).

To Cleveland Hoadley Dodge

My dear Cleve: The White House August 21, 1914

I am sure you must know what your note of sympathy meant to me. I can't say much now but I hope some day I can tell you just what your affection has meant to me. God knows that I need it now.   Affectionately yours,   Woodrow Wilson

TLS (WC, NjP).

To Robert Bridges

My dear Bobby: The White House August 21, 1914

I am sure that you know what your affection and sympathy mean to me, and they never meant more than they do now. I do not know what would become of me if I did not feel the grasp of loving hands like your own. God bless you!

Affectionately yours,   Woodrow Wilson

TLS (WC, NjP).

From John Pierpont Morgan, Jr.

Confidential

My dear Mr. President: New York. August 21st, 1914.

Referring to the question of the purchase of ships from the German flag by the United States Government or by American citizens, I feel I should inform you that, on August 18th, I received from my London firm, which is at the moment in very close touch with the British Government, a cablegram from which I quote as follows:

"* * * Our Government have privately intimated to us that such a transaction by a neutral in buying ships from a belligerent would contravene international law since the ships would be sold only to avoid capture. Therefore our Government would not hesitate to capture such ships even if sailing under American flag. This you will agree would create bad feeling between Great Britain and United States of America during the war and certain to lead to Alabama claims after the war. * * *"

I replied to the cablegram, asking if the British Government was taking the stand that it will recognize the transfer only to the British flag of ships belonging to other belligerents, and whether they would not be satisfied with bonafide transfer to a company wholly under neutral control. To this I received late last night a reply saying:

"In my opinion British Government would certainly decline admit that the transfer of German ships to neutral flag in existing circumstances would be consistent with international rules. Article 56 Declaration London makes this clear. You understand British Government quite satisfied if they know steamers were to be New York until end war and if your authorities arrange this it would be entirely satisfactory."

The balance of the cablegram consists of suggestions in regard to purchases.

I send you this information for what it is worth, appreciating very fully that your information is certainly more complete than mine, but should I be able to be of service to you in this or any other matter I trust you will let me know.

I am, my dear Mr. President,

Yours very truly,   J. P. Morgan

TLS (WP, DLC).

From Joseph Edward Davies

My dear Mr. President: Washington August 21, 1914.

It is with great hesitation that I intrude this matter upon your attention, in view of the tremendous burdens that are now upon you. I do feel, however, that you would wish that I so do, in view of the importance of the situation as affecting one of your great policies.

When I wrote you heretofore, upon this question of the narrow or broad review provided for on appeal from the orders of the proposed Trade Commission, it was on the assumption that the Senate was opposed to the narrow review, by reason of the fact that the Senate Committee on Interstate Commerce had decided to sustain Senator Pomerene's amendment. In that situation I ventured to suggest that if the broad review were settled upon, the situation would be somewhat relieved if a provision were inserted requiring new evidence adduced to be submitted to the

Commission by order of the appellate court, if it decided to permit its introduction.

The Senate has since that time *rejected* the broad review, and has gone on record in favor of a narrow review; and the question is now renewed and flatly presented in the conference committee.

The unconstitutionality of a provision providing for narrow review has been urged, and it has been insisted that unless a broad review is provided for the Commission would have no constitutional power to enter orders upon a past state of facts as to unfair competition, for the reason that it would be the exercise of a judicial function, which only judicial officers, under the Constitution, could exercise.

This question I have briefed very carefully, and I think the conclusion is a safe one that the Supreme Court would find abundant authority in its past decisions to sustain the constitutionality of a narrow review, if Congress saw fit to so provide. The character of the Commission's function is not only quasi-judicial and quasi-legislative, but it is essentially *administrative*. That last fact has been rather overlooked, apparently, in the Senate debates thus far.

The action of the Secretary of the Interior in passing upon questions of fact pertaining to land titles, of the Secretary of Labor in passing upon the past question of citizenship or present status, of the Postmaster General in passing upon a question of fact as to the character of mail matter, and many other actions of administrative officers,—all call for the exercise of a quasi-judicial function. Still, the Supreme Court has repeatedly held that where administrative officers in such situations are charged with the enforcement of a law, they must of needs exercise a quasi-judicial power in passing upon the facts to determine whether the law has been violated, as a condition precedent to the entry of their order in the enforcement of the law; and the Court has further repeatedly held that after such discretion is exercised the question of fact determined by the administrative officer will not be opened up and subjected to broad review by the courts, but that the action is final and conclusive, unless it has violated statutory authority or is entered in bad faith; and that the objection raised in these cases that it gives to administrative officers powers that are unconstitutional, because judicial in their character, would not be sustained by the courts.

Moreover, of course it is conceded that if the entry of an order commanding parties to desist from unfair competition prescribes a rule of future conduct, then the constitutionality of the Commission's power cannot be questioned, because it is a legislative function. It is submitted that the prohibition of a past act provides as much of a rule for future conduct as an affirmative declaration of what can be done in the future. Indeed, the whole body of the criminal law is prohibitory and not permissive, and, of course, is a "rule for future conduct." Upon either of the foregoing lines of decision, the Court would sustain the validity of the act, in my judgment.

Congressman Covington was of a different opinion with reference to this constitutional question, and believed rather firmly in the necessity for broad review, and I have great confidence in the ability of Congressman Covington; but I believe that in our discussions I have rather shaken his belief in this attitude. Indeed, I think that the language used in the opinions of the Supreme Court which I have at hand would have great weight to sustain the constitutionality of such provision.

Congressman Covington, however, believes firmly in the wisdom and expediency of the broad review, and this question we have discussed very frankly, and, of course, with the best of intentions and good feeling. Among other reasons for this attitude he urges the assurance which business desires upon the matter of court review.

Only the other day a New York lawyer, who has made a specialty of litigation of this kind, said to me that what the business world required, and what they wanted, and what he desired as the counsel for corporations, was a narrow review, for the reason that he desired to get the matter disposed of at one hearing on the questions of fact; that he and his clients were interested in expedition, and, of course, that if the Commission were simply "an antechamber for the courts," and simply provided a stage in the proceedings one degree farther removed from final determination, it would not materially help business, but would operate to quite the reverse. Thus the attitude of at least a portion of the business world, as expressed by this gentleman, whose clientele is very large, is in favor of the narrow review, and certainly the progressive thought of the country is overwhelmingly in favor of the narrow review.

Congressman Covington seems to think that the House is quite obdurate on this question of adherence to the broad review. Of course he is in a position to judge of the temper of the House better than am I, but I have information which leads me to believe that even on the conference committee *there is a strong feeling on the part of the House conferees in favor of the narrow review, unless it comes to them that your attitude in the matter with reference to the broad review and its necessity is voiced by Congressman Covington.* I have said to Congressman Covington frankly that I believed that if the wisdom of the narrow review, as expressed by the Senate action, were approved by you, and if he were to place his remarkable talents for effective action behind it, the House would accede to the proposition and provide for a narrow rather than a broad review.

It is suggested that the amendment providing for the reference back to the Commission of the question in the event of new testimony being taken, practically in effect provides for the narrow review. From my point of view, of course, it is better to have that provision than to have none, if the broad review is settled upon; but I cannot agree that it provides all the advantages of the narrow review. If that position is correct, however, would it not be better to expressly provide for the narrow review in terms, and get such advantages as it will bring?

Through your wonderful leadership we have embarked upon a policy that will be more far-reaching in its effect, in my judgment, than any other thing that you have thus far accomplished, with the possible exception of the reorganization of the financial system of the Government, in its effect upon the welfare of business and the people of the country. You have maintained, and do maintain, that the proper remedy in the industrial situation that confronts us is not regulation of monopoly, but the preservation of competition; and, in what appears to me great wisdom, under your direction, your administration has embarked upon a policy of administrative control to prevent monopoly from using its most potent weapon, unfair competition. In that situation, would not the best interests of the country be conserved by firmly adhering to that fundamental principle, and by then proceeding with discretion but nevertheless with constructive purpose and power, which will convince the country that we have confidence in our analysis, confidence in our proposal for remedy, and courage, coupled with discretion, and confer upon the administrative body so created for that purpose power to apply the remedies to the evils which do exist, as expeditiously as is possible?

Congressman Covington has given very remarkable and splendid service in this matter, and I feel sure that if he felt that your judgment inclined toward the narrow review in this situation, he would lend his splendid efforts successfully to bring about that situation in the conference committee negotiations.

You will, I trust, pardon the fact that I have trespassed upon your time and your energies to the extent of perpetrating this long letter upon you. I cannot but believe that it is my duty to you and to the country to submit my point of view to you in this matter, particularly inasmuch as I feel convinced from your attitude, as I know it, upon matters of this kind, that it is consonant with what you have in mind; and for the further reason that I desire that you should have such judgment as I may possess upon the constitutionality of the question before you, in a situation where, of course, you have not had the opportunity to examine into the authorities, and where the question of the constitutionality of the provision is raised. I had rather wanted to take the matter up with you personally, but in view of the tremendous pressure üpon your time and energies, with all of the burdens that you have been called upon to bear, I have felt that the better way to do probably was to submit it in this manner.

In conclusion, I cannot refrain from telling you that every mail brings to me letters containing expressions of the greatest sorrow and sympathy for you in your great bereavement and in your grief. The heart of the nation has been touched, and men are praying that you may be sustained under these tremendous burdens, and your great sorrow.

With great respect, I am,
Faithfully yours,   Joseph E. Davies.

TLS (WP, DLC).

To John Pierpont Morgan, Jr.

My dear Mr. Morgan: [The White House] August 22, 1914

Thank you sincerely for your letter of August twenty-first and for the important information which it conveys. I shall take the matter up at once with our own legal authorities in the Department of State.
Cordially and sincerely yours,   Woodrow Wilson

TLS (Letterpress Books, WP, DLC).

To Robert Lansing

My dear Mr. Lansing: The White House August 22, 1914

Surely if Mr. Morgan's information is correct as stated in the enclosed letter, the British Government is in danger of taking a very unjustifiable and high-handed action. I would very much like your carefully considered opinion on the subject.
Cordially yours,   Woodrow Wilson

TLS (SDR, RG 59, 195.1/15½, DNA).

To Charles William Eliot

My dear Doctor Eliot: The White House August 22, 1914

I am in receipt of your letter of the twentieth of August, and have carefully noted all that you say. I am glad to know that you think so well of my neutrality address.

Sincerely yours,   Woodrow Wilson

TLS (photostat in RSB Coll., DLC).

To Henry Lee Higginson

[The White House]

My dear Major Higginson: August 22, 1914

Thank you for your letter of August twentieth. I shall take pleasure in calling the attention of the Secretary of the Treasury to its important contents.

Sincerely yours,   Woodrow Wilson

TLS (Letterpress Books, WP, DLC).

From Edward Mandell House

Dear Governor: Prides Crossing, Mass. August 22nd, 1914.

Thinking that I might see you soon has caused me to hope that I might tell you in person of how splendidly I think you are meeting the difficult situations that come to you day by day.

Your Address on Neutrality is one of the finest things you have ever done and it has met with universal approbation. Every day editorials of the republican press speak of you as if you were of their party instead of being the idol of ours.

The food investigation,[1] the shipping bill, the war risk insurance bill and everything else that you are doing give the entire nation cause for constant congratulation that you are at the helm and serving it as no other man could.

Of course the war continues to be a most disturbing and uncertain element. I am sorry that Japan injected herself into the general melee, for it will place an additional strain upon us not to become involved.

The saddest feature of the situation to me is that there is no good outcome to look forward to. If the Allies win, it means largely the domination of Russia on the Continent of Europe, and if Germany wins, it means the unspeakable tyranny of militarism for generations to come.

Fundamentally the Germans are playing a role that is against their natural instincts and inclinations, and it shows how perverted man may become by habit and environment.

Germany's success will ultimately mean trouble for us. We will have to abandon the path which you are blazing as a standard for future generations, with permanent peace as its goal and a new international ethical code as its guiding star, and build up a military machine of vast proportions.

Your faithful and affectionate, E. M. House

TLS (WP, DLC).
1 Wilson had asked the Attorney General if there was anything the government could do to combat rising food prices. WW to J. C. McReynolds, Aug. 13, 1914, TLS (Letterpress Books, WP, DLC). McReynolds and Secretary Redfield set a nation-wide investigation under way. *New York Times*, Aug. 14, 1914. Nothing came of this investigation.

From Charles Allen Culberson

Dear Mr. President: Washington, D. C. August 22, 1914.

Your two letters of the 21st instant are received, one late yesterday afternoon and the other this morning.

In my judgment the provision in the bill should act only prospectively, as I said on the floor of the Senate, and that is the proper construction of the original committee amendment. It was amended, however, by the Senate, in the Committee of the Whole, to act retroactively also. An opportunity to change the retroactive feature of the amendment will be presented when the bill reaches the Senate from the Committee of the Whole, or in conference, and I will endeavor to effect the change.

The suggestions going further than this will of course have my best attention, and I will confer with members of the Committee with reference to them.

Very sincerely yours, C. A. Culberson

TLS (WP, DLC).

From Francis Griffith Newlands

Washington, D. C.
My dear Mr. President: August 22, 1914.

The conference has not proceeded as speedily as I would have wished, but many things have tended to interrupt, such as illness or absence of some of the members, the absorption of Judge Adamson in his primary, and more recently the death of a relative of Judge Covington, which called him away from the city

and prevented the continuous sessions that we had in contemplation the latter part of this week. He will not return until Sunday
night.

I send you herewith a tentative conference report, consisting
of an amalgamation of the Senate and House bills, originally prepared by Judge Covington, but recently amended at my suggestion so as to make it more acceptable to the Senate conferees. I
have not yet agreed with Judge Covington to urge this, but I think
that something approximating it will form the basis of our conference when we meet. I am now having a meeting of the Democratic members of the conference on the subject.

I fortunately escaped a contest at the primaries, but I shall
be compelled very soon to go to Nevada to undertake a
very arduous campaign. It is important, therefore, that I should
see you at as early a day as possible. Will you kindly give me an
appointment?

It is hardly necessary for me to say that I welcome at any
time any suggestion from you regarding pending legislation. I
should have sought an interview with you, but I felt that no unnecessary addition should be made to the great burden which
you have been so courageously bearing.

Most sincerely yours,   Francis G. Newlands

TLS (WP, DLC).

From Charles William Eliot

Dear President Wilson: Asticou, Maine 22 August, 1914

My letter to you of August 20th crossed in the mails yours of
August 19th to me. Yours came to hand yesterday, the 21st. I had
already come to your conclusion.

The European tangle gets more confusing every day. These last
acts of Russia towards the Russian Poles and Jews increase one's
hope that liberty will make some gains through these present
horrors. The position of England seems to me very strong—"Let
us fight for neutralization treaties and the small states, and
against the Bismarck policies for the expansion of Germany by
force!"

The Trade Commission Bill is apparently about to become a
law; and I imagine that one first-rate economist will be needed on
the Commission. I believe that Professor John H. Gray of the
University of Minnesota is the best man in the country for that
service, because of his personal qualities and the nature of his
studies. Secretary Houston must know him well. Any of the

leading economists of the United States would, I am sure, testify strongly to his fitness.

I am, with highest regard and confidence,

Sincerely yours,   Charles W. Eliot

TLS (WP, DLC).

From Josephus Daniels

Dear Mr. President: Washington. Aug. 22, 1914.

At my request the Board of Neutrality,[1] appointed by the Secretary of State and Secretary of the Navy, has given an opinion upon bills pending in Congress relating to the ownership of merchant ships by our Government in whole or in part. I thought you might like to read their views and am therefore sending the original.[2] Will you be good enough to return for our files?   Sincerely   Josephus Daniels

ALS (WP, DLC).

[1] The Joint State and Navy Neutrality Board, established by Lansing in mid-August, to serve as a central clearinghouse for legal and other problems arising from the war. Its members were James Brown Scott of the Carnegie Endowment for International Peace, who represented the State Department and served as chairman, and Captains Harry Shepard Knapp and James Harrison Oliver, who were detailed to the board by the Navy Department.

[2] Joint State and Navy Neutrality Board, "International questions arising from Government owned vessels engaged in commerce," TS memorandum (SDR, RG 59, 763.72111/7321, DNA). It advised that government ownership during wartime could easily embroil the United States in diplomatic controversies. Public vessels would be subject to restrictions while in neutral ports; there might be the inconveniences of detention; and there was the possibility of the confiscation of cargoes or of the ships themselves by the belligerents. Finally, even if immunity of private property upon the high seas became established by international law, such a privilege would hardly be extended to vessels owned by a government.

From Robert Lansing, with Enclosure

Dear Mr. President: Washington August 22, 1914.

I send you herewith a paraphrase, just handed to me by the British Chargé, of a telegram which he has received from Sir Edward Grey in regard to the purchase of German ships.

I am, Sir,   Very respectfully yours,   Robert Lansing.

TLS (WP, DLC).

E N C L O S U R E

Telegram received by Mr. Barclay from Sir Edward Grey: Paraphrase.[1]   Aug. 21, 1914.

The American Ambassador called on me today and wished to

know whether we would object to the purchase of vessels on the ground that the money would reach Germany. To this I replied that we should not object because though the money would go to the owner of the German steamship line and would keep him from becoming a bankrupt, it would not as a matter of fact in any way affect our chances of success in the present war.

I was asked by the Ambassador as to whether it would meet our objection if the ships were purchased by the United States Government and it was agreed that they would not run them to ports in Germany while a state of war existed.

I replied that I thought this would be satisfactory if the ships did not go to a neutral port near Germany, such as Rotterdam, which might become a base of supplies for the German forces.

The only object of this Government is to prevent ships of German nationality from being used in any way materially prejudicing the chances of our success in the war. If any way is found by which Great Britain can effectively guard against this risk the Government has no wish to urge technical or other objections.

T MS (WP, DLC).
 1 Of E. Grey to C. Barclay, Aug. 21, 1914, printed telegram (FO 372/578, No. 42404, PRO).

From Jessie Woodrow Wilson Sayre

Dearest, sweetest, Father: [Cornish, N. H.] Aug. 22, 1914

Frank and I arrived safely and without any mishap. New York was cool and our shopping quite successful, and Cornish is most exhilaratingly cool and fresh. It is the beginning, the earliest beginning of autumn here, no color but a feeling in the air and a look about the hills which gives promise of the beauty to come. We are hoping so eagerly that wars and Congress and all other matters will work together so that you *can* come up here this week end. Uncle Stock played golf in Hanover yesterday and enjoyed it so much that we longed for you and Dr. Grayson to be enjoying it too. If you can come we will be so grateful, and the blessing of a visit from you would last us a long time.

You know I am not urging you to come, dearest Father—you alone know what is best and wisest for the country and yourself, but we love and want you.

We are all well. You need not have the least anxiety about any of us.

Dearest Father we love and adore you so!

                              Ever devotedly   Jessie.

ALS (WP, DLC).

To Mary Allen Hulbert

Dearest Friend,   The White House 23 August, 1914.

At last I can speak a little. Until now a sort of dumb spirit seems to have had hold of my heart whenever I tried to speak to those who I knew really cared. To others I could speak, with a little effort, and tell them how I appreciated their sympathy. But whenever I tried to speak to those bound to me by affection and intimate sympathy it seemed as if a single word would open the flood-gates and I would be lost to all self-control. And so I have waited, notwithstanding I wanted, wanted *so* much, to tell you how your letters (wonderfully sweet and understanding letters) helped,—partly, I am sure, because of the evidence they have afforded me of your restored health and spirits and your happiness about Allen; for that made me very deeply grateful to God. For I cared a great deal. Write as often as you can, and give me repeatedly these glimpses of yourself, your life, and your thoughts. It will do me just the good you so sweetly wish to do me.

I never understood before what a broken heart meant, and did for a man. It just means that he lives by the compulsion of necessity and duty only and has no other motive force. Business, the business of a great country that must be done and cannot wait, the problems that it would be deep unfaithfulness not to give my best powers to because a great people has trusted me, have been my salvation; but, oh! how hard, how desperately hard, it has been to face them, and to face them worthily! Every night finds me exhausted,—dead in heart and body, weighed down with a leaden indifference and despair (so far as everything concerning myself is concerned). I am making a brave fight, the best I know how to make, to work out into the light and see my way. And I am not ungrateful: how could I be when I had her so many happy, happy years. God helping me, I shall regain command of myself and be fit for my duties again. For a little while it must be only a matter of exhausting will power.

Meanwhile my dear friends count with me more than ever. Their love and sympathy sustains me and gives me all the light and solace I have to work by. God bless you. I am deeply grateful, and am   Your devoted friend,   Woodrow Wilson

I will see if Mr. Wallace can be used. That would be fine, and I admire him for offering.   W.W.

WWTLS (WP, DLC).

To George McLean Harper

My dear Harper: [The White House] August 23, 1914

Your letter touched me very much. You really knew her. You, therefore, know in some degree what the loss must mean to me. Your letter rang so true that I am touched with a certain amount of confidence by it and am deeply grateful to you. I cannot write more now but you know what I would say if I could.

Affectionate messages to all.

Faithfully yours,   Woodrow Wilson

TLS (Letterpress Books, WP, DLC).

From Walter Hines Page

Dear Mr. President: London. 23 Augt. 1914.

It has been impossible to write lately, except by telegraph. I have been kept at work from the time I waked till 12 or 1 or 2 o'clock every night this fortnight, every minute of the time. I've seen to it—first, that no diplomatic mistake shd. be made, in this delicate situation; second, that the organization and measures for helping our stranded people were energetic and right; third, that the Embassy work proper was done when the volume of it was suddenly multiplied by ten. As I look back at this fortnight, all these tasks, I think, have been done—thanks, let me say at once, to the staff and to the very able and generous help of Americans of ability who conducted the American Relief Committee. I shall report *in extenso* on these.

The thing of great and lasting importance of course is that the diplomatic work proper be done without error and without fumbling. When this involves direct dealing with four Governments every day—well, I keep a straight path, a head not bothered with details, I get advice and—follow my own judgment. The saving fact is (and the importance of this cannot be exaggerated) that I have dealt so candidly and frankly with Sir Edw. Grey and so completely given him my confidence that his candour and confidence in me is now my shield and buckler. I could suggest no change in this relation. I have had conferences with him nearly every day these three weeks. I think he has told me every fact at every stage in this troublesome journey so far. I have seen this singularly self-contained, unemotional man weep in talking with me; I have seen him broken with care and lack of sleep—weighed down with an indescribable burden; and I have seen him roused with indignation, with a confident and invincible air. He could not be more frank or more friendly if I had known him always. That such a man shd. be in his post now is the first of our pieces of good fortune here. . . .

The dark shadow moves over the map of the continent bringing political, economic, and spiritual ruin; and again, I think, England will save Europe from itself. Turning from the awful spectacle on land and sea, it is inspiring to watch this nation— sad, dead-in-earnest, resolute, united—not a dissenting voice— silent. It will spend all its treasure and give all its men, if need be. I have never seen such grim resolution. They trust us to play our part of neutrality with scrupulous exactness & they know we will do it. It will be a hard fight, an experience of unimagined horrors. I am glad the chance comes to me to show our attitude— it calls for steadiness, clearness, frankness. These are not flashy qualities, being the brood rather of wisdom and commonsense.

Yours most heartily,   Walter H. Page.

ALS (WP, DLC).

From Mary Allen Hulbert

                                        Nantucket Massachusetts
Dearest Friend: Aug 23rd [1914]

You will be surprised to see my writing again so soon, and I am always glad of an excuse to write you. It is so very lovely this morning that I wish you and your dear ones could be here to let the still peace of this place calm your sad hearts. The only sounds are the lap of the waves on the shore, the church bells ringing softly and sweetly, and the occasional song of a bird. You are all in my thoughts so constantly that there's never a lovely sight or sound that comes to me I do not long to give you as balm. It is all such a wonderful expression of God's goodness, even in this time of stress and sorrow. I seem to intrude but you will understand why I send the enclosed.[1] It *may* help you, and it's my duty and pleasure as a grateful friend to the lender, and writer of the enclosed pages. I do wish you would send for him. His regret at being unfit for the Navy (under sized) is so deep that I think he feels there may be a recompense coming. At any rate, I want to *help*. Again God bless you.

Your friend,   Mary Allen Hulbert.

ALS (WP, DLC).
  [1] W. Wallace, T memorandum dated Aug. 21, 1914 (WP, DLC). He suggested that the government lend money to private shipping firms for the purchase of merchant vessels.

Remarks at a Press Conference

August 24, 1914

Will the purchase of these ships by the government, Mr. President, tend to encourage or discourage private capital in the future?

> I should expect that it would be encouraged. Certainly it would be encouraged by my administration in such a way as not to discourage private capital. . . .

There seems to be a general notion that, according to the newspaper statements, that this line of ships could not be used in the transatlantic trade or elsewhere because of the very nature of trade being contraband, and that it could only be used in South American trade.

> I don't know where they got that.

On the theory that they were subject to capture, just like private ships.

> They would not be. They would be under neutral flags. They would not be carrying contraband. Understand, there are two kinds of contraband. There is absolute contraband, and there is conditional contraband, which is contraband in certain circumstances. If it is being shipped to a British port, for example, if it is consigned to purchasers known, it is adjudged for belligerent governments. If it is consigned to such a place so obvious that it is intended for a belligerent area—circumstances of that sort—it makes it contraband. But in ordinary circumstances, it is not contraband.

Foodstuffs are of that class. The government's ships would not carry things of that nature?

> Certainly not. It would not be dreamed of, carrying anything that either—I mean, it wouldn't carry anything that was conditional contraband under circumstances that would make it contraband. It would accept the condition.

It would carry anything to a neutral port?

> Oh, yes. But those are questions which I think it is premature to discuss, and I hope that you won't discuss them as from the White House at all. I am perfectly willing to tell you men all that I know about it, but I think that all I ought to authorize you to discuss as a result of this interview is the purpose of the administration to push this bill.

Mr. President, we learned from the Treasury Department this morning that the situation is very rapidly being relieved as to the congestion of products in American ports.

> I think it is, at any rate, in some parts of the country. Ap-

parently it is hopeful on the North Atlantic seaboard. It is improving in New Orleans. It is not showing much improvement in Galveston. I know where there is a very great railroad warehouse congested. . . . There is a most diligent effort inside and outside—presently outside—of Mexico, to make trouble between Carranza and Villa. That effort is in the interest of those persons who would profit by intervention. We are constantly receiving direct information from those associated with Villa, and those associated with Carranza, and the reports which I see in the newspapers are false.

Can you intimate what Villa's plans are?

I am not in his confidence as to his plans. I am not in his confidence in any respect, but it is perfectly evident to me that he does not intend to present unreasonable proposals of any kind. And I think that Carranza is already showing that he knows how to manage some people in Mexico City.

Is it strictly correct, Mr. President, that John Lind is going to Mexico?

No, sir.

Mr. President, do you want to be any more specific about these people who would profit by intervention?

I don't need to be. The world knows about it.

Mr. President, have you seen Mr. Fuller since his return?

He is coming back this week from New York. I hope to see him again.

JRT transcript (WC, NjP) of CLSsh (C. L. Swem Coll., NjP).

Remarks to a Delegation Representing the Cotton Interests[1]

August 24, 1914.

Gentlemen: I am very much obliged to the Secretary of the Treasury for making the arrangements that would give me this pleasure, the pleasure of welcoming you here to put ourselves at your disposal as far as it is possible for us to do so. These conferences have led all of us to ask ourselves, What are they for? I am so much of an American that I am not willing to believe that they are intended to call upon the government to rescue men who know how to take care of themselves; but that they are called for the purpose of common counsel and for putting at the disposal of men who know how to take care of themselves every legitimate instrumentality of the government itself.

The conferences that we have held in recent weeks have done

a vast deal, first of all, to clarify the problems, and, second, and perhaps more important, to show how by cooperation we can solve the problems. Not all of these problems are going to be entirely solved, because the circumstances are of such extraordinary difficulty. But that they will come very near to being thoroughly solved I for one have no doubt—provided always we keep cool and think of these things in the same self-possessed temper that we would exercise if conditions were not extraordinary. We are not to be run away by sudden excitement; we are not to be imposed upon by unusual conditions; and the minute we sit down together I am sure that we can work things out. Our pleasure is in assisting to work them out, and I am proud to be associated with men in the several departments of government who have so thoroughly shown the spirit of cooperation and the desire of cooperation. We shall do everything that we can to make the path easy and to assist in the solution of these difficulties. My function is the very delightful one of bidding you welcome and wishing that I had a more thorough comprehension of your problems than I have so that I might put my brains at your disposal; but I find that my brains do not go 'round in the various things that I have to attend to, and I have to fall back upon such admirable deputies as the Secretary of the Treasury.

T MS (WP, DLC).
    1 A conference of bankers, planters, politicians, and representatives then meeting with McAdoo in the Pan-American Building to consider ways of dealing with the crisis occasioned by a sudden drop in cotton prices and the closing of the cotton exchanges immediately after the outbreak of the war. See Link, *The Struggle for Neutrality*, pp. 91-93.

To Francis Griffith Newlands

My dear Senator: [The White House] August 24, 1914
    I thank you warmly for your letter of August twenty-second enclosing the tentative conference report on the Trade Commission bill. I had a talk about it recently with Mr. Covington and would heartily welcome a conference with you. May I not suggest Wednesday morning at ten-thirty?
            Cordially and sincerely yours,   Woodrow Wilson

TLS (Letterpress Books, WP, DLC).

To Oswald Garrison Villard

My dear Mr. Villard: The White House August 24, 1914

It has been in my mind for many days to thank you for the group of editorials which recently appeared in the Evening Post throwing a flood of light upon public affairs not only, but throwing that light in a spirit so generous towards myself. I know that you will understand what has delayed me. I want you to know how carefully I follow the editorials of the Post and how sincerely I desire and appreciate its support and commendation.

Cordially and sincerely yours,   Woodrow Wilson

TLS (O. G. Villard Papers, MH).

From William Jennings Bryan, with Enclosures

My Dear Mr. President: Washington August 24, 1914

I am sending you herewith a translation of General Villa's letter to you and also a translation of a statement by General Villa as to the purposes and intentions of his Division of the North, together with a copy of a decree issued by General Carranza soon after he assumed the leadership of the Constitutionalist forces.[1] I am having transcribed a detailed report made by Mr. Fuller.[2] It was written upon the train and is somewhat difficult to read so I thought you would prefer to have it in typewriting. I have also received a telegram from a Mr. Semple,[3] a friend or partner of Mr. Fuller, which I am inclosing.[4] You will note his request relative to Mrs. Fuller accompanying her husband on any other trips he may make. I have no doubt you will consent to this as Mr. Fuller is serving without compensation other than the expenses of himself and his physician who accompanies him and it would seem to be proper to include Mrs. Fuller[5] in the expense account. I think that Mr. Fuller will prove a valuable man to us. His acquaintance with the Spanish enables him to talk without the need of an interpreter which is of great advantage when you desire to get into one's confidence, and his experience with Villa will be of great benefit in his meeting with Carranza.

The latest indications from Mexico are favorable. Obregon has been commissioned to proceed to Villa in an effort to restore peace in Sonora where a controversy exists between the Governor, who is friendly to Villa, and one of the Carranza Generals. I think this is a good sign. A telegram from Canova, which I inclose,[6] shows indications that Carranza is becoming more tolerant toward Villa.

Please let me know your decision in regard to Mrs. Fuller so that I may telegraph Mr. Fuller today. He is expected to be here in Washington Wednesday on his way to Mexico.[7]

I am, my dear Mr. President,

Very truly yours,   W. J. Bryan

TLS (WP, DLC).

[1] A CC MS (WP, DLC) of a decree by Carranza, dated May 10, 1913, providing for the establishment following his assumption of power in Mexico City of a commission to consider claims by Mexicans and aliens for damages sustained since the beginning of the revolution against Díaz.

[2] It is printed at Aug. 20, 1914.

[3] Lorenzo Semple, his partner in the New York law firm of Coudert Brothers. His telegram is missing.

[4] It is missing.

[5] Léonie Coudert Fuller.

[6] L. J. Canova to WJB, Aug. 22, 1914, T telegram (WP, DLC).

[7] Wilson saw Fuller and Bryan at the White House on Wednesday, August 26.

E N C L O S U R E   I

From Francisco Villa

Translation.

Very estimable Sir: Chihuahua, Mex., Aug. 18, 1914.

Your esteemed letter under date of the 9th instant was delivered to me by Mr. Paul Fuller, to whom you have the kindness to introduce me, and whose acquaintance was exceedingly pleasant to me, I having had an opportunity to speak with him at length in regard to various matters connected with the internal problems of our country, which we wish to have solved in a manner which shall be just and in accordance with the precepts of the Constitution of 1857, which governs us.

Mr. Fuller will explain to you fully the details of our interviews and the desires with which we are animated to settle our difficulties in a peaceable manner, provided always that the aspirations of the people are satisfied.

I thank you very sincerely for the good wishes which you express to me, and I avail myself of this opportunity to remain

Your obedient servant,   Francisco Villa.[1]

T translation (WP, DLC).

[1] The TLS of this letter is SDR, RG 59, 812.00/17185, DNA.

E N C L O S U R E   I I

The chief aspiration of the Division of the North, which is that of the social classes which were oppressed during the prolonged dictatorship of General Diaz and of the usurping Government of

Huerta, as well as that of the independent intellectual elements of the Republic, is the establishment of a democratic government, freely elected, without any official pressure, as the sole guarantee of the real exercise of the rights of the people and of permanent peace in Mexico.

Neither the plan of Guadalupe nor the political personality of Mr. Carranza guarantees the establishment of the National Government, for which the humble classes have been engaged in a struggle against the privileged classes, with the sacrifice of so many lives and the loss of so much property.

The *Plan of Guadalupe*,[1] formed by Mr. Carranza and a small group of his most devoted officers at the beginning of the revolutionary movement, *and without having been submitted afterwards to the approval of the numerous officers who now form the Constitutionalist Army*, is not, to sum up, more than a mere revolutionary plan, without any definite political program, and without guaranteeing the establishment of a democratic government within a specified period and on bases which insure the free casting of the popular vote.

The political personality of Mr. Carranza was revealed, while he was Governor of the State of Coahuila and afterwards as Head of the Constitutionalist Army, *as being that of a dictator, with no other counsel than his own judgment and most of the time without any other law than his own will.* In a political way he violated the sovereignty of the Ayuntamiento[2] of Torreón and of the States of Sinaloa and Sonora, being, by his arbitrary and unconstitutional acts, the one chiefly responsible for the present conflict in the last-mentioned State, between the Constitutional Governor and the revolutionary leaders supported by Mr. Carranza and elected from among the personal enemies of Mr. Maytorena, notwithstanding the written request of the Governor to appoint as commander of the troops in the State an officer with whom he could govern in harmony. In a military way he imposed his authority, without taking into account the opinion of revolutionary leaders, whose military endowments have been recognized and esteemed by everybody.

The *Division of the North*, which represents the interests of the most numerous group of armed people *and which has contributed more than any other to the triumph of the revolution*, believes that it is entitled to ask Mr. Carranza or such person as has in his hands the provisional government of the Republic, to guarantee, during his provisional administration, the realization of the means which it deems necessary for the establishment of real democracy and of peace in Mexico, founded on justice and on the satisfaction of the national needs, and it pledges itself to employ all its military forces for the upholding of the provisional government, provided it accepts the following clauses as the basis of its political program:

First.—The Division of the North, as the most powerful revolutionary element, shall be represented in the Cabinet of the Provisional President by three Secretaries elected by a majority of votes by the generals who belong to the Division.

Second.—As soon as the Cabinet has been formed, the representative of the Executive, with the advice and consent of his Ministers, shall appoint the judicial authorities, who, under the general Constitution of the Republic, are not subject to popular election either in the common or in the federal jurisdiction; and, as regards the formation of the Supreme Court of Justice and of the Superior Tribunals of the States, it shall take place under the conditions determined hereinbelow and in conformity with the general Constitution and the special constitutions of the States. The Provisional Governors of the States shall proceed at once to appoint the judges of first instance within the territory of their jurisdiction.

Third.—The person holding the office of chief federal executive and the provisional governors of the States shall appoint, provisionally, a Council composed of at least three lettered judges to take cognizance, as a court of revision, of the judgments rendered by the judges of first instance, the members forming them having the same responsibilities as are provided by law for magistrates elected according to the Constitution.

Fourth.—The Governors of the States, the Governor of the [Federal] District, and the Civil Heads of the Territories shall call Ayuntamiento elections as soon as the judicial authorities have been appointed, and the elections shall be held one month afterwards.

Fifth.—When the Ayuntamientos are installed, the President and Provisional Governors shall call elections, the former for representatives to the Congress of the Nation and Magistrates of the Supreme Court of Justice; the latter for Constitutional Governor, Deputies to the Local Legislature, and Magistrates of the Supreme Court. These elections shall be held exactly one month after the call has been issued.

Sixth.—As soon as the Constitutional Governors of the States, the Representatives to the Congress of the Nation, and those to the Local Legislatures have taken possession of their offices, the Provisional President shall call elections for President and Vice President of the Republic, which elections shall be held two months after the call has been issued. When the Chamber of Deputies has announced the result of the election, the President and Vice President of the Nation shall take possession of their elevated offices.

Seventh.—Neither the Presidency and Vice-Presidency of the Republic, nor the Governorships of the States, shall be open to those citizens who have held these offices in a provisional capacity upon the triumph of the Revolution, nor to those who may hold them from the date of the call up to the time of the election.

Eighth.—The Governors of the States shall, immediately upon entering upon the discharge of their duties, appoint a board, with its residence at the capital of the State, and composed of one representative for each district, to study the agrarian problem and prepare a plan which shall be submitted to the Congress of the State for its legal sanction.

Ninth.—The Commanding Officers of the Division of the North pledge themselves to submit to the Federal Congress, for its approval, the draft of a law according to which all persons belonging to the new National Army shall become disqualified from holding the offices of President, Vice-President, or Governor of States.

Tenth.—Mr. Carranza shall obligate himself not to dissolve the Division of the North, nor to remove any of its commanding officers, owing to the necessity of preserving its integrity, which constitutes a guarantee of the peace of the Republic.

Francisco Villa.[3]

T translation (WP, DLC).
[1] Italicization throughout this letter by Wilson.
[2] That is, the municipalities.
[3] The TS memorandum is SDR, RG 59, 812.00/17185, DNA.

From Robert Lansing

Dear Mr. President: Washington August 24, 1914.

You ask me for an opinion upon the subject of the transfer of title of German merchant ships, now in American waters, to the United States or its citizens, in connection with certain information contained in a letter to you from Mr. J. P. Morgan under date of August 21, 1914, which letter I herewith return.

I annex copies of two telegrams received by the Department from the American Ambassador at London, dated respectively August 18th and 21st, and also the paraphrase of a telegram received by the British Chargé here from Sir Edward Grey, which the former handed to me on the afternoon of August 22nd.[1]

From these communications it is manifest that there has been a very decided change of policy on the part of the British Government between the 18th and 21st. From a general attitude of opposition on legal and technical grounds to our purchase of the German ships, they now do not oppose the purchase but seek only that this Government shall guarantee that the vessels purchased shall not trade to German ports or neutral ports easily accessible to German territory.

The only condition, which Great Britain now seeks to impose on the purchase of the ships, seems to be a general requirement that their habits shall be changed, assuming of course that the transfer of title is absolute and intended to be perpetual.

The question of the legality of sale is a question of *bona fides*, and the accepted rule appears to impose the burden of proof on the parties to the sale, particularly the vendee, to establish such *bona fides*. I think that the condition, which the British Government now urge, is a reasonable one. The presumption that a sale is made to avoid the consequences of belligerent ownership is regarded as very strong if the vessel continues to follow the same trade route which it had pursued prior to the outbreak of hostilities, and as almost conclusive if the route lay between the neutral country and the ports of the belligerent, whose subjects are selling the vessel.

In one way the British condition does not go as far as the general rule, in that it does not appear to apply to trade routes other than with Germany or nearby neutral ports. On the other hand it goes beyond the rule in requiring no trade with ports of Germany or those near German territory regardless of the previous trade routes of the vessels sold.

It seems to me that the foregoing modification of the general rule in a way changes its application from the presumption created against the *bona fides* of the sale, and introduces a new element as to the violation of neutrality by the purchaser.

To illustrate, the change after sale of the trade route of a German vessel, which prior to hostilities had been running between American and German ports would remove the presumption that the sale had not been *bona fides*. On the other hand, a similar change of route by a purchased vessel formerly trading to a South American port would not be required to avoid the presumption, but the condition would be that the route could not be changed to Germany. The first case deals with the presumption of *bona fides*; the latter, with neutrality.

Nevertheless, from this point of view, I do not think the requirement unjustified or one to which this Government should seriously object, in view of the British Government's express willingness to waive all other technical grounds of objection to the sale, which I assume includes the production of evidence to establish *bona fides* in addition to the transfer papers.

In my opinion, therefore, there should be no difficulty in removing any objection by Great Britain to the purchase of German merchant vessels now in neutral harbors. As to the attitude of other belligerents we are not yet advised.

I do not think it necessary to say that in no event should we accede formally to such a condition as one which could properly be imposed. To do so might invite protest from the German Government on the ground that we were not preserving a strict neutrality. But having received notice from Great Britain of its view as to vessels so trading the American owners would naturally avoid the risk by using the vessels in other commerce.

In case you desire a more elaborate consideration of the general subject of the purchase of belligerent merchant ships by neutrals I shall be glad to furnish it.

I am, Sir,   Very respectfully yours,   Robert Lansing.

TLS (WP, DLC).
  1 WHP to WW, Aug. 18, 1914, T telegram (WP, DLC); WHP to WW, Aug. 21, T telegram (WP, DLC); E. Grey to C. Barclay, Aug. 21, 1914, T paraphrase of telegram (WP, DLC).

William Jennings Bryan to Joseph Patrick Tumulty

My dear Mr. Tumulty: Washington August 24, 1914.

I beg to quote, for the information of the President, the following telegram, dated at Mexico City August 23, 9 p.m., from Vice Consul John R. Silliman:

"I have the honor to transmit the following textual translation of a communication received by me last night."

" 'Mexico, D.F., August twenty-second, Nineteen fourteen. 'I have the honor to inform you, in order that you may kindly bring it to the notice of His Excellency the President of the United States or Woodrow Wilson, that today, in conformity with the plan of Guadalupe of the twenty-sixth of March nineteen thirteen, I have assumed the duties of the executive authority of the Mexican Republic.

'In asking that you notify your Government, it is a satisfaction to repeat the assurance of my esteemed and distinguished consideration. Signed V. Carranza. To Mister John R. Silliman,

Special Representative of the Government of the United States, present.'"
I am, my dear Mr. Tumulty,
                              Sincerely yours,   W. J. Bryan

TLS (WP, DLC).

A Message for General Villa

[c. Aug. 25, 1914]

We feel that it might prejudice the whole process of settlement if suggestions seem to come from outside sources, and we feel moreover that we are not competent here to judge of the feasibility of that part of the plan that deals with the matter and manner of selecting the provisional President. But we desire to compliment Villa upon the moderation and reasonableness of the program of reform and we feel reassured as to the spirit with which he is approaching the subject. We hope that in presenting it to Carranza he will present it in an argumentative way and not with an implication of a resort to arms which would be fatal to the Constitutionalist cause. Counter propositions should be considered in the same spirit with which Villa wishes Carranza to receive his proposals

This is reply made to Villa's representative here[1]

CLST MS (WP, DLC).
   [1] WJBhw.

To Edward Mandell House

My dear Friend: The White House August 25, 1914
    Thank you for your letter of August twenty-second. It expresses in a way that was somewhat poignant to me my feeling about the possible alternative outcomes of the war. I feel the burden of the thing almost intolerably from day to day, I think largely because there is nothing that we can as yet do or even attempt. What a pathetic thing to have this come just as we were so full of hope!
                    Affectionately yours,   Woodrow Wilson

TLS (E. M. House Papers, CtY).

To Robert Lansing

My dear Mr. Lansing: The White House August 25, 1914

Thank you sincerely for your letter of August twenty-fourth about the purchase of German ships. I think that the situation is clearing up in a very satisfactory way.

Cordially and sincerely yours,   Woodrow Wilson

TLS (SDR, RG 59, 195.1/16½, DNA).

To William Jennings Bryan

My dear Friend: The White House August 25, 1914

How shall I thank you for your letter of sympathy! Somehow a sort of dumb spirit has had possession of me of late whenever I was in the presence of those who really cared and it has been almost impossible for me to speak or even to write with self-possession. But I must not let any longer time go by without telling you how deeply I was touched by your letter of sympathy or how genuinely grateful I am for a friend who so supports me with his generous sympathy.

Cordially and sincerely yours,   Woodrow Wilson

TLS (W. J. Bryan Papers, DLC).

To Mary Eloise Hoyt

My dear Cousin Mary: The White House August 25, 1914

By some mishap or oversight your little note of August eleventh was not given to me. I found it in the Oval Room day before yesterday.

It would be a great delight to me if you could from time to time, just as you happen to remember them, jot down things that Ellen said that come back to you. I should prize them so highly because she loved you very much and I know spoke to you very intimately indeed about the things that were nearest to her. It is sweet of you to have thought of this.

It has occurred to me that if you did what I have suggested, namely, made little memoranda from time to time, you could without even copying them send them to me as they accumulated.

Things go very steady with us. Sister Annie got back safe; Cousin Mary Smith is slowly convalescing; and gradually we shall work back to as nearly a normal basis as is conceivable in the circumstances.

It was very sweet of you to write.

Affectionately yours,   Woodrow Wilson

TLS (received from William D. Hoyt, Jr.).

To Sarah Caruthers Park Hughes[1]

My dear Mrs. Hughes: [The White House] August 25, 1914

My daughter Margaret has handed me your kind letter of August fifteenth.[2] We have had a little family conference and I want to say for my daughters as well as for myself how deeply we appreciate the action of the little conference you held at Montreat[3] and how glad I am to make the suggestions you ask for.

My own judgment would be that it would be best to raise a fund which should be an endowment the interest of which should be used to pay the way through school of mountain boys and girls, because I know that this is what Mrs. Wilson would have done if she had the means and opportunity. She was paying for the education of several herself from year to year. It might be called the Ellen Wilson Fund for the Christian Education of Mountain Youth.

I cannot say how much I am touched by this action by the ladies concerned. It gives me a certain kind of joy.

Cordially and sincerely yours,   Woodrow Wilson

TLS (Letterpress Books, WP, DLC).
  [1] Mrs. Benjamin Isbell Hughes. Her husband had been an officer of the First National Bank of Rome, Georgia, since its organization in 1877.
  [2] Sarah C. P. Hughes to Margaret W. Wilson, Aug. 15, 1914, ALS (WP, DLC).
  [3] Conference center of the southern Presbyterian Church in the mountains of North Carolina.

From Elias Milton Ammons

Sir: Denver August twenty-five nineteen fourteen.

I am in receipt of your letter in relation to strike conditions in Colorado. I cannot give you in detail today as full information as I know you would desire but hope to be able to do so within a week or so and will write you further at that time. At present I can say that the Legislature, having no available monies in the treasury, authorized the issuance of $1,000,000 in bonds to take care of the insurrection expenses. A part of the certificates of indebtedness for past expenses have now been exchanged for these bonds and the balance of the certificates will be exchanged as fast as they are presented. I have a plan for taking care of the balance of the certificates. The total expenses of the insurrection up to the present time amount to $700,000 to $750,000 leaving something more than a quarter of a million worth of bonds authorized to take care of future expenditures. I think I fully appreciate your anxiety in this matter and I do not intend to cause you any further concern than I can help. The situation here has been much more difficult than the people of the East can appreciate and chiefly because they have not been given the facts. Every effort to raise money has been made with open or secret opposition. But little more than one-fourth of the state is taxable, the balance of the lands being public and you may be surprised when I tell you that 19/20ths of our taxable revenues come from 1/11th of the territory. Financial conditions have made it very hard to place our bonds and the war in Europe has intensified that condition. Notwithstanding this fact, I believe I shall as soon as the present exchanges are made be able to place sufficient bonds to take care of future expenditures. In that event I will write you at once. Because of opposition to the payment of the troops and this opposition has existed from the beginning, I was unable to raise sufficient funds to pay the men in the field and I do not believe I can possibly get men to go until these bonds are disposed of. I assure you I have allowed no unnecessary delay but am very anxious to relieve you of a burden which I know has been great and which I wish had not been placed upon you at a time when your best thoughts and energies were required in other directions.

Very sincerely yours,   E M Ammons

TLS (WP, DLC).

To Henry Cabot Lodge

My dear Senator: [The White House] August 26, 1914

I am sincerely grateful to you for your thought of me in my loss and distress. Sympathy does strengthen and sustain, and I want to say that your kind message[1] was to me a most welcome evidence of your kindness and personal thoughtfulness.

Sincerely yours,   Woodrow Wilson

TLS (Letterpress Books, WP, DLC).
[1] It is missing in both WP, DLC, and the H. C. Lodge Papers, MHi.

To Robert Lee Henry

My dear Mr. Henry: [The White House] August 27, 1914

I am very much gratified by what Mr. Tumulty tells me of the result of his conference with you and I am heartily glad that the Committee on Rules has your guidance again.

As I think Mr. Tumulty has told you, the bills that seem to me most imperatively necessary and most immediately necessary for the service of the country are the war risks insurance bill and the bill for the purchase of ships. I am going away for two or three days this afternoon for an absolutely imperative interval of rest and wanted to send you this little friendly memorandum before going. I would be very much gratified if the Committee on Rules would cooperate in any way necessary with Judge Alexander in regard to the shipping bill. I understand that unanimous consent will be refused. Very few bills that we have considered are bigger with possibilities for the country than this one.

         Cordially and sincerely yours,   Woodrow Wilson

TLS (Letterpress Books, WP, DLC).

Two Letters to James Harry Covington

My dear Mr. Covington: [The White House] August 27, 1914

I have been looking over the proposed redraft of the Trade Commission bill and want to call your attention to the proviso at line three, on page nine. May I not earnestly suggest that the House conferees urge an amendment striking out the words "or finding of the court or commission in the enforcement of this section shall be admissible as evidence in any suit, civil or criminal, brought under the anti-trust Acts, nor shall the orders," and also the word "the" on line seven and the insertion in line eight, after the word "same," of the word "shall," so that it would read "Provided, That no order of the commission or judgment of the court to enforce the same shall in any wise relieve or absolve any person, partnership, or corporation from any liability under the anti-trust Acts"?

While I do not think that the law ought to prescribe that orders and findings of the commission shall be admissable as evidence, it seems to me that it would be inconsistent with the policy adopted in the Clayton bill explicitly to provide that they shall not be. I think it would be much best to leave that to the judgment and discretion of the court in every instance.

I had yesterday a long talk with Senator Newlands and I think that if the House conferees will stand stoutly for Section V throughout, including the matter of the scope of the court review, they will win. I think I converted Senator Newlands to that view.[1]

In haste, with warmest regards,
Cordially and faithfully yours,   Woodrow Wilson

[1] Section 5, as finally enacted, provided for broad judicial review. See Link, *The New Freedom*, pp. 441-42.

My dear Mr. Covington: [The White House] August 27, 1914

I had a conversation with Senator Newlands which leads me to ask how serious the objection is in the House to providing that the Trade Commission may inquire into the trade practices abroad and allow domestic combinations in certain circumstances to meet foreign competition, or, if not so much as that, allow it after investigation to report to Congress suggested arrangements to meet the conditions of foreign competition.[1] This is a question on which my mind has changed sides several times, but while I think it would perhaps not be safe to authorize the commission to allow domestic combinations to meet foreign competition I think it might at least be very wise to authorize the commission to investigate these matters very thoroughly and report to Congress.

Cordially and sincerely yours,   Woodrow Wilson

TLS (Letterpress Books, WP, DLC).
[1] The conference committee added a paragraph to Section 6 that was a paraphrase of Wilson's words.

From Oswald Garrison Villard

My dear Mr. President,   [New York] Aug 27, 1914

I am deeply grateful for your two recent letters[1] and am, of course, very happy to feel that some of our editorials have been of service to you. At least they have come from the heart. I am truly surprised that you are able to find the time to read any expressions of newspaper opinion in these incredible times.

We feel, frankly, much worried about the shipping proposal, primarily lest it be done too hastily and frighten off genuine investors. Moreover, it will put a tremendous argument into the mouths of the Socialists. I admit, of course, that the argument and precedent are there in the Panama Railroad and the steamship company. Yet the case is different now for the Panama steamers were like the dredges—necessary for the economical construction of something that private enterprise could not undertake. Again, events in Europe are moving so quickly—the war is not four weeks old—that the problem may seem quite different two or four weeks hence.

More and more it appears as if in the end yours would be the wonderful privilege of initiating the peace measures when enough blood has been shed to permit of some sanity in Europe. I personally would ask for no greater fortune than to have a share, however small, in bringing peace to my unfortunate Fatherland.

If, therefore, there is any way in which you can use me will you bear me in mind? My knowledge of German, my German birth and my long residence abroad may be of value. You have read in my editorial "The Real Crime Against Germany"[2] something of the deep feeling I have. If the sentiments are too strongly anti-Kaiser to make me available you will know best. At any rate I should like you to feel that if there is any capacity in which I could serve you in this cause it would fulfil my highest ambitions.

May I ask for just a line to make sure this reaches your eye?
                    Sincerely yours,   Oswald Garrison Villard

ALS (WP, DLC).
    [1] WW to O. G. Villard, Aug. 14, 1914, TLS (O. G. Villard Papers, MH), and WW to OGV, Aug. 24, 1914.
    [2] New York *Evening Post*, Aug. 8, 1914, and the New York *Nation*, XCIX (Aug. 13, 1914), 181-82. Villard passionately defended the *Evening Post* and *The Nation* against charges of German sympathizers that his journals had not given "fair play" to Germany in their editorial comments since the outbreak of war. Villard stated that his papers never had and never would give allegiance to the Germany of the Kaiser and of the "autocracy of militarism." Their allegiance was to the Germany of spiritual and intellectual idealism and of scientific and commercial leadership. The "real crime" against Germany was the war into which the Kaiser and the militarists had plunged it. The only hope for the future was that a new democratic Germany might arise from the ashes of the conflict.

From William Jennings Bryan

My Dear Mr. President: Washington August 28, 1914.

We have at last received an answer from the Czar to your offer of mediation. It is as follows:

"Appreciating the humanitarian sentiments which dictated this step His Majesty has deigned to command me to transmit to the President his sincere thanks. Russia did not desire war and did everything to avoid it, but from the moment this war was imposed upon her she cannot fail to defend her rights by force of arms. Under these circumstances it seems for the moment premature to contemplate the possibility of peace.

Nevertheless I beg you to be so good as to be the interpreter to Mr. Woodrow Wilson of the thanks of His Majesty."

If you will examine the five answers received,[1] you will be reminded of that passage in the Scriptures which says "that they all with one accord began to make excuses." Each one declares he is opposed to war and anxious to avoid it and then lays the blame upon someone else. The German Ambassador this morning blamed Russia and congratulated his country that the Emporer did what he could to avoid war. He also commends the efforts of France and Great Britain to avoid war, but the Czar is charged with being the cause, his offense being the mobilization of his army after Austria had assured him that the integrity of Servia would not be disturbed.

The fact that they all declare themselves against war and express regret that it has been gone into would seem to make it easier when a way opens to present the matter again. An appeal could then be reinforced by quotations from their replies.

I hope that you are securing the rest which you so greatly need.

With assurances of high respect, I am, my dear Mr. President,
Very sincerely yours,   W. J. Bryan

TLS (EBR, RG 130, DNA).
  [1] In addition to the Czar's reply, the responses of the governments of France, Austria-Hungary, Great Britain, and Germany were conveyed in M. T. Herrick to Secretary of State, Aug. 6, 1914, *FR 1914-WWS*, p. 48; F. C. Penfield to Secretary of State, Aug. 7, 1914, *ibid.*, pp. 49-50; W. H. Page to Secretary of State, Aug. 7, 1914, *ibid.*, p. 50; J. W. Gerard to Secretary of State, Aug. 14, 1914, printed in this volume at that date.

From William Jennings Bryan, with Enclosures

[Washington, Aug. 28, 1914]

The enclosed has just been left with the Dept.

AL (WP, DLC).

E N C L O S U R E   I

Emmanuel Havenith[1] to William Jennings Bryan

Monsieur Le Secretaire d'Etat   Washington August 28 1914

I have the honour to transmit to you herewith the text of a cablegram which I have just received from my Government.

The information contained in this document will enable Your Excellency to form a judgement as to the manner in which Germany is fulfilling the obligations assumed by her in the treaty of 1839 under which she bound herself to protect Belgium.

I venture to bring these facts to your knowledge and through Your Excellency, to the Knowledge of the President of the United States for it is not only Belgium who has to mourn the massacre of her innocent sons. Such a crime as this concerns the whole world.

I beg your Excellency to accept the assurance of my highest consideration   E. Havenith

TCL (WP, DLC).
[1] Belgian Minister to the United States.

ENCLOSURE II

Telegram from the Belgian Minister for Foreign Affairs[1] to the Belgian Minister in Washington.

On Tuesday evening a body of German troops who had been driven back retired in disorder upon the town of LOUVAIN. Germans who were guarding the town thought that the retiring troops were Belgians and fired upon them. In order to excuse this mistake the Germans in spite of the most energetic denials on the part of the authorities pretended that Belgians had fired on the Germans although all the inhabitants including policemen has been disarmed for more than a week. Without any examination and without listening to any protest the commanding officer announced that the town would be immediately destroyed. All inhabitants had to leave their homes at once, some were made prisoners, women and children were put into a train of which the destination was unknown, soldiers with fire bombs set fire to the different quarters of the town; the splendid church of St Pierre, the markets the university and its scientific establishments were given to the flames and it is probable that the Hotel de Ville this celebrated jewel of Gothic art will also have disappeared in the disaster. Several notabilities were shot at sight. Thus a town of 40,000 inhabitants which since the fifteenth century has been the intellectual and scientific capital of the Low Countries is a heap of ashes. Americans many of whom have followed the courses at this illustrious alma mater and have there received such cordial hospitality cannot remain insensible to this outrage on the rights of humanity and civilization which is unprecedented in history.

TC telegram (WP, DLC).
[1] Jacques Davignon.

From Paul Fuller

New Orleans, La.

My dear Mr President: Friday morning, Aug. 28/1914

At the risk of adding, never so slightly, to the weight of your overburdened hours, I must send this line to thank you for the cordiality of your note, & to assure you of my faith in the splendid effort you are making for the lasting regeneration of our Mexican neighbors. Like all efforts that look far into the future, it must meet the doubters who look only to the selfish advantages of the day, but the stars in their courses will fight for you and at the worst we may console ourselves with Browning and remember that "not failure but low aim is crime."

Very sincerely yours   Paul Fuller

ALS (WP, DLC).

Two Letters from William Jennings Bryan

My Dear Mr. President: Washington August 29, 1914.

I am sending you a copy of a paper left with us today by the Belgian Minister,[1] and in doing so I respectfully submit that Counsellor Lansing and I agree in the opinion that it would be difficult to make an investigation at this time without danger of subjecting ourselves to severe criticism from the governments whose acts were investigated. It would be difficult enough for us to make the investigation ourselves, but the risk would be still greater if we associated ourselves with others who might, from their geographical environment, be less able to act with entire impartiality. In fact, I doubt whether any other neutral nation would be willing to join us in so delicate and difficult a task.

With assurances of high respect, I am, my dear Mr. President,
Very sincerely yours,   W. J. Bryan

[1] Minister of Foreign Affairs to E. Havenith, Aug. 28, 1914, T telegram (EBR, RG 130, DNA)', asking Havenith urgently to request President Wilson to appoint a representative to work with the Belgian commission on German atrocities, located in Antwerp.

My Dear Mr. President: Washington August 29, 1914.

I am sending you a letter written by Mr. Lansing, together with two forms of protest and a memorandum by Mr. Scott.[1]

I am so anxious that we shall avoid anything that can possibly bring us into collision with the beliggerent powers that I am not sure that we should make any protest at all. The same caution which leads me to doubt whether we should make any protest naturally leads me to favor the one least likely to raise objection.

The use of an air-ship is not forbidden by The Hague rules. At the first Hague meeting there was an agreement that they should not be used for five years, but Germany did not join in this. The second conference did not adopt any rule at all and, since the first rule has expired, there is no international law on the subject. If any protest at all is made, it must be made upon a general principle, rather than upon a specific agreement. There being no international provision which is clearly and specifically violated, we would not, I think, be justified in making a general protest simply upon humanitarian grounds, although I believe our representatives should, at the next meeting at the Hague, endeavor to secure an agreement among all the nations, and if they cannot secure an agreement among all the nations, should secure an agreement among as many as are willing to join in such. There is, in my judgment, unassailable ground upon which this can be urged, namely, that from time immemorial an attacking army must give notice of bombardment. This requirement, which comes down to us from the Bible times, has two objects, first, to permit the surrender of the city without the use of force and, second, to permit noncombatants to retire in case force is necessary. In the case of bombardment from an air-ship a notice should certainly be given to noncombatants—of this there can be no question. But how can the other condition be complied with? When an army attacks, the city can be surrendered without resistance to the attacking party. But to whom can a city be surrendered if the attack is made from air-ships? It would seem that humanity requires that the rules governing bombardment from air-ships should be as strict as those governing bombardment from sea or from land forces.

The contention that Antwerp is a fortified city cannot be regarded as sound, because the fortifications are incidental to the city and can be taken without the taking of the city. A city would seem to be different from a fortress in that noncombatants are not expected to live in a fortress, whereas a garrison constitutes but a small percentage of the residents of a city like Antwerp. The residents of Antwerp could hardly be expected to vacate without notice merely because an enemy was waging war in another part of the country.

It seems to me that the proper use of air-ships will be one of the most important subjects to be considered at the next Hague Conference, but we would hardly be justified in now basing a protest upon what should be, but is not now, international law.

As to the protest relating to our own citizens, there is some reason for taking action, for until the residents are warned to leave there is no reason why Americans residing there should abandon their residence and depart from the city. If you think it wise to make a protest at all, it might be better to make it in the form of an inquiry, so wording the inquiry as to ascertain the German version as to the facts in the case. In giving us their version they would, doubtless, state their position which would give us an opportunity to reply to any unsound argument advanced.

I hesitate to intrude upon the time which you need for rest, but you have, doubtless, been thinking of this subject and may be ready to give instructions.

With assurances of high respect, I am, my dear Mr. President,

Very truly yours,   W. J. Bryan

TLS (EBR, RG 130, DNA).
    ¹ RL to WJB, Aug. 28, 1914, TLS (EBR, RG 130, DNA), with two drafts of protest notes, and J. B. Scott to RL, Aug. 27, 1914, TLS and TLI, same file number. Lansing's letter and draft notes are printed in *FR-LP*, I, 29-32.

From the Diary of Colonel House

[Cornish, N. H.] August 30, 1914.

We arrived at Harlekendon at half past ten. The President met us at the door and insisted upon Gordon¹ remaining to lunch since his train for New York did not leave until the afternoon.

I was glad to find the President situated so delightfully. The house reminds one of an English place. The view is superb, and the arrangement and furnishings are comfortable and artistic. The President showed me my room himself. It was the one Mrs. Wilson used to occupy and was next to his with a common bathroom between. We are in one wing of the house and quite to ourselves. A small stairway leads down to his study, and it was there that we sat and discussed matters until after one o'clock when lunch was announced.

I told of my experiences in Europe and gave him more of the details of my mission. He was interested in the personalities of the people who are the governments heads, and later said my knowledge of these men and of the situation in Europe would be of great value to him.

We discussed what might be the final distribution of power

¹ His son-in-law, Gordon Auchincloss.

some centuries hence. He thought it quite possible that eventually there might be but two great nations in the world,—Russia, on the one hand, and this country on the other. I thought there would be three, China dominating Asia, Russia dominating Europe, and a part of Asia, and America dominating the Western World and perhaps the English speaking colonies.

The President spoke with deep feeling of the war. He said it made him heartsick to think of how near we had come to averting this great disaster, and he thought if it had been delayed a little longer, it could never have happened, because the nations would have gotten together in the way I had outlined.

I told in detail of my suggestion to Sir Edward Grey and other members of the Cabinet, that the surest guaranty of peace was for the principals to get together frequently and discuss matters with frankness and freedom as Great Britain and the United States were doing. He agreed that this was the most effective method and he again expressed deep regret that the war had come too soon to permit the inauguration of such procedure. He wondered whether things might have been different if I had gone sooner. I thought it would have made no difference for the reason that the Kaiser was at Corfu and it was impossible for me to approach him sooner than I did.

I expressed regret that the war did not begin before I left England, as there was a bare possibility I might have done something to have held it up long enough to have brought about a conference.

I was interested to hear him express as his opinion, what I had written him sometime ago in one of my letters from Europe, to the effect that if Germany won it would change the course of our civilization and make the United States a military nation. He also spoke of his deep regret, as indeed I did to him in that same letter, that it would check his policy for a better international ethical code.

He felt deeply the destruction of Louvain, and I found him as unsympathetic with the German attitude as is the balance of America. He goes even further than I in his condemnation of Germany's part in this war, and almost allows his feeling to include the German people as a whole rather than the leaders alone. He said German philosophy was essentially selfish and lacking in spirituality. When I spoke of the Kaiser building up the German machine as a means of maintaining peace, he said: "what a foolish thing it was to create a powder magazine and risk someone's sropping [dropping] a spark into it."

He wanted to know about the Kaiser and I gave him my

estimate of his ability and character. I showed him Zimmermann's letter[2] and asked what he had to suggest in the way of a reply. He thought to emphasize his mediation proposal and let him know that we stood ready at any time. We planned to get in direct touch with the Kaiser through Zimmermann, thinking perhaps, the Kaiser would prefer to reach the President in an unofficial way through me rather than through our Ambassador.

He thought the war would throw the world back three or four centuries. I did not agree with him. He was particularly scornful of Germany's disregard of treaty obligations, and was indignant at the German Chancellor's designation of the Belgian Treaty as being "only a scrap of paper."

I took occasion here to explain to him Sir Edward Grey's strong feeling upon the question of treaty obligation, and his belief that he, the President, had lifted international ethics to a high plane by his action in the Panama tolls question.

I explained my plan about the backward nations and of how enthusiastically it was received by the British Government, and how much they thought it would do toward bringing about a better understanding between the great powers. I believed if we had an opportunity to put this into effect, in all human probability, such a war as this would not have occurred, because with the powers meeting at regular intervals, and with such a concrete example of the good that might be accomplished by concerted action, a conflagration such as was now going on would have been impossible.

I am not giving our conversation in full for the reason I did not [most] of the talking, in order to explain the different phases of my European mission, and to tell him of the public men I met abroad.

I brought up McCombs' ambition to be Ambassador to Mexico. He replied that McCombs was not his friend and he did not want to appoint him; that he was not fitted for the place as he did not speak Spanish or have any knowledge of the Spanish people. He thought he would offer the place to Paul Fuller, if he would take it, since Fuller had all the necessary qualifications and had done well in his negotiations with Villa, and if he did as well with Carranza, he would ask him to accept the place.

We went into the Mexican situation carefully and agreed that Villa is the only man of force now in sight in Mexico. We are afraid Carranza is not equal to the situation. He is letting Car-

[2] A. Zimmermann to E. M. House, Aug. 1, 1914, TLS (E. M. House Papers, CtY), stating that the Kaiser's "strong and sincere efforts to conserve peace" had entirely failed because of Russia's mobilization, and that there was now no chance to discuss "the possibility of an understanding."

ranza know that he will not be recognized unless he maintains himself as he should, and non-recognition means failure.

We discussed the appointments of Gregory and McReynolds, news of their confirmation having just reached us. The President believed Gregory would be of much assistance in looking after Congressional affairs; he considered his Cabinet weak in this direction, McAdoo and Burleson being the only ones with any appitude [aptitude] for political work of that character.

Later, during the day, we discussed the advisability of his taking Harlekendon for another year. His inclination is to do so. I pointed out the disadvantages, one of which is that there is no hotel near by, and if he remained there for any length of time, he would be compelled to see his Cabinet and other people of importance. It would almost force him to invite them to the house as his guests, which would be rather a burden upon him. There is an hotel about sixteen miles away, but I called his attention to the fact that he would have to place an automobile at the disposal of his guests which would also be inconvenient. We allowed the question to drop for the moment to take it up later. I have a feeling that the place suits him as well or better than many suggested. He pays $2500. as rental, and he could not get such a place along the North Shore[3] for less than $6000. to $8000.

We spoke of Mr. Bryan and how responsibility sobers a man. Bryan said to him the other day "this is the greatest school either of us ever attended."

In speaking of the German military organization, it was interesting to note that this Government was spending more than Germany for its military establishment if pensions are included. He spoke of the frightful abuse of our pension system. When I was in Berlin the Kaiser called attention to the fact that our military organization, including pensions, cost more than that of Germany. "You," he said, "have nothing for it, while we have the most efficient army in the world."

In the evenings of the two days I was there, we sat around and read and talked and sometimes played pool, all of us playing equally badly, although the President managed to win a majority of the games.

The second afternoon as we were sitting on the terrace looking out over the broad Valley of the Connecticut, he began to talk of Mrs. Wilson and of what her loss meant to him personally. Tears came into his eyes, and he said he felt like a machine that had run down, and there was nothing left in him worth while.

[3] **Of Massachusetts.**

As far as he could see, he was still doing good work and his mental capacity had not been impaired by the trouble he had gone through, and yet, he looked forward to the next two years and a half with dread. He did not see how he could go through with it.

I was surprised at his desire to discuss Mrs. Wilson. He showed me photographs of her, read poems written about her, and talked of her as freely as if she were alive.

I spoke of the great work there was to do for humanity in the readjustment of the wreckage that would come from the European war, and I hoped he would console himself with this knowledge. But few men had been given the opportunity to serve as he would have. I spoke of the world having started wrongly, with brute force dominating. Later this was recognized as unjust and for the first time the beginning of law was established. It was equally wrong for the mentally [militarily?] strong to oppress the mentally deficient, and when that was recognized, another great step forward would be made, and I hoped he might prove an instrument for doing this. I laid stress upon the power of public opinion and of the advantage of having it enlisted on our side. Reforms of this sort came too slowly, and he did not have a hopeful outlook. I tried to make him see that reforms were going forward with much more celerity than heretofore, for man desired the commendation of his fellow man more than anything else, and with public opinion set toward higher purposes, individuals would naturally strive to obtain the good opinion of society.

At one time during my visit he spoke of belonging to the Clan Argyle and the Clan Campbell of Scotland, and of their being about the worst lot of freebooters Scotland had produced. He spoke of Scotch frugality, illustrating it with a story of two highwaymen who set upon a Scotchman. The Scotchman fought with such vim that he was overcome only after he had been mangled and bruised almost to extinction. The highwayman looked through his pockets and found six pence and remarked to his companion "What wad he hae doon to us had he had a shilling."

He also told of a Scotchman who said he did not like to smoke a pipe. When he used his own tobacco it was too soon over with, and when he used someone else's, he stuffed it so full it would not draw.

He related many stories of Dr. McCosh of Princeton. He spoke well of him but said he was a snob, citing the fact that he once showed him with great pride while he, Wilson, was a freshman, a letter from the Duke of Argyle. He could not understand why a man of McCosh's ability and distinction should think it was of any importance to receive a letter from a Duke who was in every way his inferior.

Dr. Patton, his predecessor, he spoke of as an "intellectual humbug, an intellectual immoral." He was very strict in his orthodoxy, but Wilson thought this true was because he wanted to give himself a mental spree, and desired to be different from others.

The President said he had a great desire to be let alone after he left office. He considered one of the drawbacks of being President was that when his term expired he could never be left to his own devices.

The second day I went over some campaign suggestions[4] which had been compiled for him regarding the Congressional campaign this Autumn. This I approved. During my visit he told many humorous stories, particularly about golf. One was the story of a rather conceited American who was playing on a course in Scotland. He told the caddie something of his prowess, and later said to him, "I expect you have seen worse players than I am." The caddie did not reply, and a little later he made the same remark. Then the caddie said "I heard you the first time, and I was a thinking."

Another story was that when the game was new in this country a friend insisted upon General Grant coming out to see him play, telling him how much good it would do him. He was somewhat nervous and after teeing the ball, he struck the ground and the ball merely rolled from the tee. This made him more nervous and the next time he missed the ball entirely. The silent General remarked, "It does seem to be good exercise, but what is the ball for?"

The last morning I was with the President he planned to play golf early enough to get back for lunch and leave on the 2.40 train for Washington. It was my intention to leave Harlekendon for Prides when he started to the golf field. This necessitated our getting up early and about the same time. He arose a half hour earlier than was necessary, merely to give me the uninterrupted use of our common bathroom. This illustrates, I think, as well as anything I could mention, his consideration for others and the simplicity of the man. I notice, too, in his relations with his family that he is always tender, affectionate and considerate.

When he bade me goodbye I thanked him for the pleasure he

4 "Programme for the Fall Campaign," undated T MS (C. L. Swem Coll., NjP), outlining a very limited presidential participation in the congressional campaign. It suggested an address before the Democratic Congressional Campaign Committee opening the campaign, followed later by a public statement detailing the administration's accomplishments and a closing speech outlining plans for the future.

had given me and he replied "I came to Harlekendon largely to be in a place where you might come to see me."

Dr Grayson had two long talks with me in which he told all the mischievous petty, White House gossip. It seem[s] impossible for the President to escape espionage concerning his most intimate personal affairs. The President's closest friends, and some members of his family often come to me concerning matters about which they hesitate to approach him, and I wonder why. They seem to stand somewhat in awe of him, and again I wonder why.

In the course of my talks with the President we discussed past and pending legislation, such as the war revenue bill, the seamans bill, the shipping registry bill, etc. etc.

Altogether it was a pleasant and profitable visit and one which I shall long remember.

James Watson Gerard to William Jennings Bryan

Berlin Via Copenhagen, Sept. 1, 1914.

Langhorne[1] requests following report forwarded Army War College.

August twenty-fourth, all was quiet in Loewen [Louvain]. On the twenty-fifth German troops advanced on Antwerp as sortie of Belgians was reported. As soon as the fighting German troops had left Loewen the whole population of the city fired treacherously from roofs and upper stories on the German soldiers who remained. This action of the inhabitants must have been organized by the Belgian Government as the residents would not all have been supplied with arms, otherwise, and the attack on the German troops was simultaneous with the Belgian sortie from Antwerp. All other reports, especially those emanating from official Belgian sources, are absolutely untrue.   Gerard.

T telegram (WP, DLC).
[1] George Taylor Langhorne, Major, U.S.A., military attaché at The Hague and Berlin.

From William Gibbs McAdoo

Dear Mr. President: Washington September 2, 1914.

For your information I beg to submit the following:

The imports from countries involved in the European conflict have shown so great a decrease as to seriously affect the revenues derived from customs duties. For the month of August, 1914, there is a decrease in the revenues collected from customs of $10,629,538.84, as compared with the corresponding month of the year 1913. The continuation of the decreases now indicated would mean a loss in customs revenues for the fiscal year ending June 30, 1915, of from $75,000,000 to $100,000,-000. It is not possible to estimate with a great degree of accuracy, because no one can foretell the extent to which the imports from the belligerant nations of Europe may be further affected by the eventualities of the war. We can, at best, make an intelligent guess only.

It is certain that this decrease in revenues from imports should be met by some form of well distributed internal revenue taxation. It is essential that the revenues of the Government shall exceed its expenditures, and that the strength of the treasury shall be maintained in order that it may continue to be a beneficial agency in the financial affairs of the country. A large part of the treasury balance, approximately $75,000,000, is on deposit with national banks distributed throughout the country. If the revenues of the Government are permitted to decline to a point where it would be necessary to recall from the national banks a considerable portion of the funds now on deposit with them, it might cause serious inconvenience or detriment to the business situation. In order to keep the treasury strong and to meet the deficiencies caused by the decline in import duties, to which I have referred, I suggest that additional revenue be raised through internal taxes to the amount of $100,000,000 per annum.   Faithfully yours,   W G McAdoo

TLS (WP, DLC).

From James Clark McReynolds

Dear Mr. President: Washington September 2, 1914.

It will be agreeable to Mr. Gregory to enter upon the duties of the Attorney General's office tomorrow—September 3d. I, therefore, have the honor hereby to tender my resignation of that office, and ask that you accept it to take effect at the close of business this day.

It is beyond me to express in words my deep appreciation of the generous consideration which you have shown me. My hope is that, by loyal and faithful service in the new position to which you have called me, I may, in a measure, indicate my deep sense of gratitude.

Please accept renewed assurance of my high and loyal admiration.   Sincerely yours,   J. C. McReynolds

TLS (WP, DLC).

To James Clark McReynolds

[The White House]

My dear Mr. Attorney General: September 2, 1914

I have your letter of September second telling me that it would be agreeable to Mr. Gregory to assume the duties of the Attorney General's office tomorrow, September third, and tendering your resignation of that office to take effect at the close of business today.

I accept your resignation of the office of Attorney General to take effect at the close of business today. In doing so, may I not congratulate you upon the conspicuous success with which you have performed the duties of Attorney General and now upon your future opportunity to serve the country as one of the Justices of the Supreme Court of the United States, and express the confident hope that the duties of your new position will bring you as much pleasure as honor?

Cordially and sincerely yours,   Woodrow Wilson

TLS (Letterpress Books, WP, DLC).

Remarks at a Press Conference

September 3, 1914

Can you tell us, Mr. President, about the conference with the German Ambassador?

> He just came to pay his respects on returning. We didn't discuss anything that the public is interested in.

Do you know whether or not, Mr. President, he has lodged any protest with reference to certain firms in this country shipping arms to England?

> No, he has not. . . .

Mr. President, there have been conflicting reports with regard to the attitude of Great Britain and France toward the proposed purchase of German ships by the United States. Has there been any complaint on the subject from them?

> No, there has not. Understand that that whole question is merely a question of bona fides. . . . Of course, that would be easy to establish in case we should purchase, but of course you also understand that the pending bill in Congress is not for the purchase of German ships. It is for the purchase of ships. We don't have to purchase anywhere.

You expect that bill to pass this session?

> Yes, certainly.

Mr. President, can you say when you will issue your proclamation on the ship registry bill?

> I am hoping to issue it tomorrow. I have got it practically ready.

Mr. President, is it a fair question, are other ships in contemplation—German, French, and English?

> I don't know the listing. I could say that they are French and English, but there are other ships in our choice.

It has been intimated, on what seems to be very good authority, that we should split up our purchases, and there would be no complaint from anybody.

> Yes.

Mr. President, can you say just to what extent these inquiries have been—

> Those—it has merely been a perfectly informal discussion between the ambassadors and the Secretary of State.

Have they laid out in any way the attitude of their governments?

> No. They expressed, I believe that they have expressed, their own opinions as to what that attitude would be, but in the most informal way, or personally so.

The view from London, Mr. President, was that Great Britain would not feel that she could be exempt from capturing ships which carried the things which the British Admiralty had announced, not necessarily as contraband, but prohibited to German commerce, and there are very few articles that can be carried by German ships.

> That is mere talk.

Mr. President, the purpose of these ships is to carry at this particular time commerce to Europe, South America, or Asia?

> To carry commerce wherever it needs to be carried.

Generally?

> Yes. Also to get our own products to market. Probably I should say just a personal opinion. The shipments to Europe will take care of themselves. That is my guess about it, because things are becoming much more normal in that field.

You mean those countries themselves are carrying it in their own ships?

> Those that have ships, yes.

Mr. President, have you any suggestion with regard to this government and violation of Chinese neutrality?

> No, sir, not so far as I know.

Mr. President, has any arrangement been made for a conference with the Belgian commissioners who are on their way to this country?[1]

No, I haven't officially learned they were on their way. I have seen that in the newspapers. So far as announcement may have reached the State Department, I haven't heard of it.

JRT transcript (WC, NjP) of CLSsh (C. L. Swem Coll., NjP).
1 Four commissioners sent by King Albert to President Wilson, to lay before him evidence of atrocities alleged to have been committed by German soldiers against Belgium and its people. The head of the commission was Henri Carton de Wiart, Envoy Extraordinary and Minister Plenipotentiary; accompanying him were Louis de Sadeleer, Paul Hymans, and Emil van de Velde, leaders of opposing political parties.

From William Jennings Bryan

My dear Mr. President: Washington September 3rd, 1914.

Before coming to the White House this morning I jotted down a number of things about which I wished to speak to you but I forgot to add one item, and an important one.

I wrote you in regard to the throwing of bombs on Antwerp. It has been repeated, although the second throwing did no great harm. They are fearful of the same danger in London, it having been rumored that the Germans intended to send their airships across the Channel and drop bombs on London.

Have you had time to think over the matter and if so to what conclusion have you come in regard to our duty in the premises? Should there be any protest—and if so, should it be based upon danger to Americans, or upon the broader ground that it is an improper method of warfare?

I enclose to you a very interesting telegram which has just been received from Page.[1]

With assurances of high respect I am, my dear Mr. President
Very sincerely yours,   W. J. Bryan

TLS (SDR, RG 59, 763.72116/18½, DNA).
1 WHP to Secretary of State, Sept. 3, 1914, FR 1914-WWS, p. 87, about British determination to deal a death blow to Germany, outrage over the destruction of Louvain and other German atrocities in Belgium, and rumors of zeppelin raids on London.

From William Gibbs McAdoo

URGENT.

Dear Mr. President: Washington September 3, 1914.

I regret very much to say that I find that the premise in the first paragraph of my letter yesterday, in relation to revenues, is wrong. It now appears that the estimated decrease in the customs revenues will amount to about $60,000,000 this fiscal year, provided European war conditions do not more seriously affect imports than now. This decrease, taken in connection with the necessary expenditures for the fiscal year ending June 30, 1915, including payments on the Panama Canal (estimated at $30,-000,000) and unavoidable expenditures occasioned by actual and contingent liabilities arising out of conditions caused by the European war, (such as war risk insurance, operation of ships, relief work) are likely to cause a deficit of $100,000,000 for the year.

Please forgive me for not having made this clearer to you yesterday, but it was not made clear to my own mind until this moment. I hope that this will not occasion you great inconvenience in altering your message to conform to these facts.

Faithfully yours,　W G McAdoo

TLS (WP, DLC).

Sir Cecil Arthur Spring Rice to Sir Edward Grey

Private & Secret.　　　　　　　Washington. 3 September 1914.

The President sent you warmest greeting and expresses his most sincere sympathy. He said: "Every thing that I love most in the world is at stake," and later "If they succeed, we shall be forced to take such measures of defence here as would be fatal to our form of Government and American ideals." He spoke of the long trial of the Civil War, and said with deep emotion that he was sure that our country would still show its powers of endurance for a high cause.

Officially, he would do all that he could to maintain absolute neutrality, and would bear in mind that a dispute between our two nations would be the crowning calamity.

The Secretary of State, whom I saw afterwards, pointed out that it would be to the common advantage that we should have Peace Commissions in working order. "If there is a dispute at sea, we could tell our people to stop talking and leave it to the Commissions."

I think that this is practical, and hope that you will authorise me to sign soon.

T telegram (E. Grey Papers, FO 800/84, PRO).

Sir Edward Grey to Sir Cecil Arthur Spring Rice

Private & Secret.   [London] 3 September 1914, 7.20 p.m.

I am most grateful for the President's message & his sympathy. If Prussian militarism succeeds the west of Europe will be no fit place for those of us who have been brought up to love liberty, humanity & good faith and I think the United States will feel the dark shadow of militarism nearer to them.

We wish in all our conduct of the war to do nothing which will be a cause of complaint or dispute as regards the U. S. Govt. Such a dispute would indeed be a crowning calamity as the President says & probably fatal to our chances of success.   E.G.

Hw telegram (E. Grey Papers, FO 800/84, PRO).

An Address to a Joint Session of Congress

[Sept. 4, 1914]

Gentlemen of the Congress: I come to you to-day to discharge a duty which I wish with all my heart I might have been spared; but it is a duty which is very clear, and, therefore, I perform it without hesitation or apology. I come to ask very earnestly that additional revenue be provided for the Government.

During the month of August there was, as compared with the corresponding month of last year, a falling off of $10,629,538 in the revenues collected from customs. A continuation of this decrease in the same proportion throughout the current fiscal year would probably mean a loss of customs revenues of from sixty to one hundred millions. I need not tell you to what this falling off is due. It is due, in chief part, not to the reductions recently made in the customs duties, but to the great decrease in importations; and that is due to the extraordinary extent of the industrial area affected by the present war in Europe. Conditions have arisen which no man foresaw; they affect the whole world of commerce and economic production; and they must be faced and dealt with.

It would be very unwise to postpone dealing with them. Delay in such a manner and in the particular circumstances in which we now find ourselves as a nation might involve consequences of the most embarrassing and deplorable sort, for which I, for one, would not care to be responsible. It would be very dangerous in the present circumstances to create a moment's doubt as to the strength and sufficiency of the Treasury of the United States, its ability to assist, to steady, and sustain the financial operations of the country's business. If the Treasury is known, or even thought, to be weak, where will be our peace of mind? The whole industrial activity of the country would be chilled and demoralized. Just now the peculiarly difficult financial problems of the moment are being successfully dealt with, with great self-possession and good sense and very sound judgment; but they are only in process of being worked out. If the process of solution is to be completed, no one must be given reason to doubt the solidity and adequacy of the Treasury of the Government which stands behind the whole method by which our difficulties are being met and handled.

The Treasury itself could get along for a considerable period, no doubt, without immediate resort to new sources of taxation. But at what cost to the business of the community? Approximately $75,000,000, a large part of the present Treasury balance, is now on deposit with national banks distributed throughout the country. It is deposited, of course, on call. I need not point out to you what the probable consequences of inconvenience and distress and confusion would be if the diminishing income of the Treasury should make it necessary rapidly to withdraw these deposits. And yet without additional revenue that plainly might become necessary, and the time when it became necessary could not be controlled or determined by the convenience of the business of the country. It would have to be determined by the operations and necessities of the Treasury itself. Such risks are not necessary and ought not to be run. We can not too scrupulously or carefully safeguard a financial situation which is at best, while war continues in Europe, difficult and abnormal. Hesitation and delay are the worst forms of bad policy under such conditions.

And we ought not to borrow. We ought to resort to taxation, however we may regret the necessity of putting additional temporary burdens on our people. To sell bonds would be to make a most untimely and unjustifiable demand on the money market; untimely, because this is manifestly not the time to withdraw working capital from other uses to pay the Government's bills; unjustifiable, because unnecessary. The country is able to pay any just and reasonable taxes without distress. And to every other form of borrowing, whether for long periods or for short, there is the same objection. These are not the circumstances, this is at this particular moment and in this particular exigency not the market, to borrow large sums of money. What we are seeking is to ease and assist every financial transaction, not to add a single additional embarrassment to the situation. The people of this country are both intelligent and profoundly patriotic. They are ready to meet the present conditions in the right way and to support the Government with generous self-denial. They know and understand, and will be intolerant only of those who dodge responsibility or are not frank with them.

The occasion is not of our own making. We had no part in making it. But it is here. It affects us as directly and palpably almost as if we were participants in the circumstances which gave rise to it. We must accept the inevitable with calm judgment and unruffled spirits, like men accustomed to deal with the unexpected, habituated to take care of themselves, masters of their own affairs and their own fortunes. We shall pay the bill, though we did not deliberately incur it.

In order to meet every demand upon the Treasury without delay or peradventure and in order to keep the Treasury strong, unquestionably strong, and strong throughout the present anxieties, I respectfully urge that an additional revenue of $100,-000,000 be raised through internal taxes devised in your wisdom to meet the emergency. The only suggestion I take the liberty of making is that such sources of revenue be chosen as will begin to yield at once and yield with a certain and constant flow.

I can not close without expressing the confidence with which I approach a Congress, with regard to this or any other matter, which has shown so untiring a devotion to public duty, which has responded to the needs of the Nation throughout a long season despite inevitable fatigue and personal sacrifice, and so large a proportion of whose Members have devoted their whole time and energy to the business of the country.[1]

Printed reading copy (WP, DLC).
[1] There is a WWsh outline of this address and a WWsh draft, with the composition date of Sept. 2, 1914, in WP, DLC.

To Frank Ellsworth Doremus

[The White House]
My dear Mr. Doremus: September 4, 1914

I have read your letter of September first[1] with a keen appreciation of its importance. It appeals to me as the leader of the party now in power with peculiar force and persuasiveness. The close of a very extraordinary session of Congress is at hand which has, I venture to say, been more fruitful in important legislation of permanent usefulness to the country than any session of Congress within the memory of the active public men of our generation. A great constructive programme has been carried through for which the country had long waited, and has been carried through with the approval and support of judicious men of all parties; and we have abundant reason to congratulate ourselves upon the record that has been made during the busy seventeen months we have devoted to our great legislative task. Certainly in ordinary circumstances, if we were free to disengage ourselves for the purpose, we would be warranted in now directing our energies to a great campaign in support of an appeal to the country to give us the encouragement of its endorsement at the autumn elections.

We could go to the country with a very sincere appeal in which there need be no pretence or boast of any kind but a plain statement of things actually accomplished which ought to be and I think would be entirely convincing. It is a record which shows us at peace with all the world; the questions which plagued business with doubt and uncertainty and irresponsible criticism out of the way, thoughtfully settled and disposed of; the apparent antagonism between government and business cleared away and brought to an end with the plain reckoning accomplished; the path for sure-footed adjustment clear ahead of us, prosperity certain to come by means which all can approve and applaud.

Moreover, there is a programme of another kind ahead of us to which it is inspiriting to look forward,—a programme free from debate except as to the best means by which to accomplish what all desire. The great questions immediately ahead of us are the building up of our merchant marine with all that that means in the development and diversification of our foreign commerce and the systematic conservation and economic use of our national resources, subjects much talked about but little acted upon. Here are other great pieces of constructive legislation waiting to be done to which we could turn without any controversy except, as I have said, as to the best ways of doing them.

I believe that ways can be found to do these things readily enough if the country will give us its generous support and trust us to do them; and it would have been a genuine pleasure to me to ask to be given again colleagues such as I have had in the two Houses of Congress during the present memorable session. I trust that there will be many occasions upon which I may have the privilege of calling the attention of my fellow-countrymen to the fine and unselfish service which has been rendered them by their present representatives, ready at all times to respond to any appeal which spoke convincingly of the public welfare.

But in view of the unlooked-for international situation our duty has taken on an unexpected aspect. Every patriotic man ought now to "stay on his job" until the crisis is passed and ought to stay where his job can best be done. We must do whatever is necessary and forego whatever is necessary to keep us in close and active concert in order to relieve in every possible way the stress and strain put upon our people during the continuance of the present extraordinary conditions. My job, I now know, can be done best only if I devote my whole thought and attention to it and think of nothing but the duties of the hour. I am not at liberty and shall not be, so far as I can now see, to turn away from those duties to undertake any kind of political canvass.

In the present emergency I am keenly aware of the two-fold responsibility I am called upon to discharge: the responsibility which devolves upon me as President of the United States and the responsibility under which I am laid as leader of a great political party. Of course, the whole country will expect of me and my own conscience will exact of me that I think first of my duties as President, responsible for exercising so far as I have the ability a constant guidance in the affairs of the country, both domestic and foreign. The labors of Congress have a natural and customary limit: the work of the Houses can be and will be finished; Congress can adjourn. But the President cannot, especially in times like these, turn away from his official work even for a little while. Too much depends upon his keeping all the threads of what is occurring in his hands.

I have, therefore, reached the conclusion that I cannot in any ordinary sense take an active part in the approaching campaign: that I must remain here to attend to the serious work sure to fill the months immediately before us,—months that will carry with them obligations, no doubt, of the most tremendous sort. I know that you will feel similarly about your own obligations: that members of Congress, too, without distinction as to party affiliations, will feel that they must remain to do their work of necessary and pressing service and bring it to a successful conclusion.

I shall, no doubt, take occasion as opportunity offers to state and perhaps restate to the country in the clearest and most convincing terms I can command the things which the Democratic party has attempted to do in the settlement of great questions which have for many a long year pressed for solution, and I earnestly hope that they will generously open their minds to what I may have to say; but I shall not allow my eagerness to win their approval or my earnest desire to be granted by their suffrages the support of another Congress to interfere with the daily performance of my official duties or distract my mind from them. The record men make speaks for itself. The country cannot be deceived concerning it and will assess it justly. What it chiefly expects and demands and what it will certainly be most surely won by is the performance of duty without fear or favor and without regard to personal consequences.

And certainly this is a time when America expects every man to do his duty without thought of profit or advantage to himself. America is greater than any party. America cannot properly be served by any man who for a moment measures his interest against her advantage. The time has come for great things. These are days big with destiny for the United States, as for the other nations of the world. A little wisdom, a little courage, a little self-forgetful devotion may under God turn that destiny this way or that. Great hearts, great natures, will respond. Even little men will rejoice to be stimulated and guided and set an heroic example. Parties will fare well enough without nursing if the men who make them up and the men who lead them forget themselves to serve a cause and set a great people forward on the path of liberty and peace.

Cordially and sincerely yours,   Woodrow Wilson[2]

TLS (Letterpress Books, WP, DLC).
[1] F. E. Doremus to WW, Sept. 1, 1914, TLS (WP, DLC), asking whether Wilson could participate in the coming campaign.
[2] There is a WWsh draft of this letter with the composition date of Sept. 3, 1914, in WP, DLC. The letter was of course given to the press and was widely reprinted.

To William Jennings Bryan

My dear Mr. Secretary: The White House September 4, 1914

I have thought a great deal about the matter of a protest with regard to the dropping of the bombs and my present judgment is that we do not know in sufficient detail the actual facts and that we ought to be very slow to make formal protests, chiefly because we shall no doubt be called upon by every one of the belligerents before the fighting is over to do something of this kind and would be in danger of becoming chronic critics of what was going forward. I think the time for clearing up all these matters will come when the war is over and the nations gather in sober counsel again.

Cordially and faithfully yours,   Woodrow Wilson

TLS (W. J. Bryan Papers, DNA).

To Oswald Garrison Villard

My dear Mr. Villard: The White House September 4, 1914

I appreciate, I think, almost as keenly as you express them the difficulties and doubts about the ship purchase proposal, and yet sitting here and hearing all sorts and varieties of suggestions it becomes clearer to me day by day that private capital is not going to undertake this thing on an adequate scale or in the most serviceable way without asking for the very kind of government backing and support to which I feel the deepest objection on principle not only, but because of some interests that would be necessarily involved.

The idea in the proposal is not that the government should permanently embark in these things, but that it should do the immediate and necessary thing.

At the same time, I realize that all the questions must be asked and, if possible, answered which are propounded in last evening's editorial in the Post. I wish I knew more but I am trying to find out all there is to get at.

With warm regard and sincere thanks for your letter of August twenty-seventh.   Cordially yours,   Woodrow Wilson

TLS (O. G. Villard Papers, MH).

To Frederic Yates

My dear Friend: The White House September 4, 1914

Thank you with all my heart for your letter of the eighteenth. Mrs. Harper was right. Words from you are not only welcome but constantly hoped for. We think of you a very great deal and with deep affection for your dear ones and yourself.

It is fine to have a hope of seeing you over here and I shall certainly try to get Senator La Follette over to see the pictures you suggest.

Thank you, my dear Fred, for your words of comfort. The thing is too poignant to speak about now to those who really care but my heart goes out to you for your loving thought of me.

God Grant that the world may soon come out of this nightmare of war!

With most affectionate messages from us all to you all three,
       Affectionately yours,   Woodrow Wilson

TLS (F. Yates Coll., NjP).

From Thomas Watt Gregory, with Enclosure

Dear Mr. President: Washington, D. C. September 4, 1914.

The conference committee on the Clayton Bill has been appointed and will meet on Wednesday next. I find that your other engagements will prevent me from seeing you until Tuesday morning.

I enclose herewith a memorandum showing five special objections to the Senate bill, and if the opportunity offers you might glance over it between now and next Tuesday. The first point is very vital to this Department, and the passage of the bill in its present shape would doubtless break up the New Haven settlement now approaching consummation, and would be likely to prevent any future settlements by the Government in proceedings under the Sherman Act.

It has occurred to me that the points suggested are of sufficient importance to justify an expression from you to the Democratic members of the conference committee, or to some one of them.

Faithfully yours,   T. W. Gregory

TLS (WP, DLC).

ENCLOSURE

September 4, 1914.

MEMORANDUM ON CLAYTON BILL, AS AMENDED BY SENATE.

Five provisions of this bill demand prompt attention.

I.

Section 4 makes judgments heretofore as well as hereafter obtained by the United States in proceedings under the Anti-Trust Act prima facie evidence against the defendant in any subsequent suit brought by any other party.

This Section should be amended so as to apply only to judgments hereafter obtained, and so as not to apply at all to judgments entered by consent before any testimony has been taken.[1]

II.

Section 6 prohibits intercorporate stockholdings amongst competing corporations, and Section 9 provides that Section 6 shall be enforced by the Interstate Trade Commission.

Since combinations and monopolies in restraint of trade prohibited by the Sherman Act are formed in most instances through intercorporate stockholdings, it is plain that Section 6 of this bill overlaps, in large part at any rate, the ground covered by the Sherman Act. This might not be particularly objectionable if Section 9 of this bill did not provide that Section 6 should be enforced by the Interstate Trade Commission. That arrangement, however, will bring about either of two results: there will be two distinct agencies, the Department of Justice and the Courts on the one hand and the Interstate Trade Commission on the other, both charged with the duty and responsibility of enforcing the statutory prohibitions against combinations in restraint of trade brought about through intercorporate stockholdings; or it will be held that the later remedy provided by this bill is an exclusive remedy and, therefore, repeals the Sherman Act in so far as it applies to combinations in restraint of trade brought about through intercorporate stockholdings.

Either of these results would be most unfortunate for obvious reasons. Both can be avoided by making the provisions of Section 6 enforceable in the courts through criminal prosecution and injunction,[2] and by eliminating so much of Section 9 as provides for the enforcement of Section 6 by the Interstate Trade Commission.[3]

III.

Section 15 of the bill would probably give private individuals the right to bring dissolution suits against corporations charged with being combinations or monopolies in restraint of trade.

This would be unfortunate in the extreme. It would open an unlimited field for blackmail. To illustrate, take the International Harvester Corporation. The court has held, in substance, that that Corporation has not been guilty of any unfair or oppressive course of conduct in trade, but that it constitutes a combination and monopoly in restraint of trade because it is a consolidation of four or five formerly competing corporations together controlling a strongly preponderating portion of the branch of trade in which they were engaged. A competitor of the Harvester Corporation, complaining that his business was threatened by loss or damage by reason of the control of the market exercised by the Harvester Corporation, would have the right under Section 15 to apply to the court for injunctive relief. The only relief which the court could administer would be dissolution, since the control of the market resulting from the size of the corporation, and not the methods of the corporation, constitute the cause of the threatened loss or damage to the competitor.[4]

IV.

Section 25 would make compulsory the appointment of receivers for every corporation adjudged a combination or monopoly in restraint of trade, and the sale of the property of such corporation and the winding up of its affairs.

This is the sort of a remedy which has an infinitely greater capacity for harm than for good. It may well be feared that its application would destroy not only combinations in restraint of trade, but the general prosperity as well.

At present there are pending suits under the Anti-Trust Act against the International Harvester Company, the United States Steel Corporation, the Reading System of railroads and coal companies, the Lehigh Valley System of railroads and coal companies, the United Shoe Machinery Company, the American Sugar Refining Company, the American Can Company, the Corn Products Company, the Southern Pacific Company, the Eastman Kodak Company, and the National Cash Register Company, among others. Under Section 25 it would be quite possible for all of these corporations, whose activities touch almost every phase of the country's commerce, to be simultaneously in the hands of receivers charged with selling their property and winding up their affairs. The perils of such a situation are plain.

The remedy provided by this Section can be exerted under existing law, in the discretion of the court, where there is no other adequate remedy; and the law should be allowed to remain that way.[5]

v.

Section 26 declares it unlawful for any corporation engaged in commerce to do business contrary to the laws of the State in which it may be doing business, &c.

If this Section has any meaning whatever, it is a clear surrender to the States of Federal power over interstate commerce.[6] Quite probably it will be declared uncons[t]itutional; but if not, it will restore all the confusion of divided control from which we are just escaping by means of such decisions as the Shreveport Rate Case.[7]

T MS (WP, DLC).

[1] Section 4 was made explicitly prospective, and consent decrees were exempted from its application.

[2] Section 6 of the Senate bill became Section 7 in the final version. It simply said that nothing in this section should be held or construed to authorize or make lawful anything heretofore prohibited or made illegal by the antitrust laws.

[3] Wilson or the conference committee did not accept this exception. In fact, the latter strengthened the commission's power in this respect.

4 This section was not changed except to make it not applicable to railroads and other common carriers.

5 The conference committee eliminated this section altogether.

6 The conference committee eliminated this section also.

7 The so-called Shreveport rate cases, 1914, in which the Supreme Court ruled that the Interstate Commerce Commission had the power to set intrastate freight rates, even when this invalidated rates set by state railroad commissions, whenever interstate and intrastate transactions of carriers were closely related.

From John Pierpont Morgan, Jr.

Personal

My dear Mr. President,   New York. September 4th, 1914.

As so much is happening, and as in view of the great pressure of work on you and also, I may add, on myself, it seems impossible to get another interview with you, I feel that I must write and advise you of the situation as I see it.

Since you were kind enough to receive me, the war in Europe is, of course, the largest event. This war, which is so dreadful in itself, has thrown a tremendous and sudden strain on American money markets, which they are facing to the best of their ability. It has increased the already pronounced tendency of European holders of American securities to sell them for whatever prices they could obtain for them, and the American investor has got to relieve the European investor of these securities by degrees and as he can. I think you will agree, therefore, that he should be encouraged to feel that his investments are safe, but, instead of such encouragement, what do we see? The Interstate Commerce Commission recently has handed down a decision in regard to the eastern freight rates. This decision practically makes it impossible for the eastern railroads to increase their earnings in any way, since the State regulations and various other things prevent their getting very much out of the passenger rate increase recommended. At the same time, the Interstate Commerce Commission issued a report of the New Haven investigation. Quite apart from any personal interest I may have had in the report, upon which I, therefore, forbear to comment, I know that, taken in conjunction with the rate decision, it has given the public a very clear idea of the attitude of the Interstate Commerce Commission to the railroads, the securities of which, heretofore, have been the most stable investments of the country.

Congress now has seen fit to pass, to nearly a final form, a bill putting all business in the hands of a political commission which has the right to pass on "fairness." The prospect of the action of the Trade Commission, in the light of the action of the Interstate Commerce Commission, can but alarm the investor still more in regard to all the investments which he has other than railroad investments; his feeling being that if one commission has done this to the railroads and their securities, what will this new commission do to the other enterprises in which he is interested?

Furthermore, the Clayton bill has now been referred to a conference committee and, if passed in anything approaching the form in which it left the Senate, will certainly increase in the minds of the American security holders the feeling which is already strongly developed, that the United States Government does not propose to allow enterprises to conduct normal business without interference. All coming together, I think everyone must see that there is material quite well at hand for the most appalling destruction of values in securities which has ever been seen in this country. Urgent sellers abroad, and frightened holders here, will flood the Stock Exchanges with selling orders at any moment that the Stock Exchanges find it possible to re-open, and they must endeavour to re-open as soon as possible. Great depreciation in the value of these securities must ensue; this in turn will throw back to the bank loans secured by them, and, as far as I can see, of necessity there will be a great tieing up of bank funds, which will interfere with the starting of the new Federal Reserve system, and produce panic conditions whenever it occurs. At such a moment as this, when all the encouragement possible is needed to induce capital to invest in American securities, and when the Government and all the financial interests are co-operating to the limit of their powers in order to tide over the present emergency and establish more favourable conditions, I must say that it seems to me most imprudent to remove from the American investor the desire to add to his holdings by the fear that those holdings are not well secured and safe. It is a matter of great regret to see our present difficulties added to by legislation which can only have one effect, namely, to reduce the enterprise and the initiative of the owners of capital in this country. The direction in which this capital should be applied cannot be controlled by legislation, except in the negative direction. You cannot, by legislation, force people to invest, but you can, by legislation, prevent them from wishing to, and this is what is being done.

And now to look foward! When we have passed through the panic period, which I fear is inevitable, and the slow process of building up begins again, the country in order to develope will require new capital. This capital it can no longer get from abroad, for there they will need all they have, and more, to replace their own losses caused by the war. The country will, therefore, have to fall back for its own development on its own capital fund, already fully invested and liable to calls from abroad for investment there and to take up American securities. Therefore, the only fund with which the country can develope itself will be that made from profits, by the slow process of saving. Let the idea once become general that profits are not to be permitted, and the development of the country will cease.

I am sure you will forgive me for putting these ideas before you in this way. I am appalled at the prospect before us, and deeply regretful that the prospect is as it is. The war, by cutting down the trade of other countries, should be a tremendous opportunity for America, but the country is not in a position to take advantage of that opportunity if it does not feel that its own capital invested in its own country is safely and remuneratively placed, and the opportunity, great as it is, must be neglected and flung on one side as long as the business of the country is under the impression of fear in which it now labours.

With great respect, I am, My dear Mr. President,

Yours very truly,   J. P. Morgan

TLS (WP, DLC).

To John Philip White and Others,[1] with Enclosure

My dear Sir: [The White House] September 5, 1914

I feel justified in addressing you with regard to the present strike situation in Colorado because it has lasted so long, has gone through so many serious stages, and is fraught with so many possibilities that it has become of national importance.

As you know, federal troops have been in the state for the purpose of maintaining order now for a long time. I have been hoping every day during that time that some light would come out of the perplexities of the situation, some indication that the mine operators and the miners who are now on strike were willing to consider proposals of accommodation and settlement, but no such indication has reached me, and I am now obliged to determine whether I am justified in using the Army of the United States indefinitely for police purposes.

Many things may come out of this situation if it is not handled with public spirit and with a sincere desire to safeguard the public as well as all others concerned, perhaps the most serious of them all the feeling which is being generated and the impression of the public that no one is willing to act, no one willing to yield anything, no one willing even to consider terms of accommodation.

As you know, two representatives of the Government of the United States have been actively engaged in investigating the whole situation and in trying to reach a dispassionate conclusion as to what it is possible to do in justice to both sides not only, but also in the interest of the public. The result of their investigations and of their very thoughtful consideration in the matter has been the drafting of the enclosed "tentative basis for the adjustment" of the strike. I recommend it to you for your most serious consideration. I hope that you will consider it as if you were acting for the whole country and I beg that you will regard it as urged upon your acceptance by myself with very deep earnestness. This is a time, I am sure you will feel, when everything should be done that it is possible for men to do to see that all untoward and threatening circumstances of every sort are taken out of the life of the people of the United States.

Sincerely yours,   Woodrow Wilson[2]

TLS (Letterpress Books, WP, DLC).
[1] Frank J. Hayes and William Green.
[2] Wilson sent this letter and its enclosure, *mutatis mutandis*, to the coal operators of Colorado.

E N C L O S U R E

DRAFT OF A TENTATIVE BASIS FOR THE ADJUSTMENT OF THE COLORADO STRIKE.

WHEREAS, the industrial conflict in the coal mining fields of Colorada has disrupted the peace of those sections of the State to the extent that a state of war has practically existed for some time, and

WHEREAS, a temporary peace is maintained by the presence of the Federal troops,

THEREFORE, there should be established a three-year-truce, subject to:

1. The enforcement of mining and labor laws of the State.

2. That all striking miners who have not been found guilty of violation of the law shall be given employment by the employer they formerly worked for, and where the place of the employee has been filled, he shall be given employment as a miner at the same or other mines of the company.

3. Intimidation of union or non-union men strictly prohibited.

4. Current scale of wages, rules and regulations for each mine to be printed and posted.

5. Each mine to have a Grievance Committee to be selected by majority ballot at a meeting called for the purpose, in which all employees (except officials of the company) have the right to participate.

Members of said committee must be employed at least six months at the individual mine before being eligible.

Married men to be in the majority on each committee.

Grievances to be first taken up individually with the proper officer of the company. Failing adjustment, they can refer to their local grievance committee for further consideration with the mine officials. Still failing adjustment, the matter shall be submitted to a Commission composed of three men to be appointed by the President of the United States and which shall be representative of each side, with the third member to act as umpire, whenever necessary. This Commission shall, during the three years of truce, serve as adjusters or referees in all disputes (whether individual or collective), affecting wages, working and social conditions.

Said Commission shall devote primarily all the necessary time to the consideration and adjustment of such disputes.

6. It is understood as a condition of the creation of said Commission, that during the life of the truce—

(a) The claim for contractual relations is to be waived, but this shall not prevent the voluntary agreement between any employer and their employees during the life of this truce.

(b) No mine guards to be employed, but this does not preclude the employment of necessary watchmen.

(c) In the establishment of the truce the presence of the Federal or State troops should become unnecessary.

(d) There shall be no picketing, parading, colonizing, or mass campaigning by representatives of any labor organization of miners that are parties to this truce, which will interfere with the working operations of any mine during the said period of three years.

(e) During said truce, the decisions of the Commission in cases submitted shall be final and binding on employers and employees.

(f) There shall be no suspension of work pending the investigation and reaching a decision on any dispute.

(g) The suspension of a mine over six consecutive days by the company may be authorized for cause satisfactory to the Commission, but not pending any dispute.

(h) Wilful violations of any of these conditions will be subject to such penalties as may be imposed by the Commission.

On account of the mutual benefits derived from the truce, the employers and employees should each pay one-half of the expenses of the Commission.

Respectfully submitted,

> [Hywel Davies, W. R. Fairley][1]
> Commissioners of Conciliation.[2]

T MS (WP, DLC).

[1] Davies was president of the Kentucky Mine Operators Association and a retired coal operator; Fairley was from Alabama and had been a member of the executive board of the United Mine Workers.

[2] The President and Secretary of Labor Wilson discussed this draft during the morning of September 4, and President Wilson approved it and agreed to submit it to the operators and union leaders. See W. B. Wilson to WW, Sept. 4, 1914, TLS (WP, DLC), enclosing "DRAFT OF A TENTATIVE BASIS . . . ," T MS (WP, DLC).

From Edward Mandell House, with Enclosures

Dear Governor: Prides Crossing, Mass. September 5th, 1914.

I am enclosing you a letter to Herr Zimmermann. If you approve, will you not have it properly sealed and sent to the German Embassy for transmission.

Please criticize it frankly and return it to me for correction if you think best.

I have a feeling that Germany will soon be glad to entertain suggestions of mediation, and that the outlook is more hopeful in that direction than elsewhere.

I am also sending you a copy of a letter I have written Page which I trust you will approve. I thought it better to let him accept my assurances without explanation.

I am still thinking of my delightful visit to Cornish, and I have been happier ever since.

> Affectionately yours,   E. M. House

TLS (WP, DLC).

E N C L O S U R E   I

Edward Mandell House to Arthur Zimmermann

My dear Herr Zimmermann: Washington, September 5, 1914

Thank you for your letter of August 1st. I gave it to The President to read, and he again expressed his deep regret that the efforts to bring about a better understanding between the great Powers of Europe had so signally miscarried. He looks upon the present war with ever increasing sorrow, and his offer of mediation was not an empty one, for he would count it a great honor to be able to initiate a movement for peace. Now that His Majesty has so brilliantly shown the power of His army, would it not be consistant with His life long endeavor to maintain peace, to consent to overtures being made in that direction?

If I could serve in any way as a medium it would be a great source of happiness to me, and I stand ready to act immediately upon any suggestion that your Excellency may convey, or have conveyed confidentially to me. With assurances of my high esteem, I am, my dear Herr Zimmermann,

Sincerely yours,   Edward M. House

ALS (Der Weltkrieg, No. 2, geheim, Vermittlungs-Aktionen, Vol. 1, pp. 3-6, GFO-Ar).

E N C L O S U R E   I I

Edward Mandell House to Walter Hines Page

Dear Page: Prides Crossing, Mass. September 4th, 1914.

I am just back from Cornish. I am glad to tell you that I left the President looking well. His short stay in the hills has done him good. I will write you further about him in another letter.

Will you not let me know just how much buckle and tongue failed to meet this year?

I think you told me that you could count on an income of about $35,000. i.e. your personal income plus your salary. If that is so, then will you not let me know how deep you had to dig into your principal the first year.

Will you not let all this be between you and me and the angels, and trust to me to find the deficiency, and in a way that will not involve you in the slightest and that may be given to the public without embarrassment to anyone should we sometime think best to do so.

With good wishes from,

Your friend,   [E. M. House]

CCL (WP, DLC).

John Reid Silliman to William Jennings Bryan

Mexico City, Mex., Sept. 5, 1914.

Following transmitted for Mr. Fuller:

"I had an interview with Carranza this morning. He disclaims any intention of prolonging interim Government or using it as a step to dictatorial power; realizes the circumscribed sphere of action of a revolutionary regime and just issued a call for a convention for Governors and Generals for October first, in accordance with the plans of Guadaloupe and Torreon to provide for organization of permanent Government; considers *dissensions* from northern section in way of adjustment which convention called for should complete.

"Zapata adjustment paralyzed by refusal of Zapata to have personal conference Carranza except at Zapata remote headquarters. Carranza considers that Jenkinson's[1] visit to Zapata has encouraged him in his unfriendly attitude, counting upon a hearing of his case by the President and the support of the United States. It would be well to have a message from the President direct sent to Zapata without delay informing him that he should immediately confer with Carranza at some place more suitable, and that his refusal must precipitate armed collision which it is his patriotic duty to avoid. This message might be sent to Silliman for personal delivery."   Silliman.

T telegram (SDR, RG 59, 812.00/13116, DNA).
  [1] Charles Jenkinson of the American Red Cross. About his visit to Zapata, see C. Jenkinson to WW, Sept. 8, 1914.

From the Diary of Colonel House

[Prides Crossing, Mass.] September 5, 1914.

The President and I settled the question of Page's expenses in London. Cleveland H. Dodge generously offers to give as much as $25,000. a year toward meeting them. The President was under the impression that Page was digging into his principal to that extent. He was relieved to find that he was running behin[d] only $12,000. to $15,000. per year.

The President asked me to take the money from Dodge and lend it to Page, taking his note therefor and afterward destroying the note. He said that he and McAdoo had concluded this was the best way to reach the matter. I have concluded to do it differently, as my letter to the President will indicate.

ADDENDA

From Robert Lewis Waring[1]

Mr. President, Sir: New York City, N. Y. May 26, 1914.

The following is submitted for your information and consideration:

The leaders of the Progressive party, National, State and County, have gotten together for the purpose of organizing a National Auxiliary to the National Committee of the above party composed of Negroes with headquarters in New York City.

This movement is forwarded by George W. Perkins, Theodore Douglas Robinson, Chairman of the State Executive Committee, Francis W. Bird, Chairman of the New York County Committee, and others, all Progressive leaders, *and the scheme is gathering strength every moment.*

Their principle argument is based on the apparent determination of your administration to ignore any and all negro democrats who seek national recognition. The presentation of this argument is having a telling effect upon the voting negro democrats throughout the country and will result in a complete exodus of negro democrats to the Progressive party unless something is done in the immediate future to off-set it.

We who have fought hard democratic battles, in the face of criticism and ostracism, now find ourselves without a leg upon which to stand, after our assertions in past campaigns, that the democratic party would be as liberal to us in Federal patronage as any other party has been.

In view of existing conditions, what are we to do? What can we say? Are we to slink out of sight, beaten by those for whom we battled? What position can we now take in the coming elections, when we are asked, what recognition has the democratic party accorded us for our loyalty? Can we again say, the democratic party will be as liberal in the future as the other parties have been in the past?

TO BE SURE THE DEMOCRATIC PARTY HAS RECOGNIZED THE NEGRO!! *By retaining negro Republicans in office!* Anderson, of New York![2] Terrell and Cobb, of Washington, D. C.![3] Johnson, of Washington, D. C. and Georgia![4] and others, *all of whom stumped the country in an endeavor to defeat the Wilson and Marshall ticket!*

In the last Mayoralty campaign in this City, Mr. Mitchell was not a favorite with the negroes generally, but those of us who craved honest government fought his battles at our own expense, AND WE ARE STILL AWAITING RECOGNITION.

WHAT IS IN STORE FOR THE HONEST NEGRO DEMOCRAT? The following are your words:

> "Whatever position I may hold it is my firm purpose to test every man by these questions—What did you do? How did you vote? With whom did you co-operate, and where did you stand?

AND NO EXPLANATION WILL CHANGE THE RECORD FOR ME."

In answer to those questions for myself, and thousands of other negro democrats, I will say—First—I fought for the democratic party—Second—I voted a straight democratic ticket—Third—I co-operated with the democratic national committee through Judge Robert S. Hudspeth, Jersey City, N. J., and Bishop Alexander Walters, New York City, N. Y., and I STOOD WITH BOTH FEET ON THE DEMOCRATIC PLATFORM AND NO EXPLANATION CAN CHANGE MY RECORD NOR THAT OF OTHER GOOD NEGRO DEMOCRATS.

Bishop Alexander Walters brought us this message from you:

> "I have always been friendly to the negroes' interests, and I assure you that in case of my election, the negroes of the country have nothing to fear from me. *I will give them a square deal.*"

All any negro asks is to be awarded according to his ability and his deeds—to be given a "square deal."

This takes us back to the object of this writing. Are we negroes being given a "square deal?" I claim not. NOT IN ANY SENSE OF THE WORD. We are being held up to the world about as the old negro in the South was, who thought he could say, "Hello Tom" to the newly elected Mayor, THE DAY AFTER ELECTION, and who was asked, "nigger don't you know the election is over?"

The humiliation of the negro democrat at this time can only be felt by those of us who had faith in the BIG PROMISES that were made us and who worked and acted accordingly.

I feel that a great wrong is being done us—not because promises are not being kept—*but that we are being studiously ignored;* because men of another party, *who reiterated upon the stump,* THAT NO NEGRO DEMOCRATS WOULD BE GIVEN FEDERAL OFFICES AND ARE BEING KEPT IN OFFICE SEEMINGLY AS A REWARD FOR THOSE UTTERANCES!

I am writing these facts not as complaints, but as obstacles which we negro democrats seek to overcome.

I AM A CANDIDATE FOR OFFICE. My application is on file in the Department of Justice and has been since December 3, 1913. The position which I seek, is one within the gift of the Attorney General and does not require the "consent" of the United States Senate.

I am herewith calling your attention to the above facts and asking that I, together with other honest negro democrats be given a "square deal" at your hands, as "no explanation can change the record for me." (us).

I have the honor to remain

Respectfully yours,   Robert Lewis Waring

TLS (WP, DLC).

[1] Lawyer and Negro Democratic leader of Harlem.

[2] Charles Williams Anderson, Collector of Internal Revenue, Second District of New York.

[3] Judge Robert H. Terrell and James A. Cobb, Special Assistant United States Attorney since 1907.

[4] Henry Lincoln Johnson, Recorder of Deeds of the District of Columbia.

To Robert Lewis Waring

My dear Mr. Waring: [The White House] June 1, 1914

I have your letter of May twenty-sixth, which I have read very carefully. I am very sorry indeed that you should feel as you do about the course of the present administration. It has been doing everything that was possible in a difficult situation.

I will take pleasure in sending your letter to the Attorney General for his consideration.

Sincerely yours,   Woodrow Wilson

TLS (Letterpress Books, WP, DLC).

From William Jennings Bryan

My Dear Mr President   [Washington, June 24, 1914]

I enclose three matters for your consideration. First a draft of treaty for Hayti. It is drawn as you will see according to Dominican form[1] except as to financial adviser & and [sic] as to (art. 9) protecting collection. Would be glad to have your opinion. 2nd I enclose a telegram from Brazilian minister about situation in Mexico City.[2] 3d Spanish Ambassador wants to know if we will make the same arrangements with Spain that we did with Great Britain about missing claims. I see no reason for objecting but will talk to you by phone about this & the message from Mexico, also about the latest telegram from Niagara Falls.[3]

   With assurances etc I am my dear Mr President

Yours truly   W. J. Bryan

ALS (WP, DLC).
  [1] It is printed at July 27, 1914, Vol. 30.
  [2] It is missing.
  [3] Printed in this volume at June 24, 1914.

To Francis Griffith Newlands

My dear Senator: [The White House] July 7, 1914
   I thank you sincerely for your letter of June sixth with its enclosures and will try to act in the most helpful way I know how in view of the information which it gives me. I hope I can be of assistance.

Cordially and sincerely yours,   Woodrow Wilson

TLS (Letterpress Books, WP, DLC).

To Francisco Villa

My dear General Villa: The White House. 9 Aug. 1914.
   The bearer of this letter, Mr. Paul Fuller, is my personal friend. He has my full confidence and knows my mind fully as regard to the matters he wishes to discuss with you. I trust him and am sure you may trust him with the utmost confidence also. Please say to him what you would wish to say to me.
   Please accept assurances of my regard and confidence and also my cordial salutations and good wishes.

Sincerely Yours,   Woodrow Wilson

HwCL (Coudert Brothers Archives).

To Paul Fuller, with Enclosure

My dear Mr. Fuller,   The White House [August 26, 1914]
   Here is the document Mr. Bryan was unable to furnish you with. I am sending it to you at his request. It bore date 12 March, 1913.[1]
   I am also enclosing the letter of introduction to General Carranza.

My warmest good wishes go with you, and I thank you with all my heart for undertaking this important mission and undertaking it in such a spirit.

With warmest regard,

Sincerely Yours,   Woodrow Wilson

WWTLS (Coudert Brothers Archives).

[1] It was a copy of his statement on Latin American policy printed at March 12, 1913, Vol. 27.

E N C L O S U R E

To Venustiano Carranza

Honoured Sir: The White House 26 August 1914

This letter will be handed you by Mr. Paul Fuller. Mr. Fuller is a trusted friend of mine, is fully in my confidence, and I commend him very warmly to your welcome and favour.

I have sent him to you in the hope that, through him, I might make you fully acquainted with my own sentiments and friendly wishes about Mexico and that you would honour him with your confidence with regard to the many matters which are of deep and lasting importance alike to Mexico and to her friend and neighbour the United States of America.

With much respect and the most sincere good wishes,

Sincerely Yours   Woodrow Wilson

HwCL (Coudert Brothers Archives).

INDEX

NOTE ON THE INDEX

THE alphabetically arranged analytical table of contents at the front of the volume eliminates duplication, in both contents and index, of references to certain documents, such as letters. Letters are listed in the contents alphabetically by name, and chronologically within each name by page. The subject matter of all letters is, of course, indexed. The Editorial Notes and Wilson's writings are listed in the contents chronologically by page. In addition, the subject matter of both categories is indexed. The index covers all references to books and articles mentioned in text or notes. Footnotes are indexed. Page references to footnotes which place a comma between the page number and "n" cite both text and footnote, thus: "624,n3." On the other hand, absence of the comma indicates reference to the footnote only, thus: "55n2"—the page number denoting where the footnote appears.

We have ceased the practice of indicating first and fullest identification of persons and subjects in earlier volumes by index references accompanied by asterisks. Volume 13, the cumulative index-contents volume is already in print. Volume 26, which will cover Volumes 14-25, will appear in the near future.

The index supplies the fullest known form of names and, for the Wilson and Axson families, relationships as far down as cousins. Persons referred to by nicknames or shortened forms of names can be identified by reference to entries for these forms of the names.

All entries consisting of page numbers only and which refer to concepts, issues, and opinions (such as democracy, the tariff, the money trust, leadership, and labor problems), are references to Wilson speeches and writings. Page references that follow the symbol △ in such entries refer to the opinions and comments of others who are identified.

INDEX

Abbott, Lyman, 407,n1

ABC powers: *see* Mexico and the United States—ABC mediation; and Argentina, Brazil, Chile

Adams, Annette Abbott (Mrs. Martin H.), 172,n1

Adamson, William Charles, 224,n1, 245, 289, 324, 348-49, 351, 433; congratulates WW on Mexican policy, 286-87

Adamson water power bill, 222-23, 224,n1, 244-45; W. Kent opposes, 217-19,n2

Address of President Wilson at Independence Hall . . . , 255n

Address of President Wilson at the Brooklyn Navy Yard . . . , 15n

Address of President Wilson at the Unveiling of the Statue to the Memory of Commodore John Barry, 36n

Address of President Wilson to the Graduating Class of the United States Naval Academy, 148n

agriculture: Smith-Lever Act, 8n1; and Clayton bill, 205-207,n2, 272; and sundry civil appropriation bill, 205, 284; effect of war on farmers, 420

Agriculture, Department of, 153, 217

Aguila Oil Co. Ltd.: *see* Mexican Eagle Oil Co.

Ahnelt, William Paul, 173n1

Alabama, U.S.S., 345, 427

Alaska, 20

Alaska development board bill, 31

Alaskan coal leasing bill, 20, 27, 31

Albert I (of Belgium), 383, 470n1

Aldrich-Vreeland Act, 325,n1, 326, 335

Aleshire, James B., 8,n1

Alexander, Joshua Willis, 223,n1, 317, 402, 454

Alsace, 190

American Can Co., 482

American Citizens' Relief Committee (London), 367, 438

American-Dominican Convention of 1907, 203,n1

American Federation of Labor: on qualities of Supreme Court justices, 309-10

American Federationist, 264

American flag, 146, 184-86, 252, 254

American Revolution, 34-36, 233

American Society in London, 367

American Sugar Refining Co., 482

American University: WW address at opening of, 89-91, 162

Ammons, Elias Milton, 37, 37-38, 45-46, 48-49, 60,n1, 422, 452-53

Anderson, Chandler Parsons, 369,n4

Anderson, Charles Williams, 491,n2

Andrew Furuseth: Emancipator of the Seamen (Weintraub), 223n1

Ángeles, Felipe, 57,n1, 97, 339, 393, 409, 413, 414, 416, 417, 418; differences with Carranza, 410

Angell, Norman, 236

Anglo-American relations: *see* Great Britain and the United States

Annapolis: *see* United States Naval Academy

Another Attack on the Banking Centres (New York *Sun*), 50,n1

antitrust legislation, 24, 44, 94, 126, 182-83, 194, 219, 243, 268, 312n1, 319n3; and H. F. Hollis, 110, 134, 187; business desire to delay, 173n1; and U.S. Chamber of Commerce, 205; and reaction of business to, 211-12; C. R. Van Hise on, 272; F. G. Newlands on, 296; and stock exchange bill, 312,n1; *see also* Clayton Antitrust Act; Federal Trade Commission Act; Sherman Antitrust Act

Antwerp, Belgium, 459n1, 460, 467, 471

Appropriations Committee (House of Reps.), 337, 337-38,n1

Appropriations Committee (Senate), 337, 337-38,n1

Archer, A. M., 165

Argentina, 23, 41-42, 121; mediation proposal to recognize provisional government in Mexico, 87; R. S. Naón on meeting with WW, 197-99; and Pan-Americanism, 271; WW's telegram of thanks to government of, 262,n1; *see also* Mexico and the United States—ABC mediation

Arlington Confederate Memorial Association, 141n2

Arlington National Cemetery, 110n1, 113,n4, 141n1

Arnold, Matthew, 22

Ashurst, Henry Fountain, 261

Asquith, Emma Alice Margaret (Margot) Tennant (Mrs. Herbert Henry), 247

Asquith, Herbert Henry, 215, 247, 258, 266

Associated Press, 203

Auchincloss, Gordon, 461,n1

Austria-Hungary: E. M. House on relations with Germany, 109; and ambassador in London, 152; and assassination of archduke, 222, 315; outbreak of war and, 314; and Germany, 323, 327; and E. Grey's attempt to prevent war with Serbia, 325; W. H. Page on causes of conflict, 330; Great Britain says no cause for war with, 368; Page fears

WOODROW WILSON

APPEARANCE

Woodrow Wilson, cont.

APPOINTMENTS

CABINET

FAMILY AND PERSONAL LIFE

Woodrow Wilson, cont.

country itself are involved, 264; It is the constant presence and pressure of great responsibility that tells, rather than the constant call of work, 276; The time has come when discrimination against particular classes of men should be absolutely laid aside and discarded as unworthy of the counsels of a great people. The effort for genuine social justice, for peace, . . . for prosperity should be a united effort without partisan prejudice or class antagonism, 299; on neutrality, 394; on the war, 450; Parties will fare well enough without nursing if the men who make them up and the men who lead them forget themselves to serve a cause and set a great people forward on the path of liberty and peace, 478

PRESS CONFERENCES

126-30, 158-60, 170-71, 181-83, 190-91, 208-209, 222-23, 243-45, 259-60, 267-71, 279-80, 296-97, 307, 317-19, 331-36, 387-90, 440-41, 469-71

PUBLIC AND POLITICAL ADDRESSES AND STATEMENTS

risks and penalties of extemporaneous speaking, 163
Statement on Latin American policy, March 12, 1913; mentioned, 494,n1
Address on Latin American policy in Mobile, Ala., Oct. 27, 1913; mentioned, 255, 272
Memorial address about servicemen killed in Veracruz, May 15, 1914, 13-15
Address on Commodore John Barry, May 16, 1914, 34-36
Address at the opening of The American University, May 27, 1914, 89-91; mentioned, 162-63
Remarks to manufacturers' associations, May 28, 1914; news report, 93-96; mentioned, 127-28
Remarks to the Princeton Alumni Association of the District of Columbia, May 29, 1914, 103-108
Memorial Day address, May 30, 1914, 110-11; mentioned, 113
Memorial address at the unveiling of a monument to Confederate dead, June 4, 1914, 141-42
Commencement address at the Naval Academy, June 5, 1914, 145-48
Remarks to the Class of 1879, June 13, 1914, 176-80
Flag Day address, June 15, 1914, 184-86

Woodrow Wilson, cont.

Remarks on the business outlook, June 25, 1914, 210-12
Remarks to a woman suffrage delegation, June 30, 1914, 226-28,n1,2,3,-4,5
Fourth of July address, July 4, 1914, 248-55; mentioned, 262
Statement on the Warburg and Jones nominations to the Federal Reserve Board, July 8, 1914, 263
Labor Day statement, July 9, 1914, 264
Special message to Congress requesting appropriations to assist Americans in Europe, Aug. 3, 1914, 337-38
Remarks to the Federal Reserve Board, Aug. 13, 1914, 376-77,n1
Remarks to a delegation of businessmen, Aug. 14, 1914, 378-79,n1
An appeal for neutrality in thought and deed, Aug. 18, 1914, 393-94; mentioned, 420, 432
Remarks to a delegation representing cotton interests, Aug. 24, 1914, 441-42,n2
Address to a joint session of Congress asking for additional revenue, Sept. 4, 1914, 473-75

RECREATION

reads poetry, 22; plays pool, 464; golf, 466

RELIGIOUS LIFE

epitaph for his father, 74; estimate of his father, 75; scholarship has usually been most fruitful when associated with religion, 90; note to J. R. Mott on his birthday, 119,-n1; But we must face the situation in the confidence that Providence has deeper plans than we could possibly have laid ourselves, 336

END OF WOODROW WILSON ENTRY

Wilson Era: Years of Peace, 1910-1917 (Daniels), 145n3
Wilson: The New Freedom (Link), 10n2, 165n1, 166n2, 191n1, 217n1, 224n1, 270n4, 273n1, 455n1
Wilson: The Struggle for Neutrality (Link), 193n1, 307n1, 325n1, 352n1, 402n1, 441n1
Windsor, Vt., 50
Wisconsin, 161, 161-62
Wisconsin Faces Reaction (Mason), 161,n1
Wise, Stephen Samuel, 144
Womack, John, Jr., 47n1
woman suffrage, 225, 226-28, 240; and national association opposed to, 257,n1